Background
for Instru

THE
BEDFORD
HANDBOOK

Sixth Edition

Glenn Blalock

Texas A&M University-Corpus Christi

Bedford/St. Martin's   Boston   ◆   New York

6   5   4   3   2   1
f   e   d   c   b   a

For information, write: Bedford/St. Martin's
75 Arlington Street, Boston, MA 02116

ISBN 0-310-39049-1

Acknowledgments

Chris M. Anson, "Distant Voices: Teaching and Writing in a Culture of Technology." From *College English* 61.3 (1999). Copyright © 1999 by the National Council of Teachers of English. Reprinted with permission.

David Bartholomae, "Inventing the University." From *When a Writer Can't Write: Studies in Writer's Block and Other Composing Problems* edited by Mike Rose. Copyright © 1985 The Guilford Press. Reprinted with permission. "The Study of Error." From *College Composition and Communication*, October 1980. Copyright © 1980 by the National Council of Teachers of English. Reprinted with permission.

Patricia Bizzell and Bruce Herzberg. "Research as a Social Act." From *The Clearing House* 60 (March 1987): 303–06. Copyright © 1987. Reprinted with permission of the Helen Dwight Reid Educational Foundation. Published by Heldref Publications, 1319 Eighteenth Street N.W., Washington, D.C. 20036-1801.

Guanjun Cai, "Texts in Contexts: Understanding Students' English Compositions." From *Evaluating Writing: The Role of Teachers' Knowledge about Text, Learning, and Culture* by Charles R. Cooper and Lee Odell, eds. Copyright © 1999 by the National Council of Teachers of English. Reprinted with permission.

Wallace Chafe, "What Good is Punctuation?" From the *Center for the Study of Writing the Occasional Paper*, Number 2, 1985. Center for the Study of Writing, Berkeley, CA. Copyright © 1985 by Wallace Chafe. Reprinted by permission of the author.

Robert Davis and Mark Shadle, "Building a 'Mystery': Alternative Research Writing and the Academic Act of Seeking." From *College Composition and Communication* 51.1. Copyright © 2000 by The National Council of Teachers of English. Reprinted with permission.

Alice Drum, "Responding to Plagiarism." From *College Composition and Communication* 37, May 1986. Copyright © 1986 by The National Council of Teachers of English. Reprinted with permission.

Acknowledgments and copyrights are continued at the back of the book on pages 474–475, which constitute an extension of the copyright page.

PREFACE

In her preface, Diana Hacker writes that she intends *The Bedford Handbook* to be useful to a wide range of students. Similarly, I intend *Background Readings for Instructors Using The Bedford Handbook,* Sixth Edition, to be useful to instructors with diverse backgrounds and different levels of experience. With this book, I want to invite new and experienced instructors to reflect carefully and critically on how and why they do what they do as writing teachers. Further, I want the readings in this book to suggest helpful, practical solutions to common problems and concerns and to provide useful and accessible references for further reading and study. I like to think that these readings will engage instructors in an ongoing professional conversation about teaching writing.

I selected the readings in this collection from among the extensive annotated bibliographical references that I provided for the *Instructor's Annotated Edition of The Bedford Handbook,* Sixth Edition. These readings are meant to complement, supplement, and enhance the teaching done in courses using *The Bedford Handbook,* and they are meant to stimulate further reading, research, and professional conversation. These selections are representative of the rich body of research that constitutes contemporary composition studies and that informs Diana Hacker's handbook.

While the organization of *Background Readings* follows that of *The Bedford Handbook,* the topics addressed in this collection are relevant to all writing courses. No matter how instructors might choose to use the handbook, they will find readings in this collection that will help them think about their courses, their assignments and activities, and their various interactions with students.

In addition to selecting the readings for this collection, I have written brief introductions for each part that explore connections between the readings and the topics addressed in that part of the handbook. And for each of the readings, introductory headnotes provide brief biographical information about the author, situate the reading in its original context, and offer a short overview of the reading. With my introductions, I attempt to provide a forum for composition scholars to share their insights with composition instructors, and I hope to invite teachers to engage in a meaningful conversation with the readings and the issues they explore.

This edition of *Background Readings* has several new features:

- Nearly one-half of the 43 readings are new to this edition and continue to represent the important ongoing work being done in composition studies.
- A new appendix, Writing in the Disciplines, includes articles that will help teachers make connections between their composition courses and courses across the curriculum.
- The updated appendix, Teaching with Technology, provides readings that continue to explore the use of instructional technology in writing classes, recognizing the ways technology and writing instruction intersect and the ways technology is changing definitions of literacy and writing instruction.
- A new section on Writing Centers, included in Part One, offers articles that discuss the role of the writing center and offer different approaches to responding to student writers and their writing.

- An updated Bibliography for Further Reading that follows the organization of *The Bedford Handbook* points out additional books and articles on topics relevant to the teaching of composition.

Acknowledgments

My work on this collection reaffirms my appreciation for the collaborative nature of composing and for the thoughtful participants of our professional community. I want to acknowledge the numerous individuals who have contributed to this book in various ways. Most obviously, without Diana Hacker's *Bedford Handbook*, this collection would have no reason to be. And as with previous editions, her insightful comments on my plans for revision have ensured that this new edition of *Background Readings* will continue to be a popular and worthy accompaniment to the handbook.

Several reviewers commented on the fifth edition of this text with thoughtful and detailed comments. Their responses invited me to reconsider many of the readings I selected and helped me recognize potential strengths and weaknesses in the book. Though I was unable to incorporate all of the reviewers' valuable suggestions, I know that this edition has benefited from their responses. I wish to thank William Archibald, University of North Dakota; Deborah Coxwell Teague, Florida State University; Richard Horvath, Fordham University; Marsha Keller, Oklahoma City University; Teresa Kynell, Northern Michigan University; Sandra Petrulionis, Pennsylvania State University, Altoona; Stephen Reid, Colorado State University; Georgia Rhoades, Appalachian State University; and Tammy Stuart Peery, Montgomery College, Germantown.

I assembled the early editions of this book while I was at the University of North Carolina at Chapel Hill, where Erika Lindemann created the environment that encouraged and valued this kind of work. She continues to inspire my work as a professional. I have been especially fortunate to find a professional home at Texas A&M University-Corpus Christi, where I am part of an active community of compositionists and dedicated, innovative teachers. I want to thank Rich Haswell, Jan Haswell, Susan Loudermilk, Robb Jackson, and the wonderful teachers in our First-Year Writing Program. They have helped to create and sustain an environment in which teaching and learning are valued, and I have relied on their presence and support while I worked on this edition. In addition to these individuals, and perhaps as important, I have to extend my thanks to the larger community of teachers and scholars who constitute the field of composition studies. As I attempted to survey the scholarly work that represents our profession, I was humbled by its quality and intellectual vitality. Without this important ongoing work, books such as *Background Readings* could not exist.

Working with Bedford/St. Martin's continues to be a wonderful and energizing experience for me, and I want to thank several individuals at Bedford for their contributions to this book. First, Joan Feinberg initially conceived of this project and trusted me to attempt it. With each revision, I have tried to repay her trust with my work on this text. I would also like to thank Anne Noonan, who oversaw the production of the book with care and patience, and Sarah Doerries for her skillful copyediting.

At Bedford/St. Martin's, I have been doubly fortunate to work on this text with the developmental editor, Ellen Thibault, and with Joanne Diaz, who served as the developmental editor for the previous edition. Ellen and Joanne deserve my highest praise and my sincere gratitude. Ellen has been especially patient, helpful, and thoughtful through the initial stages of this project. And Joanne has guided me through the final stages of the process with her usual expertise, grace, and humor. Both Ellen and Joanne have helped create an ideal working relationship: a perfect balance of professional and personal attention.

As with previous editions, I have been especially thankful for the ways that Ellen and Joanne have absorbed pressure from many different directions, and the ways they have managed skillfully and thoughtfully the complex revision process and the complicated exchanges of documents and ideas. Perhaps most important, both have been willing to listen, to read, and to respond to my ideas honestly and generously.

I owe a special acknowledgment to Dr. Laine Scales, a dedicated and caring teacher, an active scholar, a supportive partner and wife, and my best friend. Without her understanding and encouragement, I would not have been able to devote the time and energy that this project demands.

Glenn Blalock

Texas A&M University-Corpus Christi

CONTENTS

THE WRITING PROCESS

The first part of *The Bedford Handbook* introduces students to writing as a process and guides them through various stages of that process. The articles included in the first part of *Background Readings* complement that coverage by recognizing that writing is fundamentally a social activity, that composing is a complex, recursive process, and that writing instruction is an equally complex social and intellectual activity. Our understanding of writing situations and writing processes determines the choices we make as we design our courses, conduct our classes, and interact with our students and their writing. It governs the ways we introduce students to the concepts of planning, drafting, revising, and editing. It influences our approaches to assessing, responding to, and evaluating student writing.

As universities and colleges realize that writing instruction is a responsibility shared by all disciplines, and as courses across the curriculum ask students to do more writing at all levels, writing centers become more visible and more important on campuses. In many institutions, writing teachers and writing tutors work together to provide effective instruction and assistance to all students, and teachers and tutors recognize the value of shared knowledge about writing. This new edition of *Background Readings* includes selections that specifically address the unique situations of writing centers and tutors.

The articles in Part One raise a number of important questions that instructors and tutors might consider as they develop their course plans, assignments, class activities, and interactions with students.

- What are the characteristics of effective writing instruction? How can we determine "best practices"?
- How can we most effectively characterize writing situations? How can we help students assess the complex variables that constitute any given writing situation?
- How can writers think of audiences? What alternatives can students consider as they attempt to determine and analyze their audience?
- What assumptions are instructors making when they teach writing processes in a certain way?
- How can instructors help students develop more effective strategies for exploring and developing a topic? How can instructors help students consider alternative plans for their writing?
- How does revision differ from writer to writer? How can instructors help students provide and receive more effective responses to their classmates' and their own writing-in-progress?
- What are alternatives to teaching students about paragraphs? How can teachers resist the teaching of rigid patterns and prescriptive rules about development and coherence?
- What do instructors do—and what should they consider doing—as they respond to student writing?
- How can instructors help students respond to one another? How can instructors help students become more effective self-evaluators?

- What do instructors do when they assess writing? What alternatives do they have for assessing writing?
- What outcomes do we expect for our writing courses?
- What are the relationships between writing classes and writing centers? Between writing teachers and writing tutors?

FOLLOWING THE TAO

Diana Hacker

[From *Teaching English in the Two-Year College* (2000): 297–300.]

Diana Hacker has taught composition at Prince George's Community College since the late 1960s. She is the author of *A Writer's Reference* (1999), *The Bedford Handbook* (2002), *A Pocket Style Manual* (2000), and *Rules for Writers* (2000). An early version of "Following the Tao" was presented as an informal talk at the 1995 TYCA-Southwest Conference in Colorado Springs.

What do effective writing teachers do? How might we define "best practices" for teaching writing?

Hacker suggests that the Chinese classic *Tao Te Ching*, which offers advice to rulers, can benefit teachers as well. In fact, she says, many of the *Tao's* insights have become accepted wisdom in the teaching of composition over the past twenty-five years. Hacker's article is organized around five of her favorite lines from the *Tao Te Ching*: Practice nonaction. Yield and overcome; bend and be straight. In action, watch the timing. Give up learning and put an end to your troubles. Achieve greatness in little things.

Introduction

When I first encountered Lao Tsu's *Tao Te Ching*, the Chinese classic written perhaps as early as the 6th century BC, I noticed that much of its advice, intended for rulers, applied to teachers as well. My own teaching seemed to be going well when I was following the Tao, less well when I strayed from it.

Now, twenty-five years later, I am surprised to see how many of the *Tao's* insights have become accepted wisdom in the teaching of composition. Consider, for example, just five of my favorite lines from the *Tao Te Ching*:

- Practice nonaction.
- Yield and overcome; bend and be straight.
- In action, watch the timing.
- Give up learning, and put an end to your troubles.
- Achieve greatness in little things.

Practice Nonaction

Like an effective ruler, a good teacher needs to know when to do nothing. In the words of Lao Tsu, "Teaching without words and work without doing are understood by very few" (43). Certainly, we composition teachers have learned over the years that the more we are doing, the less our students are doing.

Years ago, many of us spent class time lecturing on such matters as connotation and denotation, figurative language, and the logical fallacies. We also spent time discussing and "appreciating" bellelettristic essays. This lecture/discussion/literary appreciation approach didn't work. Our students wrote badly.

It took the process movement to wake us up. The person who woke me up was Ken Macrorie, author of the rhetoric *Telling Writing*. Macrorie argued that the measure of our success is the quality of our students' writing. What a simple but profound idea! To improve the quality of my students' writing, I began to spend much more time—in class and during office hours—coaching students as they worked with their own texts. And I began including good student writing as models. I was not alone. Many of my colleagues at Prince George's, inspired not by Macrorie but by Roger Garrison, began turning their classrooms into conference-centered workshops. Similar transformations were taking place all over the country. Student writing improved dramatically, and we began to enjoy teaching composition.

Today, we continue to spend less time lecturing and more time helping students work with their own texts. And today we are less likely to appropriate or micromanage students' texts than we were twenty-five years ago. When conferencing with students, many of us follow the advice of New Hampshire teacher Chuck Annal—to sit on our hands. We agree with Donald Murray that our ambition should be "to teach as little as possible, and eventually not teach at all" (133). In other words, we should resist the temptation to interfere with the student's own learning. "The world is ruled by letting things take their course," says the *Tao*. "It cannot be ruled by interfering" (Lao Tsu 48).

Yield and Overcome; Bend and Be Straight

Lao Tsu's *Tao Te Ching* shows political rulers how to govern sometimes recalcitrant subjects, not by beating them into submission but by using more subtle means. Twenty-five years ago, some of my students could certainly be termed "recalcitrant," so I was open to any advice Lao Tsu had for me.

Years ago, many of us were too rigid. Today, we have learned to bend a bit—and paradoxically to get better results. We are less rigid in our assignments. I doubt, for example, that a book entitled *The Five Paragraph Theme* would sell well today. Now we focus on purpose and audience and give students some freedom to discover a way of reaching readers. In our description of the writing process, too, we have loosened up, acknowledging that the process is rarely linear and can vary depending on the writer and the demands of a particular writing task.

We are also more flexible when defining and evaluating writing. We once called all school writing "themes," and we rated them with a standard set of criteria. It was progress when we began calling themes "papers" or "essays," but we really progressed when we began identifying varied types of writing by name: papers and essays, to be sure, but also reports, case studies, proposals, letters, memos, newsletter articles, and even hypertext. Today we measure the success of a piece of writing not by looking to some Platonic ideal. Instead we consider purpose and audience and the conventions of the discourse community in which the writing is grounded.

Finally, we have learned to bend a bit when encountering student errors. At one time, some instructors routinely flunked an essay with even one comma splice. The result was some pretty bad "play it safe" writing—with short, choppy sentences or lots of semicolons. Today we agree with Mina Shaughnessy and David Bartholomae that some errors may be a sign of growth. Instead of getting our backs up about errors, we study them. Then we work with students on revision strategies that help them preserve the effect they were after when they wrote that fragment or comma splice in the first place.

In Action, Watch the Timing

In the past, many of us assigned papers, collected them, graded them, and told students to learn from their mistakes. Today we understand that most learning occurs during the process of writing—and we watch our timing throughout the process, offering advice when a student is most open to it.

When conferencing first became fashionable, some of my colleagues were using it for commenting on final, graded papers. What bad timing! Students aren't particularly open to advice once a paper has been graded. As Mina Shaughnessy has pointed out, writers reach closure once their work has been published or graded. That's why we shouldn't be too insulted when students glance at their grade and pay little attention to our carefully crafted comments.

Students—and indeed all writers—are much more open to advice when they are revising their drafts. Today we understand this. We also understand that when conferencing with students about those drafts we need to watch our timing. We must wait, quietly, doing little or nothing, and then strike when we see an opening.

If you think of the tactics of karate, you'll understand what Lao Tsu means by "In action, watch the timing." Let's say you're reading a student draft, silently, without pen in hand. You notice lots of shifts and pronoun agreement problems and some sexist language but say nothing. You get the student talking about the paper, and the issue of point of view comes up (though the student doesn't call it that). Then you strike because this is the moment when a discussion of point of view connects with the student's own goals. Your discussion is not just a grammar lecture but a minilesson in rhetoric, so it is likely to take hold.

What you are doing, of course, is treating the writer as a writer. You are playing the role we want our own editors to play—staying out of the way most of the time but speaking up, when necessary, to help us solve problems.

Give Up Learning and Put an End to Your Troubles

In the past, many teachers had a hard time distinguishing between two kinds of learning: what philosopher Gilbert Ryle calls "learning that" and "learning how." Too often students were asked to learn a term, such as *connotation* or *induction,* or a classification system, such as the traditional modes or the kinds of figurative language—as if this sort of learning would help them write better.

Ryle criticizes that he calls the "intellectualism legend": the idea that the first step in learning *how* is to learn *that,* i.e., to learn the rules or criteria that make for successful practice. Ryle would have loved the following story, related by novelist John Braine:

> I always have in my mind the story of W.C. Fields in his juggling days, reading Hazlitt on juggling and discovering how clever he was, how a juggler could slice a second up into a hundred different and distinct parts, how miraculous his coordination was, how the essence of juggling was a dance on the edge of disaster, or words to that effect. He read this with fascination and a growing sense of wonder: the next time he went on stage he dropped everything. (144)

When teaching writing, most of us now take a less academic approach than we did twenty-five years ago. Instead of teaching students *that* such and such is the case, we help them learn *how* to plan, draft, and revise their writing. We agree with Ryle that writers and practitioners of other skills "learn *how* by practice, schooled indeed by criticism and example, but often quite unaided by any lessons in the theory" (41).

Achieve Greatness in Little Things

A good friend of mine, Lloyd Shaw, is of the old school. He once said to me, "You don't understand, Diana, that teaching English is a religious pursuit." He's right, I don't—at least not in the composition classroom.

When teaching the skill of writing, we need to be more humble. Only a humble leader is able to do nothing, to yield and overcome, to watch the timing, and to give up learning. Grand goals—turning all of our students into great writers, changing their values in sudden and profound ways, transforming them into critical thinkers in one semester—are out of the question.

We must settle instead for those small victories that occur when we are least expecting them. And we must resist the temptation to take too much credit for these victories, for it is the writer, after all, who makes the breakthroughs. Our proper role is to stand by, encouraging and applauding those breakthroughs. In the words of Lao Tsu, "The sage does not attempt anything very big,/ And thus achieves greatness" (63).

Works Cited

Bartholomae, David. "The Study of Error." *College Composition and Communication* 31 (1980): 253–69.

Braine, John. *Writing a Novel.* New York: Coward, 1974.

Garrison, Roger. "One-to-One: Tutorial Instruction in Freshman Composition." *New Directions for Community Colleges* 2 (1974): 55–84.

Lao Tsu. *Tao Te Ching.* Trans. Gia-fu Feng and Jane English. New York: Vintage, 1972.

Murray, Donald M. *A Writer Teaches Writing: A Practical Method of Teaching Composition.* New York: Houghton, 1968.

Macrorie, Ken. *Telling Writing.* Rochelle Park: Hayden, 1970.

Ryle, Gilbert. *The Concept of Mind.* New York: Barnes, 1949.

Shaughnessy, Mina P. *Errors and Expectations: A Guide for the Teaching of Basic Writing.* New York: Oxford UP, 1979.

THE WRITING SITUATION

COMMUNITY

Joseph Harris

[From *A Teaching Subject: Composition Since 1966.* Joseph Harris. Upper Saddle River, NJ: Prentice-Hall, 1997. 97–116.]

Joseph Harris is the Director of Duke University's Center for Teaching, Learning, and Writing. Harris is the past editor of *CCC: College Composition and Communication,* and he has published numerous articles about teaching composition. His 1989 article in *CCC,* "The Idea of Community in the Study of Writing," won the Richard Braddock Award in 1990. He has authored two books: *Media Journal: Reading and Writing About Popular Culture* (1995) and *A Teaching Subject: Composition Since 1966* (1997), an innovative historical view of composition studies. He is currently at work on another book on reading as a critical practice, *Rewriting: How to Do Things With Texts.*

Since the early 1980s, compositionists have been using the concept of "community" to explain the larger contexts in which writers and readers participate and interact. In this closing chapter from *A Teaching Subject,* Harris extends his 1989 CCC article. He suggests that discussions of "community" are couched in "romantic, organic, and pastoral terms," so that members of a discourse community are often characterized as sharing similar "values and concerns." Focusing on this homogenous and largely positive rendering of community glosses over the many differences among members of a "community." Harris suggests that in addition to (or perhaps instead of) talking about "community," we introduce the concept of "public," which "refers not to a group of people (like community) but to a kind of space and process, a point of contact that needs both to be created and continuously maintained." Harris helps teachers and students to recognize the complexity of any writing situation, which can complicate notions of "audience" and "purpose."

If you stand, today, in Between Towns Road, you can see either way; west to the spires and towers of the cathedral and colleges; east to the yards and sheds of the motor works. You see different worlds, but there is no frontier between them; there is only the movement and traffic of a single city.

–Raymond Williams, *Second Generation* (9)

In *The Country and the City,* Raymond Williams writes of how, after a boyhood in a Welsh village, he came to the city, to Cambridge, only then to hear "from townsmen, academics, an influential version of what country life, country literature, really meant: a prepared and persuasive cultural history" (6). This odd double movement, this irony, in which one only begins to understand the place one has come from through the act of leaving it, proved to be one of the shaping forces of Williams' career—so that, some 35 years after having first gone down to Cambridge, he was still to ask himself: "Where do I stand . . . in another country or in this valuing city" (6)?

A similar irony, I think, describes my own relations to the university. I was raised in a working-class home in Philadelphia, but it was only when I went away to college that I heard the term *working-class* used or began to think of myself as part of it. Of course by then I no longer was quite part of it, or at least no longer wholly or simply part of it, but I had also been at college long enough to realize that my relations to it were similarly ambiguous—that here too was a community whose values and interests I could in part share but to some degree would always feel separate from.

This sense of difference, of overlap, of tense plurality, of being at once part of several communities and yet never wholly a member of one, has accompanied nearly all the work and study I have done at the university. So when, in the past few years, a number of teachers and theorists of writing began to talk about the idea of *community* as somehow central to our work, I was drawn to what was said. Since my aim here is to argue for a more critical look at a term that, as Williams has pointed out, "never seems to be used unfavourably" (*Keywords* 66), I want to begin by stating my admiration for the theorists—in particular, David Bartholomae and Patricia Bizzell—whose work I will discuss. They have helped us, I think, to ask some needed questions about writing and how we might go about teaching it.

Perhaps the most important work of these theorists has centered on the demystifying of the concept of *intention.* That is, rather than viewing the intentions of a writer as private and ineffable, wholly individual, they have helped us to see that it is only through being part of some ongoing discourse that we can, as individual writers, have things like points to make and purposes to achieve. As Bartholomae argues: "It is the discourse with its projects and agendas that determines what writers can and will do" ("Inventing" 139). We write not as isolated individuals but as members of communities whose beliefs, concerns, and practices both instigate and constrain, at least in part, the sorts of things we can say. Our aims and intentions in writing are thus not merely personal, idiosyncratic, but reflective of the communities to which we belong.

But while this concern with the power of social forces in writing is much needed in a field that has long focused narrowly on the composing processes of individual writers, some problems in how we have imagined those forces are now becoming clear. First, recent theories have tended to invoke the idea of community in ways at once sweeping and vague: positing discursive utopias that direct and determine the writings of their members, yet failing to state the operating rules or boundaries of these communities. One result of this has been a view of "normal discourse" in the university that is oddly lacking in conflict or change. Recent social views of writing have also often presented university discourse as almost wholly foreign to many of our students, raising questions not only about their chances of ever learning to use such an alien tongue, but of why they should want to do so in the first place. And, finally, such views have tended to polarize our talk about writing: One seems asked to defend either the power of the discourse community or the imagination of the individual writer.

In trying to work towards a more useful sense of *community*, I will take both my method and theme from Raymond Williams in his *Keywords: A Vocabulary of Culture and Society*. Williams' approach in this vocabulary reverses that of the dictionary-writer. For rather than trying to define and fix the meanings of the words he discusses, to clear up the many ambiguities involved with them, Williams instead attempts to sketch "a history and complexity of meanings" (15), to show how and why the meanings of certain words—*art, criticism, culture, history, literature* and the like—are still being contested. Certainly *community*, at once so vague and suggestive, is such a word too, and I will begin, then, with what Williams has to say about it:

> Community can be the warmly persuasive word to describe an existing set of relationships, or the warmly persuasive word to describe an alternative set of relationships. What is most important, perhaps, is that unlike all other terms of social organization (*state, nation, society*, etc.) it seems never to be used unfavourably, and never to be given any positive opposing or distinguishing term. (76)

There seem to me two warnings here. The first is that, since it has no "positive opposing" term, *community* can soon become an empty and sentimental word. And it is easy enough to point to such uses in the study of writing, particularly in the many recent calls to transform the classroom into "a community of interested readers," to recast academic disciplines as "communities of knowledgeable peers," or to translate standards of correctness into "the expectations of the academic community." In such cases, *community* tends to mean little more than a nicer, friendlier, fuzzier version of what came before.

But I think Williams is also hinting at the extraordinary rhetorical power one can gain through speaking of community. It is a concept both seductive and powerful, one that offers us a view of shared purpose and effort and that also makes a claim on us that is hard to resist. For like the pronoun *we*, *community* can be used in such a way that it invokes what it seems merely to describe. The writer says to his reader: "We are part of a certain community; they are not"—and, if the reader accepts, the statement is true. And, usually, the gambit of community, once offered, is almost impossible to decline—since what is invoked is a community of those in power, of those who know the accepted ways of writing and interpreting texts. Look, for instance, at how David Bartholomae begins his remarkable essay on "Inventing the University":

> Every time a student sits down to write for us, he has to invent the university for the occasion—invent the university, that is, or a branch of it, like history or anthropology or economics or English. The student has to learn *to speak our language, to speak as we do,* to try on the peculiar ways of knowing, selecting, evaluating, reporting, concluding, and arguing that define *the discourse of our community.* (134, my emphases)

Note here how the view of discourse at the university shifts subtly from the dynamic to the fixed—from something that a writer must continually reinvent to something that has already been invented, a language that "we" have access to but that many of our students do not. The university becomes "our community," its various and competing discourses become "our language," and the possibility of a kind of discursive free-for-all is quickly rephrased in more familiar terms of us and them, insiders and outsiders.

This tension runs throughout Bartholomae's essay. On one hand, the university is pictured as the site of many discourses, and successful writers are seen as those who are able to work both within and against them, who can find a place for themselves on the margins or borders of a number of discourses. On the other, the university is also seen as a cluster of separate communities, disciplines, in which writers must locate themselves through taking on "the commonplaces, set phrases, rituals and gestures, habits of mind, tricks of persuasion, obligatory conclusions and necessary connections that determine 'what might be said'"(146). Learning to write, then, gets defined both as the forming of an aggressive and critical stance towards a number of discourses, and as a more simple entry into the discourse of a single community.

Community thus becomes for Bartholomae a kind of stabilizing term, used to give a sense of shared purpose and effort to our dealings with the various discourses that make up the university. The question, though, of just who this "we" is that speaks "our language" is never resolved. And so while Bartholomae often refers to the "various branches" of the university, he ends up claiming to speak only of "university discourse in its most generalized form" (147). Similarly, most of the "communities" to which other current theorists refer exist at a vague remove from actual experience: The University, The Profession, The Discipline, The Academic Discourse Community. They are all quite literally utopias—nowheres, meta-communities—tied to no particular time or place, and thus oddly free of many of the tensions, discontinuities, and conflicts in the sorts of talk and writing that go on everyday in the classrooms and departments of an actual university. For all the scrutiny it has drawn, the idea of community thus still remains little more than a notion—hypothetical and suggestive, powerful yet ill-defined.[1]

Part of this vagueness stems from the ways that the notion of "discourse community" has come into the study of writing—drawing on one hand from the literary-philosophical idea of "interpretive community," and on the other from the sociolinguistic concept of "speech community," but without fully taking into account the differences between the two. "Interpretive community," as used by Stanley Fish and others, is a term in a theoretical debate; it refers not so much to specific physical groupings of people as to a kind of loose dispersed network of individuals who share certain habits of mind. "Speech community," however, is usually meant to describe an actual group of speakers living in a particular place and time. Thus while "interpretive community" can usually be taken to describe something like a world-view, discipline, or profession, "speech community" is generally used to refer more specifically to groupings like neighborhoods, settlements, or classrooms.[2]

What "discourse community" means is far less clear. In the work of some theorists, the sense of community as an active lived experience seems to drop out almost altogether, to be replaced by a shadowy network of citations and references. Linda Brodkey, for instance, argues that:

> To the extent that the academic community is a community, it is a literate community, manifested not so much at conferences as in bibliographies and libraries, a community whose members know one another better as writers than speakers. (12)

And James Porter takes this notion a step further, identifying "discourse community" with the *intertextuality* of Foucault—an argument that parallels in interesting ways E. D. Hirsch's claim, in *Cultural Literacy,* that a literate community can be defined through the clusters of allusions and references that its members share. In such views, *community* becomes little more than a metaphor, a shorthand label for a hermetic weave of texts and citations.

Most theorists who use the term, however, seem to want to keep something of the tangible and specific reference of "speech community"—to suggest, that is, that there really are "academic discourse communities" out there somewhere, real groupings of writers and readers, that we can help "initiate" our students into. But since these communities are not of speakers, but of writers and readers who are dispersed in time and space, and who rarely, if ever, meet one another in person, they invariably take on something of the ghostly and pervasive quality of "interpretive communities" as well.

There have been some recent attempts to solve this problem. John Swales, for instance, has defined "discourse community" so that the common space shared by its members is replaced by a discursive "forum," and their one-to-one interaction is reduced to a system "providing information and feedback." A forum is not a community, though, and so Swales also stipulates that there must be some common "goal" towards which the group is working (212–13). A similar stress on a shared or collaborative project runs through most other attempts to define "discourse community."[3] Thus while *community* loses its rooting in a particular place, it gains a new sense of direction and movement. Abstracted as they are from almost all other kinds of social and material relations, only an affinity of beliefs and purposes, consensus, is left to hold such communities together. The sort of group invoked is a free and voluntary gathering of individuals with shared goals and interests—of persons who have not so much been forced together as have chosen to associate with one another. So while the members of an "academic discourse community" may not meet each other very often, they are presumed to think much like one another (and thus also much *unlike* many of the people they deal with everyday: students, neighbors, coworkers in other disciplines, and so on). In the place of physical nearness we are given like-mindedness. We fall back, that is, on precisely the sort of "warmly persuasive" and sentimental view of community that Williams warns against.

One result of this has been, in recent work on the teaching of writing, the pitting of a "common" discourse against a more specialized or "privileged" one. For instance, Bartholomae argues that:

> The movement towards a more specialized discourse begins . . . both when a student can define a position of privilege, a position that sets him against a "common" discourse, and when he or she can work self-consciously, critically, against not only the "common" code but his or her own. ("Inventing" 156)

The troubles of many student writers, Bartholomae suggests, begin with their inability to imagine such a position of privilege, to define their views against some "common" way of talking about their subject. Instead, they simply repeat in their writing "what everybody knows" or what their professor has told them in her lectures. The result, of course, is that they are penalized for "having nothing really to say."

The task of the student is thus imagined as one of crossing the border from one community of discourse to another, of taking on a new sort of language. Again, the power of this metaphor seems to me undeniable. First, it offers us a way of talking about why many of our students fail to think and write as we would like them to *without* having to suggest that they are somehow slow or inept because they do not. Instead, one can argue that the problem is less one of intelligence than socialization, that such students are simply unused to the peculiar demands of academic discourse. Second, such a view reminds us (as Patricia Bizzell has often argued) that one's role as a teacher is not merely to inform but to persuade, that we ask our students to acquire not only certain skills and data, but to try on new forms of thinking and talking about the world as well. The problem is, once having posited two separate communities with strikingly different ways of making sense of the world, it then becomes difficult to explain how or why one moves from one group to the other. If to enter the academic community a student must "learn to speak our language," become accustomed and reconciled to our ways of doing things with words, then how exactly is she to do this?

Bizzell seems to picture the task as one of assimilation, of conversion almost. One sets aside one's former ways to become a member of the new community. As she writes:

> Mastery of academic discourse must begin with socialization to the community's ways, in the same way that one enters any cultural group. One must first "go native." ("Foundationalism" 53)

And one result of this socialization, Bizzell argues, may "mean being completely alienated from some other, socially disenfranchised discourses" (43). The convert must be born again.

While Bartholomae uses the language of paradox to describe what must be accomplished:

> To speak with authority [our students] have to speak not only in another's voice but through another's code; and they not only have to do this, they have to speak in the voice and through the codes of those of us with power and wisdom; and they not only have to do this, they have to do it before they know what they are doing, before they have a project to participate in, and before, at least in the terms of our disciplines, they have anything to say. ("Inventing" 156)

And so here, too, the learning of a new discourse seems to rest, at least in part, on a kind of mystical leap of mind. Somehow the student must "invent the university," appropriate a way of speaking and writing belonging to others.

The emphasis of Bartholomae's pedagogy, though, seems to differ in slight but important ways from his theory. In *Facts, Artifacts, and Counterfacts*, a text for a course in basic writing, Bartholomae and Anthony Petrosky describe a class that begins by having students write on what they already think and feel about a certain subject (for example, adolescence or work), and then tries to get them to redefine that thinking through a seminar-like process of reading and dialogue. The course thus appears to build on the overlap between the students' "common" discourses and the "academic" ones of their teachers, as they are asked to work "within and against" both their own languages and those of the texts they are reading (8). The move, then, is not simply from one discourse to another but towards a "hesitant and tenuous relationship" to both (41).

Such a pedagogy helps remind us that the borders of most discourses are hazily marked and often traveled, and that the communities they define are thus often indistinct and overlapping. As Williams again has suggested, one does not step cleanly and wholly from one community to another, but is caught instead in an always changing mix of dominant, residual, and emerging discourses (*Marxism* 121–27). Rather than framing our work in terms of helping students move from one community of discourse into another, then, it might prove more useful (and accurate) to view our task as adding to or complicating their uses of language.

I am not proposing such addition as a neutral or value-free pedagogy. I would instead expect and hope for a kind of useful dissonance as students are confronted with ways of talking about the world with which they are not yet wholly familiar. What I am arguing against, though, is the notion that our students should necessarily be working towards the mastery of some particular, well-defined sort of discourse. It seems to me that they might better be encouraged towards a kind of polyphony—an awareness of and pleasure in the various competing discourses that make up their own.

To illustrate what such an awareness might involve, let me turn briefly to some student writings. The first comes from a paper on *Hunger of Memory*, in which Richard Rodriguez describes how, as a Spanish-speaking child growing up in California, he was confronted in school by the need to master the "public language" of his English-speaking teachers and classmates. In her response, Sylvia, a young black woman from Philadelphia, explains that her situation is perhaps more complex, since she is aware of having at least two "private languages": A Southern-inflected speech which she uses with her parents and older relatives, and the "street talk" which she shares with her friends and neighbors. Sylvia concludes her essay as follows:

> My third and last language is one that Rodriguez referred to as "public language." Like Rodriguez, I too am having trouble excepting and using "public language." Specifically, I am referring to Standard English which is defined in some English texts as:
>
> "The speaking and writing of cultivated people . . . the variety of spoken and written language which enjoys cultural prestige, and which is the medium of education, journalism, and literature. Competence in its use is necessary for advancement in many occupations."
>
> Presently, I should say that "public language" is *becoming* my language as I am not yet comfortable in speaking it and even less comfortable in writing it. According to my mother anyone who speaks in "proper English" is "putting on airs."
>
> In conclusion, I understand the relevance and importance of learning to use "public language," but, like Rodriguez, I am also afraid of losing my "private identity"—that part of me that my parents, my relatives, and my friends know and understand. However, on the other hand, within me, there is an intense desire to grow and become a part of the "public world"—a world that exists outside of the secure and private world of my parents, relatives, and friends. If I want to belong, I must learn the "public language" too.

The second passage is written by Ron, a white factory worker in central Pennsylvania, and a part-time student. It closes an end-of-the-term reflection on his work in the writing course he was taking.

> As I look back over my writings for this course I see a growing acceptance of the freedom to write as I please, which is allowing me to almost enjoy writing (I can't believe it). So I tried this approach in another class I am taking. In that class we need to write summations of articles each week. The first paper that I handed in, where I used more feeling in my writing, came back with a (√-) and the comment, "Stick to the material." My view is, if they open the pen I will run as far as I can, but I won't break out because I have this bad habit, it's called eating.

What I admire in both passages is the writer's unwillingness to reduce his or her options to a simple either/or choice. Sylvia freely admits her desire to learn the language of the public world. Her "I understand . . . but" suggests, however, that she is not willing to loosen completely her ties to family and neighborhood in order to do so. And Ron is willing to run with the more free style of writing he has discovered, "if they open the pen." Both seem aware, that is, of being implicated in not one but a number of discourses, a number of communities, whose beliefs and practices conflict as well as align. And it is the tension between those discourses—none repudiated or chosen wholly—that gives their texts such interest.

There has been much debate in recent years over whether we need, above all, to respect our students' "right to their own language," or to teach them the ways and forms of "academic discourse." Both sides of this argument, in the end, rest their cases on the same suspect generalization: That we and our students belong to different and fairly distinct communities of discourse, that we have "our" "academic" discourse and they have "their own" "common" (?!) ones. The choice is one between opposing fictions. The "languages" that our students bring to us cannot but have been shaped, at least in part, by their experiences in school, and thus must, in some ways, already be "academic." Similarly, our teaching will and should always be affected by a host of beliefs and values that we hold regardless of our roles as academics. What we see in the classroom, then, are not two coherent and competing discourses but many overlapping and conflicting ones. Our students are no more wholly "outside" the discourse of the university than we are wholly "within" it. We are all at once both insiders and outsiders. The fear (or hope) of either camp that our students will be "converted" from "their" language to "ours" is both overstated and misleading. The task facing our students, as Min-zhan Lu has argued, is not to leave one community in order to enter another, but to *reposition* themselves in relation to several continuous and conflicting discourses. Similarly, our goals as teachers need not be to initiate our students into the values and practices of some new community, but to offer them the chance to reflect critically on those discourses—of home, school, work, the media and the like—to which they already belong.

"Alongside each utterance . . . off-stage voices can be heard," writes Barthes (21). We do not write simply as individuals, but we do not write simply as members of a community either. The point is, to borrow a turn of argument from Stanley Fish, that one does not *first* decide to act as a member of one community rather than some other, and *then* attempt to conform to its (rather than some other's) set of beliefs and practices. Rather, one is always *simultaneously* a part of several discourses, several communities, is always already committed to a number of conflicting beliefs and practices.[4] As Mary Louise Pratt has pointed out: "People and groups are constituted not by single unified belief systems, but by competing self-contradicting ones" ("Interpretive Strategies," 228). One does not necessarily stop being a feminist, for instance, in order to write literary criticism (although one discourse may try to repress or usurp the other). And, as the example of Williams shows, one does not necessarily give up the loyalties of a working-class youth in order to become a university student (although some strain will no doubt be felt).

In *The Country and the City*, Williams notes an "escalator effect" in which each new generation of English writers points to a lost age of harmony and organic community that thrived just before their own, only of course to have the era in which they were living similarly romanticized by the writers who come after them (9–12). Rather than doing much the same, romanticizing academic discourse as occurring in a kind of single cohesive community, I would urge that we instead think of it as taking place in something more like a city. That is, instead of presenting academic discourse as coherent and well-defined, we might be better off viewing it as polyglot, as a sort of space in which competing beliefs and practices intersect with and confront one another. One does not need consensus to have community. Matters of accident, necessity, and convenience hold groups together as well. Social theories of reading and writing have helped to deconstruct the myth of the autonomous essential self. There seems little reason now to grant a similar sort of organic unity to the idea of community.

The metaphor of the city would also allow us to view a certain amount of change and struggle within a community not as threats to its coherence but as normal activity. The members of many classrooms and academic departments, not to mention disciplines, often seem to share few enough beliefs or practices with one another. Yet these communities exert a very real influence on the discourses of their members. We need to find a way to talk about their workings without first assuming a consensus that may not be there. As Bizzell has recently come to argue:

> Healthy discourse communities, like healthy human beings, are also masses of contradictions. . . . We should accustom ourselves to dealing with contradictions, instead of seeking a theory that appears to abrogate them. ("What" 235)

I would urge an even more specific and material view of community: One that, like a city, allows for both consensus and conflict, and that holds room for ourselves, our disciplinary colleagues, our university coworkers, *and* our students. In short, I think we need to look more closely at the discourses of communities that are more than communities of discourse alone. While I don't mean to discount the effects of belonging to a discipline, I think that we dangerously abstract and idealize the workings of "academic discourse" by taking the kinds of rarefied talk and writing that go on at conferences and in journals as the norm, and viewing much of the other sorts of talk and writing that occur at the university as deviations from or approximations of that standard. It may prove more useful to center our study, instead, on the everyday struggles and mishaps of the talk in our classrooms and departments, with their mixings of sometimes conflicting and sometimes conjoining beliefs and purposes.

Indeed I would suggest that we reserve our uses of *community* to describe the workings of such specific and local groups. We have other words —*discourse, language, voice, ideology, hegemony*—to chart the perhaps less immediate (though still powerful) effects of broader social forces on our talk and writing. None of them is, surely, without its own echoes of meaning, both suggestive and troublesome. But none, I believe, carries with it the sense of like-mindedness and warmth that make community at once such an appealing and limiting concept. As teachers and theorists of writing, we need a vocabulary that will allow us to talk about certain forces as social rather than communal, as involving power but not always consent. Such talk could give us a fuller picture of the lived experience of teaching, learning and writing in a university today.

"I don't want no Jesuses in my promised land," is how Lester Bangs put it (259). The line comes near the end of a piece he wrote on the Clash, and to appreciate what he meant by it, you have to know that Bangs loved the Clash, admired not only their skill and energy as musicians, but also their lack of pretense, the wit and nerve of their lyrics, and, most of all, the open and democratic stance they took toward their fans. In their songs the Clash often railed against the culture and politics of Maggie Thatcher's Britain, but they had little interest in becoming the spokesmen for a cause or the leaders of a movement. But neither did they pose as celebrities or keep a distance from their fans. Instead, at least early in their career, they simply let themselves be part of the crowd, talking and drinking and hanging out with the people who came to listen to their music. Bangs saw in them what rock culture might look like if it wasn't divided into leaders and followers, stars and groupies, backstage insiders and outside nobodies. No Jesus, maybe not even a promised land, but a moment to be part of.

Like Bangs I don't want no Jesuses in my promised land either. Most talk about utopias scares me. What I value instead is a kind of openness, a lack of plan, a chance both to be among others and to choose my own way. It is a kind of life I associate with the city, with the sort of community in which people are brought together more by accident or need than by shared values. A city brings together people who do not so much choose to live together as they are simply thrown together, and who must then make the best they can of their common lot. The core values of this loose form of community, it seems to me, are a tolerance of diversity and a respect for privacy. For instance, I know very few of the people who live on my city block by name, and have at best only a vague idea of what they do for a living, much less of what their politics or beliefs or values are. And yet it is a great block to live on: People take care of their houses, shovel the snow from their walks, keep an eye out for the neighborhood kids, report prowlers, bring lost dogs back to their homes, buy church candy and Girl Scout cookies, and the like. We keep watch but we do not intrude, forming something like what Richard Sennett, also in writing about city life, has called a "community of strangers" (*Fall* 4).

Although of course such an absence of shared values has more often been viewed as a loss. There is a long tradition of lament among intellectuals about the disappearance of real community, a nostalgia for the closeness of the town or village or parish that, it is argued, has since given way to the anonymous crowds of the city. Such a yearning for community also marks many utopian dreams of reform. I know of very few utopias in film or literature that are set in large industrial cities, although many dystopias are. (Think of *Blade Runner, Robocop, Escape from New York.*) There are no Jesuses in the big city, or actually, there's often a new one on each corner, and their clamor and conflict doesn't much make for a vision of ideal community. But there is also a freedom to be had in the chaos and anonymity of city life. That has always been its allure. In the essay which begins this chapter, I argued that we have tended to talk about "discourse communities" in far too romantic, organic, and pastoral terms, that we have in effect pictured such communities more as small closely knit villages—where everyone pretty much shares the same set of values and concerns—than as large and heteroglot cities, where everyone doesn't. I want to push that contrast a little further here, to suggest how a more urban and less utopian view of social life might help us rethink the kinds of work that can go on in our classrooms.

In doing so, I want to bring a term back into our conversation that was once a key one in rhetoric but seems somehow recently to have fallen out of use or favor. Back in 1989, I cited Williams's famous remark that, alone among the words used to describe social groups, community seems "never to be used unfavourably, and never to be given any positive opposing or distinguishing term" (76). Since then no one has come up to me in order to say, why yes there is such a positive opposing term—but in continuing to read and think about the issue, I am growing more convinced that one does exist. The word is *public,* a term that does not even appear in Williams's *Keywords,* but that has been central to the work of many American intellectuals, among them John Dewey, Walter Lippmann, Hannah Arendt, C. Wright Mills, Richard Sennett, and, most recently, Kenneth Cmiel.[5] The peculiar importance of the term to these thinkers has to do with how they have tried to use it in theorizing a *large-scale* form of democracy, as a key (if troubled) means of bridging the interests of local communities and individuals with those of a state or nation. What I find most interesting and useful about this notion of a *public* is that it refers not to a group of people (like community) but to a kind of space and process, a point of contact that needs both to be created and continuously maintained.

Richard Sennett draws on a similar distinction in *The Fall of Public Man*. For Sennett, a public space is one where the members of various communities can meet to negotiate their differences. It is a site of conflict rather than consensus, of bartering rather than sharing. The classic example would be a thriving square or market in a cosmopolitan city. It makes little sense to talk of New York, for instance, as a community; it is too sprawling, diverse, heterogeneous. But there is some sense to speaking of it as a kind of public space where the representatives of various boroughs or neighborhoods, the advocates of competing interests or constituencies, can come to argue out their needs and differences. I don't mean here to argue for some idealized version of a public sphere, some free market of viewpoints and ideas. Not all communities or interests are allowed anything near a fair or equal hearing in most public debates, and some are not allowed access to them at all. I am instead thinking of a public space as a place where differences are made visible, and thus where the threat of conflict or even violence is always present. This means that we need to resist moves to romanticize conflict in order to argue for something more like *civility*, a willingness to live with difference. As Jane Jacobs puts it in her classic study of urban life, *The Death and Life of Great American Cities*, "The tolerance, the room for great differences among neighbors . . . are possible and normal only when streets of great cities have built-in equipment allowing strangers to dwell in peace together on civilized but essentially dignified and reserved terms."[6]

Thinking in terms of public rather than communal life can give us a way of describing the sort of talk that takes place *across* borders and constituencies. It suggests that we speak as public intellectuals when we talk with strangers rather than with the members of our own communities and disciplines (or of our own interdisciplinary cliques). And so what I do want to argue for here is a view of the classroom as a public space rather than as a kind of entry point into some imagined community of academic discourse. Most English classrooms are, I think, set up to move from conflict to consensus, from a diverse and competing set of readings (and maybe misreadings) to a single interpretation that teacher and students forge together as a group. The routine goes something like this: The teacher begins by asking for a reading of a certain line or passage from the text at hand and a student volunteers one. The teacher then points to a difficulty or problem with this reading (or asks another student to do so), and thus prompts an alternative reading of the passage. This second interpretation is also critiqued and then replaced by yet a third reading, and so on, until at some point the class arrives at a (more or less) common understanding of the passage. This problem-solving process is then repeated until the class builds a kind of consensual reading of the text as a whole. (A drawback of this approach is that when students are later asked to write on the text, they often feel there is nothing left for them to say about it.)

Imagine instead a class that worked not to resolve such differences in reading but to highlight them, that tried to show what might be involved in arguing for the various ways of understanding a text—as well as what might be at stake in the conflicts between them. Such a class would not try to get students to agree on what a certain text means but to see how and why various readers might disagree about what it means. And it would then ask each of them to take a stand, to commit herself to a position on the text and the issues around it. The aim of discussion in such a class would be for most people to leave thinking that just about everybody else has got it wrong, or at best only half right, and that they're going to write a paper over the weekend which shows why.

But I don't think that is likely to occur when the only alternative readings students come across are ones posed by their teacher. Many students are only too well used to coming to class only to find out, in effect, that they've blown it once again, that the poem or story they've just read doesn't mean what they thought it did—or what's probably worse, that the poem or story they couldn't figure out at all last night seems perfectly clear to their teacher. So even when we insist we are only posing an "other" way of looking at the text, many students are likely to take it (and with good reason) as the "right" way of reading it. But something else can happen when they begin to realize that other members of the class disagree with them about what a text means or how good it is. These are real people, after all. To find out that they disagree with you is both less threatening and more troubling than having your reading challenged as a matter of routine by your teacher.

This can become very clear when you have a group of students watch TV together in a classroom, for it turns what is usually a private experience into a public one. The freshman who chortles appreciatively at a sitcom line about dumb but sexy blondes, only to realize that the young woman he's been trying to impress for the last few weeks is now sitting in stony silence right next to him, suddenly has some explaining to do. And so does she, if others in the class see her response as being less correct than humorless. Similarly, the student who jokes that Roseanne Arnold is disgusting may soon find himself dealing with several others who think that actually she's pretty funny, much as the one who thinks *My So-Called Life* is moving and realistic will need to answer to those classmates who could care less about a group of whining suburban kids. What happens in such situations is that students start to hold each other to account for their readings. They begin to argue not with their teacher but among themselves about the meaning and value of what they've seen.

Let me try to give you a more detailed sense of what it might mean to set up a classroom as such a public space or zone of contact. In a previous interchapter I wrote of a beginning undergraduate class that I teach called Writing About Movies. Again, the goal of this course is not so much to introduce students to the academic study of the cinema as it is to get them thinking and writing about the ways they already have of looking at movies and TV. As a way of beginning to surface these kinds of viewing strategies, one of the first things I usually ask students to do is to locate a point where their understanding of a film breaks down, to write about a scene or image in a movie that they have trouble making sense of—that confuses or disturbs them, or that they have trouble fitting in with the rest of the film, or that just makes them angry somehow. I then ask them to recreate the scene as well as they can in their writing and to define the problem it poses for them as viewers.

One term we looked at Spike Lee's *Do The Right Thing*. Lee's movie is set in the Bed-Stuy neighborhood of Brooklyn and offers a picaresque series of glimpses into life on a city block on the hottest day of summer. Lee himself plays Mookie, a young black man who delivers pizzas for Sal (Danny Aiello), a likable Italian patriarch who owns and runs the neighborhood pizzeria, and who along with his two sons, both of whom work in his shop, are almost the only white characters we see. (City cops, a lost motorist, and a brownstoning yuppie are the only others.) Early on in the movie we see what seems a routine blowup between Sal and one of his customers, Buggin' Out, another young black man who fancies himself something of a political activist and tries to organize a neighborhood boycott of the pizzeria until Sal replaces some of the pictures of Italians—Rocky Marciano, Frank Sinatra, Al Pacino—on his "Wall of Fame" with photos of African Americans. The only support Buggin' Out is able to raise, though, comes from (even by the standards of this neighborhood) two fringe characters: Radio Raheem, a mean-looking hulk of a man with no visible occupation other than walking up and down the street blaring the rap music of Public Enemy from his giant boom box, and Smiley, a stuttering hawker of photographs of Malcolm X and Martin Luther King (which we see no one but Mookie buy). While tempers flare at a number of other points during the day, none of these exchanges come to much, and the overall mood of the film is comic and quick. So when near the end of the movie Sal decides to reopen his doors to give a few teenagers a late-night slice, it seems as if the boycott and whatever threat it might have posed to the routine peace of the block are over, that the neighborhood has managed to get through the hottest day of the year without serious incident. This isn't the case, though, as Buggin' Out, Raheem, and Smiley also take this occasion to renew their threat to close Sal down, and Sal and Raheem find themselves in a fight that erupts quickly and ends tragically. Harsh words lead to a wrestling match that sends the two men crashing into the street. Raheem pins Sal to the sidewalk and seems on the verge of strangling him when a white policeman pulls him away and, as a crowd watches in horror, chokes Raheem to death with his nightstick. Panicked, the police throw Raheem's lifeless body into a squad car and escape, leaving the enraged crowd to loot and burn Sal's pizzeria in revenge.[7]

About a third of the class that spring chose to write on this scene, and it's easy to see why, since it seems so unclear as to who if anyone "does the right thing" in it. So I decided to start our talk about the movie by looking at three of their responses to it. I began by noting that all three pieces had virtually the same concluding paragraph: a plea for greater openness and understanding among all people of all races—be they white, black, yellow, whatever. My sense was that these paragraphs had less to do with the ending of Lee's film than with how these students (and most of the others in the class) felt they were required to end a paper written for school: on a tone of moral uplift, showing that they had indeed learned a valuable lesson from this important work of art, and so on. I didn't push this point much; I simply said I was interested less in what these writers agreed on than in how and why they differed in their views of the film, which meant I wanted us to look more closely at what got said in the body of their pieces than in their official conclusions. It's like TV sitcoms, I argued; no matter what, they always end happily, with everybody loving and hugging everybody else, but if you pay attention to what goes on *before* they wrap everything up, you often find both a more tense and interesting view of work and family life. (I think most students took my point, since I read far fewer homilies at the end of their second drafts.)

And what most interested me about these three readings, why I chose them to begin our talk in class, was how each writer defines the boundaries of the scene differently, so that in each of their accounts a different action was emphasized, and a different sort of blame or responsibility is assessed. In her paper on "Radio Raheem's Death," Holly described the strangling of Raheem in detail.

> This scene starts out with a racial fight in the street between Radio Raheem, an African American youth who carries around an enormous boom box that symbolizes his power, and Sal, a white, middle-class restaurant owner. People gather around the scuttle as Raheem begins to strangle Sal. This is when the police show up at the scene. Two white policemen pull Raheem off Sal and drag him off into the street. Meanwhile, everyone is screaming in a riotous manner. The police officer, named Gary, with the fair hair and the mustache puts his nightstick around Raheem's neck. Gary then goes through some kind of racial rage and begins to put pressure on Raheem's neck. Everyone watches in terror as they see their friend and neighbor get strangled to death.

Before anyone can stop Gary (and perhaps before he fully knows what he is doing), Raheem falls dead to the ground. Then, as Holly recounts the scene,

> [The police] begin to kick him and tell him to get up. When they realized what they had done they picked up Raheem's dead body and put him in the back of a police car. Spike Lee's camera work focuses on Raheem and then out of the back window of the car at people left in the street. . . . They stare into the camera and yell murder and real names of people who were actual fatalities from police brutality cases. . . . That concludes the scene I have chosen.

From this Holly was led to conclude that the "problem . . . in my eyes, is the police brutality and how it is covered up." What bothered Samantha, though, in "Isolating One's Heritage," is the illogic of the riot that follows Raheem's death. She began her account of the scene almost exactly where Holly left off:

> As Sal's pizzeria was burning down the crowd suddenly turned around and altered all their attention toward the Korean family across the street persistantely swinging a broom at the people signalling them to stay away from their market. The Korean man was screaming don't touch my store, leave us alone we are the same as you, we are black too. One of the older men in the crowd says he's right there the same as us leave them alone. Instantly the crowd agrees and turns away with aggression yet fatigue.

This turn of events troubles Samantha, since it is made clear throughout the film that Sal treats his customers with an affection and respect that the Korean grocer lacks entirely. In trying to explain the actions of the crowd, Samantha goes on to suggest that while Sal is shown as "open-minded" through most of the film, in the end he proves "not willing to change, or 'go along' with the blacks, but the Koreans were." For her the real issue thus comes down to who gets to claim ownership of the neighborhood. "Whatever the case the blacks were still trying to make the point of saying this is our neighborhood, we have lived here for years and you think you can just come in and take over." Underlying the savagery of the riot, then, is the sort of ethnic pride that warrants the use of "violence to receive . . . social justice"—a phrasing that seems to obliquely criticize Malcolm X's famous claim, quoted at the end of the movie, that oppressed peoples have "the right to do what is necessary" in fighting for their freedom. And so while Holly's horror at the cops' brutality led her to see Lee as arguing against the racism of "the system" or "the man," Samantha read the movie instead as indicting the sort of ethnic or racial pride that can quickly devolve into simple racism and violence.

Jim offered yet a third reading of the scene that focused on the verbal duel between Sal and Raheem that leads up to the fight described by Holly and the riot discussed by Samantha. Looking at how Sal shifts suddenly from the role of friendly *pater familias* to screaming racist led Jim to conclude,

> . . . Here you saw Sal's true, hidden feelings come out. Through the entire film you see how Sal gets along with the blacks, but when confronted, he explodes physically and verbally at the blacks. . . . The film illustrates how deep nested and inevitable racism is. Though Sal accepted the blacks and was thankful for their business, that was the extent of it. As people, he didn't really respect them. . . .

And so while Jim agrees with Samantha and Holly in seeing the movie as an attack on racism, he differs with Samantha in viewing Lee's anger as directed largely against *white* racists, and unlike Holly he refuses to sharply distinguish the actions of Sal from those of the cops. In many ways, Jim gives the bleakest reading of the movie, since he sees its critique as directed at one of the most likable characters in it. If Sal is a racist, he seems to imply, then so are we all, and the inevitable result of this will be violence, either to defend "the power" or to fight it.

In leading our talk about these papers, I insisted that at first our goal would simply be to understand and describe (but not yet to evaluate) the readings of the film they offered. I thus asked the class not to compare these three readings yet, to argue right off for one or the other, but instead to think about how you might go about making the best possible case for each. Where else might you go to in the film, for instance, to support Holly's sense that Lee's anger is directed more against the "system" (as represented by the cops) than against white people in general (as represented by Sal and his sons)? Or how might you strengthen Samantha's claim that the "ethnic pride" of blacks is also being critiqued in the film? To have them do so, I broke the class into three groups (of about six or seven students), with each assigned the task of coming up with more evidence for one of these ways of reading the film.

Each of the groups proved able to come up with a striking amount of support for the view of the film they had been asked to discuss. The students who talked about Jim's paper noted several other scenes where Sal could be seen less as friendly than as patronizing; they then remarked that it was, after all, the director of the movie, Spike Lee, who plays Mookie, the character who starts the riot, which would seem to suggest that he has at least some sympathy for such actions; and they also pointed to how the last words of the film literally belong to Malcolm X, in a printed passage that speaks of the possible need for violence in a struggle for justice. In response, the group working with Holly's paper pointed out that in the scenes following the riot we see Sal and Mookie come if not to a reconciliation then at least to an uneasy truce. They also noted that, in the closing shot of the film, we hear the voice of a local radio DJ lamenting the violence that has just taken place and exhorting *political* action instead. Similarly, the group dealing with Samantha's paper had a list of scenes that poked fun (sometimes gentle and sometimes not) at the black residents of the block, and they also noted that the passage by Malcolm X at the end of the movie is preceded by one in which Martin Luther King argues *against* the use of violence. And so by the end of our talk that evening, we had developed not a single collective reading of the film but three distinct and competing views of it. This allowed me to suggest to the class that, in revising their own writings for next week, their task was not to somehow move closer to some ideal or correct understanding of the movie, but to show why, when faced with such an array of competing interpretations, they chose to read it as they did—that our aim was not to reach a consensus about the meaning or value of the text, but to enter into a critical, sustained, and public interchange of views about it.

In *A Rhetoric of Motives,* Kenneth Burke compares the give-and-take of intellectual debate to a "somewhat formless parliamentary wrangle," a "horse-trading" of ideas in which individual critics try to grab support for their own positions through whatever deals, borrowings, and alliances they can strike up with some colleagues, and whatever raids or attacks they can make on the views of others (188). While I prefer this description of intellectual work to Burke's much more often quoted metaphor of an ongoing parlor conversation, I have to admit that there also seems something slightly disreputable about it, and Burke himself points to the temptation, especially among teachers, to give form to such wrangles by placing opposing views in dialectical tension with each other, so their conflicts can then be resolved at some "higher" or "ultimate" level (188–89). The best example of this sort of dialectic can of course be found, as Burke points out, in the dialogues of Plato, which characteristically begin with Socrates facing a diverse set of opinions on a subject (what is piety? what is justice?) and then gradually leading his listeners to a consensus about what can or cannot be known about it. In Book I of *The Republic,* Socrates himself argues for the merit of this approach, saying,

> If we were to oppose him [Thrasymachus, a sophist who is his current foil in the dialogue] . . . with a parallel set speech on the blessings of the just life, then another speech from him in turn, then another from us, then we should have to count and measure the blessings mentioned on each side, and we should need some judges to decide the case. If on the other hand, we investigate the question, as we were doing, *by seeking agreement with each other,* then we ourselves can be both the judges and the advocates. (348b, my italics)

From opposing speeches to agreement, diversity to consensus, wrangle to dialogue—that is the usual progress of teaching. What I have hoped to suggest here is the value of keeping things at the level of a wrangle, of setting up our classrooms so a variety of views are laid out and the arguments for them made, but then trying *not* to push for consensus, for an ultimate view that resolves or explains the various conflicts which can surface in such talk. A problem with much teaching, it seems to me, is that the teacher often serves only too well as both judge and advocate of what gets said, pointing out the weaknesses of some positions while accenting the strengths of others. I'd like to see instead a classroom where student writings function something more like the "set speeches" that Socrates derides, that serve as positions in an argument whose blessings we can count and measure together, but whose final merits we can leave students to judge for themselves. That is, I'd rather have a wrangle, even if it is somewhat formless (or perhaps because it is), that gives students a set of chances to come to their own sense of a text or issue than a dialogue whose course has been charted in advance by their teacher. I don't want no Jesus and I don't want no Socrates either. What I do want is a sort of teaching that aims more to keep the conversation going than to lead it toward a certain end, that tries to set up not a community of agreement but a community of strangers, a public space where students can begin to form their own voices as writers and intellectuals.

Notes

[1] One might argue that there never really is a "we" for whom the language of the university (or a particular discipline) is fully invented and accessible. Greg Meyers, for instance, has shown how two biologists—presumably well-trained scholars long initiated into the practices of their discipline—had to reshape their writings extensively to make them fit in with "what might be said" in the journals of their own field. Like our students, we too must reinvent the university whenever we sit down to write.

[2] See, for instance, Dell Hymes in *Foundations in Sociolinguistics:* "For our purposes it appears most useful to reserve the notion of community for a local unit, characterized for its members by common locality and primary interaction, and to admit exceptions cautiously" (51).

[3] See, for instance, Bizzell on the need for "emphasizing the crucial function of a collective project in unifying the group" ("What" 222), and Bruffee on the notion that "to learn is to work collaboratively . . . among a community of knowledgeable peers" (646).

[4] Bruce Robbins makes much the same case in "Professionalism and Politics: Toward Productively Divided Loyalties." Fish too seems recently to be moving toward this position, arguing that an interpretive community is an "engine of change" fueled by the interaction and conflict of the various beliefs and practices that make it up. As he puts it, "Beliefs are not all held at the same level or operative at the same time. Beliefs, if I may use a metaphor, are nested, and on occasion they may affect and even alter the entire system or network they comprise" ("Change" 429).

[5] In *The Last Intellectuals,* Russell Jacoby calls on American academics to broaden the sphere of their influence. In "Making Journalism More Public," Jay Rosen both restates this call and provides a useful overview of attempts to theorize a workable notion of the "public."

[6] Readers of her work will, of course, recognize the strong influence of Jacobs on my vision here of an urban counterutopia. In revising this chapter, I was pleased to discover that Iris Marion Young also invokes this passage from Jacobs in order to make a very similar argument to my own for the city as an alternative model of social life. See her *Justice and the Politics of Difference* (226–56).

[7] Of course this scene also offers a kind of nightmare counter to my praise of urban life: the city as the site of violence, anarchy. Again, the risk of diversity will always be conflict, as advocates of organic community are usually quick to point out.

Works Cited

Bangs, Lester. "The Clash." *Psychotic Reactions and Carburetor Dung.* Ed. Greil Marcus. New York: Vintage, 1988. 224–59.

Barthes, Roland. *S/Z.* Trans. Richard Miller. New York: Hill, 1974.

Bartholomae, David. "Inventing the University." *When a Writer Can't Write: Studies in Writer's Block and Other Composing-Process Problems.* Ed. Mike Rose. New York: Guilford, 1985. 134–65.

————, and Anthony Petrosky. *Facts, Artifacts, and Counterfacts: Theory and Method for a Reading and Writing Course.* Upper Montclair, NJ: Boynton, 1986.

Bizzell, Patricia. "Foundationalism and Anti-Foundationalism in Composition Studies." *Pre/Text* 7 (1986): 37–57.

————. "What Is a Discourse Community?" *Academic Discourse and Critical Consciousness.* Pittsburgh: U of Pittsburgh P, 1992. 222–37.

Brodkey, Linda. *Academic Writing as Social Practice.* Philadelphia: Temple UP, 1987.

Bruffee, Kenneth A. "Collaborative Learning and the 'Conversation of Mankind'." *College English* 46 (Nov. 1984): 635–52.

Burke, Kenneth. *A Rhetoric of Motives.* Berkeley: U of California P, 1969.

Fish, Stanley. "Change." *South Atlantic Quarterly* 86 (1987): 423–44.

Hirsch, E. D., Jr. *Cultural Literacy: What Every American Needs to Know.* Boston: Houghton, 1987.

Hymes, Dell. *Foundations in Sociolinguistics: An Ethnographic Approach.* Philadelphia: U of Pennsylvania P, 1974.

Jacobs, Jane. *The Death and Life of Great American Cities.* 1961. New York: Modern Library, 1993.

Jacoby, Russell. *The Last Intellectuals: American Culture in the Age of Academe.* New York: Basic, 1987.

Plato. *The Republic.* Trans. G. M. A. Grube. Indianapolis: Hackett, 1974.

Porter, James. "Intertextuality and the Discourse Community." *Rhetoric Review* 5 (1986): 34–37.

Pratt, Mary Louise. "Interpretive Strategies/Strategic Interpretations: On Anglo-American Reader Response Criticism." *Boundary* 2.11 (1982–83): 201–31.

Robbins, Bruce. "Professionalism and Politics: Toward Productively Divided Loyalties." *Profession* 85 (1985): 1–9.

Rodriguez, Richard. *Hunger of Memory.* Boston: Godine, 1981.

Rosen, Jay. "Making Journalism More Public." *Communication* 12 (1991): 267–84.

Sennett, Richard. *The Fall of Public Man.* New York: Knopf, 1977.

Swales, John. "Discourse Communities, Genres, and English as an International Language." *World Englishes* 7 (1988): 211–20.

Williams, Raymond. *The Country and the City.* New York: Oxford UP, 1973.

————. *Keywords: A Vocabulary of Culture and Society.* New York: Oxford UP, 1976.

————. *Marxism and Literature.* New York: Oxford UP, 1977.

————. *Second Generation.* New York: Horizon, 1964.

Young, Iris Marion. *Justice and the Politics of Difference.* Princeton: Princeton UP, 1990.

INVENTING THE UNIVERSITY

David Bartholomae

[From *When a Writer Can't Write: Studies in Writer's Block and Other Composing Problems.* Ed. Mike Rose. New York: Guilford, 1985. 134–65.]

Professor of English and chair of the department of English at the University of Pittsburgh, David Bartholomae has been a leading scholar and a widely respected voice in composition studies for nearly two decades. With Anthony Petrosky, he coedited *Facts, Artifacts, and Counterfacts* (1986) and *Ways of Reading* (now in its 4th edition, 1996), two books that have become standards for those studying and teaching composition. Bartholomae has published numerous articles in leading journals and in important collections. He has served as chair of the annual Conference on College Composition and Communication and the second Modern Language Association conference on literacy. He is currently coeditor of the *Pittsburgh Series on Composition, Literacy, and*

Culture published by the University of Pittsburgh Press. His article "The Study of Error" (1980), which is included in Part Five of this book, won the Richard Braddock Award from CCCC in 1981.

In this now classic and often reprinted essay—written nearly ten years before Harris's *A Teaching Subject: Composition since 1966*—Bartholomae discusses academic writing situations. He argues that the writing that students do in colleges and universities takes place in a complex context of already ongoing disciplinary discourses. Bartholomae shows that assessing an academic writing situation is more complex than determining purpose and analyzing audience. Instead, students have to learn the languages of the academy, and those languages are embedded in and are the products of a complex academic culture governed in part by disciplinary and institutional conventions. Illustrating his discussion with several student essays, Bartholomae examines ways in which students attempt to join various academic discourse communities. In the process of his analyses, Bartholomae offers several solid suggestions for how teachers can more effectively engage students in purposeful writing projects, initiating them, in a sense, to the business of the academy.

Education may well be, as of right, the instrument whereby every individual, in a society like our own, can gain access to any kind of discourse. But we well know that in its distribution, in what it permits and in what it prevents, it follows the well-trodden battle-lines of social conflict. Every educational system is a political means of maintaining or of modifying the appropriation of discourse, with the knowledge and the powers it carries with it.

—Foucault, "The Discourse on Language"

Every time a student sits down to write for us, he has to invent the university for the occasion—invent the university, that is, or a branch of it, like History or Anthropology or Economics or English. He has to learn to speak our language, to speak as we do, to try on the peculiar ways of knowing, selecting, evaluating, reporting, concluding, and arguing that define the discourse of our community. Or perhaps I should say the *various* discourses of our community, since it is in the nature of a liberal arts education that a student, after the first year or two, must learn to try on a variety of voices and interpretive schemes—to write, for example, as a literary critic one day and an experimental psychologist the next, to work within fields where the rules governing the presentation of examples or the development of an argument are both distinct and, even to a professional, mysterious.

The students have to appropriate (or be appropriated by) a specialized discourse, and they have to do this as though they were easily and comfortably one with their audience, as though they were members of the academy, or historians or anthropologists or economists; they have to invent the university by assembling and mimicking its language, finding some compromise between idiosyncrasy, a personal history, and the requirements of convention, the history of a discipline. They must learn to speak our language. Or they must dare to speak it, or to carry off the bluff, since speaking and writing will most certainly be required long before the skill is "learned." And this, understandably, causes problems.

Let me look quickly at an example. Here is an essay written by a college freshman, a basic writer:

In the past time I thought that an incident was creative was when I had to make a clay model of the earth, but not of the classical or your everyday model of the earth which consists of the two cores, the mantle and the crust. I thought of these things in a dimension of which it would be unique, but easy to comprehend. Of course, your materials to work with were basic and limited at the same time, but thought help to put this limit into a right attitude or frame of mind to work with the clay.

In the beginning of the clay model, I had to research and learn the different dimensions of the earth (in magnitude, quantity, state of matter, etc.). After this, I learned how to put this into the clay and come up with something different than any other person in my class at the time. In my opinion color coordination and shape was the key to my creativity of the clay model of the earth.

Creativity is the venture of the mind at work with the mechanics relay to the limbs from the cranium, which stores and triggers this action. It can be a burst of energy released at a precise time a thought is being transmitted. This can cause a frenzy of the human body, but it depends on the characteristics of the individual and how they can relay the message clearly enough through mechanics of the body to us as an observer. Then we must determine if it is creative or a learned process varied by the individuals thought process. Creativity is indeed a tool which has to exist, or our world will not succeed into the future and progress like it should.

I am continually impressed by the patience and good will of our students. This student was writing a placement essay during freshman orientation. (The problem set to him was "Describe a time when you did something you felt to be creative. Then, on the basis of the incident you have described, go on to draw some general conclusions about 'creativity.'") He knew that university faculty would be reading and evaluating his essay, and so he wrote for them.

In some ways it is a remarkable performance. He is trying on the discourse even though he doesn't have the knowledge that makes the discourse more than a routine, a set of conventional rituals and gestures. And he does this, I think, even though he *knows* he doesn't have the knowledge that makes the discourse more than a routine. He defines himself as a researcher, working systematically, and not as a kid in a high school class: "I thought of these things in a dimension of . . ."; "had to research and learn the different dimensions of the earth (in magnitude, quantity, state of matter, etc.)." He moves quickly into a specialized language (his approximation of our jargon) and draws both a general, textbook-like conclusion ("Creativity is the venture of the mind at work . . .") and a resounding peroration ("Creativity is indeed a tool which has to exist, or our world will not succeed into the future and progress like it should"). The writer has even, with that "indeed" and with the qualifications and the parenthetical expressions of the opening paragraphs, picked up the rhythm of our prose. And through it all he speaks with an impressive air of authority.

There is an elaborate but, I will argue, a necessary and enabling fiction at work here as the student dramatizes his experience in a "setting"—the setting required by the discourse—where he can speak to us as a companion, a fellow researcher. As I read the essay, there is only one moment when the fiction is broken, when we are addressed differently. The student says, "Of course, your materials to work with were basic and limited at the same time, but thought help to put this limit into a right attitude or frame of mind to work with the clay." At this point, I think, we become students and he the teacher, giving us a lesson (as in, "You take your pencil in your right hand and put your paper in front of you"). This is, however, one of the most characteristic slips of basic writers. It is very hard for them to take on the role—the voice, the person—of an authority whose authority is rooted in scholarship, analysis, or research. They slip, then, into the more immediately available and realizable voice of authority, the voice of a teacher giving a lesson or the voice of a parent lecturing at the dinner table. They offer advice or homilies rather than "academic" conclusions. There is a similar break in the final paragraph, where the conclusion that pushes for a definition ("Creativity is the venture of the mind at work with the mechanics relay to the limbs from the cranium . . .") is replaced by a conclusion which speaks in the voice of an Elder ("Creativity is indeed a tool which has to exist, or our world will not succeed into the future and progress like it should").

It is not uncommon, then, to find such breaks in the concluding sections of essays written by basic writers. Here is the concluding section of an essay written by a student about his work as a mechanic. He had been asked to generalize about "work" after reviewing an on-the-job experience or incident that "stuck in his mind" as somehow significant: "How could two repairmen miss a leak? Lack of pride? No incentive? Lazy? I don't know." At this point the writer is in a perfect position to speculate, to move from the problem to an analysis of the problem. Here is how the paragraph continues, however (and notice the change in pronoun reference):

> From this point on, I take my time, do it right, and don't let customers get under your skin. If they have a complaint, tell them to call your boss and he'll be more than glad to handle it. Most important, worry about yourself, and keep a clear eye on everyone, for there's always someone trying to take advantage of you, anytime and anyplace.

We get neither a technical discussion nor an "academic" discussion but a Lesson on Life.[1] This is the language he uses to address the general question "How could two repairmen miss a leak?" The other brand of conclusion, the more academic one, would have required him to speak of his experience in our terms; it would, that is, have required a special vocabulary, a special system of presentation, and an interpretive scheme (or a set of commonplaces) he could use to identify and talk about the mystery of human error. The writer certainly had access to the range of acceptable commonplaces for such an explanation: "lack of pride," "no incentive," "lazy." Each would dictate its own set of phrases, examples, and conclusions, and we, his teachers, would know how to write out each argument, just as we would know how to write out more specialized arguments of our own. A "commonplace," then, is a culturally or institutionally authorized concept or statement that carries with it its own necessary elaboration. We all use commonplaces to orient ourselves in the world; they provide a point of reference and a set of "prearticulated" explanations that are readily available to organize and interpret experience. The phrase "lack of pride" carries with it its own account for the repairman's error just as, at another point in time, a reference to "original sin" would provide an explanation, or just as, in a certain university classroom, a reference to "alienation" would enable a writer to continue and complete the discussion. While there is a way in which these terms are interchangeable, they are not all permissible. A student in a composition class would most likely be turned away from a discussion of original sin. Commonplaces are the "controlling ideas" of our composition textbooks, textbooks that not only insist upon a set form for expository writing but a set view of public life.[2]

When the student above says, "I don't know," he is not saying, then, that he has nothing to say. He is saying that he is not in a position to carry on this discussion. And so we are addressed as apprentices rather than as teachers or scholars. To speak to us as a person of status or privilege, the writer can either speak to us in our terms—in the privileged language of university discourse—or, in default (or in defiance), he can speak to us as though we were children, offering us the wisdom of experience.

I think it is possible to say that the language of the "Clay Model" paper has come through the writer and not from the writer. The writer has located himself (he has located the self that is represented by the *I* on the page) in a context that is, finally, beyond him, not his own and not available to his immediate procedures for inventing and arranging text. I would not, that is, call this essay an example of "writer-based" prose. I would not say that it is egocentric or that it represents the "interior monologue of a writer thinking and talking to himself" (Flower 63). It is, rather, the record of a writer who has lost himself in the discourse of his readers. There is a context beyond the reader that is not the world but a way of talking about the world, a way of talking that determines the use of examples, the possible conclusions, the acceptable commonplaces, and the key words of an essay on the construction of a clay model of the earth. This writer has entered the discourse without successfully approximating it.

Linda Flower has argued that the difficulty inexperienced writers have with writing can be understood as a difficulty in negotiating the transition between writer-based and reader-based prose. Expert writers, in other words, can better imagine how a reader will respond to a text and can transform or restructure what they have to say around a goal shared with a reader. Teaching students to revise for readers, then, will better prepare them to write initially with a reader in mind. The success of this pedagogy depends upon the degree to which a writer can imagine and conform to a reader's goals. The difficulty of this act of imagination, and the burden of such conformity, are so much at the heart of the problem that a teacher must pause and take stock before offering revision as a solution. Students like the student who wrote the "Clay Model" paper are not so much trapped in a private language as they are shut out from one of the privileged languages of public life, a language they are aware of but cannot control.

Our students, I've said, have to appropriate (or be appropriated by) a specialized discourse, and they have to do this as though they were easily or comfortably one with their audience. If you look at the situation this way, suddenly the problem of audience awareness becomes enormously complicated. One of the common assumptions of both composition research and composition teaching is that at some "stage" in the process of composing an essay a writer's ideas or his motives must be tailored to the needs and expectations of his audience. A writer has to "build bridges" between his point of view and his readers'. He has to anticipate and acknowledge his readers' assumptions and biases. He must begin with "common points of departure" before introducing new or controversial arguments. There is a version of the pastoral at work here. It is assumed that a person of low status (like a shepherd) can speak to a person of power (like a courtier), but only (at least so far as the language is concerned) if he is not a shepherd at all, but actually a member of the court out in the field in disguise.

Writers who can successfully manipulate an audience (or, to use a less pointed language, writers who can accommodate their motives to their readers' expectations) are writers who can both imagine and write from a position of privilege. They must, that is, see themselves within a privileged discourse, one that already includes and excludes groups of readers. They must be either equal to or more powerful than those they would address. The writing, then, must somehow transform the political and social relationships between basic writing students and their teachers.

If my students are going to write for me by knowing who I am—and if this means more than knowing my prejudices, psyching me out—it means knowing what I know; it means having the knowledge of a professor of English. They have, then, to know what I know and how I know what I know (the interpretive schemes that define the way I would work out the problems I set for them); they have to learn to write what I would write, or to offer up some approximation of that discourse. The problem of audience awareness, then, is a problem of power and finesse. It cannot be addressed, as it is in most classroom exercises, by giving students privilege and denying the situation of the classroom, by having students write to an outsider, someone excluded from their privileged circle: "Write about 'To His Coy Mistress,' not for your teacher, but for the students in your class"; "Describe Pittsburgh to someone who has never been there"; "Explain to a high school senior how best to prepare for college"; "Describe baseball to a Martian."

Exercises such as these allow students to imagine the needs and goals of a reader and they bring those needs and goals forward as a dominant constraint in the construction of an essay. And they argue, implicitly, what is generally true about writing—that it is an act of aggression disguised as an act of charity. What they fail to address is the central problem of academic writing, where students must assume the right of speaking to someone who knows Pittsburgh or "To His Coy Mistress" better than they do, a reader for whom the general commonplaces and the readily available utterances about a subject are inadequate. It should be clear that when I say that I know Pittsburgh better than my basic writing students I am talking about a way of knowing that is also a way of writing. There may be much that they know that I don't know, but in the setting of the university classroom I have a way of talking about the town that is "better" (and for arbitrary reasons) than theirs.

I think that all writers, in order to write, must imagine for themselves the privilege of being "insiders"—that is, of being both inside an established and powerful discourse, and of being granted a special right to speak. And I think that right to speak is seldom conferred upon us—upon any of us, teachers or students—by virtue of the fact that we have invented or discovered an original idea. Leading students to believe that they are responsible for something new or original, unless they understand what those words mean with regard to writing, is a dangerous and counterproductive practice. We do have the right to expect students to be active and engaged, but that is more a matter of being continually and stylistically working against the inevitable presence of conventional language; it is not a matter of inventing a language that is new.

When students are writing for a teacher, writing becomes more problematic than it is for the students who are describing baseball to a Martian. The students, in effect, have to assume privilege without having any. And since students assume privilege by locating themselves within the discourse of a particular community— within a set of specifically acceptable gestures and commonplaces—learning, at least as it is defined in the liberal arts curriculum, becomes more a matter of imitation or parody than a matter of invention and discovery.

What our beginning students need to learn is to extend themselves into the commonplaces, set phrases, rituals, gestures, habits of mind, tricks of persuasion, obligatory conclusions, and necessary connections that determine the "what might be said" and constitute knowledge within the various branches of our academic community. The course of instruction that would make this possible would be based on a sequence of illustrated assignments and would allow for successive approximations of academic or "disciplinary" discourse. Students will not take on our peculiar ways of reading, writing, speaking, and thinking all at once. Nor will the command of a subject like sociology, at least as that command is represented by the successful completion of a multiple choice exam, enable students to write sociology. Our colleges and universities, by and large, have failed to involve basic writing students in scholarly projects, projects that would allow them to act as though they were colleagues in an academic enterprise. Much of the written work students do is test-taking, report or summary, work that places them outside the working discourse of the academic community, where they are expected to admire and report on what we do, rather than inside that discourse, where they can do its work and participate in a common enterprise.[3] This is a failure of teachers and curriculum designers who, even if they speak of writing as a mode of learning, all too often represent writing as a "tool" to be used by a (hopefully) educated mind.

Pat Bizzell is one of the most important scholars writing now on basic writers and on the special requirements of academic discourse.[4] In a recent essay, "Cognition, Convention, and Certainty: What We Need to Know about Writing," she argues that the problems of basic writers might be

> better understood in terms of their unfamiliarity with the academic discourse community, combined, perhaps, with such limited experience outside their native discourse communities that they are unaware that there is such a thing as a discourse community with conventions to be mastered. What is underdeveloped is their knowledge both of the ways experience is constituted and interpreted in the academic discourse community and of the fact that all discourse communities constitute and interpret experience. (230)

One response to the problems of basic writers, then, would be to determine just what the community's conventions are, so that those conventions can be written out, "demystified," and taught in our classrooms. Teachers, as a result, could be more precise and helpful when they ask students to "think," "argue," "describe," or "define." Another response would be to examine the essays written by basic writers—their approximations of academic discourse—to determine more clearly where the problems lie. If we look at their writing, and if we look at it in the context of other student writing, we can better see the points of discord when students try to write their way into the university.

The purpose of the remainder of this paper will be to examine some of the most striking and characteristic problems as they are presented in the expository essays of basic writers. I will be concerned, then, with university discourse in its most generalized form—that is, as represented by introductory courses—and not with the special conventions required by advanced work in the various disciplines. And I will be concerned with the difficult, and often violent, accommodations that occur when students locate themselves in a discourse that is not "naturally" or immediately theirs.

I have reviewed five hundred essays written in response to the "creativity" question used during one of our placement exams. (The essay cited at the opening of this paper was one of that group.) Some of the essays were written by basic writers (or, more properly, those essays led readers to identify the writers as "basic writers"); some were written by students who "passed" (who were granted immediate access to the community of writers at the university). As I read these essays, I was looking to determine the stylistic resources that enabled writers to locate themselves within an "academic" discourse. My bias as a reader should be clear by now. I was not looking to see how the writer might represent the skills demanded by a neutral language (a language whose key features were paragraphs, topic sentences, transitions, and the like—features of a clear and orderly mind). I was looking to see what happened when a writer entered into a language to locate himself (a textual self) and his subject, and I was looking to see how once entered, that language made or unmade a writer.

Here is one essay. Its writer was classified as a basic writer. Since the essay is relatively free of sentence level errors, that decision must have been rooted in some perceived failure of the discourse itself.

> I am very interested in music, and I try to be creative in my interpretation of music. While in high school, I was a member of a jazz ensemble. The members of the ensemble were given chances to improvise and be creative in various songs. I feel that this was a great experience for me, as well as the other members. I was proud to know that I could use my imagination and feelings to create music other than what was written.

Creativity to me, means being free to express yourself in a way that is unique to you, not having to conform to certain rules and guidelines. Music is only one of the many areas in which people are given opportunities to show their creativity. Sculpting, carving, building, art, and acting are just a few more areas where people can show their creativity.

Through my music I conveyed feelings and thoughts which were important to me. Music was my means of showing creativity. In whatever form creativity takes, whether it be music, art, or science, it is an important aspect of our lives because it enables us to be individuals.

Notice, in this essay, the key gesture, one that appears in all but a few of the essays I read. The student defines as his own that which is a commonplace. "Creativity, to *me*, means being free to express yourself in a way that is unique to you, not having to conform to certain rules and guidelines." This act of appropriation constitutes his authority; it constitutes his authority as a writer and not just as a musician (that is, as someone with a story to tell). There were many essays in the set that told only a story, where the writer's established presence was as a musician or a skier or someone who painted designs on a van, but not as a person removed from that experience interpreting it, treating it as a metaphor for something else (creativity). Unless those stories were long, detailed, and very well told (unless the writer was doing more than saying, "I am a skier or a musician or a van-painter"), those writers were all given low ratings.

Notice also that the writer of the jazz paper locates himself and his experience in relation to the commonplace (creativity is unique expression; it is not having to conform to rules or guidelines) regardless of whether it is true or not. Anyone who improvises "knows" that improvisation follows rules and guidelines. It is the power of the commonplace (its truth as a recognizable, and, the writer believes, as a final statement) that justifies the example and completes the essay. The example, in other words, has value because it stands within the field of the commonplace. It is not the occasion for what one might call an "objective" analysis or a "close" reading. It could also be said that the essay stops with the articulation of the commonplace. The following sections speak only to the power of that statement. The reference to "sculpting, carving, building, art, and acting" attest to the universal of the commonplace (and it attests to the writer's nervousness with the status he has appropriated for himself—he is saying, "Now, I'm not the only one here who's done something unique"). The commonplace stands by itself. For this writer, it does not need to be elaborated. By virtue of having written it, he has completed the essay and established the contract by which we may be spoken to as equals: "In whatever form creativity takes, whether it be music, art, or science, it is an important aspect of *our lives* because it enables *us* to be individuals." (For me to break that contract, to argue that *my* life is not represented in that essay, is one way for me to begin as a teacher with that student in that essay.)

I said that the writer of the jazz paper offered up a commonplace regardless of whether it was "true" or not, and this, I said, was an example of the power of a commonplace to determine the meaning of an example. A commonplace determines a system of interpretation that can be used to "place" an example within a standard system of belief. You can see a similar process at work in this essay.

During the football season, the team was supposed to wear the same type of cleats and the same type socks, I figured that I would change this a little by wearing my white shoes instead of black and to cover up the team socks with a pair of my own white ones. I thought that this looked better than what we were wearing, and I told a few of the other people on the team to change too. They agreed that it did look better and they changed their combination to go along with mine. After the game people came up to us and said that it looked very good the way we wore our socks, and they wanted to know why we changed from the rest of the team.

I feel that creativity comes from when a person lets his imagination come up with ideas and he is not afraid to express them. Once you create something to do it will be original and unique because it came about from your own imagination and if any one else tries to copy it, it won't be the same because you thought of it first from your own ideas.

This is not an elegant paper, but it seems seamless, tidy. If the paper on the clay model of the earth showed an ill-fit between the writer and his project, here the discourse seems natural, smooth. You could reproduce this paper and hand it out to a class, and it would take a lot of prompting before the students sense something fishy and one of the more aggressive ones might say, "Sure he came up with the idea of wearing white shoes and white socks. Him and Billy White-shoes Johnson. Come on. He copied the very thing he said was his own idea, 'original and unique.'"

The "I" of this text, the "I" who "figured," "thought," and "felt" is located in a conventional rhetoric of the self that turns imagination into origination (I made it), that argues an ethic of production (I made it and it is mine), and that argues a tight scheme of intention (I made it because I decided to make it). The rhetoric seems invisible because it is so common. This "I" (the maker) is also located in a version of history that dominates classroom accounts of history. It is an example of the "Great Man" theory, where history is rolling along—the English novel is dominated by a central, intrusive narrative presence; America is in the throes of a great depression; during football season the team was supposed to wear the same kind of cleats and socks—until a figure appears, one who can shape history —Henry James, FDR, the writer of the football paper—and everything is changed. In the argument of the football paper, "I figured," "I thought," "I told," "they agreed," and, as a consequence, "I feel that creativity *comes from* when a person lets his imagination come up with ideas and he is not afraid to express them." The story of appropriation becomes a narrative of courage and conquest. The writer was able to write that story when he was able to imagine himself in that discourse. Getting him out of it will be a difficult matter indeed.

There are ways, I think, that a writer can shape history in the very act of writing it. Some students are able to enter into a discourse, but, by stylistic maneuvers, to take possession of it at the same time. They don't originate a discourse, but they locate themselves within it aggressively, self-consciously.

Here is one particularly successful essay. Notice the specialized vocabulary, but also the way in which the text continually refers to its own language and to the language of others.

Throughout my life, I have been interested and intrigued by music. My mother has often told me of the times, before I went to school, when I would "conduct" the orchestra on her records. I continued to listen to music and eventually started to play the guitar and the clarinet. Finally, at about the age of twelve, I started to sit down and to try to write songs. Even though my instrumental skills were far from my own high standards, I would spend much of my spare time during the day with a guitar around my neck, trying to produce a piece of music.

Each of these sessions, as I remember them, had a rather set format. I would sit in my bedroom, strumming different combinations of the five or six chords I could play, until I heard a series which sounded particularly good to me. After this, I set the music to a suitable rhythm, (usually dependent on my mood at the time), and ran through the tune until I could play it fairly easily. Only after this section was complete did I go on to writing lyrics, which generally followed along the lines of the current popular songs on the radio.

At the time of the writing, I felt that my songs were, in themselves, an original creation of my own; that is, I, alone, made them. However, I now see that, in this sense of the word, I was not creative. The songs themselves seem to be an over-simplified form of the music I listened to at the time.

In a more fitting sense, however, I *was* being creative. Since I did not purposely copy my favorite songs, I was, effectively, originating my songs from my own "process of creativity." To achieve my goal, I needed what a composer would call "inspiration" for my piece. In this case the inspiration was the current hit on the radio. Perhaps with my present point of view, I feel that I used too much "inspiration" in my songs, but, at that time, I did not.

Creativity, therefore, is a process which, in my case, involved a certain series of "small creations" if you like. As well, it is something, the appreciation of which varies with one's point of view, that point of view being set by the person's experience, tastes, and his own personal view of creativity. The less experienced tend to allow for less originality, while the more experienced demand real originality to classify something a "creation." Either way, a term as abstract as this is perfectly correct, and open to interpretation.

This writer is consistent and dramatically conscious of herself forming something to say out of what has been said *and* out of what she has been saying in the act of writing this paper. "Creativity" begins, in this paper, as "original creation." What she thought was "creativity," however, she now calls "imitation" and, as she says, "in this sense of the word" she was not "creative." In another sense, however, she says that she *was* creative since she didn't purposely copy the songs but used them as "inspiration."

The writing in this piece (that is, the work of the writer within the essay) goes on in spite of, or against, the language that keeps pressing to give another name to her experience as a song writer and to bring the discussion to closure. (Think of the quick closure of the football shoes paper in comparison.) Its style is difficult, highly qualified. It relies on quotation marks and parody to set off the language and attitudes that belong to the discourse (or the discourses) it would reject, that it would not take as its own proper location.[5]

In the papers I've examined in this essay, the writers have shown a varied awareness of the codes—or the competing codes—that operate within a discourse. To speak with authority student writers have not only to speak in another's voice but through another's "code"; and they not only have to do this, they have to speak in the voice and through the codes of those of us with power and wisdom; and they not only have to do this, they have to do it before they know what they are doing, before they have a project to participate in and before, at least in terms of our disciplines, they have anything to say. Our students may be able to enter into a conventional discourse and speak, not as themselves, but through the voice of the community. The university, however, is the place where "common" wisdom is only of negative value; it is something to work against. The movement toward a more specialized discourse begins (or perhaps, best begins) when a student can both define a position of privilege, a position that sets him against a "common" discourse, and when he can work self-consciously, critically, against not only the "common" code but his own.

The stages of development that I've suggested are not necessarily marked by corresponding levels in the type or frequency of error, at least not by the type or frequency of sentence level errors. I am arguing, then, that a basic writer is not necessarily a writer who makes a lot of mistakes. In fact, one of the problems with curricula designed to aid basic writers is that they too often begin with the assumption that the key distinguishing feature of a basic writer is the presence of sentence level error. Students are placed in courses because their placement essays show a high frequency of such errors and those courses are designed with the goal of making those errors go away. This approach to the problems of the basic writer ignores the degree to which error is not a constant feature but a marker in the development of a writer. Students who can write reasonably correct narratives may fall to pieces when faced with more unfamiliar assignments. More importantly, however, such courses fail to serve the rest of the curriculum. On every campus there is a significant number of college freshmen who require a course to introduce them to the kinds of writing that are required for a university education. Some of these students can write correct sentences and some cannot, but as a group they lack the facility other freshmen possess when they are faced with an academic writing task.

The "White Shoes" essay, for example, shows fewer sentence level errors than the "Clay Model" paper. This may well be due to the fact, however, that the writer of that paper stayed well within the safety of familiar territory. He kept himself out of trouble by doing what he could easily do. The tortuous syntax of the more advanced papers on my list is a syntax that represents a writer's struggle with a difficult and unfamiliar language, and it is a syntax that can quickly lead an inexperienced writer into trouble. The syntax and punctuation of the "Composing Songs" essay, for example, shows the effort that is required when a writer works against the pressure of conventional discourse. If the prose is inelegant (although I'll confess I admire those dense sentences), it is still correct. This writer has a command of the linguistic and stylistic resources (the highly embedded sentences, the use of parentheses and quotation marks) required to complete the act of writing. It is easy to imagine the possible pitfalls for a writer working without this facility.

There was no camera trained on the "Clay Model" writer while he was writing, and I have no protocol of what was going through his mind, but it is possible to speculate that the syntactic difficulties of sentences like the following are the result of an attempt to use an unusual vocabulary and to extend his sentences beyond the boundaries that would be "normal" in his speech or writing:

> In past time I thought that an incident was creative was when I had to make a clay model of the earth, but not of the classic or your everyday model of the earth which consists of the two cores, the mantle and the crust. I thought of these things in a dimension of which it would be unique, but easy to comprehend.

There is reason to believe, that is, that the problem is with this kind of sentence, in this context. If the problem of the last sentence is a problem of holding together these units—"I thought," "dimension," "unique," and "easy to comprehend"—then the linguistic problem is not a simple matter of sentence construction.

I am arguing, then, that such sentences fall apart not because the writer lacks the necessary syntax to glue the pieces together but because he lacks the full statement within which these key words are already operating. While writing, and in the thrust of his need to complete the sentence, he has the key words but not the utterance. (And to recover the utterance, I suspect, he will need to do more than revise the sentence.) The invisible conventions, the prepared phrases remain too distant for the statement to be completed. The writer must get inside of a discourse he can only partially imagine. The act of constructing a sentence, then, becomes something like an act of transcription, where the voice on the tape unexpectedly fades away and becomes inaudible.

Mina Shaughnessy speaks of the advanced writer as a writer with a more facile but still incomplete possession of this prior discourse. In the case of the advanced writer, the evidence of a problem is the presence of dissonant, redundant, or precise language, as in a sentence such as this: "No education can be *total*, it must be *continuous*." Such a student, Shaughnessy says, could be said to hear the "melody of formal English" while still unable to make precise or exact distinctions. And, she says, the prepackaging feature of language, the possibility of taking over phrases and whole sentences without much thought about them, threatens the writer now as before. The writer, as we have said, inherits the language out of which he must fabricate his own messages. He is therefore in a constant tangle with the language, obliged to recognize its public, communal nature and yet driven to invent out of this language his own statements (19).

For the unskilled writer, the problem is different in degree and not in kind. The inexperienced writer is left with a more fragmentary record of the comings and goings of academic discourse. Or, as I said above, he often has the key words without the complete statements within which they are already operating.

It may very well be that some students will need to learn to crudely mimic the "distinctive register" of academic discourse before they are prepared to actually and legitimately do the work of the discourse, and before they are so-phisticated enough with the refinements of tone and texture to do it with grace or elegance. To say this, however, is to say that our students must be our students. Their initial progress will be marked by their abilities to take on the role of privilege, by their abilities to establish authority. From this point of view, the student who wrote about constructing the clay model of the earth is better prepared for his education than the student who wrote about playing football in white shoes, even though the "White Shoes" paper was relatively error-free and the "Clay Model" paper was not. It will be hard to pry the writer of the "White Shoes" paper loose from the tidy, pat discourse that allows him to dispose of the question of creativity in such a quick and efficient manner. He will have to be convinced that it is better to write sentences he might not so easily control, and he will have to be convinced that it is better to write muddier and more confusing prose (in order that it may sound like ours), and this will be harder than convincing the "Clay Model" writer to continue what he has begun.[6]

Notes

[1] David Olson has made a similar observation about school-related problems of language learning in younger children. Here is his conclusion: "Depending upon whether children assumed language was primarily suitable for making assertions and conjectures or primarily for making direct or indirect commands, they will either find school texts easy or difficult" (107).

[2] For Aristotle there were both general and specific commonplaces. A speaker, says Aristotle, has a "stock of arguments to which he may turn for a particular need."

> If he knows the *topic* (regions, places, lines of argument)—and a skilled speaker will know them—he will know where to find what he wants for a special case. The general topics, or *common*places, are regions containing arguments that are common to all branches of knowledge. . . . But there are also special topics (regions, places, *loci*) in which one looks for arguments appertaining to particular branches of knowledge, special sciences, such as ethics or politics. (154–55)

And, he says, "The topics or places, then, may be indifferently thought of as in the science that is concerned, or in the mind of the speaker." But the question of location is "indifferent" *only* if the mind of the speaker is in line with set opinion, general assumption. For the speaker (or writer) who is not situated so comfortably in the privileged public realm, this is indeed not an indifferent matter at all. If he does not have the commonplace at hand, he will not, in Aristotle's terms, know where to go at all.

[3] See especially Bartholomae and Rose for articles on curricula designed to move students into university discourse. The movement to extend writing "across the curriculum" is evidence of a general concern for locating students within the work of the university: see especially Bizzell or Maimon et al. For longer works directed specifically at basic writing, see Ponsot and Deen, and Shaughnessy. For a book describing a course for more advanced students, see Coles.

[4] See especially Bizzell, and Bizzell and Herzberg. My debt to Bizzell's work should be evident everywhere in this essay.

[5] In support of my argument that this is the kind of writing that does the work of the academy, let me offer the following excerpt from a recent essay by Wayne Booth ("The Company We Keep: Self-Making in Imaginative Art, Old and New"):

> I can remember making up songs of my own, no doubt borrowed from favorites like "Hello, Central, Give Me Heaven," "You Can't Holler Down My Rain Barrel," and one about the ancient story of a sweet little "babe in the woods" who lay down and died, with her brother.
>
> I asked my mother, in a burst of creative egotism, why nobody ever learned to sing my songs, since after all I was more than willing to learn *theirs.* I can't remember her answer, and I can barely remember snatches of two of "my" songs. But I can remember dozens of theirs, and when I sing them, even now, I sometimes feel again the emotions, and see the images, that they aroused then. Thus who I am now—the very shape of my soul—was to a surprising degree molded by the works of "art" that came my way.
>
> I set "art" in quotation marks, because much that I experienced in those early books and songs would not be classed as art according to most definitions. But for the purposes of appraising the effects of "art" on "life" or "culture," and especially for the purposes of thinking about the effects of the "media," we surely must include every kind of artificial experience that we provide for one another. . . .
>
> In this sense of the word, all of us are from the earliest years fed a steady diet of art. . . . (58–59)

While there are similarities in the paraphrasable content of Booth's arguments and my student's, what I am interested in is each writer's method. Both appropriate terms from a common discourse (about *art* and *inspiration*) in order to push against an established way of talking (about tradition and the individual). This effort of opposition clears a space for each writer's argument and enables the writers to establish their own "sense" of the key words in the discourse.

[6] Preparation of this manuscript was supported by the Learning Research and Development Center of the University of Pittsburgh, which is supported in part by the National Institute of Education. I am grateful also to Mike Rose, who pushed and pulled at this paper at a time when it needed it.

Works Cited

Aristotle. *The Rhetoric of Aristotle.* Trans. L. Cooper, Englewood Cliffs: Prentice, 1932.

Bartholomae, D. "Writing Assignments: Where Writing Begins." *Forum.* Ed. P. Stock. Montclair: Boynton/Cook, 1983. 300–312.

Bizzell, P. "The ethos of academic discourse." *College Composition and Communication* 29 (1978): 351–55.

———. "Cognition, Convention, and Certainty: What We Need to Know about Writing." *Pre/text* 3 (1982): 213–44.

———. "College Composition: Initiation into the Academic Discourse Community." *Curriculum Inquiry* 12 (1982): 191–207.

Bizzell, P., and B. Herzberg. "'Inherent' Ideology, 'Universal' History, 'Empirical' Evidence, and 'Context-Free' Writing: Some Problems with E. D. Hirsch's *The Philosophy of Composition.*" *Modern Language Notes* 95 (1980): 1181–1202.

Coles, W. E., Jr. *The Plural I.* New York: Holt, 1978.

Flower, Linda S. "Revising Writer-Based Prose." *Journal of Basic Writing* 3 (1981): 62–74.

Maimon, E. P., G. L. Belcher, G. W. Hearn, B. F. Nodine, and F. X. O'Connor. *Writing in the Arts and Sciences.* Cambridge: Winthrop, 1981.

Olson, D. R. "Writing: The Divorce of the Author from the Text." *Exploring Speaking-Writing Relationships: Connections and Contrasts.* Ed. B. M. Kroll and R. J. Vann. Urbana: National Council of Teachers of English, 1981.

Ponsot, M., and R. Deen. *Beat Not the Poor Desk.* Montclair: Boynton/Cook, 1982.

Rose, M. "Remedial Writing Courses: A Critique and a Proposal." *College English* 45 (1983): 109–28.

Shaughnessy, Mina. *Errors and Expectations.* New York: Oxford UP, 1977.

ANALYZING AUDIENCES

Douglas B. Park

[*College Composition and Communication* 37 (1986): 478–88.]

Douglas Park is professor of English at Western Washington University, where he served as department chair for ten years. He has published articles on composition and rhetoric in several journals; "Analyzing Audiences" continues an article published in *College English* in 1982.

Park recognizes that few teachers agree on how best to teach audience analysis. He offers options for expanded discussions of audience, and he emphasizes that audience analyses will be most successful if students recognize how their writing will function in a reasonable social context. As a result, Park affirms the pragmatic, functional approach to audience analysis that *The Bedford Handbook* promotes.

What do we expect analysis of audience to do for writers? What form should analysis of audience take; or, more precisely, what makes certain kinds of analysis more or less appropriate in given situations?

The centrality of audience in the rhetorical tradition and the detail with which current writing texts provide advice on analyzing an audience might suggest that the answers to such questions are well established. But they clearly are not. Side by side with the growing awareness in recent discussions that audience is a rich and complex concept exists a growing dissatisfaction with traditional audience analysis—those familiar questions about an audience's age, sex, education, and social background that form the core of most proposed heuristics. (See, for instance, Barry Kroll, "Writing for Readers: Three Perspectives on Audience," *CCC*, 35 [May 1984], 172–75; Russell Long, "Writer–Audience Relationships," *CCC*, 31 [May 1980], 221–26; Arthur Walzer, "Articles from the 'California Divorce Project': A Case Study of the Concept of Audience," *CCC*, 36 [May 1985], 155–58.)

The general import of the explicit criticism is that traditional audience analysis is too limited a tool: It works only for persuasive discourse; it seems inapplicable to discourse situations with general audiences about whom specific questions cannot be arrived at. But underneath these criticisms lies a greater uncertainty about the whole subject, characterized on the one hand by a sense that traditional analysis somehow fails altogether to provide what we now expect from audience analysis and on the other by the lack of any other widely shared way of thinking about the subject.

To address this uncertainty, we need to return to first principles and examine just what it is that we do expect audience analysis to accomplish and just how the assumptions behind traditional analysis relate to those expectations. This examination will show why traditional analysis, for all the apparent sanction of tradition, has so little practical rhetorical value for us. More important, it will provide a backdrop for a broader and, I hope, more useful view of what can go into analyzing audiences.

In a broad sense, the purpose of audience analysis is obvious enough: to aid the writer or speaker in understanding a social situation. The advice to "know your audience" carries much of the social meaning of "know" as in knowing who another person is or what that person is like. The advice to "consider your audience" suggests a deliberate weighing of the characteristics of the audience with a view to an appropriate shaping of the discourse. If we look at a set of hypothetical discourses chosen to illustrate a range of different audiences, we can describe more precisely these undifferentiated purposes for analysis. Consider

a legal argument on behalf of an accused embezzler;

a local businessman's letter to City Council protesting a zoning decision;

a grant proposal to develop computer instruction;

a memo from a provost to his university faculty arguing for annual evaluations;

a panel presentation on invention at CCCC;

an article on food in the Pacific Northwest contemplated by a freelance journalist;

an essay on rock and roll contemplated by an English 101 student.

In all but the last two cases, the most obvious specific purpose for analysis will be to understand where a given audience stands in relation to the particular aim and issues at hand. The goal is the immediately strategic one of adapting argument to audience: What are the criteria on which the grant review board makes its decisions? Why are most of the faculty so hostile to annual evaluations? What are the current issues in the discipline's discussions of invention?

In the last two cases above, however, the writers are not yet ready for this sort of strategic analysis. The freelance writer must first choose an audience—a journal such as *Sunset Magazine*—in order to be able to think about rhetorical strategy. The student, in a yet more difficult position, must somehow imagine or invent an audience in a situation where no audience naturally exists. Here the primary purpose of audience analysis becomes not the usual one of providing information about an existing audience but rather a means of actually helping students to discover an audience. And this raises the questions of just how they are to do that. What must they think about to imagine their papers as having or being capable of having an audience?

The special context of the classroom creates a peculiar purpose for audience analysis, one for which it was never intended. It does, however, usefully focus the essential question of what we mean by "having an audience." What is an audience, anyway?—as our baffled students often seem to ask. And this is just a generalized form of a need that all writers experience to understand the identity of the audience that they know they have: What does it mean to be in the situation of addressing a CCCC audience or a grant review board or a City Council? Questions of this sort are, I think, another important part of the meaning of "know your audience." They point to a purpose for analysis which lies underneath the more obvious strategic purpose of determining the audience's responses to particular issues.

Both these purposes for analysis—the fundamental identifying and defining of an audience and the strategic analysis of particular attitudes —involve describing situations, because audience is an inherently situational concept (Lisa Ede, "On Audience and Composition," *CCC*, 30 [October 1979], 294ff.). The notion of accommodating discourse to an audience is one of participating in a dynamic social relationship. And "audience" itself refers to the idea of a collective entity that can exist only in relation to a discourse; it means a group of people engaged in a rhetorical situation. Therefore if we are to identify an audience and say anything useful about it, we will have to speak in terms of the situation that brings it into being and gives it identity.

From this perspective, it becomes easy to see why traditional audience analysis so often seems unsatisfactory. What it does is to take literally the idea of "knowing" an audience as examining a group already assembled and describing any or all of the characteristics that those assembled may happen to have. In so doing it directly addresses neither the situation that has brought the audience into being as an audience nor the particular states of mind that the audience may possess in relation to the issues at hand. It tries rather to describe general traits from which rhetorically useful inferences may be drawn.

> [The elderly] are positive about nothing; in all things they err by an extreme moderation. . . . The rich are insolent and superior. . . . Now the hearer is always receptive when a speech is adapted to his own character and reflects it. (*The Rhetoric of Aristotle*, trans. Lane Cooper [Englewood Cliffs, N.J., Prentice-Hall, 1932], pp. 134–38)

> Different habits . . . and different occupations in life . . . make one incline more to one passion, another to another. . . . With men of genius the most successful topic will be fame; with men of industry, riches; with men of fortune, pleasure. (George Campbell, *The Philosophy of Rhetoric*, 2 vols. [Edinburgh, 1776], 1, 241–42)

> It is . . . to begin by recording certain information about an audience and then, on the basis of experience and research, to infer about the audience such matters as knowledge, temperament, attitudes, habits of thought, language preferences or other matters that will enter into their responses to communication. (Theodore Clevenger, Jr., *Audience Analysis* [Indianapolis, Ind.: Bobbs-Merrill, 1966], p. 43)

Clearly, both Campbell and Aristotle envision the possibility of topoi appropriate for various ages and conditions of men. If an assembled audience in a particular situation can be seen to have a salient trait or quality—what classical rhetoric calls the "character" of the audience—then various lines of argument will fit that character more or less effectively. Perhaps most of the City Council are like our letter-writer businessman "men of industry," practical men who will respond best to arguments from "riches." As a general idea—which is how audience analysis usually appears in classical rhetoric (e.g., Quintilian, *Institutio Oratoria*, III, viii, 38) —the notion seems plausible. Certainly in situations involving small, immediate audiences, most of us have had the experience of sensing the overall personality of an audience, or of dominant members in it, and the need to adjust to those qualities in a general and impressionistic way. But inflated to a social-science method of the sort that the modern description suggests, traditional analysis almost completely loses touch with rhetorical usefulness. Aside from the fact that large generalizations about the psychology of age or sex are suspect in any particular application, the accumulation of demographic facts about an audience has no clear goal or limit (Clevenger, pp. 45ff.). All it can do is amass information unlikely to add up to any sort of "character." "The characters of men," admits George Campbell, beating a retreat from the subject, "may be infinitely diversified" (243). One of our industrious business executives may also be a man of genius and education who might therefore be motivated by arguments from fame. Another is perhaps rich and therefore "insolent." Two might be in their 30's, one in his 50's, two in their 60's. Two might have high-school educations, and so on ad infinitum, the writer having no clear way to determine the relevance or weight of any of this information to the task at hand.

Of course the general assumption informing traditional audience analysis as we find it in modern speech communication texts is that it aims at the social traits held in common that shape the responses of the audience as a whole. (See, for instance, Paul Holtzman's *The Psychology of Speakers' Audiences* [Glenview, Ill.: Scott Foresman, 1970], pp. 73–79.) So we can observe that a CCCC audience will share many social traits: most will have advanced degrees in English; most will be between 25 and 65; probably at least half will be women; most will be politically liberal. Certainly all will have modest incomes. But although such facts might well interest a social scientist, they are merely symptoms of the situation that actually gives the audience its identity. If we were to send a speaker to the podium, shanghaied, blindfolded, armed only with the subject and the result of a demographic analysis, our victim would angrily or plaintively want to know, "But who is my audience?" The answer of course is "conferees attending a CCCC panel," a simple identification that compresses for someone in the know a wealth of necessary knowledge about the identity of the audience as an entity assembled for a collective purpose.

Bizarre as the case of the blindfolded speaker may be, it describes exactly the mistaken way in which traditional analysis is used to help students discover audiences by amassing detailed information about people, real or imaginary. "They [students] must construct in imagination an audience that is as nearly a replica as is possible of those many readers who actually exist in the world of reality and who are reading the writer's words" (Fred R. Pfister and Joanne F. Petrick, "A Heuristic Model for Creating a Writer's Audience," *CCC*, 30 [May 1980], 213). Following this principle, discussions commonly suggest as audiences groups with analyzable traits. "Thus a reader might be delineated as being a university administrator, over 40, male, white, etc., or a group of readers might be defined as businessmen in a small [midwestern] community" (Winifred B. Horner, "Speech-Act and Text-Act Theory: 'Theme-ing' in Freshman Composition," *CCC*, 30 [May 1979], 168). But obviously the problem that students face is not one of just visualizing hypothetical real people; it is one of grasping a situation in which real readers could constitute an "audience." In what conceivable situations, for instance, could our student writing about rock and roll be addressing a group of midwestern businessmen?

How then do we go about describing the situations that bring audiences into being and give them their identities? Or to put the question in a more basic way, how is it that discourses of any sort can have audiences? If we look at the most concrete possible image of an audience assembled to hear a speech and ask how they come to be there, the immediate answer will be that a particular occasion has brought them together. This, indeed, is the most common way we tend to think about and characterize audiences, as a particular group assembled to hear a particular speech. But a moment's reflection shows that while an audience assembles only for a particular discourse, the discourse alone cannot bring the audience into being. Lawyers do not defend their clients on street corners; passers-by do not wander into Holiday Inns to hear lectures on teaching composition; freelance journalists do not mimeograph their articles and leave them in mailboxes—unless they have become really desperate.

In brief, an audience can assemble on a particular occasion only because a social setting already exists in which a certain kind of discourse performs a recognized function. Note that the ancient classification of judicial, deliberative, and epideictic discourse follows this principle and amounts, as Chaim Perelman points out, to the identification of three basic audiences (*The New Rhetoric: A Treatise on Argumentation*, trans. John Wilkinson and Purcell Weaver [Notre Dame, Ind.: University of Notre Dame Press, 1969], p. 21). To define other audiences we need simply to amplify the principle to its broadest extent, as follows.

An audience can exist when there is (1) an established social institution or social relationship, a judicial system, a legislative process, an institutional hierarchy, a charitable foundation, a social compact of any sort, a club, a nation, even a friendship between two people; (2) and an evolved and understood function that discourse performs within and for that social relationship. Speech-act theory—and sociolinguistics in general—has taught us to see all discourse as representing action performed within and conditioned by a social situation. We can name these actions in very general terms—making statements, contracts, promises, implications, requests. But it is also important to see that all discourse, especially of the more public or formalized kind, functions in and can be described as part of a social transaction that has defined roles for both writers and readers. If I write a grant proposal, I am making a request, but I am also participating in a highly conventionalized activity evolved to enable the distribution of resources, the manipulation of tax laws, the satisfaction of political and public relations imperatives. I write as the representative of one institution. My audience exists in terms of and reads as representatives of the granting agency.

(3) Finally, for an audience to "assemble," there must be a physical setting. For written discourse, the exact analog to the place of assembly is the means of publication or distribution. Much has been made of the distance between writers and readers as opposed to the closeness of speakers and audience. Walter Ong argues that the readers of written discourse do not form an audience, a "collectivity," as do the listeners to a speech ("The Writer's Audience Is Always a Fiction," *PMLA,* 90 [January 1975], 11). In some senses this must of course be true, but because a written discourse always exists within some larger social setting and reaches its dispersed readers through a given physical means of distribution for an accepted social function, readers of prose are very much part of a collectivity. When I read a memo from the Provost in my office mail or a copy of *Sunset Magazine* in the public mail, I understand that I am participating in a social activity together with others. The major difference between speech and writing in their roles in social settings is that writing has been able to develop a wider range of functions. In the instance of popular journalism, the means of publication has been able to become a social institution in its own right. The reader of a newspaper or a magazine participates in a social relationship that has been largely created by the development of newspapers and magazines themselves.

All these intertwined elements of the social context for discourse define the terms in which the identity of an audience is best understood. This is why when we respond most directly and effectively to the question, "Who is the audience," we always respond in terms of the social institution and function that the discourse serves—a court, members of City Council, a grant review board, the college faculty, CCCC conferees, readers of *Sunset Magazine.* Unspoken but always present in any such simple identification of an audience is the whole complex of the social situation that has brought that audience into being. This unspoken presence is so compressed into the identification that it is easy to take for granted. But a writer who understands the identity of the audience grasps a wealth of tacit and explicit knowledge about the form of the discourse and the way the subject can be treated.

This knowledge informs the obvious rhetorical choices about appropriate formats, matters of tone, diction, stance toward the reader, kinds of allowable openings, structure, evidence, and argument. It also includes more subtle, crucial presuppositions about such things as how much the purpose of the discourse or the writer's own authority can be presumed or needs to be explained and justified. In many cases where the setting is subject specific—e.g., periodical journalism or scholarship—knowledge of the audience's identity also includes a great deal that the audience can be taken to know about the subject at hand. Awareness of the audience's identity provides, in short, all the sense of situation that makes it possible for a writer or speaker to proceed with a sense of being engaged in purposeful communication.

The identity of the audience, as I have described it above, constitutes, therefore, the necessary foundation for audience analysis. It constitutes as well the setting that shapes further considerations of strategy about the specific subject. For example, the lawyer pleading the case before the court will be concerned with the attitudes of the jurors toward the client and the issues of the case. But strategies to play on those attitudes will have to acknowledge the decorum of the courtroom and the jurors' own awareness of their special role as jurors. As Chaim Perelman points out, "It is quite common for members of an audience to adopt attitudes connected with the role they play in certain social institutions" (p. 21). In the case of the audience for the CCCC presentation, almost everything that one can say about their attitudes toward the subject at hand will, as Arthur Walzer suggests, have to be defined in terms of that particular "rhetorical or interpretive community" and in terms of the role that academic audiences are expected to play (p. 157).

To summarize the above discussion, I would suggest that what a writer needs to understand about an audience, what we mean by "knowing" an audience, can be adequately described by two interrelated levels of questions:

I. What is the identity of the audience?
   A. What is the institution or social relationship of writer(s) and audience that the discourse serves (or creates)?
   B. How does the discourse function in that relationship?
   C. What is the physical setting or means of distribution that brings the discourse to the audience and what are the conventions and formats associated with it?
II. How does the audience view the specific subject matter and how may it view the intentions of the discourse?
   A. What is known or can be projected about specific attitudes and knowledge in the audience that affect what the discourse will have to do in order to accomplish its purpose?
   B. To what extent are the audience's attitudes toward subject and purpose affected by or describable by reference to its collective identity as audience?

Although this outline has the appearance of a heuristic, I propose it more as a general framework for thinking about what writers may actually do when they attend to audience. How much, and at what points in the process of composing, such attention may profitably take the form of deliberate analysis of the audience are questions that I hope the above framework may help others to explore further. In particular, I think this framework helps to open a more adequate view of how different kinds of writing situations may require very different kinds of attention to audience. The elements of the audience that I have described above seem in different situations to take on different forms, to claim varying degrees of precedence and to interact in different ways.

For instance, our businessman writing to City Council probably knows the members of the Council well and has several social relationships to them— friend, enemy, fellow member of the Chamber of Commerce, and so on—any of which might be involved explicitly or implicitly in the letter. He has, therefore, a number of ways to conceive of and address his audience. But his attention seems most likely to be concentrated on their individual attitudes and predispositions toward the zoning issues. In the case of the grant proposal, by contrast, the writer's conception of the audience will be necessarily defined by their role as agents of the institution and by the conventions of grant proposals. The means of distribution for the discourse maintains distance, even anonymity, between the writer and the audience. Here, everything that can be said about the audience's attitudes will concern the kinds of argument that this particular granting agency is most responsive to. Yet again, in other kinds of institutional prose, like the provost's memo to the faculty, a piece of discourse may serve more than one function and audience—e.g., the President as well as the faculty. Much of the initial attention to audience will have to fall on actually identifying and defining these multiple audiences and then on juggling issues in recognition of all of them, while perhaps explicitly addressing only one audience. (See C. H. Knoblauch, "Intentionality in the Writing Process: A Case Study," *CCC,* 31 [May 1980], 153–59. See also Mathes and Stevenson, *Designing Technical Reports* [Indianapolis, Ind.: Bobbs-Merrill, 1976], pp. 9–23.)

In spite of the differences in the attention to audience in the above examples, all are alike in that they aim toward the second level of the audience's specific attitudes and knowledge, and the appropriate strategies to accommodate them. This is so because the general function of the writings is transactional, by which I mean that they work to produce specific actions or responses from an audience who, as members of the institution involved, have an active part to play.

The kinds of attention a writer pays to audience seem likely to alter significantly, in ways that we do not understand at all well, when the function of discourse moves away from the transactional, as it does in the typical periodical essay and in much of what we call discourse written for a general audience. The audience for such discourse is not part of an institution—members of a jury, faculty at University X—within which the discourse performs some function. The audience comes rather to the discourse to participate in the social relationship—a sort of one-sided conversation—that is offered there. Here, understanding the identity of the audience means understanding what readers expect, the nature of the "conversation," the conventions which govern that kind of prose. In particular, it usually means understanding the setting of publication, e.g. *Sunset Magazine,* that ties those conventions to a specific format or to a set of assumed interests and attitudes in readers.

In such discourse, second-level analysis of the audience in relation to the specific subject and purpose often seems almost irrelevant, or so different from the analysis in transactional discourse that we need to find other ways of talking about it. The traditional model sees the writer as assessing and accommodating specific attitudes. The discourse is an instrument of negotiation. But here the writer is in the position of offering readers a social relationship—for entertainment, for intellectual stimulation, for general information—which they may or may not choose to enter.

One familiar way to talk about this very different relationship between discourse and audience is to draw on Walter Ong's idea of the audience as a fiction evoked by the text, a series of roles that the text offers to readers, or a series of presuppositions it makes about readers that the readers can accept or not ("The Writer's Audience Is Always a Fiction," *PMLA,* 90 [January 1975], 9–21; see also Douglas Park, "The Meanings of 'Audience,'" *College English,* 44 [March 1982], 247–57). Accordingly, Russell Long suggests that young writers should not try to analyze their audiences but to ask rather "Who do I want my audience to be?" (Writer–Audience Relationships: Analysis or Invention?" *CCC,* 31 [May 1980], 225).

Although this idea has force, it has remained too undeveloped. Further, it seems clear that all discourse must in some fashion attend to the constraints imposed by the requirements of real audiences. (See Lisa Ede and Andrea Lunsford, "Audience Addressed/Audience Invoked: The Role of Audience in Composition Theory and Pedagogy," *CCC,* 35 [May 1984], 155–71.) Writers, that is to say, can set out to engage readers in conversation only by some appropriate estimate of what they are actually likely to find intelligible, credible, or interesting. In practice, the setting for publication usually yields such information. But it seems probable that what writers work with here is not precise formulations of particular attitudes or states of knowledge but rather an awareness of a range of possible viewpoints. Robert Roth, for example, describes successful student revisions that evolve by appealing to a variety of possible responses from readers, by casting a wider rather than a narrower net ("The Evolving Audience: Alternatives to Audience Accommodation," *CCC,* 38 [February 1987], 47–55). The general aim of such attention to audience might perhaps be described not as fitting discourse to audience but as making it possible for a variety of readers to become an audience.

This survey is too brief to give more than an idea of the range of considerations that can go into audience analysis. But it will do to indicate how the framework I have laid out might be used, and to indicate as well some areas that need more investigation. For teachers of writing, I hope this discussion demonstrates that analysis of audience cannot profitably be seen as a set of all-purpose questions to be tacked on to an assignment to help students invent or identify an audience. To identify an audience means identifying a situation. So the primary issue that our current concern with audience analysis poses for teachers of writing is not how we can help students analyze their audiences but, first, how and to what extent we can help them define situations for their writing. And to this question there are no simple answers.

The most obvious way to define a situation for writing is to pose hypothetical cases—Imagine you are a resident assistant writing a report for the Dean of Students; write an article for *Sports Illustrated*—or to use the composition class for "real" writing such as a letter to the hometown paper. In fact the only way to have an audience analyzable in the detail we usually envision when we speak of audience analysis is to have a situation for writing that includes a concrete setting for "publication." For such assignments, I hope this discussion will facilitate more useful analyses of audience than those evoked by traditional advice.

Most teachers, however, will resist turning their composition courses entirely over to the writing of letters for various occasions. They feel, with good reason, that too much emphasis upon specific and often imaginary situations can lead to crude pretense and mechanical emphasis on format that robs student writing of all genuineness. They want students' writing to be in some elusive but important sense real and self-generated. Unfortunately, this ideal is difficult to reconcile with the obvious need many students have for a clearer sense of audience. Well-meaning advice like, "Be your own audience," while it seems to get at a truth, can leave many students with no way to understand their writing as being for anyone or any purpose at all.

The student who escapes this limbo—perhaps our hypothetical student writing about rock and roll—will do so partly by using various conventions of written prose to evoke the shadow of a situation, by writing like a freelance journalist or a musicologist, or an encyclopedist, or a columnist, or some creative pastiche of these. The very use of a certain recognizable "register" (M. A. K. Halliday and R. Hasan, *Language as Social Semiotic* [London: Longmans, 1976], pp. 65–73)—a way of addressing the readers, of opening the subject, of organizing material, and so on—even though it is accompanied by no identifiable setting for publication, will evoke a sense of the paper's possessing an audience. If the student's paper is sufficiently like other discourse that exists in real settings for publication, then it too will be felt to some extent to have an audience. But such a sense of audience will, I would suggest, always be informed by a grasp of the social function of the prose—that is to say how it works as public discourse, what general kind of thing it offers to readers.

If we are to help students who do not have this grasp on audience, we need to learn more about it ourselves. We need, first of all, to give more attention to defining the social functions of various kinds of public discourse. It is easy enough to see that different composition courses and different teachers have preferences—too often barely conscious or impressionistically defined—for different kinds of audiences. Students in one course may be expected to write like popular journalists about their personal knowledge, in another like apprentice philosophers, in another like informal essayists in the grand tradition. The current trend to center composition courses on the varieties of academic discourse seems especially constructive because it is accompanied by an attempt to understand and make more explicit the nature of such discourse (Walzer, p. 157).

Second, we need to learn more about how different kinds of discourse written for public or "general" audiences actually work rhetorically. Recognizing that the model of audience accommodation which works for transactional prose does not apply well to all discourse situations is a starting point. Doing more to describe the conventions of such prose would also be useful, as for instance in George Dillon's *Constructing Texts* (Bloomington, Ind.: Indiana University Press, 1981). His description of how students fail to understand some of the basic conventions of expository prose gets at a fundamental part of what we mean by a sense of audience. Although it is difficult to say how far such material should be taught directly, my own experience is that students are more receptive to descriptions and discussions of writing conventions as matters of social form and function than they are to descriptions of absolute criteria for good writing.

Finally, we need to keep in mind that the culture of the classroom can be a pervasive influence on a student's ability to understand an audience. In "Collaborative Learning and the 'Conversation of Mankind'" (*College English*, 46 [November 1984], 635–52), Kenneth Bruffee provides a fine account of the way that students can learn through social interaction to internalize and then re-externalize the kind of "conversation" that defines "a community of knowledgeable peers" (p. 642). At this point the discussion may appear to have moved far from analysis of audience, but at its most basic the issue of audience in writing instruction is one of social development and maturation—of student writers learning to see themselves as social beings in a social situation. Only in such a context can the art of rhetoric and of audience analysis have any real meaning or force in our teaching of writing.

PLANNING, DRAFTING, AND REVISING

COMPETING THEORIES OF PROCESS: A CRITIQUE AND A PROPOSAL

Lester Faigley

[*College English* 48 (1986): 527–42.]

Lester Faigley is professor of English and director of the Division of Rhetoric and Composition at the University of Texas at Austin. He has also been a senior fellow at the National University of Singapore and a visiting professor at Pennsylvania State University, the University of Utah, and in the Texas Summer Program at Brasnose College, Oxford University. In 1996, he served as chair of the annual Conference on College Composition and Communication. Faigley has published numerous articles and essays on subjects that range from discourse analysis, text linguistics, and composition theory to travel literature. His 1992 book *Fragments of Rationality: Postmodernity and the Subject of Composition* won the CCCC Outstanding Book Award in 1994.

Through his wide reading about the writing process, Faigley came to see the variety of notions that have been advanced about the process. "Competing Theories of Process" is an effort to sort out those notions and to examine their intellectual backgrounds. Faigley offers an overview of the three prevailing views of composing—the expressive, the cognitive, and the social—and examines the assumptions that each view makes about writers, writing, and the composing process. The article reminds instructors that the choices they make in their course plans and daily classroom practices are informed by an implicit or explicit theory of composing. Faigley's argument is particularly valuable for its suggestive synthesis of the three competing theoretical views.

The recognition of the study of writing as an important area of research within English in North America has also led to a questioning of its theoretical underpinnings. While the teaching of writing has achieved programmatic or departmental status at many colleges and universities, voices from outside and from within the ranks question whether a discipline devoted to the study of writing exists or if those who teach writing simply assume it exists because they share common problems and interests. The convenient landmark for disciplinary historians is the Richard Braddock, Richard Lloyd-Jones, and Lowell Schoer review of the field in 1963, a survey that found a legion of pedagogical studies of writing, most lacking any broad theoretical notion of writing abilities or even awareness of similar existing studies. Contemporary reviewers of writing research point out how much happened in the years that followed, but no development has been more influential than the emphasis on writing as a process. For the last few years, Richard Young's and Maxine Hairston's accounts of the process movement as a Kuhnian paradigm shift have served as justifications for disciplinary status. Even though the claim of a paradigm shift is now viewed by some as an overstatement, it is evident that many writing teachers in grade schools, high schools, and colleges have internalized process assumptions. In the most optimistic visions, writing teachers K–13 march happily under the process banner. Slogans such as "revising is good for you" are repeated in nearly every college writing textbook as well as in many secondary and elementary classrooms. Paradigm, pre-paradigm, or no paradigm, nearly everyone seems to agree that writing as a process is good and "current-traditional rhetoric" is bad. It would seem, therefore, that any disciplinary claims must be based on some shared definition of process.

The problem, of course, is that conceptions of writing as a process vary from theorist to theorist. Commentators on the process movement (e.g., Berlin, *Writing Instruction*) now assume at least two major perspectives on composing, an *expressive view* including the work of "authentic voice" proponents such as William Coles, Peter Elbow, Ken Macrorie, and Donald Stewart, and a *cognitive view* including the research of those who analyze composing processes such as Linda Flower, Barry Kroll, and Andrea Lunsford. More recently, a third perspective on composing has emerged, one that contends processes of writing are social in character instead of originating within individual writers. Statements on composing from the third perspective, which I call the *social view*, have come from Patricia Bizzell, Kenneth Bruffee, Marilyn Cooper, Shirley Brice Heath, James Reither, and authors of several essays collected in *Writing in Nonacademic Settings* edited by Lee Odell and Dixie Goswami.

Before I contrast the assumptions of each of these three views on composing with the goal of identifying a disciplinary basis for the study of writing, I want to raise the underlying assumption that the study and teaching of writing *should* aspire to disciplinary status. In a radical critique of education in America, Stanley Aronowitz and Henry Giroux see the development of writing programs as part of a more general trend toward an atheoretical and skills-oriented curriculum that regards teachers as civil servants who dispense prepackaged lessons. Here is Aronowitz and Giroux's assessment:

> We wish to suggest that schools, especially the colleges and universities, are now battlegrounds that may help to determine the shape of the future. The proliferation of composition programs at all levels of higher education may signal a new effort to extend the technicization process even further into the humanities. . . . The splitting of composition as a course from the study of literature, [*sic*] is of course a sign of its technicization and should be resisted both because it is an attack against critical thought and because it results in demoralization of teachers and their alienation from work. (52)

While I find their conclusions extreme, their critique provokes us to examine writing in relation to larger social and political issues. Unlike most other Marxist educational theorists, Aronowitz and Giroux do not present a pessimistic determinism nor do they deny human agency. They allow for the possibility that teachers and students can resist domination and think critically, thus leaving open the possibility for a historically aware theory and pedagogy of composing.

I will outline briefly the histories of each of the dominant theoretical views of composing, drawing on an earlier book by Giroux, *Theory and Resistance in Education*, for a critical review of the assumptions of each position.[1] In the concluding section of this essay, however, I reject Aronowitz and Giroux's dour assessment of the study of writing as a discipline. Each of the theoretical positions on composing has given teachers of writing a pedagogy for resisting a narrow definition of writing based largely on "correct" grammar and usage. Finally, I argue that disciplinary claims for writing must be based on a conception of process broader than any of the three views.

The Expressive View

The beginnings of composing research in the mid-1960s hardly marked a revolution against the prevailing line of research; in fact, early studies of composing issues typically were isolated pedagogical experiments similar to those described by Braddock, Lloyd-Jones, and Schoer. One of these experiments was D. Gordon Rohman and Albert Wlecke's study of the effects of "pre-writing" on writing performance, first published in 1964. Rohman and Wlecke maintained that thinking was different from writing and antecedent to writing; therefore, teachers should stimulate students' thinking by having them write journals, construct analogies, and, in the spirit of the sixties, meditate before writing essays. Young cites the Rohman and Wlecke study as one that helped to overturn the current-traditional paradigm. What Young neglects to mention is that Rohman and Wlecke revived certain Romantic notions about composing and were instigators of a "neo-Romantic" view of process. Rohman defines "good writing" as

> that discovered combination of words which allows a person the integrity to dominate his subject with a pattern both fresh and original. "Bad writing," then, is an echo of someone else's combination which we have merely taken over for the occasion of our writing. . . . "Good writing" must be the discovery by a responsible person of his uniqueness within his subject. (107–08)

This definition of "good writing" includes the essential qualities of Romantic expressivism—integrity, spontaneity, and originality—the same qualities M. H. Abram uses to define "expressive" poetry in *The Mirror and the Lamp*.

Each of these expressivist qualities has motivated a series of studies and theoretical statements on composing. We can see the influence of the first notion—integrity—in the transmission of Rohman and Wlecke's definitions of "good" and "bad" writing. In 1969 Donald Stewart argued that the unified aim for writing courses should be writing with integrity. He illustrated his argument with a student paper titled "Money Isn't as Valuable as It Seems" that contained a series of predictable generalities. Stewart criticized the student not for failing to support his generalizations but because he "doesn't believe what he is saying. Worse yet, it is possible that he doesn't even realize he doesn't believe it" (225).[2] The problem with using integrity as a measure of value is obvious in retrospect. Not only is the writer of the paper Stewart reproduces bound by his culture, as Stewart argues, but so too are Stewart's criticisms. Stewart's charges of insincerity are based on the assumption that the student is parroting the antiestablishment idealism of the late sixties. Conversely, career-oriented students of today are so unlikely to write such a paper, that if one started an essay with the same sentences as Stewart's example ("Having money is one of the least important items of life. Money only causes problems and heartaches among one's friends and self."), a teacher likely would assume that the student believed what she was saying, no matter how trite or predictable.

Because the sincerity of a text is finally impossible to assess, a second quality of Romantic expressivism—spontaneity—became important to the process movement primarily through Peter Elbow's *Writing without Teachers,* a book that was written for a broad audience, and that enjoyed great popular success. Elbow adopted Macrorie's method of free writing, but he presented the method as practical advice for writing spontaneously, not as a way of discovering "the truth." Elbow questioned Rohman and Wlecke's separation of thinking from writing, a model he maintained led to frustration. Instead, Elbow urged that we

> think of writing as an organic, developmental process in which you start writing at the very beginning—before you know your meaning at all—and encourage your words gradually to change and evolve. Only at the end will you know what you want to say or the words you want to say it with. (15)

Elbow chose the metaphor of organic growth to describe the operations of composing, the same metaphor Edward Young used to describe the vegetable concept of genius in 1759 and Coleridge borrowed from German philosophers to describe the workings of the imagination (see Abrams 198–225). Coleridge contrasted two kinds of form—one mechanical, when we impress upon any material a predetermined form, the other organic, when the material shapes itself from within. Coleridge also realized the plant metaphor implied a kind of organic determinism. (Tulip bulbs cannot grow into daffodils.) He avoided this consequence by insisting upon the free will of the artist, that the artist has foresight and the power of choice. In much the same way, Elbow qualifies his organic metaphor:

> It is true, of course, that an initial set of words does not, like a young live organism, contain within each cell a *plan* for the final mature stage and all the intervening stages that must be gone through. Perhaps, therefore, the final higher organization in words should only be called a borrowed reflection of a higher organization that is really in me or my mind. (23)

Elbow's point is one of the standards of Romantic theory: that "good" writing does not follow rules but reflects the processes of the creative imagination.

If writing is to unfold with organic spontaneity, then it ought to expose the writer's false starts and confused preliminary explorations of the topic. In other words, the writing should proceed obliquely as a "striving toward"—a mimetic of the writer's actual thought processes—and only hint at the goal of such striving. The resultant piece of writing would then seem fragmentary and unfinished, but would reveal what Coleridge calls a progressive method, a psychological rather than rhetorical organization, unifying its outwardly disparate parts. On the other hand, insofar as a piece of writing—no matter how expressive—is coherent, it must also be mimetic and rhetorical. At times Wordsworth and to a lesser extent Coleridge seem to argue that expressivism precludes all intentionality—as if such meditations as Wordsworth's "Tintern Abbey" and Coleridge's "This Lime-Tree Bower My Prison" weren't carefully *arranged* to seem spontaneous. Peter Elbow's solution to the dilemma of spontaneity comes in *Writing with Power,* where he discusses revision as the shaping of unformed material.

A third quality of Romantic expressivism—originality—could not be adapted directly to current theories of composing because the Romantic notion of originality is linked to the notion of natural genius, the difference between the poet who is born and the poet who is made. The concept of natural genius has been replaced in contemporary expressive theory with an emphasis on the innate potential of the unconscious mind. More limited statements of this position recommend teaching creative writing to stimulate originality.[3] Stronger statements come from those expressive theorists who apply the concept of "self-actualization" from psychoanalysis to writing. Rohman says teachers "must recognize and use, as the psychologists do in therapy, a person's desire to actualize himself" (108). The implication is that personal development aids writing development or that writing development can aid personal development, with the result that better psychologically integrated people become better writers. (Case histories of twentieth-century poets and novelists are seldom introduced in these discussions.) In an essay on meditation and writing James Moffett extends the self-actualization notion introduced by Rohman, saying "good therapy and composition aim at clear thinking, effective relating, and satisfying self-expression" (235).

Giroux, however, would see Moffett's essay as emblematic of what is wrong with the expressive view. Although Giroux grants that expressive theory came as a reaction against, to use his word, the "technicization" of education, he contends the result of the quest for "psychic redemption" and "personal growth" is a turning away from the relation of the individual to the social world, a world where "social practices situated in issues of class, gender, and race shape everyday experience" (219). For Giroux, the expressive view of composing ignores how writing works in the world, hides the social nature of language, and offers a false notion of a "private" self. Before I defend the expressive position against Giroux's attack, I will move on to the cognitive view where Giroux's strongest criticisms center.

The Cognitive View

In addition to promoting expressive assumptions about composing, Rohman and Wlecke helped inspire research that led to the current cognitive view. Several researchers in the late sixties were encouraged by Rohman and Wlecke's mention of *heuristics* and their finding that students who were taught "pre-writing" activities wrote better essays. More important, Rohman and Wlecke's proposal of three linear stages in the writing process stimulated research in response. In 1964 Janet Emig first argued against a linear model of composing, and she redoubled her attack in her 1969 dissertation, later published as an NCTE research monograph. Emig was among the first writing researchers to act on calls for research on cognitive processes issued at the influential 1966 Dartmouth Seminar on English. She observed that high school writers, in contrast to standard textbook advice of the time, did not use outlines to compose and that composing "does not occur as a left-to-right, solid, uninterrupted activity with an even pace" (84). Instead, Emig described composing as "recursive," an adjective from mathematics that refers to a formula generating successive terms. While the term is technically misapplied, since writing processes do not operate this simply, the extent to which it is used by other researchers attests to Emig's influence. Another measure of Emig's influence is that denunciations of Rohman and Wlecke's *Pre-Writing, Writing, Re-writing* model became a trope for introductions of later articles on composing.

In a recent consideration of Emig's monograph, Ralph Voss credits her with developing a "'science consciousness' in composition research" (279). Emig appropriated from psychology more than the case-study approach and think-aloud methodology. Her monograph is a mixture of social science and literary idioms, with one sentence talking about a "sense of closure," the next about "a moment in the process when one feels most godlike" (44). Emig's work was well received because writing researchers wanted to enter the mainstream of educational research. For example, Janice Lauer began a 1970 article directing writing researchers to psychologists' work in problem solving with the following sentence: "Freshman English will never reach the status of a respectable intellectual discipline unless both its theorizers and its practitioners break out of the ghetto" (396). Emig provided not only a new methodology but an agenda for subsequent research, raising issues such as pausing during composing, the role of rereading in revision, and the paucity of substantial revision in student writing. Her monograph led to numerous observational studies of writers' composing behavior during the next decade.[4]

The main ingredient Emig did not give researchers was a cognitive theory of composing. When writing researchers realized Chomsky's theory of transformational grammar could not explain composing abilities, they turned to two other sources of cognitive theory. The first was cognitive-developmental psychology, which James Britton and his colleagues applied to the developing sense of audience among young writers. Britton argued that children as speakers gain a sense of audience because the hearer is a reactive presence, but children as writers have more difficulty because the "other" is not present. Consequently, a child writing must imagine a generalized context for the particular text in all but the most immediate writing situations (such as an informal letter). Britton condemned most school writing assignments for failing to encourage children to imagine real writing situations (see *Development* 63–65). Other researchers probed the notion of developmental stages in writing. Barry Kroll adapted Jean Piaget's concept of *egocentrism*—the inability to take any perspective but one's own—to explain young children's lack of a sense of audience. He hypothesized, like Britton, that children's ability to *decenter*—to imagine another perspective—develops more slowly in writing than in speaking. Andrea Lunsford extended Piaget's stages of cognitive development to college basic writers, arguing that their tendency to lapse into personal narrative in writing situations that call for "abstract" discourse indicates they are arrested in an "egocentric stage."

The second source of cognitive theory came from American cognitive psychology, which has spawned several strands of research on composing. Many college writing teachers were introduced to a cognitive theory of composing through the work of Linda Flower and John R. Hayes. Flower and Hayes' main claims—that composing processes intermingle, that goals direct composing, and that experts compose differently from inexperienced writers—all have become commonplaces of the process movement. Less well understood by writing teachers, however, are the assumptions underlying Flower and Hayes' model, assumptions derived from a cognitive research tradition. Flower and Hayes acknowledge their debt to this tradition, especially to Allen Newell and Herbert A. Simon's *Human Problem Solving*, a classic work that helped define the aims and agenda for a cognitive science research program. Newell and Simon theorize that the key to understanding how people solve problems is in their "programmability"; in other words, how people use "a very simple information processing system" to account for their "problem solving in such tasks as chess, logic, and cryptarithmetic" (870). The idea that thinking and language can be represented by computers underlies much research in cognitive science in several camps, including artificial intelligence, computational linguistics, and cognitive psychology. Newell and Simon's historical overview of this movement credits Norbert Wiener's theory of *cybernetics* as the beginnings of contemporary cognitive science.[5] The basic principle of cybernetics is the *feedback loop,* in which the regulating mechanism receives information from the thing regulated and makes adjustments.

George A. Miller was among the first to introduce cybernetic theory as an alternative to the stimulus-response reflex arc as the basis of mental activity. In

Plans and the Structure of Behavior, Miller, Eugene Galanter, and Karl Pribram describe human behavior as guided by plans that are constantly being evaluated as they are being carried out in a feedback loop. They theorize that the brain—like a computer—is divided into a *memory* and a *processing unit.* What Miller, Galanter, and Pribram do not attempt to theorize is where plans come from. To fill in this gap, Newell and Simon add to the feedback loop an entity they call the *task environment,* defined in terms of a goal coupled with a specific environment. Newell and Simon claim the resulting loop explains how people think.

If we look at the graphic representation of the Flower and Hayes model in the 1980 and 1981 versions, we can see how closely the overall design follows in the cognitive science tradition. The box labeled *Writing Processes* is analogous to the central processing unit of a computer. In the 1980 version, diagrams representing the subprocesses of composing (*planning, translating,* and *reviewing*) are presented as computer flowcharts. Like Newell and Simon's model of information processing, Flower and Hayes' model makes strong theoretical claims in assuming relatively simple cognitive operations produce enormously complex actions, and like Emig's monograph, the Flower and Hayes model helped promote a "science consciousness" among writing teachers. Even though cognitive researchers have warned that "novice writers cannot be turned into experts simply by tutoring them in the knowledge expert writers have" (Scardamalia 174), many writing teachers believed cognitive research could provide a "deep structure" theory of *the* composing process, which could in turn specify how writing should be taught. Furthermore, the Flower and Hayes model had other attractions. The placement of *translating* after *planning* was compatible with the sequence of invention, arrangement, and style in classical rhetoric. It also suited a popular conception that language comes after ideas are formed, a conception found in everyday metaphors that express ideas as objects placed in containers (e.g., "It's difficult to put my ideas into words").[6]

Giroux's response to the cognitive view of composing can be readily inferred. To begin, Giroux would be highly critical of any attempt to discover universal laws underlying writing. Writing for Giroux, like other acts of literacy, is not universal but social in nature and cannot be removed from culture. He would fault the cognitive view for collapsing cultural issues under the label "audience," which, defined unproblematically, is reduced to the status of a variable in an equation. He further would accuse the cognitive view of neglecting the content of writing and downplaying conflicts inherent in acts of writing. As a consequence, pedagogies assuming a cognitive view tend to overlook differences in language use among students of different social classes, genders, and ethnic backgrounds.

At this point I'll let Giroux's bricks fly against my windows and use an article on revision I wrote with Steve Witte as a case in point. In this study Witte and I attempt to classify revision changes according to the extent they affect the content of the text. We apply a scheme for describing the structure of a text developed by the Dutch text linguist, Teun van Dijk. What seems obviously wrong with this article in hindsight is the degree to which we assign meaning to the text. Now even van Dijk admits there are as many macrostructures for a text as there are readers. Although our conclusions criticize the artificiality of the experiment and recognize that "revision cannot be separated from other aspects of composing," the intent of the study still suffers from what Giroux sees as a fundamental flaw of cognitivist research—the isolation of part from whole.

The Social View

The third perspective on composing I identified at the beginning of this essay—the social view—is less codified and less constituted at present than the expressive and cognitive views because it arises from several disciplinary traditions. Because of this diversity a comprehensive social view cannot be extrapolated from a collection of positions in the same way I have described the expressive and cognitive views of composing. Statements that propose a social view of writing range from those urging more attention to the immediate circumstances of how a text is composed to those denying the existence of an individual author. My effort to outline a social view will be on the basis of one central assumption: human language (including writing) can be understood only from the perspective of a society rather than a single individual. Thus taking a social view requires a great deal more than simply paying more attention to the context surrounding a discourse. It rejects the assumption that writing is the act of a private consciousness and that everything else—readers, subjects, and texts—is "out there" in the world. The focus of a social view of writing, therefore, is not on how the social situation influences the individual, but on how the individual is a constituent of a culture.

I will attempt to identify four lines of research that take a social view of writing, although I recognize that these positions overlap and that each draws on earlier work (e.g., Kenneth Burke). These four lines of research can be characterized by the traditions from which they emerge: poststructuralist theories of language, the sociology of science, ethnography, and Marxism.

In the last few years, writing researchers influenced by poststructuralist theories of language have brought notions of discourse communities to discussions of composing. Patricia Bizzell and David Bartholomae, for example, have found such ideas advantageous in examining the writing of college students. Those who believe that meaning resides in the text accuse any other position of solipsism and relativism, but concepts of discourse communities provide an alternative position, offering solutions to difficult problems in interpretative theory. Reading is neither an experience of extracting a fixed meaning from a text nor is it a matter of making words mean anything you want them to in *Alice in Wonderland* fashion. Ambiguity in texts is not the problem for humans that it is for computers—not so much because we are better at extracting meaning but because language is social practice; because, to paraphrase Bakhtin, words carry with them the places where they have been.

This view of language raises serious problems for cognitive-based research programs investigating adults' composing processes. For instance, Bizzell criticizes the separation of "Planning" and "Translating" in the Flower and Hayes model. Even though Flower and Hayes allow for language to generate language through rereading, Bizzell claims the separation of words from ideas distorts the nature of composing. Bizzell cites Vygotsky, whom many cognitive researchers lump together with Piaget, but whose understanding of language is very different from Piaget's. Vygotsky studied language development as a historical and cultural process, in which a child acquires not only the words of language but the intentions carried by those words and the situations implied by them.

From a social perspective, a major shortcoming in studies that contrast expert and novice writers lies not so much in the artificiality of the experimental situation, but in the assumption that expertise can be defined outside of a specific community of writers. Since individual expertise varies across communities, there can be no one definition of an expert writer. David Bartholomae explores the implications for the teaching of college writing. He argues that writing in college is difficult for inexperienced writers not because they are forced to make the transition from "writer-based" to "reader-based" prose but because they lack the privileged language of the academic community. Bartholomae's point is similar to Bizzell's: when students write in an academic discipline, they write in reference to texts that define the scholarly activities of interpreting and reporting in that discipline. Bartholomae alludes to Barthes' observation that a text on a particular topic always has "off-stage voices" for what has previously been written about that topic. Thus a social view of writing moves beyond the expressivist contention that the individual discovers the self through language and beyond the cognitivist position that an individual constructs reality through language. In a social view, any effort to write about the self or reality always comes in relation to previous texts.

A substantial body of research examining the social processes of writing in an academic discourse community now exists in the sociology of science. Most of this research has been done in Britain, but Americans Charles Bazerman and Greg Myers have made important contributions. . . . Research in scientific writing displays many of the theoretical and methodological differences mentioned at the beginning of this section, but this literature taken as a whole challenges the assumption that scientific texts contain autonomous presentations of facts; instead, the texts are "active social tools in the complex interactions of a research community" (Bazerman 3). In the more extreme version of this argument, which follows from Rorty and other pragmatists, science itself becomes a collection of literary forms. Writing about the basis of economics, Donald McCloskey calls statistics "figures of speech in numerical dress" (98). He goes on to say that "the scientific paper is, after all, a literary genre, with an actual author, an implied author, an implied reader, a history, and a form" (105). In contrast, current British research understands a dialectical relationship between external reality and the conventions of a community. A good introduction to this field is Nigel Gilbert and Michael Mulkay's 1984 book, *Opening Pandora's Box.*[7]

A third line of research taking a social view of composing develops from the tradition of ethnography. Ethnographic methodology in the 1970s and 1980s has been used to examine the immediate communities in which writers learn to write—the family and the classroom. These researchers have observed that for many children, the ways literacy is used at home and in the world around them matches poorly with the literacy expectations of the school.[8] The most important of these studies to date is Shirley Brice Heath's analysis of working-class and middle-class families in the Carolina Piedmont. Heath found that how children learn to use literacy originates from how families and communities are structured. Another line of research using ethnographic methodology investigates writing in the workplace, interpreting acts of writing and reading within the culture of the workplace (see Odell and Goswami for examples).

Finally, I include Marxist studies of literacy as a fourth social position on composing. The essential tenet of a Marxist position would be that any act of writing or of teaching writing must be understood within a structure of power related to modes of production. A Marxist critique of the other social positions would accuse each of failing to deal with key concepts such as class, power, and ideology.[9] Giroux finds discourse communities are often more concerned with ways of excluding new members than with ways of admitting them. He attacks non-Marxist ethnographies for sacrificing "theoretical depth for methodological refinement" (98). Indeed, much Marxist scholarship consists of faulting other theorists for their lack of political sophistication.

Toward a Synthesis

At the beginning of this essay I quoted Aronowitz and Giroux's conclusion that the spread of writing programs and, by implication, the process movement itself are part of a general movement toward "atheoretical" and "skills-oriented" education in America. Now I would like to evaluate that claim. If process theory and pedagogy have up to now been unproblematically accepted, I see a danger that it could be unproblematically rejected. Process theory and pedagogy have given student writing a value and authority absent in current-traditional approaches. Each view of process has provided teachers with ways of resisting static methods of teaching writing —methods based on notions of abstract form and adherence to the "rules" of Standard English. Expressive theorists validate personal experience in school systems that often deny it. Cognitive theorists see language as a way of negotiating the world, which is the basis of James Berlin's dialogic redefinition of epistemic rhetoric (*Rhetoric and Reality*). And social theorists such as Heath have found that children who are labeled remedial in traditional classrooms can learn literacy skills by studying the occurrences of writing in the familiar world around them (see *Ways with Words,* chapter 9).

But equally instructive is the conclusion of Heath's book, where she describes how the curriculum she helped create was quickly swept away. It illustrates how social and historical forces shape the teaching of writing— relationships that, with few exceptions, are only now beginning to be critically investigated. If the process movement is to continue to influence the teaching of writing and to supply alternatives to current-traditional pedagogy, it must take a broader conception of writing, one that understands writing processes are historically dynamic—not psychic states, cognitive routines, or neutral social relationships. This historical awareness would allow us to reinterpret and integrate each of the theoretical perspectives I have outlined.

The expressive view presents one of two opposing influences in discourse— the unique character of particular acts of writing versus the conventions of language, genre, and social occasion that make that act understandable to others. The expressive view, therefore, leads us to one of the key paradoxes of literacy. When literacy began to be widespread in Northern Europe and its colonies during the eighteenth and nineteenth centuries, it reduced differences between language groups in those countries and brought an emphasis on standard usage. But at the same time linguistic differences were being reduced, individuals became capable of changing the social order by writing for a literate populace (witness the many revolutionary tracts published during the nineteenth century). Furthermore, modern notions of the individual came into being through the widespread publication of the many literary figures and philosophers associated with the Romantic movement and the later development of psychology as a discipline in the nineteenth century. Current technologies for electronic communications bring the potential for gaining access to large bodies of information from the home, yet at the same time these technologies bring increased potential for control through surveillance of communication and restriction of access. People, however, find ways to adapt technologies for their own interests. In organizations where computer technologies have become commonplace, people have taken advantage of opportunities for horizontal communication on topics of their choice through computer "bulletin boards," which function like radio call-in programs. For example, on ARPANET, the Department of Defense's computer network linking research facilities, military contractors, and universities, popular bulletin boards include ones for science fiction, movie reviews, and even a lively debate on arms control. How the possibilities for individual expression will be affected by major technological changes in progress should become one of the most important areas of research for those who study writing.

In a similar way, historical awareness would enhance a cognitive view of composing by demonstrating the historical origins of an individual writer's goals. The cognitive view has brought attention to how writers compose in the workplace. Many writing tasks on the job can be characterized as rhetorical "problems," but the problems themselves are not ones the writers devise. Writing processes take place as part of a structure of power. For instance, Lee Iacocca's autobiography reveals how writing conveys power in large organizations. Iacocca says he communicated good news in writing, but bad news orally. Surely Iacocca's goals and processes in writing are inseparable from what he does and where he works, which in turn must be considered in relation to other large corporations, and which finally should be considered within a history of capitalism.

Some social approaches to the study of discourse entail historical awareness, but a social view is not necessarily historical. The insight that the learning of literacy is a social activity within a specific community will not necessarily lead us to a desirable end. Raymond Williams observes that the term *community* has been used to refer to existing social relationships or possible alternative social relationships, but that it is always used positively, that there is no opposing term. Yet we know from the sad experiences of the twentieth century that consensus often brings oppression. How written texts become instruments of power in a community is evident in the history of colonial empires, where written documents served to implement colonial power. Some of the earliest recorded uses of writing in Mesopotamia and ancient Egypt were for collecting taxes and issuing laws in conquered territories. Written documents made possible the incident George Orwell describes in "The Hanging"—an essay frequently anthologized but rarely analyzed in writing classes for its political significance. Furthermore, in the effort to identify conventions that define communities of writers, commentators on writing processes from a social viewpoint have neglected the issue of what *cannot* be discussed in a particular community, exclusions Foucault has shown to be the exercise of power.

These questions are not mere matters of ivory-tower debate. The preoccupation with an underlying theory of the writing process has led us to neglect finding answers to the most obvious questions in college writing instruction today: why college writing courses are prevalent in the United States and rare in the rest of the world; why the emphasis on teaching writing occurring in the aftermath of the "literacy crisis" of the seventies has not abated; why the majority of college writing courses are taught by graduate students and other persons in nontenurable positions. Answers to such questions will come only when we look beyond who is writing to whom to the texts and social systems that stand in relation to that act of writing. If the teaching of writing is to reach disciplinary status, it will be achieved through recognition that writing processes are, as Stanley Fish says of linguistic knowledge, "contextual rather than abstract, local rather than general, dynamic rather than invariant" (438).

Notes

[1] Giroux directly criticizes "romantic" and "cognitive developmental" traditions of teaching literacy in *Theory and Resistance in Education.* Bruce Herzberg has extended Giroux's critique to particular composition theorists.

[2] Even more strident attacks on clichés and conventional writing assignments came from Ken Macrorie, who damned "themes" as papers "not meant to be read but corrected" (686), and from William Coles, who accused textbook authors of promoting "themewriting" by presenting writing "as a trick that can be played, a device that can be put into operation . . . just as one can be taught or learn to run an adding machine, or pour concrete" (134–42).

[3] For example, Art Young advocates having students write poems, plays, and stories in writing-across-the-curriculum classes. During the 1920s and 1930s, there were numerous appeals to incorporate creative writing into the English curriculum; see, for example, Lou LaBrant.

[4] For a bibliographic review of cognitive studies of composing, see Faigley, Cherry, Jolliffe, and Skinner, chapters 1–5.

[5] Wiener used the term *cybernetics*—derived from the Greek word for the pilot of a ship—as a metaphor for the functioning mind. He claimed as a precedent James Watt's use of the word *governor* to describe the mechanical regulator of a steam engine. Wiener's metaphor explained the mind as a control mechanism such as an automatic pilot of an airplane. For a historical overview of cybernetics and the beginnings of cognitive science, see Bell.

[6] Reddy discusses some of the consequences of the "conduit" metaphor for our understanding of language.

[7] Gilbert and Mulkay provide a bibliography of social studies of scientific discourse on 194–95.

[8] Heath includes an annotated bibliography of school and community ethnographies in the endnotes of *Ways with Words*.

[9] Richard Ohmann's *English in America* remains the seminal Marxist analysis of American writing instruction.

Works Cited

Abrams, M. H. *The Mirror and the Lamp*. New York: Oxford UP, 1953.

Aronowitz, Stanley, and Henry A. Giroux. *Education under Siege*. South Hadley, MA: Bergin, 1985.

Bartholomae, David. "Inventing the University." *When a Writer Can't Write*. Ed. Mike Rose. New York: Guilford, 1985. 134–65.

Bazerman, Charles. "Physicists Reading Physics: Schema-Laden Purposes and Purpose-Laden Schema." *Written Communication* 2 (1985): 3–23.

Bell, Daniel. *The Social Sciences since the Second World War*. New Brunswick, NJ: Transaction, 1982.

Berlin, James. *Rhetoric and Reality: Writing in American Colleges, 1900–1985*. Carbondale: Southern Illinois UP, 1984.

———. *Writing Instruction in Nineteenth-Century American Colleges*. Carbondale: Southern Illinois UP, 1984.

Bizzell, Patricia. "Cognition, Convention, and Certainty: What We Need to Know about Writing." *PRE/TEXT* 3 (1982): 213–43.

Braddock, Richard, Richard Lloyd-Jones, and Lowell Schoer. *Research in Written Composition*. Urbana: NCTE, 1963.

Britton, James, Tony Burgess, Nancy Martin, Alex McLeod, and Harold Rosen. *The Development of Writing Abilities (11–18)*. London: Macmillan, 1975.

Bruffee, Kenneth A. "Collaborative Learning and the 'Conversion of Mankind.'" *College English* 46 (1984): 635–52.

Coleridge, Samuel Taylor. "On Method." *The Portable Coleridge*. Ed. I. A. Richards. New York: Viking, 1950. 339–86.

Coles, William, Jr. "Freshman Composition: The Circle of Unbelief." *College English* 31 (1969): 134–42.

Cooper, Marilyn M. "The Ecology of Writing." *College English* 48 (1986): 364–75.

Elbow, Peter. *Writing without Teachers*. New York: Oxford UP, 1973.

———. *Writing with Power*. New York: Oxford UP, 1981.

Emig, Janet. *The Composing Processes of Twelfth Graders*, NCTE Research Report No. 13. Urbana: NCTE, 1971.

———. "The Uses of the Unconscious in Composing." *College Composition and Communication* 16 (1964): 6–11.

Faigley, Lester, Roger D. Cherry, David A. Jolliffe, and Anna M. Skinner. *Assessing Writers' Knowledge and Processes of Composing*. Norwood, NJ: Ablex, 1985.

Faigley, Lester, and Stephen P. Witte. "Analyzing Revision." *College Composition and Communication* 32 (1981): 400–14.

Fish, Stanley. "Consequences." *Critical Inquiry* 11 (1985): 433–58.

Flower, Linda, and John R. Hayes. "A Cognitive Process Theory of Writing." *College Composition and Communication* 31 (1980): 365–87.

Foucault, Michel. *Power/Knowledge: Selected Interviews and Other Writings, 1972–1977*. Ed. Colin Gordon. New York: Pantheon, 1980.

Gilbert, G. Nigel, and Michael Mulkay. *Opening Pandora's Box: A Sociological Analysis of Scientists' Discourse*. Cambridge: Cambridge UP, 1984.

Giroux, Henry A. *Theory and Resistance in Education*. South Hadley, MA: Bergin, 1983.

Hairston, Maxine. "The Winds of Change: Thomas Kuhn and the Revolution in the Teaching of Writing." *College Composition and Communication* 33 (1982): 76–88.

Hayes, John R., and Linda Flower. "Identifying the Organization of Writing Processes." *Cognitive Processes in Writing: An Interdisciplinary Approach*. Ed. Lee Gregg and Erwin Steinberg. Hillsdale, NJ: Erlbaum, 1980. 3–30.

Heath, Shirley Brice. *Ways with Words.* New York: Cambridge UP, 1983.

Herzberg, Bruce. "The Politics of Discourse Communities." Paper presented at the Conference on College Composition and Communication, New Orleans, March 1986.

Iacocca, Lee. *Iacocca: An Autobiography.* New York: Bantam, 1984.

Kroll, Barry M. "Cognitive Egocentrism and the Problem of Audience Awareness in Written Discourse." *Research in the Teaching of English* 12 (1978): 269–81.

LaBrant, Lou. "The Psychological Basis for Creative Writing." *English Journal* 25 (1936): 292–301.

Lauer, Janice. "Heuristics and Composition." *College Composition and Communication* 21 (1970): 396–404.

Lunsford, Andrea. "The Content of Basic Writers' Essays." *College Composition and Communication* 31 (1980): 278–90.

Macrorie, Ken. "To Be Read." *English Journal* 57 (1968): 686–92.

McCloskey, Donald N. "The Literary Character of Economics." *Daedalus* 113.3 (1984): 97–119.

Miller, George A., Eugene Galanter, and Karl Pribram. *Plans and the Structure of Behavior.* New York: Holt, 1962.

Moffett, James. "Writing, Inner Speech, and Meditation." *College English* 44 (1982): 231–44.

Myers, Greg. "Texts as Knowledge Claims: The Social Construction of Two Biologists' Articles." *Social Studies of Science* 15 (1985): 593–630.

———. "Writing Research and the Sociology of Scientific Knowledge: A Review of Three New Books." *College English* 48 (1986): 595–610.

Newell, Alan, and Herbert A. Simon. *Human Problem Solving.* Englewood Cliffs, NJ: Prentice, 1972.

Odell, Lee, and Dixie Goswami, eds. *Writing in Nonacademic Settings.* New York: Guilford, 1985.

Ohmann, Richard. *English in America: A Radical View of the Profession.* New York: Oxford UP, 1976.

Reddy, Michael J. "The Conduit Metaphor." *Metaphor and Thought.* Ed. Andrew Ortony. Cambridge: Cambridge UP, 1979. 284–324.

Reither, James A. "Writing and Knowing: Toward Redefining the Writing Process." *College English* 47 (1985): 620–28.

Rohman, D. Gordon, "Pre-Writing: The Stage of Discovery in the Writing Process." *College Composition and Communication* 16 (1965): 106–12.

Rohman, D. Gordon, and Alfred O. Wlecke. "Pre-Writing: The Construction and Application of Models for Concept Formation in Writing." U.S. Department of Health, Education, and Welfare Cooperative Research Project No. 2174. East Lansing: Michigan State U, 1964.

Scardamalia, Marlene, Carl Bereiter, and Hillel Goelman. "The Role of Production Factors in Writing Ability." *What Writers Know: The Language, Process, and Structure of Written Discourse.* Ed. Martin Nystrand. New York: Academic, 1982. 173–210.

Stewart, Donald. "Prose with Integrity: A Primary Objective." *College Composition and Communication* 20 (1969): 223–27.

Voss, Ralph. "Janet Emig's *The Composing Processes of Twelfth Graders:* A Reassessment." *College Composition and Communication* 34 (1983): 278–83.

Williams, Raymond. *Keywords: A Vocabulary of Culture and Society.* New York: Oxford UP, 1976.

Young, Art. "Considering Values: The Poetic Function of Language." *Language Connections.* Ed. Toby Fulwiler and Art Young. Urbana: NCTE, 1982. 77–97.

Young, Richard. "Paradigms and Problems: Needed Research in Rhetorical Invention." *Research on Composing: Points of Departure.* Ed. Charles R. Cooper and Lee Odell. Urbana: NCTE, 1978. 29–47.

Acknowledgment: Joseph Alkana, Andrew Cooper, Beth Daniell, Kristine Hansen, Greg Myers, Carolyn Miller, and Walter Reed made helpful comments on earlier drafts of this essay.

PREWRITING TECHNIQUES

Erika Lindemann

[From *A Rhetoric for Writing Teachers* by Erika Lindemann. 3rd ed. New York: Oxford UP, 1995. 105–25.]

A professor of English and current director of the writing program at the University of North Carolina at Chapel Hill, Erika Lindemann also teaches writing courses and courses for writing teachers. Her book *A Rhetoric for Writing Teachers*, first published in 1982 and with a fourth edition forthcoming, has become a standard text in composition studies. Lindemann has published numerous articles and chapters, and with Gary Tate she coedited *An Introduction to Composition Studies* (1991). Among her numerous professional awards, Lindemann has been recognized by CCCC for her service as the first editor of the Longman and CCCC Bibliographies of Composition and Rhetoric.

Recognizing that "prewriting" activities "help students assess the dimensions of a rhetorical problem and plan its solution," Lindemann suggests that teachers "involve students in several prewriting activities, not just one, for each assignment." Lindemann thinks of prewriting and of invention strategies as "keys of different shapes and sizes that grant access to experience, memory, and intuition." In this chapter from *A Rhetoric for Writing Teachers,* Lindemann presents numerous prewriting activities, including "perception exercises," "brainstorming and clustering," "freewriting," using journals, heuristics, and models. Lindemann helps teachers understand the larger complex rhetorical contexts in which these kinds of activities will be most effective.

This is the first requirement for good writing: truth; not the truth . . . but some kind of truth—a connection between the things written about, the words used in the writing, and the author's real experience in the world he knows well—whether in fact or dream or imagination.

–Ken Macrorie

The prewriting techniques discussed in this chapter help students assess the dimensions of a rhetorical problem and plan its solution. They trigger perceptual and conceptual processes, permitting writers to recall experiences, break through stereotyped thinking, examine relationships between ideas, assess the expectations of their audience, find an implicit order in their subject matter, and discover how they feel about the work.[1] Some prewriting activities enable writers to probe the subject from several perspectives; others help writers assess their relationship to an audience. Some use pictures, talk, or pantomine to generate ideas, while others ask students to write lists, notes, and scratch outlines.

As a rule, the more time students spend on a variety of prewriting activities, the more successful the paper will be. In working out the possibilities an assignment suggests, students discover what they honestly want to say and address some of the decisions they must make if the paper is to express a message effectively. Writing the first draft becomes easier because some writing—notes, list, freewriting—has already taken place. Drafting also becomes more productive because students are less preoccupied with formulating ideas from scratch and freer to discover new messages as the words appear on the page.

In many composition textbooks, the only prewriting technique discussed is the formal outline. Although writers rarely construct elaborate outlines, informal outlines serve a useful purpose. Outlining can help students shape raw material generated by other prewriting activities. Outlining also can serve revision because when students outline a draft they may discover digressions, inconsistencies, or other organizational problems to work on. Nevertheless, outlining represents only one of many prewriting activities.

Because prewriting is a means to an end, I don't grade the notes, lists, and miscellaneous scratch work my students turn in with their final drafts. I look through the material, however, to discover which students need help generating more support for their topics or making prewriting work more efficiently for them. I also involve students in several prewriting activities, not just one, for each assignment. Sequencing several kinds of prewriting activities encourages students to explore their subjects thoroughly, planning their response to an assignment gradually, moving tentatively but then more confidently toward a first draft. Eventually, students modify and combine in whatever ways work best for them the techniques discussed in this chapter. All of them offer writers places to begin, keys of different shapes and sizes that grant access to experience, memory, and intuition.

Perception Exercises

Thinking games, "conceptual blockbusting," and sense-scrambling activities encourage students to think about how they think. By analyzing the steps they go through to "have ideas" or solve problems, they discover barriers that block perceptions.[2] Much of the material in Chapter 6, including the five-of-hearts exercise, can prompt a discussion of these perceptual, cultural, emotional, and intellectual barriers. To demonstrate these principles, you might ask students to pair up and by turns lead each other blindfolded on a tour of the building or some other familiar place. Deprived of their visual orientations, they can appreciate perceptions gained through other senses: smell, touch, hearing. Students also might discuss pictures, a busy city street for example, and then draw the scene from various perspectives. What would a bird's-eye view of the picture look like? How would you draw it if you were standing at the right-hand side of the picture looking left? After students have compared their drawings and discussed the differences in perspective, the class can move on to other prewriting activities directly relevant to a particular assignment.

For many students, arts and media that don't involve writing offer a comfortable place to begin probing a subject. Pantomime and role-playing encourage students to act out a subject before translating it into written form. Especially when an issue admits several points of view or when an audience may hold diverse opinions about a subject, role-playing clarifies the options students must consider. Assignments involving argumentation can begin with impromptu debates, which might then be worked into brief written dialogues and from there into more formal kinds of discourse. Similarly, students can translate reading assignments, pictures, or music from one medium to another, then to a third and finally to a written form. The assumption behind these activities is that similar principles govern communication in various media. When students practice the "language" of pictorial art, of gesture, and of music, they also learn principles that reinforce their use of the spoken and written word. Furthermore, in responding to cartoons, music, and pantomime, students become more sensitive observers of their world.

Not every piece of writing, of course, finds a convenient beginning in art, music, or drama, but all writing can begin with speech, a comfortable means of expression for most people. As Robert Zoellner and others have suggested, talking out a rhetorical problem helps students define and solve it: "Since students have a greater fluency in speaking than in writing because they practice it more, speaking can be used as a stage prior to writing and can provide the basis for moving through increasingly adequate written versions of a unit of discourse."[3] All students, especially those whose fear of failure makes writing anything, even scratch notes, difficult, need opportunities to explain their plans to themselves or discuss them with other students, a sympathetic teacher, or even a tape recorder. Every assignment should provide several opportunities for students to discuss their work-in-progress with one another.

Brainstorming and Clustering

Brainstorming is an unstructured probing of a topic. Like free association, brainstorming allows writers to venture whatever comes to mind about a subject, no matter how obvious or strange the ideas might be. When the entire class brainstorms a topic, the teacher generally writes on the board whatever words and phrases students call out. When students brainstorm topics on their own, they list whatever details occur to them. As a rule, general or superficial observations head the list, but as students begin to examine the subject more closely, useful and interesting details begin to appear. To be useful, of course, the list must contain abundant raw material.

Sometimes, however, brainstorming yields only rambling, unfocused, or repetitive generalizations. If the teacher has presented the technique as an end in itself, students may conclude, "Okay, she wants a list of 100 details, so I'll give her a list of 100 details." The purpose of brainstorming is neither list making nor reaching a precise number of details. As Donald Murray advises in *A Writer Teaches Writing,* "The teacher must, in such lists as this, begin to encourage honesty, to have the student look into himself and into his subject with candor and vigor. The list also gives the teacher a chance to defeat the cliché and the vague generalization by saying to the student, 'What does that mean? Can you be more specific?' The teacher should praise a student when he gets a good concrete detail which has the ring of reality" (1st ed., p. 78). At least initially, students need guidance in generating *useful* details and enough of them to permit discarding those that seem irrelevant. Students also need reminding that list making serves a larger purpose, to explore the subject thoroughly and discover what makes it interesting or important.

Teachers can go over these lists with individual students in brief conferences during class. An especially rich list can be the subject of whole-class discussion, followed by groups of students reviewing their own lists with one another. What details seem most forceful? In what ways could details be grouped? What patterns have emerged in the list? What dimensions of the subject seemed to attract the writer's interest? What details must be left out at this point if the first draft is to hang together? A discussion along these lines helps students discover organizational possibilities in the raw material and suggests options for developing the paper.

Following such a discussion, students might begin clustering their material, grouping and regrouping items into a diagram such as the one in Figure 7.1. Called "mapping," "clustering," or "webbing," the process of creating such drawings helps writers explore the organizational possibilities in their material. Unlike formal outlines, with their restrictive system of Roman and Arabic numerals and their need for parallelism, cluster diagrams represent provisional representations of the relationships among topics, subtopics, and supporting evidence. If one area of the diagram looks skimpy, additional brainstorming will provide more material (or the writer may abandon it altogether). Heavy branches may need subdividing.

The clusters in Figure 7.1 grew out of a brainstorming session on the topic "campus problems." As it happened, the class creating the diagram eventually abandoned "campus problems" as the topic because the material in some of the subtopics—"alcoholism," "racism," and "apathy"—seemed more interesting. As with most cluster diagrams, any branch could be developed into a new, more detailed diagram. The purpose of clustering is to help a writer discover order in a subject and to transform lists of details into meaningful groupings, some of which eventually may find a place in a first draft.

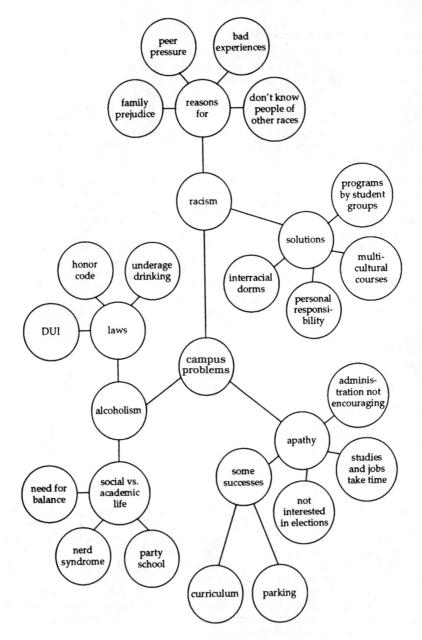

Figure 7.1 Cluster Diagram

Freewriting

Freewriting, a technique advocated by Peter Elbow and Ken Macrorie, offers students a risk-free way of getting words onto a page without having to worry about their correctness. Elbow explains the technique this way:

> The idea is simply to write for ten minutes (later on, perhaps fifteen or twenty). Don't stop for anything. Go quickly without rushing. Never stop to look back, to cross something out, to wonder how to spell something, to wonder what word or thought to use, or to think about what you are doing. If you can't think of a word or a spelling, just use a squiggle or else write, "I can't think of it." Just put down something. The easiest thing is just to put down whatever is in your mind. If you get stuck it's fine to write "I can't think of what to say, I can't think what to say" as many times as you want: or repeat the last word you wrote over and over again: or anything else. The only requirement is that you *never* stop. (*Writing without Teachers*, p. 3)

Elbow recommends that students freewrite at least three times a week. Freewritings, he insists, should *never* be graded. Their primary purpose is to get something on paper, and "it's an unnecessary burden to try to think of words and also worry at the same time whether they're the right words" (p. 5). Macrorie advocates freewriting because it produces honest writing, writing that is free from phoniness or pretension. The writer must write fast enough to use "his own natural language without thinking of his expression" (*Telling Writing*, p. 9).

Some teachers do not constrain freewriting in any way; others offer a phrase or the beginning of a sentence to help students get started. Teachers also can sequence freewriting exercises in several ways to move students closer to more formal drafts. For example, after students have completed a freewriting, they may read it aloud or silently to find words, phrases, a sentence or two that seem especially appealing. These words then offer a place to begin a second freewriting. The second freewriting may suggest ideas for a third and so on.

Murray sequences freewritings by incorporating student response at each stage.[4] First, students write freely for five minutes or so. Then, working in pairs, they discuss the freewriting by answering a question about it: "What appeared on the page that you didn't expect?" After a few minutes of discussion, students complete a second freewriting and stop to discuss it: "What idea do you want to develop in the next freewriting?" The procedure is repeated six or seven times, a new question guiding the students' discussion after each period of writing. The questions help students focus on what has appeared, on where the composing process is taking them. Teachers and students may substitute their own questions to guide the discussion, focusing on the writing but at the same time leaving students free to let their own language take charge of the page: What is the writing telling you? How do you (the writer) feel about what is appearing on the page? What do you (the reader) need to know that I haven't told you yet?

Freewriting encourages students to overcome their fear of the blank page and their stifling preoccupation with correctness. The technique encourages play with language and uses language as an aid to thinking. A freewriting represents a writer talking out an idea; it is not a polished communication intended for an outside audience. Needless to say, if teachers grade freewritings, they are no longer "free." Threatened by grades, students will shift their attention from generating and developing ideas to editing a finished product.

Journals

Journals, commonplace books, or writer's notebooks have been indispensable tools for many writers, the famous and not so famous. Some journals, like diaries, record experiences and observations meant only to be read by their authors.

Other journals, Virginia Woolf's *Writer's Diary* and Ralph Waldo Emerson's *Journals* for example, contain such significant information about an author's life and work that they reach a large public audience. Many professional writers use journals to sketch out, organize, draft, and revise their work before they submit it for publication.

The journal has several uses in a writing class. Many teachers set aside the first few minutes of every class period for journal writing. While the teacher checks the roll, returns papers, or reviews the lesson plan, students use the time to write whatever they want in their journals. The procedure settles the class down to work and gives students daily writing practice. To avoid treating the journal as inconsequential busywork, students should have opportunities to develop the material recorded in their journals into more formal assignments. Journals also can become workbooks for the course. In them, students may practice freewriting, respond to reading assignments, jot down leading ideas in preparation for class discussion, work out plans for papers, complete sentence-combining exercises, work on revisions, experiment with stylistic effects, keep track of spelling demons, and note which writing problems they have conquered and which still need work.

Unaccustomed to writing without some teacher-made assignment in front of them, students may protest that they can't think of anything to write in their journals, or they may devote several entries to deliberately "detached" topics: "I got up at eight, skipped breakfast, and went to class. Nothing much happened today." When this happens, teachers can discuss the difference between simply recording experiences and the more productive activity of reacting to or reflecting on events. They might also suggest that students capture a feeling in words or speculate about some imaginary, "what if" situation. If these open-ended, deliberately vague suggestions don't work, the following list might help, at least until students become comfortable pursuing their own interests.[5]

1. Speculate. Why do you spend so much time in a certain place? Why do you read a certain book or see a particular movie more than once?
2. Sketch in words a person who doesn't know you're watching: a woman studying her reflection in a store window, a spectator at a sports event, a student studying desperately.
3. Record some observations about a current song, book, movie, television program.
4. React to something you've read recently. Was it well written? Why or why not? What strategies did the writer use to get you to like or dislike the piece?
5. Try to capture an incident of night fear—when a bush became a bear, for example—so that a reader might feel the same way you did.
6. Explain an important lesson you learned as a child.
7. If peace were a way of life and not merely a sentiment, what would you have to give up?
8. Describe your idea of paradise or hell.
9. Write a nasty letter complaining about some product that didn't work or some service that was performed poorly.
10. Pretend you're the consumer relations official for the company in number 9. Write a calm, convincing response to your complaint.
11. If you were an administrator in this school, what's the first change you'd make? Why?
12. Tell what season of the year brings the things you like best.
13. You have been given the power to make one person, and only one, disappear. Whom would you eliminate and why?

Most teachers read their students' journals periodically, every few weeks or so. Eventually, they may assign the entire journal a percentage of the final grade;

students receive credit simply for writing regularly. Other teachers base the grade for the journal on the quantity of writing it contains, thirty entries receiving an A, twenty to twenty-nine entries earning a B, and so on. Grading individual entries in journals is counterproductive because it discourages provisional thinking and regular practice with writing. Journals offer students a place to write without fear of making mistakes or facing criticism for what they have to say. Comments on journal entries should be positive, encouraging further writing or deeper exploration of an idea: "I felt that way too when my best friend misunderstood what I said." "It must have taken courage to tell your parents this; why not write an entry as if you were telling the story from their point of view?" Students should feel free to write "Do not read" across the top of an entry they don't want anyone else to see or to fold the page over and staple it. A teacher unable to resist temptation should ask students to remove personal entries before the journals are turned in.

When I read a set of journals, occasionally I'll come across an entry full of obscenities. They're meant to shock me. Generally, I ignore them the first time around; if they appear again, I usually discuss the journal with the student. In a fit of frustration, I once asked a student to write another entry defining some of the four-letter words he'd used. He never did. Much more common are the touchingly painful accounts of personal traumas students sometimes share with their English teachers. If I ignore the entry because it makes me uncomfortable, the student will conclude that I can't handle honest, sensitive topics and prefer to read only about "safe," academic subjects. If I write some gratuitous comment in the margin, I belittle the experience. When I discover students working out difficult experiences by writing them down in a journal, I generally encourage them to tackle the problem in several entries. They may have detected an irony in the experience, a weakness or strength in themselves, or a serious flaw in their idealistic notions about people. They need to examine further what they have found, first to understand it for themselves and perhaps later to share it with a larger audience. Precisely because such entries contain honest statements about important problems, they deserve to be treated seriously.

Heuristics

Heuristics derive ultimately from the *topoi* of classical rhetoric. In Book Two of the *Rhetoric*, Aristotle discusses twenty-eight "universal topics for enthymemes on all matters," among them, arguing from opposites, dividing the subject, exploring various senses of an ambiguous term, examining cause and effect. Although the classical *topoi* represent lines of reasoning speakers might pursue to invent arguments, heuristics prompt thinking by means of questions. The questions are ordered so that writers can explore the subject systematically and efficiently, but they also are open-ended to stimulate intuition and memory as well as reason. Most students are already familiar with the heuristic procedure journalists use: Who? What? When? Where? How? These questions help reporters compose effective lead paragraphs in news stories. Conditioned by years of testing, students often think that heuristic questions must have right and wrong answers; they don't. They increase the possibilities for probing a topic thoroughly, and they usually generate provisional answers. Ideally, those tentative answers should lead students to formulate further questions.

In *Writing* (3d ed., pp. 328–29), Elizabeth Cowan Neeld presents a heuristic derived from the categories "definition," "comparison," "relationship," "testimony," and "circumstance." The author encourages students to take the questions one at a time, thoughtfully, replacing the blank with a subject they want to explore and writing brief notes to answer the questions. If students get stuck on a question, they should move on. When they have finished the entire list, they should reread their notes, starring the material that looks promising.

Definition

1. How does the dictionary define _____?
2. What earlier words did _____ come from?
3. What do *I* mean by _____?
4. What group of things does seem to belong to? How is _____ different from other things in this group?
5. What parts can _____ be divided into?
6. Did _____ mean something in the past that it doesn't mean now? If so, what? What does this former meaning tell us about how the idea grew and developed?
7. Does _____ mean something now that it didn't years ago? If so, what?
8. What other words mean approximately the same as _____?
9. What are some concrete examples of _____?
10. When is the meaning of _____ misunderstood?

Comparison

1. What is _____ similar to? In what ways?
2. What is _____ different from? In what ways?
3. _____ is superior to what? In what ways?
4. _____ is inferior to what? In what ways?
5. _____ is most unlike what? (What is it opposite to?) In what ways?
6. _____ is most like what? In what ways?

Relationship

1. What causes _____?
2. What is the purpose of _____?
3. What does _____ happen?
4. What comes before _____?
5. What comes after _____?

Circumstance

1. Is _____ possible or impossible?
2. What qualities, conditions, or circumstances make _____ possible or impossible?
3. Supposing that _____ is possible, is it also desirable? Why?
4. When did _____ happen previously?
5. Who has done or experienced _____?
6. Who can do _____?
7. If _____ starts, what makes it end?
8. What would it take for _____ to happen now?
9. What would prevent _____ from happening?

Testimony

1. What have I heard people say about _____?
2. Do I know any facts or statistics about _____? If so, what?
3. Have I talked with anyone about _____?
4. Do I know any famous or well-known saying (e.g., "A bird in the hand is worth two in the bush") about _____?
5. Can I quote any proverbs or any poems about _____?
6. Are there any laws about _____?
7. Do I remember any songs about _____? Do I remember anything I've read about _____ in books or magazines? Anything I've seen in a movie or on television?
8. Do I want to do any research on _____?

The dramatistic pentad is a heuristic derived from Kenneth Burke's rhetoric of human motives discussed in Chapter 4:

What was done? (act)

Where or when was it done? (scene)

Who did it? (agent)

How was it done? (agency)

Why was it done? (purpose)

Although Burke originally posed these questions to explore the complicated motives of human actions, most composition teachers use the heuristic with a simpler aim in mind: to help students generate descriptive or narrative material. As a prewriting technique, the pentad works well for investigating literary topics, historical or current events, and biographical subjects. The pentad gains additional heuristic power when any two of the five terms are regarded together, as "ratios." Consider, for example, how the act : scene ratio informs the plot of any murder mystery. Or how the act : purpose ratio characterizes what some people call *euthanasia* and others, *murder.*

Another series of questions, adapted from Richard Larson's problem-solving model, suggests ways to engage issues-oriented subjects, the sort teachers often assign for persuasive papers. Students also may find the heuristic useful in sorting through other problems: personal difficulties, writing problems, or the problem posed by a writing assignment.

What is the problem?

Why is the problem indeed a problem?

What goals must be served by whatever action or solution that is taken?

Which goals have the highest priority?

What procedures might attain the stated goals?

What can I predict about the consequences of each possible action?

How do the actions compare with each other as potential solutions to the problem?

Which course of action is best?

In answering these questions, students define the problem, analyze it, formulate several potential solutions, and select the best solution. "In every problem," writes Edward P. J. Corbett, "there are some things that you know or can easily find out, but there is something too that you don't know. It is the *unknown* that creates the problem. When confronted with a problem, you have to take note of all the things you do know. Then, by a series of inferences from the known, you try to form a hypothesis to determine whether your theory leads you to discover the unknown that is causing the problem" (*The Little Rhetoric and Handbook,* p. 44). Teachers too can employ the heuristic to define, analyze, and solve teaching problems or conduct research.

Because most writing teachers also teach literature courses, a heuristic for analyzing, interpreting, and evaluating literature can pose useful questions to guide students' reading or help them explore literary topics. Corbett devised the series of questions shown in Figure 7.2a–c, which have been adapted from *The Little Rhetoric and Handbook* (pp. 186–221).

Obviously, students don't need to answer all of Corbett's questions every time they read a literary work. Routinely dragging the class through each question would be boring busywork. The questions have value insofar as they guide reading, suggest new ideas to explore, or encourage a closer examination of the text. The questions can be broken apart, altered, or culled selectively. At some point, students need to frame their own questions to explain their response to the work.

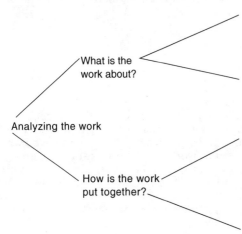

What kind of work is it? (genre)
What happens or what is said? (plot)
What is the source of conflict?

What kind of characters appear?
How does the author characterize the people in the work?

What is the work about?

Analyzing the work

What is the setting?
What is the style of the work
How is the work organized and structured?

What is the point of view from which the story is told?
Why did the author choose this point of view from which to tell the story?

How is the work put together?

Figure 7.2a

What is the theme of the work?
In what way is (a particular incident or passage related to the theme of the work?
What did (a particular character) mean when he/she said, "(quotation of the statement)"?

What did the author mean?

What is the symbolism of (a particular event or object in the work)?
What patterns do you find in the (incident characters, diction, figures of speech)?

Interpreting the work

How is the ending of the work related to other parts of the work?

What did the work mean to you?

Why did (a particular character) do what he/she did?
What kind of person is (a particular character in a story or the persona that speaks in a poem?
What attitude does the narrator have toward (a particular character) and how is the attitude revealed?

Figure 7.2b

How well does the author accomplish what he/she set out to do?

Was the work true-to-life?
Was the action plausible?

Were the characters believable and consistent?
Was the author's style clear and pleasing?
What changes would improve the work?

Evaluating the work

Did the work capture and hold your interest?
How does the work compare with other literary works you have read or with some movie, play, or television drama you have seen?

Was the work worth your time and attention?

Do you agree or disagree with what other critics have said about the work?
If you were writing a review of the work for a newspaper, what would you say to encourage others to read or not read the work?
What have you learned from reading this work that could make your life better or different?

Figure 7.2c

Because most textbooks devote little attention to audience, students may need help defining for whom they are writing and why. A heuristic for assessing the audience provides such help. Audience analysis not only generates content, depending on what a reader already knows about a subject, but it also encourages writers to think early on about their tone and point of view. The following questions, adapted from Karl R. Wallace's "*Topoi* and the Problem of Invention," ask writers to identify several characteristics of an audience:

How old is the audience?

What is the economic or social condition of the audience?

What is the educational status of the audience?

What general philosophies of government or politics does the audience hold?

What values and beliefs would be common to an audience of this age?

What economic or social values is the audience likely to hold?

What value does the audience place on education, religion, work?

Which of these values—economic, social, political, educational—is most important to the audience? Least important?

In general, how does the audience feel about its heritage or events that happened in the past? That are going on in the present? What hopes for the future does the audience hold?

In general, does the audience expect certain patterns of thought in what it reads? Should I include a lot of data to convince the audience of my point? What authorities would be most convincing? Does the audience need to see the causes and effects of my proposals? Would stories and analogies confuse my readers or encourage them to understand what I want to say? What terms will I need to define, and what terms can I assume are already understood?

What sorts of issues most frequently make the audience angry or defensive?

What things can I say without antagonizing my audience?

What options do I have for presenting unpopular opinions to my audience?

What is the most convincing appeal I could make? Should I try to convince by being reasonable and logical? Should I appeal to the emotions? Or should I demonstrate that I am an honest, trustworthy, sympathetic expert whom the audience can trust?

Have I stereotyped my audience, overlooking individuals who may hold views that are different from those the rest of my audience believes in?

Am I just saying what my audience wants to hear or am I also saying what I honestly believe to be true?

After students have grown comfortable with relatively simple prewriting techniques—brainstorming, clustering, freewriting, answering questions—they may want to use more elaborate heuristics to probe the subject even further.[6]

The following heuristic is adapted from Richard Young, Alton Becker, and Kenneth Pike's *Rhetoric: Discovery and Change* (1970) and permits us to examine a subject systematically from several perspectives. Although we customarily consider a subject from only one point of view, tagmemic invention forces us to shift mental gears to see it differently. According to Young, Becker, and Pike, anything—an object, event, concept—can be viewed from three perspectives. We usually regard an oak tree, to use their example, as an isolated, static entity, as a "thing" or particle. But we also could view the oak as a process (wave), as a participant in the natural growth cycle that begins with an acorn and ends when the tree rots or is cut into lumber. Or we may regard the tree as a system (field) of roots, trunk, branches, and leaves. These three perspectives—particle, wave, field—permit us to consider the same subject from three angles: as a static entity, as a dynamic process, and as a system.

Furthermore, in order to "know" this oak tree, we must be able to figure out three aspects of its existence (regardless of which perspective we assume):

1. *How is it unique?* As an entity, process, or system, how does it differ from everything else? Young, Becker, and Pike label this aspect "contrast."
2. *How much can it change and still be itself?* How much "variation" is possible in the oak (viewed as entity, process, or system) before it becomes something other than an oak?
3. *How does it fit into larger systems of which it is a part?* What is its "distribution"? In other words, the oak tree not only *is* a system, but it also belongs to other systems. It is affected by a system of seasonal changes; it participates in the ecosystem of the surrounding countryside; it plays a role in an economic system to which lumber production, tourism, and national parks belong.

The six concepts—particle, wave, field, contrast, variation, and distribution—can be arranged to produce a nine-cell chart, often referred to as a *tagmemic grid* or *matrix* (see *Rhetoric: Discovery and Change*, p. 127).

Although the nine-cell matrix can generate enormous amounts of material about a subject, most students need considerable practice using the technique before they find it helpful and comfortable. For this reason, you may prefer to introduce students to a simplified version of the matrix such as the one W. Ross Winterowd includes in *The Contemporary Writer* (p. 94):

The Los Angeles freeway system, for instance, can be viewed

1. *As an Isolated, Static Entity.* We ask, What features characterize it? We can draw a map of it; we can measure its total length; we can count the number of overpasses and underpasses. We can describe it in great detail. In fact, such a description could well demand a number of thick volumes. But the point is that we can view anything as an isolated, static entity and begin to find those features that characterize it.
2. *As One Among Many of a Class.* We ask, How does it differ from others in its class? From this point of view, we would compare the Los Angeles freeway system with others like it. I, for instance, immediately think of the difference between the L.A. freeway system and the turnpikes of the East and Midwest, as well as the German Autobahnen.
3. *As Part of a Larger System.* We ask, How does it fit into larger systems, of which it is a part? The L.A. freeway system would be worthless if it did not integrate with national, state, and county highway systems; therefore, its place in these larger systems is crucial.
4. *As a Process, Rather Than as a Static Entity.* We ask, How is it changing? In regard to the L.A. freeway system, this question brings up the whole problem of planning for the future, which implies the problem of history, or how the system got to be the way it currently is.
5. *As a System, Rather Than as an Entity.* We ask, What are the parts, and how do they work together? Now we are focusing on the L.A. freeways as a transportation system, each part of which must integrate and function with the whole.

Models

Discussing models for student writers to emulate is a technique as old as rhetoric itself. For centuries, teachers of rhetoric and composition have asked students to imitate noteworthy essays, aphorisms, fables, speeches, and excerpts from works by great writers. Advocates of the practice believe that it exposes students to important cultural values and helps them develop their sense of style. To imitate an excellent writer, students have to read carefully, analyze the text closely, and then use similar constructions in creating their own texts. Although close imitation is no longer a staple of contemporary writing classes, most writing teachers still present models that illustrate approaches students may take in responding to assignments.

The most common model in today's writing course is the expository essay, perhaps because it is the most frequent form of discourse students write. Despite a long tradition of using essays to teach writing, we ought to question their purpose. What kinds of models are appropriate? In what ways are they helpful? When should they be introduced? How should they be discussed?

First, the models don't always have to be essays. Letters, advertisements, reports, memoranda, newspapers, policy statements, even junk mail, can illustrate rhetorical strategies. Students themselves can bring these materials to class, providing their own examples of the kinds of writing they are practicing.

Second, the models discussed in class don't have to be written by professionals. Good student writing should serve as a model most of the time because it best exemplifies those rhetorical strategies we expect to find in students' papers. Good student writing teaches writers of similar age and experience how to plan their work, how to anticipate problems of organization and language, and how to frame their notions of audience, purpose, subject, and persona. Furthermore, student models have an important advantage over professional models: the author is sitting in the class, a live, present author who can help us sort out intended meanings or points of confusion. Student writing also represents a more realistic, attainable model than the writing of professionals. Students know that they aren't the kind of writer Montaigne or Martin Luther King, Jr., were. Nor do we want them to be. Instead, we want them to use their own voices to express their own messages, to discover their own purposes for writing. From time to time, we may even want to discuss examples of atrocious professional prose to reinforce the notion that students sometimes write better than professionals.

Third, in discussing any model, the focus should be primarily on *how* the writer solves problems. Of course, we also have some responsibility for helping students understand *what* the writer says, for teaching students to read critically and carefully. But we should avoid approaching models, especially those written by professionals, as literary works subject to intense critical analysis. In a writing course, unlike a literature course, models serve not so much as literary artifacts to interpret, but as examples of the rhetorical problems, decisions, and choices student writers confront.

Fourth, most writing teachers introduce models prematurely. The best time to discuss a model is *after* students have already completed some prewriting and perhaps an early draft. That is when they are most likely to appreciate the rhetorical problem an assignment poses and to benefit from discovering how another writer addresses similar difficulties. Students cannot value the strategies a model illustrates if their own writing projects are not yet very far along. After students understand by experience the demands an assignment makes of them, examining a model can be instructive. Then they can know firsthand what options the writer had in presenting a subject, what choices he or she made and perhaps rejected, and how the strategies evident in the model apply to the student's work-in-progress.

The value of a model is what it can teach us about our own writing projects. Consequently, we don't need to belabor their discussion. One or two models for each assignment should be plenty. Most of the time, devoting fifteen to twenty minutes of a class period for their discussion should be adequate if we ask the right questions.

What are the right questions? Robert Bain's "Framework for Judging" is a good place to begin.[7]

Framework for Judging

1. A writer promises to do something. What does this writer promise to do? Does the writer keep that promise? If not, where and why does she or he fail to do so?
2. What seems to be the writer's attitude toward the reader? Does the writer treat the audience playfully, seriously, with sarcasm? What does the writer's attitude toward the audience say about him/her and his/her subject?
3. Is the writer's attitude toward the subject convincing? Is the writer simply filling space or writing about feelings and ideas that matter? How can we tell?
4. Is there a perceivable order to the presentation? Can we follow and describe that order? If not, where does the writer lose us and why?
5. Has the writer omitted any important details or arguments that would help us understand the piece? Has the writer included details or arguments not connected with the ideas and feelings being discussed?
6. Does each paragraph signal clearly to the reader the direction in which the writer's ideas and feelings are moving? Does each paragraph develop and complete the idea it introduces? If we lose our way in a paragraph, where and why do we get lost?
7. Are the rhythms and patterns of sentences appropriate to the writer's subject and voice? If the sentences seem to be "Dick-and-Jane sen-

tences," how could the writer combine them to break up this pattern? If the sentences are so long that we get lost in them, where could the writer break sentences into shorter units? Does the writer use passive voice excessively? If so, is that usage justified?

8. Is the language of the piece appropriate to the writer's voice and subject? If the writer uses big words, is she or he showing off or trying to help us understand better? Is the language fairly free of clichés, jargon, and worn-out words and phrases? If the writer bends or breaks rules of language, making up new words or running them together, what are some reasons for doing so?

9. Has the writer observed the conventions of grammar, punctuation, spelling, and capitalization? If not, is there a good reason for not doing so?

This sequence of questions places larger rhetorical concerns first, asking students to consider subject, audience, purpose, paragraphs, and sentences before attending to matters of punctuation and usage. Bain's questions also serve several functions. Because the framework helps writers discover what they propose to do and how they intend to go about it, the questions provide an excellent heuristic for planning responses to writing assignments. They also can organize discussions of student writing or some other model. Applied to student or professional models, the framework focuses discussion on *how* the model works, on ways to solve problems in writing. The questions serve revision too. Students can work through them, on their own or in a draft workshop with other students, as they review their drafts. Not all of the questions need answering all of the time. A fifteen-minute class discussion of a student's paper, for example, might cover only the first four sets of questions; a draft workshop early in the term, only the questions in the fourth set.

Eventually, writers must stop generating answers to questions and begin organizing their raw material. They must evaluate what prewriting has yielded, identify hierarchies and classes, assign importance to some ideas and abandon others, and tentatively arrange whatever materials belong in a draft. It's difficult to say when generating material stops and shaping it begins because prewriting, writing, and rewriting don't follow a strict linear sequence. Sometimes prewriting activities generate material that reveals its own implicit organization. Sometimes writers don't discover the best way to organize their material until they've completed two or three drafts. Furthermore, as writers draft and rewrite their work, they often discover "holes" in the discourse. They stop drafting and return to prewriting, generating additional material to fill the gaps.

Most students begin drafting too soon, before they have sufficiently probed the subject, developed their own point of view, and made a commitment to the message. Their papers remain general because they haven't found enough interesting possibilities to pursue in their raw material or have failed to develop meaningful plans and goals to guide subsequent work. To address these problems, we must teach prewriting. We must give students a repertoire of planning strategies that, used in various combinations, will yield abundant raw material. Students need specific instruction in how to use a particular prewriting technique and enough practice with it to gain a sense of its potential. We can give them this practice if we structure writing assignments to move from brainstorming and freewriting to research and note-taking to responding to a heuristic, from role-playing to talking out ideas with classmates to writing them down. We also can collect scratch work and jotted notes from time to time, not merely to ensure that students give adequate time to prewriting, but also to guide them in developing more efficient, effective plans. Students should view these prewriting activities, not as isolated events, but as parts of a process that always looks ahead to drafting and revising. They are ways to let a piece of writing grow, ways to let us find a topic but also to let the topic find us.

Notes

[1] An indispensable bibliographical essay that surveys methods of invention as well as the history of the art is Richard Young, "Recent Developments in Rhetorical Invention," in *Teaching Composition: Twelve Bibliographical Essays,* ed. Gary Tate (Fort Worth: Texas Christian University Press, 1987), pp. 1–38. As Young points out, the term *prewriting* technically denotes the techniques of invention developed by D. Gordon Rohman and Albert O. Wlecke—journals, meditation, and analogy —that emphasize creative thinking and the "self-actualization" of the writer [cf. D. Gordon Rohman and Albert O. Wlecke, *Pre-Writing: The Construction and Application of Models for Concept Formation in Writing* (USOE Cooperative Research Project No. 2174; East Lansing: Michigan State University, 1964)]. However, I use *prewriting* throughout this book as a synonym for "invention," primarily because current usage among writing teachers assigns the term broader meaning than Rohman and Wlecke intended.

[2] James L. Adams, *Conceptual Blockbusting: A Pleasurable Guide to Better Problem Solving* (San Francisco: W. H. Freeman, 1974), is a useful discussion of how to cultivate thinking and problem-solving abilities. The book analyzes barriers to thinking and suggests strategies for breaking through them.

[3] Young, p. 37; cf. Robert Zoellner, "A Behavioral Approach to Writing," *College English* 30 (January 1969), 267–320.

[4] Donald Murray, workshop presentation, South Carolina English Teachers Conference, University of South Carolina, October 21, 1978. See also "The Listening Eye: Reflections on the Writing Conference," *College English* 41 (September 1979), 13–18. "Looping" and "cubing," which also depend on completing series of freewritings, are described in Elizabeth Cowan Neeld, *Writing,* 3d ed. (Glenview, IL: Scott, Foresman, 1990), pp. 20–21, and 315–16, respectively.

[5] Adapted from a list developed by Connie Pritchard, University of South Carolina, Fall 1977. See also Macrorie, *Telling Writing,* pp. 140–51.

[6] See, for example, Richard L. Larson, "Discovery through Questioning: A Plan for Teaching Rhetorical Invention," *College English* 30 (November 1968), 126–34; and Tommy J. Boley, "A Heuristic for Persuasion," *College Composition and Communication* 30 (May 1979), 187–91.

[7] The framework is adapted from Robert A. Bain, "Reading Student Papers," *College Composition and Communication* 25 (October 1974), 307–9.

Works Cited

Burke, Kenneth. *A Rhetoric of Motives.* Berkeley: University of California Press, 1969.

Corbett, Edward P. J. *The Little Rhetoric and Handbook.* 2d ed. Glenview, IL: Scott, Foresman, 1982.

Elbow, Peter. *Writing without Teachers.* New York: Oxford University Press, 1973.

Macrorie, Ken. *Telling Writing.* 4th ed. Upper Montclair, NJ: Boynton/Cook, 1985.

Murray, Donald M. *A Writer Teaches Writing.* 2d ed. Boston: Houghton Mifflin, 1985.

Neeld, Elizabeth Cowan. *Writing.* 3d ed. Glenview, IL: Scott, Foresman/Little, Brown, 1990.

Wallace, Karl R. "*Topoi* and the Problem of Invention." *The Quarterly Journal of Speech* 58 (December 1972): 387–95.

Winterowd, W. Ross. *The Contemporary Writer: A Practical Rhetoric.* 2d ed. New York: Harcourt Brace Jovanovich, 1981.

Young, Richard E., Alton L. Becker, and Kenneth L. Pike. *Rhetoric: Discovery and Change.* New York: Harcourt, Brace and World, 1970.

RIGID RULES, INFLEXIBLE PLANS, AND THE STIFLING OF LANGUAGE: A COGNITIVIST ANALYSIS OF WRITER'S BLOCK

Mike Rose

[*College Composition and Communication* 31 (1980): 389–401.]

Mike Rose is a professor in the Graduate School of Education and Information Studies at UCLA. He has produced important work in remedial reading and writing, writing across the curriculum, the cognition of composing, and the politics of literacy. In addition to many articles and essays, Rose has coedited *Perspectives on Literacy* (1988) and, with Mal Kiniry, *Critical Strategies for Academic Thinking and Writing* (3rd edition, 1998). He has written *Writer's Block: The Cognitive Dimension* (1984), *Lives on the Boundary: The Struggles and Achievements of America's Underprepared* (1989), and most recently *Possible Lives: The Promise of Public Education in America* (1996). In 1991 and 1992, articles that he coauthored won the prestigious Richard Braddock Award. His *Lives on the Boundary* has received the David H. Russell Award for Distinguished Research from the National Council of Teachers of English, the Outstanding Book Award from the Conference on College Composition and Communication, and the Mina P. Shaughnessy Prize from the Modern Language Association. Rose is also the recipient of a Guggenheim Fellowship and the Commonwealth Club of California Award for Literary Excellence.

In this article investigating causes of writer's block, Rose reports on his study of ten undergraduates, five with writer's block and five without. Rose discovered that rigid rules and inflexible plans were a significant cause of writer's block. He argues that stymied writers do not necessarily need more rules and plans, as much previous research has suggested. Rose contends instead that writers may well need different, more flexible plans and rules. He closes the article with several suggestions for helping students who suffer from writer's block.

Ruth will labor over the first paragraph of an essay for hours. She'll write a sentence, then erase it. Try another, then scratch part of it out. Finally, as the evening winds on toward ten o'clock and Ruth, anxious about tomorrow's deadline, begins to wind into herself, she'll compose that first paragraph only to sit back and level her favorite exasperated interdiction at herself and her page: "No. You can't say that. You'll bore them to death."

Ruth is one of ten UCLA undergraduates with whom I discussed writer's block, that frustrating, self-defeating inability to generate the next line, the right phrase, the sentence that will release the flow of words once again. These ten people represented a fair cross-section of the UCLA student community; lower-middle-class to upper-middle-class backgrounds and high schools, third-world and Caucasian origins, biology to fine arts majors, C+ to A– grade point averages, enthusiastic to blasé attitudes toward school. They were set off from the community by the twin facts that all ten could write competently, and all were currently enrolled in at least one course that required a significant amount of writing. They were set off among themselves by the fact that five of them wrote with relative to enviable ease while the other five experienced moderate to nearly immobilizing writer's block. This blocking usually resulted in rushed, often late papers and resultant grades that did not truly reflect these students' writing ability. And then, of course, there were other less measurable but probably more serious results: a growing distrust of their abilities and an aversion toward the composing process itself.

What separated the five students who blocked from those who didn't? It wasn't skill; that was held fairly constant. The answer could have rested in the emotional realm—anxiety, fear of evaluation, insecurity, etc. Or perhaps blocking in some way resulted from variation in cognitive style. Perhaps, too, blocking originated in and typified a melding of emotion and cognition not unlike the relationship posited by Shapiro between neurotic feeling and neurotic thinking.[1] Each of these was possible. Extended clinical interviews and testing could have teased out the answer. But there was one answer that surfaced readily in brief explorations of these students' writing processes. It was not profoundly emotional, nor was it embedded in that still unclear construct of cognitive style. It was constant, surprising, almost amusing if its results weren't so troublesome, and, in the final analysis, obvious: the five students who experienced blocking were all operating either with writing rules or with planning strategies that impeded rather than enhanced the composing process. The five students who were not hampered by writer's block also utilized rules, but they were less rigid ones, and thus more appropriate to a complex process like writing. Also, the plans these non-blockers brought to the writing process were more functional, more flexible, more open to information from the outside.

These observations are the result of one to three interviews with each student. I used recent notes, drafts, and finished compositions to direct and hone my questions. This procedure is admittedly non-experimental, certainly more clinical than scientific; still, it did lead to several inferences that lay the foundation for future, more rigorous investigation: (a) composing is a highly complex problem-solving process[2] and (b) certain disruptions of that process can be explained with cognitive psychology's problem-solving framework. Such investigation might include a study using "stimulated recall" techniques to validate or disconfirm these hunches. In such a study, blockers and non-blockers would write essays. Their activity would be videotaped and, immediately after writing, they would be shown their respective tapes and questioned about the rules, plans, and beliefs operating in their writing behavior. This procedure would bring us close to the composing process (the writers' recall is stimulated by their viewing the tape), yet would not interfere with actual composing.

In the next section I will introduce several key concepts in the problem-solving literature. In section three I will let the students speak for themselves. Fourth, I will offer a cognitivist analysis of blockers' and non-blockers' grace or torpor. I will close with a brief note on treatment.

Selected Concepts in Problem Solving: Rules and Plans

As diverse as theories of problem solving are, they share certain basic assumptions and characteristics. Each posits an *introductory period* during which a problem is presented, and all theorists, from Behaviorist to Gestalt to Information Processing, admit that certain aspects, stimuli, or "functions" of the problem must become or be made salient and attended to in certain ways if successful problem-solving processes are to be engaged. Theorists also believe that some conflict, some stress, some gap in information in these perceived "aspects" seems to trigger problem-solving behavior. Next comes a *processing period*, and for all the variance of opinion about this critical stage, theorists recognize the necessity of its existence—recognize that man, at the least, somehow "weighs" possible solutions as they are stumbled upon and, at the most, goes through an elaborate and sophisticated information-processing routine to achieve problem solution. Furthermore, theorists believe—to varying degrees—

that past learning and the particular "set," direction, or orientation that the problem solver takes in dealing with past experience and present stimuli have critical bearing on the efficacy of solution. Finally, all theorists admit to a *solution period,* an end-state of the process where "stress" and "search" terminate, an answer is attained, and a sense of completion or "closure" is experienced.

These are the gross similarities, and the framework they offer will be useful in understanding the problem-solving behavior of the students discussed in this paper. But since this paper is primarily concerned with the second stage of problem-solving operations, it would be most useful to focus this introduction on two critical constructs in the processing period: rules and plans.

Rules

Robert M. Gagné defines "rule" as "an inferred capability that enables the individual to respond to a class of stimulus situations with a class of performances."[3] Rules can be learned directly[4] or by inference through experience.[5] But, in either case, most problem-solving theorists would affirm Gagné's dictum that "rules are probably the major organizing factor, and quite possibly the primary one, in intellectual functioning."[6] As Gagné implies, we wouldn't be able to function without rules; they guide response to the myriad stimuli that confront us daily, and might even be the central element in complex problem-solving behavior.

Dunker, Polya, and Miller, Galanter, and Pribram offer a very useful distinction between two general kinds of rules: algorithms and heuristics.[7] Algorithms are precise rules that will always result in a specific answer if applied to an appropriate problem. Most mathematical rules, for example, are algorithms. Functions are constant (e.g., pi), procedures are routine (squaring the radius), and outcomes are completely predictable. However, few day-to-day situations are mathematically circumscribed enough to warrant the application of algorithms. Most often we function with the aid of fairly general heuristics or "rules of thumb," guidelines that allow varying degrees of flexibility when approaching problems. Rather than operating with algorithmic precision and certainty, we search, critically, through alternatives, using our heuristic as a divining rod— "if a math problem stumps you, try working backwards to solution"; "if the car won't start, check x, y, or z," and so forth. Heuristics won't allow the precision or the certitude afforded by algorithmic operations; heuristics can even be so "loose" as to be vague. But in a world where tasks and problems are rarely mathematically precise, heuristic rules become the most appropriate, the most functional rules available to us: "a heuristic does not guarantee the optimal solution or, indeed, any solution at all; rather, heuristics offer solutions that are good enough most of the time."[8]

Plans

People don't proceed through problem situations, in or out of a laboratory, without some set of internalized instructions to the self, some program, some course of action that, even roughly, takes goals and possible paths to that goal into consideration. Miller, Galanter, and Pribram have referred to this course of action as a plan: "A plan is any hierarchical process in the organism that can control the order in which a sequence of operations is to be performed" (p. 16). They name the fundamental plan in human problem-solving behavior the TOTE, with the initial T representing a *test* that matches a possible solution against the perceived end-goal of problem completion. O represents the clearance to *operate* if the comparison between solution and goal indicates that the solution is a sensible one. The second T represents a further, post-operation, *test* or comparison of solution with goal, and if the two mesh and problem solution is at hand the person *exits* (E) from problem-solving behavior. If the second test presents further discordance between solution and goal, a further solution is attempted in TOTE-fashion. Such plans can be both long-term and global and, as problem solving is underway, short-term and immediate.[9] Though the mechanicality of this information-processing model renders it simplistic and, possibly, unreal, the central notion of a plan and an operating procedure is an important one in problem-solving theory; it at least attempts to metaphorically explain what earlier cognitive psychologists could not—the mental procedures (see pp. 390–91) underlying problem-solving behavior.

Before concluding this section, a distinction between heuristic rules and plans should be attempted; it is a distinction often blurred in the literature, blurred because, after all, we are very much in the area of gestating theory and preliminary models. Heuristic rules seem to function with the flexibility of plans. Is, for example, "If the car won't start, try x, y, or z" a heuristic or a plan? It could be either, though two qualifications will mark it as heuristic rather than plan. (A) Plans subsume and sequence heuristic and algorithmic rules. Rules are usually "smaller," more discrete cognitive capabilities; plans can become quite large and complex, composed of a series of ordered algorithms, heuristics, and further planning "sub-routines." (B) Plans, as was mentioned earlier, include criteria to determine successful goal-attainment and, as well, include "feedback" processes —ways to incorporate and use information gained from "tests" of potential solutions against desired goals.

One other distinction should be made: that is, between "set" and plan. Set, also called "determining tendency" or "readiness,"[10] refers to the fact that people often approach problems with habitual ways of reacting, a predisposition, a tendency to perceive or function in one way rather than another. Set, which can be established through instructions or, consciously or unconsciously, through experience, can assist performance if it is appropriate to a specific problem,[11] but much of the literature on set has shown its rigidifying, dysfunctional effects.[12] Set differs from plan in that set represents a limiting and narrowing of response alternatives with no inherent process to shift alternatives. It is a kind of cognitive habit that can limit perception, not a course of action with multiple paths that directs and sequences response possibilities.

The constructs of rules and plans advance the understanding of problem solving beyond that possible with earlier, less developed formulations. Still, critical problems remain. Though mathematical and computer models move one toward more complex (and thus more real) problems than the earlier research, they are still too neat, too rigidly sequenced to approximate the stunning complexity of day-to-day (not to mention highly creative) problem-solving behavior. Also, information-processing models of problem-solving are built on logic theorems, chess strategies, and simple planning tasks. Even Gagné seems to feel more comfortable with illustrations from mathematics and science rather than with social science and humanities problems. So although these complex models and constructs tell us a good deal about problem-solving behavior, they are still laboratory simulations, still invoked from the outside rather than self-generated, and still founded on the mathematico-logical.

Two Carnegie-Mellon researchers, however, have recently extended the above into a truly real, amorphous, unmathematical problem-solving process—writing. Relying on protocol analysis (thinking aloud while solving problems), Linda Flower and John Hayes have attempted to tease out the role of heuristic rules and plans in writing behavior.[13] Their research pushes problem-solving investigations to the real and complex and pushes, from the other end, the often mysterious process of writing toward the explainable. The latter is important, for at least since Plotinus many have viewed the composing process as unexplainable, inspired, infused with the transcendent. But Flower and Hayes are beginning, anyway, to show how writing generates from a problem-solving process with rich heuristic rules and plans of its own. They show, as well, how many writing problems arise from a paucity of heuristics and suggest an intervention that provides such rules.

This paper, too, treats writing as a problem-solving process, focusing, however, on what happens when the process dead-ends in writer's block. It will further suggest that, as opposed to Flower and Hayes' students who need more rules and plans, blockers may well be stymied by possessing rigid or inappropriate rules, or inflexible or confused plans. Ironically enough, these are occasionally instilled by the composition teacher or gleaned from the writing textbook.

"Always Grab Your Audience"—The Blockers

In high school, *Ruth* was told and told again that a good essay always grabs a reader's attention immediately. Until you can make your essay do that, her teachers and textbooks putatively declaimed, there is no need to go on. For Ruth, this means that beginning bland and seeing what emerges as one generates prose is unacceptable. The beginning is everything. And what exactly is the audience seeking that reads this beginning? The rule, or Ruth's use of it, doesn't provide for such investigation. She has an edict with no determiners. Ruth operates with another rule that restricts her productions as well: if sentences aren't grammatically "correct," they aren't useful. This keeps Ruth from toying with ideas on paper, from the kind of linguistic play that often frees up the flow of prose. These two rules converge in a way that pretty effectively restricts Ruth's composing process.

The first two papers I received from *Laurel* were weeks overdue. Sections of them were well written; there were even moments of stylistic flair. But the papers were late and, overall, the prose seemed rushed. Furthermore, one paper included a paragraph on an issue that was never mentioned in the topic paragraph. This was the kind of mistake that someone with Laurel's apparent ability doesn't make. I asked her about this irrelevant passage. She knew very well that it didn't fit, but believed she had to include it to round out the paper. "You must always make three or more points in an essay. If the essay has less, then it's not strong." Laurel had been taught this rule in high school and in her first college English class; no wonder, then, that she accepted its validity.

As opposed to Laurel, *Martha* possesses a whole arsenal of plans and rules with which to approach a humanities writing assignment, and, considering her background in biology, I wonder how many of them were formed out of the assumptions and procedures endemic to the physical sciences.[14] Martha will not put pen to first draft until she has spent up to two days generating an outline of remarkable complexity. I saw one of these outlines and it looked more like a diagram of protein synthesis or DNA structure than the time-worn pattern offered in composition textbooks. I must admit I was intrigued by the aura of process (vs. the static appearance of essay outlines) such diagrams offer, but for Martha these "outlines" only led to self-defeat: the outline would become so complex that all of its elements could never be included in a short essay. In other words, her plan locked her into the first stage of the composing process. Martha would struggle with the conversion of her outline into prose only to scrap the whole venture when deadlines passed and a paper had to be rushed together.

Martha's "rage for order" extends beyond the outlining process. She also believes that elements of a story or poem must evince a fairly linear structure and thematic clarity, or—perhaps bringing us closer to the issue—that analysis of a story or poem must provide the linearity or clarity that seems to be absent in the text. Martha, therefore, will bend the logic of her analysis to reason ambiguity out of existence. When I asked her about a strained paragraph in her paper on Camus' "The Guest," she said, "I didn't want to admit that it [the story's conclusion] was just hanging. I tried to force it into meaning."

Martha uses another rule, one that is not only problematical in itself, but one that often clashes directly with the elaborate plan and obsessive rule above. She believes that humanities papers must scintillate with insight, must present an array of images, ideas, ironies gleaned from the literature under examination. A problem arises, of course, when Martha tries to incorporate her myriad "neat little things," often inherently unrelated, into a tightly structured, carefully sequenced essay. Plans and rules that govern the construction of impressionistic, associational prose would be appropriate to Martha's desire, but her composing process is heavily constrained by the non-impressionistic and non-associational. Put another way, the plans and rules that govern her exploration of text are not at all synchronous with the plans and rules she uses to discuss her exploration. It is interesting to note here, however, that as recently as three years ago Martha was absorbed in creative writing and was publishing poetry in high school magazines. Given what we know about the complex associational, often non-neatly-sequential nature of the poet's creative process, we can infer that Martha was either free of the plans and rules discussed earlier or they were not as intense. One wonders, as well, if the exposure to three years of university physical science either established or intensified Martha's concern with structure, Whatever the case, she now is hamstrung by conflicting rules when composing papers for the humanities.

Mike's difficulties, too, are rooted in a distortion of the problem-solving process. When the time of the week for the assignment of writing topics draws near, Mike begins to prepare material, strategies, and plans that he believes will be appropriate. If the assignment matches his expectations, he has done a good job of analyzing the professor's intentions. If the assignment *doesn't* match his expectations, however, he cannot easily shift approaches. He feels trapped inside his original plans, cannot generate alternatives, and blocks. As the deadline draws near, he will write something, forcing the assignment to fit his conceptual procrustien bed. Since Mike is a smart man, he will offer a good deal of information, but only some of it ends up being appropriate to the assignment. This entire situation is made all the worse when the time between assignment of topic and generation of product is attenuated further, as in an essay examination. Mike believes (correctly) that one must have a plan, a strategy of some sort in order to solve a problem. He further believes, however, that such a plan, once formulated, becomes an exact structural and substantive blueprint that cannot be violated. The plan offers no alternatives, no "sub-routines." So, whereas Ruth's, Laurel's, and some of Martha's difficulties seem to be rule-specific ("always catch your audience," "write grammatically"), Mike's troubles are more global. He may have strategies that are appropriate for various writing situations (e.g., "for this kind of political science assignment write a compare/contrast essay"), but his entire approach to formulating plans and carrying them through to problem solution is too mechanical. It is probable that Mike's behavior is governed by an explicitly learned or inferred rule: "Always try to 'psych out' a professor." But in this case this rule initiates a problem-solving procedure that is clearly dysfunctional.

While Ruth and Laurel use rules that impede their writing process and Mike utilizes a problem-solving procedure that hamstrings him, *Sylvia* has trouble deciding which of the many rules she possesses to use. Her problem can be characterized as cognitive perplexity: some of her rules are inappropriate, others are functional; some mesh nicely with her own definitions of good writing, others don't. She has multiple rules to invoke, multiple paths to follow, and that very complexity of choice virtually paralyzes her. More so than with the previous four students, there is probably a strong emotional dimension to Sylvia's blocking, but the cognitive difficulties are clear and perhaps modifiable.

Sylvia, somewhat like Ruth and Laurel, puts tremendous weight on the crafting of her first paragraph. If it is good, she believes the rest of the essay will be good. Therefore, she will spend up to five hours on the initial paragraph: "I won't go on until I get that first paragraph down." Clearly, this rule—or the strength of it—blocks Sylvia's production. This is one problem. Another is that Sylvia has other equally potent rules that she sees as separate, uncomplementary injunctions: one achieves "flow" in one's writing through the use of adequate transitions; one achieves substance to one's writing through the use of evidence. Sylvia perceives both rules to be "true," but several times followed one to the exclusion of the other. Furthermore, as I talked to Sylvia, many other rules, guidelines, definitions were offered, but none with conviction. While she *is* committed to one rule about initial paragraphs, and that rule is dysfunctional, she seems very uncertain about the weight and hierarchy of the remaining rules in her cognitive repertoire.

"If It Won't Fit My Work, I'll Change It"—The Non-blockers

Dale, Ellen, Debbie, Susan, and Miles all write with the aid of rules. But their rules differ from blockers' rules in significant ways. If similar in content, they are expressed less absolutely—e.g., "*Try* to keep audience in mind." If dissimilar, they are still expressed less absolutely, more heuristically—e.g., "I can use as many ideas in my thesis paragraph as I need and then develop paragraphs for each idea." Our non-blockers do express some rules with firm assurance, but these tend to be simple injunctions that free up rather than restrict the composing process, e.g., "When stuck, write!" or "I'll write what I can." And finally, at least three of the students openly shun the very textbook rules that some blockers adhere to: e.g., "Rules like 'write only what you know about' just aren't true. I ignore those." These three, in effect, have formulated a further rule that expresses something like: "If a rule conflicts with what is sensible or with experience, reject it."

On the broader level of plans and strategies, these five students also differ from at least three of the five blockers in that they all possess problem-solving plans that are quite functional. Interestingly, on first exploration these plans seem to be too broad or fluid to be useful and, in some cases, can barely be expressed with any precision. Ellen, for example, admits that she has a general "outline in [her] head about how a topic paragraph should look" but could not describe much about its structure. Susan also has a general plan to follow, but, if stymied, will quickly attempt to conceptualize the assignment in different ways: "If my original idea won't work, then I need to proceed differently." Whether or not these plans operate in TOTE-fashion, I can't say. But they do operate with the operate-test fluidity of TOTEs.

·True, our non-blockers have their religiously adhered-to rules: e.g., "When stuck, write," and plans, "I couldn't imagine writing without this pattern," but as noted above, these are few and functional. Otherwise, these non-blockers operate with fluid, easily modified, even easily discarded rules and plans (Ellen: "I can throw things out") that are sometimes expressed with a vagueness that could almost be interpreted as ignorance. There lies the irony. Students that offer the least precise rules and plans have the least trouble composing. Perhaps this very lack of precision characterizes the functional composing plan. But perhaps this lack of precision simply masks habitually enacted alternatives and subroutines. This is clearly an area that needs the illumination of further research.

And then there is feedback. At least three of the five non-blockers are an Information-Processor's dream. They get to know their audience, ask professors and T.A.s specific questions about assignments, bring half-finished products in for evaluation, etc. Like Ruth, they realize the importance of audience, but unlike her, they have specific strategies for obtaining and utilizing feedback. And this penchant for testing writing plans against the needs of the audience can lead to modification of rules and plans. Listen to Debbie:

> In high school I was given a formula that stated that you must write a thesis paragraph with *only* three points in it, and then develop each of those points. When I hit college I was given longer assignments. That stuck me for a bit, but then I realized that I could use as many ideas in my thesis paragraph as I needed and then develop paragraphs for each one. I asked someone about this and then tried it. I didn't get any negative feedback, so I figured it was o.k.

Debbie's statement brings one last difference between our blockers and non-blockers into focus; it has been implied above, but needs specific formulation: the goals these people have, and the plans they generate to attain these goals, are quite mutable. Part of the mutability comes from the fluid way the goals and plans are conceived, and part of it arises from the effective impact of feedback on these goals and plans.

Analyzing Writer's Block

Algorithms Rather Than Heuristics

In most cases, the rules our blockers use are not "wrong" or "incorrect"—it is good practice, for example, to "grab your audience with a catchy opening" or "craft a solid first paragraph before going on." The problem is that these rules seem to be followed as though they were algorithms, absolute dicta, rather than the loose heuristics that they were intended to be. Either through instruction, or the power of the textbook, or the predilections of some of our blockers for absolutes, or all three, these useful rules of thumb have been transformed into near-algorithmic urgencies. The result, to paraphrase Karl Dunker, is that these rules do not allow a flexible penetration into the nature of the problem. It is this transformation of heuristic into algorithm that contributes to the writer's block of Ruth and Laurel.

Questionable Heuristics Made Algorithmic

Whereas "grab your audience" could be a useful heuristic, "always make three or more points in an essay" is a pretty questionable one. Any such rule, though probably taught to aid the writer who needs structure, ultimately transforms a highly fluid process like writing into a mechanical lockstep. As heuristics, such rules can be troublesome. As algorithms, they are simply incorrect.

Set

As with any problem-solving task, students approach writing assignments with a variety of orientations or sets. Some are functional, others are not. Martha and Jane (see footnote 14), coming out of the life sciences and social sciences respectively, bring certain methodological orientations with them—certain sets or "directions" that make composing for the humanities a difficult, sometimes confusing, task. In fact, this orientation may cause them to misperceive the task. Martha has formulated a planning strategy from her predisposition to see processes in terms of linear, interrelated steps in a system. Jane doesn't realize that she can revise the statement that "committed" her to the direction her essay has taken. Both of these students are stymied because of formative experiences associated with their majors—experiences, perhaps, that nicely reinforce our very strong tendency to organize experiences temporally.

The Plan That Is Not a Plan

If fluidity and multi-directionality are central to the nature of plans, then the plans that Mike formulates are not true plans at all but, rather, inflexible and static cognitive blueprints.[15] Put another way, Mike's "plans" represent a restricted "closed system" (vs. "open system") kind of thinking, where closed system thinking is defined as focusing on "a limited number of units or items, or members, and those properties of the members which are to be used are known to begin with and do not change as the thinking proceeds," and open system thinking is characterized by an "adventurous exploration of multiple alternatives with strategies that allow redirection once 'dead ends' are encountered."[16] Composing calls for open, even adventurous thinking, not for constrained, no-exit cognition.

Feedback

The above difficulties are made all the more problematic by the fact that they seem resistant to or isolated from corrective feedback. One of the most striking things about Dale, Debbie, and Miles is the ease with which they seek out, interpret, and apply feedback on their rules, plans, and productions. They "operate" and then they "test," and the testing is not only against some internalized goal, but against the requirements of external audience as well.

Too Many Rules—"Conceptual Conflict"

According to D. E. Berlyne, one of the primary forces that motivate problem-solving behavior is a curiosity that arises from conceptual conflict—the convergence of incompatible beliefs or ideas. In *Structure and Direction in Thinking*,[17] Berlyne presents six major types of conceptual conflict, the second of which he terms "perplexity":

> This kind of conflict occurs when there are factors inclining the subject toward each of a set of mutually exclusive beliefs. (p. 257)

If one substitutes "rules" for "beliefs" in the above definition, perplexity becomes a useful notion here. Because perplexity is unpleasant, people are motivated to reduce it by problem-solving behavior that can result in "disequalization":

> Degree of conflict will be reduced if either the number of competing . . . [rules] or their nearness to equality of strength is reduced. (p. 259)

But "disequalization" is not automatic. As I have suggested, Martha and Sylvia hold to rules that conflict, but their perplexity does *not* lead to curiosity and resultant problem-solving behavior. Their perplexity, contra Berlyne, leads to immobilization. Thus "disequalization" will have to be effected from without. The importance of each of, particularly, Sylvia's rules needs an evaluation that will aid her in rejecting some rules and balancing and sequencing others.

A Note on Treatment

Rather than get embroiled in a blocker's misery, the teacher or tutor might interview the student in order to build a writing history and profile: How much and what kind of writing was done in high school? What is the student's major? What kind of writing does it require? How does the student compose? Are there rough drafts or outlines available? By what rules does the student operate? How would he or she define "good" writing? etc. This sort of interview reveals an incredible amount of information about individual composing processes. Furthermore, it often reveals the rigid rule or the inflexible plan that may lie at the base of the student's writing problem. That was precisely what happened with the five blockers. And with Ruth, Laurel, and Martha (and Jane) what was revealed made virtually immediate remedy possible. Dysfunctional rules are easily replaced with or counter-balanced by functional ones if there is no emotional reason to hold onto that which simply doesn't work. Furthermore, students can be trained to select, to "know which rules are appropriate for which problems."[18] Mike's difficulties, perhaps because plans are more complex and pervasive than rules, took longer to correct. But inflexible plans, too, can be remedied by pointing out their dysfunctional qualities and by assisting the student in developing appropriate and flexible alternatives. Operating this way, I was successful with Mike. Sylvia's story, however, did not end as smoothly. Though I had three forty-five minute contacts with her, I was not able to appreciably alter her behavior. Berlyne's theory bore results with Martha but not with Sylvia. Her rules were in conflict, and perhaps that conflict was not exclusively cognitive. Her case keeps analyses like these honest; it reminds us that the cognitive often melds with, and can be overpowered by, the affective. So while Ruth, Laurel, Martha, and Mike could profit from tutorials that explore the rules and plans in their writing behavior, students like Sylvia may need more extended, more affectively oriented counseling sessions that blend the instructional with the psychodynamic.

Notes

[1] David Shapiro, *Neurotic Styles* (New York: Basic Books, 1965).

[2] Barbara Hayes-Ruth, a Rand cognitive psychologist, and I are currently developing an information-processing model of the composing process. A good deal of work has already been done by Linda Flower and John Hayes (see p. 76 of this article). I . . . recommend . . . their "Writing as Problem Solving" (paper presented at American Educational Research Association, April 1979).

[3] *The Conditions of Learning* (New York: Holt, Rinehart and Winston, 1970), p. 193.

[4] E. James Archer, "The Psychological Nature of Concepts," in H. J. Klausmeier and C. W. Harris, eds., *Analysis of Concept Learning* (New York: Academic Press, 1966), pp. 37–44; David P. Ausubel, *The Psychology of Meaningful Verbal Behavior* (New York: Grune and Stratton, 1963); Robert M. Gagné, "Problem Solving," in Arthur W. Melton, ed., *Categories of Human Learning* (New York: Academic Press, 1964), pp. 293–317; George A. Miller, *Language and Communication* (New York: McGraw-Hill, 1951).

[5] George Katona, *Organizing and Memorizing* (New York: Columbia Univ. Press, 1940); Roger N. Shepard, Carl I. Hovland, and Herbert M. Jenkins, "Learning and Memorization of Classifications," *Psychological Monographs,* 75, No. 13 (1961) (entire No. 517); Robert S. Woodworth, *Dynamics of Behavior* (New York: Henry Holt, 1958), chs. 10–12.

[6] *The Conditions of Learning,* pp. 190–91.

[7] Karl Dunker, "On Problem Solving," *Psychological Monographs,* 58, No. 5 (1945) (entire No. 270); George A. Polya, *How to Solve It* (Princeton: Princeton Univ. Press, 1945); George A. Miller, Eugene Galanter, and Karl H. Pribram, *Plans and the Structure of Behavior* (New York: Henry Holt, 1960).

[8] Lyle E. Bourne, Jr., Bruce R. Ekstrand, and Roger L. Dominowski, *The Psychology of Thinking* (Englewood Cliffs, N.J.: Prentice-Hall, 1971).

[9] John R. Hayes, "Problem Topology and the Solution Process," in Carl P. Duncan, ed., *Thinking: Current Experimental Studies* (Philadelphia: Lippincott, 1967), pp. 167–81.

[10] Hulda J. Rees and Harold E. Israel, "An Investigation of the Establishment and Operation of Mental Sets," *Psychological Monographs,* 46 (1925) (entire No. 210).

[11] Ibid.; Melvin H. Marx, Wilton W. Murphy, and Aaron J. Brownstein, "Recognition of Complex Visual Stimuli as a Function of Training with Abstracted Patterns," *Journal of Experimental Psychology,* 62 (1961), 456–60.

[12] James L. Adams, *Conceptual Blockbusting* (San Francisco: W. H. Freeman, 1974); Edward DeBono, *New Think* (New York: Basic Books, 1958); Ronald H. Forgus, *Perception* (New York: McGraw-Hill, 1966), ch. 13; Abraham Luchins and Edith Hirsch Luchins, *Rigidity of Behavior* (Eugene: Univ. of Oregon Books, 1959); N. R. F. Maier, "Reasoning in Humans. I. On Direction," *Journal of Comparative Psychology,* 10 (1920), 115–43.

[13] "Plans and the Cognitive Process of Writing," paper presented at the National Institute of Education Writing Conference, June 1977; "Problem Solving Strategies and the Writing Process," *College English,* 39 (1977), 449–61. See also footnote 2.

[14] Jane, a student not discussed in this paper, was surprised to find out that a topic paragraph can be rewritten after a paper's conclusion to make that paragraph reflect what the essay truly contains. She had gotten so indoctrinated with Psychology's (her major) insistence that a hypothesis be formulated and then left untouched before an experiment begins that she thought revision of one's "major premise" was somehow illegal. She had formed a rule out of her exposure to social science methodology, and the rule was totally inappropriate for most writing situations.

[15] Cf. "A plan is flexible if the order of execution of its parts can be easily interchanged without affecting the feasibility of the plan . . . the flexible planner might tend to think of lists of things she had to do; the inflexible planner would have his time planned like a sequence of cause-effect relations. The former could rearrange his lists to suit his opportunities, but the latter would be unable to strike while the iron was hot and would generally require considerable 'lead-time' before he could incorporate any alternative sub-plans" (Miller, Galanter, and Pribram, p. 120).

[16] Frederic Bartlett, *Thinking* (New York: Basic Books, 1958), pp. 74–76.

[17] *Structure and Direction in Thinking* (New York: John Wiley, 1965), p. 255.

[18] Flower and Hayes, "Plans and the Cognitive Process of Writing," p. 26.

COMPOSING BEHAVIORS OF ONE- AND MULTI-DRAFT WRITERS

Muriel Harris

[*College English* 51 (1989): 174–91.]

Muriel Harris is a professor of English and director of the Writing Lab at Purdue University, where she founded and continues to edit the *Writing Lab Newsletter.* Her articles, book chapters, and conference presentations focus on individualized instruction in writing and the theory, pedagogy, and administration of writing centers. Most recently, she coordinated the development of the Purdue OWL, the Online Writing Lab, (http://owl.english.purdue.edu). She has also authored several books, including *Teaching One-to-One: The Writing Conference* (1986) and the recently published fourth edition of the *Prentice Hall Reference Guide to Grammar and Usage* (2000). Harris is widely recognized as an authority on writing centers and Writing Across the Curriculum, and she has won several teaching awards, including the National Council of teachers of English (NCTE) exemplar Award in 2000 and NCTE's Rewey Belle Inglis Award, given by the Women's Issues in Literacy and Life Assembly (WILLA), in 2000.

Harris suggests that we think of revising behaviors (and thus of revision strategies) as ranging on a continuum from writers who produce only one draft to writers who produce multiple drafts. According to Harris, one writer may exhibit several different revision behaviors, in some instances producing only one draft or doing little revision and in other instances producing multiple drafts and doing extensive revision. The variety of composing and revising behaviors, she contends, is not necessarily attributable to experience or abilities. Harris's approach to understanding revision offers instructors a powerful and flexible explanation of revising, one that accounts more fully for the variety of writing tasks that students encounter and provides them with a variety of effective composing strategies for accomplishing those tasks.

A belief shared by teachers of writing, one that we fervently try to inculcate in our students, is that revision can improve writing. This notion, that revision generally results in better text, often pairs up with another assumption, that revision occurs as we work through separate drafts. Thus, "hand in your working drafts tomorrow and the final ones next Friday" is a common assignment, as is the following bit of textbook advice: "When the draft is completed, a good critical reading should help the writer re-envision the essay and could very well lead to substantial rewriting" (Axelrod and Cooper 10). This textbook advice, hardly atypical, is based on the rationale that gaining distance from a piece of discourse helps the writer to judge it more critically. As evidence for this assumption, Richard Beach's 1976 study of the self-evaluation strategies of revisers and non-revisers demonstrated that extensive revisers were more capable of detaching themselves and gaining aesthetic distance from their writing than were non-revisers. Nancy Sommers' later theoretical work on revision also sensitized us to students' need to re-see their texts rather than to view revision as an editing process at the limited level of word changes.

A logical conclusion, then, is to train student writers to re-see and then re-draft a piece of discourse. There are other compelling reasons for helping students view first or working drafts as fluid and not yet molded into final form. The opportunities for outside intervention, through teacher critiques and suggestions or peer evaluation sessions, can be valuable. And it is equally important to help students move beyond their limited approaches and limiting tendency to settle for whatever rolls out on paper the first time around. The novice view of a first draft as written-in-stone (or fast-drying cement) can preclude engaging more fully with the ideas being expressed. On the other hand, we have to acknowledge that there are advantages in being able, where it is appropriate, to master the art of one-draft writing. When students write essay exams or placement essays and when they go on to on-the-job writing where time doesn't permit multiple drafts, they need to produce first drafts which are also coherent, finished final drafts. Yet, even acknowledging that need, we still seem justified in advocating that our students master the art of redrafting to shape a text into a more effective form.

The notion that reworking a text through multiple drafts and/or visible changes is generally a beneficial process is also an underlying assumption in some lines of research. This had been particularly evident in studies of computer-aided revision, where counts were taken of changes in macrostructure and microstructure with and without word processing. If more changes were made on a word processor than were written by hand, the conclusion was that word processors are an aid to revision. Such research is based on the premise that revision equals visible changes in a text and that these changes will improve the text.

Given this widely entrenched notion of redrafting as being advantageous, it would be comforting to turn to research results for clearcut evidence that reworking of text produces better writing. But studies of revision do not provide the conclusive picture that we need in order to assert that we should continue coaxing our students into writing multiple drafts. Lillian Bridwell's 1980 survey of revision studies led her to conclude that "questions about the relationship between revision and qualitative improvement remain largely unanswered" (199), and her own study demonstrated that the most extensively revised papers "received a range of quality ratings from the top to the bottom of the scale" (216). In another review of research on revision, Stephen Witte cites studies which similarly suggest that the amount of redrafting (which Witte calls "retranscription") often bears little relation to the overall quality of completed texts ("Revising" 256). Similarly, Linda Flower and John Hayes et al., citing studies which also dispute the notion that more re-drafting should mean better papers, conclude that the amount of change is not a key variable in revision and that revision as an obligatory stage required by teachers doesn't necessarily produce better writing. (For a teacher's affirmation of the same phenomenon, see Henley.)

Constricting revision to retranscription (i.e., to altering what has been written) also denies the reality of pre-text, a composing phenomenon studied by Stephen Witte in "Pre-Text and Composing." Witte defines a writer's pre-text as "the mental construction of 'text' prior to transcription" (397). Pre-text thus "refers to a writer's linguistic representation of intended meaning, a 'trial locution' that is produced in the mind, stored in the writer's memory, and sometimes manipulated mentally prior to being transcribed as written text" (397). Pre-texts are distinguished from abstract plans in that pre-texts approximate written prose. As the outcome of planning, pre-text can also be the basis for further planning. In his study Witte found great diversity in how writers construct and use pre-text. Some writers construct little or no pre-text; others rely heavily on extensive pre-texts; others create short pre-texts; and still others move back and forth between extensive and short pre-texts. The point here is that Witte has shown us that revision can and does occur in pre-texts, before visible marks are made on paper. In an earlier paper, "Revising, Composing Theory, and Research Design," Witte suggests that the pre-text writers construct before making marks on paper is probably a function of the quality, kind, and extent of planning that occurs before transcribing on paper. The danger here is that we might conclude that the development from novice to expert writer entails learning to make greater use of pre-text prior to transcribing. After all, in Linda Flower's memorable phrase, pre-text is "the last cheap gas before transcribing text" (see Witte, "Pre-Text" 422). But Witte notes that his data do not support a "vote for pre-text" ("Pre-Text" 401). For the students in Witte's study, more extensive use of pre-text doesn't automatically lead to better written text. Thus it appears so far that the quality of revision can neither be measured by the pound nor tracked through discreet stages.

But a discussion of whether more or fewer drafts is an indication of more mature writing is itself not adequate. As Maxine Hairston reminds us in "Different Products, Different Processes," we must also consider the writing task that is involved in any particular case of generating discourse. In her taxonomy of writing categories, categories that depict a variety of revision behaviors that are true to the experience of many of us, Hairston divides writing into three classes: first, routine maintenance writing which is simple communication about uncomplicated matters; second, extended, relatively complex writing that requires the writer's attention but is self-limiting in that the writer already knows most of what she is going to write and may be writing under time constraints; and third, extended reflective writing in which the form and content emerge as the writing proceeds. Even with this oversimplified, brief summary of Hairston's classes of writing, we recognize that the matter of when and if re-drafting takes place can differ according to the demands of different tasks and situations as well as the different skills levels of writers.

Many—or perhaps even most—of us may nod in agreement as we recognize in Hairston's classes of writing a description of the different types of writing we do. But given the range of individual differences that exist among writers, we still cannot conclude that the nature of effective revision is always tied to the writing task, because such a conclusion would not account for what we know also exists—some expert writers who, despite the writing task, work at either end of the spectrum as confirmed, consistent one-drafters or as perpetual multi-drafters. That writers exhibit a diversity of revising habits has been noted by Lester Faigley and Stephen Witte in "Analyzing Revision." When testing the taxonomy of revision changes they had created, Faigley and Witte found that expert writers exhibited "extreme diversity" in the ways they revised:

> One expert writer in the present study made almost no revisions; another started with an almost stream-of-consciousness text that she then converted to

an organized essay in the second draft; another limited his major revisions to a single long insert; and another revised mostly by pruning. (410)

Similarly, when summarizing interviews with well-known authors such as those in the *Writers at Work: The Paris Review Interviews* series, Lillian Bridwell notes that these discussions reveal a wide range of revision strategies among these writers, from rapid producers of text who do little revising as they proceed to writers who move along by revising every sentence (198).

More extensive insights into a variety of composing styles are offered in Tom Waldrep's collection of essays by successful scholars working in composition, *Writers on Writing*. Here too as writers describe their composing processes, we see a variety of approaches, including some writers who plan extensively before their pens hit paper (or before the cursor blips on their screens). Their planning is so complete that their texts generally emerge in a single draft with minor, if any, editing as they write. Self-descriptions of some experienced writers in the field of composition give us vivid accounts of how these one-drafters work. For example, Patricia Y. Murray notes that prior to typing, she sees words, phrases, sentences, and paragraphs taking shape in her head. Her composing, she concludes, has been done before her fingers touch the typewriter, though as she also notes, she revises and edits as she types (234). William Lutz offers a similar account:

> Before I write, I write in my mind. The more difficult and complex the writing, the more time I need to think before I write. Ideas incubate in my mind. While I talk, drive, swim, and exercise I am thinking, planning, writing. I think about the introduction, what examples to use, how to develop the main idea, what kind of conclusion to use. I write, revise, rewrite, agonize, despair, give up, only to start all over again, and all of this before I ever begin to put words on paper. . . . Writing is not a process of discovery for me. . . . The writing process takes place in my mind. Once that process is complete the product emerges. Often I can write pages without pause and with very little, if any, revision or even minor changes. (186–87)

Even with such descriptions from experienced writers, we are hesitant either to discard the notion that writing *is* a process of discovery for many of us or to typecast writers who make many visible changes on the page and/or work through multiple drafts as inadequate writers. After all, many of us, probably the majority, fall somewhere along the continuum from one- to multi-drafters. We may find ourselves as both one- and multi-drafters with the classes of writing that Hairston describes, or we may generally identify ourselves as doing both but also functioning more often as a one- or multi-drafter. Just as we have seen that at one end of the spectrum there are some confirmed one-drafters, so too must we recognize that at the other end of that spectrum there are some confirmed multi-drafters, expert writers for whom extensive revising occurs when writing (so that a piece of discourse may go through several or more drafts or be re-worked heavily as the original draft evolves). David Bartholomae, a self-described multi-drafter, states that he never outlines but works instead with two pads of paper, one to write on and one for making plans, storing sentences, and taking notes. He views his first drafts as disorganized and has to revise extensively, with the result that the revisions bear little resemblance to the first drafts (22–26). Similarly, Lynn Z. Bloom notes that she cannot predict at the outset a great deal of what she is going to say. Only by writing does she learn how her content will develop or how she will handle the structure, organization, and style of her paragraphs, sentences, and whole essay (33).

Thus, if we wish to draw a more inclusive picture of composing behaviors for revision, we have to put together a description that accounts for differences in levels of ability and experience (from novice to expert), for differences in writing tasks, and also for differences in the as yet largely unexplored area of composing process differences among writers. My interest here is in the composing processes of different writers, more particularly, the reality of those writers at either end of that long spectrum, the one-drafters at one end and the multi-drafters at the other. By one-draft writers I mean those writers who construct their plans and the pre-texts that carry out those plans as well as do all or most of the revising of those plans and pre-texts mentally, before transcribing. They do little or no retranscribing. True one-drafters have not arrived at this developmentally or as a result of training in writing, and they should not be confused with other writers who—driven by deadlines, lack of motivation, insufficient experience with writing, or anxieties about "getting it right the first time"—do little or no scratching out of what they have written. Multi-drafters, on the other hand, need to interact with their transcriptions in order to revise. Independent of how much planning they do or pre-text they compose, they continue to revise after they have transcribed words onto paper. Again, true multi-drafters have not reached this stage developmentally or as a result of any intervention by teachers. This is not to say that we can classify writers into two categories, one- and multi-drafters, because all the evidence we have and, more importantly, our own experience tells us that most writers are not one or the other but exist somewhere between these two ends of the continuum.

However, one- and multi-drafters do exist, and we do need to learn more about them to gain a clearer picture not only of what is involved in different revising processes but also to provide a basis for considering the pedagogical implications of dealing with individual differences. There is a strong argument for looking instead at the middle range of writers who do some writing in single drafts and others in multiple drafts or with a lot of retranscribing as they proceed, for it is very probable that the largest number of writers cluster there. But those of us who teach in the individualized setting of conferences or writing lab tutorials know that we can never overlook or put aside the concerns of every unique individual with whom we work. Perhaps we are overly intrigued with individual differences, partly because we see that some students can be ill-served in the group setting of the classrooms and partly because looking at individual differences gives us such enlightening glimpses into the complex reality of composing processes. Clinicians in other fields would argue that looking at the extremes offers a clearer view of what may be involved in the behaviors of the majority. But those who do research in writing also acknowledge that we need to understand dimensions of variation among writers, particularly those patterned differences or "alternate paths to expert performance" that have clear implications for instruction (Freedman et al. 19). In this case, whatever we learn about patterns of behavior among one- and multi-drafters has direct implications for instruction as we need to know the various trade-offs involved in any classroom instruction which would encourage more single or multiple drafting. And, as we will see when looking at what is involved in being able to revise before drafting or in being able to return and re-draft what has been transcribed, there are trade-offs indeed. Whatever arguments are offered, we must also acknowledge that no picture of revision is complete until it includes all that is known and observed about a variety of revision behaviors among writers.

But what do we know about one- and multi-drafters other than anecdotal accounts that confirm their existence? Much evidence is waiting to be gathered from the storehouse of various published interviews in which well-known writers have been asked to describe their writing. And Ann Ruggles Gere's study of the revising behaviors of a blind student gives us a description of a student writer who does not redraft but writes "first draft/final draft" papers, finished products produced in one sitting for her courses as a master's degree candidate. The student describes periods of thinking about a topic before writing. While she doesn't know exactly what she will say until actually writing it, she typically knows what will be contained in the first paragraph as she types the title. Her attention is not focused on words as she concentrates instead on images and larger contexts. A similar description of a one-drafter is found in Joy Reid's "The Radical Outliner and the Radical Brainstormer." Comparing her husband and herself, both composition teachers, Reid notes the differences between herself, an outliner (and a one-drafter), and her husband, a brainstormer (and a multi-drafter), differences which parallel those of the writers in *Writers on Writing* that I have described.

The descriptions of all of the one- and multi-draft writers mentioned so far offer a fairly consistent picture, but these descriptions do little more than reaffirm their existence. In an effort to learn more, I sought out some one- and multi-drafters in order to observe them composing and to explore what might be involved. Since my intent was not to determine the percentage of one- and multi-drafters among any population of writers (though that would be an interesting topic indeed, as I suspect there are more than we may initially guess—or at least more who hover close to either end of the continuum), I sought out experienced writers who identify themselves as very definitely one- or multi-drafters. The subjects I selected for observation were graduate students who teach composition or communications courses, my rationale being that these people can more easily categorize and articulate their own writing habits. From among the group of subjects who described themselves as very definitely either one- or multi-drafters, I selected those who showed evidence of being experienced, competent writers. Of the eight selected subjects (four one-drafters and four multi-drafters), all were at least several years into their graduate studies in English or communications and were either near completion or had recently completed advanced degrees. All had received high scores in standardized tests for verbal skills such as the SAT or GRE exams; all had grade point averages ranging from B+ to A in their graduate courses; and all wrote frequently in a variety of tasks, including academic papers for courses and journal publications, conference papers, the usual business writing of practicing academics (e.g., letters of recommendation for students, memos, instructional materials for classes, etc.), and personal writing such as letters to family and friends. They clearly earned their description as experienced writers. Experienced writers were used because I also wished to exclude those novices who may, through development of their writing skills, change their composing behaviors, and also those novices whose composing habits are the result of other factors such as disinterest (e.g., the one-drafter who habitually begins the paper at 3 a.m. the night before it's due) or anxiety (e.g., the multi-drafter who fears she is never "right" and keeps working and reworking her text).

The experienced writers whom I observed all confirmed that their composing behaviors have not changed over time. That is, they all stated that their writing habits have not altered as they became experienced writers and/or as they moved through writing courses. However, their descriptions of themselves as one- or multi-drafters were not as completely accurate as might be expected. Self-reporting, even among teachers of writing, is not a totally reliable measure. As I observed and talked with the eight writers, I found three very definite one-drafters, Ted, Nina, and Amy; one writer, Jackie, who tends to be a one-drafter but does some revising after writing; two very definite multi-drafters, Bill and Pam; and two writers, Karen and Cindy, who described themselves as multi-drafters and who tend to revise extensively but who can also produce first draft/final draft writing under some conditions. To gather data on their composing behaviors, I interviewed each person for an hour, asking questions about the types of writing they do, the activities they engage in before writing, the details of what happens as they write, their revision behaviors, the manner in which sentences are composed, and their attitudes and past history of writing. Each person was also asked to spend an hour writing in response to an assignment. The specific assignment was a request from an academic advisor asking for the writers' descriptions of the skills needed to succeed in their field of study. As they wrote, all eight writers were asked to give thinking-aloud protocols and were videotaped for future study. Brief interviews after writing focused on eliciting information about how accurately the writing session reflected their general writing habits and behaviors. Each type of information collected is, at best, incomplete because accounts of one's own composing processes may not be entirely accurate, because thinking-aloud protocols while writing are only partial accounts of what is being thought about, and because one-hour writing tasks preclude observing some of the kinds of activities that writers report. But even with these limitations I observed patterns of composing behaviors that should differentiate one-draft writers from multi-draft writers.

Preference for Beginning with a Developed Focus vs. Preference for Beginning at an Exploratory Stage

Among the consistent behaviors that one-drafters report is the point at which they can and will start writing. All of the four one-drafters expressed a strong need to clarify their thinking prior to beginning to transcribe. They are either not ready to write or cannot write until they have a focus and organization in mind. They may, as I observed Jackie and Ted doing, make some brief planning notes on paper or, as Amy and Nina did, sit for awhile and mentally plan, but all expressed a clearly articulated need to know beforehand the direction the piece of writing would take. For Nina's longer papers, she described a planning schedule in which the focus comes first, even before collecting notes. Ted too described the first stage of a piece of writing as being a time of mentally narrowing a topic. During incubation times before writing, two of these writers described some global recasting of a paper in their minds while the other two expressed a need to talk it out, either to themselves or friends. There is little resorting of written notes and little use of written outlines, except for some short lists, described by Ted as "memory jogs" to use while he writes. Amy explained that she sometimes felt that in high school or as an undergraduate she should have written outlines to please her teachers, but she never did get around to it because outlines served no useful purpose for her. Consistent throughout these accounts and in my observation of their writing was these writers' need to know where they are headed beforehand and a feeling that they are not ready to write—or cannot write—until they are at that stage. When asked if they ever engaged in freewriting, two one-drafters said they could not, unless forced to, plunge in and write without a focus and a mental plan. Ted, in particular, noted that the notion of exploration during writing would make him so uncomfortable that he would probably block and be unable to write.

In contrast to the one-drafters' preference for knowing their direction before writing, the two consistent multi-drafters, Pam and Bill, explained that they resist knowing, resist any attempt at clarification prior to writing. Their preference is for open-ended exploration as they write. They may have been reading and thinking extensively beforehand, but the topic has not taken shape when they decide that it is time to begin writing. Bill reported that he purposely starts with a broad topic while Pam said that she looks for something "broad or ambiguous" or "something small that can grow and grow." As Bill explained, he doesn't like writing about what he already knows as that would be boring. Pam too expressed her resistance to knowing her topic and direction beforehand in terms of how boring it would be. Generally, Bill will do about four or five drafts as he works through the early parts of a paper, perhaps two to four pages, before he knows what he will write about. He and Pam allow for—and indeed expect—that their topic will change as they write. Pam explained: "I work by allowing the direction of the work to change if it needs to. . . . I have to allow things to go where they need to go." When I observed them writing, Pam spent considerable time planning and creating pre-texts before short bursts of transcribing while Bill wrote several different versions of an introduction and, with some cutting and pasting, was about ready to define his focus at the end of the hour. He reported that he depends heavily on seeing what he has written in order to find his focus, choose his content, and organize. Pam also noted that she needs to see chunks of what she has transcribed to see where the piece of discourse is taking her.

The other two writers who characterized themselves as multi-drafters, Karen and Cindy, both described a general tendency to plunge in before the topic is clear. Karen said that she can't visualize her arguments until she writes them out and generally writes and rewrites as she proceeds, but for writing tasks that she described as "formulaic" in that they are familiar because she has written similar pieces of discourse, she can write quickly and finish quickly—as she did with the writing task for this study. Since she had previously written the same kind of letter assigned in this study, she did not engage in the multi-drafting that would be more characteristic, she says, of her general composing behaviors. Cindy, the other self-described multi-drafter, almost completed the task in a single draft, though as she explained with short pieces, she can revert to her "journalistic mode" of writing, having been a working journalist for a number of years. For longer papers, such as those required in graduate courses, her descriptions sound much like those of Bill, Pam, and Karen. All of these writers, though, share the unifying characteristic of beginning to write before the task is well defined in their minds, unlike the one-drafters who do not write at that stage.

Preference for Limiting Options vs. Preference for Open-ended Exploring

Another consistent and clearly related difference between one- and multi-drafters is the difference in the quantity of options they will generate, from words and sentences to whole sections of a paper, and the way in which they will evaluate those options. As they wrote, all four of the one-drafters limited their options by generating several choices and then making a decision fairly quickly. There were numerous occasions in the think-aloud protocols of three of the four one-drafters in which they would stop, try another word, question a phrase, raise the possibility of another idea to include, and then make a quick decision. When Ted re-read one of his paragraphs, he saw a different direction that he might have taken that would perhaps be better, but he accepted what he had. ("That'll do here, OK . . . OK" he said to himself and moved on.) Nina, another one-drafter, generated no alternate options aloud as she wrote.

As is evident in this description of one-drafters, they exhibited none of the agonizing over possibilities that other writers experience, and they appear to be able to accept their choices quickly and move on. While observers may question whether limiting options in this manner cuts off further discovery and possibly better solutions or whether the internal debate goes on prior to transcribing, one-drafters are obviously efficient writers. They generate fewer choices, reach decisions more quickly, and do most or all of the decision-making before transcribing on paper. Thus, three of the four one-drafters finished the paper in the time allotted, and the fourth writer was almost finished. They can pace themselves fairly accurately too, giving me their estimates of how long it takes them to write papers of particular lengths. All four one-drafters describe themselves as incurable procrastinators who begin even long papers the night before they are due, allowing themselves about the right number of hours in which to transcribe their mental constructs onto paper. Nina explained that she makes choices quickly because she is always writing at the last minute under pressure and doesn't have time to consider more options. Another one-drafter offered a vivid description of the tension and stress that can be involved in these last minute, all-night sessions.

While they worry about whether they will finish on time, these one-drafters generally do. Contributing to their efficiency are two time-saving procedures involved as they get words on paper. Because most decisions are made before they commit words to paper, they do little or no scratching out and re-writing; and they do a minimum of re-reading both as they proceed and also when they are finished. The few changes I observed being made were either single words or a few short phrases, unlike the multi-drafters who rejected or scratched out whole sentences and paragraphs. As Nina wrote, she never re-read her developing text, though she reported that she does a little re-reading when she is finished with longer papers. The tinkering with words that she might do then, she says, is counterproductive because she rarely feels that she is improving the text with these changes. (Nina and the other one-drafters would probably be quite successful at the kind of "invisible writing" that has been investigated, that is, writing done under conditions in which writers cannot see what they are writing or scan as they progress. See Blau.)

In contrast to the one-drafters' limited options, quick decisions, few changes on paper and little or no re-reading, the multi-drafters were frequently observed generating and exploring many options, spending a long time in making their choices, and making frequent and large-scale changes on paper. Bill said that he produces large quantities of text because he needs to see it in order to see if he wants to retain it, unlike the one-drafters who exhibit little or no need to examine their developing text. Moreover, as Bill noted, the text he generates is also on occasion a heuristic for more text. As he writes, Bill engages in numerous revising tactics. He writes a sentence, stops to examine it by switching it around, going back to add clauses, or combining it with other text on the same page or a different sheet of paper. For the assigned writing task, he began with one sheet of paper, moved to another, tore off some of it and discarded it, and added part back to a previous sheet. At home when writing a longer paper, he will similarly engage in extensive cutting and pasting. In a somewhat different manner, Pam did not generate as many options on paper for this study. Instead, her protocol recorded various alternative plans and pre-texts that she would stop to explore verbally for five or ten minutes before transcribing anything. What she did write, though, was often heavily edited so that at the end of the hour, she, like Bill, had only progressed somewhat through an introductory paragraph of several sentences. Thus, while Bill had produced large amounts of text on paper that were later rejected after having been written, Pam spent more of her time generating and rejecting plans and pre-texts than crossing out transcriptions.

Writing is a more time-consuming task for these multi-drafters because they expect to produce many options and a large amount of text that will be discarded. Both Bill and Pam described general writing procedures in which they begin by freewriting, and, as they proceed, distilling from earlier drafts what will be used in later drafts. Both proceed incrementally, that is, by starting in and then starting again before finishing a whole draft. Both writers are used to re-reading frequently, partly to locate what Pam called "key elements" that will be retained for later drafts and partly, as Bill explained, because the act of generating more options and exploring them causes him to lose track of where he is.

Because both Bill and Pam seem to be comfortable when working within an as-yet only partially focused text, it would be interesting to explore what has been termed their "tolerance for ambiguity," a trait defined as a person's ability to function calmly in a situation in which interpretation of all stimuli is not completely clear. (See Budner, and Frenkel-Brunswick.) People who have little or no tolerance for ambiguity perceive ambiguous situations as sources of psychological discomfort, and they may try to reach conclusions quickly rather than to take the time to consider all of the essential elements of an unclear situation. People with more tolerance for ambiguity enjoy being in ambiguous situations and tend to seek them out. The relevance here, of course, is the question of whether one-drafters will not begin until they have structured the task and will also move quickly to conclusions in part, at least, because of having some degree of intolerance for ambiguity. This might be a fruitful area for further research.

For those interested in the mental processes which accompany behaviors, another dimension to explore is the Myers-Briggs Type Indicator (MBTI), a measure of expressed preferences (i.e., not performance tasks) in four bi-polar dimensions of personality. The work of George H. Jensen and John K. DiTiberio has indicated some relationships between the personality types identified by the MBTI and writing processes. Of particular interest here is that Bill, who had independently taken the MBTI for other reasons, reported that he scored highly in the dimensions of "extraversion" and "perceiving." Extraverts, say Jensen and DiTiberio, "often leap into tasks with little planning, then rely on trial and error to complete the task" (288), and they "often find freewriting a good method for developing ideas, for they think better when writing quickly, impulsively, and uncritically" (289). Perceivers, another type described by Jensen and DiTiberio, appear to share tendencies similar to those with a tolerance for ambiguity, for perceivers "are willing to leave the outer world unstructured. . . . Quickly made decisions narrow their field of vision" (295). Perceiving types tend to select broad topics for writing, like a wide range of alternatives, and always want to read one more book on the subject. Their revisions thus often need to be refocused (296). The similarities here to Bill's writing behaviors show us that while the MBTI is somewhat circular in that the scoring is a reflection of people's self-description, it can confirm (and perhaps clarify) the relationship of writing behaviors to more general human behaviors.

The Preference for Closure vs. Resistance to Closure

From these descriptions of one- and multi-drafters it is readily apparent that they differ in their need for closure. The one-drafters move quickly to decisions while composing, and they report that once they are done with a paper, they prefer not to look back at it, either immediately to re-read it or at some future time, to think about revising it. Ted explained that he generally is willing to do one rereading at the time of completing a paper and sometimes to make a few wording changes, but that is all. He shrugged off the possibility of doing even a second re-reading of any of his writing once it is done because he says he can't stand to look at it again. All of the one-drafters reported that they hardly, if ever, rewrite a paper. This distaste for returning to a completed text can be the source of problems for these one-drafters. Forced by a teacher in a graduate course who wanted first drafts one week and revisions the next week, Nina explained that she deliberately resorted to "writing a bad paper" for the first submission in order to submit her "real" draft as the "revised" paper. Writing a series of drafts is clearly harder for one-drafters such as Nina than we have yet acknowledged.

These one-drafters are as reluctant to start as they are impatient to finish. Although they tend to delay the drafting process, this does not apply to their preparation, which often starts well in advance and is the "interesting" or "enjoyable" part for them. With writing that produces few surprises or discoveries for any of them because the generative process precedes transcription, drafting on paper is more "tedious" (a word they frequently used during their interviews) than for other writers. Said Ted, "Writing is something I have to do, not something I want to do." Even Jackie, who allows for some revising while drafting in order to develop the details of her plan, reported that she has a hard time going back to revise a paper once it is completed. She, like the others, reported a sense of feeling the paper is over and done with. "Done, dead and done, done, finished, done," concluded another of these one-drafters.

On the other hand, the multi-drafters observed in this study explained that they are never done with a paper. They can easily and willingly go back to it or to keep writing indefinitely. Asked when they know they are finished, Bill and Pam explained that they never feel they are "done" with a piece of discourse, merely that they have to stop in order to meet a deadline. As Pam said, she never gets to a last draft and doesn't care about producing "neat packages." Understandably, she has trouble with conclusions and with "wrapping up" at the end of a piece of discourse. Asked how pervasive her redrafting is for all of her writing, Pam commented that she writes informal letters to parents and friends every day and is getting to the point that she doesn't rewrite these letters as much. Bill too noted that he fights against products and hates to finish. As a result, both Bill and Pam often fail to meet their deadlines. Cindy, bored by her "journalistic one-draft writing," expressed a strong desire to return to some of her previously completed papers in order to rewrite them.

Writer-Based vs. Reader-Based Early Drafts

One way of distinguishing the early drafts produced by the multi-drafters for this study from the drafts produced by the one-drafters is to draw upon Linda Flower's distinction between Writer-Based and Reader-Based prose. Writer-Based prose, explains Flower, is "verbal expression written by a writer to himself and for himself. It is the working of his own verbal thought. In its *structure,* Writer-Based prose reflects the associative, narrative path of the writer's own confrontation with her subject" (19–20). Reader-Based prose, on the other hand, is "a deliberate attempt to communicate something to a reader. To do that it creates a shared language and shared context between writer and reader. It also offers the reader an issue-oriented rhetorical structure rather than a replay of the writer's discovery process" (20). Although Flower acknowledges that Writer-Based prose is a "problem" that composition courses are designed to correct, she also affirms its usefulness as a search tool, a strategy for handling the difficulty of attending to multiple complex tasks simultaneously. Writer-Based prose needs to be revised into Reader-Based prose, but it can be effective as a "medium for thinking." And for the multi-drafters observed in this study, characterizing the initial drafts of two of the multi-drafters as Writer-Based helps to see how their early drafts differ from those of the one-drafters.

One feature of Writer-Based prose, as offered by Flower, is that it reflects the writer's method of searching by means of surveying what she knows, often in a narrative manner. Information tends to be structured as a narrative of the discovery process or as a survey of the data in the writer's mind. Reader-Based prose, on the other hand, restructures the information so that it is accessible to the reader. Both the protocols and the written drafts produced by the two confirmed multi-drafters, Bill and Pam, reveal this Writer-Based orientation as their initial way into writing. Bill very clearly began with a memory search through his own experience, made some brief notes, and then wrote a narrative as his first sentence in response to the request that he describe to an academic counselor the skills needed for his field: "I went through what must have been a million different majors before I wound up in English and it was actually my first choice." Pam spent the hour exploring the appropriateness of the term "skills."

In distinct contrast, all four of the one-drafters began by constructing a conceptual framework for the response they would write, most typically by defining a few categories or headings which would be the focus or main point of the paper. With a few words in mind that indicated his major points, Ted then moved on to ask himself who would be reading his response, what the context would be, and what format the writing would use. He moved quickly from a search for a point to considerations of how his audience would use his information. Similarly, Amy rather promptly chose a few terms, decided to herself that "that'll be the focus," and then said, "OK, I'm trying to get into a role here. I'm responding to someone who . . . This is not something they are going to give out to people. But they're going to read it and compile responses, put something together for themselves." She then began writing her draft and completed it within the hour. Asked what constraints and concerns she is most aware of when actually writing, Amy said that she is generally concerned with clarity for the reader. The point of contrast here is that the search process was both different in kind and longer for the multi-drafters. Initially, their time was spent discovering what they think about the subject, whereas the one-drafters chose a framework within a few minutes and moved on to orient their writing to their readers. Because the transformation or reworking of text comes later for the multi-drafters, rewriting is a necessary component of their writing. The standard bit of advice, about writing the introductory paragraph later, would be a necessary step for them but would not be a productive or appropriate strategy for one-drafters to try. For the one-drafters, the introductory paragraph is the appropriate starting point. In fact, given what they said about the necessity of knowing their focus beforehand, the introductory paragraph is not merely appropriate but necessary.

Because the early stages of a piece of writing are, for multi-drafters, so intricately bound up with mental searching, surveying, and discovering, the writing that is produced is not oriented to the reader. For their early drafts, Bill and Pam both acknowledged that their writing is not yet understandable to others. When Pam commented that in her early drafts, "the reader can't yet see where I'm going," she sighed over the difficulties this had caused in trying to work with her Master's thesis committee. If some writers' early drafts are so personal and so unlikely to be accessible to readers, it is worth speculating about how effective peer editing sessions could be for such multi-drafters who appear in classrooms with "rough drafts" as instructed.

Conclusions

One way to summarize the characteristics of one- and multi-drafters is to consider what they gain by being one-drafters and at what cost they gain these advantages. Clearly, one-drafters are efficient writers. This efficiency is achieved by mentally revising beforehand, by generating options verbally rather than on paper, by generating only a limited number of options before settling on one and getting on with the task, and by doing little or no re-reading. They are able to pace themselves and can probably perform comfortably in situations such as the workplace or in in-class writing where it is advantageous to produce first-draft, final-draft pieces of discourse. Their drafts are readily accessible to readers, and they can expend effort early on in polishing the text for greater clarity. But at what cost? One-drafters are obviously in danger of cutting themselves off from further exploration, from a richer field of discovery than is possible during the time in which they generate options. When they exhibit a willingness to settle on one of their options, they may thereby have eliminated the possibility of searching for a better one. In their impatience to move on, they may even settle on options they know could be improved on. Their impulse to write dwindles as these writers experience little or none of the excitement of discovery or exploration during writing. The interesting portion of a writing task, the struggle with text and sense of exploration, is largely completed when they begin to commit themselves to paper (or computer screen). Because they are less likely to enjoy writing, the task of starting is more likely to be put off to the last minute and to become a stressful situation, thus reinforcing their inclination not to re-read and their desire to be done and to put the paper behind them forever once they have finished. And it appears that it is as hard for true one-drafters to suspend the need for closure as it is for multi-drafters to reach quick decisions and push themselves rapidly toward closure.

Multi-drafters appear to be the flip side of the same coin. Their relative inefficiency causes them to miss deadlines, to create Writer-Based first drafts, to produce large quantities of text that is discarded, and to get lost in their own writing. They need to re-read and re-draft, and they probably appear at first glance to be poorer writers than one-drafters. But they are more likely to be writers who will plunge in eagerly, will write and re-write, and will use writing to explore widely and richly. They also are more likely to affirm the value of writing as a heuristic, the merits of freewriting, and the need for cutting and pasting of text. They may, if statistics are gathered, be the writers who benefit most from collaborative discussions such as those in writing labs with tutors. Their drafts are truly amenable to change and available for re-working.

Implications

Acknowledging the reality of one- and multi-drafting involves enlarging both our perspectives on revision and our instructional practices with students. In terms of what the reality of one-drafting and multi-drafting tells us about revision, it is apparent that we need to account for this diversity of revision behaviors as we construct a more detailed picture of revision. As Stephen Witte notes, "revising research that limits itself to examining changes in written text or drafts espouses a reductionist view of revising as a stage in a linear sequence of stages" ("Revising" 266). Revision can and does occur when writers set goals, create plans, and compose pre-text, as well as when they transcribe and re-draft after transcription. Revision can be triggered by cognitive activity alone and/or by interaction with text; and attitudes, preferences, and cognitive make-up play a role in when and how much a writer revises—or is willing to revise—a text.

Yet, while recognizing the many dimensions to be explored in understanding revision, we can also use this diversity as a source for helping students with different types of problems and concerns. For students who are one-drafters or have tendencies toward single drafting, we need to provide help in several areas. They'll have to learn to do more reviewing of written text both as they write and afterwards, in order to evaluate and revise. They will also need to be aware that they should have strategies that provide for more exploration and invention than they may presently allow themselves. While acknowledging their distaste for returning to a draft to open it up again, we also need to help them see how and when this can be productive. Moreover, we can provide assistance in helping one-drafters and other writers who cluster near that end of the spectrum recognize that sometimes they may have a preference for choosing an option even after they recognize that it may not be the best one. When Tim, one of the one-drafters I observed, noted at one point in his protocol that he should take a different direction for one of his paragraphs but won't, he shows similarities to another writer, David, observed by Witte ("Pre-Text and Composing" 406), who is reluctant to spend more than fifteen seconds reworking a sentence in pre-text, even though he demonstrates the ability to evoke criteria that could lead to better formulations if he chose to stop and revise mentally (David typically does little revision of written text). This impatience, this need to keep moving along, that does not always allow for the production of good text, can obviously work against producing good text, and it is unlikely that such writers will either recognize or conquer the problem on their own. They may have snared themselves in their own vicious circles if their tendency to procrastinate puts them in a deadline crunch, which, in turn, does not afford them the luxury of time to consider new options. Such behaviors can become a composing habit so entrenched that it is no longer noticed.

As we work with one-drafters, we will also have to learn ourselves how to distinguish them from writers who see themselves as one-drafters because they are not inclined, for one reason or another, to expend more energy on drafting. Inertia, lack of motivation, lack of information about what multiple drafts can do, higher priorities for other tasks, and so on are not characteristic of true one-drafters, and we must be able to identify the writer who might take refuge behind a label of "one-drafter" from the writer who exhibits some or many of the characteristics of one-draft composing and who wants to become a better writer. For example, in our writing lab I have worked with students who think they are one-drafters because of assorted fears, anxieties, and misinformation. "But I have to get it right the first time," "My teachers never liked to see scratching out on the paper, even when we wrote in class," or "I hate making choices, so I go with what I have" are not the comments of true one-drafters.

With multiple-drafters we have other work to do. To become more efficient writers, they will need to become more proficient planners and creators of pretext, though given their heavy dependence on seeing what they have written, they will probably still rely a great deal on reading and working with their transcribed text. They will also need to become more proficient at times at focusing on a topic quickly, recognizing the difficulties involved in agonizing endlessly over possibilities. In the words of a reviewer of this paper, they will have to learn when and how "to get on with it."

Besides assisting with these strategies, we can help students become more aware of their composing behaviors. We can assist multi-drafters in recognizing that they are not slow or inept writers but writers who may linger too long over making choices. For writers who have difficulty returning to a completed text in order to revise, we can relate the problem to the larger picture, an impatience with returning to any completed task. Granted, this is not a giant leap forward, but too many students are willing to throw in the towel with writing skills in particular without recognizing the link to their more general orientations to life. Similarly, the impatient writer who, like Ted, proclaims to have a virulent case of the "I-hate-to-write" syndrome may be a competent one-drafter (or have a preference for fewer drafts) who needs to see that it is the transcribing stage of writing that is the source of the impatience, procrastination, and irritation. On the other hand, writers more inclined to be multi-drafters need to recognize that their frustration, self-criticism, and/or low grades may be due to having readers intervene at too early a stage in the drafting. What I am suggesting here is that some writers unknowingly get themselves caught in linguistic traps. They think they are making generalizations about the whole act of "writing," that blanket term for all the processes involved, when they may well be voicing problems or attitudes about one or another of the processes. What is needed here is some assistance in helping students define their problems more precisely. To do this, classroom teachers can open conferences like a writing lab tutorial, by asking questions about the student's writing processes and difficulties.

In addition to individualizing our work with students, we can also look at our own teaching practices. When we offer classroom strategies and heuristics, we need to remind our students that it is likely that some will be very inappropriate for different students. Being unable to freewrite is not necessarily a sign of an inept writer. One writer's written text may be just as effective a heuristic for that writer as the planning sheets are for another writer. Beyond these strategies and acknowledgments, we have to examine how we talk about or teach composing processes. There is a very real danger in imposing a single, "ideal" composing style on students, as Jack Selzer found teachers attempting to do in his survey of the literature. Similarly, as Susan McLeod notes, teachers tend to teach their own composing behaviors in the classroom and are thus in danger either of imposing their redrafting approaches on students whose preference for revising prior to transcribing serves them well or of touting their one- or few-draft strategies to students who fare better when interacting with their transcribed text. Imposing personal preferences, observes McLeod, would put us in the peculiar position of trying to fix something that isn't broken. And there's enough of that going around as it is.

Works Cited

Axelrod, Rise B., and Charles R. Cooper. *The St. Martin's Guide to Writing*. New York: St. Martin's, 1985.

Bartholomae, David. "Against the Grain." Waldrep I:19–29.

Beach, Richard. "Self-Evaluation Strategies of Extensive Revisers and Nonrevisers." *College Composition and Communication* 27 (1976): 160–64.

Blau, Sheridan. "Invisible Writing: Investigating Cognitive Processes in Composition." *College Composition and Communication* 34 (1983): 297–312.

Bloom, Lynn Z. "How I Write." Waldrep I:31-37.

Bridwell, Lillian S. "Revising Strategies in Twelfth Grade Students' Transactional Writing." *Research in the Teaching of English* 14 (1980): 197–222.

Budner, S. "Intolerance of Ambiguity as a Personality Variable." *Journal of Personality* 30 (1962): 29–50.

Faigley, Lester, and Stephen Witte. "Analyzing Revision." *College Composition and Communication* 32 (1981): 400–14.

Flower, Linda. "Writer-Based Prose: A Cognitive Basis for Problems in Writing." *College English* 41 (1979): 19–37.

Flower, Linda, John R. Hayes, Linda Carey, Karen Shriver, and James Stratman. "Detection, Diagnosis, and the Strategies of Revision." *College Composition and Communication* 37 (1986): 16–55.

Freedman, Sarah Warshauer, Anne Haas Dyson, Linda Flower, and Wallace Chafe. *Research in Writing: Past, Present, and Future*. Technical Report No. 1. Center for the Study of Writing. Berkeley: University of California, 1987.

Frenkel-Brunswick, Else. "Intolerance of Ambiguity as an Emotional and Perceptual Personality Variable." *Journal of Personality* 18 (1949): 108–43.

Gere, Ann Ruggles. "Insights from the Blind: Composing without Revising." *Revising: New Essays for Teachers of Writing*. Ed. Ronald Sudol. Urbana, IL: ERIC/NCTE, 1982. 52–70.

Hairston, Maxine. "Different Products, Different Processes: A Theory about Writing." *College Composition and Communication* 37 (1986): 442–52.

Henley, Joan. "A Revisionist View of Revision." *Washington English Journal* 8.2 (1986): 5–7.

Jensen, George, and John DiTiberio. "Personality and Individual Writing Processes." *College Composition and Communication* 35 (1984): 285–300.

Lutz, William. "How I Write." Waldrep I:183–88.

McLeod, Susan. "The New Orthodoxy: Rethinking the Process Approach." *Freshman English News* 14.3 (1986): 16-21.

Murray, Patricia Y. "Doing Writing." Waldrep I:225–39.

Reid, Joy. "The Radical Outliner and the Radical Brainstormer: A Perspective on Composing Processes." *TESOL Quarterly* 18 (1985): 529–34.

Selzer, Jack. "Exploring Options in Composing." *College Composition and Communication* 35 (1984): 276–84.

Sommers, Nancy. "Revision Strategies of Student Writers and Experienced Adult Writers." *College Composition and Communication* 31 (1980): 378–88.

Waldrep, Tom, ed. *Writers on Writing. Vol. 1*. New York: Random House, 1985. 2 vols.

Witte, Stephen P. "Pre-Text and Composing." *College Composition and Communication* 38 (1987): 397–425.

———. "Revising, Composing Theory, and Research Design." *The Acquisition of Written Language: Response and Revision*. Ed. Sarah Warshauer Freedman. Norwood, NJ: Ablex, 1985. 250–84.

REVISION STRATEGIES OF STUDENT WRITERS AND EXPERIENCED ADULT WRITERS

Nancy Sommers

[*College Composition and Communication* 31 (1980): 378–88.]

Nancy Sommers is the Sosland Director of Expository Writing at Harvard University, where she directs both the freshman writing program and the Harvard Writing Project. She is widely known for her work on the revision process and on responding to student writing. Sommers currently serves as the series editor for the Prentice Hall Studies in Writing and Culture. Her articles and chapters have appeared in a wide range of scholarly publications. She received the Promising Research Award from NCTE in 1979 and has twice won the Richard Braddock Award from CCCC, in 1983 and in 1993. She is currently conducting a longitudinal study, following the Harvard Class of 2001, studying the role of writing in undergraduate education.

This study was among the first to investigate with any methodological rigor the revision process of specific writers, and Sommers's findings caused writing teachers to reconsider how they present revision to their students. *The Bedford Handbook*'s extensive section on revision recognizes implicitly the results of Sommers's research, emphasizing the creative, cyclical, recursive nature of revision.

Although various aspects of the writing process have been studied extensively of late, research on revision has been notably absent. The reason for this, I suspect, is that current models of the writing process have directed attention away from revision. With few exceptions, these models are linear; they separate the writing process into discrete stages. Two representative models are Gordon Rohman's suggestion that the composing process moves from prewriting to writing to rewriting and James Britton's model of the writing process as a series of stages described in metaphors of linear growth, conception—incubation—production.[1] What is striking about these theories of writing is that they model themselves on speech: Rohman defines the writer in a way that cannot distinguish him from a speaker ("A writer is a man who . . . puts [his] experience into words in his own mind"—p. 15); and Britton bases his theory of writing on what he calls (following Jakobson) the "expressiveness" of speech.[2] Moreover, Britton's study itself follows the "linear model" of the relation of thought and language in speech proposed by Vygotsky, a relationship embodied in the linear movement "from the motive which engenders a thought to the shaping of the thought, *first* in inner speech, *then* in meanings of words, and *finally* in words" (quoted in Britton, p. 40). What this movement fails to take into account in its linear structure—"first . . . then . . . finally"—is the recursive shaping of thought by language; what it fails to take into account is *revision*. In these linear conceptions of the writing process revision is understood as a separate stage at the end of the process—a stage that comes after the completion of a first or second draft and one that is temporally distinct from the prewriting and writing stages of the process.[3]

The linear model bases itself on speech in two specific ways. First of all, it is based on traditional rhetorical models, models that were created to serve the spoken art of oratory. In whatever ways the parts of classical rhetoric are described, they offer "stages" of composition that are repeated in contemporary models of the writing process. Edward Corbett, for instance, describes the "five parts of a discourse"—*inventio, dispositio, elocutio, memoria, pronuntiatio*—and, disregarding the last two parts since "after rhetoric came to be concerned mainly with written discourse, there was no further need to deal with them,"[4] he produces a model very close to Britton's conception [*inventio*], incubation [*dispositio*], production [*elocutio*]. Other rhetorics also follow this procedure, and they do so not simply because of historical accident. Rather, the process represented in the linear model is based on the irreversibility of speech. Speech, Roland Barthes says, "is irreversible":

> A word cannot be retracted, except precisely by saying that one retracts it. To cross out here is to add: If I want to erase what I have just said, I cannot do it without showing the eraser itself (I must say: "*or rather* . . ." "*I expressed myself badly* . . ."); paradoxically, it is ephemeral speech which is indelible, not monumental writing. All that one can do in the case of a spoken utterance is to tack on another utterance.[5]

What is impossible in speech is *revision*: Like the example Barthes gives, revision in speech is an afterthought. In the same way, each stage of the linear model must be exclusive (distinct from the other stages) or else it becomes trivial and counterproductive to refer to these junctures as "stages."

By staging revision after enunciation, the linear models reduce revision in writing, as in speech, to no more than an afterthought. In this way such models make the study of revision impossible. Revision, in Rohman's model, is simply the repetition of writing; or to pursue Britton's organic metaphor, revision is simply the further growth of what is already there, the "preconceived" product. The absence of research on revision, then, is a function of a theory of writing which makes revision both superfluous and redundant, a theory which does not distinguish between writing and speech.

What the linear models do produce is a parody of writing. Isolating revision and then disregarding it plays havoc with the experiences composition teachers have of the actual writing and rewriting of experienced writers. Why should the linear model be preferred? Why should revision be forgotten, superfluous? Why do teachers offer the linear model and students accept it? One reason, Barthes suggests, is that "there is a fundamental tie between teaching and speech," while "writing begins at the point where speech becomes *impossible*."[6] The spoken word cannot be revised. The possibility of revision distinguishes the written text from speech. In fact, according to Barthes, this is the essential difference between writing and speaking. When we must revise, when the very idea is subject to recursive shaping by language, then speech becomes inadequate. This is a matter to which I will return, but first we should examine, theoretically, a detailed exploration of what student writers as distinguished from experienced adult writers *do* when they write and rewrite their work. Dissatisfied with both the linear model of writing and the lack of attention to the process of revision, I conducted a series of studies over the past three years which examined the revision processes of student writers and experienced writers to see what role revision played in their writing processes. In the course of my work the revision process was redefined as *a sequence of changes in a composition—changes which are initiated by cues and occur continually throughout the writing of a work.*

Methodology

I used a case study approach. The student writers were twenty freshmen at Boston University and the University of Oklahoma with SAT verbal scores ranging from 450 to 600 in their first semester of composition. The twenty experienced adult writers from Boston and Oklahoma City included journalists, editors, and academics. To refer to the two groups, I use the terms *student writers* and *experienced writers* because the principal difference between these two groups is the amount of experience they had in writing.

Each writer wrote three essays, expressive, explanatory, and persuasive, and rewrote each essay twice, producing nine written products in draft and final form. Each writer was interviewed three times after the final revision of each essay. And each writer suggested revisions for a composition written by an anonymous author. Thus extensive written and spoken documents were obtained from each writer.

The essays were analyzed by counting and categorizing the changes made. Four revision operations were identified: deletion, substitution, addition, and reordering. And four levels of changes were identified: word, phrase, sentence, theme (the extended statement of one idea). A coding system was developed for identifying the frequency of revision by level and operation. In addition, transcripts of the interviews in which the writers interpreted their revisions were used to develop what was called a *scale of concerns* for each writer. This scale enabled me to codify what were the writer's primary concerns, secondary concerns, tertiary concerns, and whether the writers used the same scale of concerns when revising the second or third drafts as they used in revising the first draft.

Revision Strategies of Student Writers

Most of the students I studied did not use the term *revision* or *rewriting*. In fact, they did not seem comfortable using the word *revision* and explained that revision was not a word they used, but the word their teachers used. Instead, most of the students had developed various functional terms to describe the type of changes they made. The following are samples of these definitions:

> *Scratch Out and Do Over Again:* "I say scratch out and do over, and that means what it says. Scratching out and cutting out. I read what I have written and I cross out a word and put another word in; a more decent word or a better word. Then if there is somewhere to use a sentence that I have crossed out, I will put it there."

> *Reviewing:* "Reviewing means just using better words and eliminating words that are not needed. I go over and change words around."

> *Reviewing:* "I just review every word and make sure that everything is worded right. I see if I am rambling; I see if I can put a better word in or leave one out. Usually when I read what I have written, I say to myself, 'that word is so bland or so trite,' and then I go and get my thesaurus."

> *Redoing:* "Redoing means cleaning up the paper and crossing out. It is looking at something and saying, no that has to go, or no, that is not right."

> *Marking Out:* "I don't use the word *rewriting* because I only write one draft and the changes that I made are made on top of the draft. The changes that I made are usually just marking out words and putting different ones in."

> *Slashing and Throwing Out:* "I throw things out and say they are not good. I like to write like Fitzgerald did by inspiration, and if I feel inspired then I don't need to slash and throw much out."

The predominant concern in these definitions is vocabulary. The students understand the revision process as a rewording activity. They do so because they perceive words as the unit of written discourse. That is, they concentrate on particular words apart from their role in the text. Thus one student quoted above thinks in terms of dictionaries, and, following the eighteenth-century theory of words parodied in *Gulliver's Travels,* he imagines a load of things carried about to be exchanged. Lexical changes are the major revision activities of the students because economy is their goal. They are governed, like the linear model itself, by the Law of Occam's razor that prohibits logically needless repetition: redundancy and superfluity. Nothing governs speech more than such superfluities; speech constantly repeats itself precisely because spoken words, as Barthes writes, are expendable in the cause of communication. The aim of revision according to the students' own description is therefore to clean up speech; the redundancy of speech is unnecessary in writing, their logic suggests, because writing, unlike speech, can be reread. Thus one student said, "Redoing means cleaning up the paper and crossing out." The remarkable contradiction of cleaning by marking might, indeed, stand for student revision as I have encountered it.

The students place a symbolic importance on their selection and rejection of words as the determiners of success or failure for their compositions. When revising, they primarily ask themselves: Can I find a better word or phrase? A more impressive, not so clichéd, or less humdrum word? Am I repeating the same word or phrase too often? They approach the revision process with what could be labeled as a "thesaurus philosophy of writing"; the students consider the thesaurus a harvest of lexical substitutions and believe that most problems in their essays can be solved by rewording. What is revealed in the students' use of the thesaurus is a governing attitude toward their writing: that the meaning to be communicated is already there, already finished, already produced, ready to be communicated, and all that is necessary is a better word "rightly worded." One student defined revision as "redoing"; "redoing" meant "just using better words and eliminating words that are not needed." For the students, writing is translating: the thought to the page, the language of speech to the more formal language of prose, the word to its synonym. Whatever is translated, an original text already exists for students, one which need not be discovered or acted upon, but simply communicated.[7]

The students list repetition as one of the elements they most worry about. This cue signals to them that they need to eliminate the repetition either by substituting or deleting words or phrases. Repetition occurs, in large part, because student writing imitates—transcribes—speech; attention to repetitious words is a manner of cleaning speech. Without a sense of the developmental possibilities of revision (and writing in general) students seek, on the authority of many textbooks, simply to clean up their language and prepare to type. What is curious, however, is that students are aware of lexical repetition, but not conceptual repetition. They only notice the repetition if they can "hear" it; they do not diagnose lexical repetition as symptomatic of problems on a deeper level. By rewording their sentences to avoid the lexical repetition, the students solve the immediate problem but blind themselves to problems on a textual level; although they are using different words, they are sometimes merely restating the same idea with different words. Such blindness, as I discovered with student writers, is the inability to "see" revision as a process: the inability to "re-view" their work again, as it were, with different eyes, and to start over.

The revision strategies described above are consistent with the students' understanding of the revision process as requiring lexical changes but not semantic changes. For the students, the extent to which they revise is a function of their level of inspiration. In fact, they use the word *inspiration* to describe the ease or difficulty with which their essay is written, and the extent to which the essay needs to be revised. If students feel inspired, if the writing comes easily, and if they don't get stuck on individual words or phrases, then they say that they cannot see any reason to revise. Because students do not see revision as an activity in which they modify and develop perspectives and ideas, they feel that if they know what they want to say, then there is little reason for making revisions.

The only modification of ideas in the students' essays occurred when they tried out two or three introductory paragraphs. This results, in part, because the students have been taught in another version of the linear model of composing to use a thesis statement as a controlling device in their introductory paragraphs. Since they write their introductions and their thesis statements even before they have really discovered what they want to say, their early close attention to the thesis statement, and more generally the linear model, function to restrict and circumscribe not only the development of their ideas, but also their ability to change the direction of these ideas.

Too often as composition teachers we conclude that students do not willingly revise. The evidence from my research suggests that it is not that students are unwilling to revise, but rather that they do what they have been taught to do in a consistently narrow and predictable way. On every occasion when I asked students why they hadn't made any more changes, they essentially replied, "I knew something larger was wrong, but I didn't think it would help to move words around." The students have strategies for handling words and phrases and their strategies helped them on a word or sentence level. What they lack, however, is a set of strategies to help them identify the "something larger" that they sensed was wrong and work from there. The students do not have strategies for handling the whole essay. They lack procedures or heuristics to help them reorder lines of reasoning or ask questions about their purposes and readers. The students view their compositions in a linear way as a series of parts. Even such potentially useful concepts as "unity" or "form" are reduced to the rule that a composition, if it is to have form, must have an introduction, a body, and a conclusion, or the sum total of the necessary parts.

The students decide to stop revising when they decide that they have not violated any of the rules for revising. These rules, such as "Never begin a sentence with a conjunction" or "Never end a sentence with a preposition," are lexically cued and rigidly applied. In general, students will subordinate the demands of the specific problems of their text to the demands of the rules. Changes are made in compliance with abstract rules about the product, rules that quite often do not apply to the specific problems in the text. These revision strategies are teacher-based, directed toward a teacher-reader who expects compliance with rules—with preexisting "conceptions"—and who will only examine parts of the composition (writing comments about those parts in the margins of their essays) and will cite any violations of rules in those parts. At best the students see their writing altogether passively through the eyes of former teachers or their surrogates, the textbooks, and are bound to the rules which they have been taught.

Revision Strategies of Experienced Writers

One aim of my research has been to contrast how student writers define revision with how a group of experienced writers define their revision processes. Here is a sampling of the definitions from the experienced writers:

Rewriting: "It is a matter of looking at the kernel of what I have written, the content, and then thinking about it, responding to it, making decisions, and actually restructuring it."

Rewriting: "I rewrite as I write. It is hard to tell what is a first draft because it is not determined by time. In one draft, I might cross out three pages, write two, cross out a fourth, rewrite it, and call it a draft. I am constantly writing and rewriting. I can only conceptualize so much in my first draft —only so much information can be held in my head at one time; my rewriting efforts are a reflection of how much information I can encompass at one time. There are levels and agenda which I have to attend to in each draft."

Rewriting: "Rewriting means on one level, finding the argument, and on another level, language changes to make the argument more effective. Most of the time I feel as if I can go on rewriting forever. There is always one part of a piece that I could keep working on. It is always difficult to know at what point to abandon a piece of writing. I like this idea that a piece of writing is never finished, just abandoned."

Rewriting: "My first draft is usually very scattered. In rewriting, I find the line of argument. After the argument is resolved, I am much more interested in word choice and phrasing."

Revising: "My cardinal rule in revising is never to fall in love with what I have written in a first or second draft. An idea, sentence, or even a phrase that looks catchy, I don't trust. Part of this idea is to wait a while. I am much more in love with something after I have written it than I am a day or two later. It is much easier to change anything with time."

Revising: "It means taking apart what I have written and putting it back together again. I ask major theoretical questions of my ideas, respond to those questions, and think of proportion and structure, and try to find a controlling metaphor. I find out which ideas can be developed and which should be dropped. I am constantly chiseling and changing as I revise."

The experienced writers describe their primary objective when revising as finding the form or shape of their argument. Although the metaphors vary, the experienced writers often use structural expressions such as "finding a framework," "a pattern," or "a design" for their argument. When questioned about this emphasis, the experienced writers responded that since their first drafts are usually scattered attempts to define their territory, their objective in the second draft is to begin observing general patterns of development and deciding what should be included and what excluded. One writer explained, "I have learned from experience that I need to keep writing a first draft until I figure out what I want to say. Then in a second draft, I begin to see the structure of an argument and how all the various subarguments which are buried beneath the surface of all those sentences are related." What is described here is a process in which the writer is both agent and vehicle. "Writing," says Barthes, unlike speech, "develops like a seed, not a line,"[8] and like a seed it confuses beginning and end, conception and production. Thus, the experienced writers say their drafts are "not determined by time," that rewriting is a "constant process," that they feel as if they "can go on forever." Revising confuses the beginning and end, the agent and vehicle; it confuses, *in order to find,* the line of argument.

After a concern for form, the experienced writers have a second objective: a concern for their readership. In this way, "production" precedes "conception." The experienced writers imagine a reader (reading their product) whose existence and whose expectations influence their revision process. They have abstracted the standards of a reader and this reader seems to be partially a reflection of themselves and functions as a critical and productive collaborator— a collaborator who has yet to love their work. The anticipation of a reader's judgment causes a feeling of dissonance when the writer recognizes incongruities between intention and execution, and requires these writers to make revision on all levels. Such a reader gives them just what the students lacked: new eyes to "re-view" their work. The experienced writers believe that they have learned the causes and conditions, the product, which will influence their reader, and their revision strategies are geared toward creating these causes and conditions. They demonstrate a complex understanding of which examples, sentences, or phrases should be included or excluded. For example, one experienced writer decided to delete public examples and add private examples when writing about the energy crisis because "private examples would be less controversial and thus more persuasive." Another writer revised his transitional sentences because "some kinds of transitions are more easily recognized as transitions than others." These examples represent the type of strategic attempts these experienced writers use to manipulate the conventions of discourse in order to communicate to their reader.

But these revision strategies are a process of more than communication; they are part of the process of *discovering meaning* altogether. Here we can see the importance of dissonance; at the heart of revision is the process by which writers recognize and resolve the dissonance they sense in their writing. Ferdinande de Saussure has argued that meaning is differential or "diacritical," based on differences between terms rather than "essential" or inherent qualities of terms. "Phonemes," he said, "are characterized not, as one might think, by their own positive quality but simply by the fact that they are distinct."[9] In fact, Saussure bases his entire *Course in General Linguistics* on these differences, and such differences are dissonant; like musical dissonances which gain their significance from their relationship to the "key" of the composition which itself is determined by the whole language, specific language (parole) gains its meaning from the system of language (langue) of which it is a manifestation and part. The musical composition—a "composition" of parts—creates its "key" as in an overall structure which determines the value (meaning) of its parts. The analogy with music is readily seen in the compositions of experienced writers: Both sorts of composition are based precisely on those structures experienced writers seek in their writing. It is this complicated relationship between the parts and the whole in the work of experienced writers which destroys the linear model; writing cannot develop "like a line" because each addition or deletion is a reordering of the whole. Explicating Saussure, Jonathan Culler asserts that "meaning depends on difference of meaning."[10] But student writers constantly struggle to bring their essays into congruence with a predefined meaning. The experienced writers do the opposite: They seek to discover (to create) meaning in the engagement with their writing, in revision. They seek to emphasize and exploit the lack of clarity, the differences of meaning, the dissonance, that writing as opposed to speech allows in the possibility of revision. Writing has spatial and temporal features not apparent in speech—words are recorded in space and fixed in time —which is why writing is susceptible to reordering and later addition. Such features make possible the dissonance that both provokes revision and promises, from itself, new meaning.

For the experienced writers the heaviest concentration of changes is on the sentence level, and the changes are predominantly by addition and deletion. But, unlike the students, experienced writers make changes on all levels and use all revision operations. Moreover, the operations the students fail to use—reordering and addition—seem to require a theory of the revision process as a totality—a theory which, in fact, encompasses the *whole* of the composition. Unlike the students, the experienced writers possess a nonlinear theory in which a sense of the whole writing both precedes and grows out of an examination of the parts. As we saw, one writer said he needed "a first draft to figure out what to say," and "a second draft to see the structure of an argument buried beneath the surface." Such a "theory" is both theoretical and strategical; once again, strategy and theory are conflated in ways that are literally impossible for the linear model. Writing appears to be more like a seed than a line.

Two elements of the experienced writers' theory of the revision process are the adoption of a holistic perspective and the perception that revision is a recursive process. The writers ask: What does my essay as a *whole* need for form, balance, rhythm, or communication? Details are added, dropped, substituted, or reordered according to their sense of what the essay needs for emphasis and proportion. This sense, however, is constantly in flux as ideas are developed and modified; it is constantly "re-viewed" in relation to the parts. As their ideas change, revision becomes an attempt to make their writing consonant with that changing vision.

The experienced writers see their revision process as a recursive process—a process with significant recurring activities—with different levels of attention and different agenda for each cycle. During the first revision cycle their attention is primarily directed toward narrowing the topic and delimiting their ideas. At this point, they are not as concerned as they are later about vocabulary and style. The experienced writers explained that they get closer to their meaning by not limiting themselves too early to lexical concerns. As one writer commented to explain her revision process, a comment inspired by the summer 1977 New York power failure: "I feel like Con Edison cutting off certain states to keep the generators going. In first and second drafts, I try to cut off as much as I can of my editing generator, and in a third draft, I try to cut off some of my idea generators, so I can make sure that I will actually finish the essay." Although the experienced writers describe their revision process as a series of different levels or cycles, it is inaccurate to assume that they have only one objective for each cycle and that each cycle can be defined by a different objective. The same objectives and subprocesses are present in each cycle, but in different proportions. Even though these experienced writers place the predominant weight upon finding the form of their argument during the first cycle, other concerns exist as well. Conversely, during the later cycles, when the experienced writers' primary attention is focused upon stylistic concerns, they are still attuned, although in a reduced way, to the form of the argument. Since writers are limited in what they can attend to during each cycle (understandings are temporal), revision strategies help balance competing demands on attention. Thus, writers can concentrate on more than one objective at a time by developing strategies to sort out and organize their different concerns in successive cycles of revision.

It is a sense of writing as discovery—a repeated process of beginning over again, starting out new—that the students failed to have. I have used the notion of dissonance because such dissonance, the incongruities between intention and execution, governs both writing and meaning. Students do not see the incongruities. They need to rely on their own internalized sense of good writing and to see their writing with their "own" eyes. Seeing in revision—seeing beyond hearing—is at the root of the word *revision* and the process itself; current dicta on revising blind our students to what is actually involved in revision. In fact, they blind them to what constitutes good writing altogether. Good writing disturbs: It creates dissonance. Students need to seek the dissonance of discovery, utilizing in their writing, as the experienced writers do, the very difference between writing and speech—the possibility of revision.

Notes

[1] D. Gordon Rohman and Albert O. Wlecke, "Pre-writing: The Construction and Application of Models for Concept Formation in Writing," Cooperative Research Project No. 2174, U.S. Office of Education, Department of Health, Education, and Welfare; James Britton, Anthony Burgess, Nancy Martin, Alex McLeod, Harold Rosen, *The Development of Writing Abilities* (11–18) (London: Macmillan Education, 1975).

[2] Britton is following Roman Jakobson, "Linguistics and Poetics," in T. A. Sebeok, *Style in Language* (Cambridge, Mass: MIT Press, 1960).

[3] For an extended discussion of this issue see Nancy Sommers, "The Need for Theory in Composition Research," *College Composition and Communication*, 30 (February 1979), 46–49.

[4] *Classical Rhetoric for the Modern Student* (New York: Oxford University Press, 1965), p. 27.

[5] Roland Barthes, "Writers, Intellectuals, Teachers," in *Image-Music-Text*, trans. Stephen Heath (New York: Hill and Wang, 1977), pp. 190–191.

[6] "Writers, Intellectuals, Teachers," p. 190.

[7] Nancy Sommers and Ronald Schleifer, "Means and Ends: Some Assumptions of Student Writers," *Composition and Teaching*, II (in press).

[8] *Writing Degree Zero* in *Writing Degree Zero and Elements of Semiology*, trans. Annette Lavers and Colin Smith (New York: Hill and Wang, 1968), p. 20.

[9] *Course in General Linguistics*, trans. Wade Baskin (New York: McGraw-Hill 1966), p. 119.

[10] Jonathan Culler, *Saussure* (Penguin Modern Masters Series; London: Penguin Books, 1976), p. 70.

Acknowledgment: The author wishes to express her gratitude to Professor William Smith, University of Pittsburgh, for his vital assistance with the research reported in this article, and to Patrick Hays, her husband, for extensive discussions and critical editorial help.

A CONVERSATION ABOUT SMALL GROUPS

Ruth Mirtz

[From *Small Groups in Writing Workshops: Invitations to a Writer's Life* by Robert Brooke, Ruth Mirtz, and Rick Evans. Urbana: NCTE, 1994. 172–84.]

Professor of Languages and Literature at Ferris State University, Ruth Mirtz teaches freshman composition and advanced writing. For many years Mirtz has conducted research with small groups and peer revising. She has a special interest in technology and writing and has published articles on computers and composition in *Writing on the Edge, ADE Bulletin,* and *Composition Studies and* presented her work at CCCC and MLA.

The following piece reports on three teachers' uses of small groups in their classes. In this chapter, Mirtz addresses the numerous questions that she and her coauthors have encountered when using small groups. Teachers who are unfamiliar with or skeptical about using groups in their classes will find that this chapter will answer many of their questions, and it offers suggestions for many of the problems they might encounter. The topics that Mirtz addresses include the purposes of groups, strategies for managing groups, and solutions to common problems that occur with groups. Mirtz offers practical advice and explanations, but she consistently and carefully grounds her responses in the larger theoretical contexts that inform contemporary approaches to writing instruction.

In this chapter, I'll start where I think you, our readers, are: in the middle of a course, planning a course, more certain or more confused about what you know about small groups. Just as we try to remember to start where our students are, rather than where we as teachers are, I'll try to begin with immediate questions and specific problems that trouble the people the three of us have talked to about small groups, rather than the types of narratives or descriptions with which we've structured most of this book.

Q: I still am not sure I understand the goals of small-group work in a writing class. How do you rationalize the amount of time spent in small groups in a class that ultimately seeks to improve students' writing, not their oral behavior?

A: What we do and say is largely determined by who we are, who we think we are, who we are trying to be, who we wish we were. Many of these "identity" factors take on a presence in written or spoken discourse. The need for constant direct dialogue in a writing class comes partly from the needs of writers who are trying to construct texts which simultaneously express their selves and relate to other selves, within or without. The second, but no less important, reason is that real learning takes place when one comes to understand the requirements of the role as writer, tries on new roles as writer and reader, and develops meaningfully coordinated or cooperative roles as writer, reader, friend, authority, and whatever else is needed.

Students will translate the difficulties they have finding a workable, comfortable role within our courses into like or dislike for their group members or instructor, feelings of injustice about requirements and evaluations in the course, and so on. They are accustomed to seeing their maturing and learning process (what they often call "real-world learning") as something separate from classroom or academic work.

The transformation that occurs when we see small groups and the writing process as sites of struggles among roles is that students' ability to write and respond well becomes intimately tied to their ability to resolve conflicts and to communicate with group members effectively; that ability is dynamic, constantly changing and adjusting to new situations and ideas. We change how we teach writing by incorporating the whole dimension of small-group dynamics into what we already teach about the process of inventing, revising, and responding.

These goals are the two most important ones for small groups in writing classes for us. Many times, however, small groups are more or less opportunities for (1) getting to know each other and sharing experiences; (2) warming up and reminding students of recent discussions; (3) refocusing the class on questions and issues larger than individual assignments; (4) generating more ideas and reactions faster than a large group; (5) individualizing instruction, especially participation in discussion; and (6) encouraging exposure to diverse perspectives and cultures. All six (certainly not an exhaustive list) subgoals are still sites of the struggles among the roles students take on in writing classes.

Q: I'm confused—your talk about small-group behavior keeps turning into a discussion about response to writing.

A: Because we use small groups in our writing class primarily as a way to get more direct, relevant, and quick response to students' writing, the small-group behavior we are most interested in is that which helps the response become increasingly effective for all the writers' roles students take on in our classes. Also, the structure and guidelines we set up to help small groups get along are basically response rules. Essentially, we believe nearly all small-group behavior in writing classrooms is a response to writing.

Q: I think the small groups in my classes don't work well together because of personality conflicts. If I could find a way to arrange the groups with the right people and personalities together, maybe all the small groups in my class would "work."

A: Personality differences do cause conflicts, but they don't keep us from working together in all sorts of strange situations in the world outside the classroom. Because of the power we have as teachers to move students in and out of groups, we naturally want a way (give Meyers-Briggs tests, for instance) to find out who would get along best with which others.

Outside the classroom, however, one can generally choose the personalities one wants to avoid; students can't do that, short of ignoring a member of their small group. One student may have an overbearing, excessively confrontational way of talking to strangers, while the other students in her group are uncomfortable or even unable to see this student's behavior as valuable. The others may consider her behavior impolite or downright rude. This group is likely to stop responding altogether and will certainly have difficulties unless one of the quieter students takes a stronger leadership role and balances the more aggressive personality.

It seems cruel to leave such a group intact, but in our experience, changing groups in order to find compatible personalities only causes a different set of problems. A group with very similar interests and ways of handling communication will often fall into the habit of chatting about their writing instead of responding toward significant revision.

All groups have differences and conflicts, many of which are well below the surface of the conversation and the responding you may observe or participate in. Many of us were taught from childhood to avoid talking about small-group behavior, to not question a group member's words, so even instructors, as members of a group, find that they need more conflict-resolution skills.

Q: Then what do I actually do with a small group which doesn't get along?

A: Ideally, a small group with conflicts which interfere with their ability to respond helpfully to each other's writing will find a way to work through the problems. Realistically, they will need help from their instructor, either in the form of modeling or self-monitoring.

(1) Modeling: The instructor becomes an active part of the group and shows students better ways to handle conflicts, such as asking outright about differences of opinion: "We seem to be disagreeing on this. What shall we do?" or "Since we can't seem to agree on this, let's use one of the guidelines from Tuesday." Most students respond to humor and know how to use humor to break tension. Instructors can show students how they use humor to lighten a conflict while not burying the conflict at the same time ("Gee, if we had some boxing gloves, we could take this outside and settle it like real men").

(2) Self-monitoring: The instructor can ask a small group to write letters to each other about how the group is going and what they'd like to do differently. By focusing on what other things the group could do or on creative alternatives, negative reactions about the current situation can be diplomatically left out. Reading different versions of what the small group seems to be doing in general ("Describe your small group") can be enlightening for students who don't realize how their behavior is being interpreted and perhaps completely misunderstood. An especially shy student is sometimes perceived as uninterested or indifferent when she is actually desperately trying to get a word into the conversation.

Q: You never directly intervene in a small group?

A: Of course, there are extreme cases when one member is simply out of line, refuses to try to cooperate, and is making everyone completely miserable. So there is a third method for dealing with conflicts:

(3) Intervention: Sometimes the instructor simply needs to take over the leadership of a group and spend significant amounts of time in one group (and simply hope that the other groups will function sufficiently in the interim). Some groups enjoy being labeled the "problem group" or the "slow group" because they garner attention and have a group identity provided for them. Other groups may resent the extra attention the instructor gives one group, but doing a little "floating" during each workshop allows you to explain that some groups need more help than others. Students are generally very alert to what's going on in other groups—they know, for instance, when one group is louder or quieter than other groups, when one group loses members regularly, and so on. If the instructor assumes that all groups have problems from time to time, then she will be talking to the class as a whole regularly about the problems small groups have and how to deal with them.

In rare cases, a student needs to be pulled aside and persuaded individually to resist certain ingrained communication habits, such as incessant teasing and joking or hostile, negative comments. However, giving one of these students the option of not participating in a group is not a good recourse, either, even though a terribly tempting one. This student is exactly the student who needs the time and attention paid to her small-group behavior; if the instructor lets her off the hook, the student's next instructor will merely get the task.

Q: So it really doesn't matter what method I use to form the small groups?

A: We truly suspect that we are overly concerned about how to form small groups. Whether one decides to let the students form their own groups, counts off, or uses some logical device to match or complement students doesn't seem to matter all that much. With any method, in any class, some small groups will work independently and need little modeling or monitoring, and some small groups will need intense attention and help from the instructor. No method that we have heard of will ensure perfectly formed small groups. An instructor should use the method which she is comfortable with, seems fair, and fits in the time frame and flexibility of her plans for the class. For instance, if you want to form small groups on the first day of class, you don't have time to get to know the students, and you may not even have the extra two or three minutes it takes for students to form their own groups; therefore, you'll choose a quick and easy way to form groups.

Q: Your definition of a "good" small group seems to be different than mine. I think a small group works well when they focus on drafts and follow the instructor's instructions; a small group doesn't work when they don't talk, finish early, and use their own ways of organizing themselves and responding to drafts.

A: The way we define our small groups as "working" is unusual. Actually, we are constantly reexamining our definition of a "working" small group (or a "good" small group) within the context of small groups in general. We often worry that a small group isn't "working" because they aren't obediently following directions or because they don't seem to care much for each other, and yet we see those students improving their writing as often and as much as the students in groups that do seem to value each other's writing and enjoy each other's company. What's going on?

"On-task" behavior is a trap, we have found, and just as problematic as defining a "good" student as one who plays our games according to our rules. What appears to be on-task or off-task is often the opposite; what students are learning is more important to us than whether they follow our instructions to the letter. Some groups need larger amounts of seemingly "off-task" talk in order to respond meaningfully to texts. They'll start off talking about the game on Saturday, their plans for the weekend, and half the class period will be gone before they start looking at their drafts. We don't usually worry about this form of procrastination early in the term because it helps students learn about each other, find out what interests other group members, and in general relaxes them enough to be able later to respond helpfully. They'll be the group that can look at one member's draft and make suggestions based on other stories they know the member has stored away or other talents the member has. They will be able to truly "re-envision" their texts and may sometimes have problems deciding which revisions to make and when to stop revising.

The group that seems to be made of "good students" will launch immediately into following exactly the instructions given to them, but suffer from superficial or irrelevant response because they don't know each other well enough to respond helpfully. They will be the group that gives advice too soon rather than response and reactions. They will quickly tire of the responding guidelines, and because they can't use much of the advice they get from their small group, they will rely on the instructor's response solely. They need, as much as the "off-task" group does, to monitor their group behavior and talk about how their group is functioning effectively and not so effectively.

One of the most frustrating aspects of using small groups in composition classrooms is their tendency to come up with their own ways of dealing with things. Sometimes the instructor needs to remind them of the guidelines and instructions because they really are trying to take the easy way out, while other groups are negotiating an effective way to proceed and process their own conflicts. Some groups need monitoring, but not necessarily interference.

We need to constantly examine our own definition of "working" when we talk about small groups: Do we mean following instructions, or working out differences, or helping to improve their writing, or discovering how other writers work, or experimenting with their identity as a writer?

Q: Don't all small groups go through a certain process during the semester? Shouldn't they get through these conflicts as soon as possible and then move on to the real work of the small group? Shouldn't the teacher's job be to push each group through the process as quickly as possible so that they can start working on their texts?

A: We often talk about how we deal somewhat differently with small groups early in the term than at midterm or toward the end of the term. The first few weeks of class are a time when students need more time to get to know each other, find out how each other thinks and acts, and develop functional ways of getting along despite the inevitable conflicts. By midterm, group members should be well-acquainted and ready for more difficult responding and reading tasks, ready to take more risks and experiment more boldly. By the end of term, we hope that all of our students have a rich repertoire of responding and conflict-resolution strategies that will prepare them for any other small-group experiences they have the rest of their lives.

Did you notice how conditional and wishful the last two sentences were? We can be fairly certain about what all students need during the first two or three weeks of class—structure, guidelines, time to get acquainted. But after that, each small group must be treated individually. There are no other reliable "phases" a group will go through, although happily, many groups do follow the process of development (described above). A great deal of social science research is devoted to determining the possible processes and consequently has come up with elaborate theories with fancy diagrams. Whenever we have tried to apply these theories of processes to our students, we find the actual processes much messier, more recursive, and ultimately not much help.

We stress monitoring and modeling all semester, because a small group continues to be a dynamic, constantly renegotiating location for students all semester. Some traditional-age students seem to have less tolerance for stability and routine than older adults and will work at destabilizing some small aspect of the group as soon as they feel bored. And when one student brings a much more personal draft than she has ever brought before (or much more political draft or a draft which responds to another student's draft), the small group must change its ways of responding to be sensitive to the needs of the writer's experiment. Some students are much less sure of their own identities and will need room and space to try out new roles. The student who leads confidently one week may be completely silent the next week. A group which launches into wonderfully directed response to texts one week may need half the class period the next week to talk out and rediscover themselves as peers and friends.

The constant renegotiating that takes place in all groups is what keeps many nonacademic study groups or support groups going for years. The same need makes it difficult for students to change groups during the school term and is why we suggest not changing groups during a normal fifteen- or sixteen-week semester course.

Q: So I shouldn't change the small groups at all during the term?

A: Inevitably we end up moving some members of small groups, but we don't tend to change the groups simply for variety or convenience or because students say they are bored. I often end up shuffling some members the very first day of class, before the students introduce themselves, in order to balance out the number of men and women. When I can avoid it easily, I prefer to have either groups of all women, all men, or two men with two women. The group I try to avoid is the group with a three-to-one ratio, which sometimes places a student at a disadvantage. That's one change I can make easily because I can identify the sexes easily (most of the time). Any other special needs or compatibilities are impossible to learn reliably during the first days of class.

I also change groups to keep the numbers even—three or four in each group. If enrollment changes because of drops or adds, then the small groups may have to be adjusted, but I try to warn students on the first day of class that the possibility exists.

We structure our classes so that there are many opportunities for all the students to meet and work with students besides those in their small groups, even though they may workshop their drafts and papers with the same small group all semester. Our students tell us that they enjoy working with students outside of their small group, but that they feel much more comfortable responding to drafts with a stable long-term group.

Q: What about gender differences? If one of my small groups consists of all women, they inevitably become a support group while my groups of all men become very competitive in appearing "cool" while rebellious.

A: We don't find a support group or a "cool" group as much of a problem as a group which consistently leaves one voice unheard or causes a member too much discomfort to be learning at the same time. Rather than add too many requirements to the ideal group makeup, we work with those groups who have found a real, workable group identity for themselves, to turn that "cool guy" attitude into "cool writer" attitude, or to push the support group to get past its unconditional encouragement. They are not groups in conflict as much as groups with too limited an idea of what their group can be. When we are participating in those groups, the knowledge we point out about their group problems is part of what we are making deliberate, articulate, and changeable in their group behavior.

Q: Even when I have small groups with exactly the same number of members, one group always finishes early. What do I do with them?

A: It may depend on just how early they are finishing. If a group finishes five or six minutes before the other groups, that seems a reasonable amount of time to leave them to their own conversation. Five extra minutes of getting acquainted, especially if the group members didn't pause for socializing before getting started, can only help most groups.

More than five minutes is a good time for a small group to do some writing. An excellent short writing assignment, which I often make a general rule for groups (and which sometimes ensures that they will stretch their responding time in order to finish with the other groups and avoid the extra writing) is to report on what happened in their small group. They might also start writing in their journals for the next entry, either on a suggested topic or on one of their own inspiration.

A group which consistently finishes fifteen or more minutes early needs closer monitoring. They may simply be incredibly efficient, they may have brought spectacularly short texts, or they may be completely lost about how to respond to each other's texts and not really exchanging reactions and ideas. Because my presence as a fellow writer always tends to slow down a group, I often choose to become a part-time member of the group that always finishes too early. And I often say things to them like "Are you sure that's all we can help you with?" or "But you didn't say why you thought the ending was good." I often become the social leader of those groups, too, because sometimes the quick finishers are the group of four shy nontalkers, and they need someone to engage them in conversation.

I think it's important not to "punish" small groups which finish early with the equivalent of "seat work" or expect them to sit there doing nothing, waiting for the other groups. On the other hand, I prefer not to let them leave early either, choosing rather to find a fruitful additional activity which helps them monitor themselves and their group or by modeling the kind of responding which does take time and energy.

Q: What about using small groups not only for workshopping on drafts but for collaborating on group-authored texts or for discussing assigned reading from imaginative or professional writing?

A: We find that the joys and pains of small groups responding to drafts are the same for other kinds of small groups. However, the roles students struggle with change when the goals of the group change. In a collaborative group, more unity is needed in how texts should be written—that is, more of the group members will be forced to take on unfamiliar writerly roles. In a discussion group, the status of the text is often more of a problem, causing students to work out their roles as mass reader or aesthetic critic, for example.

Q: I always thought putting students into small groups was a great way to reduce the load on the teacher.

A: Small groups can reduce the role of the teacher as an absolute authoritarian and can eliminate the need for students to write for a murky "general audience." However, using small groups in a composition class is a tremendous amount of work if the instructor intends for the groups to work as circles of fellow writers and readers.

Some teachers do use the time to mark papers or read the newspaper, but that is not a role which will ensure that the small groups will be successful. We strongly advocate an active role for the instructor during small-group workshops, either as a floating member or as a permanent member of one group. Even then, it often seems (especially to administrators) as though a teacher isn't doing anything when the small groups are meeting during class.

The instructor is constantly monitoring the groups, trying to be in at least two groups during each class session and often speaking in general with all the groups. Sometimes she will sit in on one group while listening to another group nearby. She has to make sure that each group finishes at about the same time. A group which finishes early needs an extra assignment. A group which never finishes on time needs to be pushed to either elect a timekeeper each week or become more aware of the amount of nonessential talking they do. The instructor reads, in addition to the drafts and final papers of each students, reports from each student about the small group and often responds to those additional reports. The instructor is also a fellow writer, and in that role, spends extra time each week keeping her own writing journal or notebook and drafting texts to share with the class. She also disciplines herself to read published texts and recent research in regard not only to composition, but also to small-group behavior and small-group pedagogy.

For some of us, small groups became a pedagogical method when we sought to individualize our instruction more and allow students more self-paced learning. A small group allows a student to work on her own projects at her own speed while still getting the exposure (and some mild pressure) from other students working at different levels and paces. Such individualizing of our instruction takes enormous amounts of time. First, we must keep close track of anywhere from 30 to 100 (or more) students' work separately and also counsel their choices. Then, we must find ways to draw all these separate learners together with issues which most of them have in common, although in many different ways. After more than a decade of teaching, I still find this task overwhelming.

Q: Now you've made it sound like too much work.

A: It's actually a different kind of work than most of us are accustomed to. It's also, fortunately, the kind of work that keeps us challenged as learners ourselves and provoked as teachers. The modeling we do in small groups as expert small-group members keeps us on our toes, because while we can read about research on small groups (or conduct our own), and we can predict what our small groups will do, we are usually called on to model and problem-solve on the spot, as the conflicts come up. When we join the small groups as fellow but expert writers, we get a chance to practice our own craft, to consider ourselves writers for a while.

So if it turns out to be more work, it's the kind of more work we need in order to be good teachers. Not more paperwork or grading, but more interaction with students which lets us learn more about them and about writing and learning processes.

Q: But there's so much to do already in my class, and now I have so many ideas about small-group work. It's the middle of the semester and I've already set out my goals and evaluation process. Where do I start?

A: We agree that an instructor shouldn't, under normal circumstances, suddenly make wholesale changes in a course because a better idea comes along in midstream. But we do hope you start making plans for next semester.

If you have never used small groups or haven't in a while and would like to try a limited experiment at any point in the semester, then here's a suggestion: Begin with a tightly focused, very specific writing and sharing activity which correlates with something your class has been discussing or working on, and ask the students to write an informal description of their writing process on the current assignment. Form small groups to read the descriptions out loud to each other with the rules of no apologies from the writers and no criticism from the listeners. Give the groups time to read out loud and talk about the similarities and differences between the descriptions. Then follow up by asking students to write from three to five minutes about what happened in their small group, to be handed in to you.

The more specific the tasks you give to the groups and the more naturally you can assume they will have no problem with this exercise, the more "in control" and relaxed you may feel. The follow-up responses will let you know what happened and how to adapt your instructions and expectations for the next small-group activity.

Q: Sometimes I think my students don't work well in small-group workshops because they just don't know how to work in small groups, in general. They should learn these skills in high school. Why do I have to teach them?

A: If our students came to us with no skills in small-group work, we would have written a much different book. Instead, our students come as seasoned small-group members of a different kind: they've been active in groups of friends of various sizes, clubs and committees, lab partners, and families. Those groups have provided both positive and negative experiences, though, and we draw on both kinds in college writing classes. Students don't need training in small-group behavior; they need to learn how to reapply what they already know about themselves and how they relate to people in a writing class.

Q: I've had some pretty uncomfortable experiences in small groups, myself. And I was trained to work individually and competitively as a graduate student and as a teacher. Aren't I the least likely person to make small-group work succeed in my classroom?

A: On the contrary, you are probably more sensitive to the level of comfort and discomfort your students are experiencing. For good or ill, instructors take all their educational baggage with them into the classroom. By being aware of the influence of your past experiences, you are well on the way to understanding how you want small groups to work in your own classroom. Plus, you've got some stories about how you don't think small groups should work to tell your students, who can (and should) always regale you with theirs.

Q: I'd like to find out more about small groups. What other books do you suggest?

A: We hope you will first attempt to learn more about small groups from the best source: the small groups in your classroom. Take a few notes while participating in a group. Collect and analyze the short reports your students write about how their small group is going. Look for the metaphors or other kinds of language they use to describe their group. Tape-record one small group which you aren't participating in and promise not to listen to it until after the semester is over—then *do listen to it.* See also the recommended readings in the appendix of this book.

Q: All these practical matters aside, don't you have a social agenda of some kind behind this small-group pedagogy?

A: Like most people, we don't align ourselves with any one social policy or political group. We have been influenced by such diverse thinkers as Paulo Freire, Ann Berthoff, Erving Goffman, Thomas Kuhn, the Sophists of ancient Greece, although we have probably been influenced most about small groups by the thousands of students who told us about what happened in our classrooms. We believe that both individual autonomy and interaction in groups, large and small, are necessary for developing our students' writing processes and facility, as well as their critical acumen and their sense of responsibility toward both themselves and others.

If we were to say we have a social agenda, then it would be the need for society to provide better education for all segments of that society. We believe that small groups are a part of that better education under conditions of equality and opportunity.

PARAGRAPHS

From PARAGRAPHING FOR THE READER

Rick Eden and Ruth Mitchell

[*College Composition and Communication* 37 (1986): 416–30.]

Rick Eden is a senior analyst at the RAND Corporation. He earned his doctorate in English from UCLA. Eden has published widely and has taught writing and rhetoric at UCLA, USC, California State University at Los Angeles, and the RAND Graduate School. Ruth Mitchell is author of *First Steps* (1990) and *Testing for Learning* (1992), and co-author of *Learning in Overdrive: Designing Curriculum, Instruction, and Assessment from Standards* (1997).

The following excerpt is the introduction and first part of Eden and Mitchell's article "Paragraphing for the Reader," in which they react to the prevalent method of teaching paragraphing found in many textbooks. Arguing that teaching students formulas for constructing paragraphs is ineffective, they demonstrate convincingly that we should teach writers to make paragraphing decisions in light of "purpose, audience, and rhetorical stance," always attending to readers' expectations.

The teaching of paragraphs needs a revolution. Classroom instruction offers patterns and precepts which cannot be applied to the ordinary process of writing and which, moreover, are unsupported by current research. Researchers in English like Braddock, Meade and Ellis, and Knoblauch report findings which directly contradict the textbooks' platitudes:[1] Paragraphs in admired professional writing do not necessarily contain topic sentences, they rarely follow prescribed patterns, and they seem essentially accidental, invented as the writer composes.

We have found that textbooks do not heed these warnings. Students perceive a strange disjunction between the paragraphs they read and those they are asked to write in class. Too often the latter are miniature five-element themes— introductory and concluding sentences, with three intervening sentences connected by "therefore" and "in addition."

We believe that paragraphing is best presented to student writers as an important signaling system, based on signals of two sorts, visual and substantive. To readers, the strip of indented white space separating paragraphs indicates both connection and discontinuity. It heightens their attention. To the writer, marking paragraphs offers opportunity for manipulating the reader's focus. Strategically paragraphed prose not only streamlines a message but also molds and shapes it to achieve the writer's purpose.

We shall argue for a reader-oriented theory of the paragraph.[2] In order to paragraph effectively, a writer needs to know, not the five, ten, fifteen, or twenty most common paragraph patterns that current theories enumerate, but how indentions affect the reader's perception of prose discourse. Knowing how readers perceive prose, the writer can arrange his text to mesh with their perception.

Our argument proposes (and, we hope, proves) two main theses:

1. Paragraphs depend for their effectiveness on the exploitation of psycholinguistic features—that is, of the reader's conventional expectations and perceptual patterns. For example, readers treat the first sentence of a paragraph as the orienting statement necessary for them to understand the rest, regardless of whether the writer so intended. Thus a paragraph does not "need" a topic sentence: Every paragraph has one, willy-nilly. The question for the writer is not "Where shall I put my topic sentence?" but "Do I want this initial statement to direct the reader's understanding of the paragraph?" A good deal of our argument will explicate and extend these psycholinguistic features and their consequences.
2. Paragraphing is not part of the composing but of the editing process. To think about paragraphs too early may invoke the blocking mechanisms that Mike Rose has described in "Rigid Rules, Inflexible Plans, and the Stifling of Language: A Cognitivist Analysis of Writer's Block" (*College Composition and Communication*, 41 [December 1980], 389–400) [p. 71 in this book]. Current paragraph theory has assumed that paragraphing is part of the process of generating, whereas it properly belongs with revision. It refines and shapes material already on the page.

Our argument is divided into four parts. In the first part we explain the reader's expectations of paragraphs and point out research which has clarified these expectations. Part Two demonstrates the strengths and weaknesses of the most popular current model of paragraph structure, the scheme devised by Francis Christensen to explain paragraph structure according to levels of generality. In Part Three an extended example demonstrates the power of rhetorical paragraphing. In Part Four we lay out pedagogical implications of our reader-oriented theory.[3]

1

Paragraphing for the reader means meeting the reader's expectations. These expectations are unconscious and remain so unless repeatedly disappointed. Some are rooted in cognition itself, in the reader's patterns of perception and comprehension. Others are rooted in rhetorical convention, in current practices of formatting prose.

What are these expectations?

1. Readers expect to see paragraphs when they read a piece of extended prose. They expect to see regularly spaced indentions. This is only an expectation about the appearance of the page. How frequently readers expect the indentions to appear—i.e., how long they expect the average paragraph to run—will vary according to several factors, including the size and genre of the text as a whole. Readers conventionally expect a book on philosophy to have many very long paragraphs, some filling entire pages. They do not expect the same from a modern narrow-column newspaper. Reading typescript, they need relief upon encountering pages unbroken by indentions—too many such pages make a coffee break irresistible.

   This initial, visual expectation—that prose will be indented at regular intervals—is conventional, and it changes as continually as other social conventions. In the nineteenth century, for instance, readers expected newspapers virtually to eschew indentions. The other expectations, which follow, are derived from human cognitive processes and are thus universal.
2. Readers expect paragraphs to be unified simply because they perceive them as units. Readers expect the paragraph's formal unity to signal

substantive unity and they infer one from the other as they half-find and half-fashion significance in the text.

3. Readers expect the initial sentences of a paragraph to orient them, to identify the context in which succeeding sentences are to be understood. Readers accept the initial sentences as instructions for integrating what they are about to read with what they have just read.

    These instructions do little good if readers receive them only as they finish reading a paragraph: To work effectively the instructions must appear initially. People understand material most readily when it is presented to them in a top-down fashion, with details and reasons preceded by orienting statements.[4]

4. Readers expect to find at each paragraph's peripheral points something which merits special attention, because readers naturally attend to endpoints. As they read a paragraph, their attention is greatest as they begin and end. This is simply a fact about perception—a principle of peripherality.[5] We shall show that it has implications for the rhetorical organization of paragraphs.

5. Readers expect paragraphs to be coherent, both internally and externally. The demand for external coherence is implied by the expectation for unity. To distinguish external from internal coherence, we will term the latter "cohesiveness." The reader expects each paragraph to cohere internally as well as externally, to contain a sensible sequence of thought within itself as well as to continue one begun in previous paragraphs.

Current rhetorics teach various strategies, such as repeating words and structures and supplying transitional words and phrases, to help the writer make the text cohere for the reader, and it is important that writers learn them. However, important as these strategies are in practice, in theory they have nothing to do with paragraphing. Readers expect paragraphs to be cohesive only because they expect all prose, all discourse, to be so. Rhetorics would have to teach these strategies even if we did not conventionally organize prose into paragraphs.

The same is true of the many plans of development—compare/contrast, topic/comment, question/answer, and so on—that rhetorics teach as ways to organize paragraphs internally. These patterns also have nothing inherent to do with the practice of indention. They are characterized in some texts as "types" of paragraphs simply because paragraphs provide conveniently sized forums in which to discuss, illustrate, and practice them. Francis Christensen made this point twenty years ago, but no one seems much to have heeded him:

> These methods [of paragraph development] are real, but they are simply methods of development—period. They are no more relevant to the paragraph than, on the short side, to the sentence or, on the long side, to a run of several paragraphs or to a paper as long as this or a chapter. They are the topoi of classical rhetoric. They are the channels our minds naturally run in whether we are writing a sentence or a paragraph or planning a paper. (*Notes toward a New Rhetoric*, 2nd ed. [New York: Harper & Row, 1978], p. 77)

Not many researchers have investigated how paragraphing influences the reader's interpretation of the text, but during the 1960s Koen, Becker, and Young performed a series of experiments which support our characterization of the reader's expectations.[6] They established that paragraphs are both visual and structural units. A writer sets up a paragraph by framing it with white space. He unifies its structure with three kinds of internal markers, representing the three systems which interact to produce cohesion. The lexical system depends on reiterated nouns and pronouns producing a chain of references over several sentences. These are the lexical markers. The grammatical system is signaled by inflections, the grammatical markers. The rhetorical system consists of expository patterns or modes of development—topic and illustration, for example. Its markers consist of so-called "collocational sets," that is, words whose meanings cluster round a general topic. Formal markers—such as conjunctions and transitional words and phrases—permitted subjects in Koen, Becker, and Young's experiments to recognize the systems even in nonsense passages. When prose is well paragraphed, these markers permit readers to predict paragraph boundaries in unindented passages.

The experimenters established an important principle: reparagraphing—i.e., moving indention points—is not only typographical but also substantive. Because the visual breaks direct the reader's attention, changing them changes the reader's interpretation of the text. They thus showed that paragraphs have a psychological as well as a physical reality. Their results pointed toward a reader-oriented theory of the paragraph.

More recent research, conducted by David Kieras, a psychologist at the University of Arizona, also supports our reader-oriented approach. His work corroborates our characterization of the reader's expectations for initial, orienting material. Kieras has found that "information appearing first in the passage has more influence on the reader's perception of the main idea compared to the very same information appearing later in the passage" ("How Readers Abstract Main Ideas from Technical Prose: Some Implications for Document Design," paper presented at a Document Design Center Colloquium, American Institute for Research, Washington, D.C., 17 November 1980, p. 6). These results led him to endorse the initial placement of orienting sentences: "the topic sentence of a passage really should be first, because that is where a reader expects to find the important information" (p. 7). A paragraph which violates this expectation may remain comprehensible, of course, especially if the content is familiar to the reader, but it takes longer to read and demands more work of the reader, who must revise his notion of the paragraph's main point as he proceeds.

Paragraphing is as complex as the reader's pattern of comprehension and expectation. A writer who understands these complexities commands a powerful and flexible rhetorical resource. With paragraphs, writers can shape their text so as to influence its reading. Indeed, paragraphing offers the prose writer the poet's privileges. Prose writers cannot govern the placement of sentences—where they begin and end depends on layout design, choice of typeface, size of page, and so on. But they can choose where the white indentions will indicate paragraphs. That choice offers them opportunity and responsibility, the opportunity to manipulate the reader's attention and the responsibility to do so effectively. To paragraph well, writers must exploit and reinforce the visual impact of indentions. They must provide the unity and cohesion that the paragraph's visual form promises.

Current text-oriented writing theory and pedagogy misrepresent paragraphing by oversimplifying it. Text-centered approaches abbreviate the writing process; they treat the text rather than the reader as its end point. This oversimplification creates unnecessary complications in the form of poorly motivated prescriptions (e.g., for unity) and fossilized taxonomies.

The inadequacy of these taxonomies is evident to anyone who has tried to learn or teach them. They are not and cannot possibly become exhaustive. They can't list every type of paragraph, every strategy for paragraphing. Thus, they don't give the student the flexibility he will need to handle unanticipated rhetorical demands. Nor can the taxonomies help us to evaluate paragraphs: It's impossible to know whether a paragraph which doesn't fall under one of the types is a poor paragraph or a new species.

Formal definitions of the paragraph also vitiate much research and pedagogy. Too many researchers and rhetoricians take the paragraph to be a conveniently sized, self-contained piece of prose—a sort of latter-day *chreia.* Roger C. Schank, for instance, in a paper entitled "Understanding Paragraphs" (Technical Report, Instituto per gli studi semantici e cognitivi, Castagnola, Switzerland, 1974), investigates the structures of inferences in what he calls paragraphs but what are in fact "short stories." Sharing Schank's misconception of the paragraph as a self-contained rhetorical form, composition instructors often ask students to "write a paragraph" when they mean a short story, summary, or writing sample.

Inflexible formal definitions also lie behind the frequent proscription against the one-sentence paragraph. Although student writers are commonly denied this tool by edict, any attentive reading of effective prose will demonstrate its usefulness and its frequent occurrence. A one-sentence paragraph packs a double punch: It has the normal emphasis of a sentence as well as the visual emphasis of a paragraph.

By taking into account the reader's needs, we can clear up the current muddle of principles and patterns in our theories and our texts. We can't make paragraphing appear simple, because it isn't, but we can make its complexities appear sensible and well motivated. . . .

Notes

The authors wish to thank the following colleagues who generously gave their time to criticize earlier versions of this paper: Molly Faulkner, Connie Greaser, Carol Hartzog, Richard Lanham, Alan Purves, Mike Rose, Mary Vaiana, and Joseph Williams.

[1] Richard Braddock, "The Frequency and Placement of Topic Sentences in Expository Prose," *Research in the Teaching of English,* 8 (Winter 1974), 287–302. Richard A. Meade and W. Greiger Ellis, "Paragraph Development in the Modern Age of Rhetoric," *English Journal,* 59 (February 1970), 219–26; C. H. Knoblauch, "Some Formal and Nonformal Properties of Paragraphs and Paragraph Sequences," a paper delivered in session B-12, "Revisiting the Rhetoric of the Paragraph," Conference on College Composition and Communication, Dallas, Texas, March 1981.

[2] Ruth Mitchell and Mary Vaiana Taylor laid out a reader-oriented model for composition in their article "The Integrative Perspective: An Audience-Response Model for Writing," *College English,* 41 (November 1979), 247–70. The present essay offers an extension and specific application of their model.

[3] There is a considerable history to the paragraph, documented in James R. Bennett, Betty Brigham, Shirley Carson, John Fleischauer, Turner Kobler, Foster Park, and Allan Thies, "The Paragraph: An Annotated Bibliography," *Style,* 9 (Spring 1977), 107–18. Paul C. Rodgers claimed that Alexander Bain first systematically formulated paragraph theory ("Alexander Bain and the Rise of the Organic Paragraph," *Quarterly Journal of Speech,* 51 [December 1965], 399–403). His view was modified by Ned A. Shearer ("Alexander Bain and the Genesis of Paragraph Theory," *Quarterly Journal of Speech,* 58 [December 1972], 408–17). Shearer claimed that Bain had unacknowledged predecessors and furthermore derived his paragraph theory from the unity of the sentence: a paragraph was a larger sentence, a sentence a smaller paragraph.

[4] Top-down processing means proceeding from an orienting statement to details. It applies to all units of prose larger than the sentence. A top-down arrangement presents the reader with a thesis statement which allows him to understand why he is being told what follows. But composing processes . . . often proceed bottom-up—they don't begin with an orienting statement but end with one. The consequences of top-down processing for paragraph comprehension have been investigated by Perry Thorndyke in "Cognitive Structures in Comprehension and Memory of Narrative Discourse," *Cognitive Psychology,* 9 (January 1977), 77–110, and by Bonnie Meyer in *The Organization of Prose and Its Effects on Memory* (Amsterdam: North-Holland, 1975). Perhaps the most striking example of dependence on top-down processing is supplied by J. D. Bransford and M. K. Johnson, "Considerations of Some Problems of Comprehension," in W. G. Chase, ed., *Visual Informa-*

tion Processing (New York: Academic Press, 1973). They found that experimental subjects could not understand or remember the following passage, which does not identify its orienting topic:

> The procedure is actually quite simple. First you arrange things into different groups depending on their makeup. Of course, one pile may be sufficient, depending on how much there is to do. If you have to go somewhere else due to lack of facilities, that is the next step, otherwise, you are pretty well set. It is important not to overdo any particular endeavor. That is, it is better to do too few things at once than too many. . . .

Readers must be told first that the passage describes washing clothes. Without that information, they cannot make sense of it.

[5] The principle of peripherality is well established in cognitive psychology. For a discussion of the literature see J. A. McGeoch and A. L. Irion, *The Psychology of Human Learning* (New York: Longmans Green, 1952).

[6] Frank Koen, Alton Becker, and Richard Young, "The Psychological Reality of the Paragraph, Part I," *Studies in Language and Language Behavior,* 4 (February 1967), University of Michigan; rpt. in *Technical Communication: Selected Publications by the Faculty,* Department of the Humanities, College of Engineering, University of Michigan, 1977. This article is not listed in the *Style* bibliography of the paragraph cited in note 3.

AN APPETITE FOR COHERENCE:
AROUSING AND FULFILLING DESIRES

Kristie S. Fleckenstein

[*College Composition and Communication* 43 (1992): 81–87.]

Kristie S. Fleckenstein is assistant professor of English at Ball State University. She is coeditor of the *Journal of the Assembly for Expanded Perspectives on Learning* (JAEPL), and of *Teaching Vision: Language and Imagery in the Reading-Writing Classroom.* Fleckenstein's articles have appeared in *College English, JAC, College Composition and Communication,* and *Rhetoric Review.*

Fleckenstein suggests that coherence is so difficult to teach, in part, because it is as much a "reader-based phenomenon as it is a writer-based creation." She describes a sequence of classroom activities that help students see their writing from a reader's perspective. Fleckenstein also includes examples from her students' work to illustrate how her suggestions help students become more effective at perceiving coherence (or incoherence) in their own writing. She suggests activities for individuals, peer groups, and the whole class.

The American Dream is to lose weight quickly and to keep it off without going hungry. But that's all it is: a dream. Wouldn't it be great if you could lose weight by swallowing a pill? The truth is no diet aid or diet pill will take excess weight off unless a person takes in less calories than he/she burns. Some pill packets even suggest a 1,200-calorie-a-day diet program for weight loss. How effective and safe are these diet products, though? Every year seems to bring a new drug for weight loss, and every year Americans seem to spend millions of dollars on diet aids that are ineffective and may even be dangerous.

Wouldn't it be great if you could lose weight by swallowing a pill? The American dream is to lose weight quickly and to keep it off without going hungry.

Some pill packets even suggest a 1,200-calorie-a-day diet program for weight loss. But that's all it is: a dream. The truth is no diet aid or diet pill will take excess weight off unless a person takes in fewer calories than he/she burns. Yet every year seems to bring a new drug for weight loss, and every year Americans seem to spend millions of dollars on diet aids that are ineffective and may even be dangerous.

These two introductory paragraphs, so similar but so different, demonstrate the "before" and "after" texts created by Shelly, a struggling writer in an introductory college composition course. Beyond one or two minor stylistic changes and the omission of a single sentence, the two paragraphs are identical, save in the arrangement of the sentences. And that revision in order is the difference between a coherent introductory paragraph and an incoherent introductory paragraph.

Helping students create coherent texts is one of the most difficult jobs that composition teachers have. Part of that difficulty lies in the fact that coherence is as much a reader-based phenomenon as it is a writer-based creation. As Robert de Beaugrande and Wolfgang Dressler point out in *Introduction to Text Linguistics,* writers may provide the linguistic cues, but it is the readers who fill the gaps between ideas by building relationships that bridge ideas, and who thereby create their sense of order (Longman, 1981). Form is not a product, but a process, Kenneth Burke says, "an arousing and fulfillment of desires," "the creation of an appetite in the mind of the auditor, and the adequate satisfying of that appetite" (qtd. in Sonja Foss, Karen Foss, and Robert Trapp, *Contemporary Perspectives on Rhetoric,* Waveland, 1985, 162).

No wonder it is difficult for inexpert—and expert—writers to create coherent texts, both locally, at the sentence and paragraph levels, and globally, at the full-text level. To judge the success or failure of a particular passage requires the writer to step out of his or her shoes as a writer and examine the passage as a reader. Writers need to perceive the desires or expectations their texts arouse in their projected readers and then check to see if those desires are satisfied. Such a difficult role reversal is not easy to achieve, especially for students previously taught that form, for instance the five-paragraph form, is imposed on content or for those students taught to write without a consideration of their readers.

A method that helps writers shift perspectives involves getting them outside their texts. The technique requires students to examine what they do as readers to create coherent meaning, apply those discoveries to an incoherent text, then examine their own in-progress essays for problems with coherence.

The first part of this classroom strategy demonstrates that coherence is not "in the text," but something that readers create with the aid of cues provided by the writer. Begin this process by offering students the following brief passage, instructing them to read it, noting any words or sentences they don't understand, and then, if possible, to summarize it:

> Sally first tried setting loose a team of gophers. The plan backfired when a dog chased them away. She then entertained a group of teenagers and was delighted when they brought their motorcycles. Unfortunately, she failed to find a Peeping Tom listed in the Yellow Pages. Furthermore, her stereo system was not loud enough. The crabgrass might have worked, but she didn't have a fan that was sufficiently powerful. The obscene phone calls gave her hope until the number was changed. She thought about calling a door-to-door salesman but decided to hang up a clothesline instead. It was the installation of blinking neon lights across the street that did the trick. She eventually framed the ad from the classified section.

Most students are unable to create a coherent meaning out of this passage, although they understand all the words and most of the sentences. They merely can't weave the disparate ideas into any understandable pattern. So the next step is to discuss the reasons for their difficulty. For instance, three sentences that commonly confuse my students are (1) "The crabgrass might have worked, but she didn't have a fan that was sufficiently powerful"; (2) "She thought about calling a door-to-door salesman but decided to hang up a clothesline instead"; and (3) "She eventually framed the ad from the classified section." During full-class discussions, my students complain that they can't connect crabgrass to fans in the first sample sentence. They point to a similar problem between door-to-door salesman and clothesline. Finally, in the last sample sentence, students say that they don't know what ad Sally refers to.

Following a discussion of reading frustrations, provide students with the following sentence: "Sally disliked her neighbors and wanted them to leave the area." Students discover that this sentence provides them a context to draw from. Now, they can use their background knowledge about human motivation, neighborhood irritations, and offensive strategies to build relationships within and between sentences. Thus, they are able to relate crabgrass and fan by filling the gaps with the cause-effect knowledge (1) that crabgrass is the bane of the suburbanite's lawn and (2) that the fan was meant to infest the neighbor's lawn with crabgrass. Door-to-door salesmen and clotheslines are connected in an additive relationship as ploys designed to irritate the neighbors, and the ad, associated with Sally's implied goal of driving her neighbors out, is the real estate ad announcing the sale of the neighbor's home.

These observations serve as a basis for the discovery that coherent meaning results from the relationships we as readers build between ideas. If we can't build relationships by bridging the gaps between ideas—ideas such as crabgrass and fans—we create no coherent sense of the text.

The orienting statement about Sally's sentiments can also be used to demonstrate that readers approach a text with an array of expectations already cued (including the expectation that the text confronting us is coherent). Then, as we read, we are guided by those expectations, or appetites, and sample the text to satisfy or revise those appetites. By discussing the expectations the first sentence elicits, students discover how those expectations become predictions, hypotheses, and guesses which they validate or revise as they read.

The next step of this strategy is to move students from a contemplation of themselves as readers to practical work as peer editors. Sharing and revising an incoherent text helps effect this shift from reader to writer. Using an overhead projector, project an incoherent paragraph, but separate each sentence with three to four lines of space. With a sheet of paper, cover everything except the first sentence. Ask students to write down (a) what they think the idea of the sentence is, (b) what they think will come next, and (c) what they think the entire essay will concern. Uncover the second sentence and ask the students to decide if this sentence is consistent with their expectations. Discuss differences in opinion, but without attempting to arrive at any premature closure. Then, with the first two sentences as a basis, ask students to again write down what they think the essay will be about and what will come next. Continue predicting and discussing those predictions throughout the paragraph. As the last step in the exercise, have the students pool their observations and decide, as a class, how best to revise the paragraph so that it achieves a greater sense of coherence. Ask students to make specific suggestions for revisions: what to rearrange, add, or delete.

Following this whole-class work, divide the students into small groups, pass out copies of a second paragraph, and ask each group to read, analyze, and suggest changes for that paragraph, just as they had done for the first one. Finally, ask students to take the first one or two paragraphs of their current essays-in-progress and "stretch them out"—separate each sentence by three or four lines of space—and bring them to share with their peer partners for an analysis of paragraph coherence.

During the third stage of this experience with coherence, students apply to *each other's papers* the techniques they applied previously as a group. The sample below illustrates a typical interchange between writer and peer partner. I have selected this particular interaction for a variety of reasons. First, both the writer, Trish, and the peer editor, Terry, were average writers from a developmental college writing class. Second, this sample reflects Trish's work with her first complete, formal draft of her first essay. Finally, I chose this sample because Terry did not follow the precise instructions provided in class; however, he still produced valuable reactions and advice for Trish. For instance, students were asked to (a) jot down the focus of the sentence under analysis, (b) jot down what they expect next, and (c) jot down what they expect from the entire essay. Terry frequently failed to include his expectations and the focus; instead, he explained why the sentence under examination did or did not meet his expectations, and he provided on-the-spot advice. Terry's success as a peer editor illustrates that the effectiveness of the strategy is not a product of its exact application.

1. In high school I had been in the printing class for about 3 and 1/2 years.
   a. The sentence is about printing class.
   b. Your essay's about printing class.

2. When we started out, there were 6 or 7 black students in a class that was predominately white and hispanic.
   a. It's about the kids in the class.
   b. The sentence doesn't correspond with the previous sentence. I am a bit confused.
   c. The paper is still about printing class.

3. As the years progressed and I was in my junior year there was one black student left: me.
   a. This should have been your second sentence because it corresponds with the first sentence.
   b. The problems she had in her class because she was the only black person.
   c. The essay's going to be about the problem that she had for being black.

4. I had become extremely talented with lithographic photography, which is making negatives of line copy (words), halftone pictures (regular pictures into dot form), and the PMT process (taking drawn art and making it usable for printing).
   a. This sentence doesn't fit because you started talking about being the only black and then you start explaining what you did in the class. The reader is like, the only black and so what?
   b. Being the only black gave these advantages of learning how to work the many different equipments.
   c. Learning how to work the equipment in the printing class.

5. Due to the fact I was working with light sensitive film a lot, I was in the darkroom, which is away from the rest of the class, and where I am hardly seen.
   a. This sentence doesn't fit. What does light sensitive film have to do with equipment or being the only black? About now I am confused.
   b. The sentence is about her class work.
   c. I'm not sure what the paper will be about. Discrimination in the printing class? her work?

6. This made the class look as if it was all white and hispanic, and gave the impression to the customers as well.
   a. This sort of follows because she's still talking about working out of sight, but what customers is she talking about?
   b. The customers gave all the credit to the white students.
   c. The discrimination from the printing class.

7. When I was seen in the class room, which was rare, and a customer would walk in, they would be shocked to see me.
   a. This sentence fits and your essay is starting to make sense. I think it is about being discriminated by your printing class.

8. It was then I realized the subtle prejudice of my printshop teacher, Mr. H—.
   a. I finally got the connection in your last sentence and the topic of the essay is clearer.

Suggestions for Revision I finally figured out your topic, but I still can't make all the sentences fit. Maybe you should explain about your print class and the customers. Why were you in the same class for 3 years? Maybe take out the sentence on what you did in class. I don't know how to fit it in. Can you combine the ideas in the first three sentences? Or start out with your first sentence, add a couple of sentences about the class, then explain that by your junior year you were the only black? Then say you were out of sight a lot?

Trish revised her first paragraph into the following:

In high school I had been in a printing class for about 3 and 1/2 years. The class was a production class, which meant that students could take it for a number of years and that we learned about printing by doing jobs for customers. When I started out as a freshman, there were about 6 or 7 other black students in a predominately white and hispanic class, but by my junior year I was the only black student left. Also, because I was working with light sensitive film much of the time, I was in the darkroom, away from the class and hardly seen. Customers had the impression that the class was all white and hispanic. When customers saw me in the class room, which was rare, they would be shocked. It was then that I realized the subtle prejudice of my printshop teacher, Mr. H—.

With Terry's help, Trish was able to revise her first paragraph into a much tighter introduction, one that consistently cued her topic for the entire paper and one that maintained greater unity between ideas.

Beyond the value of this technique as a revision tool, it also helps students achieve more writing control. For instance, one pedagogical goal in any writing class is to wean our students from dependence on our judgment and to foster reliance on their own judgment. This strategy for creating coherence facilitates that movement, in that it provides what Carl Bereiter and Marlene Scardamalia call executive controls: a method of determining when the composing process derails and a procedure for correcting the derailment (*The Psychology of Written Composition*, Erlbaum, 1987). This strategy does that; it can be effectively wielded by writers without access to peer partners or with less-than-satisfactory peer partners, as the following example demonstrates. The three sample paragraphs below are from the first, second, and final drafts of a paper by a writer in a developmental freshman composition class. Tina, whose peer partner frustrated her with an inconsistent performance, applied the strategy herself, as she worked through several versions of her introduction.

Draft I: Remember if you don't follow your dreams, you'll never know what's on the other side of the rainbow; you'll never know what you can find at the top of the mountain; you'll never know your journey's best. By being a pushover, you let people dictate what you can and cannot do. Letting people run over you, or pushing your thoughts aside and not caring how you feel, you'll never know what you're capable of in terms of success but the failures you possess will always carry with you. Of course the failure is being afraid to speak and tell somebody or anybody how you truly feel. By bottling up your personal frustrations that you have problems saying aloud, your insides are going to explode. That explosion can be dangerous or even fatal that you get to the point of going out and killing that person who pushes you around or develop a high blood pressure which will eventually result in a heart attack. On the other hand, you can let your frustrations out and let that weak point of your character work to your advantage. Believe me, the second choice is safer and more productive.

Draft II: For all of you pushovers out there, never let anyone tell you what to do or what's impossible for you. Remember, if you don't follow your dreams, you'll never know what's on the other side of the rainbow or what's at the top of the mountain. So always speak up for what you believe in, because if you don't do it for yourself, no one will. If you continue to be a pushover, a sucker for the rest of your life, you'll be a rug for the rest of your life. People will continue to step all over you. Believe me. I know. I was once a pushover myself. A pushover. An opponent who is easy to defeat or a victim who is capable of no effective resistance. Do not and I repeat do not subject yourself to that despicable low-life group called: the suckers.

Draft III: Pushover. An opponent who is easy to defeat or a victim who is capable of no effective resistance. Do not, and I repeat, do not subject yourself to that despicable, low-life group called the suckers. If you continue to be a sucker for the rest of your life, you'll be a rug for the rest of your life. People will continue to step all over you. Believe what I am saying. I was once a pushover myself.

Although Tina's introduction still has problems, it does reflect a tighter focus and greater coherence than do her previous two efforts.

This way to help students perceive incoherence in their writing also possesses peripheral benefits. First, it emphasizes the importance of reading in writing. To be good writers, students must also be good readers. The focus of discussions can switch easily from the students' writing process to an examination of specific cues that can help readers create the relationships the writers seemingly have in mind. Second, the strategy also offers a productive way to introduce transitions and cohesive ties as linguistic cues that signal to readers an underlying relationship. This method centers students' attention on the underlying relationship of the transitional word cues, not on the word itself. Finally, students can examine the texts of professional writers, tracing shifts and noting how these writers ensure smooth bridges between ideas, gaining a greater sense of the rhetorical conventions that govern discourse. Again, this fosters the students' growth as readers, as well as writers.

Shelly's, Trish's, and Tina's revisions are hardly problem free, but each demonstrates the increasingly effective coherence this strategy promotes. Perhaps the most rewarding outgrowth of this technique is watching students gain confidence in their own ability to create meaningful texts and to create meaning from texts without a teacher's continued intercession.

RESPONDING TO STUDENT WRITING

RESPONDING TO STUDENT WRITING

Nancy Sommers

[*College Composition and Communication* 33 (1982): 148–56.]

(For biographical information, see page 96.)

This article reports on research Sommers conducted to examine how instructors' responses to student writing actually contributed to subsequent revisions. Her findings, supported with specific examples and extensive observations, revealed discouraging tendencies in teacher responses, and her advice can help teachers avoid these problems. Teachers can apply Sommers's advice to avoid the tendency to attach responses that are too general by following *The Bedford Handbook*'s guidelines for peer reviewers (p. 55), which offer a ready-made list of features to consider while responding to student writing, encouraging text-specific comments that reinforce particular revision strategies.

More than any other enterprise in the teaching of writing, responding to and commenting on student writing consumes the largest proportion of our time. Most teachers estimate that it takes them at least 20 to 40 minutes to comment on an individual student paper, and those 20 to 40 minutes times 20 students per class, times 8 papers, more or less, during the course of a semester add up to an enormous amount of time. With so much time and energy directed to a single activity, it is important for us to understand the nature of the enterprise. For it seems, paradoxically enough, that although commenting on student writing is the most widely used method for responding to student writing, it is the least understood. We do not know in any definitive way what constitutes thoughtful commentary or what effect, if any, our comments have on helping our students become more effective writers.

Theoretically, at least, we know that we comment on our students' writing for the same reasons professional editors comment on the work of professional writers or for the same reasons we ask our colleagues to read and respond to our own writing. As writers we need and want thoughtful commentary to show us when we have communicated our ideas and when not, raising questions from a reader's point of view that may not have occurred to us as writers. We want to know if our writing has communicated our intended meaning and, if not, what questions or discrepancies our reader sees that we, as writers, are blind to.

In commenting on our students' writing, however, we have an additional pedagogical purpose. As teachers, we know that most students find it difficult to imagine a reader's response in advance, and to use such responses as a guide in composing. Thus, we comment on student writing to dramatize the presence of a reader, to help our students to become that questioning reader themselves, because, ultimately, we believe that becoming such a reader will help them to evaluate what they have written and develop control over their writing.[1]

Even more specifically, however, we comment on student writing because we believe that it is necessary for us to offer assistance to student writers when they are in the process of composing a text, rather than after the text has been completed. Comments create the motive for doing something different in the next draft; thoughtful comments create the motive for revising. Without comments from their teachers or from their peers, student writers will revise in a consistently narrow and predictable way. Without comments from readers, students assume that their writing has communicated their meaning and perceive no need for revising the substance of their text.[2]

Yet as much as we as informed professionals believe in the soundness of this approach to responding to student writing, we also realize that we don't know how our theory squares with teachers' actual practice—do teachers comment and students revise as the theory predicts they should? For the past year my colleagues, Lil Brannon, Cyril Knoblach, and I have been researching this problem, attempting to discover not only what messages teachers give their students through their comments, but also what determines which of these comments the students choose to use or to ignore when revising. Our research has been entirely focused on comments teachers write to motivate revisions. We have studied the commenting styles of thirty-five teachers at New York University and the University of Oklahoma, studying the comments these teachers wrote on first and second drafts, and interviewing a representative number of these teachers and their students. All teachers also commented on the same set of three student essays. As an additional reference point one of the student essays was typed into the computer that had been programmed with the "Writer's Workbench," a package of twenty-three programs developed by Bell Laboratories to help computers and writers work together to improve a text rapidly. Within a few minutes, the computer delivered editorial comments on the student's text, identifying all spelling and punctuation errors, isolating problems with wordy or misused phrases, and suggesting alternatives, offering a stylistic analysis of sentence types, sentence beginnings, and sentence lengths, and finally, giving our freshman essay a Kincaid readability score of eighth-grade which, as the computer program informed us, "is a low score for this type of document." The sharp contrast between the teachers' comments and those of the computer highlighted how arbitrary and idiosyncratic most of our teachers' comments are. Besides, the calm, reasonable language of the computer provided quite a contrast to the hostility and mean-spiritedness of most of the teachers' comments.

The first finding from our research on styles of commenting is that *teachers' comments can take students' attention away from their own purposes in writing a particular text and focus that attention on the teachers' purpose in commenting.* The teacher appropriates the text from the student by confusing the student's purpose in writing the text with her own purpose in commenting. Students make the changes the teacher wants rather than those that the student perceives are necessary, since the teacher's concerns imposed on the text create the reasons for the subsequent changes. We have all heard our perplexed students say to us when confused by our comments: "I don't understand how you want me to change this" or "Tell me what you want me to do." In the beginning of the process there was the writer, her words, and her desire to communicate her ideas. But after the comments of the teacher are imposed on the first or second draft, the student's attention dramatically shifts from "This is what I want to say," to "This is what *you* the teacher are asking me to do."

This appropriation of the text by the teacher happens particularly when teachers identify errors in usage, diction, and style in a first draft and ask students to correct these errors when they revise; such comments give the student an impression of the importance of these errors that is all out of proportion to how they should view these errors at this point in the process. The comments create the concern that these "accidents of discourse" need to be attended to before the meaning of the text is attended to.

It would not be so bad if students were only commanded to correct errors, but, more often than not, students are given contradictory messages; they are commanded to edit a sentence to avoid an error or to condense a sentence to achieve greater brevity of style, and then told in the margins that the particular paragraph needs to be more specific or to be developed more. An example of this problem can be seen in the following student paragraph:

You need to do more research.

wordy—be precise, which Sunday?   *comma needed*
Every year [on one Sunday in the middle of January] tens of millions of

word choice
people <u>cancel</u> all events, plans or work to watch the Super Bowl. This audience

wordy
includes [little boys and girls, old people, and housewives and men.] <u>Many</u>

Be specific—what reasons?
<u>reasons</u> have been given to explain why the Super Bowl has become so popular

and why   *what spots?*   *awkward*
that commercial spots cost up to $100,000.00. <u>One explanation is that people</u>

another what?
like to take sides and root for a team. <u>Another</u> is that some people like the

spelling
pagentry and excitement of the event. These reasons alone, however, do not

too colloquial
explain <u>a happening</u> as big as the Super Bowl.

This paragraph needs to be expanded in order to be more interesting to the reader.

In commenting on this draft, the teacher has shown the student how to edit the sentences, but then commands the student to expand the paragraph in order to make it more interesting to a reader. The interlinear comments and the marginal comments represent two separate tasks for this student; the interlinear comments encourage the student to see the text as a fixed piece, frozen in time, that just needs some editing. The marginal comments, however, suggest that the meaning of the text is not fixed, but rather that the student still needs to develop the meaning by doing some more research. Students are commanded to edit and develop at the same time; the remarkable contradiction of developing a paragraph after editing the sentences in it represents the confusion we encountered in our teachers' commenting styles. These different signals given to students, to edit and develop, to condense and elaborate, represent also the failure of teachers' comments to direct genuine revision of a text as a whole.

Moreover, the comments are worded in such a way that it is difficult for students to know what is the most important problem in the text and what problems are of lesser importance. No scale of concerns is offered to a student with the result that a comment about spelling or a comment about an awkward sentence is given weight equal to a comment about organization or logic. The comment that seemed to represent this problem best was one teacher's command to his student: "Check your commas and semicolons and think more about what you are thinking about." The language of the comments makes it difficult for a student to sort out and decide what is most important and what is least important.

When the teacher appropriates the text for the student in this way, students are encouraged to see their writing as a series of parts—words, sentences, paragraphs—and not as a whole discourse. The comments encourage students to believe that their first drafts are finished drafts, not invention drafts, and that all they need to do is patch and polish their writing. That is, teachers' comments do not provide their students with an inherent reason for revising the structure and meaning of their texts, since the comments suggest to students that the meaning of their text is already there, finished, produced, and all that is necessary is a better word or phrase. The processes of revising, editing, and proofreading are collapsed and reduced to a single trivial activity, and the students' misunderstanding of the revision process as a rewording activity is reinforced by their teachers' comments.

It is possible, and it quite often happens, that students follow every comment and fix their texts appropriately as requested, but their texts are not improved substantially or, even worse, their revised drafts are inferior to their previous drafts. Since the teachers' comments take the students' attention away from their own original purposes, students concentrate more, as I have noted, on what the teachers commanded them to do than on what they are trying to say. Sometimes students do not understand the purpose behind their teachers' comments and take these comments very literally. At other times students understand the comments, but the teacher has misread the text and the comments, unfortunately, are not applicable. For instance, we repeatedly saw comments in which teachers commanded students to reduce and condense what was written, when in fact what the text really needed at this stage was to be expanded in conception and scope.

The process of revising always involves a risk. But, too often revision becomes a balancing act for students in which they make the changes that are requested but do not take the risk of changing anything that was not commented on, even if the students sense that other changes are needed. A more effective text does not often evolve from such changes alone, yet the student does not want to take the chance of reducing a finished, albeit inadequate, paragraph to chaos—to fragments— in order to rebuild it, if such changes have not been requested by the teacher.

The second finding from our study is that *most teachers' comments are not text-specific and could be interchanged, rubber-stamped, from text to text.* The comments are not anchored in the particulars of the students' texts, but rather are a series of vague directives that are not text-specific. Students are commanded to "think more about [their] audience, avoid colloquial language, avoid the passive, avoid prepositions at the end of sentences or conjunctions at the beginning of sentences, be clear, be specific, be precise, but above all, think more about what [they] are thinking about." The comments on the following student paragraph illustrate this problem:

Begin by telling your reader what you are going to write about

↘In the sixties it was drugs, in the seventies it was rock and roll. Now in the

  avoid "one of the"

eighties, <u>one of the</u> most controversial subjects is nuclear power. The United

  elaborate

States is <u>in great need of its own</u> source of power. Because of environmentalists,

  be specific

coal is not an acceptable source of energy. [Solar and wind power have not yet

  avoid "it seems"

received the technology necessary to use them.] <u>It seems</u> that nuclear power is

the only feasible means right now for obtaining self-sufficient power. However,

too large a percentage of the population are against nuclear power claiming it is

  be precise

unsafe. <u>With as many problems</u> as the United States is having concerning

think more about your reader

Thesis sentence needed. energy, it seems a shame that the public is so quick to "can" a very feasible means

of power. Nuclear energy should not be given up on, but rather, more nuclear

plants should be built.

One could easily remove all the comments from this paragraph and rubber-stamp them on another student text, and they would make as much or as little sense on the second text as they do here.

We have observed an overwhelming similarity in the generalities and abstract commands given to students. There seems to be among teachers an accepted, albeit unwritten canon for commenting on student texts. This uniform code of commands, requests, and pleadings demonstrates that the teacher holds a license for vagueness while the student is commanded to be specific. The students we interviewed admitted to having a great difficulty with these vague directives. The students stated that when a teacher writes in the margins or as an end comment, "choose precise language," or "think more about your audience," revising becomes a guessing game. In effect, the teacher is saying to the student, "Somewhere in this paper is imprecise language or lack of awareness of an audience and you must find it." The problem presented by these vague commands is compounded for the students when they are not offered any strategies for carrying out these commands. Students are told that they have done something wrong and that there is something in their text that needs to be fixed before the text is acceptable. But to tell students that they have done something wrong is not to tell them what to do about it. In order to offer a useful revision strategy to a student, the teacher must anchor that strategy in the specifics of the student's text. For instance, to tell our student, the author of the above paragraph, to "be specific," or to "elaborate," does not show our student what questions the reader has about the meaning of the text, or what breaks in logic exist, that could be resolved if the writer supplied information; nor is the student shown how to achieve the desired specificity.

Instead of offering strategies, the teachers offer what is interpreted by students as rules for composing; the comments suggest to students that writing is just a matter of following the rules. Indeed, the teachers seem to impose a series of abstract rules about written products even when some of them are not appropriate for the specific text the student is creating.[3] For instance, the student author of our sample paragraph presented above is commanded to follow the conventional rules for writing a five-paragraph essay—to begin the introductory paragraph by telling his reader what he is going to say and to end the paragraph with a thesis sentence. Somehow these abstract rules about what five-paragraph products should look like do not seem applicable to the problems this student must confront when revising, nor are the rules specific strategies he could use when revising. There are many inchoate ideas ready to be exploited in this paragraph, but the rules do not help the student to take stock of his (or her) ideas and use the opportunity he has, during revision, to develop those ideas.

The problem here is a confusion of process and product; what one has to say about the process is different from what one has to say about the product. Teachers who use this method of commenting are formulating their comments as if these drafts were finished drafts and were not going to be revised. Their commenting vocabularies have not been adapted to revision and they comment on first drafts as if they were justifying a grade or as if the first draft were the final draft.

Our summary finding, therefore, from this research on styles of commenting is that the news from the classroom is not good. For the most part, teachers do not respond to student writing with the kind of thoughtful commentary which will help students to engage with the issues they are writing about or which will help them think about their purposes and goals in writing a specific text. In defense of our teachers, however, they told us that responding to student writing was rarely stressed in their teacher-training or in writing workshops; they had been trained in various prewriting techniques, in constructing assignments, and in evaluating papers for grades, but rarely in the process of reading a student text for meaning or in offering commentary to motivate revision. The problem is that most of us as teachers of writing have been trained to read and interpret literary texts for meaning, but, unfortunately, we have not been trained to act upon the same set of assumptions in reading student texts as we follow in reading literary texts.[4] Thus, we read student texts with biases about what the writer should have said or about what he or she should have written, and our biases determine how we will comprehend the text. We read with our preconceptions and preoccupations, expecting to find errors, and the result is that we find errors and misread our students' texts.[5] We find what we look for; instead of reading and responding to the meaning of a text, we correct our students' writing. We need to reverse this approach. Instead of finding errors or showing students how to patch up parts of their texts, we need to sabotage our students' conviction that the drafts they have written are complete and coherent. Our comments need to offer students revision tasks of a different order of complexity and sophistication from the ones that they themselves identify, by forcing students back into the chaos, back to the point where they are shaping and restructuring their meaning.[6]

For if the content of a text is lacking in substance and meaning, if the order of the parts must be rearranged significantly in the next draft, if paragraphs must be restructured for logic and clarity, then many sentences are likely to be changed or deleted anyway. There seems to be no point in having students correct usage errors or condense sentences that are likely to disappear before the next draft is completed. In fact, to identify such problems in a text at this early first draft stage, when such problems are likely to abound, can give a student a disproportionate sense of their importance at this stage in the writing process.[7] In responding to our students' writing, we should be guided by the recognition that it is not spelling or usage problems that we as writers first worry about when drafting and revising our texts.

We need to develop an appropriate level of response for commenting on a first draft, and to differentiate that from the level suitable to a second or third draft. Our comments need to be suited to the draft we are reading. In a first or second draft, we need to respond as any reader would, registering questions, reflecting befuddlement, and noting places where we are puzzled about the meaning of the text. Comments should point to breaks in logic, disruptions in meaning, or missing information. Our goal in commenting on early drafts should be to engage students with the issues they are considering and help them clarify their purposes and reasons in writing their specific text.

For instance, the major rhetorical problem of the essay written by the student who wrote the first paragraph (the paragraph on nuclear power) quoted above was that the student had two principal arguments running through his text, each of which brought the other into question. On the one hand, he argued that we must use nuclear power, unpleasant as it is, because we have nothing else to use; though nuclear energy is a problematic source of energy, it is the best of a bad lot. On the other hand, he also argued that nuclear energy is really quite safe and therefore should be our primary resource. Comments on this student's first draft need to point out this break in logic and show the student that if we accept his first argument, then his second argument sounds fishy. But if we accept his second argument, his first argument sounds contradictory. The teacher's comments need to engage this student writer with this basic rhetorical and conceptual problem in his first draft rather than impose a series of abstract commands and rules upon his text.

Written comments need to be viewed not as an end in themselves—a way for teachers to satisfy themselves that they have done their jobs—but rather as a means for helping students to become more effective writers. As a means for helping students, they have limitations; they are, in fact, disembodied re-marks—one absent writer responding to another absent writer. The key to suc-cessful commenting is to have what is said in the comments and what is done in the classroom mutually reinforce and enrich each other. Commenting on pa-pers assists the writing course in achieving its purpose; classroom activities and the comments we write to our students need to be connected. Written com-ments need to be an extension of the teacher's voice—an extension of the teacher as reader. Exercises in such activities as revising a whole text or indi-vidual paragraphs together in class, noting how the sense of the whole dictates the smaller changes, looking at options, evaluating actual choices, and then discussing the effect of these changes on revised drafts—such exercises need to be designed to take students through the cycles of revising and to help them overcome their anxiety about revising: that anxiety we all feel at reducing what looks like a finished draft into fragments and chaos.

The challenge we face as teachers is to develop comments which will provide an inherent reason for students to revise; it is a sense of revision as discovery, as a repeated process of beginning again, as starting out new, that our students have not learned. We need to show our students how to seek, in the possibility of revision, the dissonances of discovery—to show them through our comments why new choices would positively change their texts, and thus to show them the potential for development implicit in their own writing.

Notes

[1] C. H. Knoblach and Lil Brannon, "Teacher Commentary on Student Writing: The State of the Art," *Freshman English News,* 10 (Fall 1981), 1–3.

[2] For an extended discussion of revision strategies of student writers see Nancy Som-mers, "Revision Strategies of Student Writers and Experienced Adult Writers," *College Composition and Communication,* 31 (December 1980), 378–388.

[3] Nancy Sommers and Ronald Schleifer, "Means and Ends: Some Assumptions of Stu-dent Writers," *Composition and Teaching,* 2 (December 1980), 69–76.

[4] Janet Emig and Robert P. Parker, Jr., "Responding to Student Writing: Building a Theory of the Evaluating Process," unpublished paper, Rutgers University.

[5] For an extended discussion of this problem see Joseph Williams, "The Phenomenology of Error," *College Composition and Communication,* 32 (May 1981), 152–168.

[6] Ann Berthoff, *The Making of Meaning* (Montclair, N.J.: Boynton/Cook Publishers, 1981).

[7] W. U. McDonald, "The Revising Process and the Marking of Student Papers," *College Composition and Communication,* 24 (May 1978), 167–170.

RANKING, EVALUATING, AND LIKING: SORTING OUT THREE FORMS OF JUDGMENT

Peter Elbow

[*College English* 55 (1993): 187–206.]

Professor Emeritus of English at the University of Massachusetts, Amherst, Peter Elbow first gained national fame as author of the classic *Writing without Teachers* (1973). Since then he has been one of the pro-fession's most visible and prolific scholars and teachers. Among his many books, he coedited (with Pat Belanoff and Sheryl Fontaine) *Nothing Begins with N: New Investigations of Freewriting* (1990) and authored *What Is English?* published by the Modern Language Association in 1990. Elbow's numerous articles and chapters have appeared in a wide range of professional publications. Among his many awards, he won the CCCC's prestigious Richard Braddock Award in 1986. Peter Elbow retired in August 2000. He will remain in Amherst, where he plans to teach graduate seminars and continue to consult with and advise graduate students in rhetoric and composition.

Eventually, students submit their writing for a grade, no matter how much their instructors promote multiple, significant revisions. At that point instructors assess student writing—not to help guide revisions, but to decide how effectively students have achieved their goals or met assignment criteria. Elbow reflects on several alternatives available for assessing student writing, alternatives he characterizes as ranking, evaluating, and liking. He discusses the problems with ranking and the benefits of evaluating, suggesting that teachers do portfolio assessments where possible. He explores, too, the limitations of evaluation and the benefits of evaluation-free zones. Finally, Elbow discusses how simply liking students' writing—enjoying and taking a sincere interest in their work—can help motivate students and foster more effective criticism. Elbow offers several suggestions for teachers who want to explore alternative assessment strategies.

This essay is my attempt to sort out different acts we call assessment—some different ways in which we express or frame our judgments of value. I have been working on this tangle not just because it is interesting and important in itself but because assessment tends so much to drive and control *teaching*. Much of what we do in the classroom is determined by the assessment structures we work under.

Assessment is a large and technical area and I'm not a professional. But my main premise or subtext in this essay is that we nonprofessionals can and should work on it because professionals have not reached definitive conclusions about the problem of how to assess writing (or anything else, I'd say). Also, decisions about assessment are often made by people even less professional than we, namely legislators. Pat Belanoff and I realized that the field of assessment was open when we saw the harmful effects of a writing proficiency exam at Stony Brook and worked out a collaborative portfolio assessment system in its place (Belanoff and Elbow; Elbow and Belanoff). Professionals keep changing their minds about large-scale testing and assessment. And as for classroom grading, psychometricians provide little support or defense of it.

The Problems with Ranking and the Benefits of Evaluating

By ranking I mean the act of summing up one's judgment of a performance or person into a single, holistic number or score. We rank every time we give a grade or holistic score. Ranking implies a single scale or continuum or dimension along which all performances are hung.

By evaluating I mean the act of expressing one's judgment of a performance or person by pointing out the strengths and weaknesses of different features or dimensions. We evaluate every time we write a comment on a paper or have a conversation about its value. Evaluation implies the recognition of different criteria or dimensions—and by implication different contexts and audiences for the same performance. Evaluation requires going *beyond* a first response that may be nothing but a kind of ranking ("I like it" or "This is better than that"), and instead looking carefully enough at the performance or person to make distinctions between parts or features or criteria.

It's obvious, thus, that I am troubled by ranking. But I will resist any temptation to argue that we can get rid of all ranking—or even should. Instead I will try to show how we can have *less* ranking and *more* evaluation in its place.

I see three distinct problems with ranking: it is inaccurate or unreliable; it gives no substantive feedback; and it is harmful to the atmosphere for teaching and learning.

(1) First the unreliability. To rank reliably means to give a *fair* number, to find the single quantitative score that readers will agree on. But readers don't agree.

This is not news—this unavailability of agreement. We have long seen it on many fronts. For example, research in evaluation has shown many times that if we give a paper to a set of readers, those readers tend to give it the full range of grades (Diederich). I've recently come across new research to this effect—new to me because it was published in 1912. The investigators carefully showed how high school English teachers gave different grades to the same paper. In response to criticism that this was a local problem in English, they went on the next year to discover an even greater variation among grades given by high school geometry teachers and history teachers to papers in their subjects. (See the summary of Daniel Starch and Edward Elliott's 1913 *School Review* articles in Kirschenbaum, Simon, and Napier 258–59.)

We know the same thing from literary criticism and theory. If the best critics can't agree about what a text means, how can we be surprised that they disagree even more about the quality or value of texts? And we know that nothing in literary or philosophical theory gives us any agreed-upon rules for settling such disputes.

Students have shown us the same inconsistency with their own controlled experiments of handing the same paper to different teachers and getting different grades. This helps explain why we hate it so when students ask us their favorite question, "What do you want for an A?": it rubs our noses in the unreliability of our grades.

Of course champions of holistic scoring argue that they *can* get agreement among readers—and they often do (White). But they get that agreement by "training" the readers before and during the scoring sessions. What "training" means is getting those scorers to stop reading the way they normally read—getting them to stop using the conflicting criteria and standards they normally use outside the scoring sessions. (In an impressive and powerful book, Barbara Herrnstein Smith argues that whenever we have widespread inter-reader reliability, we have reason to suspect that difference has been suppressed and homogeneity imposed—almost always at the expense of certain groups.) In short, the reliability in holistic scoring is not a measure of how texts are valued by real readers in natural settings, but only of how they are valued in artificial settings with imposed agreements.

Defenders of holistic scoring might reply (as one anonymous reviewer did), that holistic scores are not perfect or absolutely objective readings but just "judgments that most readers will agree are the appropriate ones given the purpose of the assessment and the system of communication." But I have been in and even conducted enough holistic scoring sessions to know that even that degree of agreement doesn't occur unless "purpose" and "appropriateness" are defined to mean acceptance of the single set of standards imposed on that session. We know too much about the differences among readers and the highly variable nature of the reading process. Supposing we get readings only from academics, or only from people in English, or only from respected critics, or only from respected writing programs, or only from feminists, or only from sound readers of my tribe (white, male, middle-class, full professors between the ages of fifty and sixty). We *still* don't get agreement. We can sometimes get agreement among readers from some subset, a particular community that has developed a strong set of common values, perhaps *one* English department or *one* writing program. But what is the value of such a rare agreement? It tells us nothing about how readers from other English departments or writing programs will judge—much less how readers from other domains will judge.

(From the opposite ideological direction, some skeptics might object to my skeptical train of thought: "So what else is new?" they might reply. "Of *course* my grades are biased, 'interested' or 'situated'—always partial to my interests or the values of my community or culture. There's no other possibility." But how can people consent to give grades if they feel that way? A single teacher's grade for a student is liable to have substantial consequences—for example on eligibility for a scholarship or a job or entrance into professional school. In grading, surely we must not take anything less than genuine fairness as our goal.)

It won't be long before we see these issues argued in a court of law, when a student who has been disqualified from playing on a team or rejected from a professional school sues, charging that the basis for his plight—teacher grades—is not reliable. I wonder if lawyers will be able to make our grades stick.

(2) Ranking or grading is woefully uncommunicative. Grades and holistic scores are nothing but points on a continuum from "yea" to "boo"—with no information or clues about the criteria behind these noises. They are 100 percent evaluation and 0 percent description or information. They quantify the degree of approval or disapproval in readers but tell nothing at all about what the readers actually approve or disapprove of. They say nothing that couldn't be said with gold stars or black marks or smiley-faces. Of course our first reactions are often nothing but global holistic feelings of approval or disapproval, but we need a system for communicating our judgments that nudges us to move beyond these holistic feelings and to articulate the basis of our feeling—a process that often leads us to change our feeling. (Holistic scoring sessions sometimes use rubrics that explain the criteria—though these are rarely passed along to students—and even in these situations, the rubrics fail to fit many papers.) As C. S. Lewis says, "People are obviously far more anxious to express their approval and disapproval of things than to describe them" (7).

(3) Ranking leads students to get so hung up on these oversimple quantitative verdicts that they care more about scores than about learning—more about the grade we put on the paper than about the comment we have written on it. Have you noticed how grading often forces us to write comments to justify our grades?—and how these are often *not* the comment we would make if we were just trying to help the student write better? ("Just try writing several favorable comments on a paper and then giving it a grade of D" [Diederich 21].)

Grades and holistic scores give too much encouragement to those students who score high—making them too apt to think they are already fine—and too little encouragement to those students who do badly. Unsuccessful students often come to doubt their intelligence. But oddly enough, many "A" students also end up doubting their true ability and feeling like frauds—because they have sold out on their own judgment and simply given teachers whatever yields an A. They have too often been rewarded for what they don't really believe in. (Notice that there's more cheating by students who get high grades than by those who get low ones. There would be less incentive to cheat if there were no ranking.)

We might be tempted to put up with the inaccuracy or unfairness of grades if they gave good diagnostic feedback or helped the learning climate; or we might put up with the damage they do to the learning climate if they gave a fair or reliable measure of how skilled or knowledgeable students are. But since they fail dismally on both counts, we are faced with the striking question of why grading has persisted so long.

There must be many reasons. It is obviously easier and quicker to express a global feeling with a single number than to figure out what the strengths and weaknesses are and what one's criteria are. (Though I'm heartened to discover, as I pursue this issue, how troubled teachers are by grading and how difficult they find it.) But perhaps more important, we see around us a deep *hunger to rank*—to create pecking orders: to see who we can look down on and who we must look up to, or in the military metaphor, who we can kick and who we must salute. Psychologists tell us that this taste for pecking orders or ranking is associated with the authoritarian personality. We see this hunger graphically in the case of IQ scores. It is plain that IQ scoring does not represent a commitment to looking carefully at people's intelligence; when we do that, we see different and frequently uncorrelated *kinds* or *dimensions* of intelligence (Gardner). The persistent use of IQ scores represents the hunger to have a number so that everyone can have a rank. ("Ten!" mutter the guys when they see a pretty woman.)

Because ranking or grading has caused so much discomfort to so many students and teachers, I think we see a lot of confusion about the process. It is hard to think clearly about something that has given so many of us such anxiety and distress. The most notable confusion I notice is the tendency to think that if we renounce ranking or grading, we are renouncing the very possibility of judgment and discrimination—that we are embracing the idea that there is no way to distinguish or talk about the difference between what works well and what works badly.

So the most important point, then, is that *I am not arguing against judgment or evaluation*. I'm just arguing against that crude, oversimple way of *representing* judgment—distorting it, really—into a single number, which means ranking people and performances along a single continuum.

In fact I am arguing *for evaluation*. Evaluation means looking hard and thoughtfully at a piece of writing in order to make distinctions as to the quality of different features or dimensions. For example, the process of evaluation permits us to make the following kinds of statements about a piece of writing:

- The thinking and ideas seem interesting and creative.
- The overall structure or sequence seems confusing.
- The writing is perfectly clear at the level of individual sentences and even paragraphs.
- There is an odd, angry tone of voice that seems unrelated or inappropriate to what the writer is saying.
- Yet this same voice is strong and memorable and makes one listen even if one is irritated.
- There are a fair number of mistakes in grammar or spelling: more than "a sprinkling" but less than "riddled with."

To rank, on the other hand, is to be forced to translate those discriminations into a single number. What grade or holistic score do these judgments add up to? It's likely, by the way, that more readers would agree with those separate, "analytic" statements than would agree on a holistic score.

I've conducted many assessment sessions where we were not trying to impose a set of standards but rather to find out how experienced teachers read and evaluate, and I've had many opportunities to see that good readers give grades or scores right down through the range of possibilities. Of course good readers sometimes agree—especially on papers that are strikingly good or bad or conventional, but I think I see difference more frequently than agreement when readers really speak up.

The process of evaluation, because it invites us to articulate our criteria and to make distinctions among parts or features or dimensions of a performance, thereby invites us further to acknowledge the main fact about evaluation: that different readers have different priorities, values, and standards.

The conclusion I am drawing, then, in this first train of thought is that we should do less ranking and more evaluation. Instead of using grades or holistic scores—single number verdicts that try to sum up complex performances along only one scale—we should give some kind of written or spoken evaluation that discriminates among criteria and dimensions of the writing—and if possible that takes account of the complex context for writing: who the writer is, what the writer's audience and goals are, who we are as readers and how we read, and how we might differ in our reading from other readers the writer might be addressing.

But how can we put this principle into practice? The pressure for ranking seems implacable. Evaluation takes more time, effort, and money. It seems as though we couldn't get along without scores on writing exams. Most teachers are obliged to give grades at the end of each course. And many students—given that they have become conditioned or even addicted to ranking over the years and must continue to inhabit a ranking culture in most of their courses—will object if we don't put grades on papers. Some students, in the absence of that crude gold star or black mark, may not try hard enough (though how hard is "enough"—and is it really our job to stimulate motivation artificially with grades—and is grading the best source of motivation?).

It is important to note that there are certain schools and colleges that do *not* use single-number grades or scores, and they function successfully. I taught for nine years at Evergreen State College, which uses only written evaluations. This system works fine, even down to getting students accepted into high quality graduate and professional schools.

Nevertheless we have an intractable dilemma: that grading is unfair and counterproductive but that students and institutions tend to want grades. In the face of this dilemma there is a need for creativity and pragmatism. Here are some ways in which I and others use *less ranking* and *more evaluation* in teaching—and they suggest some adjustments in how we score large-scale assessments. What follows is an assortment of experimental compromises—sometimes crude, seldom ideal or utopian—but they help.

(a) Portfolios. Just because conventional institutions oblige us to turn in a single quantitative course grade at the end of every marking period, it doesn't follow that we need to grade individual papers. Course grades are more trustworthy and less damaging because they are based on so many performances over so many weeks. By avoiding frequent ranking or grading, we make it *somewhat* less likely for students to become addicted to oversimple numerical rankings—to think that evaluation always translates into a simple number—in short, to mistake ranking for evaluation. (I'm not trying to defend conventional course grades since they are still uncommunicative and they still feed the hunger for ranking.) Portfolios permit me to refrain from grading individual papers and limit myself to writerly evaluative comments—and help students see this as a positive rather than a negative thing, a chance to be graded on a body of their best work that can be judged more fairly. Portfolios have many other advantages as well. They are particularly valuable as occasions for asking students to write extensive and thoughtful explorations of their own strengths and weaknesses.

A midsemester portfolio is usually an informal affair, but it is a good occasion for giving anxious students a ballpark estimate of how well they are doing in the course so far. I find it helpful to tell students that I'm perfectly willing to tell them my best estimate of their course grade—but only if they come to me in conference and only during the second half of the semester. This serves somewhat to quiet their anxiety while they go through seven weeks of drying out from grades. By midsemester, most of them have come to enjoy not getting those numbers and thus being able to think better about more writerly comments from me and their classmates.

Portfolios are now used extensively and productively in larger assessments, and there is constant experimentation with new applications (Belanoff and Dickson; *Portfolio Assessment Newsletter; Portfolio News*).

(b) Another useful option is to make a strategic retreat from a wholly negative position. That is, I sometimes do a *bit* of ranking even on individual papers, using two "bottom-line" grades: H and U for "Honors" and "Unsatisfactory." I tell students that these translate to about A or A– and D or F. This practice may seem theoretically inconsistent with all the arguments I've just made, but (at the moment, anyway) I justify it for the following reasons.

First, I sympathize with a *part* of the students' anxiety about not getting grades: their fear that they might be failing and not know about it—or doing an excellent job and not get any recognition. Second, I'm not giving *many* grades; only a small proportion of papers get these H's or U's. The system creates a "non-bottom-line" or "non-quantified" atmosphere. Third, these holistic judgments about best and worst do not seem as arbitrary and questionable as most grades. There is usually a *bit* more agreement among readers about the best and worst papers. What seems most dubious is the process of trying to rank that whole middle range of papers—papers that have a mixture of better and worse qualities so that the numerical grade depends enormously on a reader's priorities or mood or temperament. My willingness to give these few grades goes a long way toward helping my students forgo most bottom-line grading.

I'm not trying to pretend that these minimal "grades" are truly reliable. But they represent a very small amount of ranking. Yes, someone could insist that I'm really ranking every single paper (and indeed if it seemed politically necessary, I could put an OK or S [for satisfactory] on all those middle range papers and brag, "Yes, I grade everything"). But the fact is that I am doing *much less sorting* since I don't have to sort them into five or even twelve piles. Thus there is a huge reduction in the total amount of unreliability I produce.

(It might seem that if I use only these few minimal grades I have no good way for figuring out a final grade for the course—since that requires a more fine-grained set of ranks. But I don't find that to be the case. For I also give these same minimal grades to the many other important parts of my course such as attendance, meeting deadlines, peer responding, and journal writing. If I want a mathematically computed grade on a scale of six or A through E, I can easily compute it when I have such a large number of grades to work from—even though they are only along a three-point scale.)

This same practice of crude or minimal ranking is a big help on larger assessments outside classrooms, and needs to be applied to the process of assessment in general. There are two important principles to emphasize. On the one hand we must be prudent or accommodating enough to admit that despite all the arguments against ranking, there *are* situations when we need that bottom-line verdict along one scale: which student has not done satisfactory work and should be denied credit for the course? which student gets the scholarship? which candidate to hire or fire? We often operate with scarce resources. But on the other hand we must be bold enough to insist that we do far more ranking than is really needed. We can get along not only with fewer occasions for assessment but also with fewer gradations in scoring. If we decide what the *real* bottom-line is on a given occasion—perhaps just "failing" or perhaps "honors" too—then the reading of papers or portfolios is enormously quick and cheap. It leaves time and money for evaluation—perhaps for analytic scoring or some comment.

At Stony Brook we worked out a portfolio system where multiple readers had only to make a binary decision: acceptable or not. Then individual teachers could decide the actual course grade and give comments for their own students—so long as those students passed in the eyes of an independent rater (Elbow and Belanoff; Belanoff and Elbow). The best way to begin to wean our society from its addiction to ranking may be to permit a tiny bit of it (which also means less unreliability)—rather than trying to go "cold turkey."

(c) Sometimes I use an analytic grid for evaluating and commenting on student papers. An example is given in Figure 1.

I often vary the criteria in my grid (e.g., "connecting with readers" or "investment") depending on the assignment or the point in the semester.

Grids are a way I can satisfy the students' hunger for ranking but still not give in to conventional grades on individual papers. Sometimes I provide nothing but a grid (especially on final drafts), and this is a very quick way to provide a response. Or on midprocess drafts I sometimes use a grid in addition to a comment: a more readerly comment that often doesn't so much tell them what's wrong or right or how to improve things but rather tries to give them an account of what is *happening to me* as I read their words. I think this kind of comment is really the most useful thing of all for students, but it frustrates some students for a while. The grid can help these students feel less anxious and thus pay better attention to my comment.

I find grids extremely helpful at the end of the semester for telling students their strengths and weaknesses in the course—or what they've done well and not so well. Besides categories like the ones above, I use categories like these: "skill in giving feedback to others," "ability to meet deadlines," "effort," and "improvement." This practice makes my final grade much more communicative.

(d) I also help make up for the absence of ranking—gold stars and black marks—by having students share their writing with each other a great deal both orally and through frequent publication in class magazines. Also, where possible, I try to get students to give or send writing to audiences outside the class. At the University of Massachusetts at Amherst, freshmen pay a ten dollar lab fee for the writing course, and every teacher publishes four or five class magazines of final drafts a semester. The effects are striking. Sharing, peer feedback, and publication give the best reward and motivation for writing, namely, getting your words out to many readers.

Strong	OK	Weak	
			CONTENT, INSIGHTS, THINKING, GRAPPLING WITH TOPIC
			GENUINE REVISION, SUBSTANTIVE CHANGES, NOT JUST EDITING
			ORGANIZATION, STRUCTURE, GUIDING THE READER
			LANGUAGE: SYNTAX, SENTENCES, WORDING, VOICE
			MECHANICS: SPELLING, GRAMMAR, PUNCTUATION, PROOFREADING
			OVERALL [Note: this is not a sum of the other scores.]

Figure 1.

(e) I sometimes use a kind of modified *contract grading.* That is, at the start of the course I pass out a long list of all the things that I most want students to do—the concrete activities that I think most lead to learning—and I promise students that if they do them *all* they are guaranteed a certain final grade. Currently, I say it's a B—it could be lower or higher. My list includes these items: not missing more than a week's worth of classes; not having more than one late major assignment; *substantive* revising on all major revisions; good copy editing on all final revisions; good effort on peer feedback work; keeping up the journal; and substantial effort and investment on each draft.

I like the way this system changes the "bottom-line" for a course: the intersection where my authority crosses their self-interest. I can tell them, "You have to work very hard in this course, but you can stop worrying about grades." The crux is no longer that commodity I've always hated and never trusted: a numerical ranking of the quality of their writing along a single continuum. Instead the crux becomes what I care about most: the *concrete behaviors* that I most want students to engage in because they produce more learning and help me teach better. Admittedly, effort and investment are not concrete observable behaviors, but they are no harder to judge than overall quality of writing. And since I care about effort and investment, I don't mind the few arguments I get into about them; they seem fruitful. ("Let's try and figure out why it looked to me as though you didn't put any effort in here.") In contrast, I hate discussions about grades on a paper and find such arguments fruitless. Besides, I'm not making fine distinctions about effort and investment—just letting a bell go off when they fall palpably low.

It's crucial to note that I am *not* fighting evaluation with this system. I am just fighting ranking or grading. I still write evaluative comments and often use an evaluative grid to tell my students what I see as strengths and weaknesses in their papers. My goal is not to get rid of evaluation but in fact to emphasize it, enhance it. I'm trying to get students to listen *better* to my evaluations—by uncoupling them from a grade. In effect, I'm doing this because I'm so fed up with students *following* or *obeying* my evaluations too blindly—making whatever changes my comments suggest but doing it for the sake of a grade; not really taking the time to make up their own minds about whether they think my judgments or suggestions really make sense to them. The worst part of grades is that they make students obey us without carefully thinking about the merits of what we say. I love the situation this system so often puts students in: I make a criticism or suggestion about their paper, but it doesn't matter to their grade whether they go along with me or not (so long as they genuinely revise in some fashion). They have to think; to decide.

Admittedly this system is crude and impure. Some of the really skilled students who are used to getting A's and desperate to get one in this course remain unhelpfully hung up about getting those H's on their papers. But a good number of these students discover that they can't get them, and they soon settle down to accepting a B and having less anxiety and more of a learning voyage.

The Limitations of Evaluation and the Benefits of Evaluation-free Zones

Everything I've said so far has been in praise of evaluation as a substitute for ranking. But I need to turn a corner here and speak about the *limits* or *problems* of evaluation. Evaluating may be better than ranking, but it still carries some of the same problems. That is, even though I've praised evaluation for inviting us to acknowledge that readers and contexts are different, nevertheless the very word *evaluation* tends to imply fairness or reliability or getting beyond personal or subjective preferences. Also, of course, evaluation takes a lot more time and work. To rank you just have to put down a number; holistic scoring of exams is cheaper than analytic scoring.

Most important of all, evaluation harms the climate for learning and teaching—or rather *too much* evaluation has this effect. That is, if we evaluate *everything* students write, they tend to remain tangled up in the assumption that their whole job in school is to give teachers "what they want." Constant evaluation makes students worry more about psyching out the teacher than about what they are really learning. Students fall into a kind of defensive or on-guard stance toward the teacher: a desire to hide what they don't understand and try to impress. This stance gets in the way of learning. (Think of the patient trying to hide symptoms from the doctor.) Most of all, constant evaluation by someone in authority makes students reluctant to take the risks that are needed for good learning—to try out hunches and trust their own judgment. Face it: if our goal is to get students to exercise their own judgment, that means exercising an immature and undeveloped judgment and making choices that are obviously wrong to us.

We see around us a widespread hunger to be evaluated that is often just as strong as the hunger to rank. Countless conditions make many of us walk around in the world wanting to ask others (especially those in authority), "How am I doing, did I do OK?" I don't think the hunger to be evaluated is as harmful as the hunger to rank, but it can get in the way of learning. For I find that the greatest and most powerful breakthroughs in learning occur when I can get myself and others to *put aside* this nagging, self-doubting question ("How am I doing? How am I doing?")—and instead to take some chances, trust our instincts or hungers. When everything is evaluated, everything counts. Often the most powerful arena for deep learning is a kind of "time out" zone from the pressures of normal evaluated reality: make-believe, play, dreams—in effect, the Shakespearian forest.

In my attempts to get away from too much evaluation (not from all evaluation, just from too much of it), I have drifted into a set of teaching practices which now feel to me like the *best* part of my teaching. I realize now what I've been unconsciously doing for a number of years: creating "evaluation-free zones."

(a) The paradigm evaluation-free zone is the ten-minute, nonstop freewrite. When I get students to freewrite, I am using my authority to create unusual conditions in order to contradict or interrupt our pervasive habit of always evaluating our writing. What is essential here are the two central features of freewriting: that it be private (thus I don't collect it or have students share it with anyone else); and that it be nonstop (thus there isn't time for planning, and control is usually diminished). Students quickly catch on and enter into the spirit. At the end of the course, they often tell me that freewriting is the most useful thing I've taught them (see Belanoff, Elbow, and Fontaine).

(b) A larger evaluation-free zone is the single unevaluated assignment—what people sometimes call the "quickwrite" or sketch. This is a piece of writing that I ask students to do—either in class or for homework—without any or much revising. It is meant to be low stakes writing. There is a bit of pressure, nevertheless, since I usually ask them to share it with others and *I* usually collect it and read it. But I don't write any comments at all—except perhaps to put straight lines along some passages I like or to write a phrase of appreciation at the end. And I ask students to refrain from giving evaluative feedback to each other—and instead just to say "thank you" or mention a couple of phrases or ideas that stick in mind. (However, this writing-without-feedback can be a good occasion for students to discuss the *topic* they have written about—and thus serve as an excellent kick-off for discussions of what I am teaching.)

(c) These experiments have led me to my next and largest evaluation-free zone—what I sometimes call a "jump start" for my whole course. For the last few semesters I've been devoting the first three weeks *entirely* to the two evaluation-free activities I've just described: freewriting (and also more leisurely private writing in a journal) and quickwrites or sketches. Since the stakes are low and I'm not asking for much revising, I ask for *much more* writing homework per week than usual. And every day we write in class: various exercises or games. The emphasis is on getting rolling, getting fluent, taking risks. And every day all students read out loud something they've written—sometimes a short passage even to the whole class. So despite the absence of feedback, it is a very audience-filled and sociable three weeks.

At first I only dared do this for two weeks, but when I discovered how fast the writing improves, how good it is for building community, and what a pleasure this period is for me, I went to three weeks. I'm curious to try an experiment with teaching a whole course this way. I wonder, that is, whether all that evaluation we work so hard to give really does any more good than the constant writing and sharing (Zak).

I need to pause here to address an obvious rejoinder: "But withholding evaluation is not normal!" Indeed, it is *not* normal—certainly not normal in school. We normally tend to emphasize evaluations—even bottom-line ranking kinds of evaluations. But I resist the argument that if it's not normal we shouldn't do it.

The best argument for evaluation-free zones is from experience. If you try them, I suspect you'll discover that they are satisfying and bring out good writing. Students have a better time writing these unevaluated pieces; they enjoy hearing and appreciating these pieces when they don't have to evaluate. And *I* have a much better time when I engage in this astonishing activity: reading student work when I don't have to evaluate and respond. And yet the writing improves. I see students investing and risking more, writing more fluently, and using livelier, more interesting voices. This writing gives me and them a higher standard of clarity and voice for when we move on to more careful and revised writing tasks that involve more intellectual pushing—tasks that sometimes make their writing go tangled or sodden.

The Benefits and Feasibility of Liking

Liking and disliking seem like unpromising topics in an exploration of assessment. They seem to represent the worst kind of subjectivity, the merest accident of personal taste. But I've recently come to think that the phenomenon of liking is perhaps the most important evaluative response for writers and teachers to think about. In effect, I'm turning another corner in my argument. In the first section I argued against ranking—with evaluating being the solution. Next I argued not *against* evaluating—but for no-evaluation zones in *addition* to evaluating. Now I will argue neither against evaluating nor against no-evaluation zones, but for something very different in addition, or perhaps underneath, as a foundation: liking.

Let me start with the germ story. I was in a workshop and we were going around the circle with everyone telling a piece of good news about their writing in the last six months. It got to Wendy Bishop, a good poet (who has also written two good books about the teaching of writing), and she said, "In the last six months, I've learned to *like* everything I write." Our jaws dropped; we were startled—in a way scandalized. But I've been chewing on her words ever since, and they have led me into a retelling of the story of how people learn to write better.

The old story goes like this: We write something. We read it over and we say, "This is terrible. I *hate* it. I've got to work on it and improve it." And we do, and it gets better, and this happens again and again, and before long we have become a wonderful writer. But that's not really what happens. Yes, we vow to work on it—but we don't. And next time we have the impulse to write, we're just a *bit* less likely to start.

What really happens when people learn to write better is more like this: We write something. We read it over and we say, "This is terrible. . . . But I *like* it. Damn it, I'm going to get it good enough so that others will like it too." And this time we don't just put it in a drawer, we actually work hard on it. And we try it out on other people too—not just to get feedback and advice but, perhaps more important, to find someone else who will like it.

Notice the two stories here—two hypotheses. (a) "First you improve the faults and then you like it." (b) "First you like it and then you improve faults." The second story may sound odd when stated so baldly, but really it's common sense. Only if we like something will we get involved enough to work and struggle with it. Only if we like what we write will we write again and again by choice—which is the only way we get better.

This hypothesis sheds light on the process of how people get to be published writers. Conventional wisdom assumes a Darwinian model: poor writers are unread; then they get better; as a result, they get a wider audience; finally they turn into Norman Mailer. But now I'd say the process is more complicated. People who get better and get published really tend to be driven by how much *they* care about their writing. Yes, they have a small audience at first—after all, they're not very good. But they try reader after reader until finally they can find people who like and appreciate their writing. I certainly did this. If someone doesn't like her writing enough to be pushy and hungry about finding a few people who also like it, she probably won't get better.

It may sound so far as though all the effort and drive comes from the lonely driven writer—and sometimes it does (Norman Mailer is no joke). But, often enough, readers play the crucially active role in this story of how writers get better. That is, the way writers *learn* to like their writing is by the grace of having a reader or two who likes it—even though it's not good. Having at least a few appreciative readers is probably indispensable to getting better.

When I apply this story to our situation as teachers I come up with this interesting hypothesis: *good writing teachers like student writing* (and like students). I think I see this borne out—and it is really nothing but common sense. Teachers who hate student writing and hate students are grouchy all the time. How could we stand our work and do a decent job if we hated their writing? Good teachers see what is only *potentially* good, they get a kick out of mere possibility—and they encourage it. When I manage to do this, I teach well.

Thus, I've begun to notice a turning point in my courses—two or three weeks into the semester: "Am I going to like these folks or is this going to be a battle, a struggle?" When I like them everything seems to go better—and it seems to me they learn more by the end. When I don't and we stay tangled up in struggle, we all suffer—and they seem to learn less.

So what am I saying? That we should like bad writing? How can we see all the weaknesses and criticize student writing if we just like it? But here's the interesting point: if I *like* someone's writing it's *easier* to criticize it.

I first noticed this when I was trying to gather essays for the book on freewriting that Pat Belanoff and Sheryl Fontaine and I edited. I would read an essay someone had written, I would want it for the book, but I had some serious criticism. I'd get excited and write, "I really like this, and I hope we can use it in our book, but you've got to get rid of this and change that, and I got really mad at this other thing." I usually find it hard to criticize, but I began to notice that

I was a much more critical and pushy reader when I liked something. It's even fun to criticize in those conditions.

It's the same with student writing. If I like a piece, I don't have to pussyfoot around with my criticism. It's when I don't like their writing that I find myself tiptoeing: trying to soften my criticism, trying to find something nice to say—and usually sounding fake, often unclear. I see the same thing with my own writing. If I like it, I can criticize it better. I have faith that there'll still be something good left, even if I train my full critical guns on it.

In short—and to highlight how this section relates to the other two sections of this essay—liking is not the same as ranking or evaluating. Naturally, people get them mixed up: when they like something, they assume it's good; when they hate it, they assume it's bad. But it's helpful to uncouple the two domains and realize that it makes perfectly good sense to say, "This is terrible, but I like it." Or, "This is good, but I hate it." In short, I am not arguing here *against* criticizing or evaluating. I'm merely arguing *for* liking.

Let me sum up my clump of hypotheses so far:

- It's not improvement that leads to liking, but rather liking that leads to improvement.
- It's the mark of good writers to like their writing.
- Liking is not the same as evaluating. We can often criticize something better when we like it.
- We learn to like our writing when we have a respected reader who likes it.
- Therefore, it's the mark of good teachers to like students and their writing.

If this set of hypotheses is true, what practical consequences follow from it? How can we be better at liking? It feels as though we have no choice—as though liking and not-liking just happen to us. I don't really understand this business. I'd love to hear discussion about the mystery of liking—the phenomenology of liking. I sense it's some kind of putting oneself out—or holding oneself open—but I can't see it clearly. I have a hunch, however, that we're not so helpless about liking as we tend to feel.

For in fact I can suggest some practical concrete activities that I have found fairly reliable at increasing the chances of liking student writing:

(a) I ask for lots of private writing and merely shared writing, that is, writing that I don't read at all, and writing that I read but don't comment on. This makes me more cheerful because it's so much easier. Students get *better* without me. Having to evaluate writing—especially bad writing—makes me more likely to hate it. This throws light on grading: it's hard to like something if we know we have to give it a D.

(b) I have students share lots of writing with each other—and after a while respond to each other. It's easier to like their writing when I don't feel myself as the only reader and judge. And so it helps to build community in general: it takes pressure off me. Thus I try to use peer groups not only for feedback, but for other activities too, such as collaborative writing, brainstorming, putting class magazines together, and working out other decisions.

(c) I increase the chances of my liking their writing when I get better at finding what *is* good—or *potentially* good—and learn to praise it. This is a skill. It requires a good eye, a good nose. We tend—especially in the academic world—to assume that a good eye or fine discrimination means *criticizing*. Academics are sometimes proud of their tendency to be bothered by what is bad. Thus I find I am sometimes looked down on as dumb and undiscriminating: "He likes bad writing. He must have no taste, no discrimination." But I've finally become angry rather than defensive. It's an act of discrimination to see what's good in bad writing. Maybe, in fact, this is the secret of the mystery of liking: to be able to see potential goodness underneath badness.

Put it this way. We tend to stereotype liking as a "soft" and sentimental activity. Mr. Rogers is our model. Fine. There's nothing wrong with softness and sentiment—and I love Mr. Rogers. But liking can also be hard-assed. Let me suggest an alternative to Mr. Rogers: B. F. Skinner. Skinner taught pigeons to play ping-pong. How did he do it? Not by moaning, "Pigeon standards are falling. The pigeons they send us these days are no good. When I was a pigeon. . . ." He did it by a careful, disciplined method that involved close analytic observation. He put pigeons on a ping-pong table with a ball, and every time a pigeon turned his head 30 degrees toward the ball, he gave a reward (see my "Danger of Softness").

What would this approach require in the teaching of writing? It's very simple . . . but not easy. Imagine that we want to teach students an ability they badly lack, for example how to organize their writing or how to make their sentences clearer. Skinner's insight is that we get nowhere in this task by just telling them how much they lack this skill: "It's disorganized. Organize it!" "It's unclear. Make it clear!"

No, what we must learn to do is to read closely and carefully enough to show the student little bits of *proto*-organization or *sort of* clarity in what they've already written. We don't have to pretend the writing is wonderful. We could even say, "This is a terrible paper and the worst part about it is the lack of organization. But I will teach you how to organize. Look here at this little organizational move you made in this sentence. Read it out loud and try to feel how it pulls together this stuff here and distinguishes it from that stuff there. Try to remember what it felt like writing that sentence—creating that piece of organization. Do it some more." Notice how much more helpful it is if we can say, "Do *more* of what you've done here," than if we say, "Do something *different* from anything you've done in the whole paper."

When academics criticize behaviorism as crude it often means that they aren't willing to do the close careful reading of student writing that is required. They'd rather give a cursory reading and turn up their nose and give a low grade and complain about falling standards. No one has undermined behaviorism's main principle of learning: that reward produces learning more effectively than punishment.

(d) I improve my chances of liking student writing when I take steps to get to know them a bit as people. I do this partly through the assignments I give. That is, I always ask them to write a letter or two to me and to each other (for example about their history with writing). I base at least a couple of assignments on their own experiences, memories, or histories. And I make sure some of the assignments are free choice pieces—which also helps me know them.

In addition, I make sure to have at least three conferences with each student each semester—the first one very early. I often call off some classes in order to keep conferences from being too onerous (insisting nevertheless that students meet with their partner or small group when class is called off). Some teachers have mini-conferences with students during class—while students are engaged in writing or peer group meetings. I've found that when I deal only with my classes as a whole—as a large group—I sometimes experience them as a herd or lump—as stereotyped "adolescents"; I fail to experience them as individuals. For me, personally, this is disastrous since it often leads me to experience them as that scary tribe that I felt rejected by when *I* was an eighteen-year-old—and thus, at times, as "the enemy." But when I sit down with them face to face, they are not so stereotyped or alien or threatening—they are just eighteen-year-olds.

Getting a glimpse of them as individual people is particularly helpful in cases where their writing is not just bad, but somehow offensive—perhaps violent or cruelly racist or homophobic or sexist—or frighteningly vacuous. When I know them just a bit I can often see behind their awful attitude to the person and the life situation that spawned it, and not hate their writing so much. When I know students I can see that they are smart behind that dumb behavior; they are doing the best they can behind that bad behavior. Conditions are keeping them from acting decently; something is holding them back.

(e) It's odd, but the more I let myself show, the easier it is to like them and their writing. I need to share some of my own writing—show some of my own feelings. I need to write the letter to them that they write to me—about my past experiences and what I want and don't want to happen.

(f) It helps to work on my own writing—and work on learning to *like* it. Teachers who are most critical and sour about student writing are often having trouble with their own writing. They are bitter or unforgiving or hurting toward their own work. (I think I've noticed that failed PhDs are often the most severe and difficult with students.) When we are stuck or sour in our own writing, what helps us most is to find spaces free from evaluation such as those provided by freewriting and journal writing. Also, activities like reading out loud and finding a supportive reader or two. I would insist, then, that if only for the sake of our teaching, we need to learn to be charitable and to like our own writing.

A final word. I fear that this sermon about liking might seem an invitation to guilt. There is enough pressure on us as teachers that we don't need someone coming along and calling us inadequate if we don't *like* our students and their writing. That is, even though I think I am right to make this foray into the realm of feeling, I also acknowledge that it is dangerous—and paradoxical. It strikes me that we also need to have permission to hate the dirty bastards and their stupid writing.

After all, the conditions under which they go to school bring out some awful behavior on their part, and the conditions under which we teach sometimes make it difficult for us to like them and their writing. Writing wasn't meant to be read in stacks of twenty-five, fifty, or seventy-five. And we are handicapped as teachers when students are in our classes against their will. (Thus high school teachers have the worst problem here, since their students tend to be the most sour and resentful about school.)

Indeed, one of the best aids to liking students and their writing is to be somewhat charitable toward ourselves about the opposite feelings that we inevitably have. I used to think it was terrible for teachers to tell those sarcastic stories and hostile jokes about their students: "teacher room talk." But now I've come to think that people who spend their lives teaching *need* an arena to let off this unhappy steam. And certainly it's better to vent this sarcasm and hostility with our buddies than on the students themselves. The question, then, becomes this: do we help this behavior function as a venting so that we can move past it and not be trapped in our inevitable resentment of students? Or do we tell these stories and jokes as a way of staying stuck in the hurt, hostile, or bitter feelings—year after year—as so many sad teachers do?

In short I'm not trying to invite guilt, I'm trying to invite hope. I'm trying to suggest that if we do a sophisticated analysis of the difference between liking and evaluating, we will see that it's possible (if not always easy) to like students and their writing—without having to give up our intelligence, sophistication, or judgment.

Let me sum up the points I'm trying to make about ranking, evaluating, and liking:

- Let's do as little ranking and grading as we can. They are never fair and they undermine learning and teaching.
- Let's use evaluation instead—a more careful, more discriminating, fairer mode of assessment.
- But because evaluating is harder than ranking, and because too much evaluating also undermines learning, let's establish small but important evaluation-free zones.
- And underneath it all—suffusing the whole evaluative enterprise—let's learn to be better likers: liking our own and our students' writing, and realizing that liking need not get in the way of clear-eyed evaluation.

Works Cited

Belanoff, Pat, and Peter Elbow. "Using Portfolios to Increase Collaboration and Community in a Writing Program." *WPA: Journal of Writing Program Administration* 9.3 (Spring 1986): 27–40. (Also in *Portfolios: Process and Product*. Ed. Pat Belanoff and Marcia Dickson. Portsmouth, NH: Boynton/Cook-Heinemann, 1991.)

Belanoff, Pat, Peter Elbow, and Sheryl Fontaine, eds. *Nothing Begins with N: New Investigations of Freewriting*. Carbondale: Southern Illinois UP, 1991.

Bishop, Wendy. *Something Old, Something New: College Writing Teachers and Classroom Change*. Carbondale: Southern Illinois UP, 1990.

———. *Released into Language: Options for Teaching Creative Writing*. Urbana: NCTE, 1990.

Diederich, Paul. *Measuring Growth in English*. Urbana: NCTE, 1974.

Elbow, Peter. "The Danger of Softness." *What Is English?* New York: MLA, 1990. 197–210.

Elbow, Peter, and Pat Belanoff. "State University of New York: Portfolio-Based Evaluation Program." *New Methods in College Writing Programs: Theory into Practice*. Ed. Paul Connolly and Teresa Vilardi. New York: MLA, 1986. 95–105. (Also in *Portfolios: Process and Product*. Ed. Pat Belanoff and Marcia Dickson. Portsmouth, NH: Boynton/Cook-Heinemann, 1991.)

Gardner, Howard. *Frames of Mind: The Theory of Multiple Intelligences*. New York: Basic, 1983.

Kirschenbaum, Howard, Sidney Simon, and Rodney Napier. *Wad-Ja-Get? The Grading Game in American Education*. New York: Hart, 1971.

Lewis, C. S. *Studies in Words*. 2nd ed. London: Cambridge UP, 1967.

Portfolio Assessment Newsletter. Five Centerpointe Drive, Suite 100, Lake Oswego, Oregon 97035.

Portfolio News. c/o San Dieguito Union High School District, 710 Encinitas Boulevard, Encinitas, CA 92024.

Smith, Barbara Herrnstein. *Contingencies of Value: Alternative Perspectives for Critical Theory*. Cambridge: Harvard UP, 1988.

White, Edward M. *Teaching and Assessing Writing*. San Francisco: Jossey-Bass, 1985.

Zak, Frances. "Exclusively Positive Responses to Student Writing." *Journal of Basic Writing* 9.2 (1990): 40–53.

RESPONDING TO STUDENT WRITING

Erika Lindemann

[From *A Rhetoric for Writing Teachers* by Erika Lindemann. 3rd ed. New York: Oxford UP, 1995. 216–45.]

(For biographical information, see page 55.)

In this chapter, Lindemann situates the practice of responding to student writing in the larger contexts of assessment and evaluation, helping teachers think through the several purposes and methods for responding. Lindemann suggests that teachers think of their assessments and comments as a form of teaching, and describes a step-by-step procedure that teachers can use as they consider how to respond most effectively to student writing. She concludes this chapter with a discussion of alternative assessment methods, as well as with practical advice for "handling the paper load." Lindemann's thoughtful synthesis of current research and practice will help teachers develop effective approaches for assessing and responding to their students' writing.

The writing teacher must not be a judge, but a physician. His job is not to punish, but to heal.

–Donald M. Murray

The Basics and Testing

The writing teacher's primary responsibility, Charles Cooper maintains, is to guide students through the composing process.

> To do that the teacher will have to be concerned mainly with the *essence* of compositions, rather than the *accidents* of transcriptions, to use Janet Emig's terms. Unfortunately, just as we're learning what to do about the essences, some people are using the talk about basic skills to revive misplaced concern with the accidents; but surely the *most* basic of all the writing skills are matters of persona, audience, and purpose and the word and sentence adjustments the writer makes as he tries to speak with a certain voice to a special audience on a particular topic. ("Responding to Student Writing," p. 32)

Perhaps no words have generated as much controversy among teachers, parents, and the public as "basics," "minimal competence," and "testing." For most people, each word has psychologically comfortable, positive connotations. Who can oppose what is basic? Surely none of us supports *in*competence. And how many of us mathematically inept English teachers would dispute the numbers that experts attach to tests? As a society we've learned to trust statistics. I.Q. scores reveal how smart we are. SAT and ACT scores determine whether or not we may enter college. "Leading economic indicators" tell us our dollars won't buy what they did ten years ago. Insurance figures predict how we're likely to die. Casualty figures released weekly during the Vietnam war told us we were winning.

With similar illogic, many people believe that we can solve educational problems through legislatively mandated competency tests. Test results presumably will tell us if students learn, teachers teach, and the curriculum is sound. "The effectiveness of minimum competency tests," writes Kenneth Goodman, "depends on the truth of some or all of five propositions:

1. Failure to achieve is due to a lack of school standards.
2. Student failure is largely the result of lack of teacher concern for student success, or teacher mediocrity or both.
3. Solutions for teaching-learning problems are built into current, traditional materials and methods.
4. Test performance is the same as competence; furthermore, existing tests can be used for accurate individual assessment and prediction.
5. If students are required to succeed they will.

None of these propositions, however, is true. ("Minimum Standards: A Moral View," p. 5)

For many educators, going "back to the basics" has become synonymous with going back to the secure good old days, which our selective memories usually recall as having been better than the good old present. In the main, advocates of testing programs are concerned about students, understand the problems teachers face, and want to help solve those problems. Testing students, they believe, will help resolve the literacy crisis.

Many researchers, however, insist that standardized tests aren't valid measures of writing performance. "Although widely used," write Charles Cooper and Lee Odell, "standardized tests measure only editing skills—choosing the best sentence, recognizing correct usage, punctuation, and capitalization" (*Evaluating Writing*, p. viii). Writing teachers, confronted with considerable pressure to submit to accountability-through-testing must educate themselves about the uses and abuses of tests.[1] To support teachers and encourage the responsible use of writing tests, the Conference on College Composition and Communication, a constituent organization of the National Council of Teachers of English, has adopted the following Resolution on Testing and Writing:

RESOLVED: that

1. No student shall be given credit for a writing course, placed in a remedial writing course, exempted from a required writing course, or certified for competency without submitting a piece of written discourse.
2. Responsibility for giving credit, exemption, or accreditation shall rest, not with local administrators or state officials, but with the composition faculty in each institution.
3. Tests of writing shall be selected and administered under the primary control and supervision of representatives of the composition faculty in each institution.
4. Before multiple choice or so-called objective tests are used, the complexities involved in such testing shall be carefully considered. Most important, these tests shall be examined to determine whether they are appropriate to the intended purpose.
5. Before essay tests are used, the complexities of such tests shall be carefully considered. Most importantly, topics shall be designed with great care. Also, readers of the essay tests shall be trained according to principles of statistically reliable holistic and/or analytic reading.
6. The nature and purpose of the test and the various uses of the results shall be clearly explained to all instructors and students prior to the administration of the test.
7. All possible steps shall be taken to educate the universities and colleges, the public and legislatures that, though composition faculties have principal responsibility for helping students develop writing skills, maintenance of these skills is a responsibility shared by the entire faculty, administration, and the public.
8. The officers and Executive Committee of CCCC shall make testing a major concern in the immediate future in order to provide information and assistance to composition instructors affected by a testing situation.

The impulse to assess competence in writing is not solely an educational issue. Nor is it simply a concern of writing teachers. Increasing economic and political pressures will make testing our students' writing abilities a concern well into the twenty-first century. Although high school teachers are thoroughly familiar with the impulse to "teach to the test," many college teachers have yet to discover how large-scale testing programs affect curriculum, soak up an institution's funding for writing courses, and undermine teachers' authority to assign grades. Whenever possible, teachers should involve themselves in these issues so that students, who are rarely consulted, may demonstrate their writing abilities in ways that are educationally sound and so that teachers in other disciplines will assume greater responsibility for having students write.

Describing, Measuring, Judging

The papers in Cooper and Odell's *Evaluating Writing: Describing, Measuring, Judging* (1977) provide a comprehensive discussion of techniques for evaluating students' writing. Because writing evaluations have many uses, the editors caution, "It is critical for teachers . . . to know why they are evaluating before they choose measures and procedures" (p. ix). We may evaluate writing for any one of at least eleven reasons:

Administrative

1. Predicting students' grades in English courses.
2. Placing or tracking students or exempting them from English courses.
3. Assigning public letter or number grades to particular pieces of writing and to students' work in an English course.

Instructional

4. Making an initial diagnosis of students' writing problems.
5. Guiding and focusing feedback to student writers as they progress through an English course.

Evaluation and Research

6. Measuring students' growth as writers over a specific time period.
7. Determining the effectiveness of a writing program or a writing teacher.
8. Measuring group differences in writing performance in comparison-group research.
9. Analyzing the performance of a writer chosen for a case study.
10. Describing the writing performance of individuals or groups in developmental studies, either cross-sectional or longitudinal in design.
11. Scoring writing in order to study possible correlates of writing performance.

(Evaluating Writing, p. ix)

This chapter concerns itself principally with the fourth and fifth purposes for evaluating writing. When we diagnose writing problems (item 4 in the list above), we examine students' work descriptively, not to grade it or to respond with comments that students will read, but to determine simply what strengths and weaknesses characterize the paper. "Joan organizes her paper well and knows how to support her main points," we might note, "but her evidence is skimpy, she constructs paragraphs with only two levels of generality, and she consistently misspells words with *ance/ence* and *able/ible* suffixes." Such diagnostic evaluations permit us to design a course of instruction that enhances Joan's development as a writer. For this reason, many teachers treat the first writing assignment diagnostically. It isn't graded; it's mined for information that helps us plan what to teach.

When we respond to student writing (item 5 in the list above) or encourage students to respond to one another's work, we "guide and focus feedback," helping students understand how a reader perceives the writer's message. Sometimes we provide this feedback in conferences; sometimes we train students to give their classmates good advice. Most of the time, our feedback takes the form of written comments intended to help a student revise a draft or improve a subsequent paper. Writing comments is a form of teaching, a conference on paper. Comments that enhance learning differ from traditional methods of hunting errors and identifying what's wrong with a paper. They also must point out what the student did well, why certain problems undermine effective communication, and how to improve the paper. Comments that teach help students develop effective prewriting, writing, and rewriting strategies. Comments that teach are an open-ended form of evaluation that allows students, guided by responses from their teacher and classmates, to rewrite their drafts or engage the next assignment.

Grading, however, is a closed procedure. Once we assign a grade, we've judged the paper in ways that further revision can't change. Although comments may accompany the grade, most students interpret them not as "feedback" but as justification for the judgment we've made. From the student's perspective a graded paper is "finished," and additional work won't change either the grade or their feelings about succeeding or failing. Grades represent a necessary form of evaluation, but in this chapter we'll discuss some ways in which grades and our written comments can have a less destructive impact than traditional methods promote.[2]

Diagnostic Reading

The best way to assess students' strengths and weaknesses as writers is to examine carefully samples of their work, ideally two short papers with different discourse aims. Written in class during the first week of the course, these writing samples can tell us what students have already mastered and what areas we need to emphasize. Additional diagnostic evaluations at midterm help us identify improvements students have made since the course began, new problems that emerged as students overcame previous weaknesses, and difficulties that we somehow failed to address and that now need a different approach. At the end of the course, diagnostic evaluations help us determine how students' writing has improved and where the course has failed them.

When we examine a paper diagnostically, we're concerned primarily with describing rather than judging or grading it. Although we inevitably compare it to some mental criteria for effective writing, our primary purpose isn't to determine a letter grade. Rather, we want to know how the students write, what they're having trouble with, and why. To demonstrate the procedure, let's examine David's paper, written in forty-five minutes during the second meeting of a first-semester college composition class:

Assignment: Write an essay in which you discuss the way or ways you expect your life to differ from your parents' lives.[3]

> As time changes people's views and outlooks on life change with it. My parents grew up with completely diffrent standards in a completely diffrent time. Because of the time I grew up in, and the time I live in, my life differs greatly from the lives of my parents.
> Modern society offers more aid to young people—jobs, school, financial— that my parents could never recieve. Because of this aid my life has been more free than theirs ever was. I have more free time on my hands than they ever did. My parents were, and are, always working to keep and get, the things needed for survival in this life.
> Also Because of a higher education than the education of my parents I have diffrent outlooks on life. I have a more well-rounded attitude toward life. I tend to take more things for granted that my parents never would.
> We now live in a world of entertainment. My generation has more things in which to occupy their free time that my parents never had.
> Because of the time gap separating my parents an I, I have a diffrent lifestyle than they. Lifestyles change with the change of time, and with that so do people's outlook on life.

First we need to look at the assignment. Because it doesn't specify an audience, we shouldn't be surprised to discover that David addresses his composition to his stereotype of the Teacher or to no one in particular. The assignment specifies or implies a mode ("differ" suggests contrast or classification) and a form ("essay"). The topic permits students to draw on personal experience, but it's much too broad. The aim or purpose also may be troublesome because "discuss" can imply "inform," "argue," "explain," and a host of other possibilities. The assignment offers no prewriting help or criteria for success and consequently invites a vague, general response. Given the forty-five-minute time limit, we also can assume that David spent little time prewriting or rewriting the paper.

Indeed, David handled the topic fairly generally. Most of the paragraphs contain only one or two levels of generality. Most of the nouns identify abstractions ("views and outlooks," "modern society," "young people," "well-rounded attitude," "world of entertainment," "lifestyle"). However, David does attempt some classification. He subordinates "jobs, school, financial" to "aid" in paragraph two and identifies in the three body paragraphs three ways his life differs from his parents'. More "aid" gives him free time and freedom from worry; more education gives him different outlooks on life; a world of entertainment occupies his free time. At the same time, David maintains considerable distance between himself, his subject, and his audience, a stance characteristic of most first papers. Although he probably has quite a bit to say about his life, he might not choose to say it here, certainly not in writing, a more discomfiting medium than speech, and not to a stranger, which is how he must regard his English teacher at the beginning of the term.

Although David hasn't generated enough details to develop the paper effectively, it nevertheless has a structure. He's mastered the five-paragraph formula. The first and last paragraphs repeat the idea that "time gaps" separating two generations create different lifestyles and outlooks on life. The three body paragraphs attempt to develop separate subtopics, but the material overlaps, especially when he talks about "free time." David's writing, like that of most first-year students, seems form bound. Form precedes content. David thinks first of the five-paragraph mold and then attempts to find enough material to fill it. He probably needs practice identifying several ways of organizing his work, discovering form *in*, rather than imposing it *on*, the material prewriting generates.

That David stretches himself to find enough to say, a problem prewriting could help him with, also is evident in sentence construction. Students who fear they can't meet a 500-word limit or some self-imposed length requirement often pad their sentences, especially at the end. David does too. The first sentence, for example, might have ended with *change*, but afraid that the paper won't be long enough or that he won't find its message, David adds "with it." Similarly in paragraphs two and three, "in this life" and "toward life" extend sentences that could have closed with *survival* and *attitude* respectively. David writes predominantly simple sentences, but he knows at least one kind of subordination. Four sentences begin with *because*-clauses; the first sentence, with an *as*-clause. He may be avoiding more complex constructions because they'll create additional comma problems; he plays it safe. Risk-free, ungraded sentence-combining exercises might give him greater confidence in varying sentence structures and punctuating them.

Because David writes his way around comma problems, the paper doesn't offer enough evidence to diagnose the logic governing its mispunctuation. Two introductory *because*-clauses are set off; two aren't. The comma in the last sentence correctly separates two independent clauses joined by *and*, but elsewhere, in the first two paragraphs, *and* may govern the misuse of commas. To get at the logic behind these errors, we'd need to discuss the paper with David, asking him why he thinks the misused commas belong there, then pointing out where he's used the comma conventionally and encouraging him to apply what he's done right to the mispunctuated sentences.

A conference with David also might help us understand the logic governing comparisons. David deliberately alternates the conjunction *than* with the relative pronoun *that* to complete comparisons:

That Constructions

Subject + Verb + <u>more</u> aid to young people . . . <u>that</u> my parents could (never)

receive.

Subject + Verb + to take <u>more</u> things for granted <u>that</u> my parents (never)

would.

Subject + Verb + <u>more</u> things . . . <u>that</u> my parents (never) had.

Than Constructions

Clause + Subject + Verb + <u>more</u> free <u>than</u> theirs (ever) was.

Subject + Verb + <u>more</u> free time . . . <u>than</u> they (ever) had.

Also Because of a <u>higher</u> education <u>than</u> the education of my parents.

Subject + Verb + a <u>different</u> lifestyle <u>than</u> they.

In English, we complete comparisons with *than* (or *as*), not *that*. David, however, completes negative comparisons (signaled by *never*) with *that* and positive comparisons (signaled by *ever* or by affirmative phrases and clauses) with *than*. By discussing with him the chart above, we could help him understand two strategies for rewriting the "that constructions": (1) keep *that* but get rid of *more*, or (2) keep *more* but change *that* to *than*.

The paper contains only a few misspellings. *Diffrent* (four times) and *seperating* (once) are logical transcriptions of how most speakers pronounce these words. *An* (for *and*) may not be a "pronunciation spelling" because David spells *and* correctly elsewhere; he probably just left off the *d* as he hurried to finish. In misspelling *receive* as *recieve*, he logically writes "i before e" but forgets (or never confidently learned) "except after c." We might ask him to begin a spelling log, entering these words in one column and their correct spellings in another, so that he can discover which words and sound patterns are likely to give him trouble.[4]

When I analyze a first paper, I make notes about what I've found on a separate sheet kept in each student's folder. Students never see my notes, but I refer to them throughout the term. They help me decide what writing problems each student should work on and permit me to record a student's progress. Because David can't work on everything at once without becoming frustrated, I would select only one or two areas to emphasize as he rewrites this paper or plans the next one. For David (and doubtless other members of the class), careful prewriting would effect the greatest change in future papers. Writing from an overabundance of material would lengthen paragraphs, help him better support generalizations, and perhaps remove the need to pad sentences. Prewriting also might help him find alternative patterns of arrangement in material, reducing his dependence on the five-paragraph model. In the meantime, he can begin a spelling log and practice ungraded sentence-combining exercises to expand his inventory of subordinate constructions and increase his confidence about using commas.

With practice, you can read a paper diagnostically in two or three minutes. At first it helps to describe the features in detail, but after a while, a few brief notes will remind you of problems the student has overcome, new areas to work on, and questions you need more evidence to answer. Diagnostic readings reveal not only what the student has done but also how and why, allowing you to hypothesize about the causes of writing problems. Merely to identify a paper's errors and attach a letter grade is to ignore considerable evidence that can make your teaching more effective and the student's progress surer.

Teaching through Comments

Diagnostic reading is essentially a private response to a composition. We're discussing it with ourselves, explaining its patterns of features and planning a course of instruction for the student. When we write comments, on the other hand, we're communicating with a different audience, the student. As with any communication, purpose governs how we express the message and how our audience is likely to respond. The only appropriate purpose for comments on students' papers is to offer feedback and guide learning. Some comments, however, seem written for other reasons: to damn the paper with faint praise or snide remarks, to prove that the teacher is a superior error hunter, to vent frustration with students, to condemn or disagree with the writer's ideas, to confuse the writer with cryptic correction symbols.[5] Most of us learned how to comment on papers by first surviving and then imitating the responses of teachers to our own work. Few of us, I suspect, looked forward to getting our papers back (except to learn the grade) and could probably sympathize with the following assessment of the experience:

> Confused and angry, he stared at the red marks on his paper. He had awked again. And he had fragged. He always awked and fragged. On every theme, a couple of awks and a frag or two. And the inevitable puncs and sp's. The cw's didn't bother him anymore. He knew that the teacher preferred words like courage and contemptible person to guts and fink. The teacher had dismissed guts and fink as slang, telling students never to use slang in their themes. But he liked to write guts and fink; they meant something to him. Besides, they were in the dictionary. So why couldn't he use them when they helped him say what he wanted to say? He rarely got to say what he wanted to say in an English class, and when he did, he always regretted it. But even that didn't bother him much. He really didn't care anymore.
>
> How do you keep from awking, he asked himself. The question amused him for a moment; all questions in English class amused him for a moment. He knew what awk meant; he looked it up once in the handbook in the back of the grammar book as the teacher told him to. But the illustration didn't help him much. He got more awks, and he quit looking in the handbook. He simply decided that he oughtn't awk when he wrote even though he didn't know how to stop awking.
>
> Why not frag now and then, he wondered for almost thirty seconds. Writers fragged. Why couldn't he? Writers could do lots of things. Why couldn't he? But he forgot the question almost as quickly as it entered his mind. No sense worrying about it, he told himself. You'll only live to frag again.
>
> Damn, he whispered. He knew it had to be damn. He decided that the teacher didn't have the guts to write damn when she was angry with what he wrote. She just wrote dm in the margin. She told the class it meant dangling modifier, but he was sure it meant damn.
>
> Choppy! He spat the word out to no one in particular. He always got at least one choppy. "Mature thoughts should be written in long, balanced sentences," the teacher said once. He guessed his thoughts weren't balanced. Choppy again.

But he didn't care anymore. He'd just chop his way through English class until he never had to write again.

He stared at the encircled *and* at the beginning of one of his sentences. The circle meant nothing at first. Then he remembered the teacher's saying something about never beginning sentences with a conjunction. He didn't know why she said it; writers did it. But he guessed that since he wasn't a writer he didn't have that privilege.

The rep staggered him. The teacher had drawn a red line from the red rep to the word commitment. He had used it four times. It fit, he thought. You need commitment if you believe in the brotherhood of man, he argued with himself. Why did she write the red rep? He didn't know. But there were so many things he didn't know about writing.

Why do we have to write anyway, he asked himself. He didn't know. No good reason for it, he thought. Just write all the time to show the teacher that you can't write.

Most of the time he didn't know why he was asked to write on a specific topic, and most of the time he didn't like the topic or he didn't know too much about it. He had written on the brotherhood of man four times during the last four years. He had doubts about man's brotherhood to man. People really got shook about it only during National Brotherhood Week, he had written once in a theme. The rest of the year they didn't much care about their fellow man, only about themselves, he had written. The teacher didn't like what he said. That teacher, a man, wrote in the margin: "How can you believe this? I disagree with you. See me after class." He didn't show up. He didn't want another phony lecture on the brotherhood of man.

That wasn't the only time a teacher disagreed with what he wrote. One even sent him to the principal's office for writing about his most embarrassing moment even though she had assigned the topic. She told the principal he was trying to embarrass her. But all he did was write about his most embarrassing moment, just as she had told him to. And it was a gas. Another time a teacher told him to write about how a daffodil feels in spring. He just wrote *chilly* on a piece of paper and handed it in. The teacher was furious. But he didn't care. He didn't give a dm about daffodils in spring. He didn't care much about what he did last summer either, but the teacher seemed to.

He looked for the comment at the end of the theme. Trite. Nothing else; just trite. He usually got a trite. It would probably mean a D on his report card, but he didn't care. It was hard for him not to be trite when he wrote on the brotherhood of man for the fourth time in four years. He used all the clichés. The teacher wanted them, he thought. So he gave them to her. But he was never sure just what the teacher wanted. Some kids said they had figured out just what the teachers wanted. They said they knew what kinds of words, what kinds of thoughts, and what kinds of sentences she liked. They said they had her "psyched out"; that's why they got A's. But he didn't have her psyched out, and he wasn't going to worry about it anymore.

Every week she told the class to write a theme on some topic, and he knew that she picked out the topics because she liked them. Every week—"Write a theme on such and such." Nothing else—just those instructions. So he gave the topic a few minutes' thought and wrote whatever came to mind. He thought in clichés when he tried to write for her. They were safe, he once thought. But maybe not. Trite again.

He wadded up the brotherhood of man and threw it toward the waste basket. Missed. He always missed—everything.

Drop out, fink, he told himself. Why not? He didn't know what was going on. A dropout. He smiled. Frag, he thought. Can't use dropout all alone. He knew it was a frag. At least he had learned something. The bell rang. No more awks, no more frags, no more meaningless red marks on papers. No more writing about daffodils and the brotherhood of man—until next week. (Edward B. Jenkinson and Donald A. Seybold, "Prologue," *Writing as a Process of Discovery*, pp. 3–6).

As this student's plight reveals, comments that simply point out errors or justify a grade tend to ignore the student who reads them. Formative comments, on the other hand, the kind that support learning, praise what has worked well, demonstrate how or why something else didn't, and encourage students to try new strategies. In an essay describing several approaches to formative evaluation, Mary Beaven defines six assumptions on which to base our written responses to students' writing:

1. Growth in writing is a highly individualistic process that occurs slowly, sometimes over a much longer period of time than the six-, ten-, or even fifteen-week periods teachers and researchers usually allow.
2. Through their evaluatory comments and symbols teachers help to create an environment for writing. Establishing a climate of trust, in which students feel free to explore topics of interest to them without fear that their thoughts will be attacked, is essential.
3. Risk taking, trying new behaviors as one writes, and stretching one's use of language and toying with it are important for growth in writing. As writers break out of old, "safe" composing behaviors, they often make *more* mistakes until they become comfortable with new ways of using language. Teachers must encourage and support this kind of risk taking and mistake making.
4. Goal setting is also an important process in the development of students. Goals need to be concrete and within reach, and students need to see evidence of their progress. Teachers, then, should urge students to work toward a limited number of goals at a time.
5. Writing improvement does not occur in isolation because writing is related to speaking, listening, reading, and all other avenues of communication, including the experience of living. Prewriting activities, responding to literature, class discussion, revisions, developing a sensitivity to self and others, experiences both in and out of the English classroom affect growth in writing.
6. Effective formative evaluation depends on our understanding clearly other procedures that encourage growth in writing: diagnosing what students are able to do; arranging for writing often in many modes; discussing usage, syntactical, and rhetorical deficiencies by working with the students' own writing, not by preteaching rules; giving feedback and encouragement; assessing how much growth individuals have shown, without comparing them to one another and without expecting "mastery" of some uniform class standard.

(Adapted from Evaluating Writing, pp. 136–38)

Beaven's assumptions are crucial because much research argues against commenting on students' papers—ever. Surveying this research, George Hillocks concludes: "The results of all these studies strongly suggest that teacher comment has little impact on student writing" (*Research on Written Composition,* p. 165). It makes no difference whether the comments are tape-recorded or written; appear in the margins or at the end of the paper; are frequent or infrequent; are positive, negative, or a mixture of both (though students receiving negative criticism wrote less and developed negative attitudes about themselves as writers and about writing). "Indeed, several [studies] show no pre-to-post gains for *any* groups, regardless of the type of comment" (p. 165). In the face of this evidence, writing teachers must consider whether or not they should even invest their time in commenting on students' work. I believe they should, but only under two circumstances: (1) if the comments are focused, and (2) if students also have opportunities actively to apply criteria for good writing to their own work. The studies Hillocks surveyed "indicate rather clearly that engaging young writers actively in the use of criteria, applied to their own or to others' writing, results not only in more effective revisions but in superior first drafts" (p. 160).

With these assumptions in mind, let's return to David's paper, not to read it diagnostically this time, but to respond to it as we would if we planned to return it to him. I've reproduced the paper twice so that we can compare the responses of two different teachers.

As time changes people's views and outlooks on life change with it. My

Sp parents grew up with completely <u>diffrent</u> standards in a completely <u>diffrent</u> time.
Rep.

p Because of the time I grew up in◦and the time I live in, my life differs greatly

from the lives of my parents.

Modern society offers more aid to young people—jobs, school, financial—

≠ than   *ever*
Sp that my parents could never <u>recieve</u>. Because of this aid my life has been more

cliché
free than theirs ever was. I have more free time on my hands than they ever did.

P My parents were◦and are◦always working to keep and get◦the things needed for

survival in this life.

b   *I have more education than my parents do*
Also, <u>B</u>ecause of a higher education than the education of my parents I have

cliché
diffrent outlooks on life. I have a more well-rounded attitude toward life. I tend

cliché
to take more things for granted that my parents never would.

Not a ¶   We now live in a world of entertainment. My generation has more things
awk ?

ⓘn which to occupy their free time that my parents never had.

Sp   Because of the time gap <u>seperating</u> my parents <u>an</u> I, I have a <u>diffrent</u> lifeⓢtyle

Rep. than they. Lifeⓢtyles change with the change of time, and with that so do people's

outlook on life.

Avoid clichés and be more specific.
Proofread for spelling and comma problems.

As time changes people's views and outlooks on life change with it. My

✔✔ *Beginning a paper is tough, isn't it? Notice how the sentences in this paragraph*
parents grew up with completely diffrent standards in a completely diffrent time.

repeat one idea three times. Can you tell us instead why you think these differences
Because of the time I grew up in, and the time I live in, my life differs greatly

are interesting?
from the lives of my parents.

A good point. Do you have a job? Are you on scholarship?
Modern society offers more aid to young people—jobs, school, financial—that my

✔ parents could never recieve. Because of this aid my life has been more free than

Specifically,
theirs ever was. I have more free time on my hands than they ever did. My parents

what did your parents have to worry about that you don't?
were, and are, always working to keep and get, the things needed for survival

in this life.

✔　　Also Because of a higher education than the education of my parents I

Such as? Can you give some examples of how
✔ have diffrent outlooks on life. I have a more well-rounded attitude toward life. I

your attitude or outlook differs from your parents?
tend to take more things for granted that my parents never would.

What does this phrase mean?　　　　　*Such as?*
We now live in a <u>world of entertainment</u>. My generation has more things in

What do you do with your free time? What did they do?
which to occupy their free time that my parents never had.

✔✔✔　　Because of the time gap seperating my parents an I, I have a diffrent lifestyle than they.

Lifestyles change with the change of time, and with that so do people's outlook on life.

You have a strong sense of how to organize your paper. You divide the general idea in your first and last paragraph into "aid," "education," and "entertainment," the sub-topics of your three body paragraphs. Your readers will want more specific information about each of these sub-topics. Examples would help us "see" the differences between you and your parents' "outlooks" and "life styles." Before you write your next draft, consider the questions I've written. Go back over the draft, asking of each sentence how? why? in what ways? such as? Then spend at least thirty minutes jotting down examples or incidents that might explain or support each sub-topic. Please log the spelling problems in your journal and bring it to your conference next week. Each check in the margin represents one misspelling in that line of your paper. If you can't account for all of the check marks, I'll be glad to help.

The first set of comments identifies and corrects errors. In addition to placing symbols and abbreviations in the left margin, the teacher underlines misspellings, circles punctuation problems, and rewrites some of David's prose. Comments at the end of the paper address generally what's wrong with the piece and recommend a few changes (but notice the commanding tone of the imperative verbs). For several reasons, this traditional scheme fails to teach writing. First, David may not know what the marginal abbreviations refer to. By frustrating trial and error he may have learned that *P* can mean "passive," "punctuation," "pronoun," "poor phrasing," "point?"—take your pick. *Awk* and its not-so-distant cousin *?* communicate "the teacher didn't like what I said here for some reason." David must puzzle out the reason, guess *why* the phrasing is awkward, and predict as best he can *how* to rewrite it.

Second, the comments don't help David become an independent judge of his own prose. Finding his mistakes underlined again and again, or circled, or corrected, he can easily conclude that he has no responsibility for finding problems he's previously overlooked. The teacher, he believes, will find his mistakes for him. Then, because teachers *always* discover a few errors, he can dismiss the corrections in an effort to protect himself from criticism. Such circular reasoning, which the teacher abets, won't make him a self-sufficient editor.

Third, the comments presuppose that David knew more than in fact he did. They assume that his errors result from carelessness or failure to apply the rules. Perhaps the teacher believes that David overlooked mistakes, didn't proofread his paper, or worse, defied conventions repeatedly discussed in class. David, however, didn't intend to do poorly; he probably wanted to please his teacher and earn a good grade. Except for mistakes prompted by haste, students write errors because they don't know that they *are* writing errors.

Finally, because most of the comments address problems at the level of the word, David is likely to conclude that writing well is largely a matter of "getting the words right." In failing to comment on broader concerns, the teacher promotes the view that purpose, audience, and what a writer wants to say matter very little. The teacher remains an editor, not an "aid-itor," refusing to *respond* to the piece in ways a reader would.

In *Errors and Expectations: A Guide for the Teacher of Basic Writing* (1977), Mina Shaughnessy maintains, "The errors students make . . . no matter how peculiar they may sound to a teacher, are the result not of carelessness or irrationality but of *thinking*" (p. 105). She bases this conclusion on a study of 4,000 essays written between 1970 and 1974 by students entering City College in New York, which had just opened its doors to large numbers of basic writers. She describes and classifies the problems she finds, devoting chapters of her book to problems of handwriting and punctuation; derailed syntax; common errors of tense, inflection, and agreement; spelling errors; vocabulary problems; and errors beyond the level of the sentence. She supports her discussion with copious examples from student papers.

Shaughnessy reads the unique genre called "student writing" in ways that explain how and why errors appear. "Once he grants students the intelligence and will they need to master what is being taught," she argues, "the teacher begins to look at his students' difficulties in a more fruitful way: he begins to search in what students write and say for clues to their reasoning and their purposes, and in what *he* does for gaps and misjudgments" (p. 292). Although errors may appear to us unconventional ways of using language, they are logical; they reflect unique rules and hypotheses students devise to attempt communication. Errors also are regular; they occur in deliberate, often ingenious patterns.

Instead of isolating mistakes in line after line of a student's work, Shaughnessy encourages us to examine the paper systematically for *patterns* of error, reconstructing the student's unique grammar and formulating hypotheses to explain why or how the patterns developed. What a student does right also may explain the pattern, especially when errors seem partially under control or result from mislearning or misapplying some textbook pronouncement. Whenever our own logic, the logic of the fluent writer, prevents us from discovering the rationale behind a pattern of errors, we must seek an explanation for it by discussing the evidence with the student.[6]

As the second teacher, I responded to David's paper differently. Notice that I didn't mark everything. That doesn't mean I overlooked problems; instead, I chose to address only a few manageable ones. Because David can't work on everything at once, he needs some help defining priorities. Some teachers may feel irresponsible in not marking every mistake, but with practice those pangs of guilt will diminish. Or we can redirect them by helping students log their own errors, signaled by checks in the margin. The purpose of our comments, remember, isn't to compete with other teachers in an error-hunting contest but to guide students' learning. Just as a class meeting organizes discussion around one or two topics, so too limiting the scope of our comments makes learning more efficient.

Second, the comments don't label problems; rather, they emphasize how and why communication fails. The questions create a kind of dialogue between David and me. In answering them, David must reread what he's written, eventually learning to ask similar questions of subsequent drafts. If the comments balance praise and criticism, David is more likely to read them and understand what strategies seem to have worked well. To keep lines of communication open, students can submit their own questions or comments about what concerns them, letting us know how carefully they are evaluating their work and what kinds of suggestions might help most.

Finally, in view of the research Hillocks surveyed, comments belong on students' drafts, not on final versions. If comments are to have any effect, students need opportunities to incorporate them. Commenting on drafts encourages and guides further revision. It also ensures that comments remain focused on the work-in-progress, not on the grade a student's work eventually receives.

Responding to papers in ways that enhance learning is as time-consuming as locating errors, more so until the procedure becomes comfortable and each student's problems more familiar. Although we obviously can't approach every paper in the same way, the following procedure offers some suggestions for planning written comments much as we prepare classes: (1) assess what the student needs to learn (steps 1–2), (2) plan what to teach and how (steps 3–4), (3) conduct the lesson (steps 5–10), and (4) keep notes to evaluate learning and plan future lessons (step 11).

Teaching through Comments

1. Read the paper through without marking on it.
2. Identify one or two problems. In deciding what to teach this time, view the paper descriptively, not to judge it, but to discover what the text reveals about decisions the writer made. You may want to ask yourself the following questions:
   a. Was the student committed to the assignment?
   b. What did the student intend to do? What was the purpose for writing?
   c. How did the writer define the audience for the piece?
   d. How thoroughly did the student probe the subject?
   e. How are paragraphs arranged?
   f. What are the most frequent types of sentences?
   g. What patterns of errors in spelling, punctuation, grammar, and usage does the paper contain? In what contexts do the errors appear? What makes them similar?

Examining scratch notes and earlier drafts also helps reconstruct how the student created the final draft.

3. Formulate tentative hypotheses to explain the problem you want to focus on. You can assume that there's a logic to what appears on the page, even if it isn't your logic. Try to define that logic so that your comments can turn it around or modify it. For example, "I disliked the story because it's ending confused me" assumes (logically but unconventionally) that 's marks the possessive pronoun just as it does most nouns. Students who put commas in front of every *and* may be misapplying the rule for punctuating series or conjoining independent clauses; they need to learn that a "series" of two coordinated subjects or verbs doesn't need the comma. Merely labeling the error "misplaced comma" doesn't teach students *why* and *how* your logic and theirs differ.

4. Examine what the student has done well. Can this evidence help the student solve a problem elsewhere in the paper? How can the student's strengths be used to repair weaknesses?

5. Now you are ready to begin commenting on the paper. You have examined the evidence, decided what you want to teach, and identified specific examples of the problem (and perhaps its solution) on which to base your lesson.

6. Questions can call attention to troublespots, but avoid questions that prompt simple "yes" or "no" answers. Preface questions with *why, how,* or *what* so that students must reexamine the paper and become conscious critics of their own prose ("How often have you used this kind of sentence in this paragraph?"). Avoid imperatives ("Proofread more carefully"), which identify problems but don't help students learn *how* to solve them.

7. Avoid labeling problems *unless* you also give students a way of overcoming them. If something is "unclear" or "awkward," let students know the source of your confusion ("Do you mean . . . or . . . ?"). Refer to other sections of the paper that illustrate a strategy worth repeating ("You're using abstract words here; why not give me another example as you did in paragraph 2?"). Eschew, when you can, Latinate grammatical terms, abbreviations, and private symbols. They may be clear to you—after all, you've marked hundreds of papers with them—but they might mystify the student.

8. Make praise work toward improvements. Students need to know how a reader responds to their work, but they're rarely fooled by token praise. Avoid "good" or "I like this" unless you add a noun ("Good sentence variety here") or *because* ("I like these details because they help me see Uncle Max"). Remember to commend students for progress they've made.

9. Avoid doing the student's work. Rewriting an occasional sentence can give students a model to imitate, *if* you make it clear what principle the model illustrates. Circled or underlined words (and most marginal symbols) simply locate and label errors; the student probably didn't "see" the problem and needs practice proofreading and editing. A better strategy for handling surface errors might be to place a check in the margin next to the line in which a misspelled word or punctuation problem occurs. Then ask the student to examine the entire line, locate the problem, and determine how to eliminate it. Students who can't find the error on their own should feel free to ask you what the check means. Students may log these errors and their corrections in their journals so that they develop a sense of what they're overlooking. Logs can be discussed briefly in conference to identify patterns in the errors and work out strategies for anticipating them in future papers.

10. Write out a careful endnote to summarize your comments and to establish a goal for the next draft. Endnotes can follow a simple formula:
a. Devote at least one full sentence to commending what you can legitimately praise; avoid undercutting the praise with *but* ("I like your introduction, *but* the paper is disorganized.").

    b. Identify one or two problems and explain why they make understanding the piece difficult.

    c. Set a goal for the student to work toward in the next draft.

    d. Suggest specific strategies for reaching the goal ("In your next draft, do this: . . . ").

Traditional endnotes address a paper's weaknesses, but if you want to see the strengths repeated, praise them when you find them. Silence tells students nothing. Traditional endnotes also omit goals and offer few explicit suggestions for reaching them. Including goals and strategies gives the endnote a teaching function, helps redirect a writer's energies, and reduces the amount of trial-and-error learning students must go through to improve their writing. Subsequent papers are more likely to show improvement if you explicitly define what you think needs work and how to go about it. Your suggestions also will encourage students to see connections between what they discuss in class and what they practice in their assignments, between problems they've encountered in one draft and solutions worth trying in the next.

Setting goals and offering specific solutions to writing problems can be difficult at first, especially if you don't know what to suggest to address the problem you see. But with practice, you'll find yourself developing a repertoire of goals and strategies to adapt to individual papers. State each goal positively, perhaps mentioning problems in previous papers that now have been solved or pointing to specific strengths in this paper. Instead of writing "This paper shows little thought," write "In planning your next paper, spend fifteen minutes freewriting; then fill a page with notes on your subject and decide how to group them under three or four headings." Not, "Your sentences are hopeless"; rather, "You've made considerable progress in organizing the whole essay. Now it's time to work on sentences. Read this draft aloud to hear where sentences could be combined or made less wordy. Your ideas will come across more forcefully if you avoid passive voice verbs and sentences that begin with *There are* and *It is.*" Phrase the goal in language that encourages students to experiment and take risks. Avoid prescribing additional goals until students have reached those you've already given them.

11. Write yourself a note to chart the student's progress, a reminder you can keep in the student's folder. Describe briefly what areas no longer seem to be problems, what problems you addressed this time, and what needs attention later on. If this draft enabled you to teach a principle of paragraphing, remind yourself to evaluate the next paper in light of the paragraph-goal you set. If you also noticed sentence problems this time around, a note will remind you to set a sentence-goal when paragraphs begin to look stronger.

At first reading these eleven steps seem cumbersome, but after some practice, the procedure saves time. Writing teachers expect to spend many hours commenting on papers. We do this work conscientiously because we believe that students will read what we've written and will profit from our advice. Too often, however, they don't, and consequently, we resent having devoted so much energy to an apparently pointless task. One advantage of the procedure described above is that students *will* read what we've written. They'll expect us to say "bad" things, but they'll discover that we've said "good" things about their work too. They'll read about their weaknesses as they search for comments praising the paper. Second, the procedure offers specific help with weaknesses, especially in the goal-setting endnote. If the endnote explains *how* to tackle a problem, students will attempt the strategy we've suggested at least once. If we then praise the attempt, or even notice that the writer tried something new, he or she may try it again. Focused feedback, not diffuse comments, makes learning efficient. Third, the procedure saves us time because it focuses on only one or two problems. With practice, we can develop a mental repertoire of endnotes addressing specific problems. Although the long endnote on page 156 may appear to have taken considerable time to write, it didn't. I would like my students to think so, but I drew on a stock endnote I've used many times, simply modifying it to fit the particular paper I was commenting on.

Self-evaluation

Students also must have a role in evaluating their work. They should respond to their own writing and that of other classmates for several reasons. Good writers are proficient in addressing varied audiences. Students develop this proficiency not only by writing for others but also by gaining responses to their work from audiences other than the teacher. Furthermore, because composing is highly idiosyncratic, students learn new strategies for solving writing problems by explaining their decisions to other students and hearing how they have negotiated the demands of a similar assignment. As students become progressively more independent and self-confident, their responses to one another's work become more incisive. They learn constructive criticism, close reading, and collaboration.

Writing workshops, discussed in Chapter 12, offer one way of encouraging students to respond to one another's writing. Self-evaluation encourages students to assess their own compositions. As Mary Beaven suggests, "Self-evaluation strengthens students' editing abilities, giving them control over decisions that affect their own writing growth as they learn to trust their own criteria of good writing" (*Evaluating Writing*, p. 153). Self-evaluation typically requires students to answer questions designed to elicit information about their work. Students submit their answers when they turn in a draft or final version. Although self-evaluation questions should change with each assignment to reflect the work students are doing, Beaven (p. 143) offers the following questions as a starting point:

1. How much time did you spend on this paper?
2. (After the first evaluation) What did you try to improve, or experiment with, on this paper? How successful were you? If you have questions about what you were trying to do, what are they?
3. What are the strengths of your paper? Place a squiggly line beside those passages you feel are very good.
4. What are the weaknesses, if any, of your paper? Place an X beside passages you would like your teacher to correct or revise. Place an X over any punctuation, spelling, usage, etc., where you need help or clarification.
5. What one thing will you do to improve your next piece of writing? Or what kind of experimentation in writing would you like to try? If you would like some specific information related to what you want to do, write down your questions.
6. (Optional) What grade would you give yourself on this composition? Justify it.

Self-evaluation benefits teachers as well as students. The answers to self-evaluation questions tell us what concerns students. As they become more aware of what they wanted to do and where a paper fails to realize their intentions, we can offer help, acting less like a judge and more like an experienced, trusted advisor. We discover how students perceive the composing process, what sorts of risks they're taking, and when to encourage and applaud growth. Self-evaluation realizes an important goal in a writing course: to help students become self-sufficient writers. As Beaven urges, students must have opportunities to decide for themselves "what they are going to learn, how to go about that learning process, and how to evaluate their own progress" (p. 147). Beaven recommends that students evaluate their own papers from the beginning of the course. Initially, we can comment on the quality of their assessment, modifying the goals they've set for themselves or suggesting alternatives when students seem headed in unprofitable directions. Later in the course, as students gain confidence in recognizing the qualities of good writing, we can give them more responsibility for evaluating, even grading, their work.

If answering a long list of questions begins to bore students, teachers can shift to other methods of self-evaluation. Some teachers, for example, ask students to write a paragraph or two describing the major strengths and weaknesses of a draft or final paper. These notes also might explain how students defined their purpose and audience or comment on organizational and stylistic goals that received special attention. Many teachers find these statements surprisingly perceptive and extremely useful in composing their own responses to students' work. They encourage an ongoing dialogue about writing between teacher and student.

Atomistic Evaluation

Measures of writing performance can be grouped into two categories: atomistic and holistic measures. Atomistic measures evaluate some part of the composing process, or certain features of the written product, or a skill presumed to correlate with writing ability. When teachers or administrators place students into writing courses on the basis of a vocabulary test such as the Verbal portion of the Scholastic Aptitude Test (SAT), they assume that a knowledge of words correlates with skills needed to write well. For some students it does; for others it doesn't. Students may score well on vocabulary tests yet produce ineffective compositions; they may score poorly on the test and write well. One reason is that composing involves much more than skill with words.

Editing, mechanics, and usage tests also are atomistic measures. They reveal whether or not students recognize conventions of edited American English. But because composing requires the ability to generate discourse, not merely to analyze it, editing tests can tell us only about some of the skills students use when they write. Tests of syntactic maturity are atomistic too. They enable us to evaluate the length and complexity of sentences and reveal what types of coordination and subordination students achieve in their writing.[7] This information is useful in planning instruction that enlarges students' repertoire of syntactic options. Nevertheless, because they focus primarily on the ability to construct sentences, such tests assess only one of many skills important to composing.

Atomistic measures aren't "bad" tools for evaluating student performance. They measure what they were designed to measure. Because they evaluate some activities required in composing or assess particular features in the product, they isolate problems we can help students overcome. They're misused when we mistake the part for the whole, when we ask atomistic measures to tell us everything we need to know about our students' writing ability. Writing assessments are invalid when procedures intended to evaluate only one aspect of composing are presumed to indicate "writing ability."

Holistic Evaluation

Holistic measures assume that all the features of a composition or all the skills that comprise writing ability are related, interdependent. When we grade papers holistically, we assert that their rhetorical effectiveness lies in the combination of features at every level of the discourse, that the whole is greater than the sum of its parts. Charles Cooper describes the procedure this way:

> Holistic evaluation of writing is a guided procedure for sorting or ranking written pieces. The rater takes a piece of writing and either (1) matches it with an-

other piece in a graded series of pieces or (2) scores it for the prominence of certain features important to that kind of writing or (3) assigns it a letter or number grade. The placing, scoring, or grading occurs quickly, impressionistically, after the rater has practiced the procedure with other raters. The rater does not make corrections or revisions in the paper. Holistic evaluation is usually guided by a holistic scoring guide that describes each feature and identifies high, middle, and low quality levels for each feature. (*Evaluating Writing*, p. 3)

As most teachers know, if six of us were to assign individual numbers or letter grades to the same paper, all of us might evaluate it differently. How then does holistic, "impressionistic" scoring represent an improvement over traditional methods? First of all, holistic scoring is a group activity that requires readers to agree beforehand on the criteria that will determine the ranking of papers. The readers agree to match their impressions of any particular paper to preselected model papers, a scoring guide, or a list of features that define each rank.[8] Second, before readers begin scoring the papers, they practice the procedure, using sample papers written on the same topics by the same kinds of students as those whose work they will score later. The practice session allows raters to "calibrate" themselves to the models, scoring guide, or list of features. When raters consistently agree on what rankings the sample papers should have, the actual scoring can begin. During the scoring session, each student's paper is read at least twice, by two different raters, and assigned a number or letter ranking. When raters disagree on a score, the paper is read by a third reader or given to a panel that determines the score. Because raters don't stop to mark the paper, to correct or revise the student's work, they can score a large number of papers in a short time, "spending no more than two minutes on each paper" (p. 3). And because they have practiced matching each paper against predetermined criteria, they "can achieve a scoring reliability as high as .90 for individual writers" (p. 3).

Holistic evaluation assumes, first, that written discourse communicates a complete message to an audience for a particular purpose. Consequently, "holistic evaluation by a human respondent gets closer to what is essential in such a communication than frequency counts [of errors or of word or sentence elements] do" (p. 3). Rather than single out a few features in the piece, as atomistic measures require, holistic scores recognize all the decisions students make in writing the paper.

Second, holistic measures are flexible. Working together, English teachers can define criteria consistent with a particular course or writing program. Designing and trying out the procedure requires careful work, but once the scale is in place, readers can score large numbers of papers quickly and reliably. Because raters make no comments on the papers, holistic evaluations provide no feedback for students; that is, the scores serve an administrative, not an instructional, purpose and usually help teachers make decisions about placement or final grades.

Third, holistic evaluation removes much of the subjective static that unavoidably interferes with placement and grading decisions. Although we all try to evaluate our students' work objectively, our judgments are always influenced to some degree by factors that have nothing to do with writing. Students who misbehave in class, whose socioeconomic or racial backgrounds differ from ours, whose handwriting is poor, whose past performance has already branded them as D or F students, or whose papers happen to be near the bottom of the stack may receive lower grades than their actual writing ability warrants. However, when papers are coded so that students' names don't appear, when at least two teachers must agree on the score, when all of us in the writing program participate, judgments become considerably more objective and consistent. Furthermore, in developing specific, uniform criteria to guide our scoring, we must discuss, as a faculty, what constitutes "good writing" and how the school's composition program develops the writing abilities of its students. Such questions lie at the center of all writing instruction, and working out the answers together improves both the program and our teaching.

What works for teachers works for students too. Teachers who are themselves trained in holistic scoring can teach their students to score one another's work. They give students the responsibility for assigning grades. The teacher's training is crucial; without it, teachers undermine the procedure, give responsibility with one hand while taking it away with another, and promote irresponsible grading practices. Once trained, however, teachers can help students develop a scoring guide for each assignment, explicitly defining with the class what constitutes a successful response to the assignment. The scoring guide, developed early in the students' work on an assignment, functions to clarify what the assignment requires and may serve as a revision checklist when students discuss their drafts with classmates. When students turn in their final papers, they omit their names and identify the paper with a number the teacher has assigned or with the last four digits of their social security number.

Having collected the papers, the teacher reads them quickly (without marking them), selecting two or three sample papers that meet the criteria for scores at different points in the scale established by the scoring guide. These sample papers become models discussed with the class during the practice session. During the practice session, which must be held on the same day that students score one another's papers, the students review the scoring guide again and then rate the models. The teacher discusses the ratings with the class, allowing students to "calibrate" themselves to the scoring guide. When students reach consensus on what rankings the models should have, the actual scoring begins.

During the scoring session, each student's paper receives two readings, by two different students who assign it a score that most closely matches the criteria defined by the scoring guide. To make two readings of each student's work possible, teachers may swap papers across groups (if the class is divided into permanent workshop groups) or they may require students to submit two copies of the final draft. When student raters disagree on a score by more than one point, as sometimes happens, the teacher acts as the third reader to resolve the conflict. If necessary, the teacher can convert the scores into letter grades by fiat or by discussing with the class the range of scores an assignment receives.

Because very young children can reliably score one another's work, older students, some of whom will be teachers themselves in a few years, can certainly manage the responsibility. Those who will raise the most static about the procedure tend to be students who have made good grades by learning over the years to "please the teacher." If the teacher no longer gives the grades, these students must adjust their usual definitions of success to "please the reader," an audience of classmates. Students trained to use holistic scoring rapidly learn what it means to write for a reader because they tend to see much more writing than they would in a teacher-graded class. They also become confident about how to improve their own work and offer better advice to classmates about their drafts. Letting students score one another's compositions realizes a teacher's conviction that students can learn to recognize good writing, in their own work and in the work of others, and can take active responsibility for their own learning. Teachers who share this conviction can release their control over grades and teach students to assess one another's writing carefully.

Handling the Paper Load

Both theory and practice suggest that students should write more than they do, in English classes and in other disciplines. But the size of our classes and other demands on our time work against us. Our students' work deserves a thoughtful response, but thoughtful responses take time. How can we keep up with the paper load? The question is one that both experienced and inexperienced teachers ask. Fortunately, those who ask it most have developed some of the best answers.

High school teachers, who usually teach 130 to 150 students a day, know many ways to keep students writing while simultaneously encouraging constructive responses from an interested reader.[9] They understand two important principles: the "reader" need not always be the teacher, and the writing need not always receive *written* responses.

We sometimes underestimate the value of ungraded writing assignments. Freewritings, journal entries, sentence-combining problems, and brief paragraphs can give students almost daily writing practice. They may serve several purposes: to summarize the main points of class discussion, to react to a reading assignment, to work out possibilities for future papers. We don't have to respond to these writings as we do to drafts or finished papers. Students can simply add them to their folders for review later, or they can exchange papers for a five-minute response from classmates. Or, we can collect them, skim them, and assign them a daily grade or write a few words at the top of the page. Or, we may respond orally in class by asking a few students to read their work aloud.

On longer, graded assignments, we can use other methods to save time without diminishing the quality of instruction. Many teachers find conference teaching successful. Student-teacher conferences can occur at any time during composing and offer teachers an excellent way to provide feedback when it is most useful, during planning, drafting, or rewriting. Conferences are most effective when teachers listen carefully and allow students to set the agenda. Students should begin the conference, perhaps by reading and commenting on a draft or by explaining what pleases and puzzles them most about the project they are working on. The teacher then responds to the comments, addressing the student's agenda first before raising other issues. The student ends the conference by reacting to the teacher's suggestions and summarizing what strategies will shape the next draft.

Another way to handle the paper load involves asking students to build portfolios of multiple drafts and final versions of several assignments.[10] Portfolios are collections of students' work assembled over time. They originated in fine arts departments, where students customarily select their best paintings, photographs, or drawings to submit for a grade. Although portfolios are relatively new to writing programs, they have several functions. Some institutions now use portfolios of high school writing to determine a student's placement in college writing courses. Other schools have substituted portfolios for competency exams, replacing a one-time test with writing completed in several disciplines throughout the first three years of college. The most common use of writing portfolios is the class portfolio, a collection of work students submit at the end of a single writing course.

Class portfolios permit teachers to assign a great deal of writing. Students keep all of their drafts and final versions in a folder, bring it to class and conferences, and produce an impressive quantity of work. At the end of the term (and sometimes also at midterm), students revise some of these writings yet again and submit the portfolio for a grade. Most teachers who use portfolios define some of the work that must be in the folder, let students choose the rest, and ask them to write a self-evaluation that comments on the entire collection. For example, the teacher might require four papers: a persuasive essay, an analysis of an academic text, any paper the student wishes to include, and a letter describing the contents of the portfolio and chronicling the student's development as a writer. For one of these assignments, perhaps the "student's choice," all drafts and scratchwork must accompany the final draft.

Throughout the term, students work on these assignments, just as they would in a traditional class. Teachers may write comments on drafts and discuss them in conference. Classmates also can offer feedback in writing workshops. If midterm grades are necessary, students may submit two pieces from their portfolios-in-progress at that time for grading. But they also may revise the papers again before the completed portfolio is due.

Regardless of what goes into the portfolio, teachers must define in advance what they expect it to include and how they will evaluate it. Individual pieces of writing do not receive grades; instead, teachers read the entire portfolio holistically, assigning a single comprehensive grade for all of the work. For this reason, they must develop a scoring guide in advance of receiving the portfolios, a difficult task because the portfolio comprises, by design, a diversity of writing. Although individual teachers can develop their own scoring guide independently, most teachers define the nature of the portfolio and the criteria used to judge it collaboratively. They reach consensus about what all of their students' portfolios will contain, develop a common scoring guide, and organize themselves into a review panel to evaluate one another's students' portfolios.

Portfolios demand a great deal of reading time at the end of the term and raise questions about reliably scoring such a diverse body of work; nevertheless, they have clear advantages. A carefully designed scoring guide can increase reliability, and because readers assess the portfolio as a whole, not individual papers, evaluating portfolios takes less time than grading and commenting on final drafts. Moreover, portfolios remain the best way of evaluating students' growth in writing over time. When drafts and scratchwork are included, they can document the composing process, especially rewriting. Portfolios also demonstrate to students that writing is process. Most students take greater pride and pleasure in preparing their portfolios than they do in writing individual papers for the teacher to grade. Plagiarism is virtually unheard of; while it may be tempting to cheat on one assignment, a portfolio contains so much material that must be genuine that students will find it difficult to copy someone else's work. Teachers also find their collaboration in a portfolio project rewarding. In defining the portfolio's contents and devising the standards by which it will be judged, teachers must articulate the goals of their writing courses, a conversation that reinforces convictions about the best practices for teaching writing. Portfolio projects encourage teachers to support one another in setting standards and designing courses, decisions that foster collegiality and give teachers ownership of their work.

All of these methods—in addition to class discussions of students' papers, self-evaluations, and peer responses—encourage students to write frequently, to have their work read by a variety of audiences, and to share the authority for evaluating writing. Teachers unwilling to share that authority face at least two unpleasant consequences. They feel obligated to mark too many papers (or to assign too little writing), and worse, they prevent their students from learning what the standards for effective writing are. Sharing responsibility for the paper load not only keeps us sane; it's also good teaching.

Notes

[1] For a comprehensive discussion of issues surrounding assessment, see Edward M. White, *Teaching and Assessing Writing*, 2d ed. (The Jossey-Bass Higher Education Series; San Francisco: Jossey-Bass, 1994).

[2] Although experienced teachers seem to have internalized the criteria for A, B, C, D, and F papers, beginning teachers may want a more explicit discussion of grades than they will find in this chapter. I recommend the practical advice William F. Irmscher gives in Chapter 13, "Evaluation," in *Teaching Expository Writing* (New York: Holt, Rinehart and Winston, 1979), pp. 142–78.

[3] The assignment appears among the "Placement Essay Topics" in Mina F. Shaughnessy, *Errors and Expectations: A Guide for the Teacher of Basic Writing* (New York: Oxford University Press, 1977), p. 295.

[4] An excellent discussion of types of misspellings and their causes appears in Shaughnessy, Chapter 5.

[5] A revealing study of initial and terminal comments in a sample of 3,000 papers is Robert J. Connors and Andrea A. Lunsford, "Teachers' Rhetorical Comments on Student Papers," *College Composition and Communication* 44 (May 1993), 200–223: "The teachers whose comments we studied seem often to have been trained to judge student writing by rhetorical formulae that are almost as restricting as mechanical formulae. The emphasis still seems to be on finding and pointing out problems and deficits in the individual paper, not on envisioning patterns in student writing habits or prompts that could go beyond such analysis" (p. 218). See also Chris M. Anson, ed., *Writing and Response: Theory, Practice, and Research* (Urbana, IL: NCTE, 1989).

[6] Beyond Shaughnessy's work, teachers will find helpful Elaine O. Lees, "Evaluating Student Writing," *College Composition and Communication* 30 (December 1979), 370–74; and David Bartholomae, "The Study of Error," *College Composition and Communication* 31 (October 1980), 253–69.

[7] For a description of the procedure developed by Kellogg W. Hunt, see his "A Synopsis of Clause-to-Sentence Length Factors," *English Journal* 54 (April 1965), 300, 305–9; and Kellogg W. Hunt, "Early Blooming and Late Blooming Syntactic Structures," in *Evaluating Writing*, pp. 91–104.

[8] For a description of holistic scoring using sample student papers as models, see Edward M. White, *Assigning, Responding, Evaluating: A Writing Teacher's Guide*, 2d ed. (New York: St. Martin's Press, 1990). Primary Trait Scoring, developed to score the essays for the National Assessment of Educational Progress, uses an elaborate scoring guide, described by Richard Lloyd-Jones, "Primary Trait Scoring," in *Evaluating Writing*, pp. 33–66. The best known "analytic scale" appears in Paul B. Diederich, *Measuring Growth in English* (Urbana, IL: NCTE, 1974). The prominent features of a piece of writing receive weighted numerical values, "ideas" and "organization" receiving greater weight than "handwriting" and "spelling." Diederich also constructs an attractive argument for involving the entire English faculty in evaluating writing performance so that bias doesn't unduly affect students' final grades.

[9] See the collection of practical essays compiled by the NCTE Committee on Classroom Practices in Teaching English, *How to Handle the Paper Load* (Urbana, IL: NCTE, 1979); for a valuable discussion of responding to student writing in conferences, see Donald M. Murray, *A Writer Teaches Writing*, 2d ed. (Boston: Houghton Mifflin, 1985), especially Chapter 8.

[10] For a discussion of portfolios and their uses, see *Portfolios: Process and Product*, ed. Pat Belanoff and Marcia Dickson (Portsmouth, NH: Boynton/Cook, 1991); and *New Directions in Portfolio Assessment: Reflective Practice, Critical Theory, and Large-Scale Scoring*, ed. Laurel Black, Donald A. Daiker, Jeffrey Sommers, and Gail Stygall (Portsmouth, NH: Boynton/Cook, 1994).

Works Cited

Beaven, Mary H. "Individualized Goal Setting, Self-Evaluation, and Peer Evaluation." In *Evaluating Writing: Describing, Measuring, Judging*. Ed. Charles R. Cooper and Lee Odell. Urbana, IL: NCTE, 1977. Pp. 135–56.

Cooper, Charles R. "Responding to Student Writing." In *The Writing Processes of Students*. Ed. Walter T. Petty and Patrick J. Finn. Buffalo: State University of New York, 1975. Pp. 31–39.

Cooper, Charles R., and Lee Odell, eds. *Evaluating Writing: Describing, Measuring, Judging*. Urbana, IL: NCTE, 1977.

Goodman, Kenneth. "Minimum Standards: A Moral View." In *Minimum Competency Standards: Three Points of View*. N.P.: International Reading Association, 1978. Pp. 3–5.

Hillocks, George, Jr. *Research on Written Composition: New Directions for Teaching*. Urbana, IL: ERIC Clearinghouse on Reading and Communication Skills and the National Conference on Research in English, 1986.

Jenkinson, Edward B., and Donald A. Seybold. *Writing as a Process of Discovery: Some Structured Theme Assignments for Grades Five through Twelve*. Bloomington: Indiana University Press, 1970.

Shaughnessy, Mina. *Errors and Expectations: A Guide for the Teacher of Basic Writing*. New York: Oxford University Press, 1977.

DIRECTIVE VERSUS FACILITATIVE COMMENTARY

D. R. Ransdell

[*Teaching English in the Two-Year College* (March 1999): 269–76]

D. R. Ransdell mentors first-year teaching assistants in the composition program at the University of Arizona, where she also teaches composition courses.

Since Nancy Sommers's groundbreaking research, writing teachers have become sensitive to the ways they respond to student writing. If teachers want students to make their own choices when revising and to feel a sense of ownership of their work, research and experience have shown that facilitative comments are more likely to achieve these goals than are directive comments. Ransdell recognizes the values of facilitative approaches and the dangers of directive comments, but she questions whether teachers should provide only facilitative commentary. Using examples of both kinds of commentary, Ransdell surveyed one hundred first-year writing students, asking them several questions about the kinds of comments they prefer, and when and why such comments are helpful. In this article, Ransdell shares her findings, including analyses of student responses, and recommends that teachers consider using both kinds of commentary strategically. This article reminds teachers that responding to student writing is a communicative act and an opportunity for teaching and learning.

Introduction

In recent journal articles, directive commentary—suggestions written on students' drafts of essays made in an authoritative or imperative manner—has been depicted as a dragon to be slain. Such commentary, many say, should be replaced with facilitative commentary in which the instructor helps the student rethink the paper analytically: "What do you hope your readers will understand your thesis to be?" rather than "State a clear thesis." A principal spokesperson for facilitative commentary is Richard Straub, who complains that even though we realized years ago we should not "impose our 'idealized text' on students' writing," we're still doing it ("The Concept of Control" 223). Straub asks us to use facilitative commentary rather than to take undue control; simultaneously, he asks us to write comments that are longer and more time-consuming.

Yet the situation is not clear cut: not all directive commentary is bad just as not all facilitative commentary is good. In his survey of commenting styles, Straub shows how instructors can make directive comments that don't dictate student agendas and conversely write facilitative questions that are authoritative ("The Concept of Control" 236–37). Ultimately, Straub supports the style of commentary used by Peter Elbow, since Straub uses "dissonance" to allow the student to "infer." Rather than direct the student text, Elbow explains he's not persuaded by it (244). The writer then decides whether Elbow's reactions are appropriate or whether the text needs to be changed so that it produces different ones (see also Elbow 110–20).

Elbow's advice is theoretically sound in that students should indeed make their own choices about what their texts are doing and what they want the texts to do, but not all of my first-year composition students are experienced enough to recognize what their choices are. I would like to suggest a different bottom line, that directive commentary has several legitimate uses, and that while we need to encourage students to think on their own rather than direct every step of their work, a judicious use of directive commentary can coax them into writing stronger texts. To test my own sense of commenting styles, I showed samples of both styles to my students. Below, I explain the students' thoughts on facilitative versus directive commentary and offer suggestions for choosing between them.

Early this semester, I distributed the partial "draft" to a hundred first-year composition students at Arizona State University. (I drew up two sheets; half had the directive comments on the right; the other half had them on the left.) The "draft" was an evaluation, the kind of paper the students were preparing at the time. The six "lettered" comments were directive; the six "numbered" comments were facilitative (see Figure 1).

Reactions

I asked the students to consider the comments as a set (all the lettered comments, etc.) and respond to how useful they were and how they themselves would have felt upon receiving them. (At this point in the semester, I hadn't commented on any of the students' drafts, nor had we discussed the process.) After the students recorded their responses, I asked them to form small groups and discuss their reactions. This proved interesting, for as I strolled around the room, I noticed that the responses varied drastically. While several students claimed that the comments were equally useful, and a few more stated that a combination of the sets would be the best, forty percent of the students preferred the facilitative ("numbered") set, while thirty-seven percent preferred the directive ("lettered") set. The students were so evenly divided that out of twenty-three small groups of four to five students, the members of only two groups agreed on which set they preferred.

This division led to energetic discussions as the students tried to convince one another which comments were better. Many of the students detected the rationale behind the comments, that the numbered comments were designed to help students rethink their material while the lettered comments made the job of revision easier by providing more direct instructions, but this detection only made it more difficult for them to agree on a correct method.

Once I started reading the students' written responses, I noticed patterns. In support of facilitative commentary, Michelle's response was typical:

> I would probably rather receive the numbered comments as they cause me to re-think the draft and to rework it in my own way instead of replacing my draft with the "corrected" version. The lettered comments are so direct that they don't leave room for reconsideration.

Michelle's reactions don't surprise me. As a twenty-something student with two children, she never appreciates mandates; for her argumentative paper she plans to attack my own composition department's standard attendance policy. It's interesting that she uses the phrase "replacing," as if "corrections" on past essays have required her to make changes that she saw no reason for.

I've often felt that students view suggestions as a show of authority: I'm the teacher, so do as I say. Perhaps students feel that teachers' suggestions are akin to parental orders such as "you may not use the car tonight" and see them in a similarly arbitrary light. Of course, if a draft hasn't seen much work, my comments are necessarily arbitrary. I would like to write comments that always encourage students to think hard about their writing, but sometimes they don't give me enough to work with.

When students *have* made honest attempts to think about their drafts, different problems arise. As Leah pointed out:

> Sometimes when a teacher makes such specific remarks and corrections, it creates a difficult situation if the student does not agree. Then they are faced with the dilemma of leaving it as they want or changing to adjust to the teacher.

Often when I'm too directive, it's because I assume I know what the writer's intentions are and make suggestions accordingly. But sometimes I err—in a draft it's easy to get tripped up by a phrase or sentence and assume an opposite focus. Students need to know that readers' suggestions point to something that is not working in their papers, even though they might need to discover what that "something" is by themselves. (Elbow offers a useful analysis of this situation in *Writing without Teachers* where he explains that writers need "movies of people's minds while they read" rather than specific advice (77). Such "movies" demonstrate what actually happens when people read, not the way readers would change a text to fit their own agendas.)

Leah's classmate made a similar cry for ownership. Jeff explained:

> I like the question outlook better because then it gives the writer more ways to expand. Plus if the writer chooses what to correct and what not to correct the paper is the writer's paper and not the writer and the editor's paper.

When I asked Jeff if he could expand on his written response, he explained that in high school, he and his classmates would peer-edit papers. He found it too easy to take their advice; no matter what they said, he would go along with their suggestions. Although Jeff's papers received high grades, he felt guilty about turning in work he didn't feel was his. He'd completed the assignments but lost himself as a writer.

Directive commentary also received support. Karen's comment was typical of this camp: "The numbered comments are making it more introspective to yourself. But it can leave you insecure and unsure. The 'letters' are direct; there is no guesswork." Karen is hard-working and conscientious. I'm sure she wants her papers to work out smoothly, both to please me and earn a high grade. Perhaps her comments stem from my responses to an essay draft she showed me the week before. Because I wasn't sure what she wanted to say, I kept asking her questions until we were both confused. She wanted directive commentary, but the only comments I *could* make were facilitative, and the more we talked, the more I had questions about what she was trying to say instead of suggestions to improve the writing she'd already done.

Some of my less experienced students supported directive commentary because they did not recognize a rationale for the alternate style. As Anthony wrote:

> The numbered responses don't exactly help you. They tell you something is wrong and ask why, when if the person knew why they wouldn't have wrote [sic] it in the first place. The lettered side helps you find what's wrong and how to fix it.

Anthony is assuming a model for writing as something to be corrected rather than organically grown, but his views were mirrored by several classmates. And indeed, since his writing is full of nominative uses of "me and him," I can well imagine that his previous instructors *have* viewed his writing as something to "fix." As much as I would like to concentrate on comments about substance rather than grammar, if the grammar errors are too striking, I am too distracted to follow the content.

Surprising Endings

Kevin Kline is the protagonist of the recent movie <u>In and Out</u>. In this humorous film, Kline has a job that he enjoys, but the setting makes life difficult for him. Because Kline's friends and family don't understand him, they can't help him. For these reasons, the movie is surprising all the way through.

In my opinion, Howard is the victim of circumstance. Because of the small-town environment, people are not open to new ideas. They have trouble accepting anyone who is out of the ordinary.

One of the best parts of the movie is when Howard's girlfriend is showing her anger. She is standing outside the bar, all dressed up, and yelling at the world. she doesn't know what to do because her life has been torn apart. It seems like she doesn't even have her friends support.

In the beginning of the movie, Howard is happy, he is well liked, and he is about to be married. Of course, he is in for a surprise. We can understand Howard's feelings because similar things have happened to us at one time or another. Just when we think we have our lives all figured out, some calamity or unforeseen problem changes everything in a matter of moments.

Surprising Endings

Kevin Kline is the protagonist of the recent movie <u>In and Out</u>. In this humorous film, Kline has a job that he enjoys, but the setting makes life difficult for him. Because Kline's friends and family don't understand him, they can't help him. For these reasons, the movie is surprising all the way through.

In my opinion, Howard is the victim of circumstance. Because of the small-town environment, people are not open to new ideas. They have trouble accepting anyone who is out of the ordinary.

One of the best parts of the movie is when Howard's girlfriend is showing her anger. She is standing outside the bar, all dressed up, and yelling at the world. she doesn't know what to do because her life has been torn apart. It seems like she doesn't even have her friends support.

In the beginning of the movie, Howard is happy, he is well liked, and he is about to be married. Of course, he is in for a surprise. We can understand Howard's feelings because similar things have happened to us at one time or another. Just when we think we have our lives all figured out, some calamity or unforeseen problem changes everything in a matter of moments.

Figure 1. Sample Marked Essays

Jay's comments stemmed from a sense of overload: "I usually make enough mistakes that I can't think about each one. Directly telling me what I did would help me more than frustrating me with questions." Jay is not a poor writer, but to turn initial drafts into successful final ones, he does need to spend time examining different aspects of his writing. I wonder if some of his earlier teachers have been too ambitious, if they've pressed him to make more changes per draft than he could handle. As Bob Mittan, my first teaching supervisor, impressed upon me years ago: student writers—just as apprentices in any other area—can't target all their weaknesses simultaneously. Instructors need to employ a moderate approach so students won't be so overwhelmed that they give up. Still, it's difficult for instructors to decide how much they *should* address because many students need a small push to rise to the challenge. I find it hard to restrain myself. When multiple drafting problems jump out at me, out of what is no doubt a misguided sense of duty, I feel I must address them. Perhaps some of Jay's previous teachers have shared my feelings.

Although students have different levels of tolerance for working with their writing, at some point, they all get caught in the bind of not having enough time and energy to spend on it. Optimally, students would have time to think through all their problems with the help of facilitative commentary as they slowly brainstorm for their next draft, but students do have limits. The burden is dropped on me. Am I justified in giving "answers" to some problems as long as I write thought-provoking questions that they must wrestle with for more deeply-seated ones?

Honesty also plays in. While it's important to encourage students, they need to have a realistic idea of how their writing measures up. As Marcela wrote, "The numbered comments aren't as harsh and could be easier to swallow, but the lettered comments tell it like it is." To avoid disappointing a hard-working student, I have been guilty of hiding behind comments that were masquerading as facilitative but actually represented my own inability to speak openly.

Such hedging has often led me into a bind. Even though I write "you might try" as a polite way to say "here's one way to address a problem you have," students may choose to ignore the code and interpret "might" as a conditional verb. Last year I battled Mikey on this point. On his draft I had written comments such as: "You might add a concrete example to this point" or "you might include references to current sources." Mikey took none of my suggestions: His flimsy research earned him a C–. When he questioned the grade, I asked why he hadn't added more proof. He pointed to my comments. "You wrote 'You might use more proof.' You didn't say I had to." For a moment, we were at a standstill; I wanted to be angry that he had looked for an excuse, but I wasn't positive he'd understood what I meant to say. Since the grade was at stake, Mikey eventually decided to revise his essay using my comments as a guide, but I'm not sure he was ever convinced that my comments were valid.

Further Reactions

In addition to considering the comments as a set (all the lettered comments as opposed to all the numbered ones), I asked the students to consider each pair of responses and explain why "1" was better than "A" or why "2" was better than "B." Although many students found this difficult because their inclination was to support either set as a whole (if they preferred A, they preferred B and C as well), the students did agree that the grammar comment should be straightforward; no one wanted to have to think what the rule for possessive adjectives was (and several wanted me to give them the correction rather than the rule).

The students made similar comments about 2/B. Although Michelle didn't want any of her words summarily cut, most students agreed that while "Do you need this?" was friendlier, crossing out "in my opinion" worked well enough. In both examples, the students went against Straub's claim that there is "no reason teachers cannot use open questions or reader-response comments to address grammatical flaws or matters of sentence style" ("Response" 279). They wanted quick, direct answers to concrete matters where personal choice should not be a factor.

Suggestions

At the end of each class discussion, I explained to the students what facilitative comments were and why they were favored by current theory. I said that while I would try to use such comments as often as possible, my strategies would depend on several factors, and sometimes I would lean towards the directive side. The students seemed surprised to learn that so much thought went into commenting and that people had even researched it. They appreciated the chance to explore their views and to ponder the difference between being told what to do as opposed to being encouraged to do something.

Although I haven't uncovered an unequivocal rule to guide my own commenting procedures, I can outline some general considerations and suitable tactics.

I prefer facilitative commentary when

- the student hasn't uncovered a thesis or goal for the paper and needs cues to do so.
- the draft has basic components such as a logical structure and concrete points but lacks analysis. In this case I can rarely guess the writer's intentions. Since it's possible to understand the writer's points in different ways, I must encourage elaboration.
- the draft shows little evidence of thought. I probably couldn't give good advice about a sloppy, ill-conceived draft even if I wanted to.
- the draft lacks a visible purpose. By showing the writer my confusion, I illustrate the severity of the problem.

I prefer directive commentary for

- drafts whose purpose is clear, even though elements such as organization are preventing the text from being effective at this stage.
- problems that are clear cut in terms of style or usage. I don't want to spend time explaining why the phrase is "accustomed to" rather than "accustomed for," although I might briefly list a rule in the case of a second-language student.
- drafts that have large problems in terms of thesis or structure. While it's preferable to have strong analysis, sufficient research, etc., a paper without a discernible organization or thesis won't earn a passing grade, so these problems have to be attacked vigorously. More in-depth analysis can follow once the general plan is concrete.

Conclusion

The class activity on commenting styles accomplished several purposes. It showed students the complexities of commenting on drafts. It showed them my own difficulties with commenting and proved that I wasn't, as one student had imagined, trying to "beat around the bush" by writing facilitative comments. The activity emphasized that the purpose of commenting is to help writers improve writing rather than to highlight weaknesses. However, the activity was not as successful as I thought.

During the weeks that followed the class discussion of commentary, more students came to me with questions about my comments than in previous semesters. Amanda, upset about a C grade, came in to complain. But she suspected she hadn't understood my comments, and by the time she left my office, she herself saw that the C was fair, if not generous. Peter was convinced I'd lowered his grade because I disagreed with some of his statements. I had to explain that while I wasn't convinced by all his points, I was more concerned with clarity, which is why I had written "You'll need to use clear topic sentences to be effective" at the end of his essay.

By the end of the semester, Amanda, Peter, and quite a few others used my comments to rewrite their essays and earn higher grades. They realized the importance of understanding and working with my comments rather than ignoring them. No matter the style of comments, the students profited from them, underlining Jean Chandler's claim that "What matters instead [of the kind of commentary] are the attitudes and relationship of teacher and student and whether there is a supportive constructive dialogue between them" (273). Amanda and others knew I was willing to discuss comments and interpret them. Our dialogues enabled us to analyze drafts and consider possible revisions in a positive, reasonable manner.

When I revised the students' portfolios at the end of the semester (a letter and up to two revised essays), I found that my dialogues with students had been limited. Despite the insightful comments students often made in the whole-class workshops, many revised drafts showed little revision. A majority of students had made surface changes or minor additions. If I had written "explain more here," they included an extra sentence. Time-consuming suggestions such as "How could you organize these points more deliberately?" were generally overlooked. Where had I gone wrong? As Straub points out, students often ignore our comments anyway ("Teacher" 393). Are students really so resistant to changing their texts? While a few students were too weary by the end of the semester to do more careful work, I surmise that a large number were unable to respond to my comments either because they didn't understand what the comments meant or because they didn't know how to accommodate my suggestions.

I will continue to write directive comments on students' drafts and not feel guilty for doing so because I haven't learned conclusively which comments are more useful, whether the type of commenting makes that much difference, or if the student-teacher relationship is the key factor. Perhaps better writing is simply a function of maturity, critical powers, and practice. I maintain, however, that by discussing commenting styles, students were able to make more perceptive comments about their writing and others'. But deciding among commenting styles and discussing them during a single class period is only the first step. In the future, I will repeat the activity of discussing comments, but I will follow up by encouraging students to talk about my remarks with classmates and giving them class time to brainstorm strategies for revisions. I will keep in mind that even though students make perceptive comments about one another's papers, they may need extensive help to learn to make constructive changes to their own.

Works Cited

Chandler, Jean. "Positive Control." *College Composition and Communication* 48 (1997): 273–74.

Elbow, Peter. *Writing without Teachers.* New York: Oxford UP, 1973.

Straub, Richard. "The Concept of Control in Teacher Response: Defining the Varieties of 'Directive' and 'Facilitative' Commentary." *College Composition and Communication* 47 (1996): 223–51.

———. "Response Rethought." *College Composition and Communication* 48 (1997): 277–83.

———. "Teacher Response as Conversation: More Than Casual Talk, an Exploration." *Rhetoric Review* 14 (1996): 374–98.

INDIVIDUAL STUDENT CONFERENCES AND COMMUNITY WORKSHOPS: IS THERE A CONFLICT?

Tina Lavonne Good

[From Good, Tina Lavonne, and Leanne B. Warshauer, eds. *In Our Own Voice: Graduate Students Teach Writing.* Boston: Allyn & Bacon, 2000. 221–30.]

Tina Lavonne Good completed her B.A. in English at California State University, Fresno, while tutoring and teaching composition. She is an assistant professor at Suffolk Community College, where she teaches composition and literature, including Literature of the Bible and the

Arthurian Tradition. A Ph.D. candidate at SUNY Stonybrook, Good also teaches women's studies courses. Her dissertation research focuses on assessment of writing programs and feminist pedagogical theory.

Recognizing the value of learning communities and the social aspects of writing, many writing teachers attempt to create and sustain a classroom environment that supports communities of writers. In these student-centered, active-learning classes, students have the opportunity to recognize and develop their own sense of authority as writers and readers. As teachers, we model effective interactions through our written responses, our classroom discussions, and in our individual conferences with students—another mainstay of a student-centered environment. While Good values the one-on-one interactions of individual conferences, she wants her students to become confident writers who depend not only on a teacher's prescriptive commentary, but also on peer responses. To prevent the individual conference from undercutting the authority of the peer group responses, Good suggests meeting with each group in a conference in order to help students learn how to interact more effectively. Good recommends that teachers continue to meet with students individually, too, but she offers guidelines for questioning and interacting that will help students learn to trust their own developing abilities and their growing sense of authority.

I started tutoring in the California State University, Fresno, Writing Center in the fall of 1993. I walked in to teach my first composition course the following year. Since then, I have taught and tutored composition on two coasts. I have taught at community colleges, large universities, a private engineering college, and a private business school. I have taught international students from Spain, India, Malaysia, and China; immigrants from Korea, Mexico, Vietnam, and Laos; and U.S. citizens from more ethnic groups than I can count. Some of my students have never left their homes in California or New York, while others have dodged bullets crossing the Mekong River into Thailand. They have come from a variety of families and economic groups, and they have ranged in age from seventeen to seventy-seven. They have come with interests in forestry, farming, art, interior design, criminal justice, medicine, teaching, stockbroking, and wine making. I love what I do.

Although I have held the position of teaching assistant or adjunct instructor while teaching all these students, my authority has never been doubted by my students. Challenged? Absolutely. But my role as teacher has various historical, social, and cultural resonances embedded within it for each of my students before they ever walk into the classroom. That authority has nothing to do with me as an individual teacher. Any person standing in front of the classroom would be vested with it. However, I must decide what to do with that authority. Making this decision can be an overwhelming responsibility. How I choose to manipulate that authority can determine the success or failure of the class. There are no charts to help me determine how much and what type of authority I should use for the various group dynamics that show up in my classroom. Yet I must help my students empower themselves through thinking, reading, and writing. I cannot do this if I am the undisputed locus of knowledge in the classroom; and really, how could I be, given the diverse background and interests of my students? My challenge is to help students develop their own authority and find authority in their fellow students so when they leave my classroom at the end of the semester, they know they can write something that is worthwhile. This is the authority that is questioned. This is the authority that many students do not want to assume. This is the authority that the classroom community must work to develop and sustain.

There is plenty of anecdotal evidence which denotes a student's sense of powerlessness when it comes to writing, but one story that particularly sticks out in my mind is the story told by Laurel Johnson Black in her book, *Between Talk and Teaching: Reconsidering the Writing Conference.* She writes:

> I remember a time when I was lying on a table in an emergency room getting my face stitched up, and the young woman doing this delicate work backed away in horror as I told her I taught writing. Curved needle in her hand, in control of my recovery and my appearance, still she stammered in fear and memory of humiliation that she didn't speak well. (54)

This fear and these feelings of humiliation and frustration are the primary challenges for a writing instructor. One solution is the student-centered classroom.

Many composition instructors try to decenter their authority and construct a classroom environment where a learning community can develop. The tools for constructing this environment include group work, workshops/peer review, portfolios, technology, and student conferences. But doesn't the idea underlying student conferences undermine the ideal of the student-centered classroom? If we consider the students' perspective for a moment, what motivation do they have for putting in the time and energy necessary for making workshops a time of learning and revelation if they know they are going to get the counseling they really need in an individual conference with the instructor? How can students learn to trust themselves if we force them to come see us in a one-to-one conference as a last-ditch effort to improve their papers prior to evaluation of the midterm or final portfolio? How can students have confidence in their writing if we don't?

My nine-year-old daughter was working on her homework the other night and did not understand how to answer the following question: "How do you know Matt's father has confidence in him?" This question was not as easy to explain as one might think. In fact, it put me into a tailspin of reflection for several hours. How do I show my children I have confidence in them? my husband? my students? myself? After several failed attempts at trying to explain to my daughter what to look for in her story about Matt, we had this conversation:

Me: You know how I taught you how to brush your teeth.

Sarah: Yeah.

Me: That means I had confidence in your ability to learn how to brush your teeth. If I were to stop telling you to brush your teeth, that would mean I had the confidence that you would brush your teeth without me telling you.

Sarah: So I guess you don't have confidence in me.

Me: I guess not when it comes to brushing your teeth.

Sarah: Oh.

Me: So does Matt's father do anything like that?

Sarah: I don't know—maybe. (She walked out of the room.)

Bad example. I hope her teacher does better. But do our supposedly nurturing one-to-one student conferences communicate the same message to our students? It would seem that one-to-one conferences and in-class workshops are at pedagogical, philosophical, and psychological cross purposes. Perhaps it's not conferencing in and of itself that is the problem. Perhaps it is how we use it, how we manipulate our authority within the construct of the conference setting.

Thomas Carnicelli suggests that the first principle of the conference must be that "writing should be taught as a process . . . as three stages: prewriting, writing, and re-writing" (102). Thus, if conferences are used within a process pedagogy, they will be most effective when papers are treated as drafts for potential revision rather than evaluation. They should come at a time when revision is still viable, when conversation and reflection can serve as inspiration for writing rather than have a crippling effect because of a realization that there is too much to be done in too little time. If the conference comes too late in the process, not only can a teacher "become sorely tempted to stop questioning, and listening and suggesting, and start telling the student exactly what to do" (Carnicelli 119), but the student may be too anxious to accept anything but explicit direction, thereby lessening her chance to empower her writing and feel empowered through that writing. The implication the students will be forced to draw from such a directive conference will be that she is not ready to write a finished paper without her teacher's final words. She will not have established her own writing authority.

I am reminded of my own first-year comp class when I would dutifully take my essay to the instructor, whom I admired and respected greatly. We would have coffee and discuss my paper. He would ask me questions, give me ideas, and send me out with a direction for my paper. I would always get an A on the final draft. But I could not help wonder, when would *I* know what questions to ask, when would *I* know if my writing was good or not? I felt like a fraud because I knew I could not have gotten that A without my teacher's direct advice. I felt like I was cheating. Because of this experience, I am constantly struggling to find ways instructors can inculcate within their students the self-confidence they need to confirm their own learning and to adjudicate their own work without needing to seek validation from a higher authority. Only then can it be said that a student has truly internalized the writing process.

Donald Murray extols the virtues of teaching by conference rather than through lecture in his article entitled "The Listening Eye: Reflections on the Writing Conference." He claims that his students teach themselves and that he is only there to listen and confirm what his students have learned. Yet the authority of the instructor in this setting cannot be denied. The assumed right of the instructor to "confirm what his students have learned" is an authoritative assumption. However, the construction of authority within the classroom is outside the realm of "The Listening Eye." Instead, it is opposing the lecture format as a useful pedagogical tool for the teaching of writing and offering a more personal and interactive approach. That the instructor would have less or a different sort of authority in either situation is considered only to the degree to which the student can benefit from the instructor's assumed authority. But perhaps the conference setting Murray describes even intensifies the authoritative relationship between himself and his students because of its one-to-one nature. It is up to Murray to ameliorate his own authority. There is nothing or no one else, save the student being conferenced, to mediate that authority.

Murray, Carnicelli, and others must be applauded for their great insights into teaching writing as a process through the informal conference rather than the formal lecture. They realized that the writing process must entail social interaction. Although their discussions limit that interaction to student/writing instructor, they can be credited for helping to take writing out of the tower of divine inspiration. Without them, it would have been much harder for us to develop what is now called student-centered pedagogy as an alternative to the all-encompassing authority of the instructor. Yet we must take what they have taught us and modify it to this pedagogy. We cannot conference using a different pedagogical theory than we use in the classroom.

Admittedly, I used student conferences in a similar fashion when I first began teaching composition courses. I would run workshops in my class, but to supplement the workshops, I would give extensive written comments on each draft. And just to make sure each of my students was coming along as I thought they should, right before portfolio I would have thirty-minute conferences with each student just to "firm everything up." It was a very labor-intensive approach, and I had exceptionally high pass rates. My student evaluations were positively glowing. But the small group workshops that took place in class lacked zeal. Things would fall apart, and students would note on their evaluations that workshops had note been the most productive use of time.

Clearly, the small-group workshops were not successful because my students' faith in them was no stronger than mine. I took personal responsibility for every single paper written and was devastated if a student's writing did not come along in the way that I thought it should. Although I appeared to run a student-centered classroom, I still demanded the central authority in my students' work and confirmed it with my one-to-one conferences.

It is all too easy to believe that one's conference is an equal sharing between student and instructor, but if one ever doubts the implicit authoritative relationship between instructor and student, try asking students to reflect on their conferences anonymously. I asked my students to do just this and sixteen out of twenty-five used words like "nervous," "panicked," and "intimidated," in the very first line of reflection. One student wrote,

> Before I got into Tina's office, I felt like I was going to visit with the U.S. president. I didn't know what kind of questions she was going to ask me. I didn't know how she would feel about my essay.

Another student wrote,

> When I walked into the office on the day of my conference, I felt nervous. I didn't know what to expect. What would we talk about? The thought of talking to my teacher on a one-on-one basis made me nervous. Sometimes I find it hard to do such things. Here's my chance to make a good impression. I thought, "but what if I screw up? What if I get tongue tied or run out of things to say while trying to show my teacher a great side of me." I very much dislike that feeling.

Years of socialization have developed preconceived ideas of what a teacher-student conference entails, and this socialization cannot be easily dismissed, even if we believe "My students like having conferences with me." As Black notes,

> [A conference] is, in some ways, the "back room" of teaching, where advice is given, evaluations made, and decisions rendered that usually don't occur in the classroom. There is a great deal at stake for a student: don't speak enough, speak at the wrong time, talk too much, and you can be negatively evaluated. Say the "wrong thing," and there is nowhere to hide. (40–41)

Being asked to conference with your writing instructor can be likened by students to the child being called into the principal's office. The child is powerless in this environment. Yet he must struggle to empower himself by yielding to the principal's inherent authority; OR ELSE, he could suffer even greater consequences.

Deliberate and conscious efforts must be made to decenter the authority within the conference. The instructor can take certain steps to help students assume ownership of their work, learn how to contribute to the discussion of the work, and even confirm their own authority in the writing process. Composition instructors often remark that students simply don't know how to talk about each other's papers in small group workshops. This is often true in the conference setting as well. Too often, students walk in, hand the instructor the paper, and wait for the instructor to "fix" it. One way to begin solving this problem while at the same time diffusing the anxiety felt by most students in these situations is to hold the first small-group workshop and student conference at the same time. I schedule my first workshop as a group conference to be held in my office for about an hour and a half. The group size is usually three or four people and the workshop drafts must be a minimum of three pages in length.

I ask the students to exchange copies of their papers during the class period before the conference and ask each student to read each paper and note their reader-response type of reactions to the paper. In other words, I ask them to key in to their emotional responses as they are reading. Where do they experience anger, joy, boredom, confusion, and so on? (This and many other "Sharing and Responding" ideas are more fully described in *A Community of Writers* by Peter Elbow and Pat Belanoff.) In addition, I ask the writers to be prepared to tell the group what they hoped their readers would gain as a result of reading their paper.

When the conference begins, I ask each writer to read his or her paper aloud and then we discuss the group's reactions to the paper. (Many times this is the first time I have read the paper, but of course, an instructor may wish to read through it briefly before the conference. I do not write too many comments on the paper until after the group discussion takes place because by doing so I find that my students feel I have already formed judgments about the paper, and the group work seems superfluous.) The writer discusses what he hoped to achieve, and the group decides if the paper is successful in this area. If it is, they discuss how; if not, they find possible ways to help it achieve that success. Of course, there is often disagreement on these issues, but consensus is not a goal I hold up as an ideal when discussing papers.

This approach has been successful, I think, for a number of reasons. First, my authority is immediately subsumed because quite simply, I am outnumbered in a very small room with no blackboard and no podium. In addition, the students are asked to talk about the papers using language and concepts they understand. The first conference doesn't need to discuss thesis statements, paragraph coherence, and grammar. This can and will come later and, no doubt, will be touched on at least indirectly by using this approach. Students generally leave the conference feeling that they have learned a great deal about their writing and also leave feeling like they have helped someone else. They are allowed to feel the same satisfaction instructors feel after a great day in class. In addition, it is rare that a student will shirk on his or her preparation for the conference because there are too few people to hide behind. However, if they do shirk on their responsibilities, it most generally is the last time. ·

The group also gets to know each other, and a stronger bond can begin to form among the students. If there are any problems in the group, the instructor can take note early in the semester and try to rectify the situation before it gets out of hand. Finally, the instructor will have introduced herself and her office to the students in a non-threatening way, and negative associations with student-teacher conferences can begin to subside at least a little bit.

After this initial group conference, I initiate small-group workshops in the classroom and hold individual conferences in my office. The individual conference takes place during the second drafting of an essay. I do not receive the essay in advance, and in order to qualify for a conference, the paper must be revised as a consequence of a previous group workshop. I ask the students to bring two copies of their draft so that each of us may have a copy to read.

You may ask why I even use individual conferences if group conferences are so successful. First, as bell hooks suggests, I need to get some sense of where each student is intellectually and psychically so I can get a better sense of his or her needs (78–79). It is much easier to do this on a one-to-one basis when the focus is on the individual rather than the group dynamic. Second, I want the group to be able to function in the classroom without my input and direction. If I continue to preside over the group, they will not be able to build their own authority and self-confidence. Third, as Carnicelli points out, "A teacher who reads papers at home and relies on written comments is working in a vacuum" (106). There has been much discussion about written comments and their lack of effectiveness, but for me, the destructiveness of a teacher's written comment denies the validity of the group work done in the classroom. Evaluative comments written on a paper outside the context of the classroom community imply that it doesn't really matter what happens in a peer workshop; the only thing that matters is what the teacher thinks of the paper in the end.

Written comments are only a one-way conversation. As Carnicelli notes, "a teacher reading a paper at home is deprived of two invaluable resources: the student's information and the student's opinion" (107), but more importantly, the student is deprived of the resource of a dialogue about her work with the institutionally recognized authority in the classroom. She is thereby denied the opportunity to appropriate some of that authority for herself.

Rather than using written comments to respond to student work, conferencing can work to validate the student-centered classroom in a more constructive way. Many of us simply don't feel we have done our jobs (or at least can prove to our colleagues and administrators how hard we work) until we have written comments all over student papers. But as Murray has taught us, meaningful conversation can take place in a conference where both the student and the teacher can learn and create knowledge, thereby empowering the student to write a stronger essay.

However, this type of conversation does not happen naturally in a conference, especially in a conference that takes place early in the semester. While the group conference often serves to demystify the instructor's office and humanize the instructor, the student is still very likely to feel like she is on the hot seat when she meets with the instructor one-on-one. This anxiety can be intensified if the instructor chooses to read the student's paper in front of her, leaving her to fidget and fumble while she waits for a verdict.

One way to lessen this anxiety is to have the student read her paper aloud as the instructor reads along. Not only does this practice break that awkward silence, but it allows the instructor time to critically think about the paper while forcing the student to focus on and remember what she wrote.

After the reading, it is generally agreed that an opening question is useful in beginning a dialogue, but what question? Carnicelli quite aptly points out that:

> To ask such students a question like "What do you think of your paper?" is to put them in a terrible bind. They may like a paper but refuse to admit it because they expect anything they write to be torn to pieces. They may hate a paper but not admit that, either, because they don't want to hurt their grade. The most common early-semester answer to a directly evaluative question is "I don't know." (114–15)

He suggests questions such as "What's your purpose in this paper?" "What parts of the paper do you like most?" "What parts of the paper did you have trouble with?"

I use these questions also, and I agree they can be useful, but I find they still will very likely elicit the "I-don't-know" response or heighten the anxiety of those not comfortable with their work or the environment in which they find themselves. Instead, I like to ask, "What did your group have to say about this paper?" This gives the student a tangible memory to describe. As her narrative continues, she may very well digress about the workshop itself. She may say what she agreed with or disagreed with. She may say what changes she has already made in response to the workshop. She may narrow in on only one aspect of the paper and question her group's response. I welcome these reflections.

Black warns against conferences that are "goal-driven." She says if we set agendas for the conference, "we also make clear that we are not really 'conversing,'" and that the opportunity for digression which takes place in normal conversation is obfuscated. She explains that often, "digression is exploration, is learning: reconstructing experience and knowledge" (31). By surrendering agenda to digression, we allow our students to have their teachers as an audience. Black notes that when students digress into storytelling, they have an opportunity to work their way to a point where they might feel some control over the task ahead in constructing their paper (35). This, I think, should be the "goal" for a conference within a student-centered pedagogy.

Of course, the problem with oral feedback is that it can easily be forgotten. I try to make sure that each student takes five minutes to reflect on the conference before she leaves. I write with her at this time. Black suggests that each student bring in a tape so the conference can be recorded, thereby eliminating the need for the student to take notes and enhancing the possibility for thoughtful conversation rather than dictation. I have not tried this yet, but I agree that students must take away something so they do not forget what happened in the conference when they re-approach their paper.

Thus, what I am suggesting is a reconceptualization of the purpose for one-to-one conferencing. Instead of using conferences as a means to give or confirm direction, conferences can be a time and place to encourage reflection. Although I agree with Kenneth Bruffee that "learning is a social and not an individual process" (92), the act of reflection is still an individual act. Writing is not either social or individual. To suggest it is either/or would be reductive. As Nancy Sommers writes:

> These either/or ways of seeing exclude life and real revision by pushing us to safe positions, to what is known. They are safe positions that exclude each other and don't allow for any ambiguity, uncertainty. (160)

Writing can take us away from these safe places and launch us into a world of ambiguity and uncertainty. Collaboration and reflection can help us through this journey. However, just as collaboration cannot be naturalized within a student-centered pedagogy, neither can the act of reflection.

Kathleen Blake Yancey defines reflection as

> (1) the processes by which we know what we have accomplished and by which we articulate accomplishment and (2) the products of those processes. In method, reflection is dialectical, putting multiple perspectives into play with each other in order to produce insight. (6)

The student-teacher conference can be a place where this dialectical process can be nurtured and encouraged. By seeking to achieve real conversation with students through the sharing of stories, insights, and discoveries despite the implicit power structure of the conference setting; by refusing to direct and insisting on listening; by coming out from behind the desk and relating to each other personally as professionals; by appropriating the social dialogue for the personal conversation of the conference; the student and the teacher can develop their skills of reflection and discover its value.

The instructor's role in a student-centered environment is complicated and perplexing. There is a constant negotiation of authority and power according to need and situation. The student's role is equally as complicated and such perplexity can be quite discomforting. But as John Dewey suggests, classrooms should simulate situations which allow students to experience genuine perplexity. In emphasizing the importance of perplexity in education, we can distinguish learning from assimilation. In emphasizing community in the classroom, we can create a classroom where students can step out of their private realms and contribute to a greater good. In emphasizing the individual, students can learn how to claim their own education. In Dewey's words, "Since learning is something that the pupil has to do himself and from himself, the initiative lies with the learner" (36). The composition instructor can help her students recognize that they must take an active role in their own education if she will encourage her students to discover and claim their own authority.

Works Cited

Black, Laurel Johnson. *Between Talk and Teaching: Reconsidering the Writing Conference.* Logan: Utah State UP, 1998.

Bruffee, Kenneth A. "Collaborative Learning and the 'Conversation of Mankind.'" *College English.* (Nov. 1984): 84–97.

Carnicelli, Thomas A. "The Writing Conference: A One-to-One Conversation." *Eight Approaches to Teaching Composition.* Ed. Timothy R. Donovan, and Ben W. McClelland. Urbana: NCTE, 1980. 101–31.

Dewey, John. *How We Think: A Restatement of the Relation of Reflective Thinking to the Educative Process.* Lexington: Heath, 1933.

Elbow, Peter, and Pat Belanoff. *A Community of Writers*, 2nd ed. New York: McGraw, 1995.

hooks, bell. "Toward a Revolutionary Feminist Pedagogy." *Falling into Theory: Conflicting Views on Reading Literature.* Ed. David H. Richter. Boston: Bedford, 1994. 74–79.

Murray, Donald M. "The Listening Eye: Reflections on the Writing Conference." *The Writing Teacher's Sourcebook*, 3rd ed. Ed. Gary Tate, Edward P.J. Corbett, and Nancy Myers. New York: Oxford UP, 1994. (From *College English* 41 [Sept. 1979]: 13–18.)

Sommers, Nancy. "Between the Drafts." *The Writing Teacher's Sourcebook*, 3rd ed. Ed. Gary Tate, Edward P.J. Corbett, and Nancy Myers. New York: Oxford UP, 1994. (From *College Composition and Communication* 43 [Feb. 1992]: 23–31.)

Yancey, Kathleen Blake. *Reflection in the Writing Classroom.* Logan: Utah State UP, 1998.

WPA OUTCOMES STATEMENT
FOR FIRST-YEAR COMPOSITION[1]

WPA: Writing Program Administrators

[*College English* 63 (2001): 321–25]

http://www.cas.ilstu.edu/English/Hesse/outcomes.html

http://www.mwsc.edu/~outcomes/

This Outcomes Statement, developed by the Writing Program Administrators (WPA), a national organization of composition instructors and administrators, describes the curricular goals—the "knowledge, skills, and attitudes"—that they recommend for the first-year writing course. The statement, which considers classroom practice as well as composition research and theory, is the product of four years of debate and discussion and is meant to represent the broadest range of students, teachers, programs, and institutions. The statement is intended to inform composition programs, but not to dictate standards or levels of achievement—specifics that the WPA stresses should be established by individual institutions. It has been adopted by a number of writing programs across the country. (The statement, including drafts and other WPA documents, can be read online at either of the URLs above.)

The Outcomes Statement was originally published in the organization's journal: *WPA: Writing Program Administration* 23½ (Fall/Winter 1999): 59–63. The piece that follows appeared in *College English* 63.3 (January 2000): 321–25 and features an introduction by WPA member and Clemson University professor Kathleen Blake Yancey, in which she describes how the document evolved and how it might be used as a tool for creating a common vocabulary and for realizing common goals in the composition course.

Yet what these writers should learn is, characteristic of the profession, the subject of perennial disagreement.

— Lynn Bloom

A Brief Introduction by Kathleen Blake Yancey

In the spring of 1996, several compositionists on the Writing Program Administration listserv WPA-L began to discuss four general questions:

1. Why is it that first-year composition programs seem to vary so widely?
2. Is this perception accurate? Do our programs in fact vary widely?
3. Seen another way, what might our programs have in common? What concepts and practices might our programs share?
4. Given sufficient commonality, would it be possible to articulate a general curricular framework for first-year composition, regardless of institutional home, student demographics, and instructor characteristics? Could we do this in a way that doesn't prescribe or infringe?

The short answer to the last question is yes, as embodied below in the "WPA Outcomes Statement for First-Year Composition." Getting to this answer—and this document—was an interesting and, in some ways, anomalous process. The original listserv discussants were joined by at least 25 other volunteers. Together, and in multiple venues—principally, on their own listserv and at many conferences, among them NCTE, CCCC, WPA, and Computers and Writing— this loosely confederated group began to craft a statement about what first-year students should both know and do: what we called an "Outcomes Statement." This collaborative authoring of a common set of outcomes drew on theory as well as practice, on a keen sense of language as well as an appreciation for difference, on a willingness to foreground possibility and to take a risk. Also important was this group's status, or lack thereof; unlike other such efforts, this one was neither established nor commissioned by a professional organization.

The Outcomes Group did understand, however, that if this document were to influence first-year composition programs, it would be useful to have it sanctioned by an official disciplinary organization. In part because the discussion originated on the WPA listserv, and in part because composition programs signify particularly for writing program administrators, the Outcomes Group, as the collaborative group began calling itself, asked the Council of Writing Program Administrators to adopt the statement. In April 2000, after the document was published on the Web and in the organization's journal, and after response was solicited and considered, the Executive Board of WPA adopted the Statement. That, in brief, is the document's history.

Perhaps as interesting is a question about why anyone outside of Composition Studies might be interested in this document. Several reasons are probably self-evident.

First, while first-year composition isn't always a universal requirement, it does persist as a nearly universal experience at colleges and universities across the country. Given the ubiquity of first-year comp, then, it's useful to see some common assumptions undergirding all our programs, to be able to see, in other words, how our individual programs both participate in and depart from the statement represented here.

Second, this document, particularly given its WPA-sponsorship and its publication here, takes on increasing historical value. It speaks to the nature of first-year composition at this moment in time, and it does so in a way that is unprecedented. Never in the history of American education has a disciplinary group sought to define and articulate what it is that we *expect* from students who complete first-year composition. For the first time in American postsecondary education, then, we have a document that represents fundamentals of the first-year composition curriculum.

Third, in addition to its value as an historical document, such a statement can help us think more systematically about what it is that we include in our curriculum—and what we exclude. Notably absent in the statement, for instance, is any discussion of the role of digital technology in composition programs. Currently, it's both an interesting and an open question as to whether this will change in the future.

Fourth, and very pragmatically, the Outcomes Statement has been and will continue to be used to inform composition programs. Sometimes, it is used as a context for specific programs; to create a new program, to revise an extant one. Sometimes the Statement is used to create a dialogue among different faculty, for instance those at high schools and colleges, about what it is that we expect of students. Sometimes it is used to inform others—administrators and members of the public particularly—about what is that we do in our composition classrooms.

Fifth, and not least, then, such a statement can be used politically, and it's a verbal sword that cuts both ways. As several members of the Outcomes Group have discussed, this kind of document, precisely because it seeks to make visible what we do, makes us all vulnerable—our programs and our faculty and our institutions (indeed, often the profession). Without such a statement, however, we often find ourselves equally vulnerable. Moreover, our short experience with actually using the document, to talk to administrators about the quality of the curriculum, for example, and to high school teachers about what college composition is and is not, is that it helps rather than hurts. Such a document allows us to *argue for*—the role of genre in first-year composition, for instance, and for smaller class sizes, and for the role that faculty outside of English must play in fostering student literacy—as well as to resist that which does not further the cause of student education.

What may be glaringly absent here is any discussion of the document's relationship to outcomes, to assessment, and to accreditation visits: to the general concern among all institutions of higher education about accountability. Certainly, the Statement can be used in this context as well; such a use would be entirely within the intent of the document. But this purpose was not the primary intent of the Outcomes Group as it sought to find common ground. Rather, our purpose was curricular. In calling the document an "Outcomes" Statement, however, we achieved two rhetorical advantages. We could focus on expectations, on what we want students to know, to do, to understand. And we could assign to individual campuses the appropriate authority for standards; they may determine *how well* these expectations will be met—should they choose to adopt the outcomes at all.

Ultimately, then, the Outcomes Statement is a curricular document that speaks to the common expectations, for students, of first-year composition programs in the United States at the beginning of the 21st century. Central to the document is the belief that in articulating those expectations and locating them more generally, we help students meet them, and we help assure that the conditions required for meeting them are realized.

Outcomes

Rhetorical Knowledge

By the end of first-year composition, students should

- Focus on a purpose
- Respond to the needs of different audiences
- Respond appropriately to different kinds of rhetorical situations
- Use conventions of format and structure appropriate to the rhetorical situation
- Adopt appropriate voice, tone, and level of formality
- Understand how genres shape reading and writing
- Write in several genres

Faculty in all programs and departments can build on this preparation by helping students learn

- The main features of writing in their fields
- The main uses of writing in their fields
- The expectations of readers in their fields

Critical Thinking, Reading, and Writing

By the end of first-year composition, students should

- Use writing and reading for inquiry, learning, thinking, and communicating
- Understand a writing assignment as a series of tasks, including finding, evaluating, analyzing, and synthesizing appropriate primary and secondary sources
- Integrate their own ideas with those of others
- Understand the relationships among language, knowledge, and power

Faculty in all programs and departments can build on this preparation by helping students learn

- The uses of writing as a critical-thinking tool
- The interactions among critical thinking, critical reading, and writing
- The relationships among language, knowledge, and power in their fields

Processes

By the end of first-year composition, students should

- Be aware that it usually takes multiple drafts to create and complete a successful text
- Develop flexible strategies for generating, revising, editing, and proofreading
- Understand writing as an open process that permits writers to use later invention and re-thinking to revise their work
- Understand the collaborative and social aspects of writing processes
- Learn to critique their own and others' work
- Learn to balance the advantages of relying on others with the responsibility of doing their part
- Use a variety of technologies to address a range of audiences

Faculty in all programs and departments can build on this preparation by helping students learn

- To build final results in stages
- To review work-in-progress in collaborative peer groups for purposes other than editing
- To save extensive editing for later parts of the writing process
- To apply the technologies commonly used to research and communicate within their fields

Knowledge of Conventions

By the end of first-year composition, students should

- Learn common formats for different kinds of texts
- Develop knowledge of genre conventions ranging from structure and paragraphing to tone and mechanics
- Practice appropriate means of documenting their work
- Control such surface features as syntax, grammar, punctuation, and spelling

Faculty in all programs and departments can build on this preparation by helping students learn

- The conventions of usage, specialized vocabulary, format, and documentation in their fields
- Strategies through which better control of conventions can be achieved

Note

[1] The Outcomes Statement was originally published in *WPA: Writing Program Administration* 23.1/2 (Fall/Winter 1999): 59–63 and is reprinted here by permission of the Council of Writing Program Administrators.

THE WRITING CENTER

THE IDEA OF A WRITING CENTER

Stephen North

[*College English* 46.5 (1984): 433–46.]

Professor of English at SUNY at Albany, Stephen North has directed that institution's writing program and writing center. He is the author of *The Making of Knowledge in Composition: Portrait of an Emerging Field* (1987), founding coeditor of *The Writing Center Journal,* and founding editor of the Refiguring English Studies Series. His work has appeared in numerous professional journals, including *College English* and *College Composition and Communication.* His most recent book is *Refiguring the Ph.D. in English Studies: Writing, Doctoral Education, and the Fusion-Based Curriculum* (2000). "The Idea of a Writing Center," first published in 1984, has become a classic in composition studies and is regularly cited as responsible for changing the ways the profession has conceived of writing centers.

North wrote this piece at a time when the focus of writing instruction ostensibly had shifted from the "correct product" to composition processes. As a writing center director, North addresses his colleagues in English departments, arguing that they do not understand what happens, or what should be happening, in writing centers. Instead of writing centers' being seen as the "grammar and drill center, the fix-it shop, the first aid station," North proposes a fundamental shift: that we focus not on producing better individual texts, but on producing better writers. In the first half of his essay, North establishes the historical and professional contexts in which writing centers operate, their marginal status within institutional hierarchies, and the misunderstandings about the work they do. In the second half, he explains the fuller implications of what he calls the new writing center, arguing that it should be more fully integrated into a campuswide dialogue about writing and learning. Writers would use a writing center not because they are required to; instead, the writing center would motivate their desire to talk further about writing that is meaningful to them.

This is an essay that began out of frustration. Despite the reference to writing centers in the title, it is not addressed to a writing center audience but to what is, for my purposes, just the opposite: those not involved with writing centers. Do not exclude yourself from this group just because you know that writing centers (or labs or clinics or places or however you think of them) exist; "involved" here means having directed such a place, having worked there for a minimum of 100 hours, or, at the very least, having talked about writing of your own there for five or more hours. The source of my frustration? Ignorance: the members of my profession, my colleagues, people I might see at MLA or CCCC or read in the pages of *College English*, do not understand what I do. They do not understand what does happen, what can happen, in a writing center.

Let me be clear here. Misunderstanding is something one expects—and almost gets used to—in the writing center business. The new faculty member in our writing-across-the-curriculum program, for example, who sends his students to get their papers "cleaned up" in the Writing Center before they hand them in; the occasional student who tosses her paper on our reception desk, announcing that she'll "pick it up in an hour"; even the well-intentioned administrators who are so happy that we deal with "skills" or "fundamentals" or, to use the word that seems to subsume all others, "grammar" (or usually "GRAMMAR")—these are fairly predictable. But from people in English departments, people well trained in the complex relationship between writer and text, so painfully aware, if only from the composing of dissertations and theses, how lonely and difficult writing can be, I expect more. And I am generally disappointed.

What makes the situation particularly frustrating is that so many such people will vehemently claim that they do, *really*, understand the idea of a writing center. The non-English faculty, the students, the administrators—they may not understand what a writing center is or does, but they have no investment in their ignorance, and can often be educated. But in English departments this second layer of ignorance, this false sense of knowing, makes it doubly hard to get a message through. Indeed, even as you read now, you may be dismissing my argument as the ritual plaint of a "remedial" teacher begging for respectability, the product of a kind of professional paranoia. But while I might admit that there are elements of such a plaint involved—no one likes not to be understood—there is a good deal more at stake. For in coming to terms with this ignorance, I have discovered that it is only a symptom of a much deeper, more serious problem. As a profession I think we are holding on tightly to attitudes and beliefs about the teaching and learning of writing that we thought we had left behind. In fact, my central contention—in the first half of this essay, anyway—is that the failure or inability of the bulk of the English teaching profession, including even those most ardent spokespersons of the so-called "revolution" in the teaching of writing, to perceive the idea of a writing center suggests that, for all our noise and bother about composition, we have fundamentally changed very little.

Let me begin by citing a couple of typical manifestations of this ignorance from close to home. Our writing center has been open for seven years. During that time we have changed our philosophy a little bit as a result of lessons learned from experience, but for the most part we have always been open to anybody in the university community, worked with writers at any time during the composing of a given piece of writing, and dealt with whole pieces of discourse, and not exercises on what might be construed as "subskills" (spelling, punctuation, etc.) outside of the context of the writer's work.

We have delivered the message about what we do to the university generally, and the English department in particular, in a number of ways: letters, flyers, posters, class presentations, information booths, and so on. And, as long as there has been a writing committee, advisory to the director of the writing program, we have sent at least one representative. So it is all the more surprising, and disheartening, that the text for our writing program flyer, composed and approved by that committee, should read as follows:

> The University houses the Center for Writing, founded in 1978 to sponsor the interdisciplinary study of writing. Among its projects are a series of summer institutes for area teachers of writing, a resource center for writers and teachers of writing, *and a tutorial facility for those with special problems in composition.* (My emphasis)

I don't know, quite frankly, how that copy got past me. What are these "special problems"? What would constitute a regular problem, and why wouldn't we talk to the owner of one? Is this hint of pathology, in some mysterious way, a good marketing ploy?

But that's only the beginning. Let me cite another, in many ways more common and painful instance. As a member, recently, of a doctoral examination committee, I conducted an oral in composition theory and practice. One of the candidate's areas of concentration was writing centers, so as part of the exam I gave her a piece of student writing and asked her to play tutor to my student. The session went well enough, but afterward, as we evaluated the entire exam, one of my fellow examiners—a longtime colleague and friend—said that, while the candidate handled the tutoring nicely, he was surprised that the student who had written the paper would have bothered with the Writing Center in the first place. He would not recommend a student to the Center, he said, "unless there were something like twenty-five errors per page."

People make similar remarks all the time, stopping me or members of my staff in the halls, or calling us into offices, to discuss—in hushed tones, frequently—their current "impossible" or difficult students. There was a time, I will confess, when I let my frustration get the better of me. I would be more or less combative, confrontational, challenging the instructor's often well-intentioned but not very useful "diagnosis." We no longer bother with such confrontations; they never worked very well, and they risk undermining the genuine compassion our teachers have for the students they single out. Nevertheless, their behavior makes it clear that for them, a writing center is to illiteracy what a cross between Lourdes and a hospice would be to serious illness: one goes there hoping for miracles, but ready to face the inevitable. In their minds, clearly, writers fall into three fairly distinct groups: the talented, the average, and the others; and the Writing Center's only logical *raison d'etre* must be to handle those others—those, as the flyer proclaims, with "special problems."

Mine is not, of course, the only English department in which such misconceptions are rife. One comes away from any large meeting of writing center people laden with similar horror stories. And in at least one case, a member of such a department—Malcolm Hayward of the Indiana University of Pennsylvania—decided formally to explore and document his faculty's perceptions of the center, and to compare them with the views the center's staff held.[1] His aim, in a two-part survey of both groups, was to determine, first, which goals each group deemed most important in the teaching of writing; and, second, what role they thought the writing center ought to play in that teaching, which goals it ought to concern itself with.

Happily, the writing faculty and the center staff agreed on what the primary goals in teaching writing should be (in the terms offered by Hayward's questionnaire): the development of general patterns of thinking and writing. Unhappily, the two groups disagreed rather sharply about the reasons for referring students to the center. For faculty members the two primary criteria were grammar and punctuation. Tutors, on the other hand, ranked organization "as by far the single most important factor for referral," followed rather distantly by paragraphing, grammar, and style. In short, Hayward's survey reveals the same kind of misunderstanding on his campus that I find so frustrating on my own: the idea that a writing center can only be some sort of skills center, a fix-it shop.

Now if this were just a matter of local misunderstanding, if Hayward and I could straighten it out with a few workshops or lectures, maybe I wouldn't need to write this essay for a public forum. But that is not the case. For whatever reasons writing centers have gotten mostly this kind of press, have been represented—or misrepresented—more often as fix-it shops than in any other way, and in some fairly influential places. Consider, for example, this passage from Barbara E. Fassler Walvoord's *Helping Students Write Well: A Guide for Teachers in All Disciplines* (New York: Modern Language Association, 1981). What makes it particularly odd, at least in terms of my argument, is that Professor Walvoord's book, in many other ways, offers to faculty the kind of perspective on writing (writing as a complex process, writing as a way of learning) that I might offer myself. Yet here she is on writing centers:

> If you are very short of time, if you think you are not skilled enough to deal with mechanical problems, or if you have a number of students with serious difficulties, you may wish to let the skills center carry the ball for mechanics and spend your time on other kinds of writing and learning problems. (p. 63)

Don't be misled by Professor Walvoord's use of the "skills center" label; in her index the entry for "Writing centers" reads "See skills centers"—precisely the kind of interchangeable terminology I find so abhorrent. On the other hand, to do Professor Walvoord justice, she does recommend that teachers become "at least generally aware of how your skills center works with students, what its basic philosophy is, and what goals it sets for the students in your class," but it seems to me that she has already restricted the possible scope of such a philosophy pretty severely: "deal with mechanical problems"? "carry the ball for mechanics"?

Still, as puzzling and troubling as it is to see Professor Walvoord publishing misinformation about writing centers, it is even more painful, downright maddening, to read one's own professional obituary; to find, in the pages of a reputable professional journal, that what you do has been judged a failure, written off. Maxine Hairston's "The Winds of Change: Thomas Kuhn and the Revolution in the Teaching of Writing" (*College Composition and Communication*, 33 [1982], 76–88) is an attempt to apply the notion of a "paradigm shift" to the field of composition teaching. In the course of doing so Professor Hairston catalogues, under the subheading "Signs of Change," what she calls "ad hoc" remedies to the writing "crisis":

> Following the pattern that Kuhn describes in his book, our first response to crisis has been to improvise ad hoc measures to try to patch the cracks and keep the system running. Among the first responses were the writing labs that sprang up about ten years ago to give first aid to students who seemed unable to function within the traditional paradigm. Those labs are still with us, but they're still only giving first aid and treating symptoms. They have not solved the problem. (p. 82)

What first struck me about this assessment—what probably strikes most people in the writing center business—is the mistaken history, the notion that writing labs "sprang up about ten years ago." The fact is, writing "labs," as Professor Hairston chooses to call them, have been around in one form or another since at least the 1930s when Carrie Stanley was already working with writers at the University of Iowa. Moreover, this limited conception of what such places can do—the fix-it shop image—has been around far longer than ten years, too. Robert Moore, in a 1950 *College English* article, "The Writing Clinic and the Writing Laboratory" (7 [1950], 388–93), writes that "writing clinics and writing laboratories are becoming increasingly popular among American universities and colleges as remedial agencies for removing students' deficiencies in composition" (p. 388).

Still, you might think that I ought to be happier with Professor Hairston's position than with, say, Professor Walvoord's. And to some extent I am: even if she mistakenly assumes that the skill and drill model represents all writing centers equally well, she at least recognizes its essential futility. Nevertheless—and this is what bothers me most about her position—her dismissal fails to lay the blame for these worst versions of writing centers on the right heads. According to her "sprang up" historical sketch, these places simply appeared—like so many mushrooms?—to do battle with illiteracy. "They" are still with "us," but "they" haven't solved the problem. What is missing here is a doer, an agent, a creator—someone to take responsibility. The implication is that "they" done it—"they" being, apparently, the places themselves.

But that won't wash. "They," to borrow from Walt Kelly, is *us:* members of English departments, teachers of writing. Consider, as evidence, the pattern of writing center origins as revealed in back issues of *The Writing Lab Newsletter:* the castoff, windowless classroom (or in some cases literally, closet), the battered desks, the old textbooks, a phone (maybe), no budget, and, almost inevitably, a director with limited status—an untenured or non–tenure track faculty member, a teaching assistant, an undergraduate, a "paraprofessional," etc. Now who do you suppose has determined what is to happen in that center? Not the director, surely; not the staff, if there is one. The mandate is clearly from the sponsoring body, usually an English department. And lest you think that things are better where space and money are not such serious problems, I urge you to visit a center where a good bit of what is usually grant money has been spent in the first year or two of the center's operation. Almost always, the money will have been used on materials: drills, texts, machines, tapes, carrells, headphones—the works. And then the director, hired on "soft" money, without political clout, is locked into an approach because she or he has to justify the expense by using the materials.

Clearly, then, where there is or has been misplaced emphasis on so-called basics or drill, where centers have been prohibited from dealing with the writing that students do for their classes—where, in short, writing centers have been of the kind that Professor Hairston is quite correctly prepared to write off—it is because the agency that created the center in the first place, too often an English department, has made it so. The grammar and drill center, the fix-it shop, the first-aid station—these are neither the vestiges of some paradigm left behind nor pedagogical aberrations that have been overlooked in the confusion of the "revolution" in the teaching of writing, but that will soon enough be set on the right path, or done away with. They are, instead, the vital and authentic reflection of a way of thinking about writing and the teaching of writing that is alive and well and living in English departments everywhere.

But if my claims are correct—if this is not what writing centers are or, if it is what they are, it is not what they should be—then what are, what *should* they be? What *is* the idea of a writing center? By way of answer, let me return briefly to the family of metaphors by which my sources have characterized their idea of a writing center: Robert Moore's "removing students' deficiencies," Hairston's "first aid" and "treating symptoms," my colleague's "twenty-five errors per page," Hayward's punctuation and grammar referrers, and Walvoord's "carrying the ball for mechanics" (where, at least, writing centers are athletic and not surgical). All of these imply essentially the same thing: that writing centers define their province in terms of a given curriculum, taking over those portions of it that "regular" teachers are willing to cede or, presumably, unable to handle. Over the past six years or so I have visited more than fifty centers, and read descriptions of hundreds of others, and I can assure you that there are indeed centers of this kind, centers that can trace their conceptual lineage back at least as far as Moore. But the "new" writing center has a somewhat shorter history. It is the result of a documentable resurgence, a renaissance if you will, that began in the early 1970s. In fact, the flurry of activity that caught Professor Hairston's attention, and which she mistook for the beginnings of the "old" center, marked instead the genesis of a center which defined its province in a radically different way. Though I have some serious reservations about Hairston's use of Kuhn's paradigm model to describe what happens in composition teaching, I will for the moment put things in her terms: the new writing center, far from marking the end of an era, is the embodiment, the epitome, of a new one. It represents the marriage of what are arguably the two most powerful contemporary perspectives on teaching writing: first, that writing is most usefully viewed as a process; and second, that writing curricula need to be student-centered. This new writing center, then, defines its province not in terms of some curriculum, but in terms of the writers it serves.

To say that writing centers are based on a view of writing as a process is, original good intentions notwithstanding, not to say very much anymore. The slogan—and I daresay that is what it has become—has been devalued, losing most of its impact and explanatory power. Let me use it, then, to make the one distinction of which it still seems capable: in a writing center the object is to make sure that writers, and not necessarily their texts, are what get changed by instruction. In axiom form it goes like this: Our job is to produce better writers, not better writing. Any given project—a class assignment, a law school application letter, an encyclopedia entry, a dissertation proposal—is for the writer the prime, often the exclusive concern. That particular text, its success or failure, is what brings them to talk to us in the first place. In the center, though, we look beyond or through that particular project, that particular text, and see it as an occasion for addressing *our* primary concern, the process by which it is produced.

At this point, however, the writing-as-a-process slogan tends to lose its usefulness. That "process," after all, has been characterized as everything from the reception of divine inspiration to a set of nearly algorithmic rules for producing the five-paragraph theme. In between are the more widely accepted and, for the moment, more respectable descriptions derived from composing aloud protocols, interviews, videotaping, and so on. None of those, in any case, represent the composing process we seek in a writing center. The version we want can be found only, in as yet unarticulated form, in the writer we are working with. I think probably the best way to describe a writing center tutor's relationship to composing is to say that a tutor is a holist devoted to a participant-observer methodology. This may seem, at first glance, too passive—or, perhaps, too glamorous, legitimate, or trendy—a role in which to cast tutors. But consider this passage from Paul Diesing's *Patterns of Discovery in the Social Sciences* (Hawthorne, N.Y.: Aldine, 1971):

> Holism is not, in the participant-observer method, an a priori belief that everything is related to everything else. It is rather the methodological necessity of pushing on to new aspects and new kinds of evidence in order to make sense of

what one has already observed and to test the validity of one's interpretations. A belief in the organic unity of living systems may also be present, but this belief by itself would not be sufficient to force a continual expansion of one's observations. It is rather one's inability to develop an intelligible and validated partial model that drives one on. (p. 167)

How does this definition relate to tutors and composing? Think of the writer writing as a kind of host setting. What we want to do in a writing center is fit into—observe and participate in—this ordinarily solo ritual of writing. To do this, we need to do what any participant-observer must do: see what happens during this "ritual," try to make sense of it, observe some more, revise our model, and so on indefinitely, all the time behaving in a way the host finds acceptable. For validation and correction of our model, we quite naturally rely on the writer, who is, in turn, a willing collaborator in—and, usually, beneficiary of—the entire process. This process precludes, obviously, a reliance on or a clinging to any predetermined models of "the" composing process, except as crude topographical guides to what the "territory" of composing processes might look like. The only composing process that matters in a writing center is "a" composing process, and it "belongs" to, is acted out by, only one given writer.

It follows quite naturally, then, that any curriculum—any plan of action the tutor follows—is going to be student-centered in the strictest sense of that term. That is, it will not derive from a generalized model of composing, or be based on where the student ought to be because she is a freshman or sophomore, but will begin from where the student is, and move where the student moves—an approach possible only if, as James Moffett suggests in *Teaching the Universe of Discourse* (Boston: Houghton Mifflin, 1968), the teacher (or tutor in this case) "shifts his gaze from the subject to the learner, for the subject is in the learner" (p. 67). The result is what might be called a pedagogy of direct intervention. Whereas in the "old" center instruction tends to take place after or apart from writing, and tends to focus on the correction of textual problems, in the "new" center the teaching takes place as much as possible during writing, during the activity being learned, and tends to focus on the activity itself.

I do not want to push the participant-observer analogy too far. Tutors are not, finally, researchers: they must measure their success not in terms of the constantly changing model they create, but in terms of changes in the writer. Rather than being fearful of disturbing the "ritual" of composing, they observe it and are charged to change it: to interfere, to get in the way, to participate in ways that will leave the "ritual" itself forever altered. The whole enterprise seems to me most natural. Nearly everyone who writes likes—and needs—to talk about his or her writing, preferably to someone who will really listen, who knows how to listen, and knows how to talk about writing too. Maybe in a perfect world, all writers would have their own ready auditor—a teacher, a classmate, a roommate, an editor—who would not only listen but draw them out, ask them questions they would not think to ask themselves. A writing center is an institutional response to this need. Clearly writing centers can never hope to satisfy this need themselves; on my campus alone, the student-to-tutor ratio would be about a thousand to one. Writing centers are simply one manifestation—polished and highly visible—of a dialogue about writing that is central to higher education.

As is clear from my citations in the first half of this essay, however, what seems perfectly natural to me is not so natural for everyone else. One part of the difficulty, it seems to me now, is not theoretical at all, but practical, a question of coordination or division of labor. It usually comes in the form of a question like this: "If I'm doing process-centered teaching in my class, why do I need a writing center? How can I use it?" For a long time I tried to soft-pedal my answers to this question. For instance, in my dissertation ("Writing Centers: A Sourcebook," Diss. SUNY at Albany, 1978) I talked about complementing or intensifying classroom instruction. Or, again, in our center we tried using, early on, what is a fairly common device among writing centers, a referral form; at one point it even had a sort of diagnostic taxonomy, a checklist, by which teachers could communicate to us their concerns about the writers they sent us.

But I have come with experience to take a harder, less conciliatory position. The answer to the question in all cases is that teachers, as teachers, do not need, and cannot use, a writing center: only writers need it, only writers can use it. You cannot parcel out some portion of a given student for us to deal with ("You take care of editing, I'll deal with invention"). Nor should you require that all of your students drop by with an early draft of a research paper to get a reading from a fresh audience. You should not scrawl, at the bottom of a failing paper, "Go to the Writing Center." Even those of you who, out of genuine concern, bring students to a writing center, almost by the hand, to make sure they know that we won't hurt them—even you are essentially out of line. Occasionally we manage to convert such writers from people who have to see us to people who want to, but most often they either come as if for a kind of detention, or they drift away. (It would be nice if in writing, as in so many things, people would do what we tell them because it's good for them, but they don't. If and when *they* are ready, we will be here.)

In short, we are not here to serve, supplement, back up, complement, reinforce, or otherwise be defined by any external curriculum. We are here to talk to writers. If they happen to come from your classes, you might take it as a compliment to your assignments, in that your writers are engaged in them enough to want to talk about their work. On the other hand, we do a fair amount of trade in people working on ambiguous or poorly designed assignments, and far too much work with writers whose writing has received caustic, hostile, or otherwise unconstructive commentary.

I suppose this declaration of independence sounds more like a declaration of war, and that is obviously not what I intend, especially since the primary casualties would be the students and writers we all aim to serve. And I see no reason that writing centers and classroom teachers cannot cooperate as well as coexist. For example, the first rule in our Writing Center is that we are professionals at what we do. While that does, as I have argued, give us the freedom of self-definition, it also carries with it a responsibility to respect our fellow professionals. Hence we never play student-advocates in teacher-student relationships. The guidelines are very clear. In all instances the student must understand that we support the teacher's position completely. (Or, to put it in less loaded terms—for we are not teacher advocates either—the instructor is simply part of the rhetorical context in which the writer is trying to operate. We cannot change that context: all we can do is help the writer learn how to operate in it and other contexts like it.) In practice, this rule means that we never evaluate or second-guess any teacher's syllabus, assignments, comments, or grades. If students are unclear about any of those, we send them back to the teacher to get clear. Even in those instances I mentioned above—when writers come in confused by what seem to be poorly designed assignments, or crushed by what appear to be unwarrantedly hostile comments—we pass no judgment, at least as far as the student is concerned. We simply try, every way we can, to help the writer make constructive sense of the situation.

In return, of course, we expect equal professional courtesy. We need, first of all, instructors' trust that our work with writers-in-progress on academic assignments is not plagiarism, any more than a conference with the teacher would be—that, to put it the way I most often hear it, we will not write students' papers for them. Second, instructors must grant us the same respect we grant them—that is, they must neither evaluate nor second-guess our work with writers. We are, of course, most willing to talk about that work. But we do not take kindly to the perverse kind of thinking represented in remarks like, "Well, I had a student hand in a paper that he took to the writing center, and it was *still* full of errors." The axiom, if you will recall, is that we aim to make better writers, not necessarily—or immediately—better texts.

Finally, we can always use classroom teachers' cooperation in helping us explain to students what we do. As a first step, of course, I am asking that they revise their thinking about what a writing center can do. Beyond that, in our center we find it best to go directly to the students ourselves. That is, rather than sending out a memo or announcement for the teachers to read to their classes, we simply send our staff, upon invitation, into classes to talk with students or, better yet, to do live tutorials. The standard presentation, a ten-minute affair, gives students a person, a name, and a face to remember the Center by. The live tutorials take longer, but we think they are worth it. We ask the instructor to help us find a writer willing to have a draft (or a set of notes or even just the assignment) reproduced for the whole class. Then the Writing Center person does, with the participation of the entire class, what we do in the Center: talk about writing with the writer. In our experience the instructors learn as much about the Center from these sessions as the students.

To argue that writing centers are not here to serve writing class curricula is not to say, however, that they are here to replace them. In our center, anyway, nearly every member of the full-time staff is or has been a classroom teacher of writing. Even our undergraduate tutors work part of their time in an introductory writing course. We all recognize and value the power of classroom teaching, and we take pride in ourselves as professionals in that setting too. But working in both situations makes us acutely aware of crucial differences between talking about writing in the context of a class, and talking about it in the context of the Center. When we hold student conferences in our classes, we are the teacher, in the writers' minds especially, the assigner and evaluator of the writing in question. And for the most part we are pretty busy people, with conference appointments scheduled on the half hour, and a line forming outside the office. For efficiency the papers-in-progress are in some assigned form—an outline, a first draft, a statement of purpose with bibliography and note cards; and while the conference may lead to further composing, there is rarely the time or the atmosphere for composing to happen during the conference itself. Last but not least, the conference is likely to be a command performance, our idea, not the writer's.

When we are writing center tutors all of that changes. First of all, conferences are the writer's idea; he or she seeks us out. While we have an appointment book that offers half-hour appointment slots, our typical session is fifty minutes, and we average between three and four per writer; we can afford to give a writer plenty of time. The work-in-progress is in whatever form the writer has managed to put it in, which may make tutoring less efficient, but which clearly makes it more student-centered, allowing us to begin where the writers are, not where we told them to be. This also means that in most cases the writers come prepared, even anxious to get on with their work, to begin or to keep on composing. Whereas going to keep a conference with a teacher is, almost by definition, a kind of goal or deadline—a stopping place—going to talk in the writing center is a means of getting started, or a way to keep going. And finally—in a way subsuming all the rest—we are not the teacher. We did not assign the writing, and we will not grade it. However little that distinction might mean in our behaviors, it seems to mean plenty to the writers.

What these differences boil down to, in general pedagogical terms, are timing and motivation. The fact is, not everyone's interest in writing, their need or desire to write or learn to write, coincides with the fifteen or thirty weeks they spend in writing courses—especially when, as is currently the case at so many institutions, those weeks are required. When writing does become important, a writing center can be there in a way that our regular classes cannot. Charles Cooper, in an unpublished paper called "What College Writers Need to Know" (1979), puts it this way:

> The first thing college writers need to know is that they can improve as writers and the second is that they will never reach a point where they cannot improve further. One writing course, two courses, three courses may not be enough. If they're on a campus which takes writing seriously, they will be able to find the courses they need to feel reasonably confident they can fulfill the requests which will be made of them in their academic work. . . . Throughout their college years they should also be able to find on a drop-in, no-fee basis expert tutorial help with any writing problem they encounter in a paper. (p. 1)

A writing center's advantage in motivation is a function of the same phenomenon. Writers come looking for us because, more often than not, they are genuinely, deeply engaged with their material, anxious to wrestle it into the best form they can: they are motivated to write. If we agree that the biggest obstacle to overcome in teaching anything, writing included, is getting learners to decide that they want to learn, then what a writing center does is cash in on motivation that the writer provides. This teaching at the conjunction of timing and motivation is most strikingly evident when we work with writers doing "real world" tasks: application essays for law, medical, and graduate schools, newspaper and magazine articles, or poems and stories. Law school application writers are suddenly willing—sometimes overwhelmingly so—to concern themselves with audience, purpose, and persona, and to revise over and over again. But we see the same excitement in writers working on literature or history or philosophy papers, or preparing dissertation proposals, or getting ready to tackle comprehensive exams. Their primary concern is with their material, with some existential context where new ideas must merge with old, and suddenly writing is a vehicle, a means to an end, and not an end in itself.

The essence of the writing center method, then, is this talking. If we conceive of writing as a relatively rhythmic and repeatable kind of behavior, then for a writer to improve that behavior, that rhythm has to change—preferably, though not necessarily, under the writer's control. Such changes can be fostered, of course, by work outside of the act of composing itself—hence the success of the classical discipline of imitation, or more recent ones like sentence combining or the tagmemic heuristic, all of which, with practice, "merge" with and affect composing. And, indeed, depending on the writer, none of these tactics would be ruled out in a writing center. By and large, however, we find that the best breaker of old rhythms, the best creator of new ones, is our style of live intervention, our talk in all its forms.

The kind of writing does not substantially change the approach. We always want the writer to tell us about the rhetorical context—what the purpose of the writing is, who its audience is, how the writer hopes to present herself. We want to know about other constraints—deadlines, earlier experiences with the same audience or genre, research completed or not completed, and so on. In other ways, though, the variations on the kind of talk are endless. We can question, praise, cajole, criticize, acknowledge, badger, plead—even cry. We can read: silently, aloud, together, separately. We can play with options. We can both write—as, for example, in response to sample essay exam questions—and compare opening strategies. We can poke around in resources—comparing, perhaps, the manuscript conventions of the Modern Language Association with those of the American Psychological Association. We can ask writers to compose aloud while we listen, or we can compose aloud, and the writer can watch and listen.

In this essay, however, I will say no more about the nature of this talk. One reason is that most of what can be said, for the moment, has been said in print already. There is, for example, my own "Training Tutors to Talk About Writing" (*CCC*, 33 [1982] 434–41), or Muriel Harris' "Modeling: A Process Method of Teaching" (*College English*, 45, [1983], 74–84). And there are several other sources, including a couple of essay collections, that provide some insights into the hows and whys of tutorial talk.[2]

A second reason, though, seems to me more substantive, and symptomatic of the kinds of misunderstanding I have tried to dispel here. We don't know very much, in other than a practitioner's anecdotal way, about the dynamics of the tutorial. The same can be said, of course, with regard to talk about writing in any setting—the classroom, the peer group, the workshop, the teacher-student conference, and so on. But while ignorance of the nature of talk in those settings does not threaten their existence, it may do precisely that in writing centers. That is, given the idea of the writing center I have set forth here, talk is everything. If the writing center is ever to prove its worth in other than quantitative terms—numbers of students seen, for example, or hours of tutorials provided—it will have to do so by describing this talk: what characterizes it, what effects it has, how it can be enhanced.

Unfortunately, the same "proofreading-shop-in-the-basement" mentality that undermines the pedagogical efforts of the writing center hampers research as well. So far most of the people hired to run such places have neither the time, the training, nor the status to undertake any serious research. Moreover, the few of us lucky enough to even consider the possibility of research have found that there are other difficulties. One is that writing center work is often not considered fundable—that is, relevant to a wide enough audience—even though there are about a thousand such facilities in the country, a figure which suggests that there must be at least ten or fifteen thousand tutorials every school day, and even though research into any kind of talk about writing is relevant for the widest possible audience. Second, we have discovered that focusing our scholarly efforts on writing centers may be a professional liability. Even if we can publish our work (and that is by no means easy), there is no guarantee that it will be viewed favorably by tenure and promotion review committees. Composition itself is suspect enough; writing centers, a kind of obscure backwater, seem no place for a scholar.

These conditions may be changing. Manuscripts for *The Writing Center Journal*, for example, suggest that writing center folk generally are becoming more research-oriented; there were sessions scheduled at this year's meetings of the MLA and NCTE on research in or relevant to writing centers. In an even more tangible signal of change, the State University of New York has made funds available for our Albany center to develop an appropriate case study methodology for writing center tutorials. Whether this trend continues or not, my point remains the same. Writing centers, like any other portion of a college writing curriculum, need time and space for appropriate research and reflection if they are to more clearly understand what they do, and figure out how to do it better. The great danger is that the very misapprehensions that put them in basements to begin with may conspire to keep them there.

It is possible that I have presented here, at least by implication, too dismal a portrait of the current state of writing centers. One could, as a matter of fact, mount a pretty strong argument that things have never been better. There are, for example, several regional writing center associations that have annual meetings, and the number of such associations increases every year. Both *The Writing Lab Newsletter* and *The Writing Center Journal*, the two publications in the field, have solid circulations. This year at NCTE, for the first time, writing center people met as a recognized National Assembly, a major step up from their previous Special Interest Session status.

And on individual campuses all over the country, writing centers have begun to expand their institutional roles. So, for instance, some centers have established resource libraries for writing teachers. They sponsor readings or reading series by poets and fiction writers, and annual festivals to celebrate writing of all kinds. They serve as clearinghouses for information on where to publish, on writing programs, competitions, scholarships, and so on; and they sponsor such competitions themselves, even putting out their own publications. They design and conduct workshops for groups with special needs—essay exam takers, for example, or job application writers. They are involved with, or have even taken over entirely, the task of training new teaching assistants. They have played central roles in the creation of writing-across-the-curriculum programs. And centers have extended themselves beyond their own institutions, sending tutors to other schools (often high schools), or helping other institutions set up their own facilities. In some cases, they have made themselves available to the wider community, often opening a "Grammar Hotline" or "Grammaphone"—a service so popular at one institution, in fact, that a major publishing company provided funding to keep it open over the summer.

Finally, writing centers have gotten into the business of offering academic credit. As a starting point they have trained their tutors in formal courses or, in some instances, "paid" their tutors in credits rather than money. They have set up independent study arrangements to sponsor both academic and non-academic writing experiences. They have offered credit-bearing courses of their own; in our center, for example, we are piloting an introductory writing course that uses Writing Center staff members as small group leaders.

I would very much like to say that all this activity is a sure sign that the idea of a writing center is here to stay, that the widespread misunderstandings I described in this essay, especially those held so strongly in English departments, are dissolving. But in good conscience I cannot. Consider the activities we are talking about. Some of them, of course, are either completely or mostly public relations: a way of making people aware that a writing center exists, and that (grammar hotlines aside) it deals in more than usage and punctuation. Others—like the resource library, the clearinghouse, or the training of new teaching assistants—are more substantive, and may well belong in a writing center, but most of them end up there in the first place because nobody else wants to do them. As for the credit generating, that is simply pragmatic. The bottom line in academic budget making is calculated in student credit hours; when budgets are tight, as they will be for the foreseeable future, facilities that generate no credits are the first to be cut. Writing centers—even really good writing centers—have proved no exception.

None of these efforts to promote writing centers suggest that there is any changed understanding of the idea of a writing center. Indeed it is as though what writing centers do that really matters—talking to writers—were not enough. That being the case, enterprising directors stake out as large a claim as they can in more visible or acceptable territory. All of these efforts—and, I assure you, my center does its share—have about them an air of shrewdness, or desperation, the trace of a survival instinct at work. I am not such a purist as to suggest that these things are all bad. At the very least they can be good for staff morale. Beyond that I think they may eventually help make writing centers the centers of consciousness about writing on campuses, a kind of physical locus for the ideas and ideals of college or university or high school commitment to writing—a status to which they might well aspire and which, judging by results on a few campuses already, they can achieve.

But not this way, not via the back door, not—like some marginal ballplayer— by doing whatever it takes to stay on the team. If writing centers are going to finally be accepted, surely they must be accepted on their own terms, as places whose primary responsibility, whose only reason for being, is to talk to writers. That is their heritage, and it stretches back farther than the late 1960s or the early 1970s, or to Iowa in the 1930s—back, in fact, to Athens, where in a busy marketplace a tutor called Socrates set up the same kind of shop: open to all comers, no fees charged, offering, on whatever subject a visitor might propose, a continuous dialectic that is, finally, its own end.

[1] "Assessing Attitudes Toward the Writing Center," *The Writing Center Journal*, 3, No. 2 (1983), 1–11.

[2] See, for example, *Tutoring Writing: A Sourcebook for Writing Labs*, ed. Muriel Harris (Glenview, Ill.: Scott-Foresman, 1982); and *New Directions for College Learning Assistance: Improving Writing Skills*, ed. Phyllis Brooks and Thom Hawkins (San Francisco: Jossey-Bass, 1981).

"WE DON'T PROOFREAD HERE": RE-VISIONING THE WRITING CENTER TO BETTER MEET STUDENT NEEDS

Joan Hawthorne

[*The Writing Lab Newsletter* 23.8 (1999): 1–7.]

Joan Hawthorne is the Coordinator of the Writing Center at the University of North Dakota at Grand Forks and has taught composition and education courses. Her research interests include writing center work and writing across the curriculum. Her essays and reviews have appeared in *Language and Learning across the Disciplines*, *The Writing Lab Newsletter*, and the *Journal of Teaching Writing*.

In his article, "The Idea of a Writing Center," Stephen North states that the goal of writing centers should be to produce better writers rather than better individual texts. North's axiom can be seen as part of the larger movement to avoid directive and prescriptive instruction in favor of facilitative and process-oriented instruction. Joan Hawthorne, however, sees a serious contradiction in the favoring of facilitative, process-oriented instruction in the writing center, pointing out that the ways writing center tutors talk about their work in public, professional settings is very different from their private talk. On the one hand, directive tutoring and focusing on subskills such as proofreading are clearly not acceptable; on the other hand, tutors admit that of course they help students "fix" problems, and often their advice is directive. In fact, analyses of tutoring sessions confirm that even facilitative questioning strategies that encourage writers to see their texts differently are in many ways still directive. Tutors purposefully choose questions that will focus a writer's attention on a specific feature of a text. Hawthorne explores this apparent contradiction between theory and practice, proposing that we reconsider the idea that tutors should not be directive. Instead, Hawthorne suggests that tutoring should be especially sensitive to the needs of the writer, which may mean being directive in appropriate situations. She shares two handouts she uses in tutor training, and she describes how she helps tutors learn to make decisions about when to consider directive tutoring. Hawthorne's article provides a necessary corrective to the oversimplification of North's earlier advice about the role of writing center tutors, and her handouts will be useful not only for prospective tutors but for writing instructors, too, who face a similarly complex situation when responding to students' works-in-progress.

———————

During a recent Midwest Writing Centers Association conference, I found myself noting a curious contradiction. In presentations, speakers seemed to assume that all conference attendees shared a commitment to a particular model of writing center pedagogy, a model which is often ascribed to Stephen North although Jeff Brooks more fully articulates the pedagogy in his essay on "Minimalist Tutoring." The unspoken understanding in these sessions was that tutoring is about improving the writer, not the writing; practice must follow from that premise. If our focus is on the writer, so the logic goes, directive tutoring is out. If our goal is not to improve the writing itself, editing and proofreading are inappropriate.

But informal, one-to-one conversations during the conference seemed to carry a contradictory subtext. "Of course the paper is important," was the contrasting message. "Writing center tutors work on editing and proofreading because those are important issues to teachers and students alike. Sometimes we use directive tutoring because sometimes it's the best strategy to use." In only one session did I hear these conflicts explicitly mentioned. And yet the issues at stake are bedrock for writing center directors and tutors. They address questions of who we are and how we practice. Their implications are both ethical and practical, and their impact extends to virtually every conference held within writing center doors.

Several years ago I began thinking about the difference between improving the writer and improving the writing. My interest was originally prompted by a small, "practice" project on observational research I conducted in a writing center. I watched and listened as the writing center director tutored perhaps a dozen individual students, and I rarely heard her "tell" a student what to do. Directive tutoring, she told me, was not part of her center's pedagogy—a pedagogy shaped by her familiarity with oft-cited articles like those by North and Brooks. But I noticed during my observations that her questions were usually chosen with a purpose in mind. She asked questions to help students notice and identify issues of concern that she saw in the writing. How was that different than a more openly directive style of teaching/tutoring/consulting that might allow the tutor to overtly point out a problem with organization, or to offer a potential correction of a grammatical problem?

But it was my own experience as a writing center director that really sharpened my focus on questions of tutoring pedagogy and ethics. When I became director of the University of North Dakota Writing Center, I had no immediate agenda for change. Only one writing center practice stood out in my mind as a significant concern—the habitual response to students who began a request for an appointment by asking for someone to "proofread" the paper. The writing center staff, like many tutors elsewhere, were encouraged to handle those requests with a polite but simple response that went something like this: "Well, we don't proofread here. But we could look at your paper together if you like." I flinched every time I heard that language. Students, I thought, focused on the first and negative message: "No." Furthermore, I believed that students often asked for proofreading because they lacked the vocabulary and/or experience to know what they really needed or the kind of help they wanted. And if they truly wanted to work on proofreading, I thought, tutors could at least make sure students learned something about self-editing. A friend or roommate, on the other hand, was likely to simply pencil in changes (many of which might in fact be incorrect).

So I asked our consultants to change that piece of their practice. Instead of saying "We don't proofread," consultants were asked to respond to those requests by saying something like "We'd be happy to take a look at your paper with you." In the course of the session itself, a fuller discussion about the student's needs and the limits of writing center practice could be negotiated. Over the next few months, this small change in language became the impetus for several conversations about the purpose of the writing center itself. I found myself asking questions like these during our staff meetings: What do we do in the writing center? What do our choices about what we do mean for us? What do our words about what we do convey to students? Who gets advantaged or disadvantaged by the choices we make? Who do we really serve? Of course, we were not the only writing center staff wrestling with such problematic issues. I found there was no shortage of reading material, much of it very current, to share with my tutors.

We began with the Clark and Healy piece, "Are Writing Centers Ethical?" where we found a challenge to the idea that the non-interventionist tutor is always (or perhaps even usually) the most helpful to students. A proactive new writing center ethic, they asserted, must "move beyond Stephen North's oft-quoted dictum that '[o]ur job is to produce better writers, not better writing'" (43). My next contribution to our discussion was based on a conference presentation by Nancy Grimm. As part of a call for a shift from a modernist to a post-modernist perspective on tutoring, Grimm challenged conference attendees to consider who is advantaged and who is disadvantaged by standard tutoring practices. That consideration seemed applicable to our questions about how much directivity is appropriate and how much editing can fairly be done within the collaborative structure of a writing center conference.

As my focus on these questions sharpened, I found more and more materials available to help me think about my own assumptions and those of the writing center establishment. We read the Shamoon and Burns essay, which pleaded for a broader notion of appropriate writing center practice—broad enough to include both directive and non-directive practices. We found Angela Petit's article, which argued that rigid theoretical notions of what the writing center does are unnecessarily restrictive to all of us, not least to those tutors who must depend on them (rather than years of teaching and conferencing experiences) for guidance in shaping their own practice. We reread Andrea Lunsford's early article about the three basic pedagogical stances in writing centers, and found that her criticisms of "storehouse" and "garret" centers lent further credence to our concerns about how to draw boundaries that appropriately circumscribe good writing center practice.

We returned as well to Stephen North's writing, since he is so often cited as the person responsible for anti-fix-it-shop, anti-proofreading, anti-directive pedagogies. A close reading convinced me that North offered a broad vision of tutoring pedagogy. Writing centers, North argued in an essay written for English department faculty, should be "student-centered," and tutors should "begin where the writers are, not where we told them to be" (442). Tutoring strategies can include "the classical discipline of imitation;" tutor and student can "both write. . . . We can ask writers to compose aloud while we listen, or we can compose aloud, and the writer can watch and listen" (443). In sum, I concluded that narrow interpretations of North's description of writing center pedagogies have over-simplified the case.

As the center director, I found myself looking too at tutor training materials. Manuals by Leigh Ryan and Irene Clark seemed to suggest to new tutors (by omission, if nothing else) that directive tutoring was a generally inappropriate practice. Recommended strategies instead included "active listening, facilitating by responding as a reader, silence and wait time to allow a student time to think"

(Ryan, 17). Taking a somewhat broader perspective, Clark acknowledged that editing and proofreading have a place in the writing process, and suggested that tutors might help students in that phase of the process by identifying patterns of error, teaching grammatical terminology, and recommending strategies for effective proofreading.

While puzzling over how to apply all of this in our own writing center, we talked about the similarities and differences between writing center conferences and teacher-student conferences. There, too, issues of authority and expertise are complicated, which is perhaps why so many students and teachers feel some frustration with the whole process. We concluded that conferencing is indeed complex, and that simplified answers—work on the paper, not the student—are unlikely to provide an adequate or appropriate framework for the variety of situations we encounter in the writing center. And the complexity of our ethical choices becomes clear when we look at even a few of the situations that confront us every semester.

Writing center cases: Notes from the semester

Many of us encountered a young woman from Russia, a business graduate student who frequented the center this semester. Natalia (as I'll call her) is in one sense a wonderful student to work with. She's a skilled writer who brings in clear, lucid prose—papers that are readable even to tutors who come from non-business backgrounds. Her ideas are well-organized and fully-developed. Natalia's concern is editing. Like so many ESL students, Natalia wants to "sound like an American" to readers. In truth, her writing is better than acceptable, but Natalia is a perfectionist. She is often able to identify potential errors, but, she explains, it's much more difficult to know which of several possible alternatives is "right" given a specific syntax. Is time spent with Natalia an appropriate use of writing center resources?

Many of the difficult choices we face have nothing to do with second language issues. Over about a two-week period this fall, our writing center staff saw close to 100 students from a finance class. Two teachers had chosen to offer extra-credit points to students who brought their papers to the writing center prior to turning them in. As finance students began streaming through the writing center doors, I went to the teachers to find out their rationale for the bonus points. Both teachers saw writing as an important skill for students in their discipline, and they wanted to communicate that emphasis to business undergrads. They hoped to encourage students to work on their writing in advance, so that students would develop good work habits and (ideally) learn to self-correct many of their errors in both form and content. Through offering the bonus points, these teachers told me, they thought that some of the badly constructed, poorly thought out, last-minute papers that students commonly write might be avoided.

As we dealt with the 100 junior level finance students, we realized our own academic limitations only too clearly. We were unable to bring topic expertise to the conference. If students had missed important implications or reduced complex ideas to simplified (or even inaccurate) generalizations, we didn't know about it. In other words, we couldn't tell a good idea from a bad one. On the other hand, we found that we could encourage students to work toward clarity, and to think about what they were saying and how they were presenting the information. But in many cases, the most helpful comments we could make and the most useful questions we could ask were about editing and proofreading issues. When we negotiated agendas with students, editing concerns were usually among the issues that students hoped to discuss. After the papers were due and we had time to clear our heads (and discuss the whole process at a staff meeting), we found ourselves asking difficult questions. What was the best possible use of writing center time for those students? Was it appropriate for us to see them at all, given that the primary motivation most of them had for visiting the writing center was bonus points?

Of course, tutors in our writing center also see many students with more traditional writing needs. During the past couple of months, I occasionally worked with Jason, a Comp I student who was disappointed with his college grades in writing. Formerly an A-B student, he visited the writing center because his first two college comp grades were in the C-D range. Although he brought in complete drafts, each of which represented several hours of work and multiple early drafts, we dealt with idea development, thesis, and organization. I worked with him by using questions that allowed him to figure out what he wanted to say, and more questions that asked him to figure out how that related to what he had already done and what he might want to do next. The sessions with Jason were classic writing center work. They raised no troublesome concerns about inadvertently crossing the boundaries of what is reasonable, appropriate, and ethical in terms of writing center pedagogy.

Tutor Techniques/Strategies at Your Disposal

Active Listening:
- validate via "I hear you saying"
- paraphrase to double-check understanding and show attentiveness
- question to encourage more thinking, greater comprehensiveness:
  –**OPEN** questions for rapport building, generating more background information
  –**CLOSED** questions for gathering specific information
- "I statements" to demonstrate reader reaction, need for more information
- body language to show interest, friendliness, approval

Genuine Reader Reaction:
- "I statements" regarding your expectations, understanding, reactions
- requests for more information ("Why did you say this?")
- requests for clarity ("What do you mean here?")
- questions to probe purpose, generate depth ("So what?")
- questions to generate new perspectives, develop new connections among ideas ("How are these ideas related?")
- questions to generate follow-through ("What next?" or "What would that mean?")

Silence and Wait Time:
- the pause that forces the student to think something through for him/herself
- if more wait time feels counter-productive, rephrase the question and still leave the move up to the student
- give the student more than a few seconds of think time by stepping away from the table
- provide the student with still more think time by giving a small writing or listing task and coming back to look at it in 2–5 minutes

---

Figure 1. (Adapted from Ryan, *The Bedford Guide*, pp. 17–23)

Directive Tutoring: What Can It Look Like?

- Providing (requested or not) a correction
- Providing a word or a sample sentence
- Directly answering a question about the student's writing
- Providing a variety of sample options that might work
- Modeling the writerly habit of brainstorming options and thinking them through to determine how each might shape the paper
- Showing the connection between precise language and meaning by offering sample wordings and demonstrating how meaning shifts
- Engaging in a back-and-forth discussion with the student where both of you generate ideas, meaning, ideas for organization
- For further discussion:
  - ✔ How do you know when directive tutoring is appropriate?
  - ✔ Helping students through even very minor editorial issues can be extremely slow and inefficient (and can feel patronizing) if directiveness is strictly avoided.
  - ✔ The questions we ask and the agenda-setting we do can steer students in a particular direction. Is it non-directive simply because it's in the form of a question?
  - ✔ Writing center conferences are negotiated events between the student and the consultant. There is no "right answer" or "best conference" to use as a guide. If students leave the conference (a) with a slightly better paper, (b) as a slightly better writer, and (c) feeling comfortable with the center and likely to return so you can continue the work that was begun, you've had a "good enough" conference.

Figure 2.

Sessions like those with Jason are satisfying and comfortably unproblematic, but they represent only one portion of our writing center work. Tutors need to be prepared to see someone like Jason, but they also need to be prepared—and to expect—to see students like Natalia or those in the finance classes. Especially when undergraduate tutors work in the center, it is critical to develop a training program that adequately prepares tutors for the full range of students they are likely to encounter.

Training tutors for writing center work

In preparation for my most recent tutor training workshop, I developed a handout to help us think about how we work in the writing center. On one side (see Figure 1), I included Ryan's three categories of techniques for working with students—active listening, reader response, and silence/wait time (17). During training sessions and role plays, I emphasized the importance of those techniques and made sure that each new tutor was comfortable using them. That side of the handout described conventional wisdom about how to work in the writing center.

On the other side of the handout (see Figure 2) I added a fourth category of strategies, "Directive tutoring." I went on to provide some detail about what directive tutoring might look like and how it might be used productively in a tutoring session. Then I listed key questions and issues that I suggested we needed to think about in conjunction with directive strategies. We talked specifically about editing and proofreading, since it is frequently in conjunction with those issues that tutors feel student expectations for directivity most strongly.

But we also discussed complications of easy definitions, for example, questions that become directive in their pointedness, or approaches to proofreading that leave primary responsibility in the hands of the student.

As we concluded our discussion of issues raised through the handout, I told them quite frankly that I work on editing and proofreading side-by-side with students, when that's what they feel they need most. I admitted that I am no purist, automatically rejecting tutoring strategies as directive. I also told them I expected them to rely heavily on Ryan's three suggested strategies for most of their writing center work and to decide for themselves how to deal with the complicating issues raised by our discussion of writing center taboos. And I promised them they wouldn't have to find their way through this thicket by themselves. As long as I find the questions so troubling, I said, they could expect we would continue to discuss these issues in our regular staff meetings.

This flexible approach is consistent with the overall structure of writing center sessions, as I imagine them myself and describe them for new tutors. Every session can be imagined to consist of four activities. First we develop rapport, usually through introductions and simple conversation about the course or assignment. Second, we negotiate an agenda for the 30-minute conference. During this stage, student and tutor usually negotiate fairly openly. "What brings you to the writing center?" the tutor may ask. Students might respond by saying they just want a "second opinion" or someone to "proofread" the paper. Tutors may follow up by saying something like, "What kinds of issues would you like to look at in this paper?" or "We could begin by talking about the paper as a whole and go from there, or we could focus on specific concerns that you see in the paper. What's your sense of how we could make this time most helpful to you?" In the third stage, after the student and tutor reach a consensus about agenda, attention turns to work on the paper itself. Finally, during the last few minutes of the session, tutors pull back from the paper to bring some sort of closure to the work: "OK, where do you go from here?" they may ask, or "Are you comfortable knowing what you need to do next? Is there anything else we should look at while you're here?"

Throughout stages one, two, and four, it is typical (in most writing centers, I daresay) to find student and tutor engaged in active and collaborative discussion. It seems unreasonable, then, to expect that the give and take, the mutuality, of the collaborative process should be cut off during the heart of the conference itself. A more flexible approach to writing center conferencing, guided by caution over tutor role but not unduly restricted by narrow rules about what happens in writing center sessions, is how I choose to shape my work and how I present that work to new tutors.

The growing commitment in our writing center to flexibility is further reinforced by our recognition that the choices we make about tutoring are not value-neutral (Grimm). Some of our students come from backgrounds of comparative privilege, and these students may be well placed to succeed in college-level writing no matter what pedagogical philosophy we adopt. Their family and educational backgrounds, their peer networks, their sense of entitlement to voice are among the strengths that can help them in college. Where we draw our policy lines will not make a major difference to their success as writers.

But writing center tutors see other kinds of students too. Students come here because they have no one else who can serve as a reliable second pair of eyes when proofreading important papers. Students come because they are first generation college students, with no assumption of privilege, no sense of entitlement to a voice, and no automatic entree to the language of academia. Students look to the writing center for help because they are Native Americans or immigrant Americans, because their backgrounds are emphatically working class or welfare class, because a painful degree of shyness makes it hard for them to make friends and develop support systems among their peers. When we set writing center policies and develop an ethic to tutor by, we need to make sure our policies and ethics also take these students' needs into account.

Conclusion

So where has this discussion taken us as a writing center staff? For starters, I guess, it has made us less comfortable with our practice and less sure about what is and isn't appropriate, what is and isn't ethical. We started with small changes in how we talk about our work with students, but, proving yet again that language is meaning, we've uncovered huge questions about how we actually want to do that work.

We have been forced to deal with the reality that language can get in the way of doing. Differences in meaning can actually impede our work if we allow "proofreading" to serve as code for the most negative kind of writing center practice. But the changes in language caused us to work harder to define for ourselves what we really will and won't do in practice. We do spend more time on lower-order concerns, if that's part of the student's own agenda, than we did when we began sessions by announcing that we don't do proofreading. Sometimes that makes us feel like we are turning into proofreaders. But we keep reminding ourselves that it is possible to work on proofreading issues without proofreading for the student. Students can be taught to proofread for themselves, just as they're taught to develop their own ideas and support their own theses. It's frustrating work, hardly as rewarding as deep discussions about ideas, but sometimes exactly what the student needs.

We've agreed it's not good enough to work only on improving the student: students won't use the writing center a second time if they believe their papers are no better after they've gone to the trouble of scheduling a conference. On the other hand, the student's own paper is an absolutely ideal venue for working on improving the student as writer. Nothing is more motivating than the student's own work, soon to be turned in for a grade, as part of an application to professional school, or maybe as a thesis or dissertation. Our ultimate goal of focusing on the writer rather than the writing is in no danger of changing, although the product in front of us is more forthrightly recognized as the tool we use during the session itself.

I have been pleased to learn that my instincts about students were right. Contrary to the negative student image sometimes bandied about among those who deal with student writing, most of our students really aren't looking for someone to proofread their work, and they really do want to become better writers. I recently worked with a young man who began our session by announcing that he had come to the writing center to get someone to proofread his paper. "What particularly concerns you about it?" I asked. He responded with a long explanation about the ideas he meant to include in the paper but which didn't seem clearly enough developed. He may have said "proofreading," but he meant something far more substantive.

I'm satisfied for now with the balance I've struck during tutor training and in our work in the center. I know new tutors would sometimes like clearer guidelines for right and wrong, just as the students who visit our writing center would often like clear answers about how to improve their papers. The fuzzier approach, though, is probably better. When we conduct directive sessions, we've learned to think about it but not to feel bad about it. When we spend a session focused on minor proofreading details, we've acknowledged that we may be meeting genuine needs perceived by both faculty and students. We've moved outside of a safety zone, outside of a comfort zone. But the move, we think, is an important step toward the critical goal of meeting students at the point of need. We're not always comfortable, but we're learning to live with it.

Works Cited

Brooks, Jeff. "Minimalist Tutoring: Making the Student Do All the Work." *Writing Lab Newsletter* 19.2 (Oct. 1992): 1–4.

Clark, Irene L. *Writing in the Center: Teaching in a Writing Center Setting,* 2nd ed. Dubuque, Iowa: Kendall/Hunt, 1992.

Clark, Irene L., and Dave Healy. "Are Writing Centers Ethical?" *WPA* 20.1/2 (1996): 32–48.

Grimm, Nancy Maloney. "Studying Discursive Regulation in the Writing Conference." Conference on College Composition and Communication, 1997. Phoenix.

Lunsford, Andrea. "Collaboration, Control, and the Idea of a Writing Center." *Writing Center Journal* 12.1 (1991): 3–10.

North, Stephen. "The Idea of a Writing Center." *College English* 46 (1984): 433–46.

Petit, Angela. "The Writing Center as 'Purified Space': Competing Discourses and the Dangers of Definition." *Writing Center Journal* 17.2 (1997): 111–19.

Ryan, Leigh. *The Bedford Guide for Writing Tutors.* Bedford: Boston, 1994: 17–23.

Shamoon, Linda K., and Deborah H. Burns. "A Critique of Pure Tutoring." *Writing Center Journal* 15.2 (1995): 134–51.

PART TWO

DOCUMENT DESIGN

Most students in our composition classes are already immersed in text-rich environments, exposed daily to myriad forms of documents, most designed for specific users and to accomplish particular purposes. With the ready availability of software and technology that enables writers to produce multimedia documents in print or digital form, writers must pay more attention than ever before to document design. Even though software suites provide ready-made templates and design "wizards" to guide writers through the production and publishing processes, writers need to be able to make conscious and critical document design choices. In effect, the more access students have to the tools that will assist with document design, the more important it becomes for them to understand the connection between design choices and a document's audience and purpose. Composition students need to develop visual literacy.

Building on principles of the composing process presented in Part One of the handbook, Part Two provides an effective overview of document design principles that will apply to academic writing, workplace writing, and personal writing, including e-mail and Web pages. Students and teachers must be sensitive to the idea that appropriate and effective document design is always integrally related to the larger rhetorical contexts that shape and constrain their writing and its circulation. Because few teachers of first-year composition have formal training in teaching principles of document design and visual rhetoric, the selections that follow address several questions that teachers might consider as they incorporate these issues into their courses:

- What are central principles of design that can be used in composition classes? How do these principles affect readers or users?
- What is visual rhetoric? How do the rhetorical features of a document's design relate to the rhetorical features of its text? How can teachers help students integrate the writing process and document design?
- How are planning and composing a Web page different from other forms of composition? How can teachers help students engage in this different form of composing? How can teachers evaluate writing for the Web.

VISUAL RHETORIC: A READER-ORIENTED APPROACH TO GRAPHICS AND DESIGNS

Charles Kostelnick

[*Technical Writing Teacher* 16.1 (1989): 77–88]

Professor Charles Kostelnick chairs the Department of English at Iowa State University, where he also teaches courses in advanced composition and graphic communication in business and technical writing. His articles have appeared in numerous professional journals, and he coauthored *Designing Visual Language: Strategies for Professional Communicators* (1997).

207

Recognizing that writing students need to know how to combine visual and verbal strategies to solve rhetorical problems, Kostelnick describes an approach that teachers can use to help students develop visual rhetoric. The approach he suggests has three components: (1) a matrix that teachers can use to explore the visual elements in different documents; (2) reader-oriented guidelines that writers can use to make design choices; and (3) an explanation of how teachers might integrate design decisions into the writing process. This article is especially useful for helping teachers make connections between design processes and writing processes.

Most technical writing instructors are better prepared to teach and far more experienced in verbal than visual communication. Rhetoric is practiced with words, not with visible forms. Although a few articles on teaching visual design have appeared recently, textbooks and professional writing pedagogy emphasize primarily the development of language skills, and visual thinking is often treated as a secondary cognitive mode reducible to codified rules and conventions (Barton and Barton 1985). Critics have suggested solutions to the problem: Arnheim (1969, 2–3) argues that visual thinking is central to cognition and should be developed as a general educational goal, while Barton and Barton propose applying concepts of contemporary writing pedagogy—the process approach and rhetorical theory—to instruction in visual design.

To communicate effectively in their disciplines, technical writing students need to learn how to combine visual and verbal strategies in solving rhetorical problems. By "visual rhetoric" (Bonsiepe 1965; see also Buchanan 1985) I mean the ability of the writer to achieve the purpose of a document through visual communication, at any level: for example, through the choice of a typeface (Courier, Helvetica), of graphic cues (bullets, lines, icons), of textual arrangement (lists, flow charts, trees), of data displays (a pie chart, line graph), even of the color, shape, and size of the page. By acknowledging visual rhetoric, we recognize that visual choices make a difference—in readers' attitude toward a document, in how readers process its information, and in which information they value. If the writer designs a document consistent with its purpose, visual rhetoric will enhance the communication; if not, visual cues can misdirect readers, subverting the writer's purpose. Students need to know how to write and design documents consistent with the needs and expectations of their readers.

However, to develop visual rhetoric in a writing course, we need a comprehensive model that (1) enables us to describe the variety of visual elements that comprise each document and (2) provides a framework for evaluating how these elements affect readers. The model should be compatible with the rhetorical nature of language instruction, enabling students to adapt visual design to purpose and audience. The approach to visual rhetoric outlined here has three components: a 12-cell matrix of visual communication, some reader-oriented guidelines for making design choices, and a rationale for integrating design decisions into the writing process.

Four Levels of Visual Design

Technical writing entails visual as well as verbal planning, invention, and problem-solving. To teach these activities, the instructor needs a vocabulary for describing the range of visual choices possible for each writing task. The conventional nomenclature of visual communication (graphics, visuals, layout) is too general and ambiguous to describe the visual modes, levels, and idiosyncrasies of individual documents. These generic terms impede the work of the writing teacher by suggesting that visual tasks are formulaic or performed independently by technicians or typists. Writing itself, however, is an intensely visual activity in which the writer manipulates symbols and marks on a visual field. Through the technology of print, writing becomes "thing-like" (Ong 1982), demanding the visual attention of writer and reader. Since writers create, and readers process, visual as well as linguistic cues, the instructor needs a method for planning and analyzing the design of each document in reader-oriented terms.

Unlike a plan for a building, a set of machine drawings, or an aerial photograph, technical writing is encoded largely through alphanumeric symbols. The "text" provides closure for the message, circumscribing abstract marks or pictorial images contained within, and therefore provides a reference point for the visual schema. Writers make visual choices on four levels: intra-, inter-, extra-, and supra-textual. Each level is encoded in three visual modes: alphanumeric/symbolic, spatial, and graphic. The combinations of levels and modes are plotted on the 12-Cell Matrix of Visual Communication. (See Figure 1.) Below is a brief description of each of the four levels. Further description of the matrix, especially with regard to business writing, can be found in Kostelnick (1988b, see also 1988a; for a more detailed matrix of graphic communication, see Twyman 1979).

The *Intra-textual* level (cells 1–3) governs the local design of the text. In the alphanumeric/symbolic mode, this includes typeface selection and treatment: boldface, italics, type size (10 versus 12 CPI), and upper and lower case. In the spatial mode, intra-textuality controls the linear distance between characters and semantic units, and in the graphic mode, marks that control the flow of text (punctuation) or that create emphasis (underscoring). Intra-textual choices can affect a textual particle (one word in italics) or the whole text (the selection of a typeface for a 50-page report). Governing a field of invisible points distrib-

	Alphanumerical Symbolic	Spatial	Graphic
Intra	1 variations in style, size, weight of letters, numbers, symbols	2 local spacing between textual units: picas, CPI, kerning	3 marks: punctuation, underscoring; iconic forms of letters
Inter	4 levels of headings; letters, numbers signaling textual structure	5 line endings, indentation; matrices, lists, tree configurations	6 bullets, icons; line work, arrows, geometric forms on charts, diagrams
Extra	7 legends, captions, labels; numerical description of data	8 plotting of data on X-Y axes; viewing angle, size of pictures	9 tone, texture, shading of data displays; details on pictures
Supra	10 section titles, numbers; page headers, tabs; pagination	11 placement of extra-textuals in text; page breaks, section breaks	12 marks, icons, color, line work, logos unifying pages & sections

Figure 1.   12-Cell Matrix of Visual Communication

uted across the page, intra-textuality is essentially a one-dimensional manipulation of the text.

The *Inter-textual* level (cells 4–6) generates the "access structures" (Waller 1979) that enable readers to identify relations among textual units. In the spatial mode, inter-textuality regulates line breaks (and justification) and the vertical arrangement of text. A solid block of text can be divided into paragraphs, paragraphs into lists, and lists into particles (numbers, words, phrases) that form tables, flow charts, and decision trees. In the alphanumeric/symbolic mode, inter-textuality is coded through headings, letters, and numbers, in the graphic mode through bullets, dashes, and line work (e.g., the vertical and horizontal lines on the 12-cell matrix). Through inter-textual treatment in all three modes, a text can be transformed into a hierarchical visual system "surfacing" (Herrstrom 1984, 229) the structure of the document (see also Bernhardt 1986; Twyman 1979).

The *Extra-textual* level (cells 7–9) encompasses images and systems of signs independent from the text. Like speech, textual elements can be perceived aurally. Extra-textual elements, on the other hand, are primarily seen; they may require alphanumeric coding (cell 7), but once their sign systems are understood by the viewer they are comprehended purely by the eye (Bertin 1981, 178–79). Extra-textuals range in level of abstraction from a pie chart or a stylized corporate logo to a realistic drawing or a photograph. Spatially, extra-textual sign systems are constructed on two-dimensional grids, which determine, for example, where the data are plotted (on a line graph) or the viewing angle, size, or depth of an image. Graphic coding controls the resolution of the signs: the tone, color, and fineness of marks on data displays (a dot versus a shaded bar on a graph) or of details on pictures (a stick drawing versus a photograph of workers demonstrating a task).

The *Supra-textual* level (cells 10–12) controls the global organization of a document, securing cohesion among all of its elements, both textual and extra-textual. In the spatial mode, supra-textuality arranges extra-textual elements (charts, graphs, illustrations) within the document and establishes the continuity of the text (breaks in the text between pages, pages separating major sections). In the alphanumeric mode, supra-textual elements include pagination, page headers, and chapter titles, in the graphic mode line work, color, or graphic symbols that define relations between sections, pages, or panels. Extending over several planes, the supra-textual level governs the three-dimensional design of the document. In a proposal, for example, I could use section titles and tabs to divide major units of the text (cell 10); I could design pages that folded out into larger pages (cell 11) to accommodate detailed flow charts; and I could use icons to code pages with similar functions (cell 12). These are just a few of the options I could exercise to create supra-textual cohesion.

Each document combines cells on the matrix to form a unique visual system. The two pages of sample text (see Figure 2), which exclude linguistic coding, illustrate several of the cells on the matrix, each of which is described below:

Intra:

1. Typeface selection (Palatino for text; Helvetica for the section title; Geneva for the flow chart text and for the numbers on the illustration); occasional boldface, upper case, and italic treatment of the typeface; enlarged type size for the section title on the first page.
2. Variations in the spacing between characters at the bottom of the first page.
3. Underlining of headings; various punctuation marks within the text.

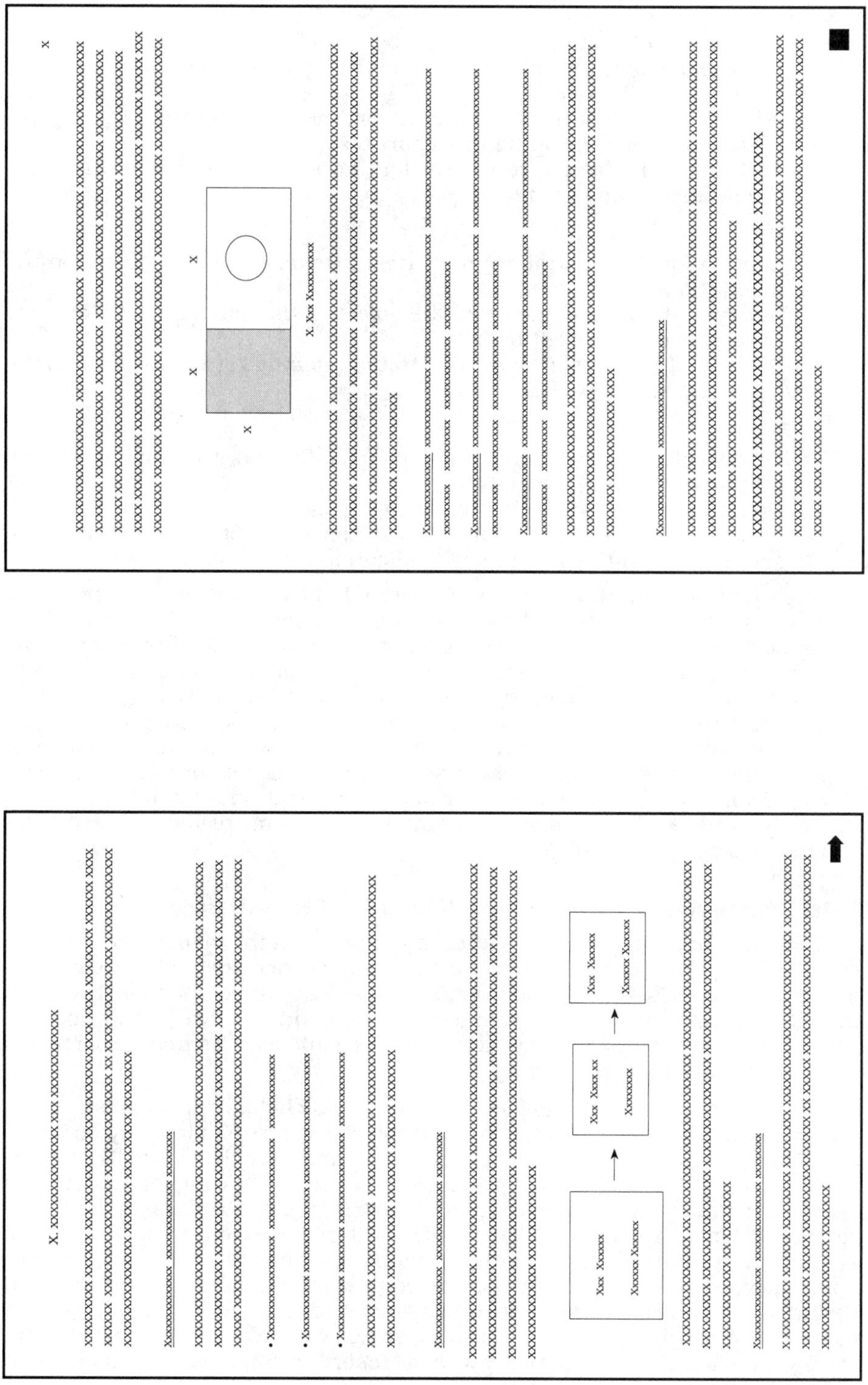

Figure 2. Sample Text

Inter:

4. Two levels of headings within the text.
5. Single spacing within paragraphs; double spacing between paragraphs; triple spacing between major headings; indentation of the list with bullets; indentation of text following the subheadings on the second page; spatial arrangement of the flow chart text.
6. Bullets cueing the list; rectilinear line work around the flow chart text; arrows connecting the rectangles.

Extra:

7. Caption for the illustration; numerical tags describing distances on the illustration.
8. Size and spatial orientation of the object in the illustration (front view, cross section of the left part).
9. Shading of the left part of the illustration; minimal graphic coding on the object (a skeletal outline only).

Supra:

10. Section title and number at the top of the first page; pagination on the second page, numbering of the illustration.
11. Break in the text at the bottom of each page.
12. Arrow icon indicating continuity between the first and second pages; square icon on the second page indicating the end of the section.

These elements are the visual raw materials of the document, which any technical writing student could execute with a modicum of desktop publishing equipment. Of course, the sample text contains only a limited number of the available options and in its present state is totally noncontextual. The four levels and three coding modes on the matrix describe a flexible visual vocabulary which the writer/designer can adapt to each communication problem. The rhetorician can use this vocabulary for various purposes—to create emphasis, stimulate reader interest, guide the reader through the text or to the most significant information, enable the reader to compare and contrast data, persuade the reader to take action—in short, for many of the same reader-oriented goals writers achieve with language.

Establishing Reader-Oriented Guidelines for Visual Design

Exercising and integrating the levels and modes on the matrix, however, are complex tasks: how do we provide students with reader-oriented guidelines for making these decisions? The instructor has at least three options: (1) deductively follow conventions outlined in textbooks, (2) inductively extract principles from actual documents and contexts, or (3) consult theories and research encompassing the visual processing of texts.

The first option is a logical place to begin: visual choices, like linguistic ones, are somewhat determined by idiom, protocol, and genre. Readers rely on previous visual experiences to process documents: a message that looks like a sales letter (visual processing always precedes linguistic processing) engenders one set of expectations; a message containing matrices, data displays, and a highly variegated text quite another. Few readers will mistake our sample text for a short story, a refusal letter, a mortgage contract, or a résumé. Generic conventions, however, cannot account for the contextual variables, both visual and rhetorical, of the communication because each document contains a unique combination of cells on the matrix as well as its own audience and purpose. Are we any more able to predict exactly what a "report" is supposed to look like than what it is supposed to *sound* like?

The second teaching method, analyzing rhetorical strategies employed in real-world texts with definable audiences, can supply the necessary contextual dimensions, preparing students to make reader-oriented decisions in their own assignments. Tebeaux (1985) and Andrews (1985) have suggested assignments for analyzing visual features of actual documents. These assignments can be used in conjunction with the matrix, which establishes a framework for the systematic visual analysis of virtually any document—an essay, advertisement, brochure, manual, or research report. Examining documents enables students to interact with real texts and to evaluate the rhetorical effects of each visual choice on the matrix. For a beginning exercise, the instructor can distribute a one- or two-page document and have students analyze each visual level or coding mode. For example, on a separate handout students can chart visual elements at each level, and the class can then discuss which elements enhance and which work against the purpose of the document.

Analytical exercises are good "predesigning" techniques that prepare students to make rhetorical choices in their own documents. Additional guidelines about how readers process visual information can be extracted from research in legibility, perception, and psychology as well as from theories of visual information processing. Empirical studies at the intra- and inter-textual levels have clearly demonstrated that readers process some text designs more easily than others (for an overview of these studies, see Benson 1985; Reynolds 1984). For example, Tinker (1963) found that a text set in lower case was more legible than one in upper case, and a relatively small range of type sizes (between 9 and 12 point) produced optimum legibility. Although readers generally preferred type styles that were the most legible, Tinker occasionally found discrepancies between preference and performance, which suggests that visual processing may be mediated by familiarity, contextual variables, or culturally influenced aesthetic norms. Moreover, the "atmosphere value" of typefaces (Spencer 1969, 29) may influence the reader's response to the text, begging the question as to whether or not *any* intra-textual choice can be excluded from rhetorical consideration.

While empirical experiments such as Tinker's establish guidelines based on the perceptual experiences of general readers, more recent studies at the inter-textual level have begun to acknowledge the contextual variables of the communication process. For example, Hartley (1980; 1984; Hartley and Trueman 1985) has conducted studies of the spatial arrangement of text (cell 5) and the use of headings (cell 4), verifying that visual cueing devices aid readers in understanding and retrieving content. Hartley's findings, however, are qualified by context—and by the ability and age of readers in the experiment and by the nature and purpose of the text. Wright (1977) has summarized similar experiments (many her own) with tables, flow charts, and decision trees. Like Hartley's experiments, these studies are sensitive to the audience's previous experience with the display device, to the complexity of the tasks being measured, and to the purpose and use of the communication. For instance, readers who are familiar with the key factors in a decision-making process can more quickly draw conclusions from scenarios presented in tables rather than in paragraph form; however, readers who are likely to consider factors not included in the visual display will probably perform better with a branching flow chart than with a table (Wright, pp. 100–02). In all cases, text designers need to analyze carefully the reader's knowledge of the subject and the display technique: inattention to either can defeat the information designer's attempt to make the text transparent. By revealing the benefits and limitations of display techniques for various readers and situations, empirical research in inter-textuality has not only generated an array of design guidelines but shown that visual communication, like language use, must always be responsive to contextual variables.

On the extra-textual level, readers "see" rather than "read" information coded in the spatial and graphic modes (Bertin 1981, 179). Whether the sign system is abstract (a bar chart) or realistic (a line drawing), guidelines must respect the perceptual nature of information processing. The numerous empirical studies investigating the perception of data displays (Macdonald-Ross 1977) and pictures (Perkins 1980) have often yielded conflicting or inconclusive results. Macdonald-Ross (1977, 369–75) narrates the controversies surrounding different methods of displaying data (e.g., bars versus circles), concluding that the research findings generally support the practices of experienced information designers. Despite all of the empirical studies on the perception of realistic images, Perkins (1980, 272) maintains that creating pictures is a "profoundly heuristic" activity guided by "tradition and invention rather than law and application."

Instructors are better served by consulting practitioners and theorists, for whom—particularly in regard to data displays—functional economy is the key reader-oriented guideline. In Bertin's semiotic theory of visual information processing, the spatial and graphic coding of quantitative data exploit the eye's ability to process numerous (possibly millions of) pieces of data simultaneously (181). According to Edward Tufte (1983), a well-designed data display presents the maximum information in the smallest area with the minimal graphic coding (51). His graphic standard of "clarity, precision, and efficiency" (51) engenders formulas (the "data-ink" and "data density" ratios) for evaluating the functional performance of charts and graphs. Tufte justifies his guidelines on aesthetic grounds as well: following the dictums of architectural design theorist Robert Venturi, he correlates complexity and structural transparency with "graphical elegance" (177).

At the supra-textual level, the laws of visual gestalt can predict the reader's global perception of the document, providing the designer with guidelines for combining visual forms. For instance, adhering to the law of "equilibrium" assures a balanced arrangement on the page (cell 11), producing visual harmony for the reader; the law of "similarity" helps the reader associate related items (cell 12 graphic cues unifying related pages); and "good figure" enables the reader to differentiate visual elements from their field or background (Bernhardt 1986, 71–72). Computer programs capable of simultaneously displaying several miniature pages of a document can increase the writer's awareness of visual gestalt, affording greater control over supra-textual cohesion. Other disciplines encompassing perception and visual display techniques can also inform supra-textual design. For example, studies derived from hemispheric brain research have found that viewers generally process verbal information more effectively in the right field of vision, visual material in the left, which may provide guidelines for integrating pictures and icons with text (Welford 1984, 14–15; for limitations of combining visual and verbal processing, see Hecht and Juhasz 1984, 133–36).

Together these sources—including empirical research, graphic communication theory, the psychology of perception, and aesthetics—furnish a wide array of concepts and empirical data (not available in technical writing pedagogy) about how readers process documents visually on all four levels of the matrix. Because context affects perception (Arnheim 1969, 54–72), guidelines extracted from these diverse disciplines must be adapted to the visual and rhetorical variables of each document. The writer must combine the cells on the matrix into a coherent visual system which advances the rhetorical goals of the communication. Discovering an optimal configuration of levels and coding modes can be as complex as discovering an optimal linguistic pattern: rhetoric, visual or verbal, resists prescription. Hence, the designer begins with the same heuristic the writer does: What is the purpose of the communication? Who are the readers? What do the readers expect? How will they use the document? The guidelines outlined above establish valid reader-oriented norms and criteria for defining rhetorical problems and for *finding* solutions rather than prescribing them a priori.

Integrating Visual and Verbal Communication

Despite the variety of visual choices writers make—especially technical writers, who have a good deal of control over in-house documents—visual design is typically regarded as a mechanical skill unrelated to the writing process (Barton and Barton 1985). However, integrating the cells on the matrix into a visual system that complements the rhetorical strategies of the linguistic text demands that the writer solve visual and verbal problems concurrently rather than sequentially. Planning, drafting, and revising require visual as well as verbal thinking: revision is a "re-seeing" guided by the eye as well as the ear, meaning discovered visually as well as linguistically. Visual and verbal thinking are cognitively interdependent, something that design theorists acknowledge in their models of the design process (see Tovey 1984).

Because writing and designing are intertwined in the same process of making meaning, the instructor can use the same principles (and nomenclature) to teach both verbal and visual problem-solving. The matrix contains a vocabulary of visual language subject to the same principles of discourse, arrangement, and style that guide linguistic choices. For example, in an assignment to design a set of instructions—say a manual for a new electronic tool sold to do-it-yourself mechanics—the student needs to consider a range of visual options encompassing several cells on the matrix:

Purpose: to motivate readers to use the document (cell 1: selection of a typeface; 8, 9: illustrations with pertinent detail; 11: size of the document that fits the carrying case); to guide readers to key information about how to solve simple operational problems (5, 6: spatial and graphic cueing devices); to highlight critical warnings that prevent readers from injuring themselves or breaking the tool (1: boldface, upper case; 3: underscoring).

Discourse Mode: narrations showing readers how to use and fix the tool (5: steps of a task segmented into a list; 6: bullets highlighting each major step of the task); forward leaps built visually into the discourse for various readers and situations (5, 6: spatial and graphic cues organizing the text into tree diagrams outlining several contingencies; 12: icons associating similar types of tasks across the whole document).

Arrangement: the steps of each task cued clearly (4: headings, lists coded with numbers; 6: graphic cues signaling a new task); clear divisions between different tasks (5: vertical spacing); illustrations revealing the most useful information (8: selection of appropriate viewing angles; 9: selection of details); cues that enable the reader to either browse through the document or quickly locate answers to questions (10: page headers; 11: illustrations placed strategically in the text).

Style: a low level of technicality (1: familiar symbols; 7: nontechnical labels identifying essential parts of the tool; 9: simple line drawings); a functional but aesthetically pleasing "gestalt" (11: balanced page designs; 12: harmony among page colors).

Tone: an informal, "friendly" document that invites reader use (1: a serif typeface in a medium point size; 3: icons that add interest; 5: ample spacing around textual units; 9: freehand drawings for illustrations); consistent coding throughout the document to avoid shifts in tone.

Readability: an integrated system of visual forms that enables the reader to find and use information with maximum ease (10–12); visual design of all 12 cells adapted to the function of the document and the conditions under which it will be used (in a home workshop or a garage, in an emergency).

Purpose, discourse mode, arrangement, style, tone, readability—these concepts pertain to aspects of the document that readers process visually as well as verbally; hence, the writer of our manual needs to make reader-oriented visual choices *during the drafting of the linguistic text.* Together, from the early planning stages, the visual and linguistic systems should simultaneously drive the rhetoric of the document. By providing a bridge between the two systems, the matrix can be applied to virtually any assignment. As the student shapes the document, recursive stages of "re-seeing," both visually and linguistically, clarify and structure meaning, and develop tone and style consistent with subject, purpose, and audience. Rather than operating as separate or hierarchical functions in the writing course, composing and designing merge into an interdependent, symbiotic process.

Conclusion

Teaching graphics and text design as bona fide, reader-oriented forms of communication enhances the basic rhetorical tenets of the technical writing course. Adapting messages to specific readers requires conscious visual thinking on several levels: the matrix is a tentative first step towards developing a comprehensive system of describing and evaluating these choices. Introducing research and theories in visual communication from various disciplines, along with analyzing actual documents, increases the student's understanding of how readers process texts visually as well as provides guidelines and criteria for visual problem-solving. To play a seminal role in supporting the rhetorical principles of the course, visual thinking must be done during each stage of the writing process. Instead of functioning as merely a specialized skill, visual design will then share with language the same rhetorical responsibilities for patterning the message to the needs of the reader.

References

Andrews, D. C. 1985. Choosing the right visuals. In *Teaching Technical Writing: Graphics*, ed. by Dixie Elise Hickman, Anthology No. 5. Association of Teachers of Technical Writing.

Arnheim, Rudolf. 1969. *Visual Thinking*. Berkeley: Univ. of California Press.

Barton, Ben F., and Marthalee S. Barton. 1985. Toward a rhetoric of visuals for the computer era. *The Technical Writing Teacher* 12:126–45.

Benson, Philippa J. 1985. Writing visually: Design considerations in technical publications. *Technical Communication* 32:35–39.

Bernhardt, Stephen A. 1986. Seeing the text. *College Composition and Communication* 37: 66–78.

Bertin, Jacques. 1981. *Graphics and Graphic Information-Processing*. Trans. William J. Berg and Paul Scott. New York: De Gruyter.

Bonsiepe, Gui. 1965. Visual/verbal rhetoric. *Ulm* 14–16:23–40.

Buchanan, Richard. 1985. Declaration by design: Rhetoric, argument, and demonstration in design practice. *Design Issues* 2:4–22.

Hartley, James. 1980. Spatial cues in text: Some comments on the paper by Frase and Schwartz. *Visible Language* 14:62–79.

———. 1984. Space and structure in instructional text. In *Information Design: The Design and Evaluation of Signs and Printed Material*, ed. by Ronald Easterby and Harm Zwaga. New York: Wiley.

Hartley, James, and Mark Trueman. 1985. A research strategy for text designers: The role of headings. *Instructional Science* 14:99–155.

Hecht, Peter, and Joseph Juhasz. 1984. Recognition memory: Implications for visual information presentation. In *Information Design: The Design and Evaluation of Signs and Printed Material*. See Hartley 1984.

Herrstrom, David Sten. 1984. Technical writing as mapping description onto diagram: The graphic paradigms of explanation. *Journal of Technical Writing and Communication* 14:223–40.

Kostelnick, Charles. 1988a. Designing for readability: An index for evaluating the visual language of technical documents. In *Proceedings of the 35th ITCC*. Washington, DC: Society for Technical Communication.

————. 1988b. A systematic approach to visual language in business communication. *The Journal of Business Communication* 25:29–48.

Macdonald-Ross, Michael. 1977. How numbers are shown: A review of research on the presentation of quantitative data in texts. *AV Communication Review* 25:359–409.

Ong, Walter J. 1982. *Orality and Literacy: The Technologizing of the Word.* New York: Methuen.

Perkins, D. N. 1980. Pictures and the real thing. In *Processing of Visible Language*, ed. by Paul A. Kolers, Merald E. Wrolstad, and Herman Bouma, vol. 2. New York: Plenum.

Reynolds, Linda. 1984. The Legibility of Printed Scientific and Technical Information. In *Information Design: The Design and Evaluation of Signs and Printed Material. See* Hartley 1984.

Spencer, Herbert. 1969. *The Visible Word.* 2nd ed. New York: Hastings.

Tebeaux, Elizabeth. 1985. Developing a heuristic approach to graphics. In *Teaching Technical Writing: Graphics. See* Andrews 1985.

Tinker, Miles. 1963. *Legibility of Print.* Ames: Iowa State Univ. Press.

Tovey, Michael. 1984. Designing with both halves of the brain. *Design Studies* 5:219–28.

Tufte, Edward. 1983. *The Visual Display of Quantitative Information.* Cheshire, CT: Graphics Press.

Twyman, Michael. 1979. A schema for the study of graphic language. In *Processing of Visible Language*, ed. by Paul A. Kolers, Merald E. Wrolstad, and Herman Bouma, vol. 1. New York: Plenum.

Waller, Robert H. 1979. Typographic access structures for educational texts. In *Processing of Visible Language. See* Twyman 1979.

Welford, A. T. 1984. Theory and application in visual displays. In *Information Design: The Design and Evaluation of Signs and Printed Material. See* Hartley 1984.

Wright, Patricia. 1977. Presenting technical information: A survey of research findings. *Instructional Science* 6:93–134.

THE CHANGING NATURE OF WRITING: PROSE OR CODE IN THE CLASSROOM

Alan Rea and Doug White

[*Computers and Composition* 16 (1999): 421–36]

Alan Rea is an assistant professor of Business Information Systems at Haworth College of Business at Western Michigan University. Rea teaches programming and Web design courses, is currently creating online courses for WMU, and is conducting research in Human Computer Interaction and Virtual Reality. Rea's work has appeared in the online journal *Kairos*. Dr. Doug White teaches networking, networking security, and programming courses for the University of Northern Colorado, and is conducting research in Web Based Data Collection and user behavior. White has published in *Simulation and Gaming, Information and Management, Simulation Digest,* and *The Journal of Social Behaviour and Personality.*

Increasingly, first-year composition courses ask students to develop their own Web pages as part of the assignment sequence. Students are usually experienced users of the Web, so engaging them in projects that ask them to write for the Web taps into their interests and helps them develop more advanced composition skills. However, the authors point out that asking students to write for the Web "is asking them to go against much of their academic training," because the Web includes forms of representation that are not all print based. As a result, inviting students to engage in these new forms of writing requires a different approach to teaching and different ways to evaluate student writing. Rea and White offer succinct explanations of the Web and of components of Web writing. Their article is most helpful with its guidelines for evaluating effective Web sites and for planning and designing a Web site, as well as for the suggestions for classroom assignments. This discussion is especially accessible because the authors assume that beginning Web writers will be using an HTML editor to create Web pages, and thus do not need to learn basic HTML scripting language before creating effective sites. This article will be especially useful as a supplement to the numerous Internet sites that guide students through the process of creating Web pages without engaging them in the kinds of critical analyses used by effective writers.

Sooner or later most Web users want to become Web writers. Working with electronic text already challenges the fixity of print with the malleability of words on the screen. Moreover, electronic text undermines cultural assumptions. Richard Lanham (1993), in *The Electronic Word: Democracy, Technology, and the Arts,* discussed the move from print to electronic forms and how "the fixed, authoritative, canonical text, simply explodes into the ether" (p. 31).

However, Web writing further heightens the distinction between our culture's privileging of print by stressing the use of graphics and other multimedia applications as equal to, or above, the use of words. Instructors should be aware that asking students to write Web pages is asking them to go against much of their academic training. George Landow (1992), in *Hypertext: The Convergence of Contemporary Critical Theory and Technology,* argued that "much of our prejudice against the inclusion of visual information in text derives from print technology" (p. 51). The more "valuable" the information in a book, the less it is illustrated. Illustrated children's books give way to elaborately written passages of prose and winding philosophical treatise as part of our maturation process. Instead of asking a student to draw or use illustrations in a writing class to enhance essays, instructors spend class time having students write passages of descriptive prose.

When instructors ask students to create Web pages incorporating graphics, colors, and fonts, they are asking students to subvert the premise on which print literacy is based (the privileging of ideas over iconic representation). This subversion can be problematic for instructors as well; they have been trained to privilege logical argument over graphic presentation.

With pictures and fonts, the glowing hyperlinks on Web pages further subvert print culture's dependence on linearity. The linear progressive argument is familiar to writing instructors. Although the five-paragraph essay may be shunned in college writing classes, instructors still look for strong thesis statements supported by various types of evidence. A student's writing is valued if it logically presents an argument and supports it with valid claims organized into recognizable units of thought. Hypertext, and the ability to link thoughts through hyperlinks, allows associations impossible given the constraints of linear prose:

> Hypertext, in other words, implements Derrida's call for a new form of hieroglyphic writing that can avoid some of the problems implicit and therefore inevitable in Western writing systems and their printed version. Derrida argues for the inclusion of visual elements in writing as a means of escaping the constraints of linearity. (Landow, 1992, p. 43)

With the increased use of powerful word-processing programs and with the ease of writing Web pages with hypertext markup language (HTML) and "what you see is what you get" (WYSIWYG) editors, students want to experiment with fonts, colors, images, and sounds. Most of the information students receive outside of the classroom is a multimedia experience (many are from the so-called MTV Generation). Asking them to use print solely for expression goes against how most communication takes place in the world outside academia. Not allowing students to experiment with these new forms of writing hampers their ability to learn effective communication skills.

Our discussion, then, focuses on how instructors can effectively teach and evaluate this "new" writing style. Focusing on teaching HTML scripting and/or Web-page writing, as well as evaluating Web pages according to basic criteria, this discussion maps a pedagogy for hypertext writing. When writing and evaluating in this medium, issues such as audience and purpose, design, and function all remain important. New issues, however, come to the forefront: contextualized hyperlinks, navigability, color schemes, and image, audio, and video integration become a part of the writing task as well. Balancing between effective presentation and sensory overload becomes a daunting task for many students as well as instructors. An improved pedagogy must be developed to assist instructors and students approach Web writing in a more structured manner.

Writing in a New Medium

To work effectively within the medium, both instructors and students need to understand the medium itself, because it is not only changing culture, but also the means through which people communicate and share information. Print allowed the dissemination of information to many people (much more than when the only source of information was manuscripts or oral tales), but with today's ever-cheaper and more powerful interactive communications technologies (email and the Web, for example), more people have the potential to express their ideas and to influence others. Instead of the select few having access to the mechanisms for book publishing, broadcast television, or radio, people can take part in the new communication possibilities available through the computer.

This radical shift carries with it a two-fold obligation. Instructors must equip students with the critical and analytical skills needed to analyze the information now being disseminated through a new medium. In addition, instructors need to help students learn how to communicate effectively with the computer (whether it be the word-processing program, desktop publishing software, electronic mail, or one of the many other Internet communication technologies).

All this change still begs the question: Why do writing instructors need to concern themselves with all of this? The answer is quite simple: All of these new communication technologies available through the computer entail writing effectively. For students to be able to participate and excel in academia and the world at large, they need to know how to communicate effectively. A large portion of this entails writing. Although most students in composition classes are not planning on making writing a career, knowing how to communicate in electronic contexts is valuable to any career path they might choose. It always has fallen to writing instructors to give students the needed foundation to communicate and express themselves clearly in their future studies. The remainder of our discussion provides instructors with the basic instruments and information to build a Web-writing pedagogy.

The World Wide Web

Much like the origin of the Internet, various histories disagree as to when the Web actually came into existence. Many histories place the beginnings of what would be called the World Wide Web in 1991, when Tim Berners-Lee released the Web on CERN (Counseil Europeen pour la Recherche Nucleaire) computers.

Although it is true that in 1991 the Web became publicly known, Robert Cal-liau (1997a), a coauthor of the original Web proposal, set the origin of the Web at 1980 in his "A Little History of the World Wide Web." According to Calliau, when Berners-Lee was consulting for CERN, the European particle physics lab in Geneva, in 1980, he wrote a notebook program, "Enquire-Within-Upon-Everything," that allowed "links to be made betwen [sic] arbitrary nodes. Each node had a title, a type, and a list of bidirectional typed links" (online). This sounds very much like the beginnings of applied hypertext.

Hypertext

Because the Web is based on the concept of hypertext, a short explanation is warranted. The Greek *hyper* meaning "over, above, concerning" does not re-ally capture the importance of hypertext. The original idea for hypertext can be traced to an idea in Vannevar Bush's 1945 *Atlantic Monthly* article. Bush called for a mechanically linked information-retrieval machine—the Memex—that would help information workers and scholars accommodate the exploding amounts of information (Bush, 1945/1999). Bush knew that effective knowl-edge building could happen only if scholars were able to access and synthesize information as they needed it. Bush argued that one of the main problems of information storage was categorization and how texts were arranged for retrieval. To work around the strict rules of organization, Bush developed (in theory) a mechanical device (the Memex) that would store all of the information on micro-film and retrieve information according to codes attached to the microfilm in-formation. Moreover, the scholar would be able to annotate and cross-reference information and annotations. The Memex would be a cognitive map of the re-search process. These associative links are, for all intent and purposes, a hyper-text trail.

Twenty years later, Bush's theories informed Ted Nelson's research during his experimentation with methods to organize his thoughts as he wrote a book of philosophy. In "Opening Hypertext: A Memoir," Nelson (1992) discussed how he broke down a "structured complex of thought" he termed a *structangle* (p. 45) and reconnected it in various ways. Eventually, Nelson's connections of the many structangles resulted in what he termed *hypertext*. In the 1960s, Nelson came up with an idea for the *docuverse*, or a vast collection of these hypertexts. For Nelson, the docuverse overcomes many of the inadequacies of information systems in database format and current library systems (vast storehouses for print accessible through electronic catalogs). Nelson's Xanadu project (started in 1985)—the docuverse in action—is creating a global hypertext of all infor-mation accessible to anyone. Organized by associative links, Xanadu might re-semble something of what the Web has become.

In 1985, Brown University's InterMedia project began to make Xanadu a re-ality; its impact on the Humanities is discussed by George Landow (1990) in "Changing Texts, Changing Readers: Hypertext in Literary Education, Criti-cism, and Scholarship." In this landmark article, Landow documented the im-portance of discoveries students made in an "English Literature from 1700 to the Present" class as they created large hypertext and hypermedia documents using InterMedia. Not only does INTERMEDIA allow students to contribute criti-cal scholarship, the contextual hypertext map creates something greater than the parts put together.

Still, hypertext had not yet truly been introduced to the world at large. Apple released Bill Atkinson's HYPERCARD in 1987 (Calliau, 1997b), but exposed this hypertext only to a small group of people (primarily Macintosh users). However, a historical timeline does not reflect the many overlapping events. Berners-Lee had been working on his interactive notebook program since 1980 and in March of 1989 he submitted "Information Management: A Proposal" with a paper entitled, "Hypertext and CERN" as background information. Robert Calliau joined Berners-Lee as a coauthor and developer. In October 1990, they presented a reformulated proposal and termed the system the *World Wide Web*. In 1991, the Web was publicly released and in 1992, the first text browser was made available by anonymous FTP, thereby allowing for its distribution (Calliau, 1997a).

Birth of the Web Browser

In 1993, Marc Andreessen, then a graduate student at University of Illinois–Chicago, presented his thesis and first alpha version of Mosaic for X: a graphical Web browser for the Internet. In 1994, Andreessen left NCSA (National Center for Supercomputing Applications) and formed the Mosaic Communication Corporation, which is now known as Netscape (Calliau, 1997a). With the release of Mosaic to the public, the Web took the Internet by storm. According to Robert Zakon (1997), in "Hobbes' Internet Timeline v2.5," the Web "proliferate[d] at a 341,634% annual growth rate of traffic in 1993" and when Netscape went public on the stock market it had the third largest NASDAQ IPO share value ever (online).

The graphical Web browser experienced a phenomenal growth rate. In 1994, the Web edged out Telnet to become the second most popular technology on the Internet (behind FTP) and in April 1995 it passed FTP. It is still the most-used technology on the Internet. What started out as 130 sites in June 1993 is now well over 250,000 and growing (Zakon, 1997).

Explanation of the Web

What Berners-Lee described in 1991 as the World Wide Web was only the beginning of what has become known as the Web. In its most basic sense, the Web is the name given to a vast collection of information, images, sounds, movies, and other forms of various resources located on various Web servers throughout the world. Moreover, each piece of data has the potential to link to another piece of data anywhere in the world through hypertext links commonly referred to as hyperlinks. A user then can access this data with a simple mouse click or a keystroke. Although the amount of Internet information accessible through the Web grows, it is only a part of the Internet—not the other way around.

Who Runs the Web?

The Web has no one governing body, either. Even though the vast collection of hyperlinks can lead people to believe that the Web is one large seamless entity, no one is in charge. There is, however, an organization called the World Wide Web Consortium, or W3 Consortium, that is led by Tim Berners-Lee, the founder of the Web. Formed in 1994, the W3's main purpose is to "develop common protocols for the evolution of the World Wide Web" (W3C, 1999). This group is not a Web, Inc. or Big Brother; rather, it is concerned with making sure all clients and helper applications conform to certain standards so that all data can be accessed and used by everyone.

Once users are able to access the data on the Web, they will understand the true dynamics of hypermedia and hypertext (many scholars distinguish between pure text and other media; it is not as necessary as some would have us believe). Many of the explanations contained in this print discussion will not do the Web justice. Moreover, much of what one needs to know about the Web can actually be found, with a little time and patience, on the Web itself. In other words, the Web is a metamedium, or a medium that can discuss what it does. The Web contains many sites (specific places on the Internet) that discuss what the Web does and how.

Scripting the Web

With the increased use of the Web for communication comes a need for trained communicators to teach students how to effectively use this medium. However, in many cases, instructors must simultaneously learn these skills with their students. To communicate effectively via the Web requires additional technical and design skills than those needed for word processing and many times instructors have not had this training. The following discussion covers many of the basic technical skills and explores many of the content and design issues that should be considered when writing and evaluating Web pages. With this information, instructors can begin to design a set of hyperheuristics to guide students in their development as Web writers.

Basic HTML

All Web pages are written in hypertext markup language (HTML). HTML is ASCII text with tags enclosed in greater-than and less-than signs (< >). This ASCII script tells a browser how the Web writer wants the Web page to look. Only a few years ago, a user had to learn HTML to write Web pages. This is no longer the case. With various HTML editors, WYSIWYG editors, and add-on features for word-processing programs, a user can script a simple Web page without ever learning HTML.

For most beginners, a WYSIWYG editor (such as Adobe PAGEMILL, Microsoft FRONTPAGE, or Netscape COMPOSER) allows a user to implement basic commands and to see what the Web page will look like as it is written. Word-processing programs, like Microsoft WORD, have HTML add-ons like INTERNET ASSISTANT that convert word-processed documents into HTML script. However, all of these programs have limitations for the time being. Eventually, many Web writers will want to know the HTML scripts behind the Web pages they find useful because sections of these scripts can be emulated and learned from.

Ultimately, the best way to learn more about HTML is to look on the Web. There are many sources that can guide a user through HTML script (references to these sites are available at http://unix.cc.wmich.edu/rea/CC/). A user also can view the source code (the HTML that creates a page) by choosing "Document Source" or "Page Source" under the "View" pull-down menu in the browser. Moreover, if users want to "experiment" with the HTML script of the page, they can choose the "source" option in the "Save as" screen under the browser's "File" pull-down menu. Then, there is a local copy (on a disk or hard drive) of the HTML that constructed the page and a Web writer can analyze the script.

When viewing code, a Web writer must remember that HTML, like any language, is a dynamic and evolving means for Web writers to communicate with browsers. In turn, these browsers are the means for others to acquire the Web writer's information in the form of Web pages. However, Web pages look different on various systems and browsers. It depends on many variables, but Web writers cannot control the type of computer used to access their Web page or the type of browser used. Moreover, HTML has gone through various revisions starting at HTML 1.0 and is currently at HTML 4.1. Older browsers cannot access many of the new features of HTML 4.x, and there is no way to know who the audience will be or what level of technology will be used. Moreover, the many variations between browser versions sometimes make it challenging to write cross-platform scripts.

Although it is impossible for Web writers to know the entire audience and their technology requirements, just as with prose, Web writers should concern themselves with who their primary audience will be. If the audience is skilled Web writers who can be expected to keep current with the technology, then there is no problem using advanced scripting features. On the other hand, if the audience is new to the Web and their equipment might be older (many schools fall into this category), Web writers might want to keep the Web presentation simple so that all computer systems might access it. A simple guideline is to place the minimum browser version needed to effectively view the Web page directly on the Web page. Moreover, the more complicated a Web page, the more need there might be to write a version accessible through text browsers (or at least older graphical browsers), so all users can have access to information or at least know what they are missing.

Evaluating Web Sites

Students will soon find that accessing information on the Web is not as much of a problem as distinguishing between valuable information and eye candy. Search engine technology is catching up with user demand, but it is still a challenge determining the validity and, ultimately, the usefulness of Web-based information.

Evaluation must also be considered from the perspective of both the organization (in this case, academia) and the individual. Organizations crave a means for assessment of work and products; hence we award grades at the end of a course. Several traditional measures are used in Web-page construction to assess this quality, such as hit counters, cookies, etc., but other more reliable means may be needed to assess the perceptions of end users of the product who are reading, researching, and using the tools produced by the organization. In this light, it may be necessary to introduce traditional, theoretical behavioral constructs that are widely known surrogates for success of information systems. Satisfaction (Doll & Torkzadeh, 1988), perceived usefulness, and perceived ease of use (Davis, 1989) are all tools that are widely accepted surrogates for success in information systems and might be used for this purpose if empirical study supports their use.

Empirical study aside, the fact remains that the power of the Web to contain a nationally known and respected organization's report next to a less than reputable group's propaganda truly can equalize the distribution of information. However, this equality can also make it difficult for students to determine the validity of the information. Familiar print standards do not appear here. Web sites can be aesthetically pleasing, yet contain no relevant information. On the other hand, a Web writer may have simply converted a groundbreaking thesis from a word processor to a text format and put it on the Web. Although the words are not aesthetically pleasing, the content might be invaluable. However, Web sites fall somewhere in between as the line between content and presentation is a permeable boundary at best.

This challenge comes to the forefront when determining source validity on the Web because not everything that looks good is necessarily a reliable source. A well-designed Web page means that the Web writer is good at writing HTML and designing an effective Web page, not that the information on that page is necessarily a reputable source for the students' needs. The following criteria for determining the validity of a Web site's content can function as a part of our Web *hyperheuristic*. (Although we discuss the application of these criteria in relation to evaluating existing Web content, many of these items can be applied to student writing as well.)

Evaluating Content

Site Location (URL). Site location can be helpful. If a page claims to be written by an organization, yet does not contain an ".org" in the domain name, then claims should be questioned. If the ".com" designation is part of the site, then business interests may skew the information. In the 1996 presidential elections there were two Bob Dole sites: one official site and one parody site. The only difference in the addresses was an ".org" for the official site and a ".com" for the parody. The sites were designed almost identically, but the content was quite different. An ".edu" designation does not necessarily make the Web writer an academic authority, but a student may be able to verify the writer's credentials by searching the academic site. Ultimately, students should consider the caliber of the information on the entire site if this is a feasible option.

Credentials. If a Web writer is unwilling to supply contact information on the Web page either for the writer or the organization sponsoring the Web site, credibility suffers. At minimum, an email contact address is necessary. Also, links to other sites, writings, etc., done by the Web writer can add to credibility (of course, those would have to be evaluated as well).

If the author is writing as part of an organization, then the organization's credibility needs to be verified. Looking for position statements and organizational goals on the site can help. Also, a student might check whether well-known organizations with similar concerns have any knowledge of the host organization. Ultimately, a student may simply need to call the organizations and ask for more information.

Quality Control/Filters. The distinctions between reputable and not-so-reputable Web sites may not be easy to make. This is especially the case with electronic journals. For example, *Kairos* has an editorial board of established academics in the computers and composition field; it puts forth review and submission guidelines, and basically follows many of the same procedures set up for scholarly journals. Many other electronic journals do not have the same reputation, yet also have editorial boards, review guidelines, etc. Students cannot determine quality unless they spend the time reading the articles and checking writers' credentials. It is an arduous, yet necessary process.

Intended Audience and Purpose. Most instructors would hope determining audience and purpose on the Web would not be a major issue for students because these topics are covered in class in connection to writing. An instructor would be safe in assuming that a student would not cite children's books about the importance of eating vegetables as part of an argument for eating a balanced diet. The American Medical Association is definitely a more reliable source than Golden Book. However, this distinction can become problematic on the Web, as the most informed professional sites are not necessarily the best-designed Web sites.

Timeliness. Although some sources can be dated on the Web—especially if they are discussing facts and figures from previous year's findings—most information changes from month to month. Given the nature of the Web, most sites need to be updated continuously. Even if the basic information on the site does not change, hyperlinks to other sites might. A recently updated Web page assures students that the Web writer at least cares enough to check the site periodically.

Tone, Register, and Bias. Given the ease of Web publication, anyone with access to a computer and a server can distribute his or her ideas and personal philosophies all over the world. Even if a site passes much of the criteria discussed above, a student still must pay attention to the reasonableness and objectivity in a Web site. This is especially true if the Web site is meant to influence users in some manner. Students must look at word choice and manner of presentation, as well as world view, to determine if information is skewed.

Documentation and Hyperlink Cross-References. Finally, a student should consider whether the site has documentation to support its assertions or findings. Then a student must determine if this documentation is reliable and if it can be verified. Is there a list of works cited? Moreover, are there other sources that support this site's findings? Another test of site reliability is to find out if it is referenced with a hyperlink from other reputable sites. A student can determine this by conducting a Web search for the site to find related hyperlink references.

Creating Web Writing

In addition to evaluating, and then applying, the concepts of content evaluation to Web sites, students and instructors must also consider presentation. In many writing contexts, the use of an approved style guide will suffice. As long as pages are formatted and sources are correctly cited, the student and instructor are able to focus on content alone. This is almost never the case with Web writing. Content and presentation always vie for attention in this medium. In many cases, presentation wins out over content as moving images and colored text are often more compelling for students than grammar and syntax. However, in Web writing both content and presentation are equally important and must share the arena. The task of the Web writer and the instructor is striking a balance between the two. Instructors must concern themselves with the HTML scripting and design of the Web pages in addition to developing content as they help students become Web writers.

Audience and Purpose

Web writing might seem to put instructors in a conundrum. Does asking students to write Web pages incorporating a mixture of images, sounds, and text go against the prose writing supposed to be the focus of a composition course? We think not. For example, the criteria of audience and purpose are still very much a part of writing Web pages. Granted, the question of audience might be difficult for students to determine, given the fact that any one of millions of users could theoretically "hit" their page on the Web. However, just as in writing prose, a Web page designed without a specific audience in mind will lack focus and be less useful than one that targets a specific audience. In most cases, students do not write Web pages only to a class audience but also to a specific audience they have discovered online in a newsgroup or a discussion list. Not only will an online audience give continual feedback on a Web page as it evolves, but such audiences can also provide the student with a specific topic to organize the Web page around.

Purpose is important as well. The existing modes of discourse now used in composition classes can be transferred to Web writing as well. For example, Web pages can inform, persuade, or entertain. Moreover, Web pages can immerse students in a dialectic with their audience (an option not always available in prose). Through email, students can receive commentary on their Web pages from a diverse audience and respond to that audience through email and Web page revisions.

Design and Function

After determining audience and purpose (and this may be part of a recursive process), design and function become a crucial aspect of Web writing. Instructors can use sections of one of the many style guides available on the Web (URLs are available at http://unix.cc.wmich.edu/rea/CC/). However, depending on the bias of the style guide author, disagreement may exist on certain issues, such as the number of hyperlinks per page. Some designers more concerned with data presentation argue for one index page full of links to every other page at the site, with no links between the various pages. Other designers opt for shorter pages with many links as opposed to one large page with a few. There is no definitive right or wrong. The following categories are organized around issues to consider in Web page design. Many overlap in concerns and all may not be applicable in any one instance, but they are all useful items to consider when writing and evaluating Web pages.

Hyperlinks

Meaningful Links. Given the power of hypertext to link passages and sites with a few keystrokes, there always is the temptation to include as many links as possible. However, the coherence of a hypertextual presentation requires that readers know that each link is meaningful and contributes to the overall site. Therefore, Web writers must make sure that all links are contextualized within the passage. Not only should it be clear where the link is going but also what the relationship to the link is. For example, each of the following links lead to the same page ("subversion.html"):

More about *hypertext.*

More about hypertext and its *relation to print culture.*

More about hypertext and its *subversion of linear prose in print culture.*

The first hyperlink leads a user to something about hypertext; the second is a bit more specific, but the third definitely gives hypertext readers an idea as to where they are going if they choose to follow this hyperlink.

Simple File Names. When writing links to separate pages in a site, Web writers should keep file names simple. Although most Web writers have no control over the domain address (e.g., most personal WMU Web pages are located at http://unix.cc.wmich.edu), they do have control over file names. Because most file names are case sensitive, it is always a good idea to keep file names in all lowercase unless capitalization helps readers with the file name (e.g., "Web-Writer.html" is easier to read than "webwriter.html"). Moreover, because one mistake in typing will result in a "file not found" (404) error, file names should be kept descriptive, but short.

Repeated Links. Another important aspect of establishing a reliable context within a Web site is avoiding the temptation to link the same word to the same site repeatedly. Although different sections of the presentation might require a repeated hyperlink to the same site, continually linking the word "subversion" or the phrase "linear prose" to "subversion.html" would be frustrating to the hypertext's audience.

Navigation. Effective contextualization of links greatly helps readers navigate Web sites. Readers new to Web navigation and the demands of hypertext especially need cues as to where they are and where they might go. Many Web writers, such as Patrick Lynch and Sarah Horton (1997) of the *Yale Style Guide*, recommend using print metaphors, such as indexes and table of contents within Web sites to orient readers. Web writers might also consider putting a link back to their home page or the page that begins the particular presentation on every page within that site. This way, lost readers are more likely to return to the site's organizing page rather than simply leave for another Web destination. Moreover, with the complexity of search engines, one of the site pages might be found without the guiding context needed for a complete understanding. A return hyperlink allows the reader to understand the entire site rather than one page taken out of context.

Most importantly, Web writers should never assume that the reader knows as much about the site as they do. It sounds simple, yet too often a Web writer forgets that the readers have not been present as each hyperlink and passage has been crafted and joined to form a coherent presentation.

Color. HTML gives Web writers the options to change the color of hyperlinks. The default selection is blue for unused links and purple (Netscape NAVIGATOR) or red (Internet EXPLORER) for used hyperlinks. If Web writers feel the need to change hyperlink colors for presentation purposes, they must weigh the aesthetic impact of these color changes with the possible confusion that may result. A reader expecting a blue link and instead getting a green may be confused as to whether the link has been used or not and choose not to follow. Worse yet, the reader might follow and find his or her expectations subverted and leave the site. No matter what the Web writer finally chooses, the hyperlink color scheme should be consistent throughout the entire site.

Color Schemes. HTML allows Web writers the ability not only to change hyperlink colors but also text colors and background colors. Web writers can use images for backgrounds as well. Most beginning Web writers will go a bit overboard with the opportunity to change every color on the Web page. A dark green background with light green text may look fine on the Web writer's monitor, but all systems display color schemes a bit differently. What may be visible on one system might not be on another. What looks to be a pleasing color scheme through one type of monitor may not be on another.

Background/Text Conflicts. Color schemes can become detrimental to presentation when the background color or image makes it impossible to read the text. In addition, Web writers must consider if they want to account for the possibility of users printing the document. Although there is an option in most browsers to disregard color schemes in favor of the default black text on gray background, most users do not know of this option (available under the "Options" pull-down menu or in "Preferences"). Even a simple Web page with white text on a black background will not show up on paper when a user tries to print it on some systems.

Font sizes and types can be problematic to presentation as well. Many of the newer browsers allow various fonts and sizes. However, a Web writer cannot always assume that a user has the newest browser. The Web writer must decide if including fonts different from the browser-set default is important enough to exclude a significant portion of a potential audience.

Images

Number. Using images and clip art on Web pages moves students closer to Lanham's (1993) *digital rhetoric.* Nevertheless, the number of images as well as their file size can greatly inhibit the effectiveness of a Web page. Images can provide wonderful illustrations to support and enhance textual points and they can act as guide markers for navigation and interaction. Arrows, email icons, and scanned photographs are just the beginnings of what a Web writer can do on a Web page. However, just as colors can be overdone, so can images. Just as every hyperlink needs to be contextualized, so does each image.

Size. Although images will not confuse users trying to navigate through the site (unless the images are also hyperlinks), they can overtax the user's system. Images require more time to download than text. Large images (100 KB and above) might take minutes depending on the speed of the user's Internet connection. Web pages that take a long time to download should be identified as such on the hyperlink leading to them. Informed users making the choice to follow a hyperlink even though they know there will be a lengthy download time are more willing to wait than uninformed users. Although it should go without saying, a responsible Web writer makes sure that the wait is worth the time invested.

Placement. Once Web writers have determined the ratio of images to text for a certain page, they must work to incorporate the images effectively. Placing all images flush left or centered is not always the best choice. Images can also be integrated effectively using height and width commands that allow the image to be resized to the Web page. However, these sizing commands distort the images depending on the original size. Finding the right combination of height and width may take some experimentation.

Sensory Overload

As browsers and HTML evolve with new versions, more options become available. Images now can be animated, text can change colors and scroll across the screen, movies and sound are more common, and JavaScript and Java Applets (forms of computer programming embedded in Web pages) can be added to make the Web page truly dynamic. Web users need to learn how much is enough and how much is too much. They must take into account download time, audience, and purpose.

Miscellaneous Items to Consider

List of Links. Anyone who has navigated (or surfed) the Web has run into many lists of links. Most of the time these are individual compilations of favorite sites or lists of sites organized around a topic. These lists can be useful if they contribute to the organization of specific information on the Web. Nevertheless, as with all hyperlinks, contextualizing each link can greatly assist a Web user.

Length of Page. Some Web writers and theorists, such as George Landow (1990, 1992), assert that short passages linked throughout a site take full advantage of hypertext and the Web medium. Pragmatists argue that a large page may take longer to download the first time, but it is less frustrating to navigate and read because the entire page is stored in the browser's cache. Both of these positions are extremes. One or two screenfulls (the amount of information appearing on a standard fifteen-inch screen) per Web page is probably more of the norm. This way, there is a large enough portion to justify a Web page (addressing the pragmatists' concerns) and still ample need for hypertextual linking (addressing Landow's concern). Web writers of a site with a substantial number of links might also consider creating a print version that may take longer to download but can be printed out as a single file if the user so desires.

Outdated Information. Web writers planning on leaving Web pages online for an extended period of time should consider whether they are willing to keep the information on their site current. Otherwise, they might consider removing outdated pages to retain the standards of the site.

Email Address. Web writers should want to hear what people think about their pages. Including an email hyperlink on every page does not guarantee that Web users will write to the Web author, but it does increase the odds. Moreover, many users are more than happy to tell a Web writer that one or more of the hyperlinks suffers from linkrot.

Practical Application

Supplied with the knowledge and the criteria needed for a hyperheuristic, the challenge then becomes classroom implementation. It is valuable for instructors to know just what to look for in a Web page, but how do they get the students to apply this information as well? In the concluding sections, we offer a sample form for writers and some pedagogical applications of our discussion in the classroom to help students become better Web writers.

We recommend that, at a minimum, instructors bring a presentation system in to show sample Web pages for discussion just as they might do with prose. However, it is also a good idea to get students into a computer classroom to practice these concepts as well.

Critique Web Sites

Using sites, such as the *Cool Site of the Day* (http://cool.infi.net), or Vincent Flander's *Web Pages That Suck* (http://www.websitesthatsuck.com), students can begin to see what other Web users deem to be good or bad. Note, however, that many of these are professionally written and may look good, but fail in other content criteria. This exercise works best if instructors supply students with specific hyperheuristics. Students may also want to look at what other students have done. The *Alliance for Computers and Writing* site at http://english.ttu .edu/acw/ includes links to student Web sites.

Students can collect three Web sites and evaluate them according to their hyperheuristics. Then, they can post the URLs and the evaluations to the class discussion list. Instructors should encourage students to look at the evaluated sites and discuss each other's evaluation either in class, on the discussion list, or both.

Design a Simple Web Page

Instructors can choose from one of the shareware HTML editors listed at http://unix.cc.wmich.edu/rea/CC/, or they can use applications available at their institution. In any case, instructors might find it easier to introduce students to Web writing if they use a WYSIWYG editor to avoid using HTML at the onset. Instructors will want to familiarize themselves with the application before bringing it into the classroom as they will, more than likely, become the help desk for students.

After students have spent some time navigating the Web and discussing issues from the hyperheuristic, they should have some idea of how Web pages can look. Instructors should then give each student a disk with a sample Web page template file. This template should consist of basic Web design items, such as bold text, hyperlinks, etc. Using this template, students can then manipulate the various format options, replace text with their own writing, and even insert images they have found on the Web. Moreover, they can begin hyperlinking various sites to their own page, thereby creating a resource for future work.

We have found that conducting this exercise well before students must focus on developing content allows them to experiment with presentation and balance the two entities later in the course.

Create a Web Resource

This activity is best suited for later in the course. It can be used to take the place of a large individual or group project. Most often, it works well as a substitute for the research paper requirement in many writing classes. Using a hyperheuristic developed for this purpose, instructors should encourage students to not only find all relevant information related to their topic on the Web and in the library, but also contextualize this information on a site. After this, students should synthesize and add to the body of knowledge. What can make this truly enticing to students is to have them actively seek input from acknowledged experts in the field via email and USENET postings.

Conclusion

This hyperaccelerated journey into Web writing is but the beginning of what the Web can provide to both students and instructors. The Web is not only a means to acquire data, but also to communicate. Unlike television or radio, which are a one-way street as far as communications go, the Web enables users to talk to one another and actively decide what will be seen and when it will be used. Moreover, the Web allows users to produce information as well. Otherwise, not many would have the chance to produce a television or radio show: The Web is more of an equal-opportunity medium.

Since its beginnings in the early 1990s, the Web has progressed and developed faster than any other technology or communication media to become part of a world culture. There are challenges that still need to be addressed, such as developing standards and providing increased access to students. Nevertheless, Web writing provides a new medium through which students can improve writing and communication skills. The Web is a research tool, a communication technology, and an expressive medium.

However, instructors need to remember that simply having the technology at one's disposal does not automatically make it an effective component of effective writing pedagogies. Instructors need to continue creating and refining guides to make the Web a viable technology of literacy. Ultimately, although the demands of Web writing instruction can be demanding, the benefits far outweigh the costs.

References

Bush, Vannevar. (1999/1945). As we may think. *Atlantic Monthly, 176*(1). Available: http://ccat.sas.upenn.edu/jod/texts/vannevar.bush.html [Accessed May 21, 1997].

Calliau, Robert. (1997a). A little history of the World Wide Web. Available: http://www.w3.org/History.html [Accessed July 5, 1999].

Calliau, Robert. (1997b). *Short history of hypertext.* Available: http://www.w3.org/History.html [Accessed July 5, 1999].

Davis, Fred D. (1989). Perceived usefulness, perceived ease of use, and user acceptance of information technology. *MIS Quarterly, 13*(4), 319–340.

Doll, William J., & Torkzadeh, Gholamreza. (1988). The measurement of end-user computing satisfaction. *MIS Quarterly, 12*(2), 259–274.

Landow, George P. (1990). Changing texts, changing readers: Hypertext in literary education, criticism, and scholarship. In Bruce Henricksen & Thais E. Morgan (Eds.), *Reorientations: Critical theories and pedagogies* (pp. 133–161). Urbana, IL: University of Illinois Press.

Landow, George P. (1992). *Hypertext: The convergence of contemporary critical theory and technology.* Baltimore, MD: The Johns Hopkins University Press.

Lanham, Richard A. (1993). *The electronic word: Democracy, technology, and the arts.* Chicago, IL: University of Chicago Press.

Lynch, Patrick J., & Horton, Sarah. (1997). *Yale style manual.* Available: http://info.med.yale.edu/caim/manual/contents.html [Accessed June 11, 1997].

Nelson, Theodor Holm. (1992). Opening hypertext: A memoir. In Myron Tuman (Ed.), *Literacy on-line: The promise (and peril) of reading and writing with computers* (pp. 43–57). Pittsburgh, PA: University of Pittsburgh Press.

W3C. (1999). About the World Wide Web Consortium (W3C). Available: http://www.w3.org/pub/WWW/Consortium [Accessed May 21, 1997].

Zakon, Robert Hobbes. (1997). Hobbes' Internet timeline v2.5. Available: http://info.isoc.org/guest/zakon/Internet/History/HIT.html [Accessed May 14, 1997].

CLEAR SENTENCES AND WORD CHOICE

Parts Three and Four of *The Bedford Handbook* offer students easy-to-understand advice about how to solve sentence-level problems, supplemented with examples that model revision possibilities. In these discussions *The Handbook* emphasizes the rhetorical impact of sentence structure and word choice, helping students understand the importance of making careful choices as they revise and edit their work.

The articles that follow will help teachers consider several alternatives for teaching students about sentences and word choice.

- How can teachers help students enlarge their repertoire of options for composing and revising sentences in the contexts of their larger rhetorical situations?
- How can teachers help students develop an awareness of sexist or discriminatory language, and how can they help students avoid using it?

TEACHING ABOUT SENTENCES

Erika Lindemann

[From *A Rhetoric for Writing Teachers*, 3rd ed. New York: Oxford UP, 1995. 158–69.]

(For biographical information, see p. 55)

Writers compose and revise sentences within larger rhetorical contexts, and effective writers make conscious choices about sentences based on their understanding of their rhetorical situation. Lindemann suggests that "[t]he goal of our teaching should be to enlarge the student's repertoire of sentence options and rhetorical choices." Synthesizing several decades of important scholarly work on syntax and discourse analysis, she offers three approaches, each one meant to help students "apply what they're learning about sentences to composing." Lindemann suggests that teachers help students recognize that readers bring a number of expectations to sentences. She also suggests that students regularly practice combining (and decombining) sentences, preferably ones from their own work in progress. As a third technique for teaching sentences, she describes how teachers can use Christensen's "generative rhetoric" to help students explore alternative sentence constructions and to help "students attend to the ways sentences express relationships among ideas." Lindemann's chapter provides teachers with theoretically consistent advice that they can apply to their work with students.

A sentence should read as if its author, had he held a plow instead of a pen, could have drawn a furrow deep and straight to the end.

–Henry David Thoreau

All of us have an intuitive understanding of sentence structures and their use. We've all been talking in sentences since childhood, rarely stopping to consider whether or not our speech represents a "complete thought," contains a subject and predicate, or shows "dependent" and "independent" clauses. Our sentences, most of which we've never heard or said before, get the message across. All native speakers *do* know what a sentence is; they can create complex sentences without knowing the names for the constructions they produce.

If that's so, why spend time in a writing class on sentences? To be sure, some types of sentence instruction do not use class time productively. Too much time spent analyzing someone else's sentences gives students too little practice generating their own. Too much attention to labeling sentence types or classifying phrases and clauses may teach terminology—*what* to call a construction—but not writing—*how* to create it. Although human beings have an intuitive competence for creating sentences, many student writers need practice translating competence into fluent performance.

A major reason why "performing" written sentences is difficult stems from differences between speech and writing. Spoken communication, which may be highly elliptical, generally succeeds without complicated syntax. Gestures, facial expressions, and the habit of taking turns reinforce the message. Although high school and college students are capable of writing complicated sentences, they're unaccustomed to using their entire syntactic repertoire, especially if they habitually write as they talk. Second, writing sentences presents considerable risk. Every word added to a sentence increases the possibility of misspellings, punctuation mistakes, or other errors that jeopardize students' grades. Short, simple sentences are safest. Third, some students have trouble with sentences because they can't depend on the eye or ear to help them identify prose rhythms. If they read poorly, rarely read for pleasure, converse infrequently with adults, or passively watch a great deal of television, they may have difficulty imagining comfortable options for sentences. Television commercials, for example, are usually scripted in sentence fragments, a style that may influence our students' "ear" for sentences to a greater extent than we realize. Finally, writing sentences requires punctuation marks that have few equivalents in speech. Yes, we pause for longer or shorter periods as we speak, but writing indicates "pauses" with a confusing array of symbols, with commas, dashes, colons, semicolons, periods, and other marks. Conversely, we don't "speak" apostrophes. Performing written sentences, then, requires confidence in manipulating symbols that have no true counterparts in spoken English.

For these reasons, students need risk-free opportunities to practice sentences, especially complex sentences. Such practice should take place in the context of composing longer stretches of discourse. When students study and practice sentences, they must be able to apply what they're learning *about* sentences to composing. They must translate knowledge into performance. Instead of analyzing sentences in a textbook, we can help students discover what kinds of sentences their own writing contains. Instead of drilling students on punctuation rules, we can encourage them to practice unfamiliar constructions and address the punctuation problems as they arise. Instead of discussing sentence patterns students have already mastered, we can help them practice types they may be avoiding for fear of making mistakes in punctuation or subject-verb agreement. The goal of our teaching should be to enlarge the student's repertoire of sentence options and rhetorical choices.

One relatively simple way to discuss sentences involves talking about readers. Readers expect sentences to conform to conventional punctuation, but they have other expectations as well.[1] Readers expect the most important information in a sentence to appear at the beginning and at the end. The beginning of a sentence names the actors and either establishes a context for information to come or links the sentence to the one before it by providing transitional, old information. The end of the sentence stresses new information. Information buried in the middle gets the least attention. Putting important information in the right slot helps readers follow along. What is "important" depends on the context in which the sentence appears. That is, writers do not compose individual sentences; they put sentences together into paragraphs and larger units of discourse. In reading the following student's paragraph, notice which words Roger has put in the most emphatic positions, the beginning and end of the sentence:

> In some cultures, <u>it is</u> the men who are more conscious of nonverbal communication than *the women are*. <u>That is</u> not true *in North America*. In our culture <u>it seems</u> that of both groups the women are more aware of body language, voice tone, and *other nonverbal messages*. <u>This was brought</u> to my attention by *a man*, but <u>it was</u> only after I became more sensitive myself that *I really believed him*.

Although Roger's paragraph is about men's awareness of nonverbal communication, *men, I* (Roger), or *nonverbal communication* rarely appear in emphatic sentence positions. The paragraph's implicit story of how Roger "became more sensitive" never gets told. Discussing such a paragraph with students shows them how to reorder sentence elements so that important information appears where a reader expects to find it. Roger's revised paragraph is more specific, shows better sentence variety, and also makes more effective use of sentence positions to advance the story of what Roger learned:

> While <u>men</u> in some cultures are more conscious than women of *nonverbal communication*, <u>I haven't always been</u>. *I learned* from my girlfriend's brother that body language, tone of voice, and gestures are less important to me than *they are to my girlfriend*. Through his advice, <u>I learned</u> *what my girlfriend's signals meant*. For example, <u>I realized</u> that when she leaned back in her chair, *she was saying, "I'm upset."* By watching my girlfriend's nonverbal messages, <u>I became</u> *more sensitive* to them.

In addition to discussing how readers regard sentences, two other techniques for teaching sentences in the context of composing are popular with writing teachers: sentence combining and generating cumulative sentences. Both techniques can increase the "syntactic fluency" of students' writing. At the same time, writing teachers must guard against the exaggerated claims of some proponents of these techniques, especially of sentence combining. Kellogg Hunt, for example, suggests structuring an entire writing course around sentence combining: "In every sense, sentence combining can be a comprehensive writing program in and of itself, for at least one semester. It is nonsense, rather than common sense, to suggest that sentence combining can't be the one and only instructional strategy, at least for one term."[2] Nonsense or not, many writing teachers and researchers *do* express misgivings about the efficacy of sentence combining as the sole instructional method in a writing course and have doubts about the syntactic gains attributed to sentence-combining practice. Some of these gains, in fact, may result from instruction in semantics and rhetoric that accompanies discussions of sentence-combining problems. More important, because composing involves more than mastering sentences, no single instructional method, including sentence combining or work with cumulative sentences, will transform poor writers into accomplished ones. Although both techniques have advantages, neither should become the exclusive focus of a writing class.

Sentence Combining

Generative-transformational theory suggests that we transform sentences intuitively by adding to, deleting from, or rearranging sentence elements. Sentence combining applies this principle to writing instruction.[3] As Charles Cooper explains, sentence-combining problems "confront the student with sentences more complex than ones he would be likely to write at that point in his development; they ask the student to write out fully-formed sentences and they provide him the content of the sentences so that his attention can remain focused on the *structural* aspects of the problem."[4] To combine the following sentences, for example, students would insert information from the indented sentence into the first sentence:

> The canary flew out the window.
>> The canary is yellow.
>
> *Student's response:* The yellow canary flew out the window.

Some sentence-combining problems offer clues about which words to add or delete:

> SOMETHING made her angry.
>> She read something in the note. (what)
>
> *Student's response:* What she read in the note made her angry.

Multiple embeddings are also possible:

> My friends and I enjoy SOMETHING.
> We race our bicycles around the paths in the park. (racing)
>> Our bicycles are lightweight.
>> Our bicycles are ten-speed.
>> The paths are narrow.
>> The paths are winding.
>
> *Student's response:* My friends and I enjoy racing our lightweight, ten-speed bicycles around the narrow, winding paths in the park.

Exercises that contain transformation cues require students to combine the sentences in a specified way. Cued exercises can give students confidence in generating syntactic structures that they may be avoiding. The cues show students *how* to combine the sentences, providing a repertoire of connectives that hold phrases and clauses together. As students work through the exercises, teachers can introduce terminology and whatever punctuation conventions a particular transformation requires.

Open-ended exercises, which offer no cues, may be more difficult for some students, but they permit more choices and encourage students to consider the rhetorical effects of possible combinations:

> The national debt concerns Americans.
> The national debt grows eight thousand dollars every second.
> The national debt totals nearly four trillion dollars.
>
> *Possible student responses, each of which achieves a different rhetorical effect:*
> The national debt concerns Americans because it grows eight thousand dollars every second and totals nearly four trillion dollars.
>
> The national debt, a concern for Americans, grows eight thousand dollars every second and totals nearly four trillion dollars.
>
> The national debt, growing eight thousand dollars every second and totaling nearly four trillion dollars, concerns Americans.
>
> Americans are concerned about the national debt, which grows eight thousand dollars every second and totals nearly four trillion dollars.
>
> Because the national debt grows eight thousand dollars every second and totals nearly four trillion dollars, it concerns Americans.

When students combine sentences in as many ways as they know how, read them aloud, and discuss which versions they like best; they're not only exercising syntactic muscles but also making rhetorical choices. Like professional writers, students develop an eye and ear for prose rhythms. "In addition to playing with transformations and making their choices," writes William Strong, "professional writers also seem to spend considerable time hearing the way sentences fit together to make up the 'melody' of their writing. They listen for the dips and swaying curves of some phrases, the hard, rhythmic, regular punch of others. They sensitize themselves to avoid sentences where meaning is almost obscured within the lengthy confines of the sentence itself; they study those sentences where pause, and momentary reflection, have their impact" (*Sentence Combining*, p. xv).

Discussing sentence-combining exercises also helps students become confident about punctuation. My own students shun participial modifiers, appositives, and relative clauses because they aren't sure how to use commas to set them off. They avoid introductory adverb clauses for similar reasons. Students who have learned to be careful about commas understandably "write around" the problem. Sentence-combining exercises illustrate how punctuation organizes sentence elements for a reader and offer risk-free opportunities to solve punctuation problems that have baffled students for years. Sometimes an exercise exposes a punctuation rule misunderstood in a previous English class. A former student of mine consistently placed commas behind words such as *because, since,* and *if* when they began a sentence: "Because, I didn't have a car I couldn't date Susan." When I asked him why he thought the comma belonged there, he explained, "My English teacher told me to set off *because* words; she called them 'introductory' something-or-other." Doubtless, his teacher encouraged him to set off the entire introductory clause, but the student had heard only part of the rule. He solved the problem by practicing a few sentence-combining exercises. My student's problem also illustrates another point: grammatical terminology sometimes creates punctuation problems. Sentence combining allows teachers to dispense with terminology altogether or, if they wish, to name constructions *after* students have practiced them.

Other students may need practice "decombining" sentences. Older students sometimes attempt such extraordinarily complicated sentences that the syntax gets twisted. They may be writing to please teachers who implicitly praise "long" sentences; nevertheless, they develop a style that obscures ideas in hopelessly convoluted syntax. Here's an example from a first-year college student's paper:

> The things that people go to the pharmacist for sometimes are just to get the pharmacist to prescribe them something for their illness, and he can not do any prescribing for anyone for medicine.

Prepositions are part of the problem here, but Kenny loses his reader by piling too much information into one sentence. When he read the sentence out loud, he said it sounded "weird," but he didn't know how to revise it. I asked him to "decombine" the sentence, breaking it into simple sentences. We came up with the following two lists, which reproduce the simple sentences embedded in his original:

- People go to the pharmacist for things.
- People go to the pharmacist sometimes.
- People just get the pharmacist to do SOMETHING. (to)
- The pharmacist prescribes them something for their illness.

and

- He cannot do any SOMETHING. (–ing)
- He prescribes for anyone.
- He prescribes medicine.

At this point, Kenny could understand why the sentence seems "weird." It lacks a single focus. Two or three subjects—"people," "pharmacist," and perhaps "things"—vie for attention. Recombining the sentences to emphasize only one subject, "people" or "pharmacist," might yield the following options:

"People" Sentences

1. People sometimes go to the pharmacist, who cannot prescribe medicine for anyone, just to get him to prescribe something for their illness.
2. Sometimes people go to the pharmacist just to get him to prescribe medicine for their illness, something he cannot do.

"Pharmacist" Sentences

1. The pharmacist cannot prescribe medicine for anyone's illness, even though people sometimes ask him to.
2. Although people sometimes ask the pharmacist to prescribe medicine for their illness, he cannot write prescriptions.

The two-step decombining and recombining procedure now gives Kenny several sentences to choose from in revising his paper.

Decombining and recombining sentences can help students untangle, tighten, and rewrite sentences too complex for a reader to follow easily. After a while, students also discover which transformations create convoluted sentences. For Kenny, beginning sentences with noun clauses and piling up infinitives creates problems. For other students, passive constructions or beginning sentences with "There are" and "It is" tangle the syntax. Different kinds of sentence-combining exercises help students detect and solve these problems.

To improve their skill in manipulating sentence structures, students need regular sentence-combining practice over a long period, ideally two or three times a week throughout the entire course of instruction. The exercises can begin as early as the fourth grade and increase in complexity through college. Inundating students with sentence-combining problems, however, turns a means into an end. Assigning too many problems too frequently bores students, who begin to regard the exercises as busywork. Because the exercises focus only on sentences, not longer stretches of discourse, and because the content of the sentences is predetermined, not invented by the student, sentence combining should supplement, not replace, students' own writing.

All the same, sentence combining has several advantages. Used correctly, the technique *does* increase students' syntactic fluency. Teachers can assign the exercises as individual homework or as in-class groupwork, students pooling their intuitive linguistic resources to solve the problems. Teachers can design their own exercises, use those available in published textbooks, or best of all, glean them from students' papers. Grading the work is inappropriate because it attaches risks to the exercises. To be effective, sentence combining must remain risk free, a way of experimenting with syntactic structures students avoid for fear of making low marks. Some teachers post or pass out answers for the problems so that students can check their sentences against the key.

Besides increasing the complexity of students' sentences, the exercises have other advantages. They demonstrate how to construct sentences without resorting to grammatical terms or singling out errors in students' papers. They permit us to avoid terminology altogether or introduce it after students understand how to perform a particular transformation. They offer plenty of examples for describing punctuation, mechanics, and conventions of edited American English in the context of writing, not isolated from it. And because students will combine sentences in many interesting ways, the exercises allow us to discuss rhetorical choices, differences in emphasis that might work more effectively in some contexts than in others. Open-ended exercises work especially well in this regard. They help students discover, not the one "right" sentence, but a range of options. Students also can apply the technique to their own drafts, rewriting sentences to emphasize ideas differently, change the focus, coordinate or subordinate material, and achieve sentence variety.

Cumulative Sentences

In *Notes toward a New Rhetoric* (1978), Francis Christensen expresses considerable dissatisfaction with traditional methods of teaching sentences. "We need," he says, "a rhetoric of the sentence that will do more than combine the ideas of primer sentences. We need one that will *generate* ideas" (p. 26). Instead of teaching sentences based on rhetorical classifications (loose, balanced, and periodic sentences) or grammatical categories (simple, compound, complex, and compound-complex sentences), Christensen offers an alternative method, generative rhetoric. It's a rhetoric that generates ideas, not words. According to Christensen, students don't need to write longer, more complex sentences simply to produce more words; rather, the sentence-as-form encourages writers to examine the ideas expressed by the words, to sharpen or add to them, and then to reproduce the idea more effectively. The "cumulative sentence," the heart of Christensen's generative rhetoric, compels writers to examine their thoughts, the meanings words convey. Consequently, generative rhetoric serves prewriting as well as rewriting.

Christensen bases his generative rhetoric on four principles derived from his study of prose style and the works of contemporary authors. He maintains, first, that "composition is essentially a process of addition"; nouns, verbs, or main clauses serve as a foundation or base to which we add details, qualifications, new meanings. Second, Christensen's "principle of modification" suggests that we can add these new meanings either before or after some noun, verb, or base clause. The "direction of movement" for the sentence changes, depending on where we've added modifiers and new meaning. When modifiers appear before the noun, verb, or base clause (which Christensen calls the "head" of the construction), the sentence "moves" forward. Modifiers placed after the noun, verb, or base clause move the sentence backward because they require readers to relate the new details, qualifications, and meanings *back* to the head appearing earlier in the sentence. Christensen's third principle states that, depending on the meanings of the words we add, the head becomes either more concrete or less so. The base word or clause together with one or more modifying additions expresses several "levels of generality or abstraction." Finally, Christensen's "principle of texture" describes and evaluates a writer's style. He characterizes style as relatively "dense" or "plain," depending on the number and variety of additions writers make to nouns, verbs, and base clauses.

We don't need to explain Christensen's four principles to students before asking them to create cumulative sentences. Native speakers form such sentences naturally. When I introduce my class to cumulative sentences, I begin by asking students to add words and phrases to the following sentence, written on the blackboard: "The horse galloped." I provide a base clause and deliberately ask the class to "load the pattern," a practice that Christensen would condemn but that gives me a starting point. After students suggest additions to the sentence for three to five minutes, it might look like the following monstrosity: "Because Farmer Brown didn't notice the swarm of bees in the apple tree and hadn't tightened the cinch on the old, brown leather saddle securely, the horse galloped off through the orchard, throwing the startled rider to the ground, terrified by the bees buzzing around his head, until he reached the weathered board fence, where he stopped."

Although the sentence is unwieldy, students seem pleased to discover that they *can* compose complicated sentences like this one. Initially, quantity not quality intrigues them. That's fine for now; we'll get to quality soon enough (and fix that misplaced modifier). Generally, students add material at the end of the base clause first. Then, prompted by prewriting questions—Who? What? When? Where? How? Why?—they begin to place modifiers at the beginning or in the middle of the sentence: appositives, participial constructions, relative clauses, adverb and adjective constructions. After they have created the sentence, we discuss the kinds of grammatical structures and relationships the sentence expresses as well as punctuation problems we have encountered. Finally, we assess its rhetorical effectiveness, concluding that writing long sentences per se isn't a virtue and that our example needs revising. So, we tighten it, rearranging and deleting elements, reading versions aloud to evaluate their rhythm, and finally, imagining the larger context of the paragraph in which revised versions of our sentence might appear. Although the sample sentence enables us to take up several grammatical, rhetorical, and mechanical concerns, we will explore them in detail for several class meetings.

In one class period, for example, we might examine the kinds of additions that expand the base clause, discussing sentences from students' papers or a reading assignment. Although I avoid grammatical terms, Christensen uses them. In contrast to traditional methods, however, he limits the number of modifiers added to base clauses to only seven grammatical constructions:

PP	Prepositional phrase
NC	Noun cluster (appositives)
VC	Verb cluster (present and past participles, infinitives)
Abs	Absolute construction (a participial construction with its own subject)
Adv	Adverb clauses
AC	Adjective clauses
Rel	Relative clauses

Each of these additions adjusts the meaning of the base clause (or other clauses added to the base). "The main or base clause," Christensen explains, "is likely to be stated in general or abstract or plural terms. With the main clause stated, the forward movement of the sentence stops: The writer instead of going on to something new shifts down to a lower level of generality or abstraction or to singular terms, and goes back over the same ground at this lower level" (p. 29).

If we indent and number the levels of generality in the sample sentence discussed earlier, it looks like this:

> 2 Because Farmer Brown didn't notice the swarm of bees/ . . . and (Adv)
> > 3 in the apple tree (PP)
>
> 2 (because he) hadn't tightened the cinch/. . . securely, (Adv)
> > 3 on the old, brown leather saddle (PP)
>
> 1 the horse galloped off
> 2 through the orchard, (PP)
> 2 throwing the startled rider (VC)
> > 3 to the ground (PP)
>
> 2 terrified (VC)
> > 3 by the bees (PP)
> > > 4 buzzing around his head, (VC)
>
> 2 until he reached the weathered board fence, (Adv)
> > 3 where he stopped. (Rel)

Christensen calls this a four-level sentence. The base clause is always numbered "level 1," regardless of where it appears in the sentence. All of the level-2 additions modify "horse" and "galloped off," words in the base or level-1 clause. The level-3 modifiers refer back to and elaborate elements of level-2 constructions; level-4 modifiers particularize elements in level 3. Indenting each level helps students see what kinds of additions have been made and where they appear (before, after, or as the slash indicates, in the middle of a group of words). The diagram also reveals whether or not groups of words are grammatically similar or parallel, and how they relate to one another by qualifying or elaborating material elsewhere in the sentence. It's not necessary that students always label the modifiers correctly or number the levels the same way. What's important is seeing how the parts of the sentence work together.

Although our Farmer Brown sentence contains four levels, it is uncharacteristically "dense." Most high school and college students write one-, or at best, two-level sentences. Their "texture" is thin or plain. They resemble lists of information that have no shape because the writer hasn't figured out what relationship the details have to some larger idea. Here's an example of a one-level sentence, written by Maria, a first-year college student who is describing an advertisement.

> 1 The background is a dull, white film while
> 1 the caption shows black type.

Because Maria had practiced expanding sentences with level-2 and -3 modifiers, she knew how and where to improve the sentence with details. Here's her revision:

> 2 Cloudy and misty, (AC)
> 1 the background looks like a soft, white film,
> 2 draped behind bold, black type, (VC)
> 3 which catches the reader's eye. (Rel)

Out of context, this revision may sound flowery, but it demonstrates the generative power of Christensen's cumulative sentence. In reviewing her first sentence, Maria was able to generate additional details about the background and caption, features of the advertisement she wanted to discuss. Her revised sentence is longer—not necessarily a virtue—but it also relates the details instead of merely listing them. It subordinates the "bold, black type" of the caption (level 2) to the background (level 1).

Generative rhetoric helps students attend to the ways sentences express relationships among ideas.

> 1 The cumulative sentence in unskillful hands is unsteady,
> 2 allowing a writer to ramble on, (VC)
> 3 adding modifier after modifier, (VC)
> 4 until the reader is almost overwhelmed (Adv)
> 5 because the writer's central idea is lost. (Adv)

Cumulative sentences are not merely multilevel constructions that string together modifiers one after another. Students also must control the placement of modifiers, drawing them out of ideas in the base clause. They must see the idea again, sharpen the image, the object, the action. In exploring the implications of what they've said, they will generate or reinvent additional meanings to express. At the level of the sentence, the new meanings become cumulative modifiers. At the level of the paragraph and whole discourse, as we've already seen, the generative principles of Christensen's rhetoric can shape new sentences, paragraphs, and sections.

Notes

[1] See Joseph M. Williams, *Style: Ten Lessons in Clarity and Grace,* 3d ed. (Glenview, IL: Scott, Foresman, 1989). I also draw on unpublished material developed by George Gopen, Duke University.

[2] Kellogg W. Hunt, "Anybody Can Teach English," in *Sentence Combining and the Teaching of Writing,* ed. Donald A. Daiker, Andrew Kerek, and Max Morenberg (Conway, AR: L & S Books, 1979), p. 156. Although I disagree with Hunt, I recommend this collection of essays for those who want to know more about sentence combining. I also recommend Stephen P. Witte's review of the book in *College Composition and Communication* 31 (December 1980), 433–37, which discusses some of the reservations writing teachers have about sentence-combining research. For a comprehensive, though dated, bibliography on the theory and practice of sentence combining, see Max Morenberg and Andrew Kerek, "Bibliography on Sentence Combining: Theory and Practice, 1964–1979," *Rhetoric Society Quarterly* 9 (Spring 1979), 97–111. A useful summary of research on sentence combining is George Hillocks, Jr., *Research on Written Composition: New Directions for Teaching* (Urbana, IL: ERIC Clearinghouse on Reading and Communication Skills and the National Conference on Research in English, 1986), pp. 141–51.

[3] Frank O'Hare, *Sentence Combining: Improving Student Writing without Formal Grammar Instruction* (NCTE Research Report No. 15; Urbana, IL: NCTE, 1973), reviews research on the relationship between grammar study and improvement in writing and describes his own investigation. O'Hare's study demonstrates that written and oral sentence-combining exercises helped seventh graders "write compositions that could be described as syntactically more elaborated or mature" and "better in overall quality" (p. 67).

[4] Charles Cooper, "An Outline for Writing Sentence-Combining Problems," *English Journal* 62 (January 1973). The next three sample problems appear in Cooper.

Work Cited

Christensen, Francis, and Bonniejean Christensen. *Notes toward a New Rhetoric.* 2d ed. New York: Harper & Row, 1978.

FROM *THE HANDBOOK OF NONSEXIST WRITING*

Casey Miller and Kate Swift

[From *The Handbook of Nonsexist Writing.* 2nd ed. New York: Harper, 1988. 1–9.]

Freelance writers and editors Casey Miller and Kate Swift have published as partners since 1970. Over the years, their work on sexism and language has been published widely, and *The Handbook of Nonsexist Writing* has been the standard recommended text on the topic since its first appearance in 1980.

In the following selection, the introduction to their book, Miller and Swift argue forcefully for continued efforts to change sexist language. The balance of the book exposes the widespread sexism in language, provides historical analyses of sexist usage, and offers practical suggestions for avoiding sexist language.

Introduction: Change and Resistance to Change

When the first edition of *The Handbook of Nonsexist Writing* appeared in 1980, efforts to eliminate linguistic sexism had already gained support from a wide assortment of national and local organizations, both public and private.

Guidelines for nonsexist usage had been issued by most major textbook publishers, and professional and academic groups ranging from the Society of Automotive Engineers to the American Psychological Association were developing their own guidelines, as were such diverse public institutions as the City of Honolulu and the University of New Hampshire. Churches and synagogues were struggling with the problems of perception raised by traditional male-oriented language; librarians were rethinking the wording of catalog entries; and groups as varied as philanthropic foundations, political councils, and consumer cooperatives were recasting their charters, bylaws, application forms, and other materials in gender-neutral terms. Advertising copy had begun to acknowledge that bankers, insurance agents, scientists, consumers at every level, farmers, and athletes are female as well as male.

By the mid-eighties the movement toward nonsexist usage had gained so much momentum that researchers who studied its impact by analyzing three recently published American dictionaries of new words were prepared to state, in the cautious phraseology of scholarship, that their results showed "a trend toward nonsexism" in written language. The data, they said, "provided a judgment of the efficacy of feminists' efforts toward nonsexist vocabulary," and they ventured the opinion that the "importance and justice of the subject have been recognized."

During the same period, a marked increase occurred in academic research into language use and its relation to women, and the number of books and articles on the subject addressed to the general public continues to grow. So extensive is this outpouring, in fact, that a newsletter established in 1976 to report on activities in the field grew in only ten years from a 4-page pamphlet to a 64-page periodical called *Women and Language*. Not all this interest has been on the side of linguistic reform, of course; opposition to the concept of nonsexist language continues and in some quarters has stiffened. But during the past ten years, some of the most influential opponents of linguistic change have been persuaded that the problem is not going to disappear as obligingly as ground fog on an autumn morning.

The increased use of nonsexist language by those in major channels of communication provides a graphic demonstration of the mysterious ways in which reality affects language and is, in turn, affected by it. For as women become more prominent in fields from which they were once excluded, their presence triggers questions of linguistic equity that, once having been asked and answered, bring new visibility to women. How does one refer to a woman who is a member of Congress, or address a woman who sits on her country's highest court or is its chief of state? What does one call a woman who flies in space? Superficial as such questions may seem, their existence brings into focus a new awareness of women's potential. When *Time* magazine named Corazon Aquino its "Woman of the Year," it paid tribute to her extraordinary achievements and, at least by implication, made two other statements: (1) the year's most newsworthy person need not be a man, and (2) some of the connotations once assumed to be communicated only by the word *man* are now attaching themselves to the word *woman*. Still to come, however, is widespread acceptance of a gender-inclusive term that, in such a context, would concentrate attention on the person's newsworthiness rather than on the irrelevant factor of gender.

Notable among recent acknowledgments of the need for more even-handed usage was the change of policy adopted by the *New York Times* regarding titles of courtesy. First the *Times* stopped prefixing women's names with honorifics in both headlines and sports stories—thereby including women under the same rubric it had followed for years with respect to men. Then the newspaper dropped its ban on the courtesy title *Ms.* because, as an Editor's Note explained, "The *Times* now believes that 'Ms.' has become part of the language." Since the *Times* moves to a majestic beat, it is not about to rush headlong into the unqualified adoption of a nonsexist lexicon, but the recognition of *Ms.* wasn't its first move in that direction, and each day brings new evidence that it was not intended to be its last.

As individuals and the media gradually work out the logic involved in each new linguistic quandary, the presence of women in government and business and in the arts and professions becomes more and more apparent. Which is not to say that as women gain positive linguistic visibility they magically gain recognition and respect. But something "magical" does happen whenever people—singly or as a class—begin to sense their potential as fully integrated members of society, and it is this "magic" that using nonsexist language helps to bring about.

One subtle, and therefore particularly harmful, linguistic practice that has not changed much in the last few years is the use of common-gender terms as though they automatically refer only to males. When a member of Congress says on a televised news program, "Any politician would have trouble running against a woman," or a newspaper reports that a man "went berserk . . . and murdered his neighbor's wife," the effect is to make women irrelevant. Politicians become, once again, an all-male breed, and a woman, denied even the identity of "neighbor," is relegated instead to that of "neighbor's wife."

The reason the practice of assigning masculine gender to neutral terms is so enshrined in English is that every language reflects the prejudices of the society in which it evolved, and English evolved through most of its history in a male-centered, patriarchal society. We shouldn't be surprised, therefore, that its vocabulary and grammar reflect attitudes that exclude or demean women. But we are surprised, for until recently few people thought much about what English—or any other language for that matter—was saying on a subliminal level. Now that we have begun to look, some startling things have become obvious. What standard English usage says about males, for example, is that they are the species. What it says about females is that they are a subspecies. From these two assertions flow a thousand other enhancing and degrading messages, all encoded in the language we in the English-speaking countries begin to learn almost as soon as we are born.

Many people would like to do something about these inherited linguistic biases, but getting rid of them involves more than exposing them and suggesting alternatives. It requires change, and linguistic change is no easier to accept than any other kind. It may even be harder.

At a deep level, changes in a language are threatening because they signal widespread changes in social mores. At a level closer to the surface they are exasperating. We learn certain rules of grammar and usage in school, and when they are challenged it is as though we are also being challenged. Our native language is like a second skin, so much a part of us we resist the idea that it is constantly changing, constantly being renewed. Though we know intellectually that the English we speak today and the English of Shakespeare's time are very different, we tend to think of them as the same—static rather than dynamic. Emotionally, we want to agree with the syndicated columnist who wrote that "grammar is as fixed in its way as geometry."

One of the obstacles to accepting any kind of linguistic change—whether it concerns something as superficial as the pronunciation of *tomato* or as fundamental as sexual bias—is this desire to keep language "pure." In order to see change as natural and inevitable rather than as an affront, we need perspective, and to gain perspective it helps to take a look at some of the changes that have already taken place in English.

To start with, if it were true that "grammar is as fixed in its way as geometry," we would still, in the twentieth century, be speaking Old English, the earliest version of the tongue we know today: Our vocabulary would be almost totally different; we would still be altering a word's form to change the meaning of a sentence instead of shifting words about—as in "Dog bites man," "Man bites dog"—to do the same thing; and we would still have "grammatical" rather than "natural" gender. The last change is important because the gender assigned to nouns and pronouns in Old English, as in most modern European languages, often had no relationship to sex or its absence. The word for "chair," for example, was masculine; the word for "table" was feminine; and the word of "ship" was neuter. In modern English we match gender with sex. That is, we reserve feminine and masculine gender for human beings and other sex-differentiated animals or, in flights of fancy, for nonliving things (like ships) onto which we project human associations. At least theoretically all other English nouns and pronouns are neuter or, in the case of agent-nouns like *teacher* and *president,* gender-neutral.

Greatly as these grammatical simplifications invigorated English, some of its special richness comes from the flexibility of its vocabulary. The English lexicon is a kind of uninhibited conglomeration put together over the centuries from related Indo-European languages and, though far less frequently, from languages as unrelated to English as Chinese, Nahuatl, and Yoruba.

Yet despite the hospitality of English to outside as well as internal influences, many people, including many language experts, become upset when confronted with new words or grammatical modifications they happen not to like. H. W. Fowler, whose widely used *Dictionary of Modern English Usage* was first published in 1926, deplored such "improperly formed" words as *amoral, bureaucrat, speedometer, pacifist,* and *coastal,* terms so commonly used today we take them for granted. His scorn for *electrocute* (formed by analogy to *execute*) pushed him beyond compassion or reason. The word, he wrote, "jars the unhappy latinist's nerves much more cruelly than the operation denoted jars those of its victims" (an emotional excess Sir Ernest Gowers, editor of the current edition of Fowler, mercifully deleted).

Lexicographers are less judgmental. In compiling dictionaries, they try to include as many commonly used words as space allows, whether the words are "properly formed" or not. Dictionaries, however, cannot help but lag behind actual usage, so they are not always reliable indicators of new or altered meanings. Merriam-Webster's Collegiate Dictionary (10th edition) defines *youth* as (among other things) "a young person; *esp:* a young male between adolescence and maturity." Essentially the same definition appears in several other current dictionaries, and some people continue to use the word in that limited sense. When film director Martha Coolidge approached a Hollywood producer about making a "low-budget youth picture," he is reported to have said, "No gays or women; it's a male subject." Actually the accepted meaning of *youth* is shifting faster than the producer realized or dictionaries can keep up with. Under the headline "Stolen Horse Is Found by Relentless Searcher," a news story in the *New York Times* referred to the horse's owner, a sixteen-year-old girl, as a youth: "After Rocky was stolen . . . the youth called every stable and horse handler she could find" and "the youth's parents brought a trailer . . . for the trip home." Though the term may once have been anomalous when used of a young woman, today it is a recognized common-gender noun, and the next round of dictionaries will no doubt add their authority to the change.

Changes in usage often occur slowly and imperceptibly, but some take place seemingly overnight. Such was the case in the 1960s when *black* replaced *Negro.* How the change occurred and something of the power of the words was described by Shirley Chisholm:

> A few short years ago, if you called most Negroes "blacks," it was tantamount to calling us niggers. But now black is beautiful, and black is proud. There are relatively few people, white or black, who do not recognize what has happened. Black people have freed themselves from the dead weight of albatross blackness

that once hung around their necks. They have done it by picking it up in their arms and holding it out with pride for all the world to see. . . . [A]nd they have found that the skin that was once seen as symbolizing their chains is in reality their badge of honor.

Although a few people are still reluctant to accept this use of *black*, the balance has clearly shifted in its favor, and the familiar alternatives *Negro*, *colored*, and *Afro-American* are heard less often.

Ironically, those who deal with words professionally or avocationally can be the most resistant to linguistic changes. Like Fowler, they may know so much about etymology that any deviation from the classical pattern of word formation grates on their ears. Or having accepted certain rules of grammar as correct, they may find it impossible to acknowledge that those particular rules could ever be superseded.

What many people find hardest to accept is that a word which used to mean one thing now means another, and that continuing to use it in its former sense— no matter how impeccable its etymological credentials—can only invite misunderstanding. When the shift in meaning happened centuries ago, no problem lingers. One may be fully aware that *girl* once meant "a young person of either sex" (as it did in Chaucer's time) and yet not feel compelled to refer to a sexually mixed group of children as girls. When the change happens in one's lifetime, recognition and acceptance may be harder.

The word *intriguing* is such a case. Once understood to mean "conniving" or "deceitful" (as a verb, *intrigue* comes through the French *intriguer*, "to puzzle," from the Latin *intricare*, "to entangle"), *intriguing* now means "engaging the interest to a marked degree," as Webster's Third New International Dictionary noted over three decades ago. People still make statements like "They are an intriguing pair" with the intention of issuing a warning, but chances are the meaning conveyed is "They are a fascinating pair," because that is how a new generation of writers and speakers understands and uses the word. In one sense precision has been lost; in another it has only shifted.

The transformation of *man* over the past thousand years may be the most troublesome and significant change ever to overtake an English word. Once a synonym for "human being," *man* has gradually narrowed in meaning to become a synonym for "adult male human being" only. Put simply in the words of a popular dictionary for children, "A boy grows up to be a man. Father and Uncle George are both men." These are the meanings of *man* and *men* native speakers of English internalize because they are the meanings that from infancy on we hear applied to everyday speech. Though we may later acquire the information that *man* has another, "generic" meaning, we do not accept it with the same certainty that we accept the children's dictionary definition and its counterparts: A girl does not grow up to be a man. Mother and Aunt Teresa are not men; they are women.

To go on using in its former sense a word whose meaning has changed is counterproductive. The point is not that we should recognize semantic change, but that in order to be precise, in order to be understood, we must. The difference is a fundamental one in any discussion of linguistic bias, for some writers think their freedom of expression and artistic integrity are being compromised when they are asked to avoid certain words or grammatical forms. Is it ever justifiable, for example, for publishers to expect their authors to stop using the words *forefathers*, *man*, and *he* as though they were sex-inclusive? Is this not unwarranted interference with an author's style? Even censorship?

No, it is not. The public counts on those who disseminate factual information—especially publishers of textbooks and other forms of nonfiction, and those who work in the mass media—to be certain that what they tell us is as accurate as research and the conscientious use of language can make it. Only recently have we become aware that conventional English usage, including the generic use of masculine-gender words, often obscures the actions, the contributions, and sometimes the very presence of women. Turning our backs on that insight is an option, of course, but it is an option like teaching children that the world is flat. In this respect, continuing to use English in ways that have become misleading is no different from misusing data, whether the misuse is inadvertent or planned.

The need today, as always, is to be in command of language, not used by it, and so the challenge is to find clear, convincing, graceful ways to say accurately what we want to say. . . .

GRAMMATICAL SENTENCES

Part Five of *The Bedford Handbook* helps students apply conventional rules for sentences and for usage as they revise. The handbook keeps these rules in perspective, presenting them in an accessible format that helps students, whatever their backgrounds, make their writing more effective.

Since Mina Shaughnessy's groundbreaking work on basic writing introduced composition specialists to error analysis (*Errors and Expectations*, 1977), instructors have become more attuned to the kinds of challenges that many students face when they attempt to compose conventional sentences and adhere to standard usage. When instructors learn to read student writing carefully and generously, and when they recognize the logical patterns of errors that appear in student writing, they are better able to offer meaningful assistance that will result in writers' growth and learning.

The selection that follows addresses central questions for teachers who want to help students with their sentence-level struggles.

- What is error analysis?
- How can it help students recognize and solve problems with sentences and usage?
- How can teachers make error analysis productive for students?

From THE STUDY OF ERROR

David Bartholomae

[*College Composition and Communication* 31 (1980): 253–69.]

(For biographical information, see page 21.)

Bartholomae wrote this article in response to instructors who felt that students' errors were signs that they couldn't write. He opens his article by surveying then current (1980) attitudes about "basic writing," the various pedagogies that instructors have adopted when confronted with "basic writers," and the results of their attempts. He argues for further research into "basic writing" and the concurrent perceptions of errors apparently inherent to basic writers. Aligning his argument with Mina Shaughnessy's groundbreaking work in *Errors and Expectations*, Bartholomae proposes error analysis as a method to better understand how writers develop and learn. The excerpt that follows begins at that point, with Bartholomae explaining error analysis and demonstrating its effectiveness with a study of one of his students' assignments in progress.

Error analysis begins with a theory of writing, a theory of language production and language development, that allows us to see errors as evidence of choice or strategy among a range of possible choices or strategies. They provide evidence of an individual style of using the language and making it work; they are not a simple record of what a writer failed to do because of incompetence or indifference. Errors, then, are stylistic features, information about *this* writer and *this* language; they are not necessarily "noise" in the system, accidents of composing, or malfunctions in the language process. Consequently, we cannot identify errors without identifying them in context, and the context is not the text, but the activity of composing that presented the erroneous form as a possible solution to the problem of making a meaningful statement. Shaughnessy's taxonomy of error, for example, identifies errors according to their source, not their type. A single type of error could be attributed to a variety of causes. Donald Freeman's research, for example, has shown that "subject-verb agreement . . . is a host of errors, not one." One of his students analyzed a "large sample of real world sentences and concluded that there are at least eight different kinds, most of which have very little to do with one another."[1]

Error analysis allows us to place error in the context of composing and to interpret and classify systematic errors. The key concept is the concept of an "interlanguage" or an "intermediate system," an idiosyncratic grammar and rhetoric that is a writer's approximation of the standard idiom. Errors, while they can be given more precise classification, fall into three main categories: errors that are evidence of an intermediate system; errors that could truly be said to be accidents, or slips of the pen as a writer's mind rushes ahead faster than his hand; and, finally, errors of language transfer, or, more commonly, dialect interference, where in the attempt to produce the target language, the writer intrudes forms from the "first" or "native" language rather than inventing some intermediate form. For writers, this intrusion most often comes from a spoken dialect. The error analyst is primarily concerned, however, with errors that are evidence of some intermediate system. This kind of error occurs because the writer *is* an active, competent language user who uses his knowledge that language is rule-governed, and who uses his ability to predict and form analogies, to construct hypotheses that can make an irregular or unfamiliar language more manageable. The problem comes when the rule is incorrect or, more properly, when it is idiosyncratic, belonging only to the language of this writer. There is evidence of an idiosyncratic system, for example, when a student adds inflectional endings to infinitives, as in this sentence, "There was plenty the boy had to *learned* about birds." It also seems to be evident in a sentence like this: "This assignment calls on *choosing* one of my papers and making a last draft out of it." These errors can be further subdivided into those that are in flux and mark a fully transitional stage, and those that, for one reason or another, become frozen and recur across time.

Kroll and Schafer, in a recent *CCC* article, argue that the value of error analysis for the composition teacher is the perspective it offers on the learner, since it allows us to see errors "as clues to inner processes, as windows into the mind."[2] If we investigate the pattern of error in the performance of an individual writer, we can better understand the nature of those errors and the way they "fit" in an individual writer's program for writing. As a consequence, rather than impose an inappropriate or even misleading syllabus on a learner, we can plan instruction to assist a writer's internal syllabus. If, for example, a writer puts standard inflections on irregular verbs or on verbs that are used in verbals (as in "I used to runned"), drill on verb endings will only reinforce the rule that, because the writer is overgeneralizing, is the source of the error in the first place. By charting and analyzing a writer's errors, we can begin in our instruction with what a writer *does* rather than with what he fails to do. It makes no sense, for example, to impose lessons on the sentence on a student whose problems with syntax can be understood in more precise terms. It makes no sense to teach spelling to an individual who has trouble principally with words that contain vowel clusters. Error analysis, then, is a method of diagnosis.

Error analysis can assist instruction at another level. By having students share in the process of investigating and interpreting the patterns of error in their writing, we can help them begin to see those errors as evidence of hypotheses or strategies they have formed and, as a consequence, put them in a position to change, experiment, imagine other strategies. Studying their own writing puts students in a position to see themselves as language users, rather than as victims of a language that uses them.

This, then, is the perspective and the technique of error analysis. To interpret a student paper without this frame of reference is to misread, as for example when a teacher sees an incorrect verb form and concludes that the student doesn't understand the rules for indicating tense or number. I want, now, to examine error analysis as a procedure for the study of errors in written composition. It presents two problems. The first can be traced to the fact that error analysis was developed for studying errors in spoken performance.[3] It can be transferred to writing only to the degree that writing is like speech, and there are significant points of difference. It is generally acknowledged, for example, that written discourse is not just speech written down on paper. Adult written discourse has a grammar and rhetoric that is different from speech. And clearly the activity of producing language is different for a writer than it is for a speaker.

The "second language" a basic writer must learn to master is formal, written discourse, a discourse whose lexicon, grammar, and rhetoric are learned not through speaking and listening but through reading and writing. The process of acquisition is visual not aural. Furthermore, basic writers do not necessarily produce writing by translating speech into print (the way children learning to write would); that is, they must draw on a memory for graphemes rather than phonemes. This is a different order of memory and production from that used in speech and gives rise to errors unique to writing.

Writing also, however, presents "interference" of a type never found in speech. Errors in writing may be caused by interference from the act of writing itself, from the difficulty of moving a pen across the page quickly enough to keep up with the words in the writer's mind, or from the difficulty of recalling and producing the conventions that are necessary for producing print rather than speech, conventions of spelling, orthography, punctuation, capitalization, and so on. This is not, however, just a way of saying that writers make spelling errors and speakers do not. As Shaughnessy pointed out, errors of syntax can be traced to the gyrations of a writer trying to avoid a word that her sentence has led her to, but that she knows she cannot spell.

The second problem in applying error analysis to the composition classroom arises from special properties in the taxonomy of errors we chart in student writing. Listing varieties of errors is not like listing varieties of rocks or butterflies. What a reader finds depends to a large degree on her assumptions about the writer's intention. Any systematic attempt to chart a learner's errors is clouded by the difficulty of assigning intention through textual analysis. The analyst begins, then, by interpreting a text, not by describing features on a page. And interpretation is less than a precise science.

Let me turn to an example. This is part of a paper that a student, John, wrote in response to an assignment that asked him to go back to some papers he had written on significant moments in his life in order to write a paper that considered the general question of the way people change:

> This assignment call on chosing one of my incident making a last draft out of it. I found this very differcult because I like them all but you said I had to pick one so the Second incident was decide. Because this one had the most important insight to my life that I indeed learn from. This insight explain why adulthood mean that much as it dose to me because I think it alway influence me to change and my outlook on certain thing like my point-of-view I have one day and it might change the next week on the same issue. So in these frew words I going to write about the incident now. My exprience took place in my high school and the reason was out side of school but I will show you the connection. The sitution took place cause of the type of school I went too. Let me tell you about the situation first of all what happen was that I got suspense from school. For thing that I fell was out of my control sometime, but it taught me alot about respondability of a growing man. The school suspense me for being late ten time. I had accummate ten dementic and had to bring my mother to school to talk to a conselor and Prinpicable of the school what when on at the meet took me out mentally period.

One could imagine a variety of responses to this. The first would be to form the wholesale conclusion that John can't write and to send him off to a workbook. Once he had learned how to write correct sentences, then he could go on to the business of actually writing. Let me call this the "old style" response to error. A second response, which I'll call the "investigative approach," would be to chart the patterns of error in this particular text. Of the approximately 40 errors in the first 200 words, the majority fall under four fairly specific categories: verb endings, noun plurals, syntax, and spelling. The value to pedagogy is obvious. One is no longer teaching a student to "write" but to deal with a limited number of very specific kinds of errors, each of which would suggest its own appropriate response. Furthermore, it is possible to refine the categories and to speculate on and organize them according to cause. The verb errors almost all involve "s" or "ed" endings, which could indicate dialect interference or a failure to learn the rules for indicating tense and number. It is possible to be even more precise. The passage contains 41 verbs; only 17 of them are used incorrectly. With the exception of four spelling errors, the errors are all errors of inflection and, furthermore, these errors come only with regular verbs. There are no errors with irregular verbs. This would suggest, then, that when John draws on memory for a verb form, he gets it right; but when John applies a rule to determine the ending, he gets it wrong.

The errors of syntax could be divided into those that might be called punctuation errors (or errors that indicate a difficulty perceiving the boundaries of the sentence), such as

> Let me tell you about the situation first of all that happen was that I got suspense from school. For thing that I fell was out of my control sometime, but it taught me alot about respondability of a growing man.

and errors of syntax that would fall under Shaughnessy's category of consolidation errors,

> This insight explain why adulthood mean that much as it dose to me because I think it alway influence me to change and my outlook on certain thing like my point-of-view I have one day and it might change the next week on the same issue.

One would also want to note the difference between consistent errors, the substitution of "situation" for "situation" or "suspense" for "suspended," and unstable ones, as, for example, when John writes "cause" in one place and "because" in another. In one case John could be said to have fixed on a rule; in the other he is searching for one. One would also want to distinguish between what might seem to be "accidental" errors, like substituting "frew" for "few" or "when" for "went," errors that might best be addressed by teaching a student to edit, and those whose causes are deeper and require time and experience, or some specific instructional strategy.

I'm not sure, however, that this analysis provides an accurate representation of John's writing. Consider what happens when John reads this paper out loud. I've been taping students reading their own papers, and I've developed a system of notation, like that used in miscue analysis,[4] that will allow me to record the points of variation between the writing that is on the page and the writing that is spoken, or, to use the terminology of miscue analysis, between the expected response (ER) and the observed response (OR). What I've found is that students will often, or in predictable instances, substitute correct forms for the incorrect forms on the page, even though they are generally unaware that such a substitution was made. This observation suggests the limits of conventional error analysis for the study of error in written composition.

I asked John to read his paper out loud, and to stop and correct or note any mistakes he found. Let me try to reproduce the transcript of that reading. I will italicize any substitution or correction and offer some comments in parentheses. The reader might first go back and review the original. Here is what John read:

> This assignment calls on *choosing* one of my incident making a last draft out of it. I found this very difficult because I like them all but you said I *had* to pick one so the Second incident was decide*d* on. Because (John goes back and rereads, connecting up the subordinate clause.) So the second incident was decided on because this one had the most important insight to my life that I indeed learn*ed* from. This insight explains why adulthood *meant* that much as it dose to me because I think it alway*s* influence*s* me to change and my outlook on certain things like my point-of-view I have one day and it might change the next week on the same issue. (John goes back and rereads, beginning with "like my point-of-view," and he is puzzled but he makes no additional changes.) So in these *few* words *I'm* going to write about the incident now. My exper*i*ence took place *because* of the type of school I went to (John had written "too.") Let me tell you about the situation (John comes to a full stop.) first of all what happen*ed* was that I got *suspended* from school (no full stop) for things that I *felt* was out of my control sometime, but it taught me a lot about *responsibility* of a growing man. The school *suspended* me for being late ten times. I had *accumulated* (for "accumate") ten *demerits* (for "dementic") and had to bring my mother to school to talk to a counselor and *the Principal* of the school (full stop) what *went* on at the meet*ing* took me out mentally (full stop) period (with brio).

I have chosen an extreme case to make my point, but what one sees here is the writer correcting almost every error as he reads the paper, even though he is not able to recognize that there *are* errors or that he has corrected them. The only errors John spotted (where he stopped, noted an error and corrected it) were the misspellings of "situation" and "Principal," and the substitution of "chosing" for "choosing." Even when he was asked to reread sentences to see if he could notice any difference between what he was saying and the words on the page, he could not. He could not, for example, see the error in "frew" or "dementic" or any of the other verb errors, and yet he spoke the correct form of every verb (with the exception of "was" after he had changed "thing" to "things" in "for things that I *felt* was out of my control") and he corrected every plural. His phrasing as he read produced correct syntax, except in the case of the consolidation error, which he puzzled over but did not correct. It's important to note, however, that John did not read the confused syntax as if no confusion were there. He sensed the difference between the phrasing called for by the meaning of the sentence and that which existed on the page. He did not read as though meaning didn't matter or as though the "meaning" coded on the page was complete. His problem cannot be simply a syntax problem, since the jumble is bound up with his struggle to articulate this particular meaning. And it is not simply a "thinking" problem—John doesn't write this way because he thinks this way—since he perceives that the statement as it is written is other than that which he intended.

When I asked John why the paper (which went on for two more pages) was written all as one paragraph, he replied, "It was all one idea. I didn't want to have to start all over again. I had a good idea and I didn't want to give it up." John doesn't need to be "taught" the paragraph, at least not as the paragraph is traditionally taught. His prose is orderly and proceeds through blocks of discourse. He tells the story of his experience at the school and concludes that through his experience he realized that he must accept responsibility for his tardiness, even though the tardiness was not his fault but the fault of the Philadelphia subway system. He concludes that with this realization he learned "the responsibility of a growing man." Furthermore John knows that the print code carries certain conventions for ordering and presenting discourse. His translation of the notion that "a paragraph develops a single idea" is peculiar but not illogical.

It could also be argued that John does not need to be "taught" to produce correct verb forms, or, again, at least not as such things are conventionally taught. Fifteen weeks of drill on verb endings might raise his test scores, but they would not change the way he writes. He *knows* how to produce correct endings. He demonstrated that when he read, since he was reading in terms of his grammatical competence. His problem is a problem of performance, or fluency, not of competence. There is certainly no evidence that the verb errors are due to interference from his spoken language. And if the errors could be traced to some intermediate system, the system exists only in John's performance as a writer. It does not operate when he reads or, for that matter, when he speaks, if his oral reconstruction of his own text can be taken as a record of John "speaking" the idiom of academic discourse.[5]

John's case also highlights the tremendous difficulty such a student has with editing, where a failure to correct a paper is not evidence of laziness or inattention or a failure to know correct forms, but evidence of the tremendous difficulty such a student has objectifying language and seeing it as black and white marks on the page, where things can be wrong even though the meaning seems right.[6] One of the hardest errors for John to spot, after all my coaching, was the substitution of "frew" for "few," certainly not an error that calls into question John's competence as a writer. I can call this a "performance" error, but that term doesn't suggest the constraints on performance in writing. This is an important area for further study. Surely one constraint is the difficulty of moving the hand fast enough to translate meaning into print. The burden imposed on their patience and short-term memory by the slow, awkward handwriting of many inexperienced writers is a very real one. But I think the constraints extend beyond the difficulty of forming words quickly with pen or pencil.

One of the most interesting results of the comparison of the spoken and written versions of John's text is his inability to *see* the difference between "frew" and "few" or "dementic" and "demerit." What this suggests is that John reads and writes from the "top down" rather than the "bottom up," to use a distinction made by cognitive psychologists in their study of reading.[7] John is not operating through the lower level process of translating orthographic information into sounds and sounds into meaning when he reads. And conversely, he is not working from meaning to sound to word when he is writing. He is, rather, retrieving lexical items directly, through a "higher level" process that bypasses the "lower level" operation of phonetic translation. When I put *frew* and *few* on the blackboard, John read them both as "few." The lexical item "few" is represented for John by either orthographic array. He is not, then, reading or writing phonetically, which is a sign, from one perspective, of a high level of fluency, since the activity is automatic and not mediated by the more primitive operation of translating speech into print or print into speech. When John was writing, he did not produce "frew" or "dementic" by searching for sound/letter/letter correspondences. He drew directly upon his memory for the look and shape of those words; he was working from the top down rather than the bottom up. He went to stored print forms and did not take the slower route of translating speech into writing.

John, then, has reached a stage of fluency in writing where he directly and consistently retrieves print forms, like "dementic," that are meaningful to him, even though they are idiosyncratic. I'm not sure what all the implications of this might be, but we surely must see John's problem in a new light, since his problem can, in a sense, be attributed to his skill. To ask John to slow down his writing and sound out words would be disastrous. Perhaps the most we can do is to teach John the slowed down form of reading he will need in order to edit.

John's paper also calls into question our ability to identify accidental errors. I suspect that when John substitutes a word like "when" for "went," this is an accidental error, a slip of the pen. Since John spoke "went" when he read, I cannot conclude that he substituted "when" for "went" because he pronounces both as "wen." This, then, is not an error of dialect interference but an accidental error, the same order of error as the omission of "the" before "Principal." Both were errors John corrected while reading (even though he didn't identify them as errors).

What is surprising is that, with all the difficulty John had identifying errors, he immediately saw that he had written "chosing" rather than "choosing." While textual analysis would have led to the conclusion that he was applying a tense rule to a participial construction, or overgeneralizing from a known rule, the ease with which it was identified would lead one to conclude that it was, in fact, a mistake, and not evidence of an approximate system. What would have been diagnosed as a deep error now appears to be only an accidental error, a "mistake" (or perhaps a spelling error).

In summary, this analysis of John's reading produces a healthy respect for the tremendous complexity of transcription, for the process of recording meaning in print as opposed to the process of generating meaning. It also points out the difficulty of charting a learner's "interlanguage" or "intermediate system," since we are working not only with a writer moving between a first and a second language, but a writer whose performance is subject to the interference of transcription, of producing meaning through the print code. We need, in general, to refine our understanding of performance-based errors, and we need to refine our teaching to take into account the high percentage of error in written composition that is rooted in the difficulty of performance rather than in problems of general linguistic competence.

Let me pause for a moment to put what I've said in the context of work in error analysis. Such analysis is textual analysis. It requires the reader to make assumptions about intention on the basis of information in the text. The writer's errors provide the most important information since they provide insight into the idiosyncratic systems the writer has developed. The regular but unconventional features in the writing will reveal the rules and strategies operating for the basic writer.

The basic procedure for such analysis could be outlined this way. First the reader must identify the idiosyncratic construction; he must determine what is an error. This is often difficult, as in the case of fragments, which are conventionally used for effect. Here is an example of a sentence whose syntax could clearly be said to be idiosyncratic.

In high school you learn alot for example Kindergarten which I took in high school.[8]

The reader, then, must reconstruct that sentence based upon the most reasonable interpretation of the intention in the original, and this must be done *before* the error can be classified, since it will be classified according to its cause.[9] Here is Shaughnessy's reconstruction of the example given above: "In high school you learn a lot. For example, I took up the study of Kindergarten in high school." For any idiosyncratic sentence, however, there are often a variety of possible reconstructions, depending on the reader's sense of the larger meaning of which this individual sentence is only a part, but also depending upon the reader's ability to predict how this writer puts sentences together, that is, on an understanding of this individual style. The text is being interpreted, not described. I've had graduate students who have reconstructed the following sentence, for example, in a variety of ways:

Why do we have womens liberation and their fighting for Equal Rights ect. to be recognized not as a lady but as an Individual.

It could be read, "Why do we have women's liberation and why are they fighting for Equal Rights? In order that women may be recognized not as ladies but as individuals." And, "Why do we have women's liberation and their fight for equal rights, to be recognized not as a lady but as an individual?" There is an extensive literature on the question of interpretation and intention in prose, too extensive for the easy assumption that all a reader has to do is identify what the writer would have written if he wanted to "get it right the first time." The great genius of Shaughnessy's study, in fact, is the remarkable wisdom and sympathy of her interpretations of student texts.

Error analysis, then, involves more than just making lists of the errors in a student essay and looking for patterns to emerge. It begins with the double perspective of text and reconstructed text and seeks to explain the difference between the two on the basis of whatever can be inferred about the meaning of the text and the process of creating it. The reader/researcher brings to bear his general knowledge of how basic writers write, but also whatever is known about the linguistic and rhetorical constraints that govern an individual act of writing. In Shaughnessy's analysis of the "kindergarten" sentence, this discussion is contained in the section on "consolidation errors" in the chapter on "Syntax."[10] The key point, however, is that any such analysis must draw upon extratextual information as well as close, stylistic analysis.

This paper has illustrated two methods for gathering information about how a text was created. A teacher can interview the student and ask him to explain his error. John wrote this sentence in another paper for my course:

I would to write about my experience helping 1600 childrens have a happy christmas.

The missing word (I would *like* to write about . . .) he supplied when reading the sentence aloud. It is an accidental error and can be addressed by teaching editing. It is the same kind of error as his earlier substitution of "when" for "went." John used the phrase, "1600 childrens," throughout his paper, however. The conventional interpretation would have it that this is evidence of dialect interference. And yet, when John read the paper out loud, he consistently read "1600 children," even though he said he did not see any difference between the word he spoke and the word that was on the page. When I asked him to explain why he put an "s" on the end of "children," he replied, "Because there were 1600 of them." John had a rule for forming plurals that he used when he wrote but not when he spoke. Writing, as we rightly recognized, has its own peculiar rules and constraints. It is different from speech. The error is not due to interference from his spoken language but to his conception of the "code" of written discourse.

The other method for gathering information is having students read aloud their own writing, and having them provide an oral reconstruction of their written text. What I've presented in my analysis of John's essay is a method for recording the discrepancies between the written and spoken versions of a single text. The record of a writer reading provides a version of the "intended" text that can supplement the teacher's or researcher's own reconstruction and aid in the interpretation of errors, whether they be accidental, interlingual, or due to dialect interference. I had to read John's paper very differently once I had heard him read it.

More importantly, however, this method of analysis can provide access to an additional type of error. This is the error that can be attributed to the physical and conceptual demands of writing rather than speaking; it can be traced to the requirements of manipulating a pen and the requirements of manipulating the print code.[11]

In general, when writers read, and read in order to spot and correct errors, their responses will fall among the following categories:

1. overt corrections—errors a reader sees, acknowledges, and corrects;
2. spoken corrections—errors the writer does not acknowledge but corrects in reading;
3. no recognition—errors that are read as written;
4. overcorrection—correct forms made incorrect, or incorrect forms substituted for incorrect forms;
5. acknowledged error—errors a reader senses but cannot correct;
6. reader miscue—a conventional miscue, not linked to error in the text;
7. nonsense—In this case, the reader reads a nonsentence or a nonsense sentence as though it were correct and meaningful. No error or confusion is acknowledged. This applies to errors of syntax only.

Corrections, whether acknowledged or unacknowledged, would indicate performance-based errors. The other responses (with the exception of "reader miscues") would indicate deeper errors, errors that, when charted, would provide evidence of some idiosyncratic grammar or rhetoric.

John "miscues" by completing or correcting the text that he has written. When reading researchers have readers read out loud, they have them read someone else's writing, of course, and they are primarily concerned with the "quality" of the miscues.[12] All fluent readers will miscue; that is, they will not repeat verbatim the words on the page. Since fluent readers are reading for meaning, they are actively predicting what will come and processing large chunks of graphic information at a time. They do not read individual words, and they miscue because they speak what they expect to see rather than what is actually on the page. One indication of a reader's proficiency, then, is that the miscues don't destroy the "sense" of the passage. Poor readers will produce miscues that jumble the meaning of a passage, as in

Text: Her wings were folded quietly at her sides.
Reader: Her wings were floated quickly at her sides.

or they will correct miscues that do not affect meaning in any significant way.[13]

The situation is different when a reader reads his own text, since this reader already knows what the passage means and attention is drawn, then, to the representation of that meaning. Reading also frees a writer from the constraints of transcription, which for many basic writers is an awkward, laborious process, putting excessive demands on both patience and short-term memory. John, like any reader, read what he expected to see, but with a low percentage of meaning-related miscues, since the meaning, for him, was set, and with a big percentage of code-related miscues, where a correct form was substituted for an incorrect form.

The value of studying students' oral reconstruction of their written texts is threefold. The first is as a diagnostic tool. I've illustrated in my analysis of John's paper how such a diagnosis might take place.

It is also a means of instruction. By having John read aloud and, at the same time, look for discrepancies between what he spoke and what was on the page, I was teaching him a form of reading. The most dramatic change in John's performance over the term was in the number of errors he could spot and correct while rereading. This far exceeded the number of errors he was able to eliminate from his first drafts. I could teach John an editing procedure better than I could teach him to be correct at the point of transcription.

The third consequence of this form of analysis, or of conventional error analysis, has yet to be demonstrated, but the suggestions for research are clear. It seems evident that we can chart stages of growth in individual basic writers. The pressing question is whether we can chart a sequence of "natural" development for the class of writers we call basic writers. If all nonfluent adult writers proceed through a "natural" learning sequence, and if we can identify that sequence through some large, longitudinal study, then we will begin to understand what a basic writing course or text or syllabus might look like. There are studies of adult second language learners that suggest that there is a general, natural sequence of acquisition for adults learning a second language, one that is determined by the psychology of language production and language acquisition.[14] Before we can adapt these methods to a study of basic writers, however, we need to better understand the additional constraints of learning to transcribe and manipulate the "code" of written discourse. John's case illustrates where we might begin and what we must know.[15]

Notes

[1] Donald C. Freeman, "Linguistics and Error Analysis: On Agency," in Donald Mc-Quade, ed., *Linguistics, Stylistics and the Teaching of Composition* (Akron, Ohio: L & S Books, 1979), pp. 143–44.

[2] Kroll and Schafer, "Error Analysis and the Teaching of Composition," *CCC*, 29 (October 1978), 243–48.

[3] In the late sixties and early seventies, linguists began to study second language acquisition by systematically studying the actual performance of individual learners. What they studied, however, was the language a learner would speak. In the literature of error analysis, the reception and production of language is generally defined as the learner's ability to hear, learn, imitate, and independently produce *sounds*. Errors, then, are phonological substitutions, alterations, additions, and subtractions. Similarly, errors diagnosed as rooted in the mode of production (rather than, for example, in an idiosyncratic grammar or interference from the first language) are errors caused by the difficulty a learner has hearing or making foreign sounds. When we are studying written composition, we are studying a different mode of production, where a learner must see, remember, and produce marks on a page. There may be some similarity between the grammar-based errors in the two modes, speech and writing (it would be interesting to know to what degree this is true), but there should be marked differences in the nature and frequency of performance-based errors.

[4] See Y. M. Goodman and C. L. Burke, *Reading Miscue Inventory: Procedure for Diagnosis and Evaluation* (New York: Macmillan, 1972).

[5] Bruder and Hayden noticed a similar phenomenon. They assigned a group of students exercises in writing formal and informal dialogues. One student's informal dialogue contained the following:

> What going on?
> It been a long time . . .
> I about through . . .
> I be glad . . .

When the student read the dialogue aloud, however, these were spoken as

What's going on?
It's been a long time . . .
I'm about through . . .
I'll be glad . . .

See Mary Newton Bruder and Luddy Hayden, "Teaching Composition: A Report on a Bidialectal Approach," *Language Learning*, 23 (June 1973), 1–15.

[6] See Patricia Laurence, "Error's Endless Train: Why Students Don't Perceive Errors," *Journal of Basic Writing*, I (Spring 1975), 23–43, for a different explanation of this phenomenon.

[7] See, for example, J. R. Frederiksen, "Component Skills in Reading" in R. R. Snow, P. A. Federico, and W. E. Montague, eds., *Aptitude, Learning, and Instruction* (Hillsdale, N.J.: Erlbaum, 1979); D. E. Rumelhart, "Toward an Interactive Model of Reading," in S. Dornic, ed., *Attention and Performance VI* (Hillsdale, N.J.: Erlbaum, 1977); and Joseph H. Denks and Gregory O. Hill, "Interactive Models of Lexical Assessment during Oral Reading," paper presented at Conference on Interactive Processes in Reading, Learning Research and Development Center, University of Pittsburgh, September 1979.

Patrick Hartwell argued that "apparent dialect interference in writing reveals partial or imperfect mastery of a neural coding system that underlies both reading and writing" in a paper, "'Dialect Interference' in Writing: A Critical View," presented at CCCC, April 1979. This paper is available through ERIC. He predicts, in this paper, that "basic writing students, when asked to read their writing in a formal situation, . . . will make fewer errors in their reading than in their writing." I read Professor Hartwell's paper after this essay was completed, so I was unable to acknowledge his study as completely as I would have desired.

[8] This example is taken from Shaughnessy, *Errors and Expectations: A Guide for the Teacher of Basic Writing* (New York: Oxford University Press, 1977), p. 52.

[9] Corder refers to "reconstructed sentences" in "Idiosyncratic Dialects and Error Analysis."

[10] Shaughnessy, *Errors and Expectations*, pp. 51–72.

[11] For a discussion of the role of the "print code" in writer's errors, see Patrick Hartwell, "'Dialect Interference' in Writing: A Critical View."

[12] See Kenneth S. Goodman, "Miscues: Windows on the Reading Process," in Kenneth S. Goodman, ed., *Miscue Analysis: Applications to Reading Instruction* (Urbana, Ill.: ERIC, 1977), pp. 3–14.

[13] This example was taken from Yetta M. Goodman, "Miscue Analysis for In-Service Reading Teachers," in Kenneth S. Goodman, ed., *Miscue Analysis*, p. 55.

[14] Nathalie Bailey, Carolyn Madden, and Stephen D. Krashen, "Is There a 'Natural Sequence' in Adult Second Language Learning?" *Language Learning*, 24 (June 1974), 235–243.

[15] This paper was originally presented at CCCC, April 1979. The research for this study was funded by a research grant from the National Council of Teachers of English.

ENGLISH AS A SECOND LANGUAGE

Part Six of *The Bedford Handbook* recognizes that increasing numbers of composition students acquire (and continue to learn) English as a second language. The purpose of this section of the handbook is to provide students with specific guidance they need to edit their writing, and to offer practical explanations and examples that relate specifically to ESL students.

Instructors encountering ESL students should recognize that language interference in student writing does not necessitate remedial exercises and drills. Instead, instructors should consider ESL variations in a developmental context: Writers struggle as they attempt to master conventions in a new language. Further, instructors must understand that ESL writers operate within several competing cultural contexts, and their home cultures may be governed by assumptions radically different from those that they encounter in and out of our classrooms. These differing cultural assumptions affect fundamentally the ways ESL writers acquire and use English, especially in their writing. Because of the complexities associated with teaching ESL writers, instructors often feel ill-equipped to help such students in writing classes. The following selections address questions that arise as a result of that uncertainty:

- What should instructors expect from ESL students? What kinds of culturally conditioned behaviors and expectations do ESL students bring to the classroom?
- How do differences in cultural contexts affect the ways students write and the ways teachers read their writing? How can teachers learn to read and assess differently? How can teachers help students learn to write in different cultural contexts?

CLASSROOM EXPECTATIONS AND BEHAVIORS
Ilona Leki

[From *Understanding ESL Writers: A Guide for Teachers* by Ilona Leki. Portsmouth, NH: Boynton, 1990. 47–57.]

Professor of English Ilona Leki is director of English as a Second Language at the University of Tennessee. Widely recognized as an authority in teaching ESL, Leki has published numerous articles and chapters. She is also the author of *Academic Writing: Techniques and Tasks*, Second Edition (1995), and she coedited (with Joan Carson) *Reading in the Composition Classroom: Second Language Perspectives* (1993).

In this chapter from *Understanding ESL Writers*, Leki offers an overview of the various expectations and behaviors that ESL students bring to the classroom, including their ideas about course work, evaluation, and student-instructor relations. Instructors who are conscious of ESL students' expectations can help make those students' learning experiences more effective and beneficial.

Most of the time ESL students are not traumatized, just surprised, surprised at the receptions they get here and surprised at some of the customs and behaviors they encounter in U.S. classrooms. International students are often hurt and insulted by American ignorance of, and disinterest in, their home countries. American undergraduates are notorious for such geographical gaffs as placing Canada on a map of Texas; Malaysia may as well be in outer space. One international student was upset to learn that his American classmate had never heard of Thailand. African students are asked if people live in houses in Africa. French students have been asked if they have refrigerators in France.

All this is disheartening coming from college students, but international students have more serious problems to face. Although many faculty members are interested in international students and friendly toward them, in disciplines and perhaps parts of the country where there are many non-natives enrolled as students, these students sometimes encounter hostility from their teachers. Certain professors build a reputation of disliking international students in their classes and of automatically giving them lower grades. How prevalent such a practice is probably cannot be determined, but certainly students believe it happens.

Students have reported other behavior on the part of some professors which is, at the very least, unbelievably insensitive, perhaps racist. One student's content-area teacher took his paper and tore it into pieces, telling the student to learn English before turning in a paper. Another student reports:

> Right at the beginning the professor said that I could not pass the course. He said, "As long as you have a Japanese mind, you can not pass 111." When he said this I thought I could not survive sometimes. I have had a Japanese mind for 30 years how can I change it? I felt so depressed. The teacher said that he had had a Korean student who had taken 111 three times in order to pass. He compared me to the Korean saying that it would take me at least that long. I felt like he thought all Asians were the same—Korean Japanese there's no difference. This felt like racial discrimination to me. (Newstetter et al., 1989)

International students fare as badly in the community. A student from Hong Kong claims that he is regularly overcharged for purchases in his conservative Southeastern community and that residual, confused resentments from the war in Vietnam cause locals to automatically take him for Vietnamese and discriminate against him. (His hilarious and ingenious solution to this problem was to announce that he was not foreign; he was just from California, a location probably as distant and exotic to many of these local residents as any place in Southeast Asia!)

Classroom Expectations

Different national groups and different individuals bring different expectations to the classroom, but many students express surprise at the same aspects of post-secondary classroom culture in the United States. Many of the surprises are pleasant. Some international students come from educational systems in which famous scholars and researchers deliver lectures to several hundred students at once, never getting to know any of them personally, or even speaking to them individually. These students are pleased to find that many of their professors here are approachable, informal, and friendly, that they set up office hours when students are welcome to discuss concerns privately. Some students are also thrilled with the flexibility of the U.S. university system and with the diversity of completely unexpected classes available, like typing or various physical education classes.

On the other hand, ESL students often remark on the apparent lack of respect for teachers here, shown in the casual clothes, sandals, even shorts, that their native classmates wear to class or in the eating and drinking that may go on in some classes. The whole teaching environment is disturbingly casual to some students. Teachers sit on the front desk while lecturing, students interrupt lectures to question or dispute what the teacher has said, teachers sometimes say they do not know the answer to a question. Any of these behaviors may jolt the expectations of non-native students.

Even something as simple as what students and teachers call each other can create confusion. Some international students feel uncomfortable calling teachers by names and prefer to use only titles, addressing their instructors simply as "Doctor" without using a name or using a first name, as in "Professor Ken," or simply using "Teacher." Students from the People's Republic of China tend to address their professors by their last names only: "Good morning, Johnson." By the same token, of course, they may expect to be addressed by their family names only and feel uncomfortable being addressed by their given names, an intimacy reserved for only a few very close family members. Even husbands and wives may refer to each other by their family names. Many of the international names are difficult for linguistically provincial Americans to pronounce, and students often resort to taking on English names while they are here. One Jordanian student writes that his name has been spelled and pronounced in so many different ways that he now responds to anything even vaguely resembling Najib: Jeeb, Nick, Nancy.

Many international university students also have a hard time adjusting to what they see as being treated like high school students. They are amazed to find teachers demanding daily attendance, assigning homework, and policing the class by testing periodically to make sure they have done the homework. These students may come from a system in which students may choose to take advantage of class lectures or not, as long as they pass a comprehensive, end-of-the-year exam. Quite a different attitude toward student responsibilities from our own!

In some countries, students may take pre-departure classes or U.S. culture classes which may cover some of the areas of difference between educational practices at home and abroad and thereby help students prepare for their experiences. But these courses cannot cover every encounter the students may have. One international student, for example, took a multiple choice test here for the first time. Having had no previous experience with this form of testing, the student assumed that multiple choice meant choosing more than one answer per item (Stapleton, 1990). Other students come from educational systems in which competing theories are presented only in order to explain the correct theory. The students are confused when they realize that their professor here assumes none of the theories is entirely correct (Krasnick, 1990). It is important to keep in mind that in addition to learning subject matter in a class, ESL students are also often learning a whole new approach to learning itself.

Classroom Behaviors

It should not come as a surprise to us, then, that these students will not always do what we expect in our classes. International students have stood up when the teacher entered the room; others have insisted on erasing the blackboard after class for the teacher. A student of mine, misconstruing the idea of office hours, complained that he had come by my office, hoping to find me by chance for a conference at 5:00 P.M. Saturday afternoon. That student said he waited for me for an hour!

Some students have a difficult time with the style of class participation they observe. While U.S. teachers may consider class participation an important sign that the students are paying attention, some ESL students will never participate unless specifically called on. They may be especially reluctant to volunteer answers to questions since they may feel that by doing so they are humiliating their classmates who cannot answer the question. A Japanese proverb says something like, "The nail that sticks up gets hammered down." Compare that to our own, "The squeaky wheel gets the oil."

ESL students may also react badly to teacher requests for opinions, especially opinions in conflict with those expressed by the teacher. Such requests may be viewed as evidence of teacher incompetence (Levine, 1983, cited in Scarcella, 1990, 94), and many ESL students are trained specifically *not* to hold opinions differing from those of their teachers. By the same token, ESL students may expect teachers to know the answers to any question they may have; these students may become embarrassed and lose confidence in teachers who honestly state that they do not know an answer but will find out. In one case, an Iranian student whose chemistry teacher had made such a statement dropped the class, explaining that he did not see the point in trying to learn from someone who did not know. In Iran, he explained, a professor would sooner fabricate an answer than admit to not knowing.

Many other types of assumptions come into conflict in culturally mixed classes. In an article on attitudes toward time, Levine (1985) describes a problem familiar to ESL teachers—ESL students' flexible attitude toward deadlines. This professor describes his first day teaching at a university in Brazil. Fearing he will be late for his first class, he asks several people the correct time and gets different answers from everyone he asks, answers differing by twenty minutes! Some of the casual strollers he asks are, he later realizes, students in the very class he was in such a rush to get to on time. Once in class, he notices students coming in fifteen minutes, thirty minutes, even an hour late, and none of them act embarrassed or chagrined or apologetic. And when the class period is over, none of them get up to leave, willing instead to stay on another fifteen, or thirty, minutes or whatever it takes to get their business done. People in many other countries are simply not driven by the clock in the way people in the United States are. As a result, even though ESL students usually know of the U.S. reputation for, they might say, fanatic devotion to punctuality, these students sometimes just cannot bring themselves to conform to class starting times and paper deadline dates. Their priorities are such that they may be unable to refuse to help a friend in need even if their term papers are due tomorrow. In one 8:00 A.M. class of mine, students from Greece, Zaire, and Palestine arrived in class every single day from five to fifteen minutes late; on the other hand, a group of students from the People's Republic of China arrived every single day from five to fifteen minutes early!

Traditional gender roles may also create problems for ESL students. For some of these students, their experience in the United States will be the first time they have been in a mixed-sex classroom. This alone may be intimidating for them. But in addition, in some parts of the world, women are expected not to speak in the presence of males at all, clearly posing a special problem of classroom participation for these students. Even if women students do not have this additional burden placed on them, they, and males from these cultures, may feel awkward working in groups together and, if given the choice, may choose to work only in groups of the same sex.

It is also the case that some of these students, particularly the males, may never have had a female professor and may need some time to adjust themselves to that new experience. ESL professionals also cite instances in which gender prejudices make male ESL students unable to take female authority figures, including teachers, as seriously as they would males. But general respect for authority and for teachers in particular apparently overrides these prejudices for the most part. These problems occur with very few students and far less often in English-speaking countries than in the students' home countries.

Language

Language óbviously creates misunderstandings. Even though ESL students may be paying careful attention to what is going on, they may actually understand only a portion of what they hear. New ESL teachers consistently register surprise at their own overestimation of how much their students understand of classroom management talk. Numbers in particular may be difficult, for example, the page numbers of reading assignments. These students may need to have directions repeated even when they claim to have understood. In fact, for students from some cultures where it seems to be taken for granted that all credit for students' learning belongs to the teacher, it may be utterly useless to ask if they understand. For cultural and linguistic reasons, they may always claim to understand even when they don't, either hesitant to bring further attention to themselves by their failure to understand or reluctant to imply that the teacher has not made a point clearly enough.

Sometimes the confusion arises because, for some cultural groups, nodding the head, which indicates agreement or at least understanding to English speakers, may merely indicate that the listener is continuing to listen, while perhaps not understanding the content of what is being said at all (Scarcella, 1990). For some Arabs, blinking the eyes indicates agreement, a gesture unlikely even to be noticed by uninformed native English speakers, and for some Indians, the gesture used is tilting the head to the side in a movement that resembles the English gesture indicating doubt! (This gesture looks like the one which might be accompanied in English by "Oh well" and a shrug.)

Some languages are spoken with a great deal more intonation or emphasis than is usual for English. If students from those language backgrounds have not learned to imitate English oral delivery style well, they may come off sounding more vehement or emotional than they intend. Other students, many Asians, for example, may seem excruciatingly shy because of the longer pauses they customarily take before answering a question put to them. An English speaker may perceive a Vietnamese speaker as not participating in a conversation because the Vietnamese speaker takes so long to reply; the Vietnamese speaker, however, may perceive a series of friendly questions as a barrage implying impatience and not permitting appropriately reflective answers (Robinson, 1985, cited in Scarcella, 1990, 103).

Another aspect of the problems caused by language, even for students who are fairly proficient in English, may occur when a student tries to make a point. The rules for turn-taking vary among languages. A person speaking English is expected to heed verbal and kinetic cues indicating that the listener is now ready to speak, cues like taking a breath or making a sound toward the end of the speaker's sentence. Non-native students may inappropriately interrupt a speaker because turn-taking is handled differently in those students' cultures and they may not yet know the correct signals to send in this culture. In some cultures, interrupting a speaker may not be rude; it may be a sign of listener attentiveness intended to show the listener's involvement in the interaction. But it is also entirely possible that while the speaker is speaking, the non-native student is rehearsing what she or he planned to say and simply has to begin speaking before the planned sentence slips away.

Language-based confusion also arises unexpectedly and in ways impossible to guard against. One example is [an] Asian student . . . who interpreted the comment "It's a shame you didn't have more time to work on this paper" to mean "You should be ashamed of this paper."

The confusion may also be on the teacher's part. Oral English proficiency, for example, including accents, can be extremely misleading. ESL students who have learned English in an environment which precluded much contact with spoken English may speak with accents very difficult to understand but may write quite well. Conversely, particularly with immigrant students, the students' oral English may sound quite native-like but their written English may be a problem. They may be quite proficient at BICS [Basic Interpersonal Communicative Skills] but may have had little experience with CALP [Cognitive Academic Language Proficiency], the language of the academy. In either case, accents cannot be equated one way or the other with proficiency.

Grades and Exams

One very important area in which cultural assumptions may differ and cause friction is evaluation. Some of these students are under tremendous pressure to get good grades either because their financial support depends on maintaining a certain average or because their pride or family honor requires excellent performance. In addition, in many countries around the world, exam results are extremely important, determining much more absolutely than we may be used to here a student's admission to certain types of educational tracks or to certain prestigious schools and ultimately to a desirable job and life style. Even exams taken at age five or six can set children on the road to a comfortable, financially secure future or to a lifetime of factory work. Students from these countries take exams extremely seriously.

Further complicating the exam issue is the fact that it is taken for granted in some countries that friends and relatives have the right to call upon each other for any help they need, and that that call must be answered. Some students feel as much obliged to share exam answers or research papers as they would to share their notes of that day's class or to share their book with a classmate. (See Kuehn, Stanwyck, and Holland, 1990, for a discussion of ESL students' attitudes towards cheating.) Knowledge may be thought of more as communal, less as individual property. The moral obligation to share, to cooperate, to help a friend or relative makes far more pressing demands on some of these students than the obligation our culture may wish to impose of individual work and competition. In other words, what we call cheating is not particularly uncommon or shocking for some of these students. It simply does not carry the onus it does here.

In places where personal relationships have more weight than they do here and adherence to impersonal rules has less weight, bureaucrats and others in authority often have a great deal more flexibility to act than they might here. As a result, arguing, persuading, and bargaining for a better deal is a part of human interaction. That includes, of course, bargaining with teachers for better grades. In situations where students are pleading for higher grades, the justification is nearly always the same: not that the student actually did better, not that the teacher's judgment was wrong, not that the student does not deserve the lower grade, but that the student *needs* a higher grade and that it is in the teacher's power to *help*. When the teacher refuses to help, the student may go away hurt and confused, personally wounded at the teacher's indifference to the student's plight. These are very painful experiences both for the student and for the teacher, but particularly for non-ESL teachers who may not understand that the student (and the teacher as well, obviously) is operating according to another set of culturally determined rules about personal interactions. Non-ESL teachers may well come to resent international students for putting them in such tense, embarrassing situations and making them feel guilty about sticking to their decisions.

In these awful confrontations, it is also not unheard of for students to exhibit more emotion than most U.S. post-secondary teachers are accustomed to dealing with. Men in other cultures, for example, are permitted to cry under a much wider range of circumstances than is permitted here. Unrestrained sobbing is sometimes a student's response to the sadness of failure or defeat.

Body Language and Socio-linguistic Snags

Other conflicting cultural styles may be less dramatic but also disconcerting. Latin American and Arab students may sit or stand too close during conferences; Vietnamese students may feel uncomfortable with a friendly pat on the shoulder; Japanese students may not look at the teacher when addressed. During a discussion of body language, I asked a class of international students whether they noticed that people use eye contact differently in the United States from the way it is used in their home countries. Several students strongly felt that this was the case. When asked to elaborate, a man from El Salvador complained that Americans refused to look him in the eye, as if they were lying, insincere, or hiding something, and a woman from Japan claimed that Americans made her feel uneasy because they seemed to insist on staring at her when they spoke, right in the eye instead of somewhere at the base of the throat, as she was accustomed to doing!

Cultural differences can cause other complications which are not strictly linguistic. One of the experiences Americans abroad often complain about is suffering the injustice of having someone butt in line and be served out of order while those in line continue to wait. But in many other cultures, people assume that those who are waiting in line are in no particular hurry and don't mind not being waited on next. If they did mind, they would be aggressively demanding attention by pushing to the front of the line and stating their desire. Students from these places, then, may feel quite comfortable crowding the teacher after class and demanding attention while other students patiently await their turns.

Other embarrassing moments may occur as a result of socio-linguistic differences among cultures. One of these areas concerns the tacit rules which govern topics of conversation. Teachers may feel intruded upon by questions which are completely normal in the students' cultures: In Asia: Are you married? How old are you? In the Arab world: How much did that cost? Do you have sons? In Eastern Europe: How much money do you make? How much do you weigh? (Wolfson, 1989). The reaction to such questions may be outrage unless we realize that the question of what is appropriate to talk about is a part of the linguistic system of a language that must be learned just as verb tenses must be learned. Just as the questions above may strike us as inappropriate, others take offense at different questions. Muslim students, for example, are offended by questions like "Why don't you drink?" or "Have you ever kissed your boyfriend?" (Wolfson, 1989). Unfortunately, socio-linguistic rules are not visible as rules, are taken for granted, and are assumed to be universal. As a result, while grammatical errors may be ignored, socio-linguistic errors brand the non-native as rude and offensive.

Notions of modesty about achievements also differ among cultures. Writing teachers may find it difficult, for example, to learn whether a writing assignment went well for given students. When asked how well they did on an assignment, Asian students invariably say they did not do a good job, that they are not good students, while Arab students seem to always reply that their paper is very good, that everything went exceedingly well.

ESL students may actually behave in ways that strike us as unusual, unexpected, or even inappropriate, but difficulties may also arise as we simply misinterpret what appears to be ordinary, recognizable behavior. The Japanese, for example, have an aversion for direct disagreement and instead of saying no to a suggestion may hedge, preferring to indicate vaguely that the decision must be postponed or further studied (Christopher, 1982, cited in Wolfson, 1989, 20). As a result, an English speaker may not recognize that the Japanese speaker has said no and may assume that the Japanese speaker really is still debating the issue. The Japanese apparently do not even like to say the word "no"; when asked whether she liked Yoko Ono, one Japanese student replied, "Yes, I hate her."

Finally, the offices of ESL teachers are often crowded with Chinese paper cuttings, Korean fans, Latin American *mulas,* and pieces of Arabic brass. Non-ESL colleagues of mine with ESL students in their classes have sometimes expressed concern that these gifts look like bribes and have wondered whether or not to accept them from their students. But this type of gift-giving is an accepted part of many cultures, and ESL students often give their teachers small gifts as tokens of respect and gratitude with no baser intentions in mind at all.

Students may misinterpret us as well or feel confused about how to interpret our signals correctly. While they may be happy to learn, for example, that professors have office hours, they may feel unsure about whether or not they are actually invited to take advantage of them. Students may be confused if the decision of whether or not to come by the office during office hours is left up to them and may conclude that an off-hand invitation to come by if they have problems, an invitation which does not *urge* or order the student to come by, is not sincere.

Conclusion

It takes some time for international students to determine exactly what their relationship with a professor is. Many of them come from cultures, such as China, in which teachers are highly respected but also are expected to behave more like mentors, to involve themselves in the students' lives, to know about them as people, and to guide them closely in moral, personal, or educational decisions. These students may then be disappointed to find this is not usually the case here.

Clearly, there is a great deal of room for both misunderstanding and resentment during confrontations involving different cultural styles. For the most part, it is the international students, outnumbered as they are, who will have to make the greater part of the adjustment to accommodate U.S. classroom expectations. But an awareness of some of these students' expectations on the part of their U.S. instructors can certainly make the adjustment easier for all. Anticipating some of the behaviors of culturally mixed groups can help us be more tolerant of them and perhaps at the same time less hesitant about pointing out, if necessary, the inappropriateness of some of these behaviors within the culture of the U.S. college classroom.

References

Krasnick, H. 1990. Preparing Indonesians for graduate study in Canada. *TESL Reporter* 23: 33–36.

Kuehn, P., D. J. Stanwyck, and C. L. Holland. 1990. Attitudes toward "cheating" behaviors in the ESL classroom. *TESOL Quarterly* 24: 313–317.

Levine, R., with E. Wolff. 1985. Social time: The heartbeat of a culture. *Psychology Today* 19 (March): 28–37.

Newstetter, W., T. Shoji, N. Mokoto, and F. Matsubara. 1989. From the inside out. Student perspectives on the academic writing culture. Paper presented at the Conference on Culture, Writing, and Related Issues in Language Teaching, Atlanta, Georgia.

Scarcella, R. 1990. *Teaching language minority children in the multicultural classroom.* Englewood Cliffs, NJ: Prentice-Hall.

Stapleton, S. 1990. From the roller coaster to the round table: Smoothing rough relationships between foreign students and faculty members. *TESL Reporter* 23 (April): 23–25.

Wolfson, N. 1989. *Perspectives: Sociolinguistics and TESOL.* New York: Newbury House.

TEXTS IN CONTEXTS: UNDERSTANDING
CHINESE STUDENTS' ENGLISH COMPOSITIONS

Guanjun Cai

[From Charles R. Cooper and Lee Odell, eds. *Evaluating Writing: The Role of Teachers' Knowledge about Text, Learning, and Culture.* Urbana: NCTE, 1999. 279–97.]

Guanjun Cai is an advisory software engineer at IBM. As an information architect, he defines product-specific publishing strategies and designs information to meet the needs of a global audience. As a Ph.D. candidate at the University of Arizona, he taught basic writing, first-year composition, advanced writing, and technical writing. He also co-edited *A Student's Guide to First-Year Composition.* Other publications include articles in *Encyclopedia of Rhetoric and Composition, Keywords in Composition Studies,* and *Theorizing Composition: A Critical Sourcebook of Theory and Scholarship in Contemporary Composition Studies.* The essay included here first appeared in *Evaluating Writing: The Role of Teachers' Knowledge about Text, Learning, and Culture.*

Too often, teachers focus on surface and sentence-level issues in the writing of ESL students, treating them as what Guanjun Cai calls "violations" of accepted conventions. In the following article, Cai argues for a different approach to working with students whose native language is not English. Instead of seeing violations, teachers should see "differences" that are "unfamiliar to composition teachers who are native speakers of English." More specifically, Cai asks teachers to recognize that they may be "making judgments within rhetorical contexts quite different from those in which the . . . students do their writing." He points out that such differences are evident in all aspects of their writing—from word and sentence to more general concerns. Teachers will be better able to help students learn English rhetorical conventions if they are familiar with the typical rhetorical strategies of the students' native cultures. Cai explains the differences between Chinese and American expectations for a typical academic essay, showing how rhetorical conventions are connected to ideological and cultural values. Using a case study of a Chinese student, Cai demonstrates how a cross-cultural perspective helps teachers analyze a student's performance and develop strategies for helping the student understand ways to revise, providing cultural and contextual reasons for those revisions. Teachers of diverse ESL students will find this article particularly useful. Even though Cai focuses specifically on Chinese students, the principles he foregrounds and illustrates will apply to students from other cultures as well.

When some English teachers see the writing of students who are native speakers of Chinese, they tend to focus on sentence-level problems, especially the absence of the "-ed" tense marker, the misuse or overuse of the definite article "the," and the frequent employment of the "although . . . but . . ." construction. Such problems are attributable to deep linguistic differences between English and Chinese. For example, while tense in an English sentence is often, though not always, revealed by the different forms its verb takes, such as the "-ed" form, past experience in Chinese is not marked by the verb itself, but indicated by an appended aspect article like *ge* or *liao.* Chinese, unlike English, does not have definite and indefinite articles, and a complex Chinese sentence in which the linked clauses speak contradictory statements requires the combined use of "although" and "but," instead of just one of them as in English. These problems and others like them are bound to arise in the English writing of Chinese students who have not yet fully understood the differences between Chinese and English.

Chinese students have to wrestle with even more substantial differences in writing to an American audience, however, as the following anecdote by Mark Salzman illustrates. In *Iron and Silk*, Salzman (1986) tells a story about helping a Chinese English instructor correct an English translation of a Chinese text. The text is a letter of application for a World Bank loan for the Chinese college where they both work. Salzman thinks the grammar is fine, but he points out to the Chinese teacher that, from a Western point of view, the content is weak and thus unacceptable as an official application for a loan. To his surprise, the Chinese teacher replies, "But this is a translation of the text written by the officials of our college. This is the Chinese way of writing this sort of thing. I am only an English teacher; I cannot presume to change it" (21). Clearly, the difference that Salzman speaks of is well beyond sentence and grammar levels in an application letter.

More important, Salzman's story indicates that some distinct features of English texts written by Chinese students may not be *violations* as they are currently marked, but at most *differences* unfamiliar to composition teachers who are native speakers of English. These features are evident at all levels of discourse, ranging from lexical choice to overall organization and rhetorical stance. "Violations" in these areas, such as "indirectness," "digressions," and "lack of transitional signals," are perceived as violations because native speakers of English make judgments within rhetorical contexts quite different from those in which the Chinese students do their writing. Within the Chinese contexts, the perceived violations may not be violations at all; they may correctly fulfill the expectations of a Chinese audience.

Teachers of English composition may better understand and analyze texts by Chinese students and, consequently, more effectively teach English rhetorical conventions to these students if the teachers themselves are familiar with the typical rhetorical strategies of Chinese academic writing, the underlying rhetorical ideologies, and the sociocultural contexts in which these strategies and ideologies are embedded. My purpose in this chapter[1] is to develop a cross-cultural perspective on writing by explaining the Chinese rhetorical contexts and then applying this perspective to the work of a Chinese student, a high school graduate in China who recently entered an American university.

A Cross-cultural Perspective on Writing

From a social constructionist standpoint, writing is a social act and takes place within a specific sociocultural context (Bruffee 1986; LeFevre 1987). The process of writing is also a process of sociocultural ideology formation (Berlin 1988; Eagleton 1991), in which the rules for a certain type of writing are set, such as what can and must be said and who gets to say it. Further, changes in political power and the associated ideologies cause drastic changes in rhetorical norms and language use (Saville-Troike 1989). Therefore, writing and rhetoric are inherently sociopolitical and ideological constructs.

In Chinese as well as in English contexts, rhetoric and academic writing have always been bound up with sociopolitical beliefs. In Chinese culture, they serve the ideological claims of the Chinese society, which greatly values social harmony and group orientation. These values are different from those in American culture, which prizes an individualism that is deeply "entrenched as a privilege and a characteristic of American society" (Hoffman 1965, 113). In China, harmony, derived from Confucianism, is still cherished. The individual is conceived as a communal being rather than an independent being in the American sense; the individual is, to borrow Regamey's term, a "harmonized collection of universals" (1968, 517). The concept of individuality may even have negative connotations, taken to mean egoism or selfishness. The sense of self is realized, not through self-fulfillment, but only when group values are recognized and accepted.

Further, in contrast to the American belief that self-expression helps minimize conflict (Van Niekerk 1987), Chinese social ideology discourages free expression of personal views. The Chinese believe that knowledge resides in collective wisdom and social norms; no ordinary individual can claim the authority of knowledge. As Fan Shen laments, "[In China] both political pressure and literary tradition require that 'I' be somewhat hidden or buried in writings and speeches; presenting the 'self' too obviously would give people the impression of being disrespectful of the Communist Party in political writings and boastful in scholarly writings" (1989, 460). In fact, personal views are often associated with wrong ways of thinking, and free self-expression is believed to cause conflict and disrupt social harmony.

For the same reasons, creative language use is discouraged. In ancient times, Confucius remarked that "artful speech and ingratiating demeanor rarely accompany virtue" (Soothill 1968, 3). Laotzu warned his disciples that "truthful words are not beautiful, beautiful words are not truthful" (1963, 79). These sages' words still influence academic writing in China. In effect, the Chinese language is planned and developed to include a large number of prescribed expressions. Classic books like *Li Ji* or *The Book of Etiquette* (Oliver 1971, 149) and more recent pamphlets like *San Jiang Si Mei Wu Re Ai* or *Three-Do's, Four-Beauties, and Five-Loves* are written to inform people of what to say and how to say it in every normally encountered situation.

Under these guiding ideologies, academic writing in China has become an appendage to politics. Discourse features, such as overall organization, topic choice, paragraph organization, sentence structure and lexical choice, self-expression and language use, and purpose for writing, are direct products of changing Chinese sociopolitical contexts. This can be seen in the practices of the eight-legged essay, the four-part essay, and the three-part essay.

The Eight-legged Essay

The eight-legged essay, known in Chinese as *ba gu wen*, was a part of the Chinese civil service examinations,[2] which were used by the Chinese ruling class to recruit local officials. It thus constituted the basic framework of expository and persuasive writing in classical Chinese and has since influenced academic writing in Taiwan, Hong Kong, Singapore, and modern China. An eight-legged essay must have the designated eight parts: (1) *po-ti;* (2) *cheng-ti;* (3) *qi-jiang;* (4) *qi-gu;* (5) *xu-gu;* (6) *zhong-gu;* (7) *hou-gu;* and (8) *da-jie* (Wang 1950), literally meaning opening up, amplification, preliminary exposition, first argument, second argument, third argument, final argument, and conclusion. The most important part was *cheng-ti,* usually consisting of two or three sentences, in which the writer introduced the chosen topic and expressed the intended thesis of the essay. In the next five parts, the writer elaborated on the topic for ten to twenty sentences by drawing from some Chinese classics. Then, the writer concluded the essay in two to four sentences. In addition, every part had to be carefully balanced by rhymed words, paired phrases, and matched length of sentences.

The structure of the eight-legged essay was reformed twice because of changes in the dominant sociopolitical ideologies. The first reform took place during the New Cultural Movement in 1919. As a result, expository and persuasive writing came to follow the *qi-cheng-jun-he* four-part organizational pattern (Zhang 1938): the introduction, the elaboration on the topic, the transition to another seemingly unrelated point, and the summing up. The second reform occurred in the 1960s when Mao Tsetung criticized the *qi-cheng-jun-he* pattern and regarded it as the "Party eight-legged essay." Mao felt that such a writing format failed to "convey the revolutionary ideologies to the people" (1967, 63).

In response, students were taught to organize their expository and persuasive essays in a somewhat *fan lun-yi lun-jie lun* three-unit progression. In the *fan-lun* or "generalization," a writer made use of a standardized statement addressing the then-ongoing political propaganda, regardless of the topic under consideration. Then, the writer proceeded to the *yi-lun* or "discussion"; in this section, the writer took up the topic and elaborated on it by giving one or two examples for brief analysis. Finally, the writer went into the *jie-lun* or "conclusion." But instead of concluding the essay, the writer actually anticipated the possible future discussion of the topic, shifting to a point seemingly irrelevant to the topic examined in the *yi-lun.*

Topic choice was also subject to the changing sociopolitical ideologies. For example, all topics for eight-legged essays were derived exclusively from such Chinese classics as the *Four Books* and the Five Classics, which convey the philosophical teachings of Confucius, setting forth the moral and ethical basis of society. During the New Cultural Movement (1919), the most-written-on topics for the four-part essays in both classrooms and professional publications came to be patriotism, the fate of the nation, and the pursuit of national awakening. The same was true during the Great Cultural Revolution (1966–1976), when school education was exclusively directed to serve the interests of the proletariat class and "the people's democratic dictatorship." As a result, academic writing focused explicitly on topics of moral and ideological education, such as self-criticism, new Party policies, and so on (Cheng 1987).

The broad rhetorical differences between Chinese and English that I have sketched are also evident in the paragraph organization of the eight-legged, the four-part, and the three-part essays. Robert Kaplan (1966) claims that most native-English-speaking writers favor a direct approach to a chosen topic. In the sense of paragraph organization, this means that English writers tend to arrange a paragraph in a hierarchical order (Fagan and Cheong 1987) in which a topic sentence is supported by other sentences. By contrast, Chinese writers tend to construct a paragraph using the *qi-cheng-jun-he* pattern (Mo 1982), the same structure for organizing an essay. In *qi*, the writer prepares the reader for the topic, and in *cheng*, he elaborates on it; after wandering into a *jun*, a seemingly unrelated point, the writer comes back and wraps up everything in a *he*. Shen describes this type of paragraph organization as peeling an onion, layer by layer, moving "from surface to the core" (1989, 462).

And finally, rhetorical differences between Chinese and English are embedded even in sentence structure and word choice. While most English writers write with "forthright, straightforward, simple expressions" and are "generally free of sentimental expressions, exaggerations, and reference to the past" (Fagan and Cheong 1987, 25), Chinese writers tend to avoid expressing personal thoughts, a tendency characteristic of the eight-legged, the four-part, and the three-part essays. The avoidance of self-expression is usually accomplished by, for example, "use of quotations and reference to the past" (25). In fact, in Chinese writing, *pang zheng bo yin and yin jing ju dian*, or quoting the classics and referring to the past, are not only considered "the height of culture" and "the mark of good breeding" (Tsao 1990, 109), but also regarded as a willingness to respect authorities and to accept traditional values, social norms, and group ideologies, and as a desire to be polite.

Moreover, English-speaking writers are trained to write with direct and explicit assertions in every part of an essay: "Tell 'em what you're going to tell 'em, tell 'em, and tell 'em what you've told 'em" (Reid 1984, 449), whereas Chinese writers are inclined to prefer "suggesting" (Leki 1992, 95) or "indirectness" (Jensen 1987, 135). That is, instead of directly "imposing" their ideas on the reader, Chinese writers tend to use rhetorical questions, metaphor and simile, analogy, and illustrative anecdotes (Gregg 1986, 356) to imply their propositions. In doing so, the writers expect the readers to "supply some significant portion of the propositional structure" (Kaplan 1988, 292), and "to work to glean meaning [on their own]" (Leki 1992, 97) from a text.

The use of all these strategies reveals the essential purpose and function of rhetoric and academic writing in the Chinese language. The primary function of Chinese rhetoric "is not to enhance the welfare of the individual speaker or listener but to promote [social] harmony" and collectivity (Oliver 1971, 261). The ultimate purpose of Chinese writing is not to argue for differences and uniqueness but to maintain the norms and traditions. Within Chinese contexts, students' writing practices are taken as a fundamental means of making a connection between classrooms and social reality, promoting harmony and collectivity, preserving social norms and traditions, and showing respect to authorities past and present (Matalene 1985, 795).

Text Analysis: A Case Study

The texts selected for the following analysis are from Fang Li's writing portfolio for English 306 at the University of Arizona. Fang (not the student's real name) is representative of millions of high school graduates in China. She started learning how to write basic academic essays in the fourth grade, under the strong influences of the eight-legged, the four-part, and the three-part essays. Like her peers, she started learning English in the seventh grade. Since English is primarily learned not for any instrumental purpose, but for such technical reasons as translating literary works and exchanging scientific information, and since English composition is not a part of the school curricula, students are not exposed to English rhetoric and academic writing. As a result, Fang is among the thousands of new Chinese students who walk into American secondary schools or universities thinking and writing English essays in the Chinese way.

Fang, now in her early twenties, has been in the United States for three and a half years, during which time she has taken five college-level writing classes, including English 306. Previously, she had taken English 106, 107, and 108, which are specially designed as a sequence of composition classes for first-year international students, and also English 308, a course emphasizing technical writing that is usually reserved for scientific or technical juniors and seniors. English 306 is intended to improve students' expository and persuasive writing skills and is open to all interested students after their first-year composition sequence (Applen, McNenny, and Ransdell 1992, 7). Fang took this course in the spring semester of 1993.

Despite her extensive contact with the English language and considerable experience with English composition, Fang's perspective on English rhetoric and composition is still significantly more Chinese than American. Most of her schematic knowledge about rhetoric and writing remains as a solid construct of the Chinese sociocultural and political contexts and her experience with Chinese academic writing, which is yet to be influenced by the English contexts. All Fang's six essays consistently show the following characteristic features of Chinese rhetoric and academic writing. Her topic choice tends to be more reliant on the given reading material than on her own imagination. As a result, her essays' content appears more a restatement of the readings than personal argument. Furthermore, the overall organization of Fang's essays seems to be more identifiable with the eight-legged or four-part pattern in Chinese writing than with the English introduction-body-conclusion linear progression, and her paragraphs demonstrate the *qi-cheng-jun-he* structure and disinterest in English cohesion. Finally, instead of directly asserting her personal views, Fang tends to develop her points by frequently employing questions, quotations, abstract wording, and word-by-word translation into English of Chinese prescribed phrasings or sayings. The detailed analysis that follows may suffice to illustrate the above features, which are not what Fang's instructor expected to see in her essays. I hope that, unlike Fang's instructor, other native-English-speaking instructors will not see these differences as violations, but recognize these features for what they are. Of course, native English speakers who have little experience with academic writing also have problems with, for instance, making their paragraphs cohesive in conventional ways and with "getting to the point." In this analysis, however, I want to compare the qualities of Fang's writing only with those of competent, native English speakers' prose.

The sociocultural ideology and political register of Chinese rhetoric are clearly evident in Fang's topic choice for all six essays. Fang and her classmates were not given any specific assignment instructions or prompts for writing these essays; rather, they were asked to read chapters from their multicultural reader, *Our Times*, by Robert Atwan (1993), and develop six arguments on any topics they felt comfortable with. However, Fang seemingly did not want to take any risk or write on subjects of her own, but decided to comment on subjects others had defined; that is, she chose topics either similar to or the same as those raised in the chapters she read. For example, after reading chapters on "Television Broadcasting: Does it Distort the News?" and "Television and Sex Roles: Is TV Defying the Stereotypes?" Fang wrote Essay #1, "For a Better Future," in which she posed exactly the same questions about mass media. Fang entitled Essay #2 "Cultural Diversity: Is It a Good Thing?" using almost the same wording as the chapter title she read: "America's Cultural Diversity: Is It a Good Thing?" In the same way, Fang's Essay #3—"Racism on Campus: Why Does It Happen?"—derived from her reading of chapters on "Racism on Campus: How Can We Explain It?"

Further, all Fang's essays address the issues of diversity, racism, and equality, which are dealt with by Atwan's book. I asked Fang why she chose to write about those topics. She explained that she was exposed to these issues when she was still in China, and the readings in English 306 reminded her of these issues. What Fang said is true. In fact, topics on problems of cultural diversity, racism, and equality are the most often used in recent Chinese political writing that criticizes Western cultures, and they are inevitably popular themes in school composition and ideology education, which warns young generations that the West is not as ideal a place as expected, and so "Going West" may not be the best choice in life. In light of her experience in China, Fang's topic selection also had clear political and moral-thematic foundations.

Moreover, Fang's topic choice is quite consistent with her perception of the function and purpose for writing, which is also reflective of Chinese rhetoric and sociocultural ideologies. Instead of intending to convince her reader of her own perspectives on the chosen topics, Fang and her writing make it clear that she has the following three common purposes in mind for all her essays. First, Fang thinks of writing in terms of demonstrating her understanding of the assigned readings to her instructor, that is, paraphrasing or repeating the authorities. Second, she intends to draw moral lessons on the chosen issues through her essays, such as in her statement: "We should try our best to eliminate racism." Finally, she sees writing as an important means for achieving or preserving social harmony. She makes this purpose clear when she claims, on the cover page to Essay #1, that "We do not want increased social conflicts and we want a peaceful future."

Fang's essays reveal some topic development strategies typical of Chinese rhetoric and sociocultural and political contexts. The overall formats or "superstructures" (Connor and Lauer 1988, 142) of Fang's six essays have a clear commonality of topic development, which is identifiable with the traditional eight-legged or four-part pattern in Chinese writing. Essay #4, below, in which Fang writes about how to achieve equality, illustrates these topic development tactics and, as my analysis will show, other rhetorical strategies characteristic of Chinese academic writing (I have numbered the paragraphs to aid in discussion).

On Equality

[1] Equality, a notion which was posed in the French Revolution two hundred years ago, has been a primary concern in most of the political movements in the last two centuries. Generations and generations of people all over the world have striven for this political ideal. However, no nation in the world has succeeded in realizing equality in their society. This failure leads people to ponder the implication of the notion itself. The debate on equality becomes a hot topic in the 1990s.

[2] In the French Revolution in the 19th century, the revolutionaries claimed that every citizen has the right to participate in the nation's politics; this is not a privilege only belonging to the nobility. In the turbulent days of revolution, various social groups—the nobility, the bourgeoisie, the urban working class and the peasants fought with each other violently for their political power, since everybody seems to believe that you are either the winner or the loser in society, and the only way to make yourself the winner is to make others the loser. However, the result of French Revolution as a whole suffered the turbulent violence of group rivalry and the old problem of inequality in the country's political, economical life had not been solved.

[3] The failure of the revolution which aims at the goal of the equality leads people to ponder what is going to be an effective way to pursue this ideal. Since human beings are born differently, some with more intelligence, some with more material wealth, some with more physical strength, the distinction among them determines that they will not achieve success in the same degree, and they will have different needs to in order to realize their goals. Because of this distinction among individuals, how the society can provide the opportunities to its members based on their different needs should be the primary concern in the process based on their divergent economic, intellectual and social conditions.

[4] Since the distribution of wealth is not equal in our society, every individual has a different economic ability to achieve their goals. A person born with several million dollars will certainly have the opportunity to receive a good education and to pursue whatever he/she decides to do in his/her life. However, people with a poor economic background will have a hard time, struggling for economic stability while they are trying their other personal goals. However, like President Kennedy said thirty years ago, "If a country cannot help the poor, it will not save a few rich." The practice of equality is to relieve the nightmare of poverty for every member of the society. It means that the poor and the economically unwell-to-do should be guaranteed the basic necessities for living, such as social security and health care, and the essential opportunity to pursue success, such as the access to a good education. Under these conditions, every individual in the society can concentrate on their career and will be more likely to succeed. At the same time, the society as a whole will benefit because the success of individuals will naturally contribute to the wealth and civilization of the society.

[5] Another crucial aspect of equality to be considered is intellectual equality. It is a matter of fact that some people are born as intellectual geniuses, and some are not. Geniuses only count a small percentage of the population; the vast majority are ordinary people like you and me. How to create opportunities so that everyone can give play to their wisdom to the highest degree is an essential factor in achieving the intellectual progress of the whole society.

[6] I feel the American higher education system has more advantages than the Chinese one because it offers more opportunities for students to pursue their education. In the Chinese system, the admission to colleges and universities totally depends on the student's score on the College Entrance Examination which is highly competitive, for only 10–30 percent of students will be accepted. A student may have been an "A" student in six years in middle school, and get sick on the day of the test, and cannot get into college for several points lower than the admission standard. One shortcoming of the Chinese higher education system is that it is not open to a large population of students, only the "perfect" students can squeeze into the door of college. In contrast, U.S. colleges have a much higher admission rate. Therefore, not only the smartest, but also the intellectually ordinary students are able to get in. In addition, after getting college, students can switch majors, which allows them to choose a field they are good at and most interested in to work on. The outcome of the flexibility of the education system and the recognition of the distinction among individual students allow more members of the society to become well-educated individuals and the society as a whole will enjoy higher level of intellectual wealth. This point can be proved by the fact that the United States is in the lead in the world's scientific and cultural fields.

[7] Social equality involves the issue of diversity. Although ethnically and culturally divergent, every citizen in the society has the right to voice their opinions. At the same time, every one has to listen to people with backgrounds different from one's own, to understand their perspectives. It is human nature that we tend to like people that are the same as us and mistrust people different from us. However, if everyone sticks to this point, the whole society will become the battle ground of various social groups. The dialogue with other members in society will allow us to examine and reexamine our notions about people different from us and gradually eliminate various kinds of social stereotypes which are the stumbling blocks to social equality.

[8] My own experience shows how important it is to listen to the divergent point of view instead of only listening one side of the argument. When I had just arrived at the University of Arizona, I used to hear some Chinese students talking about blacks in a despising tone. Not having had any contact with blacks before, that was the first impression that I got about blacks. However, after living here for two years, because of the everyday contact with black students, I found out that black people are remarkable individuals, and what I have heard about them are just racial stereotypes.

[9] The search for equality is a formidable path, because we have to deal with economic, intellectual, and social diversities which are complicated issues. However, there is hope if we recognize the difference among individuals and respect people unlike ourselves. In this way, we will not necessarily be rivals of each other, but there is the possibility that everybody can become a winner on his/her life. That is the real implication of equality and it is what we should strive for.

In Paragraph #1, Fang appears to define the notion of equality. But because the paragraph is so abstract and general, it falls short of explaining what equality is and seemingly has little to do with the thesis implied in Paragraphs #2 and #3, which is, in her own words: "The failure of the revolution which aims at the goal of equality leads people to ponder what is going to be an effective way to pursue this ideal." As a result, Paragraph #1 appears to be the *po-ti* in the eight-legged pattern, the *qi* in the four-part format, and the *fan-lun* in the three-unit pattern, which all offer a grand opening up to an essay.

Fang proceeds to the part of *cheng-ti* (the amplification) or *cheng* (the elaboration) in the next four paragraphs by taking up the proposed thesis in Paragraphs #2 and #3 and offering general solutions to the problem in economic, intellectual, and sociopolitical contexts. Then, in Paragraph #8, she suddenly turns to a short discussion of her own experience with "racial stereotypes," which seems to have little relevance to the subject under consideration: "I found out that black people are remarkable individuals." Finally, she ends the essay by tying everything together, not "logically" in a Western sense, but simply by repeating her main point in general terms: "The search for equality is a formidable path . . . and it is what we should strive for."

The apparent irrelevance of Paragraph #1 to the rest of the essay, the abrupt transitions from topic to topic, and the brief mention of her own experience also come to the notice of Fang's instructor. In his endnote to the final draft of this essay, Fang's instructor remarks: "Ultimately, the paper is not very cohesive. The topic you <u>start</u> discussing isn't very well connected to the topic at the <u>end</u> of the essay." He characterizes this disconnection, not as a *difference,* but as a clear *violation* of English's rhetorical norms. He underlines both "start" and "end" to bring what he considers the incoherence of her ideas to Fang's attention, and he repeated this view to me when I asked him about it. More important, without knowledge of alternate rhetorical traditions, he does not point out to Fang in his endnote why he considers the incohesive topics as something absolutely wrong and not merely different from the rules Fang follows.

At the intersentential level, Fang tends to structure her paragraphs in the *qi-cheng-jun-he* progression that Mo and Tsao speak of rather than the more straightforward topic-support structure of English paragraphs. Paragraph #4 provides examples. Fang introduces her reader to the paragraph with the statement that "every individual has a different economic ability to achieve their goals." This statement, which is the *qi* part, does not necessarily have the same function as a topic sentence in English does because, unlike an assertive topic sentence, the *qi* statement is, rather, a general comment on the *implied* theme of the paragraph.

Then, Fang proceeds to the *cheng* part and comments in the next two sentences on the implied theme that inequality in wealth hinders many individuals' pursuit of personal goals. Before ending the paragraph with *he* in the last sentence, Fang leaves the theme with the *jun*, turning to government responsibility and welfare, topics only loosely related to the general theme. Fang offers a brief "However" warning of this turn, but it is not enough to keep her native English-speaking readers on the track. Her instructor, who again does not see the *difference,* writes his frustration on the margin: "I don't understand the significance of the quote."

In addition to their typical topic-support structure, English paragraphs also display coordinate or subordinate relationships between sentences. These relationships are often enhanced by the use of external cohesion devices. Fang's paragraphs, by contrast, illustrate the Chinese perception of cohesion and coherence. In Chinese writing, the semantic chain of each sentence to the other is more important than the syntactic and lexical cohesion to the concerned topic, in part because the Chinese language is more "tolerant" of lexical absence (Tsao 1990, 101–5). This can be seen in Paragraph #5, in which Fang does not use any lexical cohesive device (e.g., "but" or "however") to help shift from Sentence #2 to Sentence #3 in the way that an English writer might. The semantic relation between these two sentences is, however, strong and clear to Fang and her Chinese readers, who are instilled with the ideology that geniuses are rare and that the only way to succeed is to "work hard and make progress everyday."

As regards topic development at the sentence level, features of Fang's self-expression and language use are worth noting. Fang's self-expression tends to be general, impersonal, and less direct than what American academic writing expects. First, instead of direct assertions, Fang often employs questions to imply her points. The following example is from Paragraph #2 of Fang's Essay #2:

> Facing this situation, some people begin to doubt: Is cultural diversity a good thing? Is it a mistake of the founders of this country to allow every race and nationality to move into America? Is separation of different groups and encouraging them to live in their own community a way to reduce ethic conflicts?

On the surface, there seems nothing inappropriate about the use of these questions. But these questions are not just rhetorical gestures. Placed in the introduction, and clearly intended as the thesis statement for the whole essay, these sentences are a way of stating a thesis without direct imposition of an opinion.

Second, Fang frequently uses quotations and references to other sources in order to avoid expressing personal views, but without "citing references" in the Western style. In Paragraph #2 of Essay #4 above, for example, Fang makes substantial reference to the French Revolution, suggesting the origin and history of the concept of equality. Also, Fang does not credit the source of the information—the assigned readings in Atwan's book. This is permissible in Chinese academic writing because *pang zheng po yin* or *yin jing ju dian* does not necessarily require the writer to provide full citation information. Similarly, in Essay #2, Fang writes that:

> As a major instrument to propagate the dominant ideology for the society, the mass media always picks upon the minority groups because they usually do not have enough strength to fight back and therefore are the perfect target. Stereotypes against various groups, such as Blacks, Indians, Asians, and other unpopular groups are all of the same nature: the crucification of these groups as the scapegoat of social pathology.

In addition to taking phrases such as "social pathology," "unpopular groups," and "to propagate the dominant ideology" directly from the assigned readings, Fang also paraphrases several passages from them in writing this segment. This causes her instructor to be concerned, for he is not sure why Fang does what she does. When I asked about this, he explained that Fang "got more help than she should," suggesting that she used others' ideas without properly crediting them. But instead of explaining this to Fang, he writes next to the segment in an almost sarcastic tone: "This sounds like very sophisticated language."

Finally, Fang tends to address her topics in general, abstract, and impersonal terms. For example, in defining equality in Essay #4, Fang uses such abstract terms as "primary concern," "political ideal," "privilege," "goal," "opportunities," "distribution of wealth," "economic stability," and "intellectual geniuses" vs. "ordinary people," and so on. Without knowing her intention, Fang's instructor runs out of patience during his reading of Paragraph #3 and literally begs: "As a reader, I am desperate for details at this point of your essay." Again, he underlines his concern and request.

Other aspects of Fang's language reflect her view of language not as a vehicle of individual expression, but as part of a communal store of accepted notions. For example, Fang's language use tends to be both impersonal (in the sense of being not "individualized") and prescribed (rather than "original"). Even though Fang uses the personal pronoun "I" in every one of her essays—especially in personal anecdotes—impersonal pronouns, such as "we" or "us," "you," "one person," "everyone," "everybody," "people," "our society," "they" or "their," and "every individual," are usually among her first choices when taking a stand. In addition, many of Fang's sentences are direct translations of prescribed sayings in *si xiang jiao yu* ("ideology education") pamphlets in China, for example;

1. Generations and generations of people all over the world have strived for this political ideal.

2. You are either the winner or the loser in society, and the only way to make yourself the winner is to make others the loser.
3. Since human beings are born differently . . .
4. That is the real implication of equality, and that is what we should strive for. (numbers added)

Sometimes Fang's translation relies too much on Chinese wording, word order, and sentence structure to be understood by her instructor. Once again, considering what Fang does as being absolutely unacceptable, he marks the following sentences with phrases like "awkward expression," "What do you mean?" and in one place, simply a question mark:

1. *The search for equality is a formidable path.*
2. The society as whole will benefit because the success of individuals will naturally contribute to *the wealth and civilization of the society.*
3. Its negative portrayal of minority groups efficiently promotes social stereotype and turns out to be *a public health hazard.* (numbers and emphasis added)

While these sentences make little sense to Fang's instructor, they ring with meaning for Chinese speakers. The first sentence is a direct translation of a popular Chinese saying: *xun zao ping den shi yi tiao jian kou de dao lou.* The phrases of "the wealth and civilization of society" in the second sentence and "a public health hazard" in the third render *shi hui de chai fu yu wen ming* and *da zhong wei sheng de yin huan* in Chinese.

Conclusion: Implications for Composition Teachers

The foregoing theoretical discussion and textual analysis suggest the following two principal implications for understanding English compositions by Chinese students. First, ESL composition teachers need to realize that rhetoric and writing are direct products of sociocultural and political contexts; they are schematic representations of the writer's experience and interactions within the given sociocultural context. Therefore, English composition teachers should be aware that Chinese students may write in accordance with a set of rhetorical norms that differ from those of English. The ultimate goal of such awareness is acknowledgment of and respect for rhetorical traditions outside of the West. As Jensen (1987) states,

> We have exhausted ourselves probing the Western rhetorical heritage, which honors verbal expression, reason, cause and effect linear linkages, directions, clear organization, unadorned style, and the debating of opposing views so that truth will emerge more purely from the clash. We have overlooked the rhetorical heritage of the East, which honors non-expression, silence, the nonverbal, the softness and subtlety of ambiguity and indirectness, the insights of intuition, and the avoidance of clash of opinion in order to preserve harmony. We have not fully appreciated communication which highly values reasoning from authority and example, which relies heavily on analogy and metaphor. With our devotion to individualism we have not fully appreciated communicative behavior which puts groups above the individual, which greatly respects relationships with others based on age, relative status, and tradition. (135)

Teachers should examine Chinese students' English compositions by first considering the Chinese contexts. In doing so, teachers will be able to find out why students compose a text as they do, identify those schemata typical of Chinese ideology, and eventually better understand the students' writing. More important, teachers will be able to acknowledge students' strengths as writers and then help them modify and make the Chinese rhetorical schemata in their English compositions more in turn with those of English.

The second primary implication of my discussion is that, being aware of rhetoric and writing as sociocultural constructs, teachers need to help Chinese students get to know English contexts and audience expectations for English com-positions. That is, Chinese students should not be taught isolated composition skills (e.g., establishing a thesis up front, being straightforward or original); rather, they need to be taught English rhetorical norms and the broader socio-cultural contexts in which these norms are embedded. If teachers want Chinese ESL students to organize their English compositions along the "Introduction-Body-Conclusion" three-part pattern, the students should be explicitly taught that this pattern represents an implicit agreement between the writer and the reader in the English language; that the writer uses this pattern to fulfill the reader's expectations; and that English culture and academic writing value lin-earity over other thought patterns. Similarly, if teachers want Chinese ESL stu-dents to "Be original" or "Be yourself" in their writing, these students should be taught that individuality is encouraged and appreciated in English culture and that free expression of personal views and thinking is essential in English aca-demic writing. By the same token, Chinese ESL students should be reassured that although a direct, straightforward approach to a topic may give their read-ers the impression of "imposing," it will eventually promote intellectual under-standing between themselves and their English-speaking audience. Only such explicit teaching of English discourse ideologies can produce changes in the discourse strategies in ESL students' writing, because change in language use comes from change in guiding ideologies and expectations. In other words, only when Chinese ESL students understand the underlying discourse schemata shared by American academics are they able to compose properly and accept-ably in English.

Further Sources

Teachers can turn to recent research in contrastive rhetoric and second-language writing to learn more about the English writing of Chinese students and, most important, about strategies for helping those students with their writing. These include several of the studies that I mentioned earlier, particu-larly those done by Kaplan, Matalene, and Shen. Kaplan's "Cultural Thought Patterns in Inter-cultural Education" (1966) and other numerous writings will help familiarize teachers with the notion of contrastive rhetoric. Kaplan argues that rhetoric is a culturally coded phenomenon and that different languages embody different rhetorical norms and conventions for writing. He suggests that teachers take note that writing in a second language will be influenced by the rhetorical preferences in the first language.

In "Contrastive Rhetoric: An American Writing Teacher in China," Matalene reminds teachers that Chinese students may not only write, but also think the Chinese way in their English classes. She indicates that teachers may need to take the initiative to explain their comments, such as "Use new language," be-cause "Chinese students are too puzzled and too polite to point this out—and they are certainly not in the habit of questioning teachers" (1985, 92). On the other hand, Shen's "The Classroom and the Wider Culture: Identity as a Key to Learning English Composition" offers other ways of helping Chinese stu-dents with their writing. Shen explains that, in his English essays, he was using the Chinese approach of *yi-jing*, creating a mental picture that went along with the abstract meaning he was trying to argue. He suggests that, in order for him to write good English essays, his English professors had to help him "get rid of" this approach and, instead, use "Western logical critical ap-proaches" (1989, 460). Finally, teachers may find Ulla Connor and Robert B. Kaplan's *Writing Across Languages: Analysis of L2 Text* (1987), Donna M. Johnson and Duane H. Roen's *Richness in Writing: Empowering ESL Students* (1989), and Ilona Leki's *Understanding ESL Writers: A Guide for Teachers* (1992) very helpful.

Notes

[1] I wish to thank my fellow graduate student Clyde Moneyhun, who offered me guidance throughout the writing process; this chapter would not have been possible without his generous help. I would also like to express my gratitude to my professors, Clair Bernhardt Brohaugh, Muriel Saville-Troike, Rudolph Troike, and Tilly Warnock; my editors, Charles Cooper and Lee Odell; and my wife, Jie Liang, for their insightful comments and suggestions for improvement.

[2] This civil system was invented in the Warring States Period (475 B.C.E.–221 B.C.E.), officially implemented in the Tang Dynasty (618–907 C.E.), and fully developed during the Ming (1368–1644) and Qing (1645–1911) dynasties. It consisted of three basic parts: the examination, the appointment, and the evaluation. It was the examination part that required the eight-legged writing since the Ming dynasty. For more information on this system, consult Jinfan Zhang's (1990) "A Comprehensive Discussion of China's Ancient Civil Service System," *Social Sciences in China* 2: 35–58.

Works Cited

Applen, J. D., Gerri McNenny, and D. R. Ransdell, eds. 1992. *A Teacher's Guide to Composition,* 1992–93 Edition. Tucson: The University of Arizona, Composition Program. [Photocopy.]

Atwan, Robert. 1993. *Our Times/3: Reading from Recent Periodicals.* Boston: St. Martin's Press.

Berlin, James. 1988. "Rhetoric and Ideology in the Writing Class." *College English* 50:477–94.

Bruffee, Kenneth A. 1986. "Social Construction, Language, and the Authority of Knowledge: A Bibliographical Essay." *College English* 48 (8): 773–90.

Cheng, Bixiang. 1987. *Xian Dai Hanyu Yuyan Jiaoyu Fa Zhan Shi* (A Dynamic History of Modern Chinese Language Education). Kunming, PRC: Yunnan Educational.

Connor, Ulla, and Robert B. Kaplan. 1987. *Writing Across Languages: Analysis of L2 Text.* Reading, MA: Addison-Wesley.

Connor, Ulla, and Janice Lauer. 1988. "Cross-Cultural Variation in Persuasive Student Writing." In *Writing Across Languages and Cultures: Issues in Contrastive Rhetoric,* ed. Alan C. Purves, 138–59. Newbury Park, CA: Sage.

Eagleton, Terry. 1991. *Ideology: An Introduction.* New York: Verso.

Fagan, Edward R., and Peggy Cheong. 1987. "Contrastive Rhetoric: Pedagogical Implications for the ESL Teacher in Singapore." *RELC: A Journal of Language Teaching and Research in Southeast Asia* 18 (1): 19–31.

Gregg, Joan. 1986. Comments on "Academic Writing and Chinese Students: Transfer and Developmental Factors." *TESOL Quarterly* 20 (2): 354–58.

Hoffman, Frederick J. 1965. "Dogmatic Innocence: Self-Assertion in Modern American Literature." In *Innocence and Power: Individualism in Twentieth-Century America,* ed. Gorden Mills, 112–25. Austin: University of Texas Press.

Jensen, Vernon J. 1987. "Teaching East Asian Rhetoric." *Rhetoric Society Quarterly* 17 (2): 135–49.

Johnson, Donna M., and Duane H. Roen. 1989. *Richness in Writing: Empowering ESL Students.* New York: Longman.

Kaplan, Robert B. 1988. "Contrastive Rhetoric and Second Language Learning: Notes Toward a Theory of Contrastive Rhetoric." In *Writing Across Languages and Cultures: Issues in Contrastive Rhetoric,* ed. Allan C. Purves, 275–304. Newbury Park, CA: Sage.

———. 1966. "Cultural Thought Patterns in Inter-cultural Education." *Language Learning* 17 (1/2): 1–20.

Laotzu. 1963. *Dao De Jing.* Trans. D. C. Lau. Harmondworth, England: Penguin.

LeFevre, Karen. 1987. *Invention as a Social Act.* Urbana, IL: National Council of Teachers of English.

Leki, Ilona. 1992. *Understanding ESL Writers: A Guide for Teachers.* Portsmouth, NH: Boynton/Cook.

Mao, Tsetung. 1967. "Oppose Stereotyped Party Writing." In *Selected Works of Mao Tsetung,* Trans. and ed., 53–68 Foreign Languages Press. Beijing, PRC: People's.

Matalene, Carolyn. 1985. "Contrastive Rhetoric: An American Writing Teacher in China." *College English* 47 (8): 789–808.

Mo, J. C. 1982. "A Study of English Reading Comprehension from the Point of View of Discourse Function." *English Teaching and Learning* 6 (3): 39–48.

Oliver, Robert T. 1971. *Communication and Culture in Ancient India and China.* Syracuse, NY: Syracuse University Press.

Regamey, Constantin. 1968. "The Individual and the Universal in East and West." In *The Status of the Individual in East and West,* ed. Charles A. Moore, 503–18. Honolulu: University of Hawaii Press.

Reid, Joy M. 1984. "ESL Composition: The Linear Product of American Thought." *College Composition and Communication* 35 (4): 449–52.

Salzman, Mark. 1986. *Iron and Silk.* New York: Vintage.

Saville-Troike, Muriel. 1989. *The Ethnography of Communication: An Introduction.* 2nd ed. New York: Blackwell.

Shen, Fan. 1989. "The Classroom and the Wider Culture: Identity as a Key to Learning English Composition." *College Composition and Communication* 40 (4): 459–66.

Soothill, William E., trans. 1968. *The Analects of Confucius.* New York: Paragon.

Tsao, Feng-fu. 1990. "Linguistics and Written Discourse in Particular Languages: Contrastive Studies: English and Chinese (Mandarin)." *Annual Review of Applied Linguistics* 11: 99–117.

Wang, Chun. 1950. *Zuo Wen Zha Ji* (A Miscellany on Composition). Beijing, PRC: The Worker.

Van Niekerk, Barend. 1987. *The Cloistered Virtue: Freedom of Speech and the Administration of Justice in the Western World.* New York: Praeger.

Zhang, Jinfan. 1990. "A Comprehensive Discussion of China's Ancient Civil Services." *Social Sciences in China* 2: 35–58.

Zhang, Yiping. 1938. *Zuo Wen Jiang Ping* (Lectures on Composition). Shanghai, PRC: Beixian.

PUNCTUATION AND MECHANICS

The parts of *The Bedford Handbook* on punctuation and mechanics present explanations of how these conventions affect writers' goals. Students typically encounter rules for punctuation or mechanics only when they have not used them appropriately, and too often instructors ask students to learn how to use them through exercises, drills, and rote memorization. The handbook's presentation of these conventions suggests that students should avoid the counterproductive approach of trying to apply all of the rules every time they write. Instead, students should consider ways to focus on appropriate use of conventions at particular stages of the revision process.

Writing teachers regularly face the challenge of convincing students to attend to conventional uses of punctuation and mechanics, even after teachers have conducted "error analyses" and determined the most effective strategies that students might consider as they revise. The following selection offers one example of an effective way to think about sentence-level conventions: consider them in the larger rhetorical contexts of purposeful writing for particular audiences. In particular, the article included below challenges teachers to reconsider their perceptions about teaching the basics and asks them to consider the following questions:

- How can teachers invite students to think differently about conventions such as punctuation or mechanics?
- How can teachers reconsider teaching methods? What approaches can they consider?

WHAT GOOD IS PUNCTUATION?

Wallace Chafe

[Center for the Study of Writing Occasional Paper No. 2. Berkeley: Center for the Study of Writing, 1985. ERIC ED 292 120.]

A professor in the Department of Linguistics at University of California–Santa Barbara, Wallace Chafe is coauthor (with Jane Danielewicz) of "Properties of Spoken and Written Language," a chapter in *Comprehending Oral and Written Language* (1987). His most recent work is *Discourse, Consciousness, and Time: The Flow and Displacement of Conscious Experience in Speaking and Writing* (1994). An expanded version of the selection that follows appeared in *Written Communication* in 1988 under the title "Punctuation and the Prosody of Written Language."

Both articles resulted from Chafe's research on the differences between speaking and writing. He suggests that instructors consider supplementing their presentation of punctuation rules by teaching students to relate punctuation to the "sound of written language." This would encourage students to be more conscious of punctuation as a stylistic option that can contribute to the effectiveness of their writing.

There are few people whose heart will skip a beat at the thought of punctuation. For sheer excitement, punctuation ranks well below spelling, which at least lends itself to interesting games and contests. At best, it seems to be a necessary evil. Since it is present in all normal English writing, anyone who is going to write English needs to learn to use it in an acceptable way, but it is seldom mentioned as an important ingredient of good writing. Interestingly, in the early nineteenth century those in the printing profession believed they knew more about how to punctuate than their authors did. A book called *The Printers' Manual* published in London in 1838 "laments the ignorance of most writers in the art of punctuation and fantasizes about a world in which authors turn in manuscripts with no punctuation at all, leaving that chore to the professional competence of the compositors" (Shillingsburg, 1986, p. 60).

Even if we might now be willing to admit that punctuation is not exactly in a class with setting type, and that authors are best allowed to have some control over it, it continues to suffer from a popular reputation as something that is arbitrary, unmotivated, and governed by rules that make no particular sense. In short, it is in a class with "grammar." Perhaps it is even a part of grammar, but certainly not one of the more interesting parts.

There is a centuries old debate over whether, or to what extent, punctuation is in fact determined by grammar, or whether its primary function is rather to signal the "prosody"—the patterns of pitch and stress and hesitations—that authors have in mind when they write and that readers attribute to a piece of writing. Prosody is an obvious property of *spoken* language, where it takes only a moment of listening to confirm the presence of pitch changes, stresses, and hesitations. But what could it mean to say that these same features are present in written language too? Is not writing something that we see, rather than hear?

Some who have reflected on their own personal experiences in reading and writing have concluded that written language does actually involve a mental image of sound. Just as people can imagine what some familiar piece of music sounds like, readers and writers seem to be able to imagine how writing sounds. Eudora Welty, in her autobiographical book *One Writer's Beginnings*, put it this way: "Ever since I was first read to, then started reading to myself, there has never been a line read that I didn't *hear*. As my eyes followed the sentence, a voice was saying it silently to me. . . . My own words, when I am at work on a story, I hear too as they go, in the same voice that I hear when I read in books. When I write and the sound of it comes back to my ears, then I act to make my changes. I have always trusted this voice." If we can assume that Welty's observations capture something real and important, then the ways writers manage prosody can have an important effect on their writing.

To return to the debate over whether punctuation reflects grammar or whether it has more to do with the prosody of this inner voice, one reason for the inconclusiveness of the debate is the fact that, in the majority of cases, prosody and grammar support each other. Whether the period at the end of a sentence means, "This is the end of a sentence" (signaling something grammatical), or whether it means, "This is where there is a falling pitch and a pause" (signaling something prosodic) may be difficult to decide, since usually both things are true. There are some cases, to be sure, where grammar dictates the presence or absence of punctuation, whereas prosody does the reverse. When one looks at such cases in actual writing, one finds that sometimes grammar has its way, sometimes prosody. There is no clear answer to which predominates, but it is prosody that gives expression to that inner voice.

If we listen a little more carefully to spoken language and its prosody, we find that it is typically produced in brief spurts, each showing a coherent pitch contour and usually followed by a pause. (For more on these spurts and their significance, see Chafe, 1987a.) It is of some interest that these spoken "intonation units" are nicely reflected in the punctuation units of much good writing. (By "punctuation unit" I mean the stretches of language that are separated by punctuation marks.) Notice how Herman Melville used commas, semicolons, and periods to create this effect in *Moby Dick*. I have written the punctuation units on separate lines to emphasize their nature:

1. The prodigious strain upon the mainsail had parted the weather-sheet,
2. and the tremendous boom was now flying from side to side,
3. completely sweeping the entire after part of the deck.
4. The poor fellow whom Queequeg had handled so roughly,
5. was swept overboard;
6. all hands were in a panic;
7. and to attempt snatching at the boom to stay it,
8. seemed madness.
9. It flew from right to left,
10. and back again,
11. almost in one ticking of a watch,
12. and every instant seemed on the point of snapping into splinters.

This example typifies much nineteenth-century writing by including instances of punctuation that are not in accord with grammatically based rules. Most obvious is the fact that the commas and the ends of lines 4 and 7 separate a subject from a predicate, where conventional grammar would not countenance such a separation. But if one thinks of how this passage *sounds* as one reads it to oneself, and presumably as Melville imagined it to himself, the punctuation quite plausibly reflects his prosodic intentions.

Other literature, however, provides us with many examples where punctuation, or the lack of it, seems not to reflect the way the writing sounds. Take, for example, the following long unpunctuated sequence from James Agee's *A Death in the Family*, where a reader may have some difficulty restraining the impulse to insert a few prosodic boundaries:

> He has been dead all night while I was asleep and now it is morning and I am awake but he is still dead and he will stay right on being dead all afternoon and all night and all tomorrow while I am asleep again and wake up again and go to sleep again and he can't come back home again ever any more but I will see him once more before he is taken away.

Doubtless Agee was trying to achieve an effect of breathlessly tumbling, silent ideas. That kind of effect, however, is possible only in writing, and it removes writing from the link with spoken prosody that is so clear in Melville.

The Melville and Agee examples were produced about a hundred years apart, but we can easily find examples of contemporary writing that differ in similar ways. To illustrate with two extremes, there is a marked contrast between the punctuation of the text of a recent automobile advertisement in *Time*:

> Town road.
> The longest straightaway on the course.
> The 16-valve,
> intercooled,
> turbocharged engine,
> capable of doing 130 and more on a test track,
> reaches its mandated maximum of 35 mph and purrs nicely along at that speed.

and the punctuation of a recent scholarly article regarding "paleodemography":

> Persons familiar with the problems inherent in the estimation of demographic parameters for living human groups characterized by small size and a lack of census records should scarcely be surprised to find that paleodemography is controversial.

We can see, then, that writers of different periods as well as of different contemporary styles use punctuation in different ways. Is this because their prosodic intentions are so different, or is it because they differ in the degree to which they make use of punctuation to express their intentions? Both factors undoubtedly play a role, but I will focus here on the second: the assertion that styles of writing are distinguished by the degree to which their punctuation captures the prosody of the inner voice.

Putting things in this way implies that we can have some independent knowledge of the prosody of inner voice, so that we can compare it with a writer's punctuation in order to determine whether that punctuation expresses it well or badly. But how can we know about the inner voice except through punctuation? One way to make it overt might be through reading aloud. In a sense, reading aloud turns written language into spoken language, giving it a prosody that anyone can hear. To see what a systematic investigation along these lines would offer, we listened to tape recordings of a number of people reading aloud various passages of different styles (see Chafe, 1987b, for further details). It was found that they divided the passages into intonation units much like those of normal speech, regardless of how the passages had been punctuated. For example, the Agee passage was divided in the following way by most oral readers:

> He has been dead all night,
> while I was asleep,
> and now it is morning,
> and I am awake,
> but he is still dead,
> and he will stay right on being dead,
> all afternoon,
> and all night,
> and all tomorrow,
> while I am asleep again,
> and wake up again,
> and go to sleep again,
> and he can't come back home again,
> ever any more.
> But I will see him once more,
> before he is taken away.

The average length of these intonation units was just under five words. Five or six words is the typical length for intonation units in ordinary spoken English.

If oral readers create intonation units much like those of speech, regardless of how a passage was punctuated, they show us the degree to which an author punctuated in a spoken-like way. Thus, the automobile advertisement quoted above could be said to be very spoken-like in its punctuation, whereas the Agee passage was very unspoken-like in this respect. Reading aloud can also show associations between specific punctuation marks and specific pitch contours. For example, periods are almost always read aloud as falling pitches (suggesting the end of a declarative sentence), whereas commas are usually read aloud as nonfalling pitches (suggesting that more is to follow).

But it is not necessarily the case that people read something aloud the same way they read it to themselves. Reading aloud is subject to various constraints, both physical and psychological. A speaker has to breathe, for example, and there is a practical limit on how fast one can say something. There seem also to be some mental limitations on the speed with which one can process speech. The inner voice of written language may be freer of these constraints, with the result that more can be included in a written punctuation unit than in a spoken intonation unit. We asked some other readers, instead of reading these passages aloud, to "repunctuate" them, that is, to insert their own punctuation into versions from which the original punctuation had been removed. These repunctuated versions showed us the extent to which the authors had punctuated in ways their readers regarded as appropriate. They also provided clues as to how readers chose between the dictates of grammar and prosody.

The difference between those who read the passages and those who repunctuated them can be illustrated with a brief excerpt from Henry James (taken from *The Turn of the Screw*). James wrote at one point:

> We were to keep our heads if we should keep nothing else—

Most of the people who read this little excerpt aloud, in spite of the fact that they were looking at the original punctuation, inserted a prosodic boundary after the word "heads." That is, they read it as if the punctuation had been:

> We were to keep our heads, if we should keep nothing else—

In splitting this fragment into two six-word segments, these oral readers were adhering to the five- or six-word limit of spoken intonation units. But the silent readers who repunctuated this passage, even though they did not see the original punctuation, agreed with James: Most of them left the passage whole.

Why did both James and his silent readers prefer a punctuation unit twelve words long, twice the normal length of a spoken intonation unit? They probably were not just being slaves to punctuation rules. In another study writers were found to insert commas before subordinate clauses about 40 percent of the time (Chafe, 1984). Probably it is relevant that very little in this excerpt was "new," in the sense of information being brought up for the first time. Just before this James had written:

> . . . we were of a common mind about the duty of resistance to extravagant fancies.

To then write "we were to keep our heads" was to repeat the idea of a "resistance to extravagant fancies," clarifying it and reinforcing it by wording it in a different way. And then to add "if we should keep nothing else" was only to emphasize the resolve by saying that this was the one essential thing to do. The passage in question does little more than strengthen an idea that had already been expressed in the passage before it. In writing, it seems that passages which express little in the way of new information can be all of a piece. Silent readers can absorb them without the need to split them apart. Speakers, locked into the more rigid requirements of spoken language, are more comfortable with a prosody that keeps things shorter. If, among the silent readers, some wish to follow a more leisurely pace, they are free in this example to interpret the conjunction "if " as a prosodic boundary in their own inner prosody. But neither James nor most of his readers saw any need to make this option explicit by inserting a comma.

What does such a study suggest with regard to the teaching of writing? Above all, it suggests how important it is for writers to pay attention to their inner voices. Good writers, whether or not they realize it, *listen to what they write*. They listen while they are writing, and even more importantly they listen while they are reading what they wrote in order to make changes. Paying attention to the sound of written language is absolutely essential to the effective use of punctuation.

It may be a little harder to be a writer these days than it was in the days of Thoreau and Melville. Then, writers were skilled in imagining how something would sound if it were read aloud, and they punctuated accordingly. The trick was to use punctuation marks as if they were stage directions for effective oral presentation. Whether or not these authors specifically intended their works to be read aloud, they punctuated as if that were their intention.

Reading aloud is not so much in fashion any more, nor is punctuation that is based on what reading aloud would sound like. If, as is currently assumed, most reading is going to take place silently and rapidly, more language can be assimilated within single acts of comprehension. A result is the current tendency for longer punctuation units, and for leaving more of a prosodic interpretation up to the reader, allowing the grammar to give prosodic options. This is the style often referred to nowadays as "open" punctuation.

Contemporary writing actually exhibits a broad variety of punctuation styles, so that accomplished writers need to be able to punctuate in ways that are appropriate to whatever kinds of writing they may be doing. An advertising copy writer who punctuated like a professor would soon be out of work, and a professor who punctuated like a nineteenth-century novelist would find journal editors deleting commas right and left.

Students, in addition to being sensitized to their inner voices, will benefit from knowing the range of punctuating options that are available, and from being shown, through examples, what is most appropriate to one style and another. They can learn from practice in writing advertising copy as well as the more academic kinds of exposition, and from experimenting with fiction that mimics the very different punctuation styles of, say, Melville and Agee. At the same time, developing writers need to know that there are certain specific rules for punctuating that violate the prosody of their inner voices, and that simply have to be learned. These arbitrary rules are few in number and well defined, and to learn them need be no burden. The rules themselves may be appropriate to some styles and not to others. For example, the rule against placing a comma between a subject and predicate, violated so often by nineteenth-century writers, was also safely ignored by the person who wrote the following for the outside of a cereal box:

> Two cups of Quaker 100% Natural Cereal mixed with a little of this and a little of that, make the best cookies you've tasted in years.

The bottom line is that punctuation contributes substantially to the effectiveness of a piece of writing, and that its successful use calls for an awareness of something that is, for this and other reasons, essential to good writing: a sensitivity to the sound of written language.

References

Chafe, Wallace. 1984. "How People Use Adverbial Clauses." *Proceedings of the Tenth Annual Meeting of the Berkeley Linguistics Society.*

Chafe, Wallace. 1987a. "Cognitive Constraints on Information Flow." In Russell Tomlin (ed.), *Coherence and Grounding in Discourse.* Amsterdam: John Benjamins.

Chafe, Wallace. 1987b. "Punctuation and the Prosody of Written Language." Technical Report No. 11, Center for the Study of Writing, Berkeley.

Shillingsburg, Peter L. 1986. *Scholarly Editing in the Computer Age: Theory and Practice.* Athens: University of Georgia Press.

Welty, Eudora. 1983. *One Writer's Beginnings.* New York: Warner Books.

PART NINE

CRITICAL THINKING

Although the overall theoretical approach to writing and to writing instruction that informs *The Bedford Handbook* invites students to exercise their critical-thinking skills throughout the composing process, Part Nine of the Handbook focuses specifically on several of the more prominent dimensions of critical thinking. The idea of teaching critical thinking, of promoting and enabling critical literacy, has gained considerable visibility and credibility over the past two decades, especially with the ever increasing quantity of text and images that circulate through electronic media, including the Internet. But thinking critically has been part of the rhetorical tradition from the beginning. Critical analyses of rhetorical situations, purposeful and judicious choices of argumentative strategies, careful construction of reasonable arguments—these are only a few of the ways that contemporary approaches to teaching composition encourage writers to develop their critical-thinking faculties.

The readings included below address questions that confront teachers who are trying to help students become careful, critical readers and recognize and employ responsible argumentation strategies, both of which are important and necessary components for developing critical consciousness.

- How can teachers help students develop critical reading skills? How can teachers help students approach their reading (and writing) as though they were engaging authors and readers in conversation?
- How can teachers help students expand their understanding of *argument* to include not only confrontation and conflict but also critical inquiry, sustained deliberation, and responsible cooperation? How can teachers help students think of argumentation as a deliberative and generative process?
- How does technology affect the teaching of critical-thinking skills and strategies?

CONVERSATIONS WITH TEXTS:
READING IN THE TEACHING OF COMPOSITION

Mariolina Salvatori

[*College English* 58 (April 1996): 440–54.]

Associate professor of English at the University of Pittsburgh, Mariolina Salvatori teaches and does research in hermeneutics, composition, literacy, and pedagogy. She is particularly interested in exploring the transactions of knowledge and the relations between teachers, students, and texts that different theories of reading make possible. She has published numerous articles and chapters on composition and teaching and has written on twentieth-century Italian literature, literary perceptions of aging, and the immigrant experience. Most recently Salvatori has studied the iconographic literacy of ex-votos and reading difficulties students experience as sources of potential understanding. She is the author of *Pedagogy: Disturbing History, 1819–1929* (1996) and coeditor of *Reader: Essays in Reader-Oriented Theory,* and *Pedagogy;* since 1999, she has been a Carnegie Scholar.

Engaging students in active critical thinking helps them think of reading and writing as conversation with readers and writers. In this article, Salvatori builds on the notion of critical reading as conversing with a text, observing that readers have the "tremendous responsibility of giving a voice, and therefore a sort of life, to the text's argument." Writers have "the responsibility of writing a text that asks (rather than answers) questions, that proposes (rather than imposes) arguments, and that therefore makes a conversation possible." In a teacher-student relationship, teachers have a responsibility to converse with students' writing; but students have a responsibility to make that conversation possible. After providing a brief historical context, Salvatori traces the theoretical connections between reading and writing, and then she offers an example of how she teaches the interconnectedness of reading and writing.

> The art of dialectic is not the art of being able to win every argument. . . . Dialectic, as the art of asking questions, proves itself only because the person who knows how to ask questions is able to persist in his questioning. . . . The art of questioning . . . i.e. the art of thinking . . . is called "dialectic," for it is the art of conducting a real conversation. . . . To conduct a conversation means to allow oneself to be conducted by the object to which the partners in the conversation are directed. It requires that one does not try to out-argue the other person, but that one really considers the weight of the other's position . . .
>
> – Hans-Georg Gadamer, *Truth and Method* (330)

Here Gadamer is writing about face-to-face conversations; but he does so in order to articulate the rules and the workings of other inaudible conversations, those that readers make happen as they read. Gadamer theorizes reading as a "hermeneutical conversation with a text"—a conversation that can only begin and be sustained if and when the reader/interlocutor reconstructs and critically engages the "question," or the argument, that the text itself might have been occasioned by or be an answer to. He writes, "Texts . . . have to be *understood,* and that means that one partner in the hermeneutical conversation, the text, is expressed only through the other partner, the interpreter" (349; emphasis added). This view of reading enables us to imagine a text's argument not as a position to be won and defended by one interlocutor at the expense of another, but rather as a "topic" about which interlocutors generate critical questions that enable them to reflect on the meaning of knowledge and on different processes of knowledge formation. Thus a text's argument can function as a fulcrum that brings parties (reader and text) together. But for this to happen a reader must accept and carry out the tremendous responsibility of giving a voice, and therefore a sort of life, to the text's argument. Although Gadamer does not point it out explicitly, a corollary to the reader's responsibility is the writer's responsibility, the responsibility of writing a text that asks (rather than answers) questions, that proposes (rather than imposes) arguments, and that therefore makes a conversation possible. And although Gadamer's subjects are expert readers and writers, what he has to offer those of us who teach as yet inexperienced readers and writers is, I believe, very valuable. Gadamer's emphasis on the reader's responsibility, for example, makes me think of the tremendous and delicate responsibility I have as reader of my students' arguments. But it also makes me think of the corollary to my responsibility, a student's responsibility to write argument in ways that allow a reader to converse with it. To teach students to assume and to exercise this responsibility is indeed very difficult. Nevertheless, I will suggest, they can learn to exercise this sophisticated practice of writing in the process of learning to understand and to appreciate the effects of writing on themselves as readers.

What follows is an argument on behalf of the theoretical and practical appropriateness of using "reading" as a means of teaching "writing." The word "argument" has multiple resonances here: my essay enters an ongoing argument or debate about the place of reading in the composition classroom (see for instance Gary Tate's and Erika Lindemann's recent essays in *College English*), and the arguments of texts are at the same time central to the particular understanding of reading and of teaching reading that I propose.

Historical Context

In 1974, in *Teaching Composing: A Guide to Teaching Writing as a Self-Creating Process*, William E. Coles argued against the use of reading in the composition classroom. He wrote:

> So we decided to get rid of everything that teachers and students alike are tempted to look at writing from behind or through or under. The anthology went; so did the standard plays, novels, poems. (2)

I remember, when I read these lines for the first time in the early 1980s, how struck I was by what seemed a peculiar and arbitrary decision. In 1992, in the process of composing a paper to be delivered at the Conference on College Composition and Communication, I returned to Coles's text and for reasons that have to do with the kind of work I had done in the interim—mainly, my historical research in pedagogy, and my work with hermeneutics and the phenomenology of reading—I was able to read and to respond to this passage differently. In that paper (of which this essay is a revision) I myself returned to a subject that, though central to my intellectual formation as a compositionist, and central to my undergraduate and graduate teaching, I had not written about for some time. The paper was my attempt to understand which theoretical and institutional forces had led first to the separation and subsequently to the integration of the activities of reading and writing in the composition classroom. Focusing on the juncture of the theoretical and the institutional gave me a vantage point from which I was able to conjecture and to reconstruct the "argument" that had led Coles to make what had seemed to me such an iconoclastic gesture. This time, rather than judging Coles's statement as a blanket and arbitrary indictment of the presence of "reading" in composition classrooms, I began to see in his gesture a specific denunciation of what reading had been reduced to within *the teaching of composition* (but also within the teaching of literature, which problematically was and remains the model for much of the teaching of reading done in composition classrooms). I began to see that what Coles was indicting was a particularly enervated, atrophied kind of reading. A reading immobilized within textbooks, and reduced therein to sets of disparate simplifying practices that, separated from the various theories that motivate them, turn into meaningless and arbitrary exercises: reading for "the main idea," for "plot," for "argument," for "point of view," for "meaning," for "message"—interchangeably and without knowing what for. Or reading texts, especially literary texts, as inscrutable and unquestionable "models" of style or rhetorical strategies. Or as "blueprints" for linguistic theories, or political programs, or philosophies of language. I began to see, *through* Coles, the effects of practices that restrain students and teachers from asking questions of a text other than the ones the textbooks have already "gridded." I began to see, *with* Coles, why the kind of writing that these texts and their "facilitating" questions would foster could be nothing but "canned" or "theme" writing. This I understood to be the "problem" of reading that Coles was attacking, and for which he proposed, as a "pharmakon," getting rid of antho-logies, plays, novels, poems, and replacing them with the text of the assignments and of the writing that students did in response to them.

Considering the position of composition in the academy in 1974, both inside and outside departments of English; considering the available work force of teachers of composition at the time; considering that the services of composition were in growing demand; considering the perceived need for compositionists to define their discipline on their own terms—considering all this, Coles's appar-ently "disciplinarian" act can be read, perhaps, as a stern act of self-discipline. That act, set in motion by a confluence of institutional needs, theoretical posi-tions, and programmatic divisions, had a lasting influence. Moreover, in complex ways, it encouraged or catalyzed other compositionists' felt need for a theory and practice of the reading-writing relation that would include the teacher's reading of student writing.

In the 1980s, Coles's move was challenged by some compositionists who shared his concern for student writing as the center of attention in the composition classroom. Rather than turning away from reading, however, these composi-tionists turned *to* theories of reading that seemed to offer fresh perspectives.

A 1985 essay by John Clifford and John Schilb, "Composition Theory and Literary Theory," reviewed the work of literary theorists who made it possible to imagine the teaching of literature and composition, reading and writing, as in-terconnected disciplines. Clifford and Schilb assessed the influence of reader-response poststructuralist theories and rhetoric and examined the work of those compositionists and literary critics who, they argued, offered ways of thinking about reading and writing that would elide programmatic and disci-plinary separations (to name a few: Susan Miller, Richard Lanham, Ross Win-terowd, Wayne Booth, Nancy Comley and Robert Scholes, and Terry Eagleton). Though remarkably different from one another, these theorists share a concern with *acts* rather than *facts* of reading (Ray). Instead of being seen as an intru-sion onto the field of composition, or a pretext for paying attention to something other than students' writing, as in the thinking of the 1970s, reading, re-seen in the 1980s through new theories and practices, was now appealed to as a means of "bridging the gap" between the two activities and disciplines, a way of paying attention to reading and writing *differently*. But, I wish to argue, to set the two arguments side by side is to realize what either position may in debate unwittingly end up obscuring: that "the question of reading in the teaching of composition" is not merely the question of whether reading should or should not be used in the composition classroom. The issue is *what kind of reading* gets to be theorized and practiced. (Even if it were true that certain aspects of reading would always remain mysterious, teachers would still need to attend most closely to those aspects of reading which are not cloaked but can be made visible.) This issue cannot be critically and reflexively engaged apart from the following interconnected questions: (1) Which theories of reading are better suited to teaching reading and writing as interconnected activities? (2) What is the theoretical justification for privileging that interconnectedness? (3) How can one teach that interconnectedness?

Theories of Reading and Writing as Interconnected Activities

Not all theories of reading are suited to uncovering and enacting the inter-connectedness of reading and writing. Among those least suited to doing so are those that construct writers as visionary shapers of meanings, and their works as venerable repositories for those meanings (such theories generally discourage or consider inappropriate a reader's critical response to a text, particularly the response of an inexperienced reader); theories that construct as mysterious and magical the complicated processes of thinking on which writing imposes provisional order and stability (I am thinking here of critics/theorists as different as Benedetto Croce and Georges Poulet); and theories with unquestioned and unquestionable interpretive frames reducing texts to various thesis statements—cultural, political, religious, and so on. What I find objectionable in these theories is that they make it possible to cover over the processes by which knowledge and understanding are produced. By making it impossible to recapture and learn from the complex processes that have given a written text its particular shape, these theories, in different ways and for different reasons, simultaneously glorify reading and proclaim its unteachability. In classrooms where these theories of reading are unreflexively performed *for* students, where reading materials are used as mere pretexts for writing exercises, a *student's* reading of those materials may become *secondary* in at least two ways: it may become less important than the writing it produces; it may be constructed as needing to rely on a series of simplifying practices generated by somebody else. Such uses of reading as a means of teaching writing can indeed be arbitrary, questionable, even counterproductive.

In contrast with these notions about reading are theories that posit the possibility and the advantages of exploring the complex processes by which "reading" gives a voice to an otherwise mute "writing"; theories that turn texts and readers into "interlocutors" of each other; theories that interrogate rather than mystify the "naturalness," the mystery; and the interpretive "framing" both of the reading and of the writing processes. Such theories make it possible to claim not only that reading can be taught, but also that it can be taught as an opportunity to investigate knowledge-producing practices. Rather than divining a text's meaning or making a text subservient to preestablished significations, such theories construct reading as an activity by means of which readers can engage texts responsibly and critically. *Responsibly,* that is, in ways that as far as possible make *those* texts speak, rather than speak *for* them or make them speak *through* other texts. And *critically*—in ways, that is, that demand that readers articulate a reflexive critique both of the argument they attribute to those texts and of the argument they compose as they respond to those texts. (Among theorists of reading who, in different ways, provide such possibilities are Hans-Georg Gadamer, Wolfgang Iser, M. M. Bakhtin, and Paul de Man.) However, it does not follow that these theories automatically and necessarily lead to their own rigorous enactment.

Two of the texts that in the 1980s advocated a programmatic and theoretical rapprochement of reading and writing and their attendant domains of expertise and performance—literature and composition—demonstrate what I would call a perplexing inattentiveness to moving from theorizing the interconnectedness of reading and writing to making it visible and teaching it. The texts are *Composition and Literature: Bridging the Gap,* edited by Winifred Bryan Horner, and *Writing and Reading Differently,* edited by Douglas Atkins and Michael Johnson. With a few notable exceptions (the essays by Sharon Crowley, Barbara Johnson, and Jasper Neel in *Writing and Reading Differently*), in these volumes reading and writing as interconnected activities are constructed as something that teachers do either *to* and *for* their students or for themselves and equally enlightened others—rather than something teachers do *with* their students to open up the areas of investigation that this particular focus makes possible. The interconnectedness of reading and writing (that virtual, provisional interaction between two extremely complex, invisible, imperceptible processes that can nevertheless be used to test and to foreground each other's moves) tends to be constructed as something either obvious or authorized by such an illustrious tradition—from Plato to Derrida—as not to require much explanation or articulation.

The advantages for the teaching of writing that this understanding of reading promises are ultimately invalidated. Teaching the reading/writing interconnection becomes another kind of hermetic performance, one that hides rather than reveals the processes of cognition that should be the subject of investigation and reflection. Paradoxically, these two texts end up reconfiguring the very situation that Coles was trying to avoid—approaching students' writing, and reading, "from behind or through or under" something else. Perhaps, though, what I perceive as a regrettable shortcoming of otherwise praiseworthy projects can serve an important function: it can remind us that although certain theories of reading *are* more conducive than others to teaching reading and writing as interconnected activities, to foreground and to teach—rather than just to understand—that interconnectedness is a highly constructed, unnatural, obtrusive activity—one that requires a particular kind of training that historically our educational systems and traditions have neither made available nor valorized.

Theoretical Justifications for Focusing on the Interconnectedness of Reading and Writing

I wish to suggest at least two justifications for privileging this interconnectedness. First, insofar as reading is a form of thinking (Gadamer calls it "an analogue for thinking"), written accounts of it, however approximate, can provide us with valuable insights into the ways we think. Second, learning to recapture in one's writing that imperceptible moment when our reading of a text began to attribute to it—began to produce—a particular "meaning" makes it possible to consider what leads us to adopt and to deploy certain interpretive practices. In other words, although the processes that constitute our reading and writing are essentially invisible, those processes are, in principle, accessible to analysis, scrutiny, and reflection. "The ways we think" need neither be kept shrouded in mystery, nor be reduced, in the interest of demystifying the reading process, to a bunch of technical, predictive, or authoritarian formulas. The possibility of gaining access to these processes by no means implies that they can be completely controlled or contained. Nor should they be. But through such access one might learn to account for, however approximately, and to understand, however imperfectly, how certain meanings, certain stories, certain explanations, certain interpretive frames come to be composed or adopted. Expert readers and writers have developed a kind of introspective reading that allows them to decide—as they read and as they write—when to pursue, when to revise, when to abandon a line of argument, and when to start afresh. They have devised a method of reading that, in Coleridge's words, functions as "a way or path of transit" that allows their minds "to classify" and "to appropriate" the events, the images, the thoughts they think as they read. Part of the challenge confronting us as teachers is to learn how to make it possible—within the time and institutional constraints that bind us—for students to learn to perform this kind of introspective reading. To think about reading and the teaching of reading in these terms—to think of reading, that is, as an analogue for thinking about one's own and others' thinking, about how one's thinking ignites and is ignited by the thoughts of others, justifies the presence of reading in composition classrooms not as a pretext but as a context for writing.

Teaching the Interconnectedness of Reading and Writing

It is one thing to say that, even to articulate how, reading and writing are interconnected (as most of the authors featured in *Bridging the Gap* and *Writing and Reading Differently* do); and it is another to imagine and to develop teaching practices that both enact and benefit from that interconnectedness. This approach to teaching, one that requires teachers' and students' relentless attention and reflexivity, is difficult both to initiate and to sustain. Over the years, as a teacher of both composition and literature, I have learned to deploy certain teaching strategies that simultaneously enable and force me and my students to reflect on the moves we make as readers, writers, and thinkers. I do not consider these strategies as mere applications or implementations of somebody else's theories, and as I proceed to describe some of them I do not offer them as such. Nor—an important caveat—can these strategies be lifted out of the theoretical framework I have articulated here and seen as transportable tips or prescriptions; like all strategies, they make sense, that is, are plausible and justifiable, only within the particular approach to teaching that my understanding of "the act of reading" and its connections with writing calls for. I think of these strategies as means a teacher has of exposing (that is, of making visible as well as making available to reflection and critique—her own and others') the *nexus* between the theory she espouses and the practices that theory demands.

To foreground and to exploit the interconnectedness of reading and writing, I make a point of framing reading and writing activities (formal assignments, in-class writings, journals) that ask students first to write their response to a text, second to construct a reflective commentary on the moves they made as readers and the possible reasons for them, and third to formulate an assessment of the particular text their reading produced (an adaptation of Ann E. Berthoff's double-entry journal). By means of this triadic (and recursive) sequence, I try to teach readers to become conscious of their mental moves, to see what such moves produce, and to learn to revise or to complicate those moves as they return to them in light of their newly constructed awareness of what those moves did or did not make possible. This "frame" is my attempt to imagine strategies that enact what Gadamer sees as the three pivotal and interconnected phases of reading—*erkennen, wiedererkennen,* and *berauserkennen.* It is important to note that this frame is not a "grid." Insofar as readers bring their own "presuppositions of knowledge" to the texts they read, the situations they find themselves in, and the experiences they live, and insofar as those presuppositions of knowledge will differ from one person to another, readers' readings of a text will vary.

Initially, my assignments generate considerable resistance on the part of students, mainly because they are not accustomed to performing this kind of introspective reading. When I ask of a point they made, "what made you think that?" or "how did you come to that conclusion?" they often hear reproach in my questions, in spite of my repeated efforts to explain my rationale for this approach. Occasionally students do readily learn to hear my questions as I intend them. But often they don't, and in this case I try to be extremely sensitive to any clues they offer that might make it possible for me to develop a strategy that answers the need of the moment. Here is an example.

Several years ago, one of the first times I taught Charlotte Perkins Gilman's "The Yellow Wall-Paper," I was temporarily silenced by a female student's defense of "the doctor." She was very articulate about all that the doctor had said and done, and she had come to the conclusion that the text made an argument for men's (as opposed to women's) inclination for science (medicine), and for what women had to lose when they did not abide by men's counsel. As I tried to collect myself enough to formulate a question that might make her reflect on what she had just said and why, the book in front of her caught my attention. It was highlighted, rather sparsely. I picked it up, flipped through it, and in a rare moment of extraordinary clarity I noticed that what she had marked in the text, what she had chosen to pay attention to, was everything in the text that had to do with "the doctor." She had paid little or no attention to anything else. I asked to be shown how other students had marked the text. Many had left it untouched (their reasons varied from not wanting to mark their books so that they could sell them to assuming that putting pen to page would interrupt their concentration, arrest their speed). Others had highlighted it, some methodically, others erratically. What became evident to me was that "making a mark" on a text (Bartholomae and Petrosky) was a way of reading they had been taught *not* to perform. (A historical antecedent for my attempt to read the marks on the page as traces of a method could be found in the Renaissance "adversaria" [see Sherman].)

The rest of the period was spent first discussing the marks in the text as indicating what a reader chooses to be attentive to as she or he reads a text and then focusing on three representative samples: one by the student who mainly paid attention to the character of the doctor; one by a student who chose to focus on the narrator; and one by a student who, after an initial rather random system of marking the text, focused on the various characters' responses to the wallpaper. That class made it possible for me to turn a rather mechanical "study habit"—the highlighting of a text—into a strategy, one that can make "visible" the number and the intricacy of strands in a text's argument that a reader (or an interlocutor) pays attention to, and that can show how the selection, connection, and weaving of those strands affects the structuring of the argument a reader constructs. Like any strategy, this is not effective by itself. It is a tool to be used at the appropriate moment, more as a commentary on an incipient awareness of what it means to read an argument than as a means of instructing a reader how to pay attention to somebody else's argument.

A less local strategy, one less contingent on a particular context, is the assignment of what I call the "difficulty paper." (My article "Towards a Hermeneutics of Difficulty" articulates a theoretical framework for such an assignment; note also that Dave Bartholomae and Anthony Petrosky have developed a sequence of assignments around the generative force of difficulty.) Before we discuss a text collectively, I ask students to write a detailed one-page description of any difficulty the text they have been assigned to read might have posed for them. I photocopy what I consider a representative paper and distribute it for class discussion. Then, what I try to do is guide the discussion toward an assessment of the kind of reading that names a particular feature of a text as "difficult." Does difficulty arise because a reader's expectations blind her to a text's clues? Or because the method of reading a reader is accustomed to performing will not work with this particular text? Is it exacerbated when inexperienced readers assume that difficulties are an indictment of their abilities rather than characteristic features of a text? I have repeatedly relied on this kind of assignment, not as a means to expose my students' inadequacies, but as a reflexive strategy that eventually allows them to recognize that what they perceive as "difficult" is a feature of the text demanding to be critically engaged rather than ignored. What is remarkable about this approach is that students' descriptions of difficulties almost inevitably identify a crucial feature of the text they are reading and contain *in nuce* the interpretive move necessary to handle them. They might say for example that they had "difficulty" with a text because it presented different and irreconcilable positions on an issue—their "difficulty" being in fact an accurate assessment of that text's argument.

The focus on difficulty can also be profitably used as a means of directing students' attention to the assignments by means of which many teachers suggest a possible reading of a text. Students can be asked to reflect on the kind of argument that the assignment's frame invites readers to construct about the text—and the kinds of arguments that it simultaneously closes off. Thus the focus will be not only on the difficulty of doing justice to a complex text, but also on the difficulty of adequately representing the complexity of one's response to a complex text. This exercise can help foster habits of rigorous attention to one's reading of others' positions and to one's re-presentations of them; and it can teach students (and remind teachers) to read assignments as more than sets of injunctions.

There are many ways of encouraging students to practice recursive and self-monitoring readings, and they will vary according to context, the rapport that teachers can establish with their students, the configuration of the group, the "feel" of the classroom . . . I am partial to those that can contribute to making what is imperceptible—thinking—at least dimly perceptible. Let's assume, for example, that a student writer has begun to compose a reading of a text (whether in response to an assignment, or to the "difficulty paper" instructions, or as a response of his own) that the teacher thinks might benefit from a second, more attentive reading. Perhaps the student has produced a hasty generalization or an inaccurate conclusion or an overbearingly biased and unexamined pre-understanding that made her oblivious to a text's argument. To ask that student to account for the steps she took to compose that reading, to ask her to actually *mark* which places in the text she "hooked up with" and which she merely scanned, can yield a dramatic visualization of how much of a text's argument can be erased because of preestablished conclusions or inattentiveness to the construction of that argument. Another way of putting students in a position to see the limits and the possibilities of how they choose to structure an argument is to set up a comparative analysis of two or three different papers. Focusing on the papers' introductory moves as simultaneously points of entry into a text (reading) and tentative beginnings for the arguments they will formulate (writing) helps to illuminate what difference it makes to begin a discussion of a text *there* rather than *elsewhere,* or to begin, say, with a question rather than an evaluative comment. It also helps teachers avoid interventions that focus on mistakes, on deficiencies, on what's wrong with this or that way of thinking.

The strategies I have cursorily described here represent some of the ways I choose to participate in and respond to my students' reading/thinking/writing activities. What is significant about these strategies is that they function simultaneously as heuristic devices for students (through them they learn how to perform certain reflexive moves) and as constant reminders to me that as a teacher I must demonstrate in my reading of my students' words the responsiveness and the responsibility with which I expect them to engage texts. (This does not mean that I am always successful in doing so.) It is also significant that these strategies deliberately foreground "moments of reading" to show how these determine the writing students produce, and that they privilege places that can serve as points of critical reflection on the connection between reading and writing.

Countering Objections

I want now to turn to two of the most frequently articulated academic objections to the theory and practice of reading/writing interconnectedness I have outlined. I find these objections compelling and challenging, so much so that I keep returning to them to assess how they can help me understand better the assumptions about reading that subtend them. Insofar as for the past ten years these objections have consistently complicated and forced me to reexamine my positions on reading, on writing, on teaching, on education, I cannot exclude them from an argument of which they are such an integral part.

Using the names of the programs in my department whose theoretical orientations these objections could be said to represent, I will call them the "creative writing" and the "cultural studies" positions. What follows is a composite sketch of these objections that I have gleaned from three graduate courses I teach—the "Seminar in the Teaching of Composition," "Literacy and Pedagogy," and "Reception Theories." These courses lend themselves extremely well to engaging the issue of the intellectual and programmatic division of which the question of reading in the teaching of composition is both a cause and a consequence.

In the name of (a version of) "creativity" that is constructed as *being,* and *needing to remain,* beyond analysis, some of the representatives of the "creative writing" position articulate their opposition to the rigorous introspection that the interconnectedness of reading and writing requires. When as a group we grope for ways of describing not only *what* happens when we read, but also *how* it is that we tend to construct one and not another critical response to a text, some of the graduate students who align themselves with the "creative writing" position seem willing to engage the first but not the second line of inquiry. Their descriptions of reading are often magical, mysterious. They recollect, lyrically and convincingly, scenes of instruction within which—as children or adolescents—they taught themselves to read, with passion and imagination as their motives and guides. In response to questions about the context that favored their auto-didacticism, some will describe households replete with books and talk about books—a kind of oasis of family discourse that "naturally" fostered a love of reading and writing. Others, however, will describe settings that are exactly the opposite, within which they performed a sort of heroic, individually willed—and therefore "natural" in quite a different sense of the word—form of self-education.

My aim in interrogating these moving accounts is not to devalue them or discredit their veracity, but to point out that these notions of reading may lead to approaches to teaching that are potentially elitist and exclusionary. (I develop this argument in "Pedagogy and the Academy," and more fully in *Pedagogy: Disturbing History*.) What happens when students show little cultural, emotional, or intellectual predisposition for this mystical love of reading? What kinds of responses will they write to a text they did not *love* reading? How can a teacher teach her students to perform a kind of reading that she has herself learned to perform mysteriously and magically? It is significant, I think, that when some of the readers who describe their reading processes as dream-like or intuitive are asked to read back those processes so as to gain insight into their habitual cognitive strategies, they often declare their suspicion of a process they name "critical dissecting."

The "cultural studies" position, on the other hand, objects to the focus on critical self-reflexivity as "nostalgic, reactionary, humanistic," and ultimately an ineffective educational practice. Such a focus, it is claimed, on the one hand can foster the illusion of human beings as independent, self-relying subjectivities; on the other hand, it can disseminate a pernicious account of knowledge-formation, one that exploits self-reflexivity, or a focus on method, as a tactic of avoidance, derailment, deflection. A teacher's commitment to enacting ways of reading that make it both possible and necessary for readers to reflect on and to be critically aware of how arguments—their own and others'—are constructed becomes within this critique a structured avoidance of more substantial issues. According to this critique, to focus, for example, on *how* John Edgar Wideman in "Our Time," or Alice Walker in "In Search of Our Mothers' Gardens," or Gloria Steinem in "Ruth's Song (Because She Could Not Sing It)" construct their narratives, is potentially a way of avoiding the ideological issues of race, class, and gender.

Insofar as it does not reduce "critical reflexivity" to an intentionally depoliticizing attention to form, the cultural studies position provides a salutary warning. Insofar as it does not reduce it to a version of necrophilia, the creative writing position on critical self-reflexivity as a potential blockage to action—creative or political—is compelling. But why is it that at their most oppositional, these and other critiques of self-reflexivity are predicated on a construction that turns it into an unnecessary, arbitrary, or stultifying practice?

What is so disturbing and uncomfortable about critical reflexivity? Why do the critical questioning and the introspective analysis it requires generate such suspicion and anxiety? How are we to read these responses? Do they indicate that the project of teaching reading and writing as interconnected activities is unreasonable, utopian, oblivious to the material circumstances within which it is to be carried out? Should we decide, as Coles did in the 1970s, that it might be opportune to scale down this project of reading in the composition classroom from reading the interconnectedness of reading and writing to the reading of the assignments and student papers? (What does this suggest about teachers' and students' ability to engage this task?) Does my critique of the ways most "integrationists" in the 1980s carried out the project of eliding the schism between reading and writing, literature and composition, confirm the wisdom of Coles's solution?

I see how it might be possible to answer all these questions in the affirmative. And I become despondent. My current historical work in pedagogy, work that I undertook to understand what as a foreigner I found puzzling and disturbing, namely the separation of reading from writing, the proliferation of specialized programs within departments, the reduction of pedagogy from a philosophical science to a repertoire of "tips for teaching," shows that our educational system has consistently opted for simplifying solutions every time it has been confronted with the inherent and inescapable complexity of educational issues. What I find disturbing is that decisions often made for teachers, without the participation of teachers, are subsequently read as indictments of teachers' inadequate intellectual and professional preparation. (One of the most frequently voiced reservations to my project is that "it is too difficult" to carry it out without sacrificing writing to reading.) We cannot afford not to come to terms with the consequences of these streamlining interventions. We need to acknowledge that, for reasons whose complexity we cannot deny but that we can certainly call into question, our scheme of education has consistently and repeatedly skirted the responsibility of nurturing one of the most fundamental human activities—critical self-reflexivity.

Every time I teach reading and writing as interconnected activities, I begin by declaring, by making visible, my teaching strategies and by exposing their rationale. And yet every time it is a struggle for students to see this approach to teaching not as a cynical tendency to tear apart and to discredit the ways they read and write, as an exercise in dissection, or as a paralyzing threat, but rather, the way it is meant, as an attempt at promoting engagement in the kind of self-reflection and self-awareness that they are so often expected to demonstrate but are so seldom given an opportunity to learn.

In *On Literacy,* Robert Pattison argues that the project of developing the critical mind requires "another kind of training not generally available in the American scheme of education" (176). I agree with him, and I believe that we can and must find ways of providing that kind of training even within institutional environments that are opposed to it. Let me suggest that teaching reading and writing as interconnected activities, teaching students how to perform critically, and self-reflexively, those recuperative acts by means of which they can conjecture an argument and can establish a responsible critical dialogue with it, as well as with the text they compose in response to it, might be an approach appropriate to developing the critical mind—an approach that might mark the difference between students' participating in their own education and their being passively led through it.

Works Cited

Atkins, Douglas G., and Michael L. Johnson, eds. *Writing and Reading Differently: Deconstruction and the Teaching of Composition and Literature.* Lawrence, KS: U of Kansas P, 1985.

Bakhtin, M. M. *The Dialogic Imagination: Four Essays by M. M. Bakhtin.* Ed. Michael Holquist. Trans. Caryl Emerson and Michael Holquist. Austin: U of Texas P, 1981.

Bartholomae, David, and Anthony Petrosky. *Ways of Reading: An Anthology for Writers.* 2d ed. Boston: Bedford Books, 1990.

Clifford, John, and John Schilb. "Composition Theory and Literary Theory." *Perspectives on Research and Scholarship in Composition.* Ed. Ben W. McClelland and Timothy R. Donovan. New York: Modern Language Association, 1985.

Coleridge, Samuel Taylor. "On Method." *The Portable Coleridge.* Ed. I. A. Richards. New York: Viking, 1950.

Coles, William E. *Teaching Composing: A Guide to Teaching Writing as a Self-Creating Process.* Rochelle Park, NY: Hayden, 1974.

De Man, Paul. *Blindness and Insight: Essays in the Rhetoric of Contemporary Criticism.* Minneapolis: U of Minnesota P, 1983.

Gadamer, Hans-Georg. *Truth and Method.* New York: Continuum, 1975.

———. *Philosophical Hermeneutics.* Trans. and ed. David E. Linge. Berkeley: U of California P, 1976.

Horner, Winifred Bryan, ed. *Composition and Literature: Bridging the Gap.* Chicago: U of Chicago P, 1983.

Iser, Wolfgang. *The Act of Reading: A Theory of Aesthetic Response.* Baltimore: Johns Hopkins UP, 1978.

———. *The Fictive and the Imaginary: Charting Literary Anthropology.* Baltimore: Johns Hopkins UP, 1993.

Lindemann, Erika. "Freshman Composition: No Place for Literature." *College English 55* (March 1993): 311–16.

———. "Three Views of English 101." *College English 57* (March 1995): 287–302.

Pattison, Robert. *On Literacy: The Politics of the Word from Homer to the Age of Rock.* New York: Oxford UP, 1982.

Salvatori, Mariolina. "Towards a Hermeneutics of Difficulty." *Audits of Meaning: A Festschrift in Honor of Ann E. Berthoff.* Ed. Louise Z. Smith. Portsmouth, NH: Boynton/ Cook, 1988.

———. "Pedagogy and the Academy: 'The Divine Skill of the Born Teacher's Instincts.'" *Pedagogy in the Age of Politics: Writing and Reading (in) the Academy.* Ed. Patricia A. Sullivan and Donna J. Qualley. Urbana: NCTE, 1994.

———. *Pedagogy: Disturbing History, 1819–1929.* Pittsburgh: U of Pittsburgh P, 1996.

Ray, William. *Literary Meaning: From Phenomenology to Deconstruction.* New York: Basil Blackwell, 1984.

Sherman, William. *John Dee: The Politics of Reading and Writing in the English Renaissance.* Amherst: U of Massachusetts P, 1995.

Tate, Gary. "A Place for Literature in Freshman Composition." *College English 55* (March 1993): 317–21.

———. "Notes on the Dying of a Conversation." *College English 57* (March 1995): 303–09.

MOMENTS OF ARGUMENT: AGONISTIC INQUIRY AND CONFRONTATIONAL COOPERATION

Dennis A. Lynch, Diana George, and Marilyn M. Cooper

[*College Composition and Communication* 48 (February 1997): 61–84.]

Dennis A. Lynch is an assistant professor of rhetoric and composition, director of writing programs, and a member of the graduate committee at Michigan Technological University. Most recently, his work has appeared in *Rhetoric Review.* Diana George is an associate professor in the Department of Humanities at MTU, where she teaches courses in composition pedagogy and theory, cultural studies and composition, visual representation, popular culture, and British literature. She has published many articles and chapters in composition studies, and is the author of *Reading Culture* (1995). Marilyn Cooper is an associate professor of English and director of Graduate Teaching Assistant Education at MTU. She, too, has published widely in composition studies, and her work has most recently appeared in the *Journal of Advanced Composition.*

Students often have difficulty developing responsible arguments that employ the fullest range of critical-thinking strategies. Too often, the kind of argumentation that students learn and use is one that reduces complex issues to artificial dualities, which Deborah Tannen describes as "two, and only two, diametrically opposed positions." Recognizing that this view of argument will not prepare "students to participate in serious deliberations on issues that face all of us every day," the authors of this article explore "a way of reconceiving argument that includes both confrontational and cooperative perspectives, a multifaceted process that includes moments of conflict and agonistic positioning as well as moments of understanding and communication." Their explanations and descriptions are useful, and help teachers "to see argumentation as a crucial social responsibility—an activity that requires us to position ourselves within complicated and interconnected issues."

Writing teachers have been teaching argument for decades. As a profession, we have taken generations of students through the laws of logic, the etiquette of dispute, and the lessons of preparedness only to receive in return the same stale and flat arguments on the big issues: abortion rights, gun control, affirmative action, and others just as large and just as canned. In their writings, our students fall easily into one of two camps: for or against. They cling to their original positions as if those were sacred to home, country, and spiritual identity. Too frequently absent from these debates is any real knowledge of the issue at hand as anything more than a pointless argument among people who do not care very much about the outcome—except that it is always better, in the classroom as in many other arenas, to be on the winning rather than the losing side.

We don't blame our students. Schooled, as so many of us are lately, on the heated but shallow public debates raging on such television programs as *Firing Line* and *Crossfire,* or the broadside attacks of Rush Limbaugh, or even the sleepy This-Side-Then-That-Side interviews of *MacNeil/Lehrer Newshour,* our students merely follow their models. Students have learned to argue vigorously and even angrily, but not think about alternatives, or listen to each other, or determine how their position may affect others, or see complexities, or reconsider the position they began with, or even to make new connections across a range of possible disagreements. Louis Menand points out that "[o]ne of the techniques we've perfected for screaming at one another—as the linguist Deborah Tannen has recently been complaining—is to divide every discussion, 'Crossfire'-style, into two, and only two, diametrically opposed positions, and to have the representatives of each side blast away at each other single-mindedly until interrupted by a commercial" (76). Hardly a style that will generate new, productive lines of action.

Iris Marion Young locates one source of this pattern of public discourse in what she calls interest-group pluralism. All debates over public policy in our society, she argues, are reduced to debates over the distribution of wealth, income, and material goods, and interest groups are formed to ensure that particular interests get their fair share. "Public policy dispute is only a competition among claims, and 'winning' depends on getting others on your side" (72). This distributive paradigm forces even arguments for ending nonmaterially based oppression and dominance to look like arguments to attain the selfish desires of a particular interest group. Thus, for example, arguments for affirmative action programs appear not as attempts to change unconscious stereotypes that underlie biased hiring practices but as attempts to get more jobs for minorities. Young concludes, "This process that collapses normative claims to justice into selfish claims of desire lacks the element of public deliberation that is a hallmark of the political. A politicized public resolves disagreement and makes decisions by listening to one another's claims and reasons, offering questions and objections, and putting forth new formulations and proposals, until a decision can be reached" (72–73).

What we want to work out in this essay is a way of understanding and teaching argument that prepares students to participate in serious deliberations on issues that face all of us every day. It sometimes seems, in recent arguments over argument, that we must choose between two contrasting styles of argument, competitive or collaborative, but such a decision is unnecessarily abstract and ignores the historical development of thought about argument and its role in social democratic processes. Throughout most of this century, as Andrea Lunsford and Lisa Ede argue (39), we have steadily moved away from argumentation as competition and contest. Since I. A. Richards defined rhetoric as the study of misunderstanding (thereby bringing rhetoric closer to hermeneutics), the prevailing sentiment has been in favor of a more cooperative conception of rhetoric. The ultimate aim of rhetoric should be communication, not persuasion, we are told. And later, the idea that rhetoric is epistemic and the correlate notions of rhetoric as inquiry and of writing to learn have continued the same general effort to expand rhetoric's horizons while diminishing or eliminating altogether the nasty clash of individual intentions that marks much traditional rhetorical practice and its theory.

More recently, though, some rhetoricians have begun to suspect that the whole point of argumentation is being lost in our talk about cooperation and collaboration, that we are losing the value of challenging, opposing, and resisting "the interplay of social, cultural and historical forces" that structure our lives (Bizzell, *Discourse* 284). Susan Jarratt, for example, calls for composition instructors to rethink their objections to agonistic rhetoric and conflict-based pedagogy. She acknowledges that, at this historical juncture, those who advocate a "nurturing, nonconflictual composition classroom" may feel uneasy with her suggestion ("Feminism" 120). Indeed, as bell hooks points out (*Talking Back* 53), students may not leave the class feeling all that comfortable, either. Nevertheless, Jarratt and others (among them Bizzell, Bauer, Berlin, and Fitts and France) continue to argue that teachers should take a stronger, less nurturing, and more confrontational role in the classroom—especially if the aim is to prepare students to take action in a bureaucratized world that resists change.

Peter Elbow has argued that we neutralize potential hostility by emphasizing the believing game over the doubting game. While this position encourages students to listen to each other and to think about alternatives, Jarratt points out that it also leaves unexamined the social origins of difference and untouched the existing structures of privilege and authority ("Feminism" 116–17). Students—as well-schooled in the ideology of pluralism as in the habits of popular debate—are eager to grant the right of everyone to their own opinion. A theoretical openness to other perspectives is, though, easily reversed in practice, especially when the situatedness of perspectives within established power structures is ignored, as when whites insist that blacks, or men insist that women, be more open to and accepting of their perspectives.

What we are seeking is a way of reconceiving argument that includes both confrontational and cooperative perspectives, a multifaceted process that includes moments of conflict and agonistic positioning as well as moments of understanding and communication. We want to see argument as agonistic inquiry or as confrontational cooperation, a process in which people struggle over interpretations together, deliberate on the nature of the issues that face them, and articulate and rearticulate their positions in history, culture, and circumstance. And thus we join with Jarratt in hoping for writing courses where "instructors help their students to see how differences emerging from their texts and discussions have more to do with those contexts than they do with an essential and unarguable individuality" ("Feminism" 121). Such a conception can remove argument from the (televised) boxing ring and return it not to the private domestic sphere but to the many ambiguous public spaces—meeting rooms, hallways, cafeterias, and, yes, classrooms—where it has a chance to become more productive. The question that confronts us now is, what exactly might such a conception of argument look like? What kind of activity are we trying to suggest by the admittedly difficult (if not oxymoronic) expressions "agonistic inquiry" and "confrontational cooperation"?

A New Articulation

Before we describe two different courses in which we attempted to put into practice our understanding of how argument might best be approached in first-year composition, we would like to briefly articulate the theoretical perspective that emerged as we tried to find a new paradigm for the teaching of argument.

Our concern from the start was that, without knowledge of the history behind an issue or those affected or potentially affected by it, or of the complex material causes and potential real effects of the decisions being made, classrooms could easily drive students back into a narrower kind of arguing. Jarratt, in "Feminism and Composition," shows her awareness of such a potential problem when she argues for a distinction between "eristic wrangling" and "disputation." Wrangling takes place, according to Jarratt, between people who position themselves from the start as enemies, whereas disputation acknowledges that conflict also plays a role among friends who argue with one another out of good will. Disputation, which draws on the "ability to move into different positions," should then open up the space needed for more considered judgments and disagreements.

However, the point of Jarratt's distinction often seems on the edge of slipping away, for instance, when she quotes bell hooks urging us to establish in the classroom ". . . an atmosphere where [students] may be afraid or see themselves at risk" ("Feminism" 120). If we emphasize the fear and the risk, we can see the aggressive and agonistic qualities of traditional debate returning to the classroom, together with its narrowness and simplicity. The weight placed by Jarratt on conflict, on the necessary emergence of real differences, and especially on the need for students who have been disempowered to become more "self-assertive" in the classroom may push students toward strategies of simplification as a matter of survival. But if instead we emphasize, as Jarratt later does, a classroom "in which students argue about the ethical implications of discourse on a wide range of subjects and, *in so doing, come to identify their personal interests with others,* understand those interests as implicated in a large communal setting, and advance them in a public voice" ("Feminism" 121, emphasis added), then we hear an echo of John Gage and what we have called a cooperative rhetoric of inquiry.

In an essay that in some interesting ways anticipates Jarratt's position, "An Adequate Epistemology For Composition," Gage suggests that we might clarify our disagreements over the best way to teach argument by attending to the epistemological bases of the modes of argumentation we are considering. Toward this end, he offers his own distinction among three views of argument. The first two views disconnect rhetoric from knowledge—either skeptically or positivistically—and turn it into an artifice or a vehicle. An argument, under both of these views, becomes a mere formal exercise. In the first case, unencumbered by any sense of truth or right, one concentrates on learning and employing those forms that will help one to win or survive. In the second case, one has recourse to rhetorical forms because ideas—truths—still need to be embodied and communicated: argument thus becomes a mere vehicle for leading an audience to a truth known independently of the rhetorical process. The third view, in contrast to the other two, connects rhetoric to dialectic and to the social production of knowledge, and, as we might expect, Gage associates this view with Aristotle:

> From this perspective, rhetoric aims at knowledge, or makes it available. Rather than producing persuasion without reference to truth, rhetoric aims at producing mutual understandings and therefore becomes the basis for inquiry into sharable truths. "The function of rhetoric," Aristotle asserted, "is to deal with things about which we deliberate, but for which we have no rules." ("Adequate Epistemology" 153–55)

Gage thus seeks to contain the eristic impulses within argumentation by linking argument to the production of knowledge—though disagreeing, people cooperate to make connections in the construction of "sharable truths." This is not knowledge in the modernist sense—objective and timeless truth—but a knowledge that is true only insofar as it emerges from the social, cooperative process of argumentation.

People argue, according to Gage, in order to negotiate conflicts and differences. We do not argue in order to express our inner selves or as a fun exercise, though we can approach argument in this way if we so choose. The primary function of argument, therefore, the one Young argues is necessary for public deliberation and that Gage would have us consider as teachers of writing, is to get something done in the world, including the academic world. And given the kinds of issues we tend to discuss in the academic world, according to Gage, we cannot and should not expect to rely on truths or independent formal guarantees that would render the negotiation process mechanical and easy. All we can do is come together (in some fashion), articulate our differences, listen, try hard to understand, acknowledge how thoroughgoing the differences may be, and—and here is Gage's main contribution, as he sees it—not just formulate reasons that defend our initial position, but reformulate those very positions through a process of argument ("Adequate Epistemology" 162). In other words, the real conflicts are already there at the outset of a disagreement, in the way we define the issues and set up our purposes, and thus when teachers ask students to establish their position *before* they interact with those with whom they disagree, teachers inadvertently push students to reproduce their disagreements rather than moving towards negotiated and temporary resolutions of disagreements.

Gage's approach to argument perhaps sounds closer than it probably is to the work of Jarratt, Bizzell, and others who have been critical of a humanist tradition (with its connections to Aristotle) and who look instead to postmodern theories or look behind Aristotle to the sophists. Yet even so, a lingering concern might remain for many who would read (or reread) Gage's work in the present context of composition studies: careful as he is to emphasize the thoroughly social and dialectical nature of his approach to argument, his account still lacks a fully social and political dimension. This is perhaps most visible in his characterization of conflict. When Gage sets his students up to argue with one another, the aim that he assumes will govern their efforts *is* to negotiate conflict—but the conflicts he imagines are what he calls "conflicts of knowledge." What is at stake in any argumentative situation for Gage is the current state of one's knowledge or beliefs, and even though he is careful to stress that people, not ideas, are in conflict—the "real people" that he reaches for in his account of argument often seem at the last minute to gently dissolve into mere place holders for the ideas they are committed to. The effect is especially apparent when one recalls that the conflicts our students experience are reflected in the structure of our social, political, and economic conditions—and thus are not contained in the minds of individual students. Put otherwise, the social production of knowledge that Gage so engagingly argues for remains a mostly abstract and intellectual affair because the extent to which his students enter into their arguments already positioned unequally itself remains unquestioned.

But if we hesitate to embrace the limited sense of "social" in Gage's social rhetoric of inquiry, neither are we fully satisfied with Jarratt's pedagogy of "productive conflict." In this regard, we intend our provisional and somewhat playful notion of "agonistic inquiry" to delineate an activity that is a social process of negotiating, not "conflicts of knowledge," so much as conflicts of positioning and power—conflicts in which students can discern that something is at stake, someone is affected, and someone has been silenced for reasons that can be determined.

Indeed, the differences among Gage's, Jarratt's, and our positions can perhaps better be seen in the manner in which we each describe the kind of risks we anticipate our students will face in our classrooms. In Gage's contribution to *What Makes Writing Good,* for instance, he asks his students to "risk committing yourself, if only for the time being, to an idea," and he sees such a commitment as a risk because it "means that there will be people who will not agree with you" (100). To argue is to commit yourself, not to others, but to an idea, and to be committed to an idea ensures that you will run into conflicts and disagreements with others. The risk for students, in other words, is that by connecting with an idea they will isolate themselves, which of course is what has motivated Gage's argument from the start: by risking disagreement, we stand to recoup our loss on another level, that of the social production of knowledge.

The strong focus on knowledge that Gage adopts thus threatens to hold students within a temporary state of isolation while they carefully work and rework their thesis-statements. True enough, the consideration a student gives to her opponent's position overcomes some of the effects of that isolation—but only certain intellectual effects. The fact that argumentative activity has been cut off from that which differentiates us—especially from our histories, our cultures, our various positions of power within institutions and social practices—all serves to decrease the chance that our students will feel or find new connections with those affected by an issue, especially with those whose "interests" are not readily observable within the issue as it has been divided up and handed to us historically. The possibility that traditional argumentation, even reconfigured as a rhetoric of inquiry, might still isolate students more than it connects them is finally what led Lester Faigley, in part, to explore the potential of networked classrooms—in spite of or perhaps because of their admitted messiness: "while electronic discourse explodes the belief in a stable, unified self, it offers a means of exploring how identity is multiply constructed and how agency resides in the power of connecting with others and building alliances" (199). We believe that argumentation can and should be approached in a manner that will allow this form of agency to emerge in the classroom, rather than be constrained by a particular epistemological model.

The risk Jarratt's students face is similar to the one Gage anticipates, though it is tinged with a much stronger sense of loss or threat. She also asks her students to accept the risk of encountering disagreement, to risk a public display of difference, but she anticipates much more in such a risk—much more struggle, tension, confusion, anger, embarrassment, condescension, reprisal, intractability. When Jarratt calls for a renewed commitment to "serious and rigorous critical exchange" between students, and also between teachers and students, we sense that her aim is not just to get her students to reconsider a few beliefs or opinions. Her aim is to position students in a manner that will challenge who they are—positions they might enjoy or suffer. The risk of not being connected with others, of learning that others disagree with you, thus becomes intensified for Jarratt's students, increasing the likelihood that disagreement will turn into direct challenge.

Because we are sympathetic to Jarratt's concerns—especially regarding the "unequal positioning" some people enjoy over others when arguing within institutional settings—we appreciate the urge to intensify the risks her students might experience in her classroom and the desire to make differences and disagreements more real and more risky. From our perspective, though, the risk is not merely that your social position and identity may be challenged, or not merely that someone may disagree with your intellectual position, or not even that you may lose the argument; the risk is also that you may become different than you were before the argument began. Serious argumentation requires a willingness to see things differently and to be changed in and through the dialogic process. As Gage points out, argumentation enables us to reformulate our positions through our interactions with those with whom we are in conflict; as Jarratt emphasizes, those positions are not just intellectual ones but positions of power and identity that come out of real histories.

This kind of change is not easy. In *Teaching to Transgress*, bell hooks acknowledges the pain in this process and the consequent need for teachers to show compassion:

> There can be, and usually is, some degree of pain involved in giving up old ways of thinking and knowing and learning new approaches. I respect that pain. And I include recognition of it now when I teach, that is to say, I teach about shifting paradigms and talk about the discomfort it can cause. (43)

Eloise Buker points out that the change we go through in order to understand another person or perspective is "often accomplished only through struggle," and the threat of struggle always carries with it the reflex action of retrenchment, a retreat back into isolation and defended difference. We believe that students will risk such changes only when argumentation is perceived as a social activity through which they, first and foremost, *connect* with others.

We have seen that aspects of the kind of argumentation to which we have been pointing can be found within both Gage's and Jarratt's fully articulated positions: Gage moves us toward an understanding of rhetoric as something that requires us to connect and interact with those with whom we disagree; and Jarratt insists that when we do so we must squarely confront the differences among us. Yet the pressure each puts on argumentation—as the production of knowledge (finding a sharable thesis) or as the last hope in a world of unspeakable injustices—tends to obscure these insights and thus to reduce, rather than to enhance, the chance that students will experience how argument can facilitate our "ability to move into different positions," generate new relations with others, and thus change both the inner and outer landscapes of our initial disagreements and conflicts.

Our quest to develop a new approach to teaching argumentation began, however, not with these theoretical considerations but rather developed as we together designed courses that tried to instantiate a revised sense of argument as inquiry. The two courses we describe below differ from each other in outline and content, but each course takes as its primary goal to engage students in a kind of writing that moves beyond the "opposing viewpoints," disputatious, display type of argumentation. Both courses avoid, as much as possible, rushing students to defend sides or to decide on a position. Instead, we sought to give students more time to learn and think about the issues they were engaging, with the idea in mind that in the process they will recognize that the positions we take—especially the first, easy positions that we have "accepted"—usually have been socially, culturally, and historically determined and, not coincidentally, usually have unforeseen consequences for others, others whose positions are often not even represented by the manner in which the issues are handed down to us ("pro and con").

At the same time, we wanted students to have the chance to discover that complex issues have the potential to involve us in unexpected alliances through which we can open ourselves to new possibilities and responsibilities. What we are about to offer, we acknowledge, is not so much a specific method of teaching argument that can be followed, step by step, as an approach, or a loose affiliation of approaches. Our discussion is instead meant as a part of an ongoing project we share with others to rethink the role of argument in the writing curriculum, especially as we attempt to answer the demand that our writing courses help prepare students to deal with the real conflicts that face all of us in society today.

What's Wrong with the Washington Redskins?

> What the government did to the Cherokee Indians was cruel and unusual punishment. No one should be forced off their land and then forced to travel hundreds of miles. On top of this one third of their population died along the way. Even though this type of thing would never happen in modern day, we can look back now and critique the action of the government. I feel sorry for the Indians, but if the government had not done this, America would not be what it is today. If Indians still owned most of the United States, America would be a third world country.

The first-year MTU student whose work is excerpted above is not exceptional in his assessment that bad things just happen on the road to progress. This is the sort of comment that is normal in many courses, at least in Michigan's Upper Peninsula, that deal with issues of American Indian rights or the history of westward expansion. This student was not taking such a course, however. He was in a second term composition course and was asked to write a short response to a passage from *The Education of Little Tree*. That he chose to stake out a position is less interesting to us, in our discussion of argument, than the sense we have that he feels that there is no real issue at hand. History is history. Bad things happen to good people. Let's get on with our lives. The course we will describe in the next few pages was designed partially in response to that easy way in which first-year students often seem to dismiss the many issues that surround them daily, in the news, in classes, in work situations, even in the most mundane kinds of arenas—like what to name a football team.

In this writing course, which focused on the issue of using Indian mascot names and logos for sports teams, we began working essentially from argument out: we asked students to read and to summarize two extremely opposed positions presented in two articles: "Indians Have Worse Problems," by syndicated columnist Andy Rooney, and "Crimes Against Humanity," by Cherokee activist and critic Ward Churchill. Many students found Rooney's arguments (even such claims as "American Indians were never subjected to the same kind of racial bias that blacks were," or, "While American Indians have a grand past, the impact of their culture on the world has been slight") as reasonable, even persuasive. By contrast, many were offended by Ward Churchill's charge that "the use of native names, images and symbols as sports team mascots and the like is, by definition, a virulently racist practice" (43). But by far, the most consistent response of the class, an honors section, was that the question of Indian mascot names was a non-issue. Several students, for example, wrote that demonstrations over mascot names were publicity stunts from a radical group of Indians who did not represent the majority. Moreover, the class made the charge that this issue was just another example of PC at work. Why should anyone care what a team calls itself?

It seemed to us that this was a good start for the approach to argument we had in mind. The question, "Why should anyone care?" was precisely the kind of question we wanted students to ask—and answer. Yet, at this moment in the course we also had to contend with the fact that our students were oscillating in their relation to the issue, oscillating between disengaging from the issue—calling it PC and a non-issue—and throwing themselves into a heated defense of using Indian mascot names. Clearly Ward Churchill's charges had threatened something very close to them, perhaps their loyalties to school, team, tradition, even national identity. Since team and school mascot names function to unite students' and fans' identities, in effect building both public and private loyalties, the issue of changing the name of a team can easily become tied to those and other loyalties. Such an issue threatens to polarize students as they take sides and doggedly defend their "camp"—which is precisely the behavior we had hoped to avoid. That attachment to "what is" over a willingness to debate "what might be the implications of" accounts, at least in part, for the sort of positioning we see in the passage above. To that student, America is fine as it is. This is his country. If anything else had happened, we would have some other, some less developed country—a country not his. Loyalty is a complicated bit of the puzzle of human reasoning.

What is more, an issue like the mascot one seems, for many students, to hit at political loyalties. As we noted above, by the second day of this assignment, students were already dismissing its relevance as simply another "PC debate." This turn was perhaps inevitable, for, as Gerald Graff points out, "In literature and the humanities, cultural nationalism has been the main organizing principle since the romantic period, when the doctrine became established that the quality of a nation's language and literature was the touchstone of its greatness as a nation" (151). This kind of loyalty plays itself out easily enough every time we bring cultural studies, cultural critique, or a multicultural agenda to the writing class. Such an agenda threatens nationalism. As Graff reminds us, "The rule seems to be that any politics is suspect except that kind that helped us get where we are, which by definition does not count as politics" (156). Thus, our students' easy initial acceptance of Rooney's column and their discomfort with Churchill's article. They found Rooney abrasive but acceptable and Churchill merely abrasive. (We might add here that both are openly abrasive.)

This is, of course, a paradoxical predicament for a class given over to the study of argumentation. The presumed goal is to critically examine not just one's beliefs but the decisions that are being made in our communities. The more those decisions touch students' loyalties, though, the more likely students are to retrench, not listen to others, resort to quips, and as a result lose sight of the complexity of the issue under consideration. We chose this moment of oscillation, then, to ask the students to write out (in their notebooks) their own position in this debate. Then we asked them to put that position statement away and to start a different kind of work.

At the end of the term, when they did share with their instructor that initial notebook entry, students' own inability to see any issue worth discussing here was clear. The most common reaction was anger: Indians, one student wrote, just "have to have something to cry about." They should, "GROW UP, STOP CRYING, AND GET ON WITH LIFE!" Others echoed that attitude. One admitted that when she thought of Indians, she got a picture of fat, lazy drunkards who live off the government. The class, as a whole, certainly gave the impression that they felt those arguing over mascot names were "making a big deal out of nothing." They didn't understand why anyone could get upset over such a topic. And, they felt that American Indians were simply holding onto a past they no longer had a right to. One student, for example, wrote that he lives in Keweenaw Bay, where one band of Ojibway is located, and he resents the fact that the Indians there can haul "thousands of pounds of lake trout from Keweenaw Bay with motorized boats, instead of canoes and commercially made nets, instead of hand woven ones." A few stated very simply that Indian people ought to assimilate and get it over with. Many agreed with the student who said, during class discussion, that the Indians have lost the big battle, and they have to understand what it means to lose. The instructor, by contrast, was not convinced that her students knew the many consequences of "losing." The class seemed comfortable with the status quo, unwilling to poke around into an argument they wished had never been brought up in the first place.

These vigorously negative stereotypes might surprise a few readers who see more romanticized images as the current media stereotype, especially from such recent popular programs and films as *Northern Exposure, Dr. Quinn: Medicine Woman, Pocahontas, Dances with Wolves,* and *The Last of the Mohicans,* to name a few. Jeffrey Hanson and Linda Rouse explain this kind of contradictory stereotyping of American Indians as common. They discovered that, although the students they studied reported that most of the information they have about American Indians came from the media, the stereotype they eventually formed depended on where they were living. If they lived in areas where American Indians were not a visible minority and were not competing for resources, the stereotype tended to be overwhelmingly positive and romanticized. If they lived in a region (such as South Dakota, Wisconsin, or Minnesota), where Indian people did constitute a visible minority and might compete for resources, the stereotypes were severely negative. Our students' responses to this issue are typical of the kinds of responses Rouse and Hanson discovered among students living in this part of the country.

For this section of the term, then, the class sometimes angrily argued that we had entered into a silly, even meaningless debate. They claimed no interest in and, several of them, no knowledge of the ways each side might argue their position. And, yet, when asked to list arguments from both sides of the discussion, students found it much easier to outline the position represented by Rooney than that represented by Churchill. For the instructor, that meant that either Rooney's position was the position most available in the popular press, or that students' own loyalties or stereotypes were interfering with their ability to understand other positions.

The next step in this assignment, then, was to begin investigating the many issues, questions, and concerns that surround the arguments set forth in Rooney's and Churchill's articles. In an attempt to get students beyond polarized debate, we asked them not to look for more arguments for or against using Indian mascot names. Instead, we wanted them to ask different questions— questions that would direct their attention more broadly to the people involved in the discussion, what matters to those people, and how the debate got to the Rooney-Churchill level. Then we asked them to start looking for some possible answers to these questions: Why would anyone argue over something as seemingly harmless as a name? Why does anyone think it is an issue at all? Obviously, it wasn't just an issue with Indian people, or Andy Rooney, the Cleveland Indian fans, and others would not be so resolute in their determination to keep what they considered theirs. The argument came from somewhere, and it was about something more than naming teams. Where did it come from? What was it about? Our first strategy, then, was to ask students to question the concepts they were using (the significance of naming), to situate the issue historically (how did the problem develop?), and to find analogous problems from the past in order to resist coming to closure too quickly.

For the next six weeks, the students did research that might have seemed far afield of the initial argument. Goaded by Rooney's assertion that American Indians had contributed little to contemporary culture, they learned and wrote about separate Indian cultures. In response to Churchill's question of why it seems so much easier these days to use Indian names in ways we would not use other group names, they did research on reservation schools and acculturation—along the way learning what Richard Henry Pratt meant when he declared it a necessity that "[t]he Indian must die as an Indian in order to live as a man." During this part of the course, several students did work on stereotyping and its effects. As a result, one student compared the arguments over Indian mascot names and symbols to arguments in the sixties and seventies when a number of African American stereotyped product names and logos were changed. Another student ran across articles detailing the controversy over Crazy Horse Malt Liquor and was prompted by that controversy to learn more about Crazy Horse. He had heard the name all his life and knew nothing of the man. The student who shouted in all caps to Indian people to GROW UP! found there was much more to get over than he had anticipated. After watching *In the White Man's Image*, this student wrote,

> After watching the tape on the Indian school, I was shocked when I heard an Indian voice say that after the school, they wanted to be good and live in wood houses and settle down. They taught the Indians that their old ways were bad.
> I think this is horrible. It helps to destroy the heritage of the Indians.

In his paper, he acknowledged the truth that most team supporters quite honestly do not intend to demean Indian people with mascot names, but he pointed out that the intention is not necessarily the effect. He quoted Indian activist and songwriter John Trudell who told the class, "There are a million ways to put a people down and using their names and rituals is just one way." What this student did, then, was to try to understand why some people might defend the status quo while others see it as "a virulently racist practice" (Churchill).

At the end of the term, students wrote about the experience of using argument as a tool of intellectual inquiry. In portfolio cover letters, most said they had not really changed their initial position on the argument (though now most simply said that if a name offends the group named, it ought to be dropped), and they still thought the argument was a trivial one. What had changed, however, was why they thought it trivial. In the process of questioning the issue— what matters? why does naming seem both so serious and so trivial?—they felt they had discovered other, more significant (historically and culturally informed) issues within this one. They weren't ready to give either Andy Rooney or Ward Churchill the nod in terms of who they thought had "won" this debate, but they did see something much more profound embedded within the terms of the debate. One student wrote that, far from learning to keep his opinion to himself (as he had been taught to do in high school), this work had taught him that he had to more carefully understand his position and its consequences. He wrote, "[t]he research I did for essay 3 made me want to run and tell the world how I felt about the mascot issue. So I did. I was rewarded when upon reading my paper in front of the class, everyone seemed interested in it." This was the student who had done his work on Crazy Horse.

We should add that these students did not feel compelled to take the Indians' side in this debate, either. Despite fears expressed by some that introducing political dispute into the classroom is a way of forcing students to accept the instructor's politics, our experience has been that such acceptance is neither easy nor likely. For example, in this course, one student who began the class angrily declaring that Indians had to accept the fact that they were the ones who lost, wrote,

> I feel I have succeeded in showing that one of the reasons that this topic is an issue is that the American mainstream and the Indians are two separate cultures. The two most important things that I have learned from this course [are] that it is all right to think for yourself and form educated opinions . . . [and] that you have to look at every issue from many different perspectives.

He remained steadfast in his belief that the only way for this issue to be resolved would be for Indian people to accept assimilation as a goal (a position that certainly did not reflect the instructor's politics), but he no longer thought of assimilation as an easy or natural consequence of having lost the big battle. He had, in other words, uncoupled his conclusion that Indians must accept assimilation from the myth of the big battle and reconnected it to his emerging thoughts about culture and cultural conflicts. What he makes of that achievement may well take years to fully realize.

It is true that what these students ended up writing might look less like argument, as we have come to know it, and more (depending on the student's choice of topic) like analysis. And, yet, the course does not avoid argument, either. The kind of assignment we have been describing acknowledges the flat debate then leaves it alone. At the same time, the assignment leads students to an understanding that a more complex argument might be made possible through ongoing inquiry. Too many classroom strategies, too many textbooks, insist that students learn to take hold of and argue a position long before they understand the dimensions of a given issue. We would much rather our students learn to resist doggedly defending their position too soon in the discussion. That is not to suggest that students do not hold positions very early in this process. Certainly, they do, and they most likely want to defend and keep intact those positions. We won't deny that. For the students in this class, however, their initial position statements were never used during whole-class discussion. Those early statements remained theirs to do with as they pleased. Primarily, students seemed to use them as a starting point for their research or as a way to identify questions within the broader topic of the course. As their instructors, we were more interested (and we believe the class was, too) in what students learned about the issues surrounding this debate than which side they initially took in it. Moreover, we were interested in helping students realize the complications embedded in discussions on even seemingly uncomplicated issues like what to name a football team.

A River Runs Through It

> Eventually, all things merge into one, and a river runs through it. The river was cut by the world's great flood and runs over rocks from the basement of time. On some of the rocks are timeless raindrops. Under the rocks are the words, and some of the words are theirs. I am haunted by waters.
>
> –Norman MacLean, *A River Runs Through It* (113)

Generally speaking, water is not a topic people in the upper midwest spend a lot of time thinking about, much less arguing about. Except in bad winters when water mains freeze, we don't worry much about where our water is coming from and whether we will have enough. So, when we announced to a first-year writing class that the topic we would be focusing on for the quarter was water resources, they were distinctly nonplused. But a few weeks into the course, many of them wrote comments like the following:

> Before entering HU 101, water resources rated just as high as the Royal Family on my list of importance. Now, after reading a few articles on the subject, I think about it quite often. What amazes me most about water resource management is its complexity.

Like the rivers of North America, the issue of water resources flows through a complex array of political positions and priorities in our society. From the James Bay hydroelectric project in Quebec to the California aqueduct, from the draining of the Everglades to proposals for a pipeline to pump Alaskan water to Texas, the questions of who owns the water in North America and how it should be used are the concern of agribusiness, golfers, small farmers, white-water rafters, mining companies, American Indians, fishermen, electrical companies,

environmentalists, and urban residents, among others, and the conflicting demands of these interests result in strange and shifting alliances among groups
who are often opposed on other issues. In arguing in this arena, students find
it hard to locate preconstructed positions they can accept and argue for. Instead, they must sort through and negotiate competing concerns in order to
construct a position they feel is justified and they want to defend.

Of course, any issue, including water resources, can be cast in the point-
counterpoint argument mode: America's Rivers—Should we dam them for
power or let them run free? When differences of opinion are polarized and sen-
sationalized in this way, the emphasis in argument shifts from the issue to the
skills and personalities of the combatants and the formal structures of argumentation. And while these are always a part of argument, and contribute a lot
to the enjoyment some people find in argument, focusing on stark controversies
at the expense of the complexities of an issue is also a way of evading or cover-
ing up the painful and complex problems that face us and that we must resolve
if we want to have a society that's worth living in. We wanted to show students
that arguments do matter, that the positions they take matter to them in their
daily lives, and that argument serves a useful function in society, the function
of helping us all make better decisions, together. We called the kind of writing
they would be doing deliberative discourse, not to take the focus off the differences that lead to disputation but to emphasize that such differences are legitimate and deeply felt and must be talked about in a serious way.

We were again, in this course, concerned to not push students prematurely
into taking a position on issues they knew little about and thus cared little
about. Certainly, the aim of argument is to influence specific decisions in a specific context, to recommend a particular course of action, and certainly it is the
pressure imposed by the need for specific decisions—should we enact NAFTA?
should we raise the sales tax or the income tax to finance public schools?—that
sometimes leads us to simplify what we know are complicated issues and to
wrangle over them heatedly. But this is only one moment in the activity of arguing, and in many ways the end of argument. To see this moment as the whole
of argumentative writing is to risk seeing all decisions as final, all positions as
absolute or even natural, to see argument, paradoxically, as somehow anti-
thetical to change.

It takes time to learn about an issue, to learn what you really think about it
and how it affects your life and the lives of others. On the first day, we talked
about all the ways water was important to us: in raising crops and in otherwise
providing us with food; in mining resources; in manufacturing products; in dis-
posing of waste; in transporting people and products; in providing electrical
power; in providing habitats for other species, recreational opportunities, and
spiritual relaxation; and in simply sustaining our lives. We then handed out the
assignments for the course. We asked them to write four related papers in
which they were to construct a position they believed in on a specific issue of
their choice involving water resources. The assignments were designed to give
students a chance to reflect on their ideas and arguments as they wrote and
read and discussed and rewrote; in essence, the first three papers were simply
drafts, albeit "good" drafts, steps in the process of developing a carefully considered argument for a carefully constructed position in the fourth and final
paper.

The first assignment asked them simply to explore the general issue of water
resources and their reactions to it, to find what aspects of this issue interested
them. Some of the questions we asked them to think about in this paper were:
What aspects of this issue relate to your interests and plans and how do they
relate? What experiences have you had that shape how you feel about this
issue? What aspects of the issue do you find interesting at this point and why?

What surprised you in what we have read and discussed? What else would you like to find out about this issue? The purpose here was for them to find some way to connect to the issue, whether intellectually, experientially, or emotionally.

Many of our midwestern students who personally experienced the decline of farming in this region were struck by one of Marc Reisner's conclusions in *Cadillac Desert:* "In a West that once and for all made sense, you might import a lot more meat and dairy products from states where they are raised on rain, rather than dream of importing those states' rain" (517). One student who grew up on a farm in Michigan explained that his stepfather had committed suicide when the price of milk declined and he couldn't repay his bank loans. His experience clearly affected how he responded to much of the material we looked at in the course: he was especially sympathetic to the plight of the long-term small rancher in Nevada who lost his water to the newly irrigated large farms down the valley, to the situation of the olive farmer in California who was put out of business by Prudential Insurance's cornering the market with their five-thousand acre farm near Bakersfield, and to the Hispanic farmers in *The Milagro Beanfield War* in their fight against the developers.

Other students found less heart-rending personal connections to the issues involving water. A student who lived on a lake investigated the state laws that allowed the owner of the water rights of the lake to manipulate the water level to maximize the hydroelectric power his dam could produce. A student with a passion for golf looked into water conserving designs for the abundant golf courses in western deserts. Some students were simply moved by a question of fairness: several wrote about the treatment of the Cree Indians by the developers of the James Bay hydroelectric project. And others were interested in the technological problems involved, like the students who wrote about new methods of irrigation and power generation. The students' level of commitment to the issue—and then to the position they constructed—thus varied in strength and nature, but all understood that deliberative discourse required some kind of commitment on their part.

The second assignment asked students to begin to stake out a position they found persuasive on a specific issue, although we cautioned them to discuss *all* the positions that they found persuasive and to explain how these positions might conflict with one another and how these conflicts might be resolved. We also emphasized, both in the instructions and in comments on their drafts, that this paper was only the beginning of the process of constructing a position, that they would next need to look at the position they had stated and think about such things as whether it really represented what they believed in, what sort of actions would follow from this position, whether they really found these actions to be possible and desirable, and what questions their position raised that they would need to investigate further.

When one student, a very skilled writer, handed in the first draft of this second paper, he told the instructor he had the outline of his final paper, and all he would have to do in the rest of the course was to add in a little more information from the library. He had formulated a logical problem-solution argument: since irrigated farming in the west made no economic sense, the government should buy out western agricultural concerns and subsidize the development of more agriculture in the midwest and east. When we suggested that there were a couple of serious problems with his solution, namely that the federal government most assuredly did not have the money in these times of national debt to finance such a plan, and that people who had lived and farmed in the west for generations might not appreciate having their livelihoods eliminated in this way, he said that he was ignoring these aspects of the situation for the purposes of his argument. We said that a solution that wouldn't work isn't a solution at all, that there was more to taking a position than constructing a clear thesis and a logically argued paper.

He seemed somewhat taken aback; clearly, this strategy of quickly taking stock of the issue and offering a novel and definitive solution had worked well for him in past writing courses. We pressed our questions because we wanted to push him (and the other students) beyond the form of argument that ignores real conflicts by turning them into abstract problems to be solved or managed. In his second draft of the second paper and in the third paper, he analyzed the complexities of the situation more thoroughly. He discovered that financial incentives for more efficient use of water by farmers could and were being paid for by urban water users in the west rather than the federal government. He discovered that zoning, the establishment of agricultural districts, and cluster residential development were possible solutions to the increasing pressure of development that drives up the property values of agricultural land beyond the levels where farming is economically feasible in the midwest.

The third assignment asked students to reconsider their initial positions from the point of view of someone who would not agree with them. We told students that the reason to look at opposing positions when constructing an argument was not so much to anticipate and counter objections as it was to learn more about the issue and thus to make your own position more reasonable and practical, to take into account not only your own interests and desires and experiences but also those of others.

We had a chance to make this point clearer one day in another class that was similarly structured but focused on a different topic. A female student stated unequivocally that it was essential that one parent in a family not work so that someone would be home when the kids got back from school; a male student countered that both his parents worked and that he had not suffered at all from coming home to an empty house. The two debated this issue rather heatedly for about five minutes with the rest of the class throwing in encouraging comments or reactions. She argued that she would have felt insecure and unloved in his position; he countered that he developed a strong sense of independence and still felt close to his parents because of the time they did find to spend together. When he finally said it was clear he couldn't win this argument because she always had something to say in response, we instead asked the class to look at what had happened differently, not as simply an argument to be won or lost but as an opportunity to learn about different perspectives—to learn that your experiences and needs are not necessarily the same as those of others and that there are benefits and drawbacks to the differing decisions made by parents.

In composing this third assignment we reminded ourselves that the risk in argument is not that you may lose but rather that you may change. We asked them to think about the concerns of someone who held a position that they did not find to be persuasive and explain why someone might hold this position. Then we asked them to discuss what they might learn from this position: What beliefs and feelings did they find they could sympathize with, even if they did not agree with them? What experiences did they learn about that might help them see new aspects of the issue? How did some of the concerns expressed relate to some of their concerns? We asked these questions knowing full well that our students were in the midst of working and reworking their relations to the world around them and that our questions might contribute to that work by asking them to connect with others' concerns and needs. We also knew full well the rhetorical force of the questions we asked; thoughtfully pursued, these questions could and did prompt changes in our students.

The student who was so concerned with the plight of small farmers began his writing by adamantly opposing corporate farming, but he really did not know why he opposed corporate farming—except that it put small traditional farmers out of business and he thought that this was unfair. In the course of his work on his papers, he came across a statement by René Dubos in an essay by Edward Abbey ("farming as a way of life is a self-sustaining, symbiotic relationship between man and earth") that gave him a way of talking about the difference in attitude toward the land and toward their work he felt between traditional small farmers and corporate agribusinesses. But at the same time, he developed an understanding of the place of corporate farming in the economic system of the country. In a statement he wrote at the end of the course, he explained:

> My position on the topic of water at first was corporate farms are no good and we shut them down completely. As we read articles and wrote papers I slowly learned how complex our economic system is. I didn't realize all the jobs that would be lost and how it would affect California's economic system. Also I finally realized the fact that corporate farms just didn't appear out of nowhere. They developed over time. . . . The corporate farms that should be kept after and be taxed super high are conglomerates like Prudential, [which] would possibly force them to sell their land to people who care and respect the land and soil. These are the corporate farms that don't care for the land and if the land becomes worthless they just buy land somewhere else and they say "oh well we lost a couple of acres of land we can just write it off as a loss." I guess I'm still against corporate farms but mostly only them being owned by conglomerates.

The student who lived on a lake came to sympathize with the owner of the water rights' desire to make a living through the sale of hydroelectric power, and he connected this situation to that of a western water dispute between a rancher and alfalfa farmers. Instead of recommending government regulation, as he had started out doing, he argued instead that people need to learn to work together so that all can make a living and be satisfied that their water is being used efficiently.

The last assignment asked students to pull together all that they had learned from writing and rewriting the first three papers, from their readings, and from our work in class. By then they had all learned a lot—and so had we—not only about the specific issue they had been researching and analyzing, but also about different attitudes toward water issues in general and different concerns that needed to be taken into account. They had lots of their own writing to read over and reflect on, to revise and reuse. They had, in short, a good place from which to begin constructing a thoughtful and informed argument. Constructing a position, we told them, means sorting through for yourself the various questions and problems and values involved in an issue and coming to a decision you can stand up for.

What this sequence of assignments allowed students to do, then, was to take some time with a single issue, to really think about it, to investigate what was involved, to respond to it in more than one way, to make assertions about it and then reconsider those assertions, to risk changing how they thought about the things that mattered to them and what they might do in the future. And students did, for the most part, change their thinking about the issues they dealt with, although, as with the students in the course discussing mascot names, they did not simply shift sides or take on the instructor's position. Despite a great deal of skepticism expressed by the instructor, the golf aficionado still argued that the desert was a good place to situate golf courses, as long as they were correctly designed. The student who first proposed that western agriculture be abandoned still argued in his final paper that we must reverse the trend toward dependence on western agriculture, but the solution he offered was much more complex—and much more realistic. In a statement about his paper, he observed, "I initially thought that farming in the desert was completely ludicrous and had no place in crop production. I've since learned that, if done correctly, irrigating farming can be a part of American farming for a long time." In his paper, he argued that "irrigating farmers in the American southwest are going to have to adapt to their regions pending water shortages," and that "planned rural developments" in the midwest "are needed to ensure that these lands remain available for farming." Almost all of the students in this class arrived at extremely complex positions, often so complex that they had to struggle hard to express them in any coherent way. But also, more importantly, students developed positions that mattered to them and that dealt with real world problems in a realistic way.

Pushing students to develop positions that take into account the complexities of real world issues not only moves argumentative writing into a more serious realm, away from display or eristic debate, it also gives them a sense of how their academic work can connect with and help them understand their everyday lives. One of the number of students who wrote about the impact of the James Bay hydroelectric project on the lifestyle of the Cree Indians attended a local round table discussion about sustainable development as part of her preparation for writing her final paper. What she learned there was more than just support for her position: "When I went to the Round Table Meeting on Monday night my thoughts about this paper strengthened even more. My feelings were really true, they weren't made up by reading about the subject in magazine articles."

Asking students to research issues and to learn from people they disagree with does not prevent them from taking strong positions, though it does result in positions that are more reasonable and thoughtful. Their work is a form of collaborative inquiry, but it is still argument, too, in that it negotiates serious differences and recommends a course of action. We also found that bringing conflicts into the classroom does not necessarily mean turning the classroom into a site of conflict. When students are aware that the differences of opinion between them exist in a broader arena—that these differences are not just their own opinions but arise from historical, social, and cultural conditions—they do not feel they need to argue so fiercely and single-mindedly, and they can take the time to listen to other voices and rethink their positions.

By Way of a Conclusion

Perhaps the most frustrating, though not surprising, thing we learned from our two courses was that the very things we set out to resist—two-sided issues, the rush to assert a thesis, and the concentration on forms—returned again and again, if we were not careful. Just as so many argument readers tell students that pro-and-con arguments are too facile and yet go on to organize their chapters in terms of pro-and-con (or speak in ways that assume students "want to take a side"), we found ourselves worrying whether our students' "positions" were clear enough, or whether they had a controversial enough "thesis." Even our examples betray the obvious, namely, that once you ask students to write through their interest in an issue, the assumption becomes that they will have a position that stands against, is differentiated from, someone else's position. And it is easier to grasp one's position, think it through, and present it to others if it is conceived in terms of an opposition.

We thus saw (and tried to understand) the forces that drove us and our students to simplify and to formalize the argumentative situation, and this is why, in the first course, we were not concerned that the papers we received did not all look argumentative. We understood that the initial disagreement (between Rooney and Churchill) would contextualize, for them and for their readers, their effort to answer questions that seemed only tangentially related to the disagreement. Their research did not preclude argument; it was infused with the initial sense of argument, and, what is most important, their answers served to modify the initial simplicity of the disagreement.

In the second class, on water resources, similar doubts arose. Although we asked students to articulate their "positions," the decision to see their positions as solutions to problems, together with the scrutiny given the solutions offered (and together with the relatively "untopical" nature of the issue), encouraged students to reconfigure the conflicts, to bring in other perspectives, other complications, which then served to decenter the original disagreement in a fresh (and more complex) direction. Thus, in one case the issue shifted from "irrigated farming in the western states: yes or no?" to "how can we tilt the balance of farming back to the midwestern states (which have a natural supply of water) in a manner that increases the efficiency of western farming and discourages the selling off of good farm land to developers in the midwest?"

In our approach to argument, we share concerns with both cooperative and neosophistic rhetorics. Although we too want to teach the conflicts, at the same time we do not want to turn the classroom into the place where conflicts between students or between students and teachers erupt—not because we are reticent to allow emotion or turmoil into our classrooms, and not because we think all classrooms should be nurturing, but because we suspect, for now at any rate, that the desire to see results in the form of "critical action," when pressed too single-mindedly, may backfire and reduce a much needed understanding of the complexity of those conflicts. Wanting to have something to say and (desperately) needing to have something to say in self-defense can be productive under certain circumstances. But when arguments are entered into hastily, the complexity of the issues is often lost, and with it (we might add) the basis for introducing important, higher level concepts such as ideology, multiple subjectivity, and contingent foundations.

Neither do we wish to ignore or banish the different experiences and commitments that students bring with them into the classroom, for the expression and investigation of these differences is crucial to understanding the complexities of the problems we want to do something about. Conflicts have histories and are embedded in more or less permanent power structures; decisions affect different people differently and have consequences that go beyond immediate situations; differences are rarely (if ever) brought permanently into consensus. What is important, to our minds, in teaching students to deal with conflict is that they experience the process of constructing a complex, historically knowledgeable position in light of what matters to, and what will result for, those affected by the positions taken.

If we believe that the writing classroom is a place to engage in serious intellectual inquiry and debate about the questions that trouble our everyday lives, we need to think again about our approach to argument. We need to see argumentation as a crucial social responsibility—an activity that requires us to position ourselves within complicated and interconnected issues. We need to see it as a complex and often extended human activity, or, rather, as an array of human activities, including institutionalized formal debate, legal trials, shouting matches that threaten to end in fistfights, conversational games of one-upsmanship, disagreements among friends, and extended deliberations within a community over what course of action to pursue. We need to see it not just as a matter of winning or losing but as a way to connect with others which may lead to change, not only in the world but also in ourselves. But, most of all, we need to see it as a means of coming to decisions, a way of getting things done in the world, that includes moments of agonistic dispute, moments of inquiry, moments of confrontation, and moments of cooperation.

Works Cited

Bauer, Dale M. "The Other 'F' Word: The Feminist in the Classroom," *College English* 52 (1990): 385–97.

Berlin, James. *Rhetorics, Poetics, and Cultures.* Urbana: NCTE, 1996.

Bizzell, Patricia. *Academic Discourse and Critical Consciousness.* Pittsburgh: U of Pittsburgh P, 1992.

————. "Power, Authority, and Critical Pedagogy." *Journal of Basic Writing* 10 (1991): 54–70.

Buker, Eloise A. "Rhetoric in Postmodern Feminism: Put-Offs, Put-Ons, and Political Plays." *The Interpretive Turn: Philosophy, Science, Culture.* Ed. David R. Hiley, James F. Bohman, and Richard Shusterman. Ithaca: Cornell UP, 1991. 218–45.

Churchill, Ward. "Crimes Against Humanity." *Z Magazine* March 1993: 43–48.

Elbow, Peter. "The Doubting Game and the Believing Game." *Writing Without Teachers.* New York: Oxford UP, 1973. 147–91.

Faigley, Lester. *Fragments of Rationality: Postmodernity and the Subject of Composition.* Pittsburgh: U of Pittsburgh P, 1992.

Fitts, Karen and Alan W. France, eds. *Left Margins: Cultural Studies and Composition Pedagogy.* New York: State U of New York P, 1995.

Gage, John. "John Gage's Assignment." *What Makes Writing Good: A Multiperspective.* Ed. William E. Coles, Jr., and James Vopat. Lexington: Heath, 1985. 98–105.

————. "An Adequate Epistemology for Composition: Classical and Modern Perspectives." *Essays on Classical Rhetoric and Modern Discourse.* Ed. Robert J. Connors, Lisa S. Ede, and Andrea A. Lunsford. Carbondale: Southern Illinois UP, 1984. 152–70.

Graff, Gerald. *Beyond the Culture Wars: How Teaching the Conflicts Can Revitalize American Education.* New York: Norton, 1993.

Hanson, Jeffery R., and Linda P. Rouse. "Dimensions of Native American Stereotyping." *American Indian Culture and Research Journal* 11 (1987): 33–58.

hooks, bell. *Talking Back: Thinking Feminist, Thinking Black.* Boston: South End, 1989.

————. *Teaching to Transgress: Education as the Practice of Freedom.* New York: Routledge, 1994.

Jarratt, Susan C. *Rereading the Sophists: Classical Rhetoric Refigured.* Carbondale: Southern Illinois UP, 1991.

————. "Feminism and Composition: The Case for Conflict." *Contending with Words: Composition and Rhetoric in a Postmodern Age.* Ed. Patricia Harkin and John Schilb. New York: MLA, 1991. 105–24.

Lunsford, Andrea A., and Lisa S. Ede. "On Distinctions between Classical and Modern Rhetoric." *Essays on Classical Rhetoric and Modern Discourse.* Ed. Robert J. Connors, Lisa S, Ede, and Andrea A. Lunsford. Carbondale: Southern Illinois UP, 1984. 37–50.

MacLean, Norman. *A River Runs Through It.* New York: Pocket, 1992.

Menand, Louis. "The War of All against All." *The New Yorker* (14 March 1994): 74–85.

Pratt, Richard H. "Remarks on Indian Education." *Americanizing the American Indians: Writings by the "Friends of the Indian" 1880–1900.* Ed. Francis Paul Prucha. Cambridge: Harvard UP, 1973. 277–80.

Reisner, Marc. *Cadillac Desert.* New York: Viking, 1986.

Rooney, Andy. "Indians Have Worse Problems." *Chicago Tribune* 14 March 1991: 14, 92.

Rouse, Linda P., and Jeffery R. Hanson. "American Indian Stereotyping, Resource Competition, and Status-based Prejudice." *American Indian Culture and Research Journal* 15 (1991): 1–17.

Young, Iris Marion. *Justice and the Politics of Difference.* Princeton: Princeton UP, 1990.

CRITICAL THINKING IN WEB COURSES: AN OXYMORON?

David Lang

[*Syllabus* 14.2 (2000): 20–24]

Assistant professor and past chair of the English Department at Golden Gate University, David Lang teaches writing both on the Web and in traditional, face-to-face classes.

A common critique of Web-based instruction is that it lacks the energy and spontaneity of face-to-face classroom interactions and that students are less motivated to engage course materials in sophisticated ways that would help them develop critical-thinking skills. Lang disagrees. Though he doesn't dismiss the challenges posed by asynchronous, online interactions among students and between students and teachers, he argues that Web-based classes offer "the opportunities, the means, and the motivation for thinking critically." He points specifically to the focus on writing, the time lags in online conversations, and the absence of nonverbal communication as features that actually contribute to the development of critical thinking. Lang's article will be useful for teachers using technology, whether their interactions with students are wholly or partially online.

How many subtleties of a class discussion, and indeed the very structure of its development, rely on sight and sound: raised eyebrows, excited hand movements, the shrug of a shoulder, varying tones of voice? Without these signals, isn't an online discussion missing essential channels of communication? Isn't it just too impersonal to be effective?

When a face-to-face (FTF) discussion goes well, there's often an emotional energy in the room, a feeling of excitement and discovery. Tuning into this energy, participants bounce ideas off each other, building a structure of propositions and counter-propositions interspersed with questions and comments in an exchange of ideas that can be rich, thoughtful, and fresh. But how can this experience possibly manifest in an environment where the participants are not only invisible to each other, but are posting their comments on a computer at all times of the day and night? Where is the spontaneity and excitement of a discussion when, instead of responding immediately to a comment, participants must first log on, find and read a comment (one among, say, thirty other comments), and then write and post a response, which the recipient may or may not read and respond to for several days?

To faculty unfamiliar with online teaching, this and other limitations of asynchronous discussions can lead to the conclusion that online discussions are a poor substitute for FTF discussions. Can sophisticated critical thinking be fostered in an asynchronous environment? Are students really engaged with the material and with each other's ideas? Is there really such a thing as a good online discussion?

Critical thinking, defined broadly as a dialogical process that produces an increasingly sound, well-grounded, and valid understanding of a topic or issue, involves participants developing and examining their ideas as fully as possible, presenting them clearly and credibly to others, and examining and challenging the ideas of others. In other words, critical thinking happens in good discussions. While the problems of asynchronous discussions do not go away, their reliance on writing, their time lags, and the absence of nonverbal communication present both students and faculty with the opportunities, the means, and the motivation for thinking critically.

Online Features for Critical Thinking

For years, proponents of Writing-Across-the-Curriculum (WAC) have been saying that students learn when they formulate their ideas in writing. Although the extent to which faculty have adopted WAC approaches has been limited, suddenly, without any push from WAC adherents, students and faculty in online discussions find themselves in a WAC paradise.

Unlike speech, writing is reviewable. The words do not disappear, but are recorded. Thus writers can read, reread, and revise their comments—in the process discovering and developing what they mean—all before the reader sees them. In other words, writers don't need to "say" anything until their words are thoughtful and clear. Furthermore, unlike FTF participants, who are often competing for the attention of the moderator, online participants have an equal opportunity to "speak." The opportunity itself can last a week instead of just a few moments. And the participants cannot be interrupted. Thus, while the time lag of asynchronous courses can certainly reduce the spontaneity of a discussion, it can also provide opportunities and means for thoughtful exchanges.

But are participants motivated to write well, aside from the incentive of earning favorable reviews and high grades? One motivational factor is the need people have to represent themselves favorably to others. People want—Maslow would say need—both to be accepted and to excel. In FTF discussions, the major channels through which people meet these needs are nonverbal. Online, however, the nonverbal channels are not available, so in order to represent oneself favorably to others, one must write well. In addition, because online writing is published and can remain "on the public record" for weeks, the significance of the writing increases.

Of course, writing also takes place in FTF classes (usually for homework assignments and term papers), but is often not perceived as "real world" communication. It is, instead, seen as a method of communication whose purpose is limited to students' demonstrating knowledge and thinking skills only to the instructor, who probably already knows the topic very well. Papers may even be delivered to the instructor, only to disappear completely or to be returned with a few marginal comments and a grade—barely dialogical.

In an online discussion, however, writing is very much dialogical. In addition to the instructor, there is an audience of peers whose role is not to evaluate for a grade but to explore and develop ideas together. They are interested in discussing ideas to further their understanding. This communicative purpose in the writing process is what many composition teachers aim for in having students share their writing in small groups, for there students take more care with—and therefore think more carefully about—writing that has a real purpose for a live audience. Online, that purpose and that audience are an integral part of the environment.

Instructors in online classes also can divide participants into small groups, and even though all the conversations are happening simultaneously, the instructor can be present in all the groups at the same time. What effect does this "omniscient" instructor have on the quality of discussions? The effect will likely be to raise the level of focus and the quality of thinking in the small groups. In an FTF class divided into small groups, the instructor has limited time and opportunity to answer questions and requests for help from the various groups. Online, however, there are fewer limitations. The instructor can respond to each group's concerns, analyze the quality and direction of work, and guide the groups individually.

Finally, there is the fact that the Web is a marvelous resource. Although students in FTF classes can just as easily log on and research the Web when they are writing a paper out of class, students online have the time to incorporate any resource—Web-based or traditional—into their comments in the middle of a discussion. This opportunity enables participants to present more credible, richer, and more thoughtful contributions to online discussions than they might in FTF courses.

Strategies that Encourage Critical Thinking

Perhaps the most balanced conclusion one can come to about the quality of thinking in online discussions is that the potential is there for both success and failure. Some discussions fail miserably, while others are spectacularly successful. The probability of success, and thus of quality thinking by students will likely be increased if the instructor is a skilled facilitator.

Much has been written in the literature about facilitation skills. The following checklist selected from *Learning Networks* by Harasim, Hiltz, Teles, and Turoff (from "Teaching at an Internet Distance") is a useful summary of advice for online facilitators:

- Do not lecture
- Be clear about expectations of the participants
- Be flexible and patient
- Be responsive
- Do not overload
- Monitor and prompt for participation.

For assignments, set up small groups and assign tasks to them.

Also:

- Be a process facilitator
- Write weaving [summarizing] comments every week or two
- Organize the interaction
- Set rules and standards for good etiquette
- Establish clear norms for participation and procedures for grading
- Assign individuals or small groups to play the roles of teacher and of moderator for portions of the course
- Close and purge moribund conferences in stages
- Adopt a flexible approach toward curriculum integration on global networks.

Facilitating a Dialogical Process

The basic challenge for teachers in asynchronous discussions and teachers in FTF discussions is the same: to facilitate the engagement of students in a dialogical process that produces increasingly sound, well grounded, and valid understanding of a topic or issue. While online discussions are relatively new environments featuring time lags, writing, and the absence of nonverbal channels of communication, they are not environments inimical to facilitation. In fact, they present a special combination of means, opportunities, and motivation, which can encourage in both students and faculty substantial critical thinking.

Resources

Bonk, C. J., Cummings, Jack A., Hara, Noriko, Fischler, Robert B., Lee, Sun Myung. "A Ten Level Web Integration Continuum for Higher Education: New Resources, Partners, Courses, and Markets." (March 22, 2000).

Funaro, Gina M. "Pedagogical Roles and Implementation Guidelines for Online Communication Tools." *Asynchronous Learning Networks Magazine* 3.2 (1999). (March 22, 2000).

Picciano, Anthony G. "Developing an Asynchronous Course Model at a Large, Urban University." *Journal of the Asynchronous Learning Networks* 2.1 (1998). (April 6, 1999).

"Teaching at an Internet Distance: The Pedagogy of Online Teaching and Learning: The Report of a 1998–1999 University of Illinois Faculty Seminar." (December 7, 1999).

Wegner, Scott B. "The Effects of Internet-based Instruction on Student Learning." *Journal of the Asynchronous Learning Networks* 3.2 (1999). (March 22, 2000).

ONLINE STRATEGIES FOR TEACHING THINKING

William Peirce

[*Syllabus* 14.2 (2000): 21, 24]

William Peirce is a professor at Prince George's Community College, where he is also Coordinator of Reasoning Across the Curriculum. He has designed and teaches two Web courses for the University of Maryland University College.

Peirce shares eight active-learning strategies that can be used with online classes or courses. His explanations and examples will provide teachers with a full range of activities that are meant to engage students in course content and critical thinking.

In an online course, teachers can employ many traditional classroom active-learning strategies to encourage good thinking, engage students in the course content, and promote intellectual development.

1. Design self-testing quizzes and tutorials on basic chapter content.

In a Web course, the usual source of course content is a textbook and teacher-written text, so it is important for students to self-test understanding of their reading. If test-writing software is not available, an easy method is to post questions in one file and post models of good and poor answers (with commentary) in another file. Instructors can use the quiz as a gateway to the online discussion, allowing only those students who pass the quiz into the discussion.

2. Apply the concepts of the textbook chapters to cases or issues every week.

Asking students to apply course concepts in informal writing tasks such as homework assignments is probably the most obvious and frequently used approach to promoting thinking. Responses can be written by groups or individuals, posted publicly in the conference, or collected in a student's assignment portfolio. In small groups where there is a single written response to teacher-posed problems, thinking is clarified as students consider several perspectives and negotiate the language to articulate their response.

Informal writing tasks on course-based topics are especially good for promoting course-based thinking. Private, personal applications can be placed in assignment folders; less personal topics can be placed in a public conference. Colleges with writing across the curriculum programs are likely to have a rich collection of tasks available through their teaching and learning centers. Asking 25 students to respond individually to one scenario or topic in a conference may result in thoughtful responses from the first three responders and "I think so, too" from the remaining 22. To avoid boring repetition, variations of the scenario or topic can be posed to a smaller group of three or four students. For example, ask for individual responses to Scenario 1 from students whose last names begin with A–C, to Scenario 2 from D–G, and so on.

3. Pose well-designed questions for asynchronous discussion.

Here is the ubiquitous Bloom higher-order thinking taxonomy and typical objectives within the categories:

- **Knowledge.** Identification and recall of information: tell who, what, when, where, how; describe.
- **Comprehension.** Organization and selection of facts and ideas: retell, state the main idea.
- **Application.** Use of facts, rules, principles: use example, relate, explain significance.
- **Analysis.** Separation of a whole into component parts: break down into features, classify, outline or diagram, compare/contrast, present evidence.
- **Synthesis.** Combination of ideas to form a new whole: predict/infer, add ideas to, create/design, combine, suggest solutions.
- **Evaluation.** Development of opinions, judgments, or decisions: agree/disagree, explain, prioritize, decide, assess.

4. Create cognitive dissonance: provoke discomfort, unsettle confirmed notions, uncover misconceptions, inspire curiosity, pose problems.

The point here is not to befuddle students, but to dispel complacency by creating cognitive dissonance. Accompanying a disorienting intellectual situation is a wish to resolve it. Students who experience a gap in their knowledge will seek to fill it. For example, an instructor can design a task that uses students' prior knowledge but also requires new information or procedures that the students do not know. Students become aware of a gap between the task's goal and what they need to know or do to achieve it; creating this need to know in students is a basic strategy underlying inquiry learning and problem-based learning. Socratic questioning is a variation on this theme; its basic structure begins with inquiry, leads to perplexity, and ends with enlightenment.

5. Ask students to write reflective responses to the course content and to consider their learning processes in private journals.

Improving students' metacognitive abilities is crucial to improving their thinking; reflecting on one's learning processes is crucial to becoming a better learner. Students can move toward both goals by writing in private journals. For example, one can grade journals holistically on the criteria of thoroughness and responsiveness to the instructor's questions.

6. Conduct opinion polls/surveys as pre-reading activities before assigned readings to arouse interest in issues or topics.

Like everyone else, students have opinions on any issue, whether or not they are well informed. To generate interest in assigned readings, an instructor can conduct a survey of students' opinions on the issue or test their prior knowledge of the facts presented in the readings. Another pre-reading strategy is to mix data from the assigned readings with wrong data that the instructor invents and then ask students which facts are true and which are false.

7. Present activities that require considering opposing views.

In asynchronous discussions or as formal or informal assignments, ask students to consider opposing views, methods, data, principles, concepts, definitions, interpretations, and conclusions. Dialectical thinking (sometimes called dialogical thinking) is one of the best ways to engage students' minds and personalities, challenge their previously held beliefs, promote openmindedness, defer the rush to judgment, and move them to higher intellectual stages. Adopting a position and explaining why it is better than the alternative requires knowledge, reasoned judgment, and intellectual criteria.

8. Assign a mediatory argument promoting a resolution acceptable to both sides.

This strategy comes from *The Aims of Argument* by Timothy W. Crusius and Carolyn E. Channell. The purpose of the argument to mediate or negotiate is to seek consensus within an audience polarized by differences in a context where there is a need to cooperate and to preserve good relations. The mediatory argument uses reasons and evidence to persuade opposing sides to resolve an issue in a way that satisfies both sides, an approach that can extend students' thinking beyond their simply supporting one side of a dichotomy.

PART TEN

RESEARCHED WRITING

The Bedford Handbook recognizes the essential connections between research and much of the writing students will do in school and beyond. Typically, a substantial research assignment has been central in first-year writing courses. However, many writing teachers and professional librarians have been emphasizing the need for students to develop "information literacy," especially as more information becomes available and accessible through electronic resources, and as more of it is unregulated, not necessarily screened through traditional print-publication processes or library acquisition procedures. In other words, writing teachers and their colleagues across the curriculum are recognizing the need to emphasize information literacy, research strategies, and researched writing throughout their assignment sequences.

The selections that follow focus on several questions that teachers should consider as they plan how to introduce students to researched writing:

- How do we define *research* and how is it related to *inquiry*? How do the answers to these questions affect our courses and our teaching?
- If many teachers consider the traditional research paper as dysfunctional, what alternative forms of researched writing can replace the traditional model?
- How can teachers help students understand and avoid plagiarism?

RESEARCH AS A SOCIAL ACT
Patricia Bizzell and Bruce Herzberg

[*The Clearing House* 60 (1987): 303–06.]

Patricia Bizzell is a professor of English and director of the honors program at the College of the Holy Cross, where she directed the writing program for ten years, founded the peer tutoring workshop, and started the writing across the curriculum program. A frequent speaker at professional meetings, Bizzell has published many articles on basic writing, writing across the curriculum, and rhetorical theory in such journals as *College English, College Composition and Communication, PRE/TEXT*, and *Rhetoric Review,* and in the anthology *Contending with Words* (1991). She is also the author of *Academic Discourse and Critical Consciousness* (1992), a collection of her articles. Bruce Herzberg is a professor of English at Bentley College, where he is director of the expository writing program and the writing across the curriculum program. A regular speaker at CCCC and other conferences, Herzberg has published articles on composition in the journals *MLN, College Composition and Communication,* and *Rhetoric Review,* and in the anthologies *The Politics of Writing Instruction* (1991) and *Contending with Words* (1991). Bizzell and Herzberg have collaborated on several successful books: *The*

Rhetorical Tradition (1990)—now in its second edition (2001)—was the winner of the Outstanding Book Award from the CCCC, *The Bedford Bibliography for Teachers of Writing*—now in its fifth edition and available on the World Wide Web at http://www.bedfordstmartins.com, and *Negotiating Difference: Cultural Case Studies for Composition*.

Bizzell and Herzberg observe that instructors typically define research in two ways: as discovery or as recovery. Both definitions, they argue, are inadequate and contribute to ineffective assignments and teaching strategies. The authors ask instructors to recognize that research is a "social, collaborative act that draws on and contributes to the work of a community that cares about a given body of knowledge," and they suggest a range of activities to engage students as active participants in knowledge communities.

"Research" can be defined in several ways. First, it may mean discovery, as in the discovery of new information about the world by a researcher. We often call this work "original" research and think of the researcher as a solitary genius, alone in a study or, more likely, a laboratory. Second, "research" may mean the recovery from secondary sources of the information discovered by others. This is often the way we think of student research: students go to the library to extract information from books for a research paper. These two definitions call for some examination.

The first kind of research—discovery—seems more valuable than the second kind—recovery. Discovery adds to the world's knowledge, while recovery adds only to an individual's knowledge (some might add, "if we're lucky"). No matter how we protest that both kinds of research are valuable, there is a distinctly secondary quality to recovery. After all, recovery is dependent entirely upon discovery, original research, for its materials. Discovery actually creates new knowledge, while recovery merely reports on the results of the work of those solitary geniuses.

Common sense tells us that students, with rare exceptions, do not do original research until graduate school, if then. Students and teachers quite naturally share the feeling that research in school is, thus, mere recovery. Consequently, students and teachers often conclude that students are not likely to produce anything very good when they do this kind of research. Indeed, one cannot be doing anything very good while piling up the required number of facts discovered by others. Research-as-recovery seems to justify writing a paper by copying others' accounts of what they have discovered.

If we try, however, to remedy the defects of the research paper by calling for actual discovery, we run into more problems. Those who hope to do original research must know, before anything else, where gaps exist in current knowledge. And, of course, knowing where the holes are requires knowing where they are not. For most (perhaps all) students, this takes us back to research-as-recovery, that plodding effort to find out some of what others have already figured out.

Even research that evaluates sources of information, relates the accounts of information to one another, frames an argument that ties them together, and either reveals something important about the sources themselves or develops into a new contribution on the same topic requires, like discovery, a grasp of a field of knowledge that students cannot be expected to have.

The problem with both kinds of research, then, hinges on knowledge itself. The popular image of the solitary researcher in the lab or the library does not hint at the problem of knowledge—that these people are workers in knowledge who need knowledge as a prerequisite to their work. According to the popular image, they simply find facts. If that were all, presumably anyone could find them. But we know that is hardly the case.

What successful researchers possess that our students typically do not is knowledge, the shared body of knowledge that helps scholars define research projects and employ methods to pursue them. Invariably, researchers use the work of others in their field to develop such projects and consult others in the field to determine what projects will be of value. In short, all real research takes place and can only take place within a community of scholars. Research is a social act. Research is always collaborative, even if only one name appears on the final report.

This, then, is the third definition of research: a social, collaborative act that draws on and contributes to the work of a community that cares about a given body of knowledge. This definition is also a critique of the popular images that we have been examining. For, by the social definition of research, the solitary researcher is not at all solitary: the sense of what can and should be done is derived from the knowledge community. The researcher must be in constant, close communication with other researchers and will likely share preliminary results with colleagues and use their suggestions in further work. Her or his contributions will be extensions of work already done and will create new gaps that other researchers will try to close. Finally, his/her work of discovery is impossible without continuous recovery of the work of others in the community.

The social definition also allows us to revise the notion of research-as-recovery, for the recoverer in a community of knowledge is not merely rehashing old knowledge or informing himself/herself about a randomly chosen topic—he/she is interpreting and reinterpreting the community's knowledge in light of new needs and perspectives, and in so doing creating and disseminating new knowledge. The activity of interpretation reveals what the community values and where the gaps in knowledge reside. "Study knows that which yet it doth not know," as Shakespeare recognized long ago.

In many fields, the activities of synthesis and interpretation are primary forms of research. Think, for example, of the fields of history, philosophy, art and literary criticism, even sociology, economics, and psychology. But the important point is that no field of knowledge can do without such work. Clearly, the lab-science image of research is inaccurate, unrepresentative, and unhelpful. Research as a social act makes far more sense.

This new definition of research changes what it means for students to do research in school. In what ways do students participate in knowledge communities? One well-known and successful research assignment—the family history—suggests that in this very real community, student researchers find material to be interpreted, contradictions to be resolved, assertions to be supported, and gaps to be filled. They share the information and interpretations with the rest of the community, the family, who do not possess such a synthesis and are grateful to get it. But how do students fit into academic knowledge communities that are so much larger and colder than the family?

First, we must recognize that secondary and middle level students are novices, slowly learning the matter and method of school subjects. But they need not master the knowledge of the experts in order to participate in the subcommunity of novices. They will need to know what other students know and do not know about a subject that they are all relatively uninformed about. In other words, they need to have a sense of what constitutes the shared body of knowledge of their community and a sense of the possible ways to increase that knowledge by useful increments. Imagine the classroom as a neighborhood in the larger academic community. Students contributing to the knowledge of the class are engaged in research in much the same way that expert researchers contribute to the larger community. They find out what is known—the first step in research—and identify what is unknown by sharing their knowledge amongst themselves. Then, by filling in the gaps and sharing what they find, they educate the whole community.

There are several practical implications for reimagining research in this way:

1. The whole class must work in the same area of inquiry—not the same topic, but different aspects of the same central issue. A well-defined historical period might do: by investigating work, play, social structure, literature, politics, clothing styles, food, and so on, students would become local experts contributing to a larger picture of the period. We will look at other examples later.

2. Students will need some common knowledge, a shared text or set of materials and, most of all, the opportunity to share with each other what they may already know about the subject. By collaborating on a questionnaire or interviewing each other, students learn valuable ways of doing primary research.

3. They will need to ask questions, critically examine the shared knowledge, and perhaps do some preliminary investigation to determine what the most tantalizing unknowns may be. Here again, some free exchange among class members will be helpful.

4. The exchange of ideas must continue through the process of discovery. Like expert researchers, students need to present papers or colloquia to the research community, distribute drafts and respond to feedback, and contribute to the work of others when they are able. Finally, their work must be disseminated, published in some way, and made available to the group. The early framework of the research community ought not to be reduced to a way to introduce the regular old term paper.

A perfectly good way to choose the general area of research for a class is simply to choose it yourself. Teachers represent the larger community and can be expected to know something about the topic at hand and provide guidance, so if the topic interests the teacher, all the better. Of course, the teacher can lean toward topics that may interest the class. Students may be asked to choose from among several possibilities suggested by the teacher, but it is likely to be needlessly daunting to the students to leave the whole selection process to them. Among the possibilities for class topics: utopia, Shakespeare's England, Franklin's America, the jazz age, the death of the dinosaurs, the year you were born, images of childhood, the idea of school, work and play, wealth and poverty, country and city, quests and heroes, creativity—it's easy to go on and on.

Central texts can be books, photocopied selections, a film, or videotapes. More's *Utopia* might work for some classes, but a utopian science fiction book might be better for others, and the description of the Garden of Eden, a well-known utopia, is only three pages long. Shakespeare plays are easy to come by, as is Franklin's *Autobiography* or selections from it. Not every topic will require such materials, of course. For some topics, the students' interviews or other initial responses might be compiled into the central text.

The shared knowledge of the group might be elicited through alternate writing and discussion sessions, the students answering questions like "what do you know about x?" or "what would you like to know about x?" Interviews and questionnaires also work, as noted. All of this preliminary reading, writing, and discussion will help to create a sense of community and give students a jump-start on writing for the group, rather than for the teacher. Needless to say, the teacher ought not to grade and need not even read such preliminary work, beyond requiring that it be done.

Identifying a gap in the group's knowledge and choosing a topic for individual research may still be difficult, and it helps to be armed with suggestions if the students run out of ideas or need to be focused. Have a list of questions about utopias, a list of attempted utopian communities, the names of prominent figures in the period under discussion, some key ideas or events or issues to pursue, and so on. Students may not see, in the central text, problems like class differences in opportunities for schooling, or assumptions about the place of women, or attitudes linked to local or historical circumstances. If discussion and preliminary research do not turn them up, the teacher can reasonably help out. We need not pretend that we are inventing a new field of inquiry, but we must beware of the temptation to fall back on assigned topics.

Having students share drafts and give interim reports takes time, but it is usually time well spent. Students can learn to provide useful feedback to other students on drafts of papers—teachers should not read every draft. Students acting as draft-readers can respond to set questions (what did you find most interesting? what do you want to learn more about?) or work as temporary collaborators in attacking problem areas or listen to drafts read aloud and give oral responses. Other kinds of sharing may be worthwhile. Annotated bibliographies might be compiled and posted so that resources can be shared. Groups might lead panel discussions to take the edge off formal presentations. Reading aloud and oral reporting are good ways, too, of setting milestones for writing, and public presentation is important for maintaining the sense of community. Oral reports, by the way, tend to be better as drafts than as final presentations—the feedback is useful then, and anxiety about the performance is muted. Publishing the final results is the last step—copies of the papers might be compiled with a table of contents in a ring binder and put on reserve in the school library, for example.

These activities do not eliminate problems of footnote form and plagiarism, but in the setting of a research community, the issues of footnoting and plagiarism can be seen in a fresh light. Students should be able to articulate for themselves the reasons why members of a community would want to enforce among themselves (and their novices) a common and consistent method of citation. When knowledge exists to be exchanged, footnotes facilitate exchange. So too with plagiarism: members of the community would love to see themselves quoted and footnoted, but not robbed.

An excellent way to teach citation and reinforce community cohesion is to ask students to cite each other. How do you cite another student's paper, especially in draft form? How do you cite an oral report? How do you thank someone for putting you onto an idea? These citation forms may be used rarely, but they are good ways to stir up interest in the need for and uses of footnotes.

If the students are discovering the process of drafting, peer-review, and interim reports for the first time, the problems of discussing work-in-progress may come up in that context. Many students have learned that it is "wrong" to look at someone else's paper and will just be learning about the way professionals share and help each other with their work. A good place to see how collaboration works is to look at the pages of acknowledgments in books. Students will find, in all of their textbooks, long lists of people who are acknowledged for help in the process of writing. Writing their own acknowledgments will allow students to talk about how their ideas were shaped by others, especially by those who cannot reasonably be footnoted.

If the social act of research is successful, students have the opportunity to learn that knowledge is not just found, but created out of existing knowledge. And if people create knowledge, it is reasonable to expect knowledge to change. What people regard as true may be something other than absolute fact. Indeed, it may be only a temporary formulation in the search for better understanding. We can hope that our students will develop ways to evaluate knowledge as a social phenomenon and progress toward a critical consciousness of all claims to knowledge.

"BUILDING A MYSTERY": ALTERNATIVE RESEARCH WRITING AND THE ACADEMIC ACT OF SEEKING

Robert Davis and Mark Shadle

[*CCC* 51.1 (2000): 417–41]

Robert Davis and Mark Shadle are associate professors of English and writing at Eastern Oregon University in La Grande, where Davis heads the Writing Program and Shadle directs the Writing Lab. Their teaching and research interests include writing in multiple genres, disciplines, cultures, and media. Currently, they are at work on a textbook on research writing that presents traditional forms alongside less conventional forms.

Davis and Shadle point out that in spite of regular critiques, the research paper continues to be a mainstay of first-year writing programs, and the approaches to researched writing have remained relatively stable. The authors argue that the explosion of and access to information has made the research process more complex, and that traditional approaches need to be reconsidered. Davis and Shadle argue for four specific alternatives to the traditional research paper—alternatives that they believe will help students to think of research in terms of "uncertainty, passionate exploration, and mystery." This piece offers a brief history of the traditional research paper, a description of the proposed four alternatives, and strategies for teaching them.

Research writing is disrespected and omnipresent, trite and vital, central to modern academic discourse, yet a part of our own duties as teachers of writing that we seldom discuss.[1] For nearly thirty years, the conventional construct of research writing, the "research paper," has seemed ready to collapse, undercut by the charge that it is an absurd, "non-form of writing" (Larson). Still, the research paper goes on. In a 1982 survey, James Ford and Dennis R. Perry found that the research paper is taught in 84 percent of first-year composition courses and 40 percent of advanced composition courses (827). The survey has not been repeated, but our own informal research suggests that the research paper is still taught in most composition curriculums, typically at the end of a first-year composition course or course sequence, and thus it is positioned as the final, even climactic, step for students entering the communities of academic discourse.[2]

This notable status has not kept the research paper from being notoriously vacant, clichéd, and templated. Research writing textbooks, despite their earnest good intentions, tend to reinforce unoriginal writing by providing students not only with maps through the conventional routes of academic research, but also a standardized concept of how academic research writing should look and sound; textbooks typically provide sample papers, and stock advice on the "rules" of logical argumentation, linear organization, acceptable evidence, and the proper way to cite sources.

In this essay, we will present a series of alternatives to the modernist research paper: the argumentative research paper, the personal research paper, the research essay, and the multi-genre/media/disciplinary/cultural research paper. Part of our purpose is practical—we want to suggest new choices to teachers and students of research writing. However, we are also interested in the theoretical implications of alternative research writing strategies. We see in these strategies movement away from the modernist ideals of expertise, detachment, and certainty, and toward a new valuation of uncertainty, passionate exploration, and mystery. We also see an increased rhetorical sophistication. Alternative research writing often asks students to compose within a large range of strategies, genres, and media. Our students, whose work we will highlight at the end of this essay, create research projects that use, and mix, not only multiple genres and media, but also multiple disciplines and cultures. This work overcomes not only students' fear of, and boredom with, traditional research writing, but also some of the false oppositions prevalent in composition studies and academic culture. These include the divisions between: academic and expressive writing; competing canons; fiction and nonfiction; high, pop, and folk culture; and the methods and jargons of different fields.

Escaping Posusta

Research writing instruction in its current state has begun to spawn parasitic parodies. What "Cliff Notes" has done for literature, Steven Posusta's *Don't Panic: The Procrastinator's Guide to Writing an Effective Term Paper (You know who you are)* does for research writing manuals. Posusta is a snowboarder and mountain biker with an M. A. who tutored at UCLA. His book is at once a spoof of other research writing texts; an exposé of the emptiness of "academic discourse," at least as practiced by cynics; and perhaps the best guide to research writing in that it makes full, explicit use of the value that hovers at the edges of other, more polite, texts: sheer efficiency. The writing "process" Posusta outlines can be completed in just one night, although he admits that two are best.

This efficiency took time to develop. Posusta recounts his own painful lessons as an academic outsider learning to, in David Bartholomae's phrase, "invent the university":

> Writing papers for college or university professors can be terrifying. The first paper I ever wrote came back to me flowing with red ink. A note on the first page read: "Why did you ignore my instructions? Rewrite!" I had unfortunately interpreted the professor's instructions as mere suggestions. Papers are personal, aren't they? If I answer the question and speak my mind, I'll do fine, right? Wrong. (7)

To better invent, Posusta had to learn the academy's customs, rules, and practices. He eventually did this well enough to become a writing tutor, where he encountered students like the one he had been, struggling to write in the ways of the academy. Further, he found that most students put off their writing until the last minute. Rather than attempt to help them enact longer writing processes, he instead suggested methods for quickly creating acceptable discourse.

His book is a continuation of his tutoring. At a sleek 62 pages (with large print), it claims a special ability to help students quickly get up to speed. Devices such as the Instant Thesis Maker help:

The Instant Thesis
#1. Although _____,
    (general statement, opposite opinion)
#2. nevertheless _____.
    (thesis, your idea)
#3. because _____.
    (examples, evidence, #1, #2, #3, etc.) (12)

The only thing more efficient would be to let an expert like Posusta or a computer program do the work for you, filling in the blanks in the Instant Thesis, Body, and Conclusion. Posusta, however, stands guard against forms of cheating even he considers too efficient. He cannot keep students from downloading research papers from the Internet, but he can foil their plans to pass off as their own the sample paper provided in *Don't Panic*. While other authors blather about the evils of plagiarism, Posusta takes protective measures. Instructors reading the photocopies of his sample paper, handed in by students who have failed to read it, will find the following sentence in the midst of the competent prose: "I am plagiarizing, please fail me" (9).

As the many cases of plagiarism and Posusta's Instant Book suggest, the research paper has become a stationary target. We would like to believe that research writing teaches valuable skills and encourages students to commit to the academic ideals of inquiry and evidentiary reasoning. However, it may be as often the case that the research paper assignment teaches students little more than the act of producing, as effortlessly as possible, a drab discourse, vacant of originality or commitment.

Defenses of the research paper often rely on its preparatory function. We must teach the research paper, the argument goes, because students are likely to encounter it again in other courses across the disciplines. While this argument has validity, it can be countered by noting that teaching the research paper as the sole example of research writing will fail to prepare students for a myriad of other research-based writings: lab reports, case studies, news stories, position papers, take-home exams, and research proposals. Further, one can argue, the research paper is solely academic. In a culture overrun with data, the public often remains uninterested in the detached perspective of the modernist research paper. As Sharon Crowley and Debra Hawhee point out, facts take on meaning within networks of interpretation, which enable and shape cultural debates (6).

Richard Larson's well-known criticism goes further, charging that, theoretically speaking, the research paper does not exist:

> Research can inform virtually any writing or speaking if the author wishes it to do so; there is nothing of substance or content that differentiates one paper that draws on data from outside the author's own self from another such paper— nothing that can enable one to say that this paper is a "research paper" and that paper is not. (Indeed even an ordered, interpretive reporting of altogether personal experiences and responses can, if presented purposively, be a reporting of research.) I would assert therefore that the so-called "research paper," as a generic, cross-disciplinary term, has no conceptual or substantive identity. If almost any paper is potentially a paper incorporating the fruits of research, the term "research paper" has virtually no value as an identification of a kind of substance in a paper. Conceptually, the generic term "research paper" is for practical purposes meaningless. (813)

Larson's erasure of the research paper's grounding, however, reveals the omnipresence and importance of research writing. He opens his essay with a defense of research-based learning as part of any literate education:

> Let me begin by assuring you that I do not oppose the assumption that student writers in academic and professional settings, whether they be freshmen or sophomores or students in secondary school or intend to be journalists or lawyers or scholars or whatever, should engage in research . . . and that appropriately informed people should help them learn to engage in research in whatever field these writers happen to be studying. (811)

Larson is joined by advocates of research writing, and the authors of sincere, non-Posusta research writing textbooks, in stressing the importance of research in our infoculture and the necessity of teaching research skills. Research writing, we are told, should teach students about how data is generated and expertise gained. It should also allow them to cultivate their intellectual curiosity and expand their knowledge. The issue becomes method and form—how to do research and how to write it in ways that will allow students to embrace academic ideals and escape the cynicism of Posusta.

In alternative research writing, Larson's claim that research can inform nearly all discourse becomes the ground on which research writing is re-made. The models of composing we will present often involve choosing among, mixing, and juxtaposing a grand variety of discourses. The field of composition is here constituted as the study of all utterances—communicative, persuasive, expressive—in any genre, media, discipline, or culture. Seen in this light, research writing begins to enact the vision of composition theorist Derek Owens:

> Feasibly, taken in this broadest sense, composition studies is a crossroads discipline, a catalytic zone where a motley assemblage of discourse communities and arenas for intellectual exploration converge, metamorphose, and regenerate. At the same time, we cannot study multiple disciplines without being brought back somehow to the art of composing: musically, syntactically, lexically, orally, dialogically, socially, politically, poetically. (160)

As well as a broadened field for composing, the practices of alternative research writing enact a revised understanding of the purposes of academic work. According to its original ideal, modern research writing was to inscribe an act of seeking by presenting the knowledge the act secured. Seeking was made to consist of creating the conditions under which knowledge could present itself to the mind ready to receive it. But, as critiques of modernism have shown, knowledge cannot "present itself" to the mind because the mind and the world around it cannot be separated. Research has never been the hollow act of recording dead facts in a static world, and research writing has never been a mirror of nature. As James Elkins says in *The Object Stares Back: On the Nature of Seeing,* the gaze into the mirror is always an act of desire:

> When I say, "Just looking," I mean I am searching, I have my "eye out" for something. Looking is hoping, desiring, never just taking in light, never merely collecting patterns and data. Looking is possessing or the desire to possess—we eat food, we own objects, and we "possess" bodies—and there is no looking without thoughts of using, possessing, repossessing, owning, fixing, appropriating, keeping, remembering and commemorating, cherishing, borrowing, and stealing. I cannot look at *anything*—any object, any person—without the shadow of the thought of possessing that thing. Those appetites don't just accompany looking: they are looking itself. (22)

In the modern academy, the possessive gaze is expressed as the desire for expertise, which hides the passionate need to control the world. Werner Muensterberger has seen a similar drive in exacting and prestigious collectors. In *Collecting: An Unruly Passion,* he writes:

> I have followed the trail of these emotional conditions in the life histories of many collectors. . . . They like to pose or make a spectacle of their possessions. But one soon realizes that these possessions, regardless of their value or significance, are but stand-ins for themselves. And while they use their objects for inner security and outer applause, their deep inner function is to screen off self-doubt and unassimilated memories. (13)

Alternative research writing may offer hope for resisting the will to possess without returning to illusory claims to detachment, objectivity, and pure reflection. Such research writing does not seek claims to constant truth or an unassailable perspective, but instead asks us to take comfort in contingency, and thrill at mystery. Desire here is enacted as a restlessness reversing the libidinal economy of ownership; instead of wanting to possess, or even "know" the other, we want to sustain the experiential excitement of not knowing, the seductive wonder we feel at discovering that the other is beyond us, unknown, inexhaustible. The ideal of alternative research writing is exploration freed from its historical weight of conquest and enslavement.

Alternative research writing then, is not only a set of pedagogic strategies, but also a series of expressions of an altered conception of inquiry. Knowledge here plays leapfrog with mystery; meanings are made to move beyond, and writing traces this movement. Research becomes seeking as a mode of being. As academic seekers, we journey toward a state of understanding that subsumes both ignorance and knowledge, a state in which we "know" more deeply our own incapacity for certainty and find that it is uncertainty that keeps us alive and thinking. Alternative research writing is what William Covino calls a form of wondering: a way not to end thinking, but to generate and sustain it.[3] This discursive inquiry has a literal parallel in many world cultures. Whether we think of Australian aborigines on walkabout or East Indian men on sunyata, intellectual wondering is enacted as physical wandering.

Alternative research writing is intensely academic, but it also strives to reconstitute the academy by reaching beyond the disciplinary thinking, logos-dominated arguing, and nonexpressive writing we have come to call "academic." Alternative research writing inscribes an inclusive cross-disciplinary academy, which mixes the personal and the public and values the imagination as much as the intellect. Such writing thus helps us to regather creative work as inquiry, recalling, for instance, the moral charge Milan Kundera has given the novel: it must operate within the unknown to rediscover our world and ourselves. The plight of the alternative research writer is like the one Donald Barthelme sees in the novelist beginning a work:

> Writing is a process of dealing with not-knowing, a forcing of what and how. We have all heard novelists testify to the fact that, beginning a new book, they are utterly baffled as to how to proceed, what should be written and how it might be written, even though they've done a dozen. At best there's a slender intuition, not much greater than an itch. (486)

Student research writers may be working on a writing project that is, in some ways, different from a novel—still, we want them to have, and heed, an itch.[4] We want them to use research writing to follow questions wherever they lead and write this winding trail in discourse that is dialogic, Protean, and playful, while also passionately engaged—in the act of seeking itself, the work of the restless, wandering mind.

Ours, then, is an Instant Thesis after vitamins:

1. The research paper may be a vacant (non) form;
2. nevertheless, research writing remains a valuable activity, central to the academy in an infoculture—
3. as evidenced by alternative research writing strategies, which we will discuss here.
4. Further, we want to suggest, these alternative strategies may be read as inscriptions of the field of composition and academic culture revising themselves, reclaiming mystery as the heart of academic experience and discourse.

The research paper as modernism diminished

But first, #0, some history. We will trace the research paper as a historical construct, in part to attach it to a modern era, now passing. We also want to suggest, however, a more complicated set of relations, in which the ghost of the original modern spirit lives on, rekindled in alternative research writing. At the advent of modern research writing, we find an egalitarian respect for the act of seeking, a desire to inscribe the passage into the unknown. Research writing was conceived in the modern era as a way of writing the making of knowledge, and this writing was, at least in theory, open to all.[5] Anyone, according to this modern mythology, was capable of making a breakthrough, given the right disposition, intelligence, and training. The research paper as we now teach it, like many things modern, scarcely lives up to this promise. It is, typically, an apprentice work, not making knowledge as much as reporting the known.

Curricular histories cast the research paper as the product of the modern American university and modern society. In *Writing in the Academic Disciplines, 1870–1990*, David R. Russell notes, "The research paper, like the American university itself, is a grafting of certain German traditions onto what was originally a British system of college education" (79). The idea of requiring students to do text-based scholarship, a thesis or dissertation, began to take hold in the United States as early as the 1860s. In many cases, theses supplanted the earlier forensic speechmaking toward which much of undergraduate education was geared. The change in forms signaled a change in values as well: "Oral performance for a local academic community demanded only a *display* of learning, but the new text-based standards demanded an *original contribution* to a disciplinary community in written form: a research paper" (Russell 80).

Research writing prospered in a climate favoring originality and calling for the creation of knowledge. Such writing was to demonstrate the writer's place in the society of knowers by increasing the society's store of knowledge. As a written embodiment of modernist values, research writing proliferated. By the early 20th century, it was central to college writing courses. Its widespread adoption in these courses, however, may have stemmed from motivations very different from the stress on knowledge-making with which modern research writing began. In *Composition-Rhetoric*, Robert Connors writes:

> The rise of the "research paper" as a genre in freshman composition is another way teachers tried to transcend the personal writing that occupied the early stages of any course. Library research—often unconnected to any writing purpose other than amassing brute facts for regurgitation into a "research" paper—became very popular around 1920 and has remained a staple in writing courses since. (321)

The research paper came to be chiefly a vehicle for training—not in the creation of knowledge, but in the recording of existing knowledge. Connors describes the state-of-being of the student research paper writer:

> He is, finally, a medium, not an originator. His task is to explore the library or the words of the world, not timeless wisdom or his own experience. He is to be trained to pick and choose carefully among myriad facts, coming ideally to that selfless position of knowing secondary materials so well that he merges with them. As Canby et al. wrote in 1933, "Now if your paper is to be worth reading this must be the expression of information that has finally become so thoroughly digested that it truly comes from your own storehouse" (Canby et al., 300–01). The research writer is meant, in other words, to give himself up absolutely to a discourse community. (322–23)

A student writer given over to a discourse community may be ready for originality, ready to make the knowledge that will take the community to a new place. However, this potential was often lost in a tangle of legalistic concerns. Freshman research writing was not only to introduce students to the already known, it also sought to enforce a set of rules about the ownership of the known. As Connors notes, the research paper assignment "meant to teach the entire process of 'ethical' research—giving proper space to varied sources and proper crediting of sources. These concerns were just a formalization of the growing concern with intellectual property that had become a notable part of nine-teenth-century law and jurisprudence" (321). The emerging conventions of the research paper "presented teachers with a grateful mass of practical formal material for which they could hold students responsible—the minutiae of formats, footnotes, bibliographies, citation forms, and so on" (322).

Russell notes that teacher/regulators saw poor writing as caused by poor thinking, and saw poor thinking as a threat to the academy:

> The "undisciplined" gropings of student prose were of course far from the research ideal held up by the disciplines. As faculty never tired of pointing out, student papers were replete with ignorance and errors of all sorts, which could seem-ingly never be entirely eradicated. Because faculty tended to regard poor writing as evidence of poor thinking, not as evidence of a student's incomplete assimi-lation into a disciplinary community, faculty sensed that the discipline's "store of knowledge," acquired at great sacrifice, was "tarnished" by poor writing. (74)

The writing teacher thus becomes part guard, part dishwasher: "'Scouring' stu-dent writing for 'mistakes of fact and expression' became the goal, and writing instruction 'professional scullery'" (Wolverton 407, quoted in Russell, 74).

The history of research writing in the American university is one of failed promise for students, teachers, and discourse. Begun with the egalitarian ideal of the making of knowledge, modern research writing has become the fallen "re-search paper," an apprentice work piecing together what is known, and pre-senting this piecing in a form that is also known, at least by the teacher. The teaching of research writing has remained tied to a contrived and templated way of writing, and to the self-imposed charge of safeguarding the university's store of knowledge—from those who do not know, and may never know, the words and thoughts that will grant them admittance to the society of knowers.

Some students seem to experience the culture of expertise as Kafka's land surveyor does the castle—as impenetrable, governed either by inexplicable whims or rules that defy surveying. Those students who learn the rules, how-ever, often suffer another dilemma—an apparent unwillingness or inability to think imaginatively or originally. Many of the teachers we know complain that even advanced students are content to do what they know how to do: present the knowledge made by others, write within set conventions, and produce what they have been conditioned to believe teachers want. The teaching of research writing is often part of this conditioning: by asking students to stick to research-ing the known, we teach them to fear the unknown. We also make possible Steven Posusta, who would make the research process and product generic, re-peatable, and instant.

The alternative ways of researching writing we survey below challenge the conditioned fear of the unknown and the banalities of "efficient" research writing. These methods embrace the modernist value of collegial work within the un-known. At least two of the methods, the research essay and the multi-genre/media/disciplinary/cultural research project, recall the intellectual wandering of early modernists, such as Montaigne. As ways of working within contingency, methods that use multiple genres and media may seem in sync with postmod-ern literature and art.

Beyond this entwinement of the modern and postmodern, we prefer, how-ever, to see these methods as neither modern nor postmodern, but instead of historical time-travelers, regathering habits of mind and ways of writing, while attempting to stage intellectual experience as seeking and saying in the heart of mystery.[6] Inside "heart" is the "ear" and "hear"; it is thus what we heed in lis-tening to poet Charles Olson's call to pay attention to the life passing through us mysteriously. Throughout *The Special View of History*, Olson also reminds us of the consequences of practicing Herodotus's original translation of "istorin" as "to find out for yourself." Such a perspective need not lead to a postmodern nihilism and relativism; instead, in an ever-changing world where every person is imperfect, and each event is an incomplete palimpsest we select or build from the shards at our disposal, the importance of the rhetorical process and critical thinking are amplified. When no researcher can have the "best facts of interpretations," it becomes crucial to carefully assess the audience, occasion, message, purpose, and logic of our writing.

In teaching alternative research writing, we ask our students to practice not only this rhetorical sophistication, but also the gathering and syncretism found in so many cultures pre-dating and leaking into Western Civilization. In his novel *The Mapmaker's Dream*, James Cowan has his Italian Renaissance mapmaker monk, while researching the geography of earth, describe this syncretism of an either/and (rather than either/or) world/consciousness in these words:

> Every man who had ever lived became a contributor to the evolution of the earth, since his observations were a part of its growth. The world was thus a place entirely constructed from thought, ever changing, constantly renewing itself through the process of mankind's pondering its reality for themselves. (60)

Similarly we recall the "nomadic" thought of Deleuze and Guattari, which inscribes "plateaus" of intense conductivity without center or fixed form. This is the kind of practice we envision for, and begin to see enacted by, alternative research writing. Like the surprising transformation of traditional nomadic life into the itinerancy of our own, we see such research writing as committed, its practitioners engaged in a sustained, "lifelong" learning in which the spirit is always at stake precisely because the individual's journey does matter in a world that is always changing and uncertain.[7]

Survey of alternative research writing methods

When taken in turn, the alternative research writing methods we will present—the research argument, research essay, personal research paper, and multi-genre/media/disciplinary/cultural research project—enact a gradual reopening of the purpose of research writing, reminiscent of a closed fist opening finger-by-finger. Viewed consecutively, these methods trace a movement away from the templated discourse of the research paper and into an increasingly complex world of rhetorical choices. This movement also performs what Zygmunt Bauman calls a "re-enchantment of the world," supplanting the will to power with a sense of playfulness and wonder.[8] Alternative research writing, as we read and enact it, inscribes an enchanted world that is a continual source of wonder. The stunted will to know is here eclipsed by its shadow: the academic act of seeking inspired by the endless seductions of mystery and the shimmering promise of syncretic mapping.

The research argument

Research writing has always *argued;* persuasion is needed, even in discourses aimed at exposition, to hold the writing together, and provide an understanding of what the data means. Robert E. Schwegler and Linda K. Shamoon, however, argue that research papers may contain arguments, but are nonetheless distinct from persuasive writing. Instead, they claim, the overall structure and aim of research papers fit the category James Kinneavy called scientific discourse: "writing that makes interpretive statements about some aspect of reality . . . and demonstrates the validity of these statements" (Kinneavy 88–89, quoted in Schwegler and Shamoon 818).

Still, most research writing textbooks now include some elements of argumentation, often in complex relation to the informational and interpretive intents of the modern research paper. In *The Craft of Research*, Wayne C. Booth,

Gregory G. Colomb, and Joseph M. Williams suggest that copious notes and collections of facts take on meaning only when writers discover the claims they want to make. These authors then provide an explication of the Toulminian scheme of claims, warrants, qualifications, and evidence. They further note that arguing in research writing can shift the emphasis of the paper from the information presented to the significance of the information, and even the authorial self projected on the page. The authors recommend that research writers imagine themselves in conversation with their readers: ". . . you making claims, your readers asking good questions, you answering them as best you can" (89).

In *Doing Research: The Complete Research Paper Guide,* Dorothy Seyler delineates three modes of research writing: the expository research paper, the analytic research paper, and the argumentative research essay. Each is animated by different kinds of questions and yields different sorts of discourse. She suggests the differences in a list of topics:

Expository:
Report on debate over relationship of modern birds to dinosaurs.
Report on recent literature on infant speech development.

Analytic:
Account of the processes used to identify and classify animals based on the fossil record.
Explanation of process of infant speech development.

Argumentative:
Support of claim that modern birds descended from dinosaurs.
Argument for specific actions by parents to aid infant speech development. (6)

Seyler's first argumentative topic would allow its writer to enter a current debate about evolution; far from reporting the known, this paper would stake a claim in a hotly contested area. The second topic functions on a personal level; it appeals to the parent, and/or future parent in its writer and reader. In each case, we can easily imagine that the student writer's claims would not be seen as pure knowledge, or even accepted as correct. Others in the class might suggest that birds evolved from another source, or that evolution does not make new families, phyla, or species. Advice about speech development could be supplemented or challenged by other research or the experience of the reader. Research and writing, here, become fodder for continuing debate.

The "research argument" constructs the academy as a site for informed conversation. Writers of the research argument seek to become experts, taking in the research they need to formulate and support an intelligent position. They are not, however, charged with ending dialogue and establishing set truth. Instead, their responsibility is to use research to inform debate and to position themselves as reasonable persuaders.

Further, the research argument can call on students to consider, and use, a range of rhetorical strategies. While some books may stress a fairly rigid approach to argumentation—stressing, for instance, the appeal to reason, using factual evidence or probabilities—teachers and students can also adopt a more varied approach, stressing diverse appeals and showing how they can be integrated.[9]

The research argument pushes toward, then, an academic environment that values debate, and calls for the appropriate and strategic use of a wide rhetorical repertoire. However, the research argument can also be criticized for requiring the defense of a claim or position, rather than a detached examination of data, as in the modernist research paper, or a more open exploration of a series of claims, as in the alternative methods of research writing explicated below. These methods allow writers to examine a range of viewpoints, but without forcing them to adopt a single position to defend. They make conversations not only communal, but also internal.

The personal research paper

While the research argument asks students to at least stimulate informed entry into public debate, the personal research paper allows students to research and inscribe a personal issue. In his textbook *Research: The Student's Guide to Writing Research Papers,* Richard Veit suggests that the advantage of the personal research paper is that it allows students to formally think about subjects to which they feel intimately connected. Veit acknowledges that his personal research paper is Macrorie's "I-Search" paper renamed and offers the same opportunity to answer existential, or practical needs; Veit and Macrorie's samples include papers on choosing the right camera and becoming a creative writer. Research sources include both written materials and interviews with those who can shed light on the question being pursued. In form, personal research papers often use a narrative structure and chronological order to recreate the writer's unfolding search. The papers typically end with either a tentative, perhaps temporary, conclusion, or the redirection of the question: "Should I be a writer?" becomes "Are the rewards of writing worth the sacrifices?"

The personal nature of these papers, it seems, might lead to writing that means much to the writer but little to readers. Veit and Macrorie, however, each stress that lively writing makes these papers captivating. Perhaps so, but the well-known criticism of Macrorie's approach—that it largely misses the social dimension of writing—still has force, even if the I-Search does seem a powerful method for helping students direct their own lives.[10.]

Approaches are needed that preserve the spirit of the I-Search in discourse that explores questions that are more explicitly intellectual and public. For instance, recasting "Should I be a disc jockey?" as "Why does radio fascinate?" may lead to interdisciplinary research that is both library- and interview-based and writing that is more likely to apply to readers as well as its writer. Such public/private work preserves the notion that learning is autobiographical, while also sustaining one of the chief lessons of rhetoric—that even the personal scripts in which we think we are socially constructed and keep us connected to a shared, if conflicted, world. It also seems wise to preserve, while transforming, the idea that open questions are to be pursued and explored, rather than avoided, or terminally answered. As Theodore Zeldin argues in *An Intimate History of Humanity,* the ability and willingness to hold an open and continuing conversation is a defining act of consciousness, necessary for becoming human. We might add that it is what we may most need to escape from the current barbarisms in which our world abounds.

The alternative methods of research writing described below typically make use of open-ended questions that are both personal and public. These methods are notably inclusive, allowing writers to use material from different kinds of research as well as personal experience. Further, they are syncretic discourses— using a variety of modes, genres, and, in some cases, media, and bringing together material from a number of disciplines and perspectives. We cannot claim that any of these methods will save the world, but done well, they can help enliven the worlds of the students who use them.

The research essay

We refer to essaying in the Montaignian sense of attempting, wondering, or as Scott Russell Sanders puts it, creating "experiments in making sense of things" (*Paradise* xiii):

> The "essay is the closest thing we have, on paper, to a record of the individual mind at work and play . . . [it is] the spectacle of a single consciousness making sense of a part of the chaos" of experience. The essay works by "following the zigzag motions of the inquisitive mind. . . . The writing of an essay is like finding

one's way through a forest without being quite sure what game you are chasing, what landmark you are seeking." ("Singular" 660, quoted in Heilker 89)

Paul Heilker argues that the essay counters the "thesis/support form," which he finds restrictive to students' development as thinkers and writers, and in conflict with current theories of social epistemology and rhetoric. These theories, he notes, tend to see truth and reality as multiple, provisional, dialogic, and dialectical. The essay better fits such theories in that it allows for multiple viewpoints, puts these viewpoints into dialogue with one another, and arrives, like the I-Search, at a provisional conclusion to be questioned in the dialectic's next round, or a recasting of the question.

Potentially, the essay can include all of experience. As Susan Griffin suggests in "The Red Shoes," and enacts in many of her works, essays can make the private public, erasing the lines we draw between parts of our experience. In this way, Griffin says, the essay is like the novel, which she finds to have discovered the legitimacy of private worlds for public writing. In form, the essay also resembles the novel by being varied in structure and often radically mixed in form. As Lydia Fakundiny notes, "Every essay is the only one of its kinds. There are no rules for making beginnings, or middles, or endings; it is a harder, a more original discipline that than" (2). Further, essays typically collect many different kinds of discourse: personal narratives, philosophic speculations, textual interpretations, parables, legends, folk wisdom, jokes, dialogues, complaints, rants, and arguments. Essay writing requires fluid thinking, rhetorical flexibility, and the ability to orchestrate.

The essay is brought to research writing in the work of Bruce Ballenger. In *The Curious Researcher,* Ballenger says that students who write research essays shape, and are shaped by, the information they encounter. A broad range of topics is possible, since the writer is not limited to arguing a single position. Topic development often leads to the expansion of thinking as the writer takes in and reflects on various viewpoints. It also offers an element of risk, as writers must mediate between views and work toward their own developing understanding. However, with risk can come intellectual growth—as well as academic enculturation. By inscribing themselves in the midst of a dialogue, debate, or search, students cast themselves within a culture of seeking.

An objection to assigning the research essay stems from compositionists' concerns with preparing students for college writing. Students are unlikely to write this hybrid, post-Montaignian, research-enhanced form (or collection of forms) in other courses. It may be, however, that the research essay prepares students for the diverse literacies of the academy precisely through its variety of information and discourse. It can be used to teach students various modes and genres, while also showing how this variety can function together. The research essay can prepare students for further academic and intellectual work by helping them to cultivate the ability and desire to engage multiple perspectives on issues that remain open for further inquiry.[11]

The multi-genre/media/disciplinary/cultural research project

The final alternative strategy we survey here, the multi-genre/media/disciplinary/cultural research project, further expands the field of seeking. Here, students explore topics of interest or fascination and use a variety of sources to inform projects that combine multiple genres and, in some cases, different media, disciplines, and cultures. These projects often resist, suspend, and/or decenter the master consciousness or central perspective inscribed in the essay as a unifying voice. They instead suggest a wandering consciousness, the traces of which we read in the various, linked, echoing pieces it has left behind for us to find.

These traces may come in the form of words, or in other media. In *The Electronic Word*, Richard Lanham calls print "an act of perceptual self-denial," and says that electronic textuality makes us aware of that self-denial "at every point and in all the ways in which print is at pains to conceal" (74). Multi-media research writing also points out these denials, but offering a full world of expression and communication in which the visual arts, video, music, noise, textures, even smells and tastes work in complex relations with writing. Like Web sites and other electronic discourses, multi-media research writing enacts a process of intertextual linking that erases the boundaries between texts, and between author and audience. Multi-media research projects gather material from many sources and often inspire readers to contribute more, or to do related work.

The act of gathering can also go beyond genres and media. The wandering, and wondering, consciousness is connected to the traits Julie Thompson Klein ascribes to interdisciplinary thinkers: "reliability, flexibility, patience, resilience, sensitivity to others, risk-taking, a thick skin, and a preference for diversity and new social roles" (182–83). Klein also claims that "the tendency to follow problems across disciplinary boundaries" is ". . . a normal characteristic of highly active researchers" (183). The wandering/wondering consciousness knows no boundaries because its focus is on the questions it pursues. Such pursuit is not careless, for it requires great concentration as well as openness. Enacting such a mind is a sign of great "discipline," but not that which requires us to stick to bounded fields.

A combination of flexibility and focus is also often seen in the multicultural codeswitchers who have finally begun to gain recognition as the margins of culture become central sites for intellectual study. In *Borderlands/La Frontera*, Gloria Anzaldúa writes of the new *mestiza*, who "operates in a pluralistic mode—nothing is thrust out, the good, the bad and the ugly, nothing rejected, nothing abandoned. Not only does she sustain contradictions, she turns the ambivalence into something else" (79).

This "something else" is a state of consciousness and discourse that the multi-genre/media/disciplinary/cultural research project begins to work toward. Such projects can create intellectual spaces that allow for various information, mindsets, and ideas—as well as diverse methods of thinking and ways of expressing, arguing, and communicating—to question and deepen one another and together make a greater, but still dissonant, whole. These projects work by making, but not forcing, connections: as such, they model the holistic learning that most formal schooling, with its disciplinary structure and many exclusions, too often works against.

David Jolliffe's work on multi-genre inquiry offers a starting point for considering how to enact multi-genre/disciplinary/cultural research writing. Jolliffe asks students to make an "inquiry contract" in which they agree to research and write several different pieces about a subject. Example topics, listed in Jolliffe's *Inquiry and Genre: Writing to Learn in College*, include the history of the seeding system in tennis, the relationship between the stock market and the defense industry, and the roles of women in American wars. Students pursue their topics using a range of rhetorical strategies, including: the contract proposal; the clarification project, in which students write reflectively about what they already know; the information project, in which they report on things they learn; the exploration project, with an essay raising additional questions; and the working documents project, which results in public writing designed to change people's minds.

Pieces within Jolliffe's method are reminiscent of the expository modernist research paper, the research argument, and the research essay, and—since each project begins with students' own interests—the overall agenda is similar to that of the personal research paper. By using these varied strategies, students strive to build a rhetorical repertoire. They also learn how to better recognize that their thinking is conditioned by the genres they write in, and that inquiry can extend across a range of singular, but related, texts.

Tom Romano describes multi-genre research projects that are potentially even more student-driven and open-ended. Romano's idea for what he came to call the Multi-Genre Research Paper surfaced after reading Michael Ondaatje's multi-genre "novel," *The Collected Works of Billy the Kid,* the reading of which Romano compared to listening to jazz: ". . . the reader feels something satisfying and meaningful, but may not be able to articulate what it is right away" (124). Romano asked his high school students to make biographical research projects using a style similar to Ondaatje's. The students wrote on subjects including Elvis Presley, Jimi Hendrix, Jim Thorpe, Marilyn Monroe, and Maya Angelou. Romano reports on the results:

> I have never read anything like these papers. Although four or five [of 26] were disappointing, showing little depth, breadth, or commitment, the rest were good, genuinely interesting in style and content, with seven or eight papers astonishingly superior. The visions were complex, the writing versatile. (130–31)

These students' projects are portfolios of diverse writing on a common subject. Each piece echoes the others, as an inner dynamic or theme emerges. A sample paper on John Lennon focuses especially on Lennon's love for Yoko Ono. The project is linked, in part, by a continuing series of poems about Lennon's murder called "Unfinished Music." It also contains other genres, including a news story, several narratives, and a meditation on the number "9" and its repeating presence in John and Yoko's lives. The author, Brian McNight, calls the project a "play," perhaps because it manages multiple voices (132–37).

Our students at Eastern Oregon University have gone beyond the multi-genre research paper to compose research projects that incorporate multiple genres, media, disciplines, and cultures. This approach originated in a 200-level Applied Discourse Theory course. It came out of long meditation on the way our students often found research sterile and theory either incomprehensible or dry. While initial resistance to the multi-genre/media/disciplinary/cultural approach was great—as the only thing more terrifying than slavery is sometimes freedom—students quickly found the excitement in research and theory directed toward projects that linked their academic and personal lives.

"Multi-writing," as we have come to call it, has now spread at our university to a 400-level capstone seminar in English/Writing; 300-level courses in Writing Theory, Electronic Literacy, and American Folklore; 200-level courses in Argumentation and Methods of Tutoring Writing; and a 100-level Exploratory Writing course. It has also expanded to courses in other disciplines, including a 100-level American Government course, and a 300-level Spanish Literature course. Next year, the university is planning a holistic revision of general education that will cast multi-writing as a central method for helping students to learn across disciplines and connect academic issues to their personal concerns. We see this sort of work early in college as an important retention effort, as well as a way of breaking intellectual ground for further work at the higher levels.

Through conference presentations and workshops, multi-writing has now been taken up on other campuses in our state and nationally and has moved into K–12 classes, especially those taught by fellows of the Oregon Writing Project, many of whom have participated in multi-writing workshops. At the primary and secondary levels, multi-writing helps students generate rich work samples, demonstrating multiple proficiencies for assessment.[12]

In teaching multi-writing in our discourse theory course, we first open students up to a sense of either a multi-dimensional self or multiple selves, in order to create in a postmodern world. We have used texts like Daniel Halpern's *Who's Writing*

This?, where dozens of famous writers rewrite the little self-portrait of Jorge Luis Borges in their own surprisingly different ways. Often students move from writing traditional and summative autobiographical pieces, where the older and wiser narrator looks back, to multi-cultural and generative ones, where the writer creates a new incarnation to grow into. Also successful has been a variation of autoethnography where students interview three people about themselves, then affirm or rebut the comments. We even invented two new kinds of multi-autobiography: "ought-to" and "want-to" biography—where students with a difficult childhood they would rather not delve into can imagine a different past: struggling artist in Paris, Tibetan monk, Earth Goddess, architect, blues musician.

In our most recent term of teaching, multi-autobiography projects included: Frank Kaminski's recycling box of personal obsessions from banal pop culture (*Star Wars*, the *Dukes of Hazzard*, the *Alien* movies); Katie McCann's cast-a-way project in which she imagines she is stranded on an island (her writings and drawings are contained in bottles); and Cara Kobernik's project on shoes. Shoes have been an important part of the author's life since she was baby, due originally to medical problems with her feet. The project includes a mock shoe catalogue and an illuminated manuscript called "Shoe Stories," as well as a beloved pair of sandals. In another memorable project, Lisa Rodgers split her self into three emanations with very different personalities and had the three escape from the dictatorial "Lisa" and journey on an improbable adventure, reminiscent of *Thelma and Louise*.

To keep the self from becoming too abstract and imaginary, we then require a mini-body project. Texts like Diane Ackerman's *A Natural History of the Senses* help students see how to combine facts with stylish prose. Student projects on the body often counter the typical images of the body prevalent in our culture, searching for other, richer views. Recent examples include Aubree Tipton's study of the relation of mind to disease and Sherry McGeorge's elaborate project on a feminist philosophy of belly dancing.

Finally, students create their own "multi-research project" on a theme they select. Some of these projects are biographical, like those of Romano's students. Subjects of recent "multi-biographies" include Adrienne Rich, Howard Hughes, Georgia O'Keefe, and Kurt Cobain. Other students find different themes, including: angels, Schoedinger's cat experiment, theories of the end of the world, massage, autism, the mysteries of tea, the Grand Canyon, the color blue, the Shroud of Turin, the Taiwanese language/dialect, the religion of television, masks, islands, Proppian interpretation of dreams, the concept of the "soulmate," the birth of punk rock, and debates over the literary canon.

The works show remarkable syncretism. Aubree Tipton's project on the Grand Canyon brings together courses she has taken in history, geology, and literature. Linnea Simon's project on tea is a cross-cultural dialogue, while Jakob Curtis studies Taiwan as a multiculture. Shirley Crabtree's interdisciplinary/multicultural project on fleas inscribes the history of this tiny but durable animal as part of a wider narrative of attempts by various imperial and fascistic entities to kill those seen as lesser.

The projects are widely varied in form. Like Romano's students, ours typically employ a range of genres: narratives, interpretive essays, letters, poems, wills, employment applications, lab reports, ethnographic and archeological field notes, prophecies, aphorisms, monologues, and dialogues, to name just a few. Cara Kobernik's project on the meaning of spring includes poems, personal and historical narratives, myths, folktales, monologues (including one by the Easter bunny), scripture and scriptural exegesis, aphorisms, science writing, philosophic reflection, and recipes.

Various media also abound. Judith Darrow's project on the fresco includes several original paintings in a style that might be called postmodern gothic.

Kobernik's project on Spring is very nearly a coffeetable book, with many photographs and drawings and an elegant design, as well as a lovely, floral smell. Nearly all of Jan Harris' project on blue is displayed in blue, on blue. The Grand Canyon project includes music, as does the project on blue, and many others. Videos are also common. Project containers are often interesting. We have received projects in folders, books, albums, boxes, crates, ovens, and even the back of a pickup truck. The project on blue comes in a binder covered with a blue suit. Eric Hutchinson's project on train travel is contained in its own kerchief-and-pole hobo bag. McGeorge's project on belly dancing comes wrapped in a beautiful scarf.

Some of the projects include strong elements of parody, often with serious intent: Sherri Edvalson's "A Feminist Education for Barbie" explores the effectiveness of gender theory and pedagogy in a continually sexist culture; it is enacted through a series of mock assignments for various courses and contained in a Barbie bookbag. Sue Ruth's EmpTV Guide, which is written in the form of a mock *TV Guide,* includes substantial research on television programming and cultural criticism, as well as scripts for mock commercials and Barnie's appearance on the Home Shopping Network. The project shows us locked into a media culture from which even parody cannot quite grant us escape.

In the midst of a grand variety of possible subjects, purposes, and forms, choices must be made. In his project on Houdini, Randy Kromwall saw and wanted to show intensity, obsession, awe, and passion in the magician's relationship to one of his most famous and dangerous tricks, the Water Torture Cell. Kromwall crafted a discourse that is part dialogue, part interior monologue, part lyric poem. The machine speaks, claiming that it is loved, and Houdini answers: "Yes, I love you / But you also terrify me. . . ." Kromwall gives his project a sensational tone and circus-like aura through the use of gothic type and several colorful posters advertising Houdini.

In her project on theories of good and evil, Judy Cornish used genres and media creatively to represent the ways in which her sources, and Cornish herself, have seen the two forces interlocking, and even becoming one. Her project design employed only black, white, and gray for its many images from high art and pop culture. Cornish made some images from scratch, and processed others into collages and striking juxtapositions. Among her writings is a dialogue in which the Kenpo concept of "push/pull," a way of absorbing violence, is explicated by a master and absorbed by a student, physically and spiritually. At the end, a provisional peace is realized when master and student redirect violence in a dance of acceptance.

In a reflective essay we typically assign at the end of a project, Cornish writes that her work on good and evil grew from her own hard life choices, which have made her question whether she was "good" or "evil," or if these words refer to anything real. Her project makes use of views on good and evil from writers of various time periods and cultures, including Toni Morrison, John Barth, Niccolo Machiavelli, and Kitaro Nishida. Cornish has told us that her personal connection to the material not only prompted the project, but pushed her toward doing more research and writing, even after she had clearly gone far beyond the requirements of the assignment. She was intellectually exploring a question that she was also urgently living.

A similar personal impetus motivates many of our students' projects, and sometimes leads them to work beyond the project. For Michelle Skow, a project on the Japanese American Internment grew into a larger capstone project, to which she has continued to add, even now that she has graduated. Skow realized that her own identity was deeply entwined with her grandparents' experience during the Internment. In her reflective essay, she wrote:

The Japanese American Internment experience is something my grandparents rarely discuss. When they do, they refer to their internment as "camp"—a euphemism for unlawful incarceration. Both claim to remember little of what happened during this time, even though my grandma was eleven and my grandpa was fourteen. . . . I have urged them to share, in-depth, this part of their lives with me, but they cling tightly to their vow of silence. I cannot say I disagree with their desire to forgive and forget, but I feel a part of me is missing.

Skow's project became an act of historical memory and re-creation. It begins dramatically, with a stark copy of the internment order (see Figure 1).[13] The project also includes: a conventional historical narrative about the Internment; found texts, such as James Masao Mitsui's poems written from photographs; Skow's own poems; diary entries written by Skow from the point of view of her grandparents during the Internment; photographs; and a poster announcing Executive Order 9066, the Internment order.

At times, we are taken to the camps; at other times, we are looking back at them. Gradually, Skow comes to better understand not only the Internment, but also her older relatives' attitude about it. She writes:

I want to forget Okasan as she sits,
Silently crocheting doily after doily,
Tablecloth after tablecloth.
Her nymph-like hands, cracked and withered
From the burning sun and stinging dust.
Working consciously, stitching a contract of silence:
Never forsake, never look back, never forget.

She has circled back to her grandmother's silence, with a new understanding. But not a full one. Skow followed up her first "multi-project" with another on first-generation Japanese Americans that grew into a capstone for her English/History double major. Now that she has graduated, she continues to tell us about new reading and writing that she has done, including essays on her "third generation" cultural heritage, and more writings from her grandparents' point of view. She says that she sees herself trying to mesh the first-generation world view and her own.

As well as asking students to write reflectively about (and, often, within) their projects, we also ask students to refract, to think about projects deflected from the original, threads left hanging, questions remaining, or questions not yet asked.[14] Several of our students have followed Skow in creating linked projects. Michael McClure began with an autobiographic project, modeled after Gregory Ulmer's concept of "mystory," held in a trunk full of texts and objects supposedly recovered in an archeological dig.[15] McClure followed this project with another on the artist Joseph Cornell, who made art in and from boxes, cases, and trunks. McClure's project includes a Cornellesque box of found and made objects, including an old gold watch, and several expository, interpretive, and creative writings, including a meditation on archeological time in Cornell's work.

These projects continue to evolve in the minds of their viewers/readers as well as their makers. We return to them again and again, trying to understand them in full, but also finding pleasure in knowing that we will not, that they will remain fertile mysteries. This is an experience far different from reading modernist research papers, where all meanings are to be made immediately clear, and the product is considered acceptable in large measure because it follows the rules. In multi-writing, "rules" are few. Students are shown some of the earlier projects, then asked to do something better. We assess them according to what they demonstrate as researchers, writers, and thinkers. We ask them to find a variety of sources, show us some of their range and depth as a rhetor, and reach for a philosophic understanding of their subject and their own

**WESTERN DEFENSE COMMAND AND FOURTH ARMY
WARTIME CIVIL CONTROL ADMINISTRATION**
Presidio of San Francisco, California
April 1, 1942

INSTRUCTIONS
TO ALL PERSONS OF
JAPANESE
ANCESTRY
Living in the Following Area:

All that portion of the City and County of San Francisco, State of California, lying generally west of the north-south line established by Junipero Serra Boulevard, Worchester Avenue, and Nineteenth Avenue, and lying generally north of the east-west line established by California Street, to the intersection of Market Street, and thence on Market Street to San Francisco Bay.

All Japanese persons, both alien and non-alien, will be evacuated from the above designated area by 12:00 o'clock noon Tuesday, April 7, 1942.

No Japanese person will be permitted to enter or leave the above described area after 8:00 a. m., Thursday, April 2, 1942, without obtaining special permission from the Provost Marshal at the Civil Control Station located at:

1701 Van Ness Avenue
San Francisco, California

The Civil Control Station is equipped to assist the Japanese population affected by this evacuation in the following ways:

1. Give advice and instructions on the evacuation.

2. Provide services with respect to the management, leasing, sale, storage or other disposition of most kinds of property including: real estate, business and professional equipment, buildings, household goods, boats, automobiles, livestock, etc.

3. Provide temporary residence elsewhere for all Japanese in family groups.

4. Transport persons and a limited amount of clothing and equipment to their new residence, as specified below.

The Following Instructions Must Be Observed:

1. A responsible member of each family, preferably the head of the family, or the person in whose name most of the property is held, and each individual living alone, will report to the Civil Control Station to receive further instructions. This must be done between 8:00 a. m. and 5:00 p. m., Thursday, April 2, 1942, or between 8:00 a. m. and 5:00 p. m., Friday, April 3, 1942.

2. Evacuees must carry with them on departure for the Reception Center, the following property:

(a) Bedding and linens (no mattress) for each member of the family;

(b) Toilet articles for each member of the family;

(c) Extra clothing for each member of the family;

(d) Sufficient knives, forks, spoons, plates, bowls and cups for each member of the family;

(e) Essential personal effects for each member of the family.

All items carried will be securely packaged, tied and plainly marked with the name of the owner and numbered in accordance with instructions received at the Civil Control Station.

The size and number of packages is limited to that which can be carried by the individual or family group.

No contraband items as described in paragraph 6, Public Proclamation No. 3, Headquarters Western Defense Command and Fourth Army, dated March 24, 1942, will be carried.

3. The United States Government through its agencies will provide for the storage at the sole risk of the owner of the more substantial household items, such as iceboxes, washing machines, pianos and other heavy furniture. Cooking utensils and other small items will be accepted if crated, packed and plainly marked with the name and address of the owner. Only one name and address will be used by a given family.

4. Each family, and individual living alone, will be furnished transportation to the Reception Center. Private means of transportation will not be utilized. All instructions pertaining to the movement will be obtained at the Civil Control Station.

Go to the Civil Control Station at 1701 Van Ness Avenue, San Francisco, California, between 8:00 a. m. and 5:00 p. m., Thursday, April 2, 1942, or between 8:00 a. m. and 5:00 p. m., Friday, April 3, 1942, to receive further instructions.

J. L. DeWITT
Lieutenant General, U. S. Army
Commanding

CIVILIAN EXCLUSION ORDER NO. 5

Figure 1. The [internment order poster] as it appeared in 1942. The full text is repeated in Note 13.

project that will allow the work to hang together and make each piece part of the same web.

Less efficiency, more mystery

It would be possible, perhaps even desirable, to reconstruct the progression we have presented. One could easily cast the alternatives listed above as simply a series of possibilities to be mixed and matched, as supplements of, or replacements for, the modernist research paper. It might be quite sound pedagogically, for instance, to ask students to write a research paper, then a research argument, essay, or multi-writing research project; or to continue teaching the research paper at the 100-level, and then move on to alternative methods later; or to use alternative methods in introductory courses to get students started researching with fervor, and then require the research paper as they progress toward graduation. Such methods would satisfy consciences that believe the modernist paper ought still to be taught, but also allow students valuable new experiences.

For our purposes, however, establishing a progression is vital, for it shows the purpose and nature of research writing changing to meet the demands of a fluid world of complex relationships. If we want to describe a fixed world as others have described it, the modernist research paper will do. The research argument allows us to move beyond exposition of the unchanging to inscribe a human world continually remade by argument, in which research supports the will to stake and defend a claim. The personal research paper allows an inward turn from this culture of conflict, asking its writer to explore and mediate personal conflicts, contradictions, and questions.

The research essay provides an important reconnection with the social scene of writing, taking as its purpose the personal exploration of an issue or theme of collective concern. The essay can be seen as a discourse of the question, in which a variety of genres of writing are used to wander the terrain of a subject matter through which the writer may have tread before, but which she or he cannot claim to finally "know." The research essay thus foregrounds a shift in priorities—begun in the research argument and personal research paper—away from claims to, or descriptions of, verifiable knowledge, and toward a more open stance on the part of writers aware of uncertainty and contingency.

The multi-writing research project makes visible use of possibilities implicit in the research essay. Here, the trail of a question or questions leads through a range of connected material, including different genres of writing and, in some cases, different media, disciplines, and cultures. The maker of the multi-writing project is a collector, but not in the way of Muensterberger's collector/possessor. Instead, the intent here is to lay out a portion of what is potentially an inexhaustible, and radically open, network, to which the project's maker, and its readers/viewers, can add. One can imagine an infinite multi-writing which would call into its fold, bit by bit, all of discourse. Even the other methods of research writing—the research paper, the research argument, the personal research paper, the research essay—would be subsumed by this syncretic, ravenous multi-text.

Are we arguing that facts are useless, or that the discourses of expository intent, such as the modernist research paper, be abandoned? No. We are suggesting, however, that facts and expository writing have limits; they allow only certain types of inquiry to take place. What we envision, finally, is a discourse that will not have limits, that will allow for various kinds and levels of inquiry to echo, question, and deepen one another. Cornish's Kenpo scene may end with a brief bit of peace, but her project on good and evil settles nothing. Theories are both upheld and negated, as they challenge, question, and dance with one another. And yet, something important has happened. A student, an intellectual, a person has (re-)engaged an important, open question—one of the fascinations/terrors/ joys through which she shapes, repeatedly and anew, her examined life.

Above all, we want our students to view mystery as a source of inquiry, research, and writing. Mystery is an academic value; what good would an institute of inquiry be if everything was already known? A collective appreciation of mystery can also be a basis for revising the academy, making it truly a place of free inquiry, where the unknown is approached from many directions, using a variety of ways of thinking, writing, and making. In this academy, we envision the research writer learning many traditions of inquiry and discourse, while also learning to use these traditions syncretically in the composition classroom. Here, students can begin to write the eclectic and multiple texts of their learning; they can, in singer Sarah McLachlan's oxymoronic words, mix craft and inspiration, and "build a mystery."

Notes

[1] James E. Ford notes that the 1995 volume he edited, *Teaching the Research Paper: From Theory to Pedagogy, from Research to Writing*, is the first book on research paper instruction. His introduction provides additional counts: only 2 sessions on research writing have been presented at the MLA Convention, only 1 published bibliography has appeared on the subject (1). Further "[Research paper instruction] has been ignored in the periodic overview of the profession conducted by the MLA, NCTE, and CEA. . . . The annual and semiannual bibliographies published in the major writing journals omit it completely" (2). This inattention is striking, especially given Ford's estimate that 56 percent of first-year composition teachers devote an average of 29 percent of their time to research paper instruction (1–2).

[2] In Oregon, for instance, the research paper is most often taught in the third of a three-course sequence in first-year writing.

[3] See Covino's *Forms of Wondering: A Dialogue of Writing, for Writers*, a textbook on writing enacted through a series of dialogic forms. For Covino's re-reading of the Western rhetorical and philosophic tradition as a series of wonderings, see *The Art of Wondering*.

[4] See Kundera's *The Art of the Novel*.

[5] Of course, the practices of the modern academy were exclusionary—sexist, racist, and classist. Still, the direction of the academy at this stage was, roughly, toward greater inclusion.

[6] Historian Daniel J. Boorstin identifies seeking as the great communal human act: ". . . While the finding, the belief that we have found the Answer, can separate us and make us forget our humanity, it is the seeking that continues to bring us together" (1). Philosopher Steven R. L. Clark brings together seeking and saying: ". . . the pursuit of knowledge through the exchange of ideas is something that we must assume we have been about since we were talking beasts" (4).

[7] For examples of nomadic thought, see especially Deleuze and Guattari's *A Thousand Plateaus: Capitalism and Schizophrenia*.

[8] Bauman identifies this reenactment with postmodernity, seeing it as a way of relating to the world that comes after the tragic history of modernism, in which power-supported structures of cultural meaning are repeatedly erected only to be demolished.

[9] A work such as Sharon Crowley and Debra Hawhee's *Ancient Rhetorics for Contemporary Students*, while not nominally a research-writing text, could be helpful in showing students the range of argumentative strategies.

[10] James Berlin's "Contemporary Composition: The Major Pedagogical Theories" and Lester Faigley's "Competing Theories of Process: A Critique and a Proposal" brand Macrorie's work "expressionist." Berlin argues that expressionist pedagogies typically encourage students to use writing to reach toward a deep, personal truth. While students in expressionist classrooms often work together, the purpose of this collaboration is for students to help each other come to realizations that are finally individual. Expressionist practices are thus reminiscent of Platonic dialectics.

In *Textual Carnivals*, Susan Miller carries the critique of expressionism further, suggesting that such pedagogic strategies perpetuate the dominant order by enacting writing as an individual act, separate from social concerns and constraints.

Expressionist discourse fares better, however, in Geoffrey Sirc's "Never Mind the Tagmemics: Where's the Sex Pistols?" Here, Macrorie is cast as something of a punk compositionist, whose work is finally devalued because it does not ask students to bow to the dominant discursive order of academic convention.

[11] If our suggestions of the value of wondering and the uses of mystery seem to suggest a purely humanistic or philosophic viewpoint on research writing, consider an episode of *Nova* in which scientists confront the thrilling mysteries of the planet Venus. Venus, these scientists say, was traditionally thought to be very similar to Earth, close in size and, probably, composition. It was even thought that Venus might have oceans and rich oil deposits. Data from various probes, however, suggest not only that Venus is not like Earth, but that things happen there that could not happen on Earth, at least given our current understanding of natural processes and laws. The Earth's surface, for instance, is thought (and verifiably proven) to have been made over time, through the mechanics of volcanic eruption and plate tectonics. The surface of Venus appears to be all one age. By Earthly standards, this can't be.

[12] For more on using multi-writing to meet proficiency standards, see "Multi-Genre Writing and State Standards," an article in the *Oregon English Journal*, which we wrote with high school teachers Tom Lovell, Jennifer Pambrun, and John Scanlan.

[13] The text of [the Western Defense Command internment order] is as follows:

Instructions to All Persons of Japanese Ancestry Living in the Following Area:

All that portion of the City and County of San Francisco, State of California, lying generally west of the north-south line established by Junipero Serra Boulevard, Worchester Avenue, and Nineteenth Avenue, and lying generally north of the east-west line established by California Street, to the intersection of Market Street, and thence on Market Street to San Francisco Bay.

All Japanese persons, both alien and non-alien, will be evacuated from the above designated area by 12:00 o'clock noon Tuesday, April 7, 1942.

No Japanese person will be permitted to enter or leave the above described area after 8:00 a.m., Thursday, April 2, 1942, without obtaining special permission from the Provost Marshall at the Civil Control Station located at:
1701 Van Ness Avenue
San Francisco, California

The Civil Control Station is equipped to assist the Japanese population affected by this evacuation in the following ways:

1. Give advice and instructions on the evacuation.
2. Provide services with respect to the management, leasing, sale, storage or other disposition of most kinds of property including: real estate, business and professional equipment, buildings, household goods, boats, automobiles, livestock, etc.
3. Provide temporary residence elsewhere for all Japanese in family groups.
4. Transport persons and a limited amount of clothing and equipment to their new residence, as specified below.

The Following Instructions Must Be Observed:

1. A responsible member of each family, preferably the head of the family, or the person in whose name most of the property is held, and each individual living alone, will report to the Civil Control Station to receive further instructions. This must be done between 8:00 a.m. and 5:00 p.m., Thursday, April 2, 1942, or between 8:00 a.m. and 5:00 p.m., Friday, April 3, 1942.
2. Evacuees must carry with them on departure for the Reception Center, the following property:
   (a) Bedding and linens (no mattress) for each member of the family;
   (b) Toilet articles for each member of the family;
   (c) Extra clothing for each member of the family;
   (d) Sufficient knives, forks, spoons, plates, bowls and cups for each member of the family;
   (e) Essential personal effects for each member of the family.

All items carried will be securely packaged, tied and plainly marked with the name of the owner and numbered in accordance with instructions received at the Civil Control Station.

The size and number of packages are limited to that which can be carried by the individual or family group.

No contraband items as described in paragraph 6, Public Proclamation No. 3, Headquarters Western Defense Command and Fourth Army, dated March 24, 1942, will be carried.

3. The United States Government through its agencies will provide for the storage at the sole risk of the owner of the more substantial household items, such as iceboxes, washing machines, pianos and other heavy furniture. Cooking utensils and other small items will be accepted if crated, packed and plainly marked with the name and address of the owner. Only one name and address will be used by a given family.

4. Each family and individual living alone, will be furnished transportation to the Reception Center. Private means of transportation will not be utilized. All instructions pertaining to the movement will be obtained at the Civil Control Station.

Go to the Civil Control Station at 1701 Van Ness Avenue, San Francisco, California, between 8:00 a.m. and 5:00 p.m., Thursday, April 2, 1942, or between 8:00 a.m. and 5:00 p.m., Friday, April 3, 1942, to receive further instructions.

J. L. DeWITT
Lieutenant General, U.S. Army, Commanding

[14] A similar view of revision as refraction is held by Nancy Welch in *Getting Restless*. Welsh argues that composition teachers have failed to ask questions such as "something missing, something else?" in responding to student drafts, instead conceiving of revision mainly as a way to narrow foci, correct inappropriate tones, and achieve clarity. For Welch, revision should strive not to eliminative dissonance, but instead use it as "the start of a reproductive struggle that can lead to a change of direction, a change of thesis, a real re-envisioning of the text, its meaning and intentions" (30).

[15] Ulmer presents "mystory" as a writing-after-video that combines personal, professional, and historic elements and utilizes the jump-cut logic of television. Ulmer's own mystory, "Derrida at Little Bighorn," can be seen as a work of personal and public research writing for the electronic age.

Works Cited

Ackerman, Diane. *A Natural History of the Senses.* New York: Random House, 1990.

Anzaldúa, Gloria. *Borderlands/La Frontera: The New Mestiza.* San Francisco: Aunt Lute Books, 1991.

Ballenger, Bruce. *The Curious Researcher: A Guide to Writing Research Papers.* Boston: Allyn and Bacon, 1994.

Barthelme, Donald. "Not-Knowing." *The Art of the Essay.* Ed. Lydia Fakundiny. Boston: Houghton Mifflin, 1991. 485–97.

Bartholomae, David. "Inventing the University." *When a Writer Can't Write: Studies in Writer's Block and Other Composing-Process Problems.* Ed. Mike Rose. New York: Guilford P, 1985. 134–65.

Bauman, Zygmunt. *Intimations of Postmodernity.* London: Routledge, 1992.

Berlin, James. "Contemporary Composition: The Major Pedagogical Theories." *College English* 44 (1982): 343–48.

Boorstin, Daniel J. *The Seekers: The Story of Man's Continuing Quest to Understand His World.* New York: Random House, 1998.

Booth, Wayne C., Gregory G. Colomb, and Joseph M. Williams. *The Craft of Research.* Chicago: U of Chicago P, 1995.

Canby, Henry S., et al. *English Composition in Theory and Practice.* 3rd ed. New York: Macmillan, 1933.

Clark, Steven R. L. "Ancient Philosophy." *The Oxford History of Western Philosophy.* Ed. Anthony Kenny. Oxford: Oxford UP, 1994. 1–54.

Connors, Robert J. *Composition-Rhetoric: Backgrounds, Theory, and Pedagogy.* Pittsburgh: U of Pittsburgh P, 1997.

Covino, William A. *The Art of Wondering: A Revisionist Return to the History of Rhetoric.* Portsmouth, NH: Heinemann, 1988.

———. *Forms of Wondering: A Dialogue of Writing, for Writers.* Portsmouth, NH: Heinemann, 1990.

Cowan, James. *A Mapmaker's Dream: The Meditations of Fra Mauro, Cartographer to the Court of Venice.* New York: Warner, 1996.

Crowley, Sharon, and Debra Hawhee. *Ancient Rhetorics for Contemporary Students.* 2nd ed. Boston: Allyn and Bacon, 1999.

Davis, Robert L., Tom Lovell, Jennifer Pambrun, John Scanlan, and Mark Shadle. "Multi-Genre Writing and State Standards." *Oregon English Journal* 20.2 (1988): 5–10.

Deleuze, Gilles, and Félix Guattari. *A Thousand Plateaus: Capitalism and Schizophrenia.* Trans. Brian Massumi. Minneapolis: U of Minnesota P, 1987.

Elkins, James. *The Object Stares Back: On the Nature of Seeing.* New York: Simon and Schuster, 1996.

Faigley, Lester. "Competing Theories of Process: A Critique and a Proposal." *College English* 48 (1986): 527–42.

Fakundiny, Lydia. "On Approaching the Essay." *The Art of the Essay.* Ed. Lydia Fakundiny. Boston: Houghton Mifflin, 1991. 1–19.

Ford, James E. "Introduction: The Need for *The Research Paper.*" *Teaching the Research Paper: From Theory to Practice, from Research to Writing.* Ed. James E. Ford. Metuchen, NJ: Scarecrow, 1995. 1–5.

Ford, James E., and Dennis R. Perry. "Research Paper Instruction in Undergraduate Writing Programs: National Survey." *College English* 44 (1982): 825–31.

Griffin, Susan. "The Red Shoes." *The Eros of Everyday Life: Essays on Ecology, Gender, and Society.* New York: Doubleday, 1995. 161–76.

Halpern, Daniel, ed. *Who's Writing This?: Notations on the Authorial I, with Self-Portraits.* Hopewell, NJ: Ecco P, 1995.

Heilker, Paul. *The Essay: Theory and Pedagogy for an Active Form.* Urbana, IL: NCTE, 1996.

Jolliffe, David A. *Inquiry and Genre: Writing to Learn in College.* Boston: Allyn and Bacon, 1999.

Kafka, Franz. *The Castle.* Trans. Edwin and Willa Muir. New York: Knopf, 1941.

Kinneavy, James. *A Theory of Discourse.* Englewood Cliffs, NJ: Prentice-Hall, 1971.

Klein, Julie Thompson. *Interdisciplinarity: History, Theory and Practice.* Detroit: Wayne State UP, 1990.

Kundera, Milan. *The Art of the Novel.* Trans. Linda Asher. New York: Grove P, 1988.

Lanham, Richard. *The Electronic Word: Democracy, Technology, and the Arts.* Chicago: U of Chicago P, 1993.

Larson, Richard L. "The 'Research Paper' in the Writing Course: A Non-Form of Writing." *College English* 44 (1982): 811–16.

Macrorie, Ken. *The I-Search Paper.* Portsmouth, NH: Heinemann, 1988.

Miller, Susan. *Textual Carnivals: The Politics of Composition.* Carbondale: Southern Illinois UP, 1991.

Muensterberger, Werner. *Collecting: An Unruly Passion: Psychological Perspectives.* Princeton, NJ: Princeton UP, 1994.

Olson, Charles. *The Special View of History.* Berkeley: Oyez, 1970.

Ondaatje, Michael. *The Collected Works of Billy the Kid.* New York: Norton, 1974.

Owens, Derek. "Composition as the Voicing of Multiple Fictions." *Into the Field: Sites of Composition Studies.* Ed. Anne Ruggles Gere. New York: MLA, 1993. 159–75.

Posusta, Steven. *Don't Panic: The Procrastinator's Guide to Writing an Effective Term Paper (You know who you are).* Santa Barbara: Bandanna, 1996.

Romano, Tom. *Writing with Passion: Life Stories, Multiple Genres.* Portsmouth, NH: Heinemann, 1995.

Russell, David R. *Writing in the Academic Disciplines 1870–1990: A Curricular History.* Carbondale: Southern Illinois UP, 1991.

Sanders, Scott Russell. *The Paradise of Bombs.* Athens: U of Georgia P, 1987.

———. "The Singular First Person." *Sewanee Review* 96 (1988): 658–72.

Schwegler, Robert E., and Linda K. Shamoon. "The Aims and Process of the Research Paper." *College English* 44 (1982): 817–24.

Seyler, Dorothy U. *Doing Research: The Complete Research Paper Guide.* 2nd ed. Boston: McGraw-Hill, 1999.

Sirc, Geoffrey. "Never Mind the Tagmemics: Where's the Sex Pistols?" *College Composition and Communication* 48 (1997): 9–29.

Ulmer, Gregory. *Teletheory: Grammatology in the Age of Video.* New York: Routledge, 1989.

Veit, Richard. *Research: The Student's Guide to Writing Research Papers.* 2nd ed. Boston: Allyn and Bacon, 1998.

"Venus Unveiled." *Nova.* PBS. Oct. 17, 1995.

Welch, Nancy. *Getting Restless: Rethinking Revision in Writing Instruction.* Portsmouth, NH: Heinemann-Boynton/Cook, 1997.

Wolverton, S. F. "Professional Scullery." *Educational Review* 60 (1920): 407.

Zeldin, Theodore. *An Intimate History of Humanity.* New York: Harper, 1996.

RESPONDING TO PLAGIARISM

Alice Drum

[*College Composition and Communication* 37 (1986): 241–43.]

Vice president of the College and Dean at Franklin and Marshall College in Lancaster, Pennsylvania, Alice Drum has published numerous articles and reviews in professional journals, including *College Literature, College Composition and Communication, Journal of Higher Education,* and *World Literature Written in English.* She is coauthor of *Funding a College Education,* published by the Harvard Business School Press.

Drum wrote the following article as a response to a plagiarism case that was especially troubling to her. After the case was over she surveyed composition texts to see how they presented plagiarism. She concluded that many of the presentations were inadequate and that introductory writing courses needed to do more to prevent plagiarism. With its thorough coverage on pages 576–80, *The Bedford Handbook* answers Drum's call for more emphasis on teaching students how to avoid plagiarism.

Plagiarism is a disease that plagues college instructors everywhere. I believe that our reliance on the classic argument against plagiarism may be one of the reasons for its continued virulence. That argument reads something like this: Plagiarism is both legally and morally wrong because it involves the appropriation of words or ideas that belong to someone else and the misrepresentation of them as one's own. Unfortunately, we tend to place a great deal of emphasis on the first part of the process, the simple act of taking ideas, and very little on the second stage, the more complicated act of passing them off as one's own. In our conferences with students suspected of plagiarism, we carefully point out the legal and ethical implications of what they have done, but we neglect to mention the pedagogical implications of what they have not done—completed an assignment. As the continuing practice of plagiarism testifies, this emphasis on the legalistic rather than the pedagogical consequences of plagiarism has proved an ineffectual way of dealing with the problem. In its place, I would recommend a holistic approach, a recognition that plagiarism involves a student, an instructor, and the structure within which the two interact.

In the first place, we must admit that many students do not know how to avoid plagiarism, that most rhetoric textbooks are of little help in this respect, and that many college composition classes deal inadequately with the problem. The greatest weakness is with the textbooks. A random survey of thirty popular texts reveals that many provide no reference to plagiarism in the index, and that most contain at best a paragraph of explanation and definition. Most textbooks say, in effect, "Do not plagiarize," but they refuse to do much more than remonstrate against the practice. They seldom contain useful writing exercises on the paraphrase, the summary, and the precis, although such exercises would indicate to students that there are varied ways of avoiding plagiarism. Instead, the standard handbook emphasizes the mechanics of documentation—the presentation of footnotes and bibliography in the currently accepted form.

In the classroom, we take our cue from the handbooks and concentrate on rules rather than on the various ways of integrating source materials in a text. Avoiding plagiarism is not simply a matter of following accepted rules, however. If a student changes Harold Bloom's description of Milton, "the severe father of the sublime mode" (*Poetry and Repression,* p. 21), to "a severe father of sublimity," that student has not repeated more than three words in a row, thus adhering to one popular formula on how to avoid plagiarism. On the other hand, the student has not added anything that is original; clearly, the sentence needs a footnote. Occasionally, footnotes are omitted through oversight, but generally the need for documentation is clear to students, once they understand that avoiding plagiarism does not simply involve adhering to a formula but also involves dealing carefully with the style and the content of the original.

In my composition classes, to help students understand this principle, a research paper is due only after I have assigned and returned three or four preliminary assignments and after the students have participated in several research writing workshops. The preliminary assignments may include an abstract, a summary, a brief background paper. The writing workshops include sessions where the students analyze the style and the content of a selected passage and then attempt to put that passage in a different form. They may work on creating an effective paraphrase of a brief article; they may take a single sentence and rewrite it a number of times, making as many stylistic changes as possible without changing the content; they may rewrite a brief passage—an article from *Newsweek*—in the style of a well-known writer. The aim of these exercises is twofold: to help the students understand that writers do give an identity to their words, and to give students confidence in their own ability to create a style of their own in their writing.

These exercises are designed to correct unconscious plagiarism, but we all know that many acts of plagiarism are conscious ones. In regard to these cases, we must examine the myth that plagiarism has everything to do with some anonymous "other"—a critic, an expert—and nothing to do with the teacher of the class, who has, after all, made the assignment which the student has failed to complete. Because written assignments involve at least one, and probably all, of the steps of the cognitive process, they test the student's ability to collect evidence, make inferences, and render judgments. The professor's response in the form of a grade or a written commentary is a means of communicating his or her opinion of the student's intellectual maturity. When students fail to comply honestly with an assignment, the pedagogical process breaks down.

For this reason, the instructor—not deans, chairpersons, nor commissions—should handle initial cases of plagiarism. There are a number of benefits to be derived from this procedure. An important one is that we would not be perpetuating the myth that plagiarism has nothing to do with the instructor and the course. Another benefit is that students are more likely to be concerned about the response of a professor who represents a familiar face than they are about the response of a dean who represents anonymous authority. And professors, only too aware of the difficulties of dealing with bureaucracy, may be more inclined to confer with a student than to involve themselves in the time-consuming procedure of reporting plagiarism to someone else.

Instead, the penalty for plagiarism, at least for initial cases in introductory courses such as composition, should be meted out by the instructor. With initial cases, we can reasonably assume that either the students do not know how to avoid plagiarism or that they have been led to believe that it does not matter. We can assure them that the latter is not true, and we can provide instructions on how to avoid plagiarism in the future. Some persons may argue that the individual professor may not be harsh enough, that stringent punishments are needed to stop the widespread cheating on campuses today. But it can, also, be argued that legalistic punishments have not proved particularly effective, and that they necessitate extensive protections for the student and increasing complications for the professor who attempts to prove plagiarism. I am not arguing for permissiveness in regard to plagiarism, but rather for a recognition that it is at least as much a pedagogical offense as a legalistic one. Certainly, we must insist that we will not tolerate plagiarism, that students will receive significantly lowered grades when they plagiarize. But we should also admit that students may learn more from a second chance to complete an assignment than from an automatic failure in a course. With this alternative procedure, there should be added penalties and added work, but there would, also, be an opportunity for the student to learn how to deal with research material with integrity. And that, after all, is one of the reasons that we assign library papers.

PART ELEVEN

GRAMMAR BASICS

Though writing teachers no longer consider direct grammar instruction to be central to the teaching of writing, they recognize that students need understandable definitions of grammatical terms and concepts as they revise and edit. Part Eleven of *The Bedford Handbook* offers a straightforward explanation of the basics of grammar, providing students with an easy-to-use reference source.

The following article explores questions that teachers might confront as they consider how to encourage students to use the handbook's information on grammar:

- What are different definitions of *grammar*? How might these definitions help writing teachers? How can the different kinds of grammar contribute to the teaching of writing?
- How can teachers provide students with the information they need about grammar without hindering their development as writers?

GRAMMAR, GRAMMARS, AND THE TEACHING OF GRAMMAR

Patrick Hartwell

[*College English* 47 (1985): 105–27.]

Patrick Hartwell, professor of English at Indiana University of Pennsylvania, is interested in error analysis, basic writing, and literacy. His articles have appeared in *College English, Rhetoric Review,* and *Research in the Teaching of English.*

In the following article, Hartwell enters the ongoing debate about the role of grammar instruction in writing courses, observing that this is actually a debate about the sequence of instruction in composition classes: should teachers address word- and sentence-level concerns first, or should they use a "top-down" approach, attending first to issues of meaning and purpose? In his attempt to clarify the debate, Hartwell analyzes what we might mean by *grammar* and describes at least five meanings for the term. His discussion of those meanings can help new and experienced teachers be more specific in their use of grammar instruction and can help them understand more fully what they might or might not want to accomplish when presenting grammar to students.

For me the grammar issue was settled at least twenty years ago with the conclusion offered by Richard Braddock, Richard Lloyd-Jones, and Lowell Schoer in 1963.

In view of the widespread agreement of research studies based upon many types of students and teachers, the conclusion can be stated in strong and unqualified terms: the teaching of formal grammar has a negligible or, because it usually displaces some instruction and practice in composition, even a harmful effect on improvement in writing.[1]

Indeed, I would agree with Janet Emig that the grammar issue is a prime example of "magical thinking": the assumption that students will learn only what we teach and only because we teach.[2]

But the grammar issue, as we will see, is a complicated one. And, perhaps surprisingly, it remains controversial, with the regular appearance of papers defending the teaching of formal grammar or attacking it.[3] Thus Janice Neuleib, writing on "The Relation of Formal Grammar to Composition" in *College Composition and Communication* (23 [1977], 247–50), is tempted "to sputter on paper" at reading the quotation above (p. 248), and Martha Kolln, writing in the same journal three years later ("Closing the Books on Alchemy," *CCC*, 32 [1981], 139–51), labels people like me "alchemists" for our perverse beliefs. Neuleib reviews five experimental studies, most of them concluding that formal grammar instruction has no effect on the quality of students' writing nor on their ability to avoid error. Yet she renders in effect a Scots verdict of "Not proven" and calls for more research on the issue. Similarly, Kolln reviews six experimental studies that arrive at similar conclusions, only one of them overlapping with the studies cited by Neuleib. She calls for more careful definition of the word *grammar*—her definition being "the internalized system that native speakers of a language share" (p. 140)—and she concludes with a stirring call to place grammar instruction at the center of the composition curriculum: "our goal should be to help students understand the system they know unconsciously as native speakers, to teach them the necessary categories and labels that will enable them to think about and talk about their language" (p. 150). Certainly our textbooks and our pedagogies—though they vary widely in what they see as "necessary categories and labels"—continue to emphasize mastery of formal grammar, and popular discussions of a presumed literacy crisis are almost unanimous in their call for a renewed emphasis on the teaching of formal grammar, seen as basic for success in writing.[4]

An Instructive Example

It is worth noting at the outset that both sides in this dispute—the grammarians and the anti-grammarians—articulate the issue in the same positivistic terms: what does experimental research tell us about the value of teaching formal grammar? But seventy-five years of experimental research has for all practical purposes told us nothing. The two sides are unable to agree on how to interpret such research. Studies are interpreted in terms of one's prior assumptions about the value of teaching grammar: their results seem not to change those assumptions. Thus the basis of the discussion, a basis shared by Kolln and Neuleib and by Braddock and his colleagues—"what does educational research tell us?"—seems designed to perpetuate, not to resolve, the issue. A single example will be instructive. In 1976 and then at greater length in 1979, W. B. Elley, I. H. Barham, H. Lamb, and M. Wyllie reported on a three-year experiment in New Zealand, comparing the relative effectiveness at the high school level of instruction in transformational grammar, instruction in traditional grammar, and no grammar instruction.[5] They concluded that the formal study of grammar, whether transformational or traditional, improved neither writing quality nor control over surface correctness.

> After two years, no differences were detected in writing performance or language competence; after three years small differences appeared in some minor conventions favoring the TG [transformational grammar] group, but these were

more than offset by the less positive attitudes they showed towards their English studies. (p. 18)

Anthony Petrosky, in a review of research ("Grammar Instruction: What We Know," *English Journal*, 66, No. 9 [1977], 86–88), agreed with this conclusion, finding the study to be carefully designed, "representative of the best kind of educational research" (p. 86), its validity "unquestionable" (p. 88). Yet Janice Neuleib in her essay found the same conclusions to be "startling" and questioned whether the findings could be generalized beyond the target population, New Zealand high school students. Martha Kolln, when her attention is drawn to the study ("Reply to Ron Shook," *CCC*, 32 [1981], 139–151), thinks the whole experiment "suspicious." And John Mellon has been willing to use the study to defend the teaching of grammar; the study of Elley and his colleagues, he has argued, shows that teaching grammar does no harm.[6]

It would seem unlikely, therefore, that further experimental research, in and of itself, will resolve the grammar issue. Any experimental design can be nit-picked, any experimental population can be criticized, and any experimental conclusion can be questioned or, more often, ignored. In fact, it may well be that the grammar question is not open to resolution by experimental research, that, as Noam Chomsky has argued in *Reflections on Language* (New York: Pantheon, 1975), criticizing the trivialization of human learning by behavioral psychologists, the issue is simply misdefined.

> There will be "good experiments" only in domains that lie outside the organism's cognitive capacity. For example, there will be no "good experiments" in the study of human learning.
>
> This discipline . . . will, of necessity, avoid those domains in which an organism is specially designed to acquire rich cognitive structures that enter into its life in an intimate fashion. The discipline will be of virtually no intellectual interest, it seems to me, since it is restricting itself in principle to those questions that are guaranteed to tell us little about the nature of organisms. (p. 36)

Asking the Right Questions

As a result, though I will look briefly at the tradition of experimental research, my primary goal in this essay is to articulate the grammar issue in different and, I would hope, more productive terms. Specifically, I want to ask four questions:

1. Why is the grammar issue so important? Why has it been the dominant focus of composition research for the last seventy-five years?
2. What definitions of the word *grammar* are needed to articulate the grammar issue intelligibly?
3. What do findings in cognate disciplines suggest about the value of formal grammar instruction?
4. What is our theory of language, and what does it predict about the value of formal grammar instruction? (This question—"what does our theory of language predict?"—seems a much more powerful question than "what does educational research tell us?")

In exploring these questions I will attempt to be fully explicit about issues, terms, and assumptions. I hope that both proponents and opponents of formal grammar instruction would agree that these are useful as shared points of reference: care in definition, full examination of the evidence, reference to relevant work in cognate disciplines, and explicit analysis of the theoretical bases of the issue.

But even with that gesture of harmony it will be difficult to articulate the issue in a balanced way, one that will be acceptable to both sides. After all, we are dealing with a professional dispute in which one side accuses the other of "magical thinking," and in turn that side responds by charging the other as "alchemists." Thus we might suspect that the grammar issue is itself embedded in larger models of the transmission of literacy, part of quite different assumptions about the teaching of composition.

Those of us who dismiss the teaching of formal grammar have a model of composition instruction that makes the grammar issue "uninteresting" in a scientific sense. Our model predicts a rich and complex interaction of learner and environment in mastering literacy, an interaction that has little to do with sequences of skills instruction as such. Those who defend the teaching of grammar tend to have a model of composition instruction that is rigidly skills-centered and rigidly sequential: the formal teaching of grammar, as the first step in that sequence, is the cornerstone or linchpin. Grammar teaching is thus supremely interesting, naturally a dominant focus for educational research. The controversy over the value of grammar instruction, then, is inseparable from two other issues: the issues of sequence in the teaching of composition and of the role of the composition teacher. Consider, for example, the force of these two issues in Janice Neuleib's conclusion: after calling for yet more experimental research on the value of teaching grammar, she ends with an absolute (and unsupported) claim about sequences and teacher roles in composition.

> We do know, however, that some things must be taught at different levels. Insistence on adherence to usage norms by composition teachers does improve usage. Students can learn to organize their papers if teachers do not accept papers that are disorganized. Perhaps composition teachers can teach those two abilities before they begin the more difficult tasks of developing syntactic sophistication and a winning style. ("The Relation of Formal Grammar to Composition," p. 250)

(One might want to ask, in passing, whether "usage norms" exist in the monolithic fashion the phrase suggests and whether refusing to accept disorganized papers is our best available pedagogy for teaching arrangement.)[7]

But I want to focus on the notion of sequence that makes the grammar issue so important: first grammar, then usage, then some absolute model of organization, all controlled by the teacher at the center of the learning process, with other matters, those of rhetorical weight—"syntactic sophistication and a winning style"—pushed off to the future. It is not surprising that we call each other names: those of us who question the value of teaching grammar are in fact shaking the whole elaborate edifice of traditional composition instruction.

The Five Meanings of "Grammar"

Given its centrality to a well-established way of teaching composition, I need to go about the business of defining grammar rather carefully, particularly in view of Kolln's criticism of the lack of care in earlier discussions. Therefore I will build upon a seminal discussion of the word *grammar* offered a generation ago, in 1954, by W. Nelson Francis, often excerpted as "The Three Meanings of Grammar."[8] It is worth reprinting at length, if only to re-establish it as a reference point for future discussions.

> The first thing we mean by "grammar" is "the set of formal patterns in which the words of a language are arranged in order to convey larger meanings." It is not necessary that we be able to discuss these patterns self-consciously in order to be able to use them. In fact, all speakers of a language above the age of five or six know how to use its complex forms of organization with considerable skill; in this sense of the word—call it "Grammar 1"—they are thoroughly familiar with its grammar.
>
> The second meaning of "grammar"—call it "Grammar 2"—is "the branch of linguistic science which is concerned with the description, analysis, and formulization of formal language patterns." Just as gravity was in full operation before

Newton's apple fell, so grammar in the first sense was in full operation before anyone formulated the first rule that began the history of grammar as a study.

The third sense in which people use the word "grammar" is "linguistic etiquette." This we may call "Grammar 3." The word in this sense is often coupled with a derogatory adjective: we say that the expression "he ain't here" is "bad grammar." . . .

As has already been suggested, much confusion arises from mixing these meanings. One hears a good deal of criticism of teachers of English couched in such terms as "they don't teach grammar any more." Criticism of this sort is based on the wholly unproven assumption that teaching Grammar 2 will improve the student's proficiency in Grammar 1 or improve his manners in Grammar 3. Actually, the form of Grammar 2 which is usually taught is a very inaccurate and misleading analysis of the facts of Grammar 1; and it therefore is of highly questionable value in improving a person's ability to handle the structural patterns of his language. (pp. 300–301)

Francis' Grammar 3 is, of course, not grammar at all, but usage. One would like to assume that Joseph Williams' recent discussion of usage ("The Phenomenology of Error," *CCC*, 32 (1981), 152–168), along with his references, has placed those shibboleths in a proper perspective. But I doubt it, and I suspect that popular discussions of the grammar issue will be as flawed by the intrusion of usage issues as past discussions have been. At any rate I will make only passing reference to Grammar 3—usage—naively assuming that this issue has been discussed elsewhere and that my readers are familiar with those discussions.

We need also to make further discriminations about Francis' Grammar 2, given that the purpose of his 1954 article was to substitute for one form of Grammar 2, that "inaccurate and misleading" form "which is usually taught," another form, that of American structuralist grammar. Here we can make use of a still earlier discussion, one going back to the days when *PMLA* was willing to publish articles on rhetoric and linguistics, to a 1927 article by Charles Carpenter Fries, "The Rules of the Common School Grammars" (42 [1927], 221–237). Fries there distinguished between the scientific tradition of language study (to which we will now delimit Francis' Grammar 2, scientific grammar) and the separate tradition of "the common school grammars," developed unscientifically, largely based on two inadequate principles—appeals to "logical principles," like "two negatives make a positive," and analogy to Latin grammar; thus, Charlton Laird's characterization, "the grammar of Latin, ingeniously warped to suggest English" (*Language in America* [New York: World, 1970], p. 294). There is, of course, a direct link between the "common school grammars" that Fries criticized in 1927 and the grammar-based texts of today, and thus it seems wise, as Karl W. Dykema suggests ("Where Our Grammar Came From," *CE*, 22 (1961), 455–465), to separate Grammar 2, "scientific grammar," from Grammar 4, "school grammar," the latter meaning, quite literally, "the grammars used in the schools."

Further, since Martha Kolln points to the adaptation of Christensen's sentence rhetoric in a recent sentence-combining text as an example of the proper emphasis on "grammar" ("Closing the Books on Alchemy," p. 140), it is worth separating out, as still another meaning of *grammar*, Grammar 5, "stylistic grammar," defined as "grammatical terms used in the interest of teaching prose style." And, since stylistic grammars abound, with widely variant terms and emphases, we might appropriately speak parenthetically of specific forms of Grammar 5— Grammar 5 (Lanham); Grammar 5 (Strunk and White); Grammar 5 (Williams, *Style*); even Grammar 5 (Christensen, as adapted by Daiker, Kerek, and Morenberg).[9]

The Grammar in Our Heads

With these definitions in mind, let us return to Francis' Grammar 1, admirably defined by Kolln as "the internalized system of rules that speakers of a language share" ("Closing the Books on Alchemy," p. 140), or, to put it more simply, the grammar in our heads. Three features of Grammar 1 need to be stressed: first, its special status as an "internalized system of rules," as tacit and unconscious knowledge; second, the abstract, even counterintuitive, nature of these rules, insofar as we are able to approximate them indirectly as Grammar 2 statements; and third, the way in which the form of one's Grammar 1 seems profoundly affected by the acquisition of literacy. This sort of review is designed to firm up our theory of language, so that we can ask what it predicts about the value of teaching formal grammar.

A simple thought experiment will isolate the special status of Grammar 1 knowledge. I have asked members of a number of different groups—from sixth graders to college freshmen to high-school teachers—to give me the rule for ordering adjectives of nationality, age, and number in English. The response is always the same: "We don't know the rule." Yet when I ask these groups to perform an active language task, they show productive control over the rule they have denied knowing. I ask them to arrange the following words in a natural order:

French   the   young   girls   four

I have never seen a native speaker of English who did not immediately produce the natural order, "the four young French girls." The rule is that in English the order of adjectives is first, number, second, age, and third, nationality. Native speakers can create analogous phrases using the rule—"the seventy-three aged Scandinavian lechers"; and the drive for meaning is so great that they will create contexts to make sense out of violations of the rule, as in foregrounding for emphasis: "I want to talk to the French four young girls." (I immediately envision a large room, perhaps a banquet hall, filled with tables at which are seated groups of four young girls, each group of a different nationality.) So Grammar 1 is eminently usable knowledge—the way we make our life through language— but it is not accessible knowledge; in a profound sense, we do not know that we have it. Thus neurolinguist Z. N. Pylyshyn speaks of Grammar 1 as "autonomous," separate from common-sense reasoning, and as "cognitively impenetrable," not available for direct examination.[10] In philosophy and linguistics, the distinction is made between formal, conscious, "knowing about" knowledge (like Grammar 2 knowledge) and tacit, unconscious, "knowing how" knowledge (like Grammar 1 knowledge). The importance of this distinction for the teaching of composition— it provides a powerful theoretical justification for mistrusting the ability of Grammar 2 (or Grammar 4) knowledge to affect Grammar 1 performance—was pointed out in this journal by Martin Steinmann, Jr., in 1966 ("Rhetorical Research," *CE*, 27 [1966], 278–285).

Further, the more we learn about Grammar 1—and most linguists would agree that we know surprisingly little about it—the more abstract and implicit it seems. This abstractness can be illustrated with an experiment, devised by Lise Menn and reported by Morris Halle,[11] about our rule for forming plurals in speech. It is obvious that we do indeed have a "rule" for forming plurals, for we do not memorize the plural of each noun separately. You will demonstrate productive control over that rule by forming the spoken plurals of the nonsense words below:

thole   flitch   plast

Halle offers two ways of formalizing a Grammar 2 equivalent of this Grammar 1 ability. One form of the rule is the following, stated in terms of speech sounds:

a. If the noun ends in /s z š ž č ǰ/, add /ɨz/;
b. otherwise, if the noun ends in /p t k f Ø/, add /s/;
c. otherwise, add /z/.

This rule comes close to what we literate adults consider to be an adequate rule for plurals in writing, like the rules, for example, taken from a recent "common school grammar," Eric Gould's *Reading into Writing: A Rhetoric, Reader, and Handbook* (Boston: Houghton Mifflin, 1983):

> *Plurals* can be tricky. If you are unsure of a plural, then check it in the dictionary.
>
> The general rules are:
>
> Add *s* to the singular: *girls, tables*
>
> Add *es* to nouns ending in *ch, sh, x* or *s: churches, boxes, wishes*
>
> Add *es* to nouns ending in *y* and preceded by a vowel once you have changed *y* to *i: monies, companies.* (p. 666)

(But note the persistent inadequacy of such Grammar 4 rules: here, as I read it, the rule is inadequate to explain the plurals of *ray* and *tray*, even to explain the collective noun *monies*, not a plural at all, formed from the mass noun *money* and offered as an example.) A second form of the rule would make use of much more abstract entities, sound features:

> a. If the noun ends with a sound that is [coronal, strident], add /ɨz/;
> b. otherwise, if the noun ends with a sound that is [non-voiced], add /s/;
> c. otherwise, add /z/.

(The notion of "sound features" is itself rather abstract, perhaps new to readers not trained in linguistics. But such readers should be able to recognize that the spoken plurals of *lip* and *duck*, the sound [s], differ from the spoken plurals of *sea* and *gnu*, the sound [z], only in that the sounds of the latter are "voiced"— one's vocal cords vibrate—while the sounds of the former are "non-voiced.")

To test the psychologically operative rule, the Grammar 1 rule, native speakers of English were asked to form the plural of the last name of the composer Johann Sebastian *Bach*, a sound [x], unique in American (though not in Scottish) English. If speakers follow the first rule above, using word endings, they would reject a) and b), then apply c), producing the plural as /baxz/, with word-final /z/. (If writers were to follow the rule of the common school grammar, they would produce the written plural *Baches*, apparently, given the form of the rule, on analogy with *churches*.) If speakers follow the second rule, they would have to analyze the sound [x] as [non-labial, non-coronal, dorsal, non-voiced, and non-strident], producing the plural as /baxs/, with word-final /s/. Native speakers of American English overwhelmingly produce the plural as /baxs/. They use knowledge that Halle characterizes as "unlearned and untaught" (p. 140).

Now such a conclusion is counterintuitive—certainly it departs maximally from Grammar 4 rules for forming plurals. It seems that native speakers of English behave as if they have productive control, as Grammar 1 knowledge, of abstract sound features (± coronal, ± strident, and so on) which are available as conscious, Grammar 2 knowledge only to trained linguists—and, indeed, formally available only within the last hundred years or so. ("Behave as if," in that last sentence, is a necessary hedge, to underscore the difficulty of "knowing about" Grammar 1.)

Moreover, as the example of plural rules suggests, the form of the Grammar 1 in the heads of literate adults seems profoundly affected by the acquisition of literacy. Obviously, literate adults have access to different morphological codes: the abstract print *-s* underlying the predictable /s/ and /z/ plurals, the abstract print *-ed* underlying the spoken past tense markers /t/, as in "walked," /əd/, as in "surrounded," /d/, as in "scored," and the symbol /Ø/ for no surface realization, as in the relaxed standard pronunciation of "I walked to the store." Literate adults also have access to distinctions preserved only in the code of print (for example, the distinction between "a good sailer" and "a good sailor" that Mark Aranoff points out in "An English Spelling Convention," *Linguistic Inquiry*, 9 [1978], 299–303). More significantly, Irene Moscowitz speculates that the ability of third graders to form abstract nouns on analogy with pairs like *divine: :divinity* and *serene: :serenity*, where the spoken vowel changes but the spelling preserves meaning, is a factor of knowing how to read. Carol Chomsky finds a three-stage developmental sequence in the grammatical performance of seven-year-olds, related to measures of kind and variety of reading; and Rita S. Brause finds a nine-stage developmental sequence in the ability to understand semantic ambiguity, extending from fourth graders to graduate students.[12] John Mills and Gordon Hemsley find that level of education, and presumably level of literacy, influence judgments of grammaticality, concluding that literacy changes the deep structure of one's internal grammar; Jean Whyte finds that oral language functions develop differently in readers and non-readers; José Morais, Jesús Alegria, and Paul Bertelson find that illiterate adults are unable to add or delete sounds at the beginning of nonsense words, suggesting that awareness of speech as a series of phones is provided by learning to read an alphabetic code. Two experiments—one conducted by Charles A. Ferguson, the other by Mary E. Hamilton and David Barton—find that adults' ability to recognize segmentation in speech is related to degree of literacy, not to amount of schooling or general ability.[13]

It is worth noting that none of these investigators would suggest that the developmental sequences they have uncovered be isolated and taught as discrete skills. They are natural concomitants of literacy, and they seem best characterized not as isolated rules but as developing schemata, broad strategies for approaching written language.

Grammar 2

We can, of course, attempt to approximate the rules or schemata of Grammar 1 by writing fully explicit descriptions that model the competence of a native speaker. Such rules, like the rules for pluralizing nouns or ordering adjectives discussed above, are the goal of the science of linguistics, that is, Grammar 2. There are a number of scientific grammars—an older structuralist model and several versions within a generative-transformational paradigm, not to mention isolated schools like tagmemic grammar, Montague grammar, and the like. In fact, we cannot think of Grammar 2 as a stable entity, for its form changes with each new issue of each linguistics journal, as new "rules of grammar" are proposed and debated. Thus Grammar 2, though of great theoretical interest to the composition teacher, is of little practical use in the classroom, as Constance Weaver has pointed out (*Grammar for Teachers* [Urbana, Ill.: NCTE, 1979], pp. 3–6). Indeed Grammar 2 is a scientific model of Grammar 1, not a description of it, so that questions of psychological reality, while important, are less important than other, more theoretical factors, such as the elegance of formulation or the global power of rules. We might, for example, wish to replace the rule for ordering adjectives of age, number, and nationality cited above with a more general rule—what linguists call a "fuzzy" rule—that adjectives in English are ordered by their abstract quality of "nouniness": adjectives that are very much like nouns, like *French* or *Scandinavian*, come physically closer to nouns than do adjectives that are less "nouny," like *four* or *aged*. But our motivation for accepting the broader rule would be its global power, not its psychological reality.[14]

I try to consider a hostile reader, one committed to the teaching of grammar, and I try to think of ways to hammer in the central point of this distinction, that the rules of Grammar 2 are simply unconnected to productive control over Grammar 1. I can argue from authority: Noam Chomsky has touched on this point whenever he has concerned himself with the implications of linguistics for language teaching, and years ago transformationalist Mark Lester stated unequivocally, "there simply appears to be no correlation between a writer's study of language and his ability to write."[15] I can cite analogies offered by others: Francis Christensen's analogy in an essay originally published in 1962 that for-

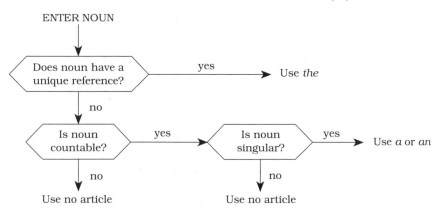

ENTER NOUN

Does noun have a unique reference? — yes → Use *the*

no

Is noun countable? — yes → Is noun singular? — yes → Use *a* or *an*

no → Use no article

no → Use no article

mal grammar study would be "to invite a centipede to attend to the sequence of his legs in motion,"[16] or James Britton's analogy, offered informally after a conference presentation, that grammar study would be like forcing starving people to master the use of a knife and fork before allowing them to eat. I can offer analogies of my own, contemplating the wisdom of asking a pool player to master the physics of momentum before taking up a cue or of making a prospective driver get a degree in automotive engineering before engaging the clutch. I consider a hypothetical argument, that if Grammar 2 knowledge affected Grammar 1 performance, then linguists would be our best writers. (I can certify that they are, on the whole, not.) Such a position, after all, is only in accord with other domains of science: the formula for catching a fly ball in baseball ("Playing It by Ear," *Scientific American*, 248, No. 4 [1983], 76) is of such complexity that it is beyond my understanding—and, I would suspect, that of many workaday center-fielders. But perhaps I can best hammer in this claim—that Grammar 2 knowledge has no effect on Grammar 1 performance—by offering a demonstration.

The diagram above is an attempt by Thomas N. Huckin and Leslie A. Olsen (*English for Science and Technology* [New York: McGraw-Hill, 1983]) to offer, for students of English as a second language, a fully explicit formulation of what is, for native speakers, a trivial rule of the language—the choice of definite article, indefinite article, or no definite article. There are obvious limits to such a formulation, for article choice in English is less a matter of rule than of idiom ("I went to college" versus "I went to a university" versus British "I went to university"), real-world knowledge (using indefinite "I went into a house" instantiates definite "I looked at the ceiling," and indefinite "I visited a university" instantiates definite "I talked with the professors"), and stylistic choice (the last sentence above might alternatively end with "the choice of the definite article, the indefinite article, or no article"). Huckin and Olsen invite non-native speakers to use the rule consciously to justify article choice in technical prose, such as the passage below from P. F. Brandwein (*Matter: An Earth Science* [New York: Harcourt Brace Jovanovich, 1975]). I invite you to spend a couple of minutes doing the same thing, with the understanding that this exercise is a test case: you are using a very explicit rule to justify a fairly straightforward issue of grammatical choice.

Imagine a cannon on top of _____ highest mountain on earth. It is firing cannonballs horizontally. _____ first cannonball fired follows its path. As cannonball moves, _____ gravity pulls it down, and it soon hits ground. Now _____ velocity with which each succeeding cannonball is _____ fired is increased. Thus, _____ cannonball goes farther each time. Cannonball 2 goes farther than _____ cannonball 1 although each is being pulled by _____ gravity toward the earth all _____ time. _____ last cannonball is fired with such tremendous velocity that it goes completely around _____ earth. It returns to _____ mountaintop and continues around the earth again and again. _____ cannonball's inertia causes it to continue in motion indefinitely in _____ orbit around earth. In such a situation, we could consider cannonball to be _____ artificial satellite, just like _____ weather satellites launched by _____ U.S. Weather Service. (p. 209)

Most native speakers of English who have attempted this exercise report a great deal of frustration, a curious sense of working against, rather than with, the rule. The rule, however valuable it may be for non-native speakers, is, for the most part, simply unusable for native speakers of the language.

Cognate Areas of Research

We can corroborate this demonstration by turning to research in two cognate areas, studies of the induction of rules of artificial languages and studies of the role of formal rules in second language acquisition. Psychologists have studied the ability of subjects to learn artificial languages, usually constructed of nonsense syllables or letter strings. Such languages can be described by phrase structure rules:

$$S \Rightarrow VX$$
$$X \Rightarrow MX$$

More clearly, they can be presented as flow diagrams, as below:

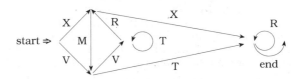

This diagram produces "sentences" like the following:

VVTRXRR.	XMVTTRX.	XXRR.
XMVRMT.	VVTTRMT.	XMTRRR.

The following "sentences" would be "ungrammatical" in this language:

*VMXTT.	*RTXVVT.	*TRVXXVVM.

Arthur S. Reber, in a classic 1967 experiment, demonstrated that mere exposure to grammatical sentences produced tacit learning: subjects who copied several grammatical sentences performed far above chance in judging the grammaticality of other letter strings. Further experiments have shown that providing subjects with formal rules—giving them the flow diagram above, for example—remarkably degrades performance: subjects given the "rules of the language" do much less well in acquiring the rules than do subjects not given the rules. Indeed, even telling subjects that they are to induce the rules of an artificial language degrades performance. Such laboratory experiments are admittedly contrived, but they confirm predictions that our theory of language would make about the value of formal rules in language learning.[17]

The thrust of recent research in second language learning similarly works to constrain the value of formal grammar rules. The most explicit statement of the value of formal rules is that of Stephen D. Krashen's monitor model.[18] Krashen divides second language mastery into *acquisition*—tacit, informal mastery, akin to first language acquisition—and formal learning—conscious application of Grammar 2 rules, which he calls "monitoring" output. In another essay Krashen uses his model to predict a highly individual use of the monitor and a highly constrained role for formal rules:

> Some adults (and very few children) are able to use conscious rules to increase the grammatical accuracy of their output, and even for these people, very strict conditions need to be met before the conscious grammar can be applied.[19]

In *Principles and Practice in Second Language Acquisition* (New York: Pergamon, 1982) Krashen outlines these conditions by means of a series of concentric circles, beginning with a large circle denoting the rules of English and a smaller circle denoting the subset of those rules described by formal linguists (adding that most linguists would protest that the size of this circle is much too large):

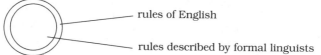

rules of English

rules described by formal linguists

Krashen then adds smaller circles, as shown below—a subset of the rules described by formal linguists that would be known to applied linguists, a subset of those rules that would be available to the best teachers, and then a subset of those rules that teachers might choose to present to second language learners:

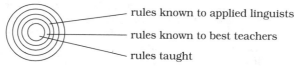

rules known to applied linguists

rules known to best teachers

rules taught

Of course, as Krashen notes, not all the rules taught will be learned, and not all those learned will be available, as what he calls "mental baggage" (p. 94), for conscious use.

An experiment by Ellen Bialystock, asking English speakers learning French to judge the grammaticality of taped sentences, complicates this issue, for reaction time data suggest that learners first make an intuitive judgment of grammaticality, using implicit or Grammar 1 knowledge, and only then search for formal explanations, using explicit or Grammar 2 knowledge.[20] This distinction would suggest that Grammar 2 knowledge is of use to second language learners only after the principle has already been mastered as tacit Grammar 1 knowledge. In the terms of Krashen's model, learning never becomes acquisition (*Principles*, p. 86).

An ingenious experiment by Herbert W. Seliger complicates the issue yet further ("On the Nature and Function of Language Rules in Language Learning," *TESOL Quarterly*, 13 [1979], 359–369). Seliger asked native and non-native speakers of English to orally identify pictures of objects (e.g., "an apple," "a pear," "a book," "an umbrella"), noting whether they used the correct form of the indefinite articles *a* and *an*. He then asked each speaker to state the rule for choosing between *a* and *an*. He found no correlation between the ability to state the rule and the ability to apply it correctly, either with native or non-native speakers. Indeed, three of four adult non-native speakers in his sample produced a correct form of the rule, but they did not apply it in speaking. A strong conclusion from this experiment would be that formal rules of grammar seem to have no value whatsoever. Seliger, however, suggests a more paradoxical interpretation. Rules are of no use, he agrees, but some people think they are, and for these people, assuming that they have internalized the rules, even inadequate rules are of heuristic value, for they allow them to access the internal rules they actually use.

The Incantations of the "Common School Grammars"

Such a paradox may explain the fascination we have as teachers with "rules of grammar" of the Grammar 4 variety, the "rules" of the "common school grammars." Again and again such rules are inadequate to the facts of written language; you will recall that we have known this since Francis' 1927 study.

R. Scott Baldwin and James M. Coady, studying how readers respond to punctuation signals ("Psycholinguistic Approaches to a Theory of Punctuation," *Journal of Reading Behavior,* 10 [1978], 363–383), conclude that conventional rules of punctuation are "a complete sham" (p. 375). My own favorite is the Grammar 4 rule for showing possession, always expressed in terms of adding -'s or -s' to nouns, while our internal grammar, if you think about it, adds possession to noun phrases, albeit under severe stylistic constraints: "the horses of the Queen of England" are "the Queen of England's horses" and "the feathers of the duck over there" are "the duck over there's feathers." Suzette Haden Elgin refers to the "rules" of Grammar 4 as "incantations" (*Never Mind the Trees,* p. 9: see note 3).

It may simply be that as hyperliterate adults we are conscious of "using rules" when we are in fact doing something else, something far more complex, accessing tacit heuristics honed by print literacy itself. We can clarify this notion by reaching for an acronym coined by technical writers to explain the readability of complex prose—COIK: "clear only if known." The rules of Grammar 4— no, we can at this point be more honest—the incantations of Grammar 4 is COIK. If you know how to signal possession in the code of print, then the advice to add -'s to nouns makes perfect sense, just as the collective noun *monies* is a fine example of changing -*y* to -*i* and adding -*es* to form the plural. But if you have not grasped, tacitly, the abstract representation of possession in print, such incantations can only be opaque.

Worse yet, the advice given in "the common school grammars" is unconnected with anything remotely resembling literate adult behavior. Consider, as an example, the rule for not writing a sentence fragment as the rule is described in the best-selling college grammar text, John C. Hodges and Mary S. Whitten's *Harbrace College Handbook,* 9th ed. (New York: Harcourt Brace Jovanovich, 1982). In order to get to the advice, "as a rule, do not write a sentence fragment" (p. 25), the student must master the following learning tasks:

Recognizing verbs.

Recognizing subjects and verbs.

Recognizing all parts of speech. (*Harbrace* lists eight.)

Recognizing phrases and subordinate clauses. (*Harbrace* lists six types of phrases, and it offers incomplete lists of eight relative pronouns and eighteen subordinating conjunctions.)

Recognizing main clauses and types of sentences.

These learning tasks completed, the student is given the rule above, offered a page of exceptions, and then given the following advice (or is it an incantation?):

> Before handing in a composition, . . . proofread each word group written as a sentence. Test each one for completeness. First, be sure that it has at least one subject and one predicate. Next, be sure that the word group is not a dependent clause beginning with a subordinating conjunction or a relative clause. (p. 27)

The school grammar approach defines a sentence fragment as a conceptual error—as not having conscious knowledge of the school grammar definition of *sentence*. It demands heavy emphasis on rote memory, and it asks students to behave in ways patently removed from the behaviors of mature writers. (I have never in my life tested a sentence for completeness, and I am a better writer— and probably a better person—as a consequence.) It may be, of course, that some developing writers, at some points in their development, may benefit from such advice—or, more to the point, may think that they benefit—but, as Thomas Friedman points out in "Teaching Error, Nurturing Confusion" (*CE,* 45 [1983], 390–399), our theory of language tells us that such advice is, at the best, COIK. As the Maine joke has it, about a tourist asking directions from a farmer, "you can't get there from here."

Redefining Error

In the specific case of sentence fragments, Mina P. Shaughnessy (*Errors and Expectations* [New York: Oxford University Press, 1977]) argues that such errors are not conceptual failures at all, but performance errors—mistakes in punctuation. Muriel Harris' error counts support this view ("Mending the Fragmented Free Modifier," *CCC*, 32 [1981], 175–182). Case studies show example after example of errors that occur *because* of instruction—one thinks, for example, of David Bartholomae's student explaining that he added an -*s* to *children* "because it's a plural" ("The Study of Error," *CCC*, 31 [1980], 262). Surveys, such as that by Muriel Harris ("Contradictory Perceptions of the Rules of Writing," *CCC*, 30 [1979], 218–220), and our own observations suggest that students consistently misunderstand such Grammar 4 explanations (COIK, you will recall). For example, from Patrick Hartwell and Robert H. Bentley and from Mike Rose, we have two separate anecdotal accounts of students, cited for punctuating a *because*-clause as a sentence, who have decided to avoid using *because*. More generally, Collette A. Daiute's analysis of errors made by college students shows that errors tend to appear at clause boundaries, suggesting short-term memory load and not conceptual deficiency as a cause of error.[21]

Thus, if we think seriously about error and its relationship to the worship of formal grammar study, we need to attempt some massive dislocation of our traditional thinking, to shuck off our hyperliterate perception of the value of formal rules, and to regain the confidence in the tacit power of unconscious knowledge that our theory of language gives us. Most students, reading their writing aloud, will correct in essence all errors of spelling, grammar, and, by intonation, punctuation, but usually without noticing that what they read departs from what they wrote.[22] And Richard H. Haswell ("Minimal Marking," *CE*, 45 [1983], 600–604) notes that his students correct 61.1 percent of their errors when they are identified with a simple mark in the margin rather than by error type. Such findings suggest that we need to redefine error, to see it not as a cognitive or linguistic problem, a problem of not knowing a "rule of grammar" (whatever that may mean), but rather, following the insight of Robert J. Bracewell ("Writing as a Cognitive Activity," *Visible Language*, 14 [1980], 400–422), as a problem of metacognition and metalinguistic awareness, a matter of accessing knowledges that, to be of any use, learners must have already internalized by means of exposure to the code. (Usage issues—Grammar 3—probably represent a different order of problem. Both Joseph Emonds and Jeffrey Jochnowitz establish that the usage issues we worry most about are linguistically unnatural, departures from the grammar in our heads.)[23]

The notion of metalinguistic awareness seems crucial. The sentence below, created by Douglas R. Hofstadter ("Metamagical Themas," *Scientific American*, 235, No. 1 [1981], 22–32), is offered to clarify that notion; you are invited to examine it for a moment or two before continuing.

Their is four errors in this sentence. Can you find them?

Three errors announce themselves plainly enough, the misspellings of *there* and *sentence* and the use of *is* instead of *are*. (And, just to illustrate the perils of hyperliteracy, let it be noted that, through three years of drafts, I referred to the choice of *is* and *are* as a matter of "subject-verb agreement.") The fourth error resists detection, until one assesses the truth value of the sentence itself—the fourth error is that there are not four errors, only three. Such a sentence (Hofstadter calls it a "self-referencing sentence") asks you to look at it in two ways, simultaneously as statement and as linguistic artifact—in other words, to exercise metalinguistic awareness.

A broad range of cross-cultural studies suggest that metalinguistic awareness is a defining feature of print literacy. Thus Sylvia Scribner and Michael Cole, working with the triliterate Vai of Liberia (variously literate in English, through schooling; in Arabic, for religious purposes; and in an indigenous Vai script, used for personal affairs), find that metalinguistic awareness, broadly conceived, is the only cognitive skill underlying each of the three literacies. The one statistically significant skill shared by literate Vai was the recognition of word boundaries. Moreover, literate Vai tended to answer "yes" when asked (in Vai), "Can you call the sun the moon and the moon the sun?" while illiterate Vai tended to have grave doubts about such metalinguistic play. And in the United States Henry and Lila R. Gleitman report quite different responses by clerical workers and PhD candidates asked to interpret nonsense compounds like "house-bird glass": clerical workers focused on meaning and plausibility (for example, "a house-bird made of glass"), while PhD candidates focused on syntax (for example, "a very small drinking cup for canaries" or "a glass that protects house-birds").[24] More general research findings suggest a clear relationship between measures of metalinguistic awareness and measures of literacy level.[25] William Labov, speculating on literacy acquisition in inner-city ghettoes, contrasts "stimulus-bound" and "language-bound" individuals, suggesting that the latter seem to master literacy more easily.[26] The analysis here suggests that the causal relationship works the other way, that it is the mastery of written language that increases one's awareness of language as language.

This analysis has two implications. First, it makes the question of socially nonstandard dialects, always implicit in discussions of teaching formal grammar, into a non-issue.[27] Native speakers of English, regardless of dialect, show tacit mastery of the conventions of Standard English, and that mastery seems to transfer into abstract orthographic knowledge through interaction with print.[28] Developing writers show the same patterning of errors, regardless of dialect.[29] Studies of reading and of writing suggest that surface features of spoken dialect are simply irrelevant to mastering print literacy.[30] Print is a complex cultural code—or better yet, a system of code—and my bet is that, regardless of instruction, one masters those codes from the top down, from pragmatic questions of voice, tone, audience, register, and rhetorical strategy, not from the bottom up, from grammar to usage to fixed forms of organization.

Second, this analysis forces us to posit multiple literacies, used for multiple purposes, rather than a single static literacy, engraved in "rules of grammar." These multiple literacies are evident in cross-cultural studies.[31] They are equally evident when we inquire into the uses of literacy in American communities.[32] Further, given that students, at all levels, show widely variant interactions with print literacy, there would seem to be little to do with grammar—with Grammar 2 or with Grammar 4—that we could isolate as a basis for formal instruction.[33]

Grammar 5: Stylistic Grammar

Similarly, when we turn to Grammar 5, "grammatical terms used in the interest of teaching prose style," so central to Martha Kolln's argument for teaching formal grammar, we find that the grammar issue is simply beside the point. There are two fully-articulated positions about "stylistic grammar," which I will label "romantic" and "classic," following Richard Lloyd-Jones and Richard E. Young.[34] The romantic position is that stylistic grammars, though perhaps useful for teachers, have little place in the teaching of composition, for students must struggle with and through language toward meaning. This position rests on a theory of language ultimately philosophical rather than linguistic (witness, for example, the contempt for linguists in Ann Berthoff's *The Making of Meaning: Metaphors, Models, and Maxims for Writing Teachers* [Montclair, N.J.: Boynton/Cook, 1981]); it is articulated as a theory of style by Donald A. Murray and, on somewhat different grounds (that stylistic grammars encourage overuse of the monitor), by Ian Pringle. The classic position, on the other hand, is that we can find ways to offer developing writers helpful suggestions about prose style, suggestions such as Francis Christensen's emphasis on the cumulative sentence, developed by observing the practice of skilled writers, and Joseph Williams' advice about predication, developed by psycholinguistic studies of comprehension.[35] James A. Berlin's recent survey of composition theory (*CE*, 45 [1982], 765–777) probably understates the gulf between these two positions and the radically different conceptions of language that underlie them, but it does establish that they share an overriding assumption in common: that one learns to control the language of print by manipulating language in meaningful contexts, not by learning about language in isolation, as by the study of formal grammar. Thus even classic theorists, who choose to present a vocabulary of style to students, do so only as a vehicle for encouraging productive control of communicative structures.

We might put the matter in the following terms. Writers need to develop skills at two levels. One, broadly rhetorical, involves communication in meaningful contexts (the strategies, registers, and procedures of discourse across a range of modes, audiences, contexts, and purposes). The other, broadly metalinguistic rather than linguistic, involves active manipulation of language with conscious attention to surface form. This second level may be developed tacitly, as a natural adjunct to developing rhetorical competencies—I take this to be the position of romantic theorists. It may be developed formally, by manipulating language for stylistic effect, and such manipulation may involve, for pedagogical continuity, a vocabulary of style. But it is primarily developed by any kind of language activity that enhances the awareness of language as language.[36] David T. Hakes, summarizing the research on metalinguistic awareness, notes how far we are from understanding this process:

> the optimal conditions for becoming metalinguistically competent involve growing up in a literate environment with adult models who are themselves metalinguistically competent and who foster the growth of that competence in a variety of ways as yet little understood. ("The Development of Metalinguistic Abilities," p. 205: see note 25)

Such a model places language, at all levels, at the center of the curriculum, but not as "necessary categories and labels" (Kolln, "Closing the Books on Alchemy," p. 150), but as literal stuff, verbal clay, to be molded and probed, shaped and reshaped, and, above all, enjoyed.

The Tradition of Experimental Research

Thus, when we turn back to experimental research on the value of formal grammar instruction, we do so with firm predictions given us by our theory of language. Our theory would predict that formal grammar instruction, whether instruction in scientific grammar or instruction in "the common school grammar," would have little to do with control over surface correctness nor with quality of writing. It would predict that any form of active involvement with language would be preferable to instruction in rules or definitions (or incantations). In essence, this is what the research tells us. In 1893, the Committee of Ten (*Report of the Committee of Ten on Secondary School Studies* [Washington, D.C.: U.S. Government Printing Office, 1893]) put grammar at the center of the English curriculum, and its report established the rigidly sequential mode of instruction common for the last century. But the committee explicitly noted that grammar instruction did not aid correctness, arguing instead that it improved the ability to think logically (an argument developed from the role of the "grammarian" in the classical rhetorical tradition, essentially a teacher of literature—see, for example, the etymology of *grammar* in the *Oxford English Dictionary*).

But Franklin S. Hoyt, in a 1906 experiment, found no relationship between the study of grammar and the ability to think logically; his research led him to conclude what I am constrained to argue more than seventy-five years later, that there is no "relationship between a knowledge of technical grammar and the ability to use English and to interpret language" ("The Place of Grammar in the Elementary Curriculum," *Teachers College Record*, 7 [1906], 483–484). Later studies, through the 1920s, focused on the relationship of knowledge of grammar and ability to recognize error; experiments reported by James Boraas in 1917 and by William Asker in 1923 are typical of those that reported no correlation. In the 1930s, with the development of the functional grammar movement, it was common to compare the study of formal grammar with one form or another of active manipulation of language; experiments by I. O. Ash in 1935 and Ellen Frogner in 1939 are typical of studies showing the superiority of active involvement with language.[37] In a 1959 article, "Grammar in Language Teaching" (*Elementary English*, 36 [1959], 412–421), John J. DeBoer noted the consistency of these findings.

> The impressive fact is . . . that in all these studies, carried out in places and at times far removed from each other, often by highly experienced and disinterested investigators, the results have been consistently negative so far as the value of grammar in the improvement of language expression is concerned. (p. 417)

In 1960 Ingrid M. Strom, reviewing more than fifty experimental studies, came to a similarly strong and unqualified conclusion:

> direct methods of instruction, focusing on writing activities and the structuring of ideas, are more efficient in teaching sentence structure, usage, punctuation, and other related factors than are such methods as nomenclature drill, diagramming, and rote memorization of grammatical rules.[38]

In 1963 two research reviews appeared, one by Braddock, Lloyd-Jones, and Schorer, cited at the beginning of this paper, and one by Henry C. Meckel, whose conclusions, though more guarded, are in essential agreement.[39] In 1969 J. Stephen Sherwin devoted one-fourth of his *Four Problems in Teaching English: A Critique of Research* (Scranton, Penn.: International Textbook, 1969) to the grammar issue, concluding that "instruction in formal grammar is an ineffective way to help students achieve proficiency in writing" (p. 135). Some early experiments in sentence combining, such as those by Donald R. Bateman and Frank J. Zidonnis and by John C. Mellon, showed improvement in measures of syntactic complexity with instruction in transformational grammar keyed to sentence combining practice. But a later study by Frank O'Hare achieved the same gains with no grammar instruction, suggesting to Sandra L. Stotsky and to Richard Van de Veghe that active manipulation of language, not the grammar unit, explained the earlier results.[40] More recent summaries of research—by Elizabeth I. Haynes, Hillary Taylor Holbrook, and Marcia Farr Whiteman—support similar conclusions. Indirect evidence for this position is provided by surveys reported by Betty Bamberg in 1978 and 1981, showing that time spent in grammar instruction in high school is the least important factor, of eight factors examined, in separating regular from remedial writers at the college level.[41]

More generally, Patrick Scott and Bruce Castner, in "Reference Sources for Composition Research: A Practical Survey" (*CE*, 45 [1983], 756–768), note that much current research is not informed by an awareness of the past. Put simply, we are constrained to reinvent the wheel. My concern here has been with a far more serious problem: that too often the wheel we reinvent is square.

It is, after all, a question of power. Janet Emig, developing a consensus from composition research, and Aaron S. Carton and Lawrence V. Castiglione, developing the implications of language theory for education, come to the same conclusion: that the thrust of current research and theory is to take power from the teacher and to give that power to the learner.[42] At no point in the English curriculum is the question of power more blatantly posed than in the issue of formal grammar instruction. It is time that we, as teachers, formulate theories of language and literacy and let those theories guide our teaching, and it is time that we, as researchers, move on to more interesting areas of inquiry.

Notes

[1] *Research in Written Composition* (Urbana, Ill.: National Council of Teachers of English, 1963), pp. 37–38.

[2] "Non-magical Thinking: Presenting Writing Developmentally in Schools," in *Writing Process, Development and Communication*, Vol. II of *Writing: The Nature, Development and Teaching of Written Communication*, ed. Charles H. Frederiksen and Joseph F. Dominic (Hillsdale, N.J.: Lawrence Erlbaum, 1980), pp. 21–30.

[3] For arguments in favor of formal grammar teaching, see Patrick F. Basset, "Grammar— Can We Afford Not to Teach It?" *NASSP Bulletin*, 64, No. 10 (1980), 55–63; Mary Epes et al., "The COMP-LAB Project: Assessing the Effectiveness of a Laboratory-Centered Basic Writing Course on the College Level" (Jamaica, N.Y.: York College, CUNY, 1979) ERIC 194 908; June B. Evans, "The Analogous Ounce: The Analgesic for Relief," *English Journal*, 70, No. 2 (1981), 38–39; Sydney Greenbaum, "What Is Grammar and Why Teach It?" (a paper presented at the meeting of the National Council of Teachers of English, Boston, Nov. 1982) ERIC 222 917; Marjorie Smelstor, *A Guide to the Role of Grammar in Teaching Writing* (Madison: University of Wisconsin School of Education, 1978) ERIC 176 323; and A. M. Tibbetts, *Working Papers: A Teacher's Observations on Composition* (Glenview, Ill.: Scott, Foresman, 1982).

For attacks on formal grammar teaching, see Harvey A. Daniels, *Famous Last Words: The American Language Crisis Reconsidered* (Carbondale: Southern Illinois University Press, 1983); Suzette Haden Elgin, *Never Mind the Trees: What the English Teacher Really Needs to Know about Linguistics* (Berkeley: University of California College of Education, Bay Area Writing Project Occasional Paper No. 2, 1980) ERIC 198 536; Mike Rose, "Remedial Writing Courses: A Critique and a Proposal," *College English*, 45 (1983), 109–128; and Ron Shook, Response to Martha Kolln, *College Composition and Communication*, 34 (1983), 491–495.

[4] See, for example, Clifton Fadiman and James Howard, *Empty Pages: A Search for Writing Competence in School and Society* (Belmont, Cal.: Fearon Pitman, 1979); Edwin Newman, *A Civil Tongue* (Indianapolis, Ind.: Bobbs-Merrill, 1976); and *Strictly Speaking* (New York: Warner Books, 1974); John Simons, *Paradigms Lost* (New York: Clarkson N. Potter, 1980); A. M. Tibbets and Charlene Tibbets, *What's Happening to American English?* (New York: Scribner's, 1978); and "Why Johnny Can't Write," *Newsweek*, 8 Dec. 1975, pp. 58–63.

[5] "The Role of Grammar in a Secondary School English Curriculum." *Research in the Teaching of English*, 10 (1976), 5–21; *The Role of Grammar in a Secondary School Curriculum* (Wellington: New Zealand Council of Teachers of English, 1979).

[6] "A Taxonomy of Compositional Competencies," in *Perspectives on Literacy*, ed. Richard Beach and P. David Pearson (Minneapolis: University of Minnesota College of Education, 1979), pp. 247–272.

[7] On usage norms, see Edward Finegan, *Attitudes toward English Usage: The History of a War of Words* (New York: Teachers College Press, 1980), and Jim Quinn, *American Tongue in Cheek: A Populist Guide to Language* (New York: Pantheon, 1980); on arrangement, see Patrick Hartwell, "Teaching Arrangement: A Pedagogy," *CE*, 40 (1979), 548–554.

[8] "Revolution in Grammar," *Quarterly Journal of Speech*, 40 (1954), 299–312.

[9] Richard A. Lanham, *Revising Prose* (New York: Scribner's, 1979); William Strunk and E. B. White, *The Elements of Style*, 3rd ed. (New York: Macmillan, 1979); Joseph Williams, *Style: Ten Lessons in Clarity and Grace* (Glenview, Ill.: Scott, Foresman, 1981); Christensen, "A Generative Rhetoric of the Sentence," *CCC*, 14 (1963), 155–161; Donald A. Daiker, Andrew Kerek, and Max Morenberg, *The Writer's Options: Combining to Composing*, 2nd ed. (New York: Harper & Row, 1982).

[10] "A Psychological Approach," in *Psychobiology of Language*, ed. M. Studdert-Kennedy (Cambridge, Mass.: MIT Press, 1983), pp. 16–19. See also Noam Chomsky, "Language and Unconscious Knowledge," in *Psychoanalysis and Language: Psychiatry and the Humanities*, Vol. III, ed. Joseph H. Smith (New Haven, Conn.: Yale University Press, 1978), pp. 3–44.

[11] Morris Halle, "Knowledge Unlearned and Untaught: What Speakers Know about the Sounds of Their Language," in *Linguistic Theory and Psychological Reality*, ed. Halle, Joan Bresnan, and George A. Miller (Cambridge, Mass.: MIT Press, 1978), pp. 135–140.

[12] Moscowitz, "On the Status of Vowel Shift in English," in *Cognitive Development and the Acquisition of Language*, ed. T. E. Moore (New York: Academic Press, 1973), pp. 223–260; Chomsky, "Stages in Language Development and Reading Exposure," *Harvard Educational Review*, 42 (1972), 1–33; and Brause, "Developmental Aspects of the Ability to Understand Semantic Ambiguity, with Implications for Teachers," *RTE*, 11 (1977), 39–48.

[13] Mills and Hemsley, "The Effect of Levels of Education on Judgments of Grammatical Acceptability," *Language and Speech*, 19 (1976), 324–342; Whyte, "Levels of Language Competence and Reading Ability: An Exploratory Investigation," *Journal of Research in Reading*, 5 (1982), 123–132; Morais et al., "Does Awareness of Speech as a Series of Phones Arise Spontaneously?" *Cognition*, 7 (1979), 323–331; Ferguson, *Cognitive Effects of Literacy: Linguistic Awareness in Adult Non-readers* (Washington, D.C.: National Institute of Education Final Report, 1981) ERIC 222 857; Hamilton and Barton, "A Word Is a Word: Metalinguistic Skills in Adults of Varying Literacy Levels" (Stanford, Cal.: Stanford University Department of Linguistics, 1980) ERIC 222 859.

[14] On the question of the psychological reality of Grammar 2 descriptions, see Maria Black and Shulamith Chiat, "Psycholinguistics without 'Psychological Reality,'" *Linguistics*, 19 (1981), 37–61; Joan Bresnan, ed., *The Mental Representation of Grammatical Relations* (Cambridge, Mass.: MIT Press, 1982); and Michael H. Long, "Inside the 'Black Box': Methodological Issues in Classroom Research on Language Learning," *Language Learning*, 30 (1980), 1–42.

[15] Chomsky, "The Current Scene in Linguistics," *College English*, 27 (1966), 587–595; and "Linguistic Theory," in *Language Teaching: Broader Contexts*, ed. Robert C. Meade, Jr. (New York: Modern Language Association, 1966), pp. 43–49; Mark Lester, "The Value of Transformational Grammar in Teaching Composition," *CCC*, 16 (1967), 228.

[16] Christensen, "Between Two Worlds," in *Notes toward a New Rhetoric: Nine Essays for Teachers*, rev. ed., ed. Bonniejean Christensen (New York: Harper & Row, 1978), pp. 1–22.

[17] Reber, "Implicit Learning of Artificial Grammars," *Journal of Verbal Learning and Verbal Behavior*, 6 (1967), 855–63; "Implicit Learning of Synthetic Languages: The Role of Instructional Set," *Journal of Experimental Psychology: Human Learning and Memory*, 2 (1976), 889–94, and Reber, Saul M. Kassin, Selma Lewis, and Gary Cantor, "On the Relationship Between Implicit and Explicit Modes in the Learning of a Complex Rule Structure," *Journal of Experimental Psychology: Human Learning and Memory*, 6 (1980), 492–502.

[18] "Individual Variation in the Use of the Monitor," in *Principles of Second Language Learning*, ed. W. Richie (New York: Academic Press, 1978), pp. 175–85.

[19] "Applications of Psycholinguistic Research to the Classroom," in *Practical Applications of Research in Foreign Language Teaching*, ed. D. J. James (Lincolnwood, Ill.: National Textbook, 1983), p. 61.

[20] "Some Evidence for the Integrity and Interaction of Two Knowledge Sources," in *New Dimensions in Second Language Acquisition Research*, ed. Roger W. Andersen (Rowley, Mass.: Newbury House, 1981), pp. 62–74.

[21] Hartwell and Bentley, *Some Suggestions for Using Open to Language: A New College Rhetoric*. (New York: Oxford University Press, 1982), p. 73; Rose, *Writer's Block: The Cognitive Dimension* (Carbondale: Southern Illinois University Press, 1983), p. 99; Daiute, "Psycholinguistic Foundations of the Writing Process," *RTE*, 15 (1981), 5–22.

[22] See Bartholomae, "The Study of Error"; Patrick Hartwell, "The Writing Center and the Paradoxes of Written-Down Speech," in *Writing Centers: Theory and Administration*, ed. Gary Olson (Urbana, Ill.: NCTE, 1984), pp. 48–61; and Sondra Perl, "A Look at Basic Writers in the Process of Composing," in *Basic Writing: A Collection of Essays for Teachers, Researchers, and Administrators* (Urbana, Ill.: NCTE, 1980), pp. 13–32.

[23] Emonds, *Adjacency in Grammar: The Theory of Language-Particular Rules* (New York: Academic, 1983); and Jochnowitz, "Everybody Likes Pizza, Doesn't He or She?" *American Speech*, 57 (1982), 198–203.

[24] Scribner and Cole, *Psychology of Literacy* (Cambridge, Mass.: Harvard University Press, 1981); Gleitman and Gleitman, "Language Use and Language Judgment," in *Individual Differences in Language Ability and Language Behavior*, ed. Charles J. Fillmore, Daniel Kemper, and William S. Y. Wang (New York: Academic Press, 1979), pp. 103–126.

[25] There are several recent reviews of this developing body of research in psychology and child development: Irene Athey, "Language Development Factors Related to Reading Development," *Journal of Educational Research,* 76 (1983), 197–203; James Flood and Paula Menyuk, "Metalinguistic Development and Reading/Writing Achievement," *Claremont Reading Conference Yearbook,* 46 (1982), 122–32; and the following four essays: David T. Hakes, "The Development of Metalinguistic Abilities: What Develops?," pp. 162–210; Stan A. Kuczaj, II, and Brooke Harbaugh, "What Children Think about the Speaking Capabilities of Other Persons and Things," pp. 211–27; Karen Saywitz and Louise Cherry Wilkinson, "Age-Related Differences in Metalinguistic Awareness," pp. 229–50; and Harriet Salatas Waters and Virginia S. Tinsley, "The Development of Verbal Self-Regulation: Relationships between Language, Cognition, and Behavior," pp. 251–277; all in *Language, Thought, and Culture,* Vol. II of *Language Development,* ed. Stan Kuczaj, Jr. (Hillsdale, N.J.: Lawrence Erlbaum, 1982). See also Joanne R. Nurss, "Research in Review: Linguistic Awareness and Learning to Read," *Young Children,* 35, No. 3 (1980), 57–66.

[26] "Competing Value Systems in Inner City Schools," in *Children In and Out of School. Ethnography and Education,* ed. Perry Gilmore and Allan A. Glatthorn (Washington, D.C.: Center for Applied Linguistics, 1982), pp. 148–71; and "Locating the Frontier between Social and Psychological Factors in Linguistic Structure," in *Individual Differences in Language Ability and Language Behavior,* ed. Fillmore, Kemper, and Wang, pp. 327–40.

[27] See, for example, Thomas Farrell, "IQ and Standard English," *CCC,* 34 (1983), 470–484, and the responses by Karen L. Greenberg and Patrick Hartwell, *CCC,* in press.

[28] Jane W. Torrey, "Teaching Standard English to Speakers of Other Dialects," in *Applications of Linguistics: Selected Papers of the Second International Conference of Applied Linguistics,* ed. C. E. Perren and J. L. M. Trim (Cambridge, Mass.: Cambridge University Press, 1971), pp. 423–428; James W. Beers and Edmund H. Henderson, "A Study of the Developing Orthographic Concepts among First Graders," *RTE,* 11 (1977), 133–48.

[29] See the error counts of Samuel A. Kirschner and C. Howard Poteet, "Non-Standard English Usage in the Writing of Black, White, and Hispanic Remedial English Students in an Urban Community College," *RTE,* 7 (1973), 351–55; and Marilyn Sternglass, "Close Similarities in Dialect Features of Black and White College Students in Remedial Composition Classes," *TESOL Quarterly,* 8 (1974), 271–83.

[30] For reading, see the massive study by Kenneth S. Goodman and Yetta M. Goodman, *Reading of American Children Whose Language Is a Stable Rural Dialect of English or a Language Other than English* (Washington, D.C.: National Institute of Education Final Report, 1978) ERIC 175 754; and the overview by Rudine Sims, "Dialect and Reading: Toward Redefining the Issues," in *Reader Meets Author/Bridging the Gap: A Psycholinguistic and Sociolinguistic Approach,* ed. Judith A. Langer and M. Tricia Smith-Burke (Newark, Del.: International Reading Association, 1982), pp. 222–232. For writing, see Patrick Hartwell, "Dialect Interference in Writing: A Critical View," *RTE,* 14 (1980), 101–118; and the anthology edited by Barry M. Kroll and Roberta J. Vann, *Exploring Speaking-Writing Relationships: Connections and Contrasts* (Urbana, Ill.: NCTE, 1981).

[31] See, for example, Eric A. Havelock, *The Literary Revolution in Greece and Its Cultural Consequences* (Princeton, N.J.: Princeton University Press, 1982); Lesley Milroy on literacy in Dublin, *Language and Social Networks* (Oxford: Basil Blackwell, 1980); Ron Scollon and Suzanne B. K. Scollon on literacy in central Alaska, *Interethnic Communication: An Athabascan Case* (Austin, Tex.: Southwest Educational Development Laboratory Working Papers in Sociolinguistics, No. 59, 1979) ERIC 175 276; and Scribner and Cole on literacy in Liberia, *Psychology of Literacy* (see note 24).

[32] See, for example, the anthology edited by Deborah Tannen, *Spoken and Written Language: Exploring Orality and Literacy* (Norwood, N.J.: Ablex, 1982); and Shirley Brice Heath's continuing work: "Protean Shapes in Literacy Events: Ever-Shifting Oral and Literate Traditions," in *Spoken and Written Language,* pp. 91–117; *Ways with Words: Language, Life and Work in Communities and Classrooms* (New York: Cambridge University Press, 1983); and "What No Bedtime Story Means," *Language in Society,* 11 (1982), 49–76.

[33] For studies at the elementary level, see Dell H. Hymes et al., eds., *Ethnographic Monitoring of Children's Acquisition of Reading/Language Arts Skills In and Out of the Classroom* (Washington, D.C.: National Institute of Education Final Report, 1981) ERIC 208

096. For studies at the secondary level, see James L. Collins and Michael M. Williamson, "Spoken Language and Semantic Abbreviation in Writing," *RTE*, 15 (1981), 23–36. And for studies at the college level, see Patrick Hartwell and Gene LoPresti, "Sentence Combining as Kid-Watching," in *Sentence Combining: A Rhetorical Perspective*, ed. Donald A. Daiker, Andrew Kerek, and Max Morenberg (Carbondale: Southern Illinois University Press, 1985).

[34] Lloyd-Jones, "Romantic Revels—I Am Not You," *CCC*, 23 (1972), 251–271; and Young, "Concepts of Art and the Teaching of Writing," in *The Rhetorical Tradition and Modern Writing*, ed. James J. Murphy (New York: Modern Language Association, 1982), pp. 130–41.

[35] For the romantic position, see Ann E. Berthoff, "Tolstoy, Vygotsky, and the Making of Meaning," *CCC*, 29 (1978), 249–55; Kenneth Dowst, "The Epistemic Approach," in *Eight Approaches to Teaching Composition*, ed. Timothy Donovan and Ben G. McClellan (Urbana, Ill.: NCTE, 1980), pp. 65–85; Peter Elbow, "The Challenge for Sentence Combining"; and Donald Murray, "Following Language toward Meaning," both in *Sentence Combining: A Rhetorical Perspective* (1985; see note 33); and Ian Pringle, "Why Teach Style? A Review-Essay," *CCC*, 34 (1983), 91–98.

For the classic position, see Christensen's "A Generative Rhetoric of the Sentence" and Joseph Williams' "Defining Complexity," *CE*, 41 (1979), 595–609; and his *Style: Ten Lessons in Clarity and Grace* (see note 9).

[36] Courtney B. Cazden and David K. Dickinson, "Language and Education: Standardization versus Cultural Pluralism," in *Language in the USA*, ed. Charles A. Ferguson and Shirley Brice Heath (New York: Cambridge University Press, 1981), pp. 446–468; and Carol Chomsky, "Developing Facility with Language Structure," in *Discovering Language with Children*, ed. Gay Su Pinnell (Urbana, Ill.: NCTE, 1980), pp. 56–59.

[37] Boraas, "Formal English Grammar and the Practical Mastery of English." Diss. University of Illinois, 1917; Asker, "Does Knowledge of Grammar Function?" *School and Society*, 17 (27 January 1923), 109–11; Ash, "An Experimental Evaluation of the Stylistic Approach in Teaching Composition in the Junior High School," *Journal of Experimental Education*, 4 (1935), 54–62; and Frogner, "A Study of the Relative Efficacy of a Grammatical and a Thought Approach to the Improvement of Sentence Structure in Grades Nine and Eleven," *School Review*, 47 (1939), 663–75.

[38] "Research on Grammar and Usage and Its Implications for Teaching Writing," *Bulletin of the School of Education*, Indiana University, 36 (1960), pp. 13–14.

[39] Meckel, "Research on Teaching Composition and Literature," in *Handbook of Research on Teaching*, ed. N. L. Gage (Chicago: Rand McNally, 1963), pp. 966–1006.

[40] Bateman and Zidonis, *The Effect of a Study of Transformational Grammar on the Writing of Ninth and Tenth Graders* (Urbana, Ill.: NCTE, 1966); Mellon, *Transformational Sentence Combining: A Method for Enhancing the Development of Fluency in English Composition* (Urbana, Ill.: NCTE, 1969); O'Hare, *Sentence-Combining: Improving Student Writing without Formal Grammar Instruction* (Urbana, Ill.: NCTE, 1971); Stotsky, "Sentence-Combining as a Curricular Activity: Its Effect on Written Language Development," *RTE*, 9 (1975), 30–72; and Van de Veghe, "Research in Written Composition: Fifteen Years of Investigation," ERIC 157 095.

[41] Haynes, "Using Research in Preparing to Teach Writing," *English Journal*, 69, No. 1 (1978), 82–88; Holbrook, "ERIC/RCS Report: Whither (Wither) Grammar," *Language Arts*, 60 (1983), 259–63; Whiteman, "What We Can Learn from Writing Research," *Theory into Practice*, 19 (1980), 150–156; Bamberg, "Composition in the Secondary English Curriculum: Some Current Trends and Directions for the Eighties," *RTE*, 15 (1981), 257–66; and "Composition Instruction Does Make a Difference: A Comparison of the High School Preparation of College Freshmen in Regular and Remedial English Classes," *RTE*, 12 (1978), 47–59.

[42] Emig, "Inquiry Paradigms and Writing," *CCC*, 33 (1982), 64–75; Carton and Castiglione, "Educational Linguistics: Defining the Domain," in *Psycholinguistic Research: Implications and Applications*, ed. Doris Aaronson and Robert W. Rieber (Hillsdale, N.J.: Lawrence Erlbaum, 1979), pp. 497–520.

APPENDIX A

WRITING ACROSS THE CURRICULUM

One of the goals of the first-year composition course is to prepare students for the kinds of writing they will be asked to do during their academic careers. Academic writing will be required in almost every course they complete, and within the sphere of different disciplines. During their college experience, students will be asked to write not only about literature, but to apply specific strategies to write about readings in various genres, in other courses. Students will be asked to think critically and to develop and support arguments. They will be asked to write persuasively, with consideration of audience and purpose, whether in a business memo or other document related to their field of study.

As colleges and universities develop writing across the curriculum (WAC) initiatives to address the student's writing experience, both inside and outside of the academy, the composition course will be required to introduce students to the demands of writing in different disciplines, in different situations, for different purposes, and for different audiences. Instructors at schools where there is a WAC focus can inform their teaching by becoming familiar with the goals and theoretical principles of the WAC movement and the specific approaches favored by their department. For example, some departments prefer the "writing to learn" approach which is meant to increase students' engagement with and learning of a subject through writing. Others favor the "learning to write" approach, in which students learn to write as members of specific discourse communities, within their disciplines.

The articles in this appendix address questions and issues that composition instructors face as they prepare students to be effective and versatile writers and readers in courses across the curriculum, such as:

- What is WAC and what are its origins? What does it mean to teach WAC? How can instructors learn more about it?
- How can instructors incorporate WAC principles in their writing courses? What kinds of assignments will help students learn about different disciplinary approaches to inquiry, research, or genre?
- How can instructors interest students in approaching literature from different critical perspectives? Given the sophistication of current critical theory and the complexity of various interpretive approaches to literature, how can instructors teach writing about literature without introducing confusion and despair?
- How can composition instructors prepare students for the kinds of writing they will do in business and professional situations?

WRITING ABOUT LITERATURE

WRITING FOR THE IGNORANT READER

Susan G. LeJeune

[*Teaching English in the Two-Year College* (December 1998): 163–67.]

Susan G. LeJeune is an associate professor of English at Louisiana State University at Eunice where she teaches first-year composition and British literature.

Focusing on her second-semester courses in Composition and Literature, LeJeune explains how she uses the idea of "the ignorant reader" to help her students consider more carefully the potential audiences for their writing. The article offers several detailed suggestions for introducing and using this concept in writing classes.

Being a teacher of composition is not easy these days. With the public outcry for literate, coherent communication and the demands of the academy for "academic" writing, what's a teacher to do? These approaches to prose certainly don't seem to be one and the same. Try reading an article in *Cosmopolitan* and one in *PMLA* and you'll see what I mean. Although I prefer the straightforward *Cosmo* style myself, there are many who feel obligated to teach academic writing and some who actually prefer it.

Regardless of personal preferences, we writing teachers, especially those who teach that neither-fish-nor-fowl second-semester course, Composition and Literature, find ourselves in a quandary. Should we continue the direct, personalized writing of the initial composition course, or should we train our students to examine literature using the style and language of the academy?

Academic writing forms the core of most college composition/literature courses, extending from the second semester all the way to the baccalaureate and beyond. It also produces some turgid prose that impedes communication. Fledgling writers who try their hands at academic writing often adopt new and strange voices that don't speak clearly.

How do we solve the problem of teaching students to write in a relaxed manner about inherently unnatural material (at least to them), literary texts? This is one time that teachers of composition can have it both ways. It is possible to create academic writing that is clear, readable, and appealing to the "average reader," whatever that is, and at the same time have writing that is logical and supported by clear examples in the best analytical/persuasive style. Writing should convey the human being behind the pen without degenerating into touchy-feely prose. The kind of academic writing I once taught muffled and distorted student voices and produced some mind-numbingly boring or incomprehensible stuff. Then something happened.

Several years ago, I noticed that, while working in collaborative groups, the students communicated ideas effectively to each other orally, even under intense time pressure. We were doing an activity that I called "the ignorant reader." Students asked a question that would clarify a problem with the reading but one that they couldn't answer on their own. No question was too stupid to ask. The only requirement was that it be brief and direct. The response, too, was to be brief and direct, considering that all questions were to be asked and answered in five minutes total.

I was amazed at how well the students responded to peer questioning. They cut to the chase, wasted no words, answered simple questions asked by their peers with direct responses supported by clear examples.

The key to their success lay in the focus: communicating to that ignorant reader who had asked the simple question. He needed the answer; he needed to understand why that answer was valid; he had no time to spare on any fluff. I decided that the key to writing about literature lay in that audience, the ignorant reader with his stupid question. To create a vital, breathing academic prose that isn't smothered by high-blown phrasing and convoluted sentence structure, try the ignorant reader as the audience.

Who is this ignorant reader—the perfect audience for the developing academic writer or those who have been writing for years. The ignorant reader is the one who has read the work and knows what's in it like the back of her hand, so she doesn't need a plot summary. She also knows all the definitions, so she needn't be told them again. However, she has a question that must be answered. She is rather obtuse, so the answer must be clear and well-explained. She is also skeptical, so she demands support for every point.

How does the ignorant reader function as an audience for writing about literature? He asks the initial question that stimulates the creation of a paper. For example, after reading "A Rose for Emily," he might ask this question: "How does the setting allow Emily to get away with murder?" For "Araby," he'd ask, "Why was the kid so disappointed at the end of the story?" Each of these questions lends itself to writing about the work. All the essayist must do is answer the question—clearly and with support to prove his point.

The ignorant reader also browbeats the writer for the why's. An answer to the Emily question like "It's a small town" won't be clear to the ignorant reader. He'll ask why the size of the town matters, forcing the writer to explain why it makes a difference. A response to the "Araby" question saying, "He lost his dreams," wouldn't be adequate. The ignorant reader would want to know *why* the kid lost his dreams—and by the way, what *were* his dreams? He needs a clear explanation, thus forcing the writer to use a "because" clause, or something like it, to give the ignorant reader the reason.

The ignorant reader demands to be shown as well as told. "How do you know?" is a typical question the ignorant reader asks. As a result, the writer must find supporting examples. "Show me what you're talking about" compels the writer to use tangible proofs, the kind of support that lies in the concrete example. ("No ideas but in things" is a great motto for those who write about literature.) In a character analysis, for example, the ignorant reader asks, "How do you know the mother is hard-working? Where can I see her act in a hard-working manner?"

The ignorant reader is carried around with the writer on the writer's shoulder, like a good angel. Once a student begins to think like her ignorant reader, she will begin to address any possible question this artificial entity could ask. If she anticipates the questions as she writes and formulates proofs while fashioning her essay, she will be communicating clearly and effectively with you, the omniscient teacher.

The ignorant reader has a place in every classroom that demands analytical or argumentative writing of any kind, but it serves a particularly valuable function in the literature/composition classroom. It is in this arena that most students lose the ability to communicate clearly. Possibly the demands of a work of literature are intrinsically more difficult. Perhaps the students begin to feel that they must sound like literary critics to convey ideas. Whatever the reason, the problem remains the same: some mighty poor writing that doesn't reach the goal set by the assignment.

So how can you get this ignorant reader audience to work miracles in *your* classroom? Here are my suggestions.

First, introduce the ignorant reader to the students prior to their writing their first literary analysis. An appropriate time follows a small group discussion that demands intragroup questions and answers. Explain that the ignorant reader is very much like any typical student in the class. She has read the assignment, familiarized herself with terminology. She doesn't need a plot summary nor does she need definitions of terms in the course of the paper. Yet, she has one little question that must be answered. It is usually a somewhat stupid question, something she should be able to answer, but for some reason she just doesn't get it.

Give the class an example pertaining to the coming assignment. If the essay will be an analysis of conflict in "To Build a Fire," the ignorant reader question (IRQ) might be "What is the man's major adversary?" Obvious, isn't it? Keep the question simple at first. The students will pooh-pooh it, of course, as just too ridiculous to bother with. Remind them that this reader is slow. Her questions are simple. All the writer must do is answer the simple question.

Next, show the students how to answer that simple question by pretending to be an ignorant reader (IR) yourself as the class outlines a sample paper addressing a typical IRQ. If the answer to "What is the major adversary?" in "To Build a Fire" is nature, the IR will demand proof. "Where do you see it?" is her next question. From that question come the tangible examples that prove the answer is correct. With you playing the ignorant reader, the students will generate proof without realizing what they're doing.

At this point, you've generated one body paragraph (at least) with multiple examples of the conflict. Thus, you've written a skeletal outline.

The IR isn't satisfied yet, though. As the students write the paper, giving the answer with supporting examples, they must also explain the ideas from time to time because the IR doesn't always catch on. Here is an example using just a few sentences from a typical essay using the ignorant reader audience.

> The first conflict evident in the story is man versus nature. [This is the answer to the original question about the conflict.] An example of this struggle occurs when the man removes his gloves to eat lunch without having first built a fire. [This is a supporting example prompted by the "Where do you see it?" question. Note that there is no re-telling of the story, simply a brief mention of the incident.] Because it is so cold, seventy-five below zero, his hands begin to freeze immediately, making him aware for the first time of the threat the weather poses. [This is the explanatory material that should be considered for virtually every example. Notice that it makes clear the conflict implied by the example.]

Does all of this seem like unnecessary effort? It isn't. Papers become clearer and clearer as the semester goes on. After a while students begin to speak orally to the ignorant reader when they answer questions posed during class. Recently, a student explicated a sonnet orally using that imaginary audience without realizing it. Her explication was as clear an analysis of that sonnet as anything I've ever heard. Working in a group, her collaborators had asked one ignorant reader question after another until her final explanation for the entire class addressed every potentially confusing point clearly and succinctly.

Writing for the ignorant reader can eliminate many of the problems we find in student academic prose. First, the technique offers students a ready-made audience in the ignorant reader. Better yet, the ignorant reader is someone like them.

For those who think that students should write for an audience unlike them, think back to the convoluted prose resulting from writing for "the teacher." Students who are uncertain of audience will try to sound like they *think* a critic sounds to convey erudition. They end up sounding like visitors from another planet who are unfamiliar with basic sentence structure and the connotation of words. They also fill their papers with extraneous information that they feel obligated to include, as well as the clutter of adjectives and adverbs.

When students write for the ignorant reader, they envision a confused individual—someone like them. They want to make this person understand a simple concept by answering his simple question. In designing their papers, they will speak to him, perhaps using an occasional contraction and maybe even an "I" or two. These stylistics might not be part of traditional academic writing, but they can easily be eliminated later, if you insist, once the student understands the clear communication of ideas to a person who needs an answer. Frankly, I'm a fan of the first person and contractions.

The ignorant reader also demands complete clarity not only in the ideas but also in the diction conveying them. Students rarely misuse unfamiliar words when writing to this audience because they don't use them. They assume the IR wouldn't catch on to those fifty-dollar words anyway, so they use their own vocabularies and never fall into the thesaurus trap. If you feel simple is less effective, think back to the last time a first-year student used "cognition" for "understanding" and you'll remember a student losing his or her voice.

The second built-in advantage of the ignorant reader as audience is that it creates a clear focus for the paper from the outset. The students know that they must answer a question with their papers. Thus, the "Where do I go from here?" problem is solved before it begins. The student can plan a response working from a ready-made thesis, a simple restatement of the IRQ making it a declarative sentence. The question "What kind of person is Mama in Alice Walker's 'Everyday Use'?" becomes "Mama in Alice Walker's 'Everyday Use' is _____, _____, and _____," in a primitive but crystal clear thesis statement.

Working from the restated IRQ, the student must design a paper to offer the answers. I often suggest the companion IRQ "How do you know?" as a guide to designing the body of the essay. The students simply think of the elements in the story that made the answer clear to them and work these examples into a paper.

The quantity and quality of the examples composing the support are fringe benefits of using the ignorant reader. The student soon realizes that the only way to help the IR understand a point is to give an illustration. The ignorant reader must be shown everything in concrete images she can understand. To a statement like "Mama is hard-working," the ignorant reader will respond, "How do you know?" The writer then must convey the abstraction in a manner that even the most ignorant reader can understand and, so he will gravitate toward concrete examples. The "no ideas but in things" concept guides the construction of all essays written for this audience.

As the students become attuned to the needs of the ignorant reader, they will understand the need for planning before writing, the third benefit of using this audience. They begin jotting down ideas, if not creating detailed outlines. Because the ignorant reader asks very simple questions, there is no need to digress. Every body paragraph should relate directly to the IRQ; furthermore, every example within the paragraph should support the topic sentence. If not, the IR will definitely become confused.

Students soon realize that planning is a must. The ignorant reader insists that an essay lead from point to point with specific examples that support each point. To demonstrate how clear and well-organized writing must be for the ignorant reader, I ask students to read their rough drafts orally to small groups of peers. Listeners are not allowed to look at the draft at any time. If the listeners are confused after hearing the paper read aloud, the writer has lost sight of the ignorant reader. A well-constructed IR paper should be as readily understood by a listener as by a reader. If a point needs to be expanded or explained more clearly, the ignorant listener will notice the problem, as would the ignorant reader.

Another advantage of the ignorant reader as audience is that this audience transfers readily to writing in other disciplines. Soon students begin writing history essays for the ignorant history student, chemistry essays for the ignorant chemistry student. Because they are no longer writing for the "teacher," students clarify their diction, omit extraneous information and actually answer the question in readable prose. For teachers in all disciplines who venture to add a discussion or essay question to an objective test, the ignorant reader can be a blessing.

Still skeptical? Introduce the ignorant reader as a new audience for your students in just one class. I'd suggest you start with your poorest, least coherent writers. You will be amazed at the metamorphosis in their writing. None of them will sound like literary critics, but should they? They will, however, be communicating ideas and persuading readers in clear, direct prose. Come to think of it, some of us pedants might try writing for the ignorant reader, too. What is a heuristic anyway? Do I really need to know?

A PASSAGE INTO CRITICAL THEORY

Steven Lynn

[*College English* 52 (1990): 258–71.]

Steven Lynn is the Louise Fry Scudder Professor of Liberal Arts and director of the first-year English program at the University of South Carolina. He has published numerous essays and three books: *Texts and Contexts* (2000), which is in its third edition and extends the approach taken in the essay reprinted here; *Samuel Johnson after Deconstruction* (1992); and *A Brief Guide to Writing* (1997). He is a contributing editor of *The Year's Work in English Studies*.

In the introduction to "A Passage into Critical Theory," Lynn describes the situation that prompted the article: When he attempted to introduce instructors to contemporary literary criticism, they became confused and frustrated. This difficulty is analogous to the problems students have when their instructors try to teach the concept of differing critical perspectives. Lynn's overview demystifies various critical approaches and complements *The Bedford Handbook*'s discussion on being an active reader by offering teachers expanded options for helping student writers engage literary texts.

She might have deplored the sentiment, had it come from one of her students. "What we need," she was saying, trying hard not to whine, "is a short cut, a simple guide, a kind of recipe for each of these theories, telling us step by step how to make a particular reading." It was the second week of a three-week institute dedicated to the proposition that all teachers were created equal and that therefore all should share in the excitement and challenge of the ongoing transformation of literary criticism. But these teachers, it was clear, were just on the verge of saying, "Let's just pretend that nothing important has happened since, oh, 1967." I had whipped them into an evangelistic fever at the outset of the institute, ready to receive the spirit of critical theory; and they had read so much and worked so hard. But I nodded. She was right. They were mired in complexity and subtleties. I realized, of course, that no one whose loaf was fully sliced would seriously attempt an overview of recent critical theory in a few pages. But all they needed was to get their bearings, and then the confusion of ideas bouncing around in their heads would probably start falling into some comprehensible order. So I came up with the briefest of guides to some of the recent critical theory, an overview that would succeed when its users began to understand its limitations.

My strategy was to show how a single passage might be treated by a handful of different critical theories—certainly not every theory available, but enough to show how theory shapes practice and to help my students with those most puzzling them. Although multiple readings of the same work are easy to assemble and useful, my effort not only had the virtue of a calculated simplicity and brevity, it also displayed the same reader attempting to act as the extension of various different interpretive codes. The passage I chose, a wonderful excerpt from Brendan Gill's *Here at the New Yorker,* is itself brief, but also rich. In offering these notes I am assuming that my reader, like those teachers, knows enough about recent critical theory to be confused. Obviously, my theorizing will be alarmingly reductive, and the examples won't illustrate what any student at any level can produce, given a sketch of this or that theory. They illustrate only what I can do to provide in a very small space an example of a particular kind of critical behavior. But my teacher/students, as well as my student/students, have found these discussion/examples helpful, and so I'll proceed immediately to Gill's text and then mine, before anyone gets cut on any of these slashes.

Here's Gill's text:

> When I started at *The New Yorker,* I felt an unshakable confidence in my talent and intelligence. I revelled in them openly, like a dolphin diving skyward out of the sea. After almost forty years, my assurance is less than it was; the revellings, such as they are, take place in becoming seclusion. This steady progress downward in the amount of one's confidence is a commonplace at the magazine—one might almost call it a tradition. Again and again, some writer who has made a name for himself in the world will begin to write for us and will discover as if for the first time how difficult writing is. The machinery of benign skepticism that surrounds and besets him in the form of editors, copy editors, and checkers, to say nothing of fellow-writers, digs a yawning pit an inch or so beyond his desk. He hears it repeated as gospel that there are not three people in all America who can set down a simple declarative sentence correctly; what are the odds against his being one of this tiny elect?
>
> In some cases, the pressure of all those doubting eyes upon his copy is more than the writer can bear. When the galleys of a piece are placed in front of him, covered with scores, perhaps hundreds, of pencilled hen-tracks of inquiry, suggestion, and correction, he may sense not the glory of creation but the threat of being stung to death by an army of gnats. Upon which he may think of nothing better to do than lower his head onto his blotter and burst into tears. Thanks to the hen-tracks and their consequences, the piece will be much improved, but the author of it will be pitched into a state of graver self-doubt than ever. Poor devil, he will type out his name on a sheet of paper and stare at it long and long, with dumb uncertainty. It looks—oh, Christ—his name looks as if it could stand some working on.
>
> As I was writing the above, Gardner Botsford, the editor who, among other duties, handles copy for "Theatre," came into my office with the galleys of my latest play review in his hand. Wearing an expression of solemnity, he said, "I am obliged to inform you that Miss Gould has found a buried dangling modifier

in one of your sentences." Miss Gould is our head copy editor and unquestionably knows as much about English grammar as anyone alive. Gerunds, predicate nominatives, and passive periphrastic conjugations are mother's milk to her, as they are not to me. Nevertheless, I boldly challenged her allegation. My prose was surely correct in every way. Botsford placed the galleys before me and indicated the offending sentence, which ran, "I am told that in her ninth decade this beautiful woman's only complaint in respect to her role is that she doesn't have enough work to do."

I glared blankly at the galleys. Humiliating enough to have buried a dangling modifier unawares; still more humiliating not to be able to disinter it. Botsford came to my rescue. "Miss Gould points out that as the sentence is written, the meaning is that the complaint is in its ninth decade and has, moreover, suddenly and unaccountably assumed the female gender." I said that in my opinion the sentence could only be made worse by being corrected—it was plain that "The only complaint of this beautiful woman in her ninth decade . . ." would hang on the page as heavy as a sash-weight. "Quite so," said Botsford. "There are times when to be right is wrong, and this is one of them. The sentence stands."

New Criticism

I'll start with New Criticism because modern literary study arguably begins with New Criticism, and because it is probably, even today, the most pervasive way of looking at literature. It emerged in the struggle to make literary criticism a respectable profession, which for many scholars meant making it more rigorous, more like the sciences—a goal embodied in Wellek and Warren's landmark *Theory of Literature* in 1949. Wellek's chapter on "The Mode of Existence of a Literary Work of Art" is crucial: "The work of art," Wellek asserts, is "an object of knowledge," "a system of norms of ideal concepts which are intersubjective" (p. 156). What Wellek means by this difficult formulation, at least in part, is that "a literary work of art is in exactly the same position as a system of language" (p. 152). Because the work has the same sort of stable and "objective" status as a language, existing in a "collective ideology," governed by enduring "norms," critical statements are not merely opinions of taste: "It will always be possible to determine which point of view grasps the subject most thoroughly and deeply," as "All relativism is ultimately defeated." This assumption is important, because although New Critics in practice have not always ignored authors, genres, or historical contexts, the purpose of their analysis of particular works, their "close reading," has been finally to reveal how the formal elements of the literary work, often thought of as a poem, create and resolve tension and irony. Great works control profound tensions, and therefore New Criticism's intrinsic analysis, dealing with the work in isolation, is implicitly evaluative.

Common sense might suggest that the function of criticism is to reveal the meaning of a work, but New Criticism attends to *how* a work means, not *what*, for a simple reason: As Cleanth Brooks puts it, the meaning of a work is "a controlled experience which has to be *experienced*, not a logical process" (p. 90). The meaning cannot, in other words, be summed up in a proposition, but the system of norms that constructs a reader's experience can be analyzed. So, the New Critic focuses on "the poem itself" (rather than the author, the reader, the historical context), asking, "What elements are in tension in this work?" and "What unity resolves this tension?"

In Gill's story, the most obvious tension might be seen as that between right and wrong (or editor versus writer, or the world versus *The New Yorker*, or grammar versus style, or confidence versus doubt, or something else). Whatever the basic tension is determined to be, it must somehow be resolved if the text succeeds, and New Criticism is inevitably teleological: Endings are crucial. Thus a New Critical reading of Gill's passage might well focus on the reconciliation at the end, when Botsford pronounces "right is wrong." The New Critic would then consider, "How does this idea fit into the system of the work's tensions, and how is the tension ordered and resolved?" The following paragraph briefly suggests the sort of discussion that might be produced in response:

> In Gill's story of the dangling modifier, Botsford solves the conflict between Miss Gould's rules and Gill's taste with a paradox that unifies the work: Sometimes "right is wrong." Miss Gould was right to spot the error, but Gill was right to be wrong, to have written the sentence as he did. The irony of this solution is reinforced by various paradoxical images: For example, the dolphin is "diving skyward," an action that in its simultaneously downward ("diving") and upward ("skyward") implications embodies the same logic as a wrong rightness. The "progress downward" of the writer, and even his "becoming seclusion" (appealing to others; unknown to others), convey the same image. In larger terms, the writer's "unshakable confidence" that quickly becomes a "dumb uncertainty" suggests the reversal that informs the story's truth. In such an upside-down world, we would expect to find the imagery of struggle and violence, and such is indicated by the "yawning pit" and the "army of gnats." Such tension is harmonized by Gill's brilliant conclusion: In writing, conducted properly, the demands of correctness and style are unified by the writer's poetic instincts, just as the story itself is resolved by the notion of a correct error.

Structuralism

At first glance, structuralism might appear to be simply the enlargement of New Criticism's project. But instead of focusing on the formal elements that create the experience of a particular work, structuralism aspired to deal, as Terry Eagleton says, "with structures, and more particularly with examining the general laws by which they work" (p. 94). In other words, the structuralist looks at a surface manifestation and theorizes about a deep structure, or s/he interprets surface phenomena in terms of this underlying structure.

In its most ambitious moments, structuralism may aspire to reveal anything from the structure of the human mind itself to the conventions of a literary form. Structuralists have tried, for instance, not only to isolate the conventions of certain kinds of narrative, such as the fantastic and science fiction, but also to determine what features allow us to identify a text as a story. Is Gill's passage a self-contained story, an entity in itself, or is it an excerpt, a fragment, a part of *Here at the New Yorker*? If we consider how we decide whether something is a story, we might well agree that a passage becomes a story when it fits our ideas of what a story is, when it satisfies certain general laws of discourse regarding a story. If we use a very simple and ancient notion of narrative structure, most readers would probably agree that Gill's text does have a beginning, a middle, and an end, moving from harmony, to complication and crisis, and finally to resolution. Readers might also agree it has a hero (the writer, who appears to be Gill), a helper (Botsford), and a villain (Miss Gould), features that Vladimir Propp finds, interestingly enough, in fairy tales. We can identify these elements, which we might argue are essential to a story, because we can relate this story to other ones and to a paradigm of stories. We can imagine (and perhaps even recall) other stories involving a confident neophyte who encounters destructive forces, descends into despair and near helplessness, and then finds an unexpected helper and vindication. Such structuralist analysis moves into the realm of archetypal criticism (as in Northrop Frye's work) when it seeks the universal patterns, the "archetypes" which are the foundation of the system of "literature," rather than isolating the structures and relationships within a particular system of discourse.

To produce a structuralist reading, then, exposing a text's conventions and operations, we must first identify the elements of the text—the genre, the agents, the episodes, the turning points, whatever. Structuralists are naturally attracted to charts and diagrams because these are helpful in reducing the complexity of a text to some understandable pattern, which can be compared to other patterns, or their transmutation, or absence. This concern with conventions rather than discrete works means that structuralism, unlike New Criticism, is not implicitly evaluative. *Gulliver's Travels* and *Gilligan's Island* are equally worthy of analysis, at least structurally: They may, in fact, illuminate one another, since textual conventions appear in the relationship of texts. If all the stories in our culture, regardless of characters or plot, end with a pack of multicolored dogs going off to hunt antelopes, as is indeed apparently the case in one African culture (Grimes, p. vii), then we recognize such an event as a discrete element: the ending element. In the case of Gill's text, one convention of a literary work that we surely recognize as missing is a beginning operation: a title. Does this lack alone disqualify this text as a literary story? If so, could we then add a title (what would it be?) and make the text into a story? If so, who would be the author of this story that didn't exist until we titled it? (We might also consider the status of this story before it was extricated from Gill's book.)

Because students' experience of literature may be limited, it's often helpful to supply comparable texts or to ask students to invent a comparable text, thus making the textual conventions easier to imagine. Here is my very limited attempt to think structurally about this excerpt, offering also another story to highlight the postulated form.

> The structure of Gill's text involves the repetition of an underlying sequence, in which a central figure encounters a contrary force that reverses his fortunes: x + y Æ anti-x. This sequence, which we see in the first two paragraphs, might be represented this way:
>
> 1. Unrealistic confidence ("unshakable confidence") + critical forces (editors, copy editors, and checkers) Æ unrealistic doubt ("dumb uncertainty").
>
> The same underlying structure appears in the last two paragraphs, except this time a particular example of the pattern is presented:
>
> 2. Specific instance: Unrealistic confidence ("boldly challenged her allegation") + critical force (Miss Gould) Æ unrealistic doubt ("Still more humiliating").
>
> In the final paragraph the pattern is inverted, as confidence becomes doubt, antagonistic forces become helpful, and doubt becomes confidence. This inversion, which is perhaps a common occurrence in the concluding element of a series, heightens by contrast the effect of the hero's success:
>
> 3. Unrealistic doubt (helpless to "disinter it") + a helpful force (Botsford) Æ realistic confidence (Gill's bold challenge, stoutly maintained, is upheld).
>
> The same underlying pattern can be seen in the following plot:
>
> 1. Dreaming of future glory as an artist, a student comes to study at the university and discovers that art professors systematically show students how incompetent they are.
> 2. The art student turns in a project, and one faculty member explains in public how the project is grossly wrong. The student did not realize that he had departed from the assignment.
> 3. The chairman of the department then responds to the faculty member's criticism, saying that the assignment was a foolish one, and the student has demonstrated admirable creativity in revising the professor's directions and producing a good project.

Deconstruction

New Criticism, like its sibling philosophy of writing instruction, Current-Traditional Rhetoric, is product-oriented. It is perhaps then not surprising that my New Critical reading of Gill's piece focuses on the centrality of error, one of

C-T Rhetoric's fundamental concerns. At first glance, Gill's story may appear to deflate Error's terror, since being wrong turns out to be right. If we press this close reading, however, asking if the text might say something other than what it appears to say, we move into the realm of deconstruction. Composition students in particular might be sensitive to the way Botsford's paradox reverses itself, unravelling Gill's grammatical triumph and plunging "the writer" finally into an even dumber and darker uncertainty. It's bad enough for the writer at *The New Yorker,* not to mention the composer in Freshman English, if the rules of writing are so complex that not even three people in America "can set down a simple declarative sentence correctly," if an experienced and accomplished writer can commit a major blunder without knowing it and without being able to fix it when he does know it. But it's even worse if the rules obtain in one case and not in another, and the rules for determining such exceptions don't seem to exist but are rather invented and applied by whoever happens to be in charge. Basic writing students, mystified by the rules of Standard English, live in just such a nightmare, I suspect.

If we look again at Botsford's vindication, we see it is deceptive, for he does not actually say that sometimes right is wrong and wrong is right. He only says that sometimes "right is wrong." Certainly wrong is also occasionally wrong, and perhaps it is always wrong. But Botsford's apparent reversal of the dismantling of authors at *The New Yorker* is finally ambiguous, since we never know if the writer is ever correct, no matter what he does. "The sentence stands" indeed, but it stands with its error intact, a monument to Gill's inability and the inevitable error of writing—the way language masters us. The passage thus complements the deconstructive commonplace that reading is always misreading.

Although it has been asserted that poststructuralism is not an applicable method (see Tompkins), I am, I think, just applying some basic deconstructive moves to Gill's text, which seems especially receptive, given its overt oppositions and emphasis on language. And despite the reluctance of some theorists to risk the spectacle of defining deconstruction (an action that deconstruction, by definition, renders futile), useful and clear explanations are available. For example, Barbara Johnson says that deconstruction proceeds by "the careful teasing out of warring forces of signification within the text itself" (p. 5). Jonathan Culler says that "to deconstruct a discourse is to show how it undermines the philosophy it asserts, or the hierarchical oppositions on which it relies" (p. 86). This teasing out or undermining might be described as a three-step process: First, a deconstructive reading must note which member of an opposition in a text appears to be privileged or dominant (writers versus editors, error versus correctness, men versus women, etc.); second, the reading shows how this hierarchy can be reversed within the text, how the apparent hierarchy is arbitrary or illusory; finally, a deconstructive reading places both structures in question, making the text ultimately ambiguous. For students to deconstruct a text, they need to locate an opposition, determine which member is privileged, then reverse and undermine that hierarchy. Such activity often makes central what appears to be marginal, thereby exposing "hidden" contradictions. Deconstruction seems to me especially worthwhile because it encourages creativity (my students often enjoy the imaginative playfulness and punning of much poststructuralist criticism) and scrutiny (in order to deconstruct a work, one at least must read it carefully).

Thus, if structuralism shows how the conventions of a text work, then poststructuralism, in a sense, points out how they fail. In our time, the genres fiction and nonfiction have proved especially interesting. Gill's passage would appear to be nonfiction, since Gill really did work at *The New Yorker,* and his book obviously employs the operations of autobiography. But look at Miss Gould's uncannily apt name: She is a Miss Ghoul, having unearthed a "buried" dangling modifier, decomposing Gill's sentence; Botsford, perhaps played by

Vincent Price, enters with "an expression of solemnity," carrying this mutilated modifier that the author finds himself unable to "disinter." Miss Gould may not drink human blood, but she does have some strange nutritional ideas: "gerunds, predicate nominatives, and passive paraphrastic conjugations are mother's milk to her." Fortunately, the editor, a gardener, or rather a Gardner, who has the final responsibility for nurturing, pruning, and harvesting the writer's sentences, knows how to deal with buried modifiers. A Botsford, he knows how to get over the unavoidable errors of prose, how to ford the botches of writing (ouch!). Thus, although we initially may place this piece into the nonfiction category, deconstruction calls such placement into question. People in nonfiction usually don't have symbolic numbers—do they? Of course, there was that White House spokesperson named Larry Speakes. And then my allergist in Tuscaloosa, whose name, prophetically enough, was Dr. Shotts. And a hundred other folks I've known with strangely meaningful names. Deconstruction typically leaves us in uncertainty, but with a richer understanding of the categories we have put in motion—thereby unavoidably functioning as a kind of cultural criticism, or at least a prelude to cultural criticism.

Although deconstructive critics may well deal with pervasive, basic issues, they may also choose some marginal element of the text and vigorously explore its oppositions, reversals, and ambiguities. In fact, for some critics, deconstruction is simply a name for "close reading" with a vengeance. The deconstructive critic, for example, might well decide to concentrate on the arguably marginal assertion that because of the editors' merciless correction, "the piece will be much improved." The New Critic, I think, would not be very likely to consider this assertion central, the key to the passage. Yet, proceeding from deconstructive assumptions, bringing the marginal to the center, here is what happened when I turned on this assertion:

> Gill's anecdote clearly sets the world's writers against the editors, and the latter control the game. The editors and their henchmen, the checkers and copy editors, get to say what is wrong. They get to dig the "yawning pit" in front of the helpless writer's desk; they determine the "tiny elect" who can write correctly; they make the scores and hundreds of "hen-tracks" on the writer's manuscript, which serve as testimony to the incompetence of writers, the near-impossibility of writing, and the arbitrary power of the editor. To be sure, it is acknowledged that these editorial assaults upon the writer serve their purpose, for "Thanks to the hen-tracks and their consequences, the piece will be much improved." But the cost is clearly terrible. Not only is the writer unable to write his own name with any confidence, he has become a "Poor devil," outside "the elect." In delivering his writing over to the editors, conceding their dominance, the writer inevitably places his own identity, perhaps even his own soul, in jeopardy, as the expostulation "oh Christ!" comes to be an invocation to the only power who can save the writer from the devil and the editor's destructive forces.
>
> In fact, this story of the errors of writing actually reveals that the kingdom of editors is based upon a lie: It simply is not true, despite the beleaguered writer's admission under torture, that "the piece will be much improved" by editorial intervention. Miss Gould's enormous grammatical lore does not improve the piece at all; her effort nearly made it "worse." And Botsford's contribution involves simply leaving the piece as it was written—a strange method of improvement. This instance, in other words, suggests that the writer need not approach dissolution in order to compose his writing. At the same time, Gill can never become again like the gill-less dolphin of the first paragraph, confidently "diving skyward," for the dangling modifier remains, a part of the sea of language the author cannot leave. In the end, both writer and editor are defeated by their inability to control their language, as the status of the writer at *The New Yorker* becomes a paradigm for the alarming status of writing itself: deceptive, mute, and intractable, "The sentence stands," neither improved nor made worse.

Psychological Criticism

In its most commonsensical form, a psychological approach to a text simply involves focusing attention on the motivations and relationships involved in the text's production or consumption. The mental processes of author, character, and/or reader may be involved in such considerations. My students, who have seen their own writing covered by "pencilled hen-tracks of inquiry, suggestion, and correction," are easily interested in what Gill's passage implies about the emotional effects of criticism and why writers react so unconstructively and painfully to correction and advice. Whereas reader-response criticism would build a "reading" from such subjective reaction, psychological criticism would be more interested in analyzing (rather than expressing) the passage's effects. Obviously, terms like "ego," "anxiety," "unconscious," and "obsessive," would be handy in such an analysis, although an introduction to psychological concepts could quickly engulf a course in criticism. And one could easily spend several semesters exploring different psychological schools and the various ways they might influence our reading. My minimal (but still challenging) goal in an introduction to theory is to give my students an extremely basic understanding of some essential Freudian ideas and their application.

Many of my students think they already understand Freud: He's the guy who thought of everything in terms of sex. Freud did of course think that sexuality (in a large sense) pervades our lives, but it is also always in conflict with opposing forces. So that we can function in society, our drive toward pleasure is necessarily contained and suppressed, relegated in part to the unconscious, where it does not slumber peacefully away, but rather asserts itself indirectly, in dreams, jokes, slips of the tongue, creative writing. For instance, dreams of water, Freud tells us, harken back to "the embryo in the amniotic fluid in the mother's uterus"; dreams of diving into water may be expressing a desire to return to the womb (*Lectures*, p. 160). Repression of such desires becomes a problem when the unconscious enlarges its domain, creating hysterical, obsessional, or phobic neuroses that insistently express the desire while still disguising it. If the power of the unconscious begins to take over reality, creating delusion, then we have a psychosis.

This economy of desire is based on Freud's most outrageous (and undeniable) claim: That even infants are sexual beings. Freud's theory of the central sexual phenomenon of early childhood, admittedly based on the development of males, is laid out in a brief and accessible paper, "The Dissolution of the Oedipus Complex." Focusing first on the mother's breasts, the young boy invests his desire in his mother—he "develops an object-cathexis" for her, Freud says. As the boy's "sexual wishes in regard to his mother become more intense," his father is increasingly "perceived as an obstacle to them," thus originating what Freud calls "the simple positive Oedipus complex" (p. 640). The desire to supplant his father and join with his mother cannot be acted out, and it must be repressed, turned away from, put out of sight. This "primal repression" initiates the unconscious, engendering a "place" for repressed desires. If no more than a repression is achieved, however, the Oedipus complex "persists in an unconscious state in the id and will later manifest its pathogenic effect." This "pathogenic effect" can be avoided, Freud says, by "the destruction of the Oedipus complex," which "is brought about by the threat of castration" (p. 664). This threat is embodied in the father and perpetuated by the formation of the superego, which "retains the character of the father" (p. 642) and comes to stand for the restraints of "authority, religious teaching, schooling and reading." This constraining law in Lacan's reading of Freud is ultimately the system of language.

Even the most glimmering understanding of Freud, I would argue, can be useful: The idea of the unconscious, for instance, dispenses with the second-most-often-asked question in introductory courses—"Do you think the author really intended to mean any of that?" Further, my students generate thin and uninteresting readings more out of caution and a poverty of options than a plenitude of possibilities, and after an exposure to Freud, what interpretation can be immediately rejected as absurd? Even a basic understanding of "The Dissolution of the Oedipus Concept" opens up Gill's passage in ways my students have found liberating, comic, and revealing. For example, one of the most interesting problems in this passage is the apparent disparity between the emotional content and the actual events. We see a writer bursting into tears, hiding his head on his blotter; a writer who considers himself humiliated, who glares "blankly"; we even see a writer who is unsure of his very name. And what is the cause? A grammatical error? The scene makes so little logical sense that we may well wonder if it makes more psychological sense. The following reading tries to see what might happen when the Oedipal triangle, the unconscious, the super-ego, and the castration complex get Gill's passage on the couch:

> The dolphin diving skyward at the beginning of Gill's passage is an obvious Freudian image of birth, and an important clue to the psychic problems being addressed here. The writer moves from the buoyant amniotic ocean of pure pleasure and unthreatened ego, the world of "unshakable confidence," into the difficult reality of *The New Yorker,* the world of the anxious, neurotic writer. Gill's longing for an impossible return to the uncomplicated indulgence of an animal state, symbolized by the dolphin, conflicts with his unavoidable status in a parental society of traditions, gospels, grammatical rules, and "editors, copy editors, and checkers." The ambiguity of the image, "diving skyward," reflects this troubled position, suspended between the id's impossible nostalgia and the super-ego's stern correction. Gill's symbol for himself, the dolphin, is an interesting (and no doubt unconscious) play on his name: a "gill" is naturally associated with a fish, which becomes the dolphin; a dolphin, however, does not have a "gill," thus marking again the gulf between the burdened Gill and the free-floating dolphin.

> Does Freud's model of psychosexual development also help to explain how this loss of innocence leads to Gill's unexpectedly emotional reaction? Yes, startlingly well in fact, for analysis reveals how Gill's scene reenacts the traumatic dissolution of the Oedipal complex. To see how the Oedipal triangle shapes Gill's passage, how Gill's response bears the emotional charge of reworking his way through this complex, we should first note the writer's special relationship to his editors: He owes his existence, as a writer anyway, to his editors. The union of Miss Gould and Gardner Botsford, in this case, allows "Brendan Gill" to appear. Miss Gould, the copy editor, the symbolic mother, stands for grammatical correctness. At *The New Yorker,* the writer's first desires must be for her "yes." But this identification with Miss Gould, or rather what she represents, is unavoidably frustrated. Like the child who desires union with his mother, the writer is ill-equipped to satisfy Miss Gould: not even one of the "tiny elect," the writer cannot possibly fill in the "yawning pit" of error.

> But the writer, like the developing child, must also face the law of the father. Gardner Botsford, the symbolic father, the senior editor, must ultimately direct the writer's attention away from Miss Gould toward the proper object of his attention, outside *The New Yorker* family—the reader. We see that Gill does in fact reveal a turning away from Miss Gould, using in fact the same focus as the child who turns initially from the mother's breasts as an object of desire: Gill finds Miss Gould's "mother's milk," the predicate nominatives and such, distasteful. The way Gill chooses to present her name (not "Gloria Gould" but "Miss Gould") marks his recognition of her as a "Miss." As a by-the-book grammarian, she may also be a ghoul, bringing a deadly stiffness to what he handles. Gill's development as a writer thus requires him to reject her.

> To see how this rejection is accomplished, again in terms of the Oedipus complex, we must observe how the writer's identification with his writing contributes to his extraordinary anxiety and its symptomatic distortions. Threats to

his writing endanger his identity, his ego. Thus we see that although it is the writer's galleys that are covered with "inquiry, suggestion, and correction," Gill shifts these impressions to the writer, and further transforms them from "pencilled hen-tracks" into stings. It is not, as we might suppose, the particular work that may be attacked so much it dies, but instead the writer who may be "stung to death by an army of gnats." In reality, gnats do not, of course, have stingers; they bite, if anything. The dreamlike alteration here again substantiates the threat to his identity that the author has perceived: Being bitten to death by gnats is absurd, but being stung to death is a terrifying prospect.

At this point Freud's assertion that the dissolution of the Oedipus complex is accomplished by the threat of castration is especially helpful. Gardner Botsford, Gill's senior editor, his symbolic father, poses this threat. To see how Botsford plays this role, we must consider what he is threatening to remove. Botsford enters the scene with Gill's play review "in his hand," and we discover eventually that a part of this review has been illegitimately "buried," and may subsequently be removed, although Gill himself cannot see how to "disinter it." This threat to Gill's writing is charged by the fear of castration precisely because the writer identifies with his writing. It is no accident that the writer's "dumb uncertainty" becomes a paralyzed silence that threatens to erase the most public sign of his identity, as "his name looks as if it could stand some working on." His name, his signature, organizes the evidence of his potency, his ability (in a sense) to reproduce and promulgate himself. Thus, the writer may well "stare" at his name "long and long," once he realizes he may lose it if he cannot control the prose to which it is attached. Gill realizes that the editorial parents may correct and improve his "piece," but the cost may be terrible, as the piece may be separated from the writer, taken over by the authorities who control the emissions of his pen. Gill's image for what he has lost, the dolphin, thus becomes a rather blatant phallic symbol, reemerging as the pen (the grammatical penis) that the "dumb," unnamed writer loses. In other words, the writer must give up his "piece" to be published, to survive as a writer—but then he is no longer the writer. He cannot get himself into print, so he submits to the authorities of culture, propriety, and correctness, having realized that the self may be cut off from the sign of its identity.

We now may see the fittingness of the error Miss Gould finds: A structure that is "dangling." The writer may see his own fate in the sentence that sticks out, for it suddenly has "assumed the female gender." We would have to agree that the writer who focuses his desire upon grammar and correctness will be impotent, emasculated. The writer, in order to thrive, must get beyond the desire to please the Miss Goulds of the world. We may also see now the fittingness of "Gardner" as the name for the symbolic father: So close to "gardener," Gardner is the one who has the power to prune, to root out, the writer who is stuck on the mother's milk of Miss Gould, grammar. Thus, Gill's story draws on his psychosexual development and an apparently unresolved Oedipus complex to rehearse in powerful terms the advantages of accepting the values of the father and shifting his desire to the reader. Gill evades symbolic castration. "The sentence stands," the father says, saving the writer's pen(is).

Feminist Criticism

I have only recently stopped being amazed at how easily and enthusiastically my students take to feminist criticism. Part of its appeal, I suppose, is its simplicity, at least on the surface: To practice feminist criticism, one need only read as a woman. Such a procedure quickly turns out to have a profound effect on the reader and the text—an effect that hardly can avoid being political. Whatever students' sexual politics might be, feminist criticism unavoidably involves them in significant, timely issues. I do not mean to say that feminist criticism is invariably easy: Reading as a woman, even if one is a woman, may be extremely difficult, requiring the reader to dismantle or discard years of learned behavior. And, of course, I am leaping over the difficult question of what "as a woman" actually means. Since we can't reasonably discuss, as Cheryl Torsney claims, "a single female sexuality" (p. 180), isn't it absurd to assume there is a distinctly feminine way of reading? How can a man even pretend to read "as a woman"?

But these questions need not be answered in order for students to attempt to undo their sexual assumptions, try out new ones, or simply sensitize themselves to the sexual issues present in a work. Feminist criticism thus involves students in reader-response and political criticism. Not all texts, of course, lend themselves easily to feminist criticism, but it is difficult to find one that completely resists a feminist stance. I have found that Gill's passage easily supports a familiar feminist observation, that language itself is phallocentric, as Hélène Cixous and Luce Irigaray have insistently argued. But the passage also repays a more aggressive and perhaps even outrageous (or outraged) approach. Both appear in the following analysis:

> We know not all the writers at *The New Yorker* were men, even some years ago during Brendan Gill's tenure. So, when Gill speaks of "some writer who has made a name for himself in the world," and about the editorial "machinery" that besets "him," Gill is of course referring to writers in the generic sense. One may still assert today, although less confidently than in 1975, that "himself" and "him" in this passage include "herself" and "her." Such a claim, that one sexual marker includes its opposite, is feeble—as if "white" included "black," or "totalitarian" included "democratic." But the motivations for such a claim are revealed even in this brief passage, for Gill's story not only contains this obvious pronominal bias, still accepted by some editors and writers; the story also conveys more subtle messages about sexuality and sexual roles. It is, in fact, a not-so-subtle attack on the image of women.
>
> Miss Gould functions as a familiar stereotype: the finicky spinster, a Miss Thistlebottom, who has devoted her life to English grammar and its enforcement. She is a copy editor, subservient to the male editor and writer, and her lack of imagination and taste testify to the wisdom of this power structure. This division of labor—male/creative, female/menial—is subtly reinforced by reference to the "hen-tracks" (not rooster tracks) that cover the writer's galley, thus further associating petty correction with the feminine, even though surely some copy editors could have been male. These "hen-tracks" are more than an aggravating correction, as they even come to threaten the writer's very identity. The effects of these hen-tracks, feminine marks of correction, allow Gill to assert the disabling consequences of the feminine upon the masculine: The writers become emotional, and even effeminately hysterical, crying on their blotters. Gill receives comfort and approval from the man, Botsford, but Miss Gould lacks the penetrating insight to deal properly with a problem as small as a grammatical error.
>
> Gill's misogyny influences the passage in other ways. The metaphorical threat to the writer is distinctly gynecological, a "yawning pit." Miss Gould's shortcoming is that she fails maternally, providing indigestible "mother's milk." Even the error that Miss Gould locates is subtly connected to the feminine, for the problem with the sentence is that part of it has "assumed the female gender," which may be seen as the underlying problem for Gill: Something has assumed the female gender. That part of the sentence Miss Gould complains of, naturally, is a "complaint"—which, Gill and Botsford determine, should retain its feminine nature. The complaint itself seems strange: In the mode of feminine busybodies like Miss Gould, the nonagenarian laments not having "enough work to do." Miss Gould, similarly overzealous, has herself done more work than is reasonable, and Botsford's pronouncement that "The sentence stands" returns her to her place, negating her feminine fussiness, reasserting masculine mastery of the phallocentric world of writing.

Conclusion

One might want to point out, I suppose, that in offering this rehearsal of critical "approaches," I am assuming that plurality is better than unity, that the relative is better than the absolute (or even a quest for the absolute). And, given what I think we know about language and knowing, it seems silly to me to assume otherwise: As Jane Tompkins says, articulating a current commonplace, we are not "freestanding autonomous entities, but beings that are culturally constituted by interpretive frameworks or interpretive strategies that our culture makes available to us" (p. 734). In other words, the texts we read—when we look at books, at our world, at ourselves—are likewise constituted by these frameworks or strategies. Obviously, if this "reading" of meaning is correct, plurality offers us a richer universe, allowing us to take greater advantage of the strategies our culture makes available—strategies that do not approach a text, but rather make it what we perceive. Our students therefore should learn how to inhabit the theories mentioned here—and a good many others.

To be sure, such plurality is not always comfortable. Furthermore, if we should agree that the more strategies students can deploy (or be deployed by), the more power and insight they can potentially wield, then must we also agree there are no limits? Are all readings welcome, the more the merrier? My initial impulse is to say, "Yes, we can learn from any reading, from any set of interpretive assumptions. Come one, come all." We can see how readings that seem severely inattentive might offer useful insights: Robert Crosman reveals, for example, how one student's reading completely missed the significance of the hair on the pillow at the end of "A Rose for Emily," and yet this reading, comparing Emily to the student's grandmother, profoundly enlarged Crosman's understanding of Faulkner's story. We can even imagine how ludicrous errors might stimulate our thinking: My student who thought *The Hamlet* was by Shakespeare did lead me to ask (mostly in an attempt to ease his embarrassment) about Shakespeare's influence on Faulkner—perhaps *The Hamlet* in some sense is by Shakespeare, or is shaped by *Hamlet*. But we must admit that most readings in violation of shared interpretive strategies will usually be seen as inferior, if not wrong, and that finding insight in such violations often seems an act of kindness, a salvage operation.

I can also imagine theoretical possibilities that would not be welcome in my critical home, should they ever appear: Nazi criticism, racist criticism, electroshock criticism, for example. In other words, if we are not freestanding autonomous entities, we are also not entirely helpless, simply the products of the interpretive operations we inherit, "a mere cultural precipitate," as Morse Peckham puts it (p. xviii). I would like to think we can resist; we can change; we can grow; we can, perhaps, in some sense, even get better. We can, that is, attempt to evaluate ways of making meaning, and their particular applications—and if we are very clever and very lucky, we may even modify interpretive frameworks, or possibly even invent new ones.

But only if we have some awareness that such frameworks exist.

References

Brooks, Cleanth. *The Well-Wrought Urn*. New York: Harcourt Brace, 1947.
Crosman, Robert. "How Readers Make Meaning." *College Literature* 9 (1982): 207–15.
Culler, Jonathan. *On Deconstruction: Theory and Criticism after Structuralism*. Ithaca, N.Y.: Cornell University Press, 1982.
Eagleton, Terry. *Literary Theory: An Introduction*. Minneapolis: University of Minnesota Press, 1982.
Freud, Sigmund. "The Dissolution of the Oedipus Complex." *The Freud Reader*. Ed. Peter Gay. New York: Norton, 1989, pp. 661–66.

———. *Introductory Lectures on Psychoanalysis*. Trans. and ed. James Strachey. New York: Norton, 1966.

Frye, Northrop. *Fables of Identity*. New York: Harcourt, 1951.

Gill, Brendan. *Here at the New Yorker*. New York: Random, 1975.

Grimes, Joseph. *The Thread of Discourse*. Paris: Mouton, 1975.

Johnson, Barbara. *The Critical Difference: Essays in the Contemporary Rhetoric of Reading*. Baltimore: Johns Hopkins University Press, 1980.

Peckham, Morse. *Explanation and Power: The Control of Human Behavior*. New York: Seabury, 1979.

Propp, Vladimir. *The Morphology of the Folktale*. Austin: University of Texas Press, 1968.

Tompkins, Jane. "A Short Course in Post-Structuralism." *College English* 50 (Nov. 1988): 733–47.

Torsney, Cheryl. "The Critical Quilt: Alternative Authority in Feminist Criticism." *Contemporary Literary Theory*. Ed. G. Douglas Atkins and Laura Morrow. Amherst: University of Massachusetts press, 1989, pp. 180–99.

Wellek, Rene, and Austin Warren. *Theory of Literature*. 1942. New York: Harcourt, 1977.

BUSINESS AND PROFESSIONAL WRITING

THE TROUBLE WITH EMPLOYEES' WRITING MAY BE FRESHMAN COMPOSITION

Elizabeth Tebeaux

[*Teaching English in the Two-Year College* (1988): 9–19.]

Elizabeth Tebeaux, a professor of English, teaches undergraduate and graduate courses in technical communications at Texas A&M University. She has published widely on technical writing, including articles, chapters, and textbooks. Tebeaux authored *Design and Business Communications: The Process and the Product* (1990) and coauthored *Reporting Technical Information* (9th ed., 2000). She has also published articles in *Written Communication, Issues in Writing, Journal of Business and Technical Communication,* and the *Technical Communications Quarterly.*

Because many students do not take any writing courses after freshman composition, they may find themselves underprepared for jobs that require them to write for a variety of specific purposes. Tebeaux describes her experience as a writing consultant in business and government, observing that many problems employees have in their writing result from writing strategies they learned in first-year composition courses. Tebeaux suggests changes in the design of composition courses—changes that will help students become more effective writers in the "real world." Her argument makes explicit the vital connections between what we ask students to do in writing classrooms and what those same students will do when they write at work.

In the past two decades, programs in rhetoric and composition have expanded in size as well as in range of studies offered. Yet literacy still remains a serious national problem, and business and industry continue to report problems in their employees' ability to write effectively. A number of large corporations are attempting to handle the problem in one of two ways: (1) by developing in-house writing courses that are included as part of company training programs; and (2) by hiring college writing teachers to design and to teach in-house writing courses. After having taught eleven workshops for three large corporations during the past three years and having served as a writing consultant to a large county government for two additional years, I have observed a number of employee writing problems that are traceable to writing strategies learned in freshman composition. While my findings will certainly not be new to technical writing teachers, my purpose here is to share these findings with teachers of freshman composition.

During this five-year period, I have worked with approximately 250 writers in either business organizations or county government. I found that 218 of 250 participants (87 percent) reported that traditional freshman composition was the only writing instruction they had received in college. Of that 250, 91 percent held at least one college degree, and 31 percent had a master's degree. Participants had been out of college 2 to 26 years, although most had been out of college fewer than 10 years. Those who had not earned a four-year degree had completed two years of junior college. Nearly all of these writers (234) reported that they had taken one or two courses in freshman composition. Only 37 reported having taken any kind of course in professional, technical, or business writing, although a course in business letter writing was the most frequent professional writing course mentioned. Forty-four participants reported that spelling, usage, and punctuation errors were marked in some courses in their major field of study. But the most revealing statement was that 87 percent of the employee-participants said that what they knew about how to write they gained in freshman composition.

Designing the Organizational Short Course

Prior to beginning the short courses, I asked employee-participants (all were there because they knew they needed help) to complete a background questionnaire (from which I derived the information given above) and to submit two samples of writing that they knew had been ineffective or that their supervisors had deemed "bad." To each example they submitted, they were asked to answer the following questions:

1. How did you determine that this piece of writing is "bad" writing?
2. Why did you write it the way you did?
3. What was the purpose of the document? What were the circumstances that led to your writing this document?

Prior to planning each workshop, which consisted of four two-hour settings, I examined these samples and discussed them with the manager who had retained me to design the workshop. Based on the problems discovered in analyzing the samples and talking to each manager, I designed an instructional approach to deal efficiently with the problems. The kinds of problem reports employees submitted were similar to Figure 1. [See next page.] Basically, this memorandum looks just like a freshman essay. The opening paragraph states the purpose. The second and third paragraphs provide support, and the final paragraph concludes by asking for the reader's cooperation.

From the perspective of a reader in an organization who is inundated with routine paperwork like this, the report reveals a number of problems that make it "bad" writing:

- Lack of clearly revealed organization;
- Lack of deductive presentation strategy that gives the reader the main information first;

Figure 1.   *Original Sample*

Company Policy on Interduct

The Company's previous position has been not to place interduct direct buried for fiber optic cable. This directive reemphasizes this policy and explains why it is still in effect.

There has recently been a company pursuing sales of interduct for this purpose, stating that their interduct will allow placing of fiber optic cable. Several demonstrations were held that showed the duct being buried and a similar size cable being pulled into the duct with some success.

A recent real life trial of this direct buried interduct was very unsuccessful. It was found that after placing the interduct and allowing the ground to settle for several days, the interduct conformed to the high and low spots in the trench. When these numerous small bends are introduced into the interduct, it becomes impossible to pull more than 400 to 600 feet of fiber optic cable into the interduct before the 600-pound pulling tension is exceeded.

Interduct itself offers little or no advantage as protection to a direct buried fiber optic cable. In fact, it has a negative advantage, in that it will allow the cable to be pulled and fibers shattered or cracked for much greater distances.

As a result of this trial and previous recommendation, there should be no interduct placed for direct buried.

Please direct further questions to H. L. Rogers at 6727. We will appreciate your cooperation in enforcing this matter.

- Lack of visual presentation techniques for revealing organization and content;
- Lack of analysis of the reader's needs concerning the topic being discussed.

During the workshop, participants were asked to analyze and then revise the two reports they knew to be poorly written. After reviewing the report in Figure 1 with the four problem areas in mind, the writer admitted that the main information he wanted to emphasize was not easy to find, much less remember. But after studying visual presentation techniques, the rationale for deductive organization, and the importance of designing any writing with the readers' needs dictating the organization and the visual design, the engineer who wrote Figure 1 submitted the revision in Figure 2.

The most striking aspect of the revision is the effective way in which the writer has visually displayed the information. Through use of visual strategies, the readers have various options for reading the report: they can read the boldface subject line and overview sentence for each reason given and be able to grasp the essential meaning of the report. Or, they can read the subject line, the opening paragraph, the overview sentence for each supporting point, and perhaps as much detail pertaining to each point as they deem necessary. Note, too, that the revision contains more specific reasons for not using interduct than the original version. During analysis of the sample, the writer stated that in designing the message deductively, and in listing each reason for not using interduct, he discovered, in his original, that he had failed to provide all reasons for not using interduct. Thus, the revision is not only visually effective, it is more complete.

Another sample (Figure 3) illustrates the same problems as the previous one; i.e., the report looks like an essay. The report opens with a paragraph stating the thesis. The second and third paragraphs elaborate on that thesis. The final sentence reiterates the thesis statement.

After the discussion on the importance of deductive organization, visual display of information, and the importance of designing writing with readers' needs in mind, the writer stated that she could now see why the MISS Worksheets were not being corrected and/or returned. First, she had not anticipated her readers' needs, particularly that they would not know how to deal with the Profiles and Worksheets. Second, she had not given a date by which she wanted the materials returned to her and additional information that would help readers respond as she wished them to. Third, she had not organized the instructions and presented them on the page so that they could be easily followed. As a result, most profiles had not been returned; she had received numerous calls asking for clarification; several profiles that had been returned were incorrect or had notes attached indicating that the reader was not sure if changes had been done correctly.

In revising her original, the writer places important information first, establishes hierarchies of key information with headings, uses these headings to guide inclusion of information that will make verification easier for readers, and displays all information so that it is visually accessible.

Figure 2.   *Revised Sample*

TO: Harlan Stevenson, Manager—Customer Services, BIRMINGHAM

SUBJECT: Company Policy: Interduct shall not be placed for buried lightweight cable.

Contrary to the alleged claims of some overzealous vendors, the above policy remains unchanged.

A field trial was recently conducted where the interduct was buried and cable placement was attempted several days later. The negative observations were as follows:

1. **Cable lengths are reduced between costly splices.**
   The interduct conformed to the high and low spots in the trench. These numerous bends introduced added physical resistance against the cable sheath during cable pulling. Even with application of cable lubricant, the average length pulled was 500 feet before the 600 pound pulling tension was exceeded.

2. **Maintenance liability is increased.**
   Due to shorter cable lengths, the number of splices increases. As the number of splices increases, maintenance liability increases.

3. **Added material costs are counterproductive.**
   Interduct, while adding 16% to the material cost, offers little or no mechanical protection to buried fiber optic cable. In fact, when an occupied interduct was pulled at a 90 degree angle with a backhoe bucket, the fibers were not broken only at the place of contact, as would have been with a direct buried cable. Instead, due to the stress being distributed along the interduct, the fibers shattered and cracked up to 100 feet in each direction.

4. **Increased labor costs are unnecessary.**
   In about the same amount of time required to place interduct, the fiber optic cable could be placed. The added 28% of labor hours expended to pull cable after the interduct is placed cannot be justified.

Please insure that this policy is conveyed to and understood by your construction managers. If you have questions, please call me at 817 334-2178.

                                        John Doe
                                        Corporate Engineering Manager

---

Figure 3.   *Original Sample*

MISS

Employee Profiles and Employee Worksheets

The purpose of the following is to explain how the MISS Employee Profiles and Employee Worksheets are to be verified. Your group's worksheets are attached.

The Employee Profiles need to be verified for accuracy before they are filed in the employee's Personal History File. If a change needs to be made that was our error, mark the profile and return it with the Worksheet so that a new profile can be generated. If you are making a change, mark the profile and have it signed and concurred and return both the profile and the Employee Worksheet. After the Employee Profile has been verified, please return the Employee Worksheet to me for my records.

Please note that only information that appeared on the Worksheet was keyed into the MISS data base. Information other than what is on the worksheet is furnished by other data bases. For example, the title is generated by the title code. The title code suffix is generated by the job evaluation number. There have been problems with the title suffix being incorrect. If this is the only correction, please note this on the Employee Profile and worksheet. Please advise me by attaching a note to the employee worksheet when you return it to me. Also, please verify that any other information that may appear to be incorrect is not due to a recent change on payroll records.

If you have problems, please contact me at 6512.

Jane Doe
MISS Administrator

In analyzing the revision by emphasizing the reader's response, other employees observed that the revision was easy to see, easy to follow. In addition, the importance of the message was now apparent.

The essay technique, as applied to short reports and memoranda, the most commonly written documents in business organizations, was apparent in nearly every employee's submission. In fact, the most common answer to Question 2 on the Trouble Analysis Sheet—Why did you write this document the way you did?—yielded some version of the following answers on over 200 samples:

1. this is the way we were taught to write in college;
2. this is the only way I have ever written anything;
3. I don't know any other way to write.

Given the fact the employees in business have too much to read, that they seldom read all of any document, that they "skim" or "search" read most routine writing, participants soon realized why documents, like Figure 3, were not being read or not being read correctly. That is, because of lack of deductive organization to give the reader the "news" immediately and visual presentation technique to reveal organization and content, the memorandum was not "readable"[1] in the sense that the intended audience did not find the document easy to access and process. The revision, Figure 4, however, was deemed a document that would be read because it is visually accessible. You can see organization and content at a glance.

The final assignment required participants to revise some kind of document, usually a policy, which I selected from each organization's policy binder. Like the reports that participants brought to the workshop, many policies too often were not clearly organized and were too visually dense to be read quickly. Figure 5 is one vacation policy statement that participants were asked to revise.

Figure 4.   *Revised Sample*

TO: Jane Doe

FROM: MISS Administrator

SUBJECT: Procedures for Reviewing MISS Employee Profiles by
May 22, 1986

If any information is inaccurate on the attached MISS profiles, please return those for correction within the next two weeks.

Each employee should have a MISS profile placed in his/her history file. The profile will replace the SW-1006 in the near future. In addition, all departments within Fabrico's five-state area will be pulling MISS profiles to fill vacancies within their departments.

Procedures for Reviewing MISS Employee Profiles

1. If a change is required because information was keyed incorrectly, mark the profile and return it with the worksheet. A new profile will be sent to you.
2. If you are making a change, mark the profile and have it signed and concurred at the next higher level. Return both the profile and the worksheet. A new profile will be sent to you for review.
3. After the profile has been verified, please return the worksheet to me for my records.

Incorrect Information That May Appear on the MISS Employee Profile

The information that appeared on the worksheet shows the only items that were keyed into MISS. The MISS data base is merged with other data bases to produce the profile.

1. Incorrect title—The title is generated by the title code from the MERT data base. Please check this code on the last PCR and allow one week for the PCR to be worked.
2. Incorrect title code suffix—The title code suffix is generated by the JE number from the Atlanta job evaluation data base. Please note an incorrect title suffix on the worksheet and profile, as I will be working with Atlanta on this problem.
3. Incorrect payroll information—Please allow one week for the last PCR submitted to be worked and merged with new data.

Please call me if you have any questions about how to make changes.

After having revised two of their own reports, participants yielded interesting versions of policies. Figure 6 is one revision of the policy shown in Figure 5. It is concise and clear mainly because it is visually accessible.

Analysis of Samples—Implications for Basic Composition

The opportunity I have had to observe the writing problems and the writing instruction backgrounds of these employees has led me to several initial conclusions which I believe are worth sharing with other composition teachers:

(1) If my experience during the past five years is even partially representative of the kinds of problems many employee writers are experiencing, then, more than likely there are many other employees who are attempting to write at work by applying techniques learned in freshman composition to the kinds of writing they are required to do on the job. Yet, traditional freshman composition, as it is usually taught, does not provide adequate preparation for writing at work. While the goal of freshman composition has traditionally been to help students write better in school, too many students and even faculty within English departments and other college departments have assumed that "good writing" is

Figure 5.   *Original Policy*

Joint Practice 27: Vacation Days for Management

General

The purpose of this Joint Practice is to outline the vacation treatment applicable to Management employees.

Eligibility

Vacations with pay shall be granted during the calendar year to each management employee who shall have completed six months' employment since the date employment began. Vacation pay will not be granted if the employee has been dismissed for misconduct. Vacation allowed will be determined according to the following criteria: (a) One week's vacation to any such management employee who has completed six months or more but less than twelve months of service. (b) Two weeks' vacation to any such management employee who has completed twelve months of service but who could not complete seven years of service within the vacation year. Two weeks will be allowed if the employee initially completes six months' service and twelve months' service within the same vacation year. (c) Three weeks' vacation to any management employee who could complete seven or more but less than fifteen years' service within the vacation year and to District level who shall have completed six months' employment within the vacation year. (e) Five weeks' vacation to any management employee who completes twenty-five or more years of service within the vacation year and to Department head level and higher management who shall have completed a period of six months' employment within the vacation year.

The criteria described above are Net Credited Service as determined by the Employees' Benefit Committee. Where eligibility for a vacation week under (a) or (b) above first occurs on or after December 1 of a vacation year, the vacation week may be granted in the next following vacation year if it is completed before April 1 and before the beginning of vacation for the following year. When an authorized holiday falls in a week during which a management employee is absent on vacation, an additional day off (or equivalent time off with pay) may be taken in either the same calendar year or prior to April 1 of the following calendar year. When the additional day of vacation is Christmas Day, it may be granted immediately preceding the vacation or prior to April 1 of the following calendar year.

"good writing," and that the student who writes well in school will write well on the job. Too many people outside the ranks of technical writing teachers are unaware of the differences between writing in academe and writing in nonacademic settings. English teachers assume, perhaps too optimistically, that what we teach in freshman composition and in writing across the curriculum programs will automatically transfer to nonacademic settings.

(2) Even though technical and business communication programs have grown steadily in the past decade,[2] they are apparently not reaching enough students. In other words, freshman composition is still the main and only "writing instruction" for many students.

(3) Well-meaning faculty in non-English disciplines are not "teaching writing" by assiduously marking errors in spelling, usage, and punctuation and implying that mechanically correct writing is good writing. The problems I found—the previous samples illustrate these—were not mechanical ones; they stemmed from:

- failing to determine what the audience needed to know so that the writer's purpose (to instruct, persuade, or inform) was achieved;
- failing to organize deductively to reveal the main information first to readers who have more to read than they can and will read carefully;

- failing to use visual design to produce documents that are visually accessible and therefore easy to read;
- failing to understand the importance of creating a visually accessible document and believing that messages that are important to the writer will be important to the reader, and therefore, will be read thoroughly.

The most common problem attributed by any supervisor to the employees attending the workshops was not mechanics; it was lack of clarity and "getting the point across,"[3] both of which, my experience suggests, can be corrected to a great extent by using deductive organization of information and visual design to reveal hierarchies, or levels, of information. Even in original samples that contained a large number of comma splices and nonstandard usage, participants during peer review of each other's work did not think that the main "problem" was mechanics. Employees, in skim- or search-reading routine documents, read holistically. They are looking for answers to the following questions: What is this? Why am I getting this? What am I supposed to do now? The effectiveness of the routine business document is determined by how quickly the reader can answer these questions, not by the mechanical correctness of the content. Correctness becomes an issue if problems in usage, sentence construction, or punctuation hinder the audience's ability to find and process the message.

Figure 6. *Revised Policy*

Joint Practice 27: Vacation Time Allowed Management Employees

The following schedule describes the new vacation schedule approved by the company. This schedule is effective immediately and will remain in effect until a further update is issued.

Vacation Eligibility

1. Vacation with pay shall be granted during the calendar year to each management employee who has completed 6 months' service since the date of employment. Employees who have been dismissed for misconduct will not receive vacation with pay.

Net Credited Service	Eligible Weeks
6 mos.–12 mos.	1
12 mos.–7 yrs.	2
7 yrs.–15 yrs. and to District Level with 6 mos. service	3
15 yrs.–25 yrs. and to Division Level with 6 mos. service	4
25 yrs. or more and to Department Head or higher management with 6 mos. service	5

Net Credited Service is determined by the Employee Benefits Committee

2. If eligibility occurs on or after December 1 of a vacation year,
    - vacation may be granted in the next following year if it is taken before April 1.

3. If an authorized holiday falls in a vacation week,
    - an additional day may be taken in either calendar year or before April 1 of the following year.

4. If the additional day of vacation is Christmas day,
    - it may be taken immediately preceding the vacation or before April 1 of the following year.

Reorienting Freshman Composition—Five Recommendations

I am not suggesting that freshman composition be replaced by courses in technical or business writing. Students clearly need the preparation that freshman composition gives them for writing in college. I am suggesting, however, that we need to impress our freshman students and our colleagues in other disciplines with the importance of a course in professional writing to prepare these students for writing in nonacademic contexts. We need to emphasize to students and colleagues that writing at work is not like writing in the classroom and that students need preparation in both areas.

There are, however, some changes that could be implemented in freshman composition programs to make our basic composition courses more relevant to students after they leave school without damaging the basic mission of freshman composition:

(1) Visual design strategies—presenting content in visually effective ways—need to be introduced in composition.[4] Much of the writing in the world of work (brochures, technical reports, articles for publication, advertisements) uses visual rhetoric in making messages persuasive and clear. Why pretend any longer that visual appeal is not an important rhetorical device? Students need to be introduced, even in freshman composition, to basic concepts in producing visually accessible, visually pleasing documents. They need to understand that visual accessibility (one aspect of the difficult area of readability) is as crucial a quality in writing as coherence, unity, and structure. They also need to understand that teachers are the only people who are committed to reading everything students write, that in a work context audiences will read a document only if they believe it will benefit them and if it is easy to access and understand.

(2) The importance of deductive writing in developing "reader-based" prose needs to be emphasized more in freshman composition. In learning to write research papers, students should be taught that placing the conclusions after the introduction is an acceptable organizational method. Students should also be required to use clearly worded informative headings throughout research papers. Doing so enforces the point that developing the outline into headings and subheadings helps the reader follow the presentation and helps the writer organize the discussion, eliminate irrelevant information, and generally "stay on track."

(3) The essay needs to be deemphasized as the main, if not the sole, teaching form in freshman composition. (How many people ever write essays after they graduate from college?) Students may benefit from studying effectively designed sets of instructions, which incorporate visual design. Students may also benefit from writing instructions and then evaluating them for clarity and visual access during peer review.

(4) Freshman composition should be redefined as Introduction to Writing, to emphasize to our colleagues in other disciplines and to our freshmen that students need more than an introduction to writing to prepare them for the writing they will do after college. We need to explain to students throughout freshman composition how writing in school differs from writing at work, that the standards of "good" writing will ultimately change, that they cannot write on the job the way they have written in the classroom. More freshman composition texts, such as *Four Worlds of Writing*,[5] would be helpful in giving students a perspective on how writing is used beyond the classroom.

(5) To develop competencies that will be valuable outside academic writing, the paradigm in freshman composition needs to be integrated with the paradigm in technical writing. That is, in every writing course, students should have to write for specifically defined audiences; students should have a purpose to

achieve with that audience; they should learn to deal with tone, voice, organization, and visual presentation commensurate with that purpose. But ultimately, students need to understand that these common rhetorical elements control all writing, whether it is expressive, referential, literary, or informative.[6]

Conclusion

Much of the published scholarship that fills the pages of rhetoric and composition journals underscores the problem I continue to confront in teaching industrial short courses: little concern is expressed for the usefulness of freshman composition after college, for the differences in which writing in school differs from writing at work, for designing writing curricula to ensure that writing instruction is relevant during students' college years and afterward in nonacademic settings. Basic composition theory, in its emphasis on expressive discourse, continues to foster the traditional goals of writing as learning and writing as thinking, with little attention to ways by which these competencies can be sustained and applied in nonacademic writing environments. The problem, I suspect, stems from the fact that few composition teachers, unless they also teach technical writing, understand, or even care about the relevance of their instruction. However, my consulting experience suggests that we should care and that achieving relevance is not only possible but necessary if our composition instruction is to provide any long-lasting solution to the literacy problem.

Notes

[1] For useful approaches to the design of readable texts, see the following essays in *New Essays in Technical and Scientific Communication: Research, Theory, Practice*, ed. Paul V. Anderson, R. John Brockmann, Carolyn R. Miller (Farmingdale: Baywood, 1983); Lester Faigley and Stephen P. Witte, "Topical Focus in Technical Writing," (pp. 59–68); Jack Selzer, "What Constitutes a 'Readable' Style?" (pp. 71–89); Thomas N. Huckin, "A Cognitive Approach to Readability," (pp. 90–98). Also, Daniel B. Felker, ed. *Document Design: A Review of the Relevant Research* (Washington, DC: American Institutes for Research, 1979), Chapters 1, 2, and 4; Lee Odell and Dixie Goswami, *Writing in Nonacademic Settings* (New York: Guilford, 1985), Chapters 2 and 3.

[2] William E. Rivers, "The Current Status of Business and Technical Writing Courses in English Departments," *ADE Bulletin* 82 (Winter 1985): 50–54.

[3] A number of studies suggest the paramount importance of clarity as the most desirable quality in employee writing: Donna Stine and Donald Skarzenski, "Priorities for the Business Communication Classroom: A Survey of Business and Academe," *Journal of Business Communication* 16 (Summer 1979): 15–30; Robert R. Bataille, "Writing in the World of Work: What Our Graduates Report," *CCC* 32 (Oct. 1982): 276–280; Lester Faigley and Thomas P. Miller, "What We Learn from Writing on the Job," *College English* 44 (Oct. 1982): 567–569; Gilbert Storms, "What Business School Graduates Say about the Writing They Do at Work: Implications for the Business Communication Course," *ABCA Bulletin* 46 (Dec. 1983): 13–18; Carol Barnum and Robert Fischer, "Engineering Technologists as Writers: Results of a Survey," *Technical Communication* 31 (Second Quarter, 1984): 9–11.

[4] The Document Design Center has generated a number of studies on visual design which are available for purchase through DDC. However, only two articles in rhetoric and composition journals have yet dealt with the importance of visual rhetoric as a pedagogical consideration: Robert J. Conners, "*Actio:* A Rhetoric of Manuscripts," *Rhetoric Review* 2.1 (Sept. 1983): 64–73; and Stephen Bernhardt, "Seeing the Text," *CCC* 37 (Feb. 1986): 66–78.

[5] Janice M. Lauer and others, *The Four Worlds of Writing* (New York: Harper, 1985).

[6] For a discussion of linking all writing, see Harry P. Kroitor and Elizabeth Tebeaux, "Bringing Literature Teachers and Writing Teachers Closer Together," *ADE Bulletin* 78 (Summer 1984): 28–34.

WRITING IN THE DISCIPLINES

THE PEDAGOGY OF WRITING ACROSS THE CURRICULUM

Susan McLeod

[From Gary Tate, Amy Rupiper, and Kurt Schick, eds. *A Guide to Composition Pedagogies*. New York: Oxford UP, 2000. 149–64.]

Susan McLeod is Professor of English at Washington State University, where she teaches graduate and undergraduate courses and facilitates faculty writing across the curriculum seminars. At WSU she has served in various administrative capacities, including director of composition, chair of the English Department, and associate dean of the College of Liberal Arts. As a member of the board of consultants of the National Network of Writing Across the Curriculum Programs, she has consulted nationally and internationally with other universities seeking to build WAC programs. Her publications include *Strengthening Programs for Writing Across the Curriculum* (1992), *Writing Across the Curriculum: A Guide to Developing Programs* (1992), and *Notes on the Heart: Affective Issues in the Writing Classroom* (1997), as well as articles on writing across the curriculum and writing program administration. Her current project, a coedited collection titled *WAC for the New Millennium*, is in press.

McLeod offers a comprehensive overview of WAC, including its origins, current definitions, approaches to teaching, strategies for working with colleagues in other disciplines, and future developments. This article will be especially useful for teachers who want to integrate WAC principles into their courses. McLeod offers numerous suggestions for further reading and resources, and provides solid theoretical contexts for the pedagogical approaches she explains. In addition, her succinct discussion of how to plan and conduct a workshop to introduce other teachers to WAC principles will be useful to teachers who are interested in collaborating with colleagues across the campus.

Origins of WAC

Chances are good that if you are in the field of rhetoric and composition, you have heard of writing across the curriculum. As an educational reform movement, it has been around more than twenty-five years—about as long as the National Writing Project,[1] its counterpart in elementary and secondary schools. It was born in the 1970s during a time of curricular and demographic change in higher education, when college teachers found themselves with students who struggled with college writing tasks. The widespread use of the "objective" multiple-choice/true-false test in public education meant that many students had little practice with extended writing tasks by the time they got to college; at the same time, the rapid growth of higher education coupled with open admissions at some institutions brought a new population of first-generation college students to the institution. Faced with what looked like declining skills, faculty felt the need to do something, anything, about the state of student writing. The first WAC faculty seminar came about in 1969–70 at Central College in Pella, Iowa (Russell, *Writing* 283), when Barbara Walvoord's Chaucer seminar didn't make; to fill the void she organized a regular meeting of faculty to discuss issues of student writing. She went on to write the first book on teaching writing that was aimed at faculty in the disciplines, *Helping Students Write Well: A Guide for Teachers in All Disciplines,* first published in 1982. This book, now in its second edition, is still the standard reference for teachers in fields outside of English who need a guidebook to help them understand how to assign and respond to student writing. True to its title, the book is for those who want to help students learn to write well, as most faculty do.

All of us who have been involved in WAC since its beginnings have a story to tell about how we got started facilitating faculty seminars. The story usually involves faculty colleagues like Barbara's who were at their collective wits' end trying to deal with the student writing problems they were encountering. Here's mine. One day I was cornered just outside my office by a friend who taught history, who was furious with me and with (it appeared) not only the English Department but the entire discipline of English. "Why can't you people teach these students how to write?" he thundered. I was defensive—of course I was teaching them how to write. I had stacks of papers waiting to be graded to prove it. After we had both finished harumphing and started to listen to each other, I asked to see the papers he was so distressed about. Among them was a paper from a former student of mine, one who had done reasonably well in my freshman comp class the previous semester. He was right; it was abysmal. He had asked for analysis and discussion of historical data, and she had responded with vague generalities and personal opinion. Like all progressive writing teachers at that time, I was trying to help my students find their authentic voices. But my history colleague was not interested in this student's authentic voice; he wanted her to try to think and write like a historian. My class, based as it was on literary notions of what good writing was, had not helped her figure out how to do that. Out of cross-disciplinary faculty conversations like this one, out of seminars like the one Walvoord started, the WAC movement was born.

What Is WAC?

Like the term *general education, writing across the curriculum* has come to have an aura that is vaguely positive, something that is good for students. Like general education programs, WAC programs are defined in part by their intended outcomes—helping students to become critical thinkers and problem-solvers as well as developing their communications skills. But unlike general education, WAC is uniquely defined by its pedagogy. Indeed, one might say that WAC has been, more than any other recent educational reform movement, one aimed at transforming pedagogy at the college level, at moving away from the lecture mode of teaching (the "delivery of information" model) to a model of active student engagement with the material and with the genres of the discipline through writing, not just in English classes but in all classes across the university. WAC draws on many pedagogical techniques used in general composition classes, but unlike those classes (for example, freshman composition) it focuses around a particular body of information. Where freshman composition might focus on teaching the general features of what we term "academic discourse," WAC focuses not on writing skills per se, but on teaching both the content of the discipline and the particular discourse features used in writing about that content.

When we speak of WAC pedagogy, we are talking about two somewhat different approaches: we may think of these under the headings of "writing to learn" and "writing to communicate."[2] The former is the pedagogy most identified with WAC programs, one that caught on quickly in the form of one of its most popular assignments, the journal. Based on the theories of language and learning articulated by James Britton and by Janet Emig in her article "Writing as a Mode of Learning," this pedagogy encourages teachers to use ungraded writing (writing to the self as audience) in order to have students think on paper, to objectify their knowledge and therefore to help them discover both what they know and what they need to learn. The latter approach, writing to communicate, is pedagogically more complex. It is based on theories of the social construction of knowledge, best summarized in Kenneth Bruffee's article "Collaborative Learning and the 'Conversation of Mankind.'" The most obvious pedagogical manifestation of this approach is the use of peer groups in the classroom and approaches to teaching that take into account analysis of the discourse of the disciplines and genre theory. The rest of this essay will be devoted to these two pedagogical approaches for classrooms—writing to learn and writing to communicate—and will in addition consider the appropriate pedagogy for one of the most important elements of a WAC program, the faculty workshop.

Before reviewing these approaches, however, I feel it necessary to warn readers away from a view of writing to learn and writing to communicate somehow in conflict with each other. There are two articles in the WAC literature that present such a view: C. A. Knoblauch and Lil Brannon's "Writing as Learning Through the Curriculum," and more recently, Daniel Mahala's "Writing Utopias: Writing Across the Curriculum and the Promise of Reform." The former article appeared in *College English* before it became a refereed journal; it presents a vision of then-existing WAC programs as being largely "grammar across the curriculum," a claim that is not backed by any proof and certainly not borne out by the results of national WAC surveys that I have now twice conducted (McLeod; Miraglia and McLeod). The authors' discussion of the textbook *Writing in the Arts and Sciences* by Elaine Maimon and her colleagues (mentioned below) is a good example of what I see as a false dichotomy, characterizing that text as an introduction to mere forms and formats and opposing it to "writing to learn." The same approach is taken by Mahala, who sets up a dichotomy between "American formalism" and "British expressivism," again misrepresenting the approach of Maimon and colleagues by quoting out of context from their work in order to argue his case. Neither of these articles is taken seriously by the WAC discourse community at large. On the contrary, most of us who have been involved in WAC programs from the beginning see "writing to learn" and "writing to communicate" as two complementary, even synergistic, approaches to writing across the curriculum.

Writing to Learn

Writing to learn pedagogy encourages teachers to use writing as a tool for learning as well as a test for learning, or as James Moffett would say at workshops, "writing to *know* as well as to *show*." This branch of WAC has its roots in the language across the curriculum movement in British secondary schools, sparked by James Britton and his colleagues and associated in the United States with Toby Fulwiler and his colleagues at Michigan Technological University. In *Language and Learning*, Britton argued that language is central to learning because it is through language that we organize our representations of the world (214). His research called for the use of more "expressive" writing in the curriculum—writing that will help students explore and assimilate new ideas, create links between the unfamiliar and the familiar, mull over possibilities, explain things to the self before explaining them to others. The analog for this kind of student writing is the expert's notebook—the scientist's lab book, the engineer's notebook, the artist's and architect's sketchbook (the journals of Thomas Edison and of Leonardo da Vinci are prototypical examples). It is not polished work intended for an outside audience; sometimes it is comprehensible only to the writer.

For such writing to be useful in the classroom as a tool for learning, it must be ungraded. The teacher does respond, but as a facilitator and coach rather than as a judge. As I mentioned earlier, the most popular writing to learn assignment, one that caught on very quickly across the curriculum, is the journal. In *The Journal Book*, Toby Fulwiler has gathered together more than forty accounts from teachers across the disciplines who use journals in their classrooms. The actual assignments vary. Ann Berthoff describes the dialectical notebook—a double-entry notebook, with summaries of readings or passages copied out on one side and the student's responses (or metacomments) on the facing page (11–18). Jana Staton discusses the dialogue journal, in which elementary school students comment and the teacher responds, creating a private conversation between teacher and student about course content (47–63). French teacher Karen Wiley Sandler describes the use of the journal in the foreign language class as a place to experiment and make mistakes (as we all do when learning a language) without fear of penalty; the journal becomes a place to approximate, to play with the new language (312–20). Catherine Larson and Margaret Merrion describe the music journal, used to help students understand and describe the aesthetic experience of listening to music (254–60). Stephen BeMiller describes the mathematics notebook, in which students do their practice work—explorations of possible solutions to problems, discussions of the course challenges, questions, outlines of concepts, and self-tests of comprehension (359–66). All the descriptions have one thing in common: student use of informal, speculative, personal writing to make sense of the course material with the teacher acting as prompter and guide.

Of course, the journal is not the only assignment teachers have integrated into their pedagogical repertoire. Another way to facilitate writing as a mode of learning is the "quick write" or "focused freewrite" that has become popularized by Thomas Angelo and K. Patricia Cross in *Classroom Assessment Techniques*[3] as the "minute paper" (148–58). Where the journal is more suitable for smaller classes in which the teacher can collect and respond to student writing periodically, the minute paper has been used successfully in classes of all sizes, including large lecture classes. The technique is simple: at some point in the class, the students write for one minute answering a question that asks them to evaluate their learning in some way. For example, at the end of a lecture, students might be asked to jot down the two or three most important points of the lecture, and also what puzzled them about the material. These jottings, usually no more than half a page, give the teacher instant feedback as to the success of the lecture and show her what issues may need clarification. Angelo and Cross give this example: a history teacher might ask students two questions: "What is the single most significant reason that Italy became a center of the Renaissance?" and "What one question puzzles you about Italy's role in the Renaissance?" Because they are writing anonymously, students are free to express their genuine puzzlement, and the teacher can see immediately how to address their confusion about cause and effect in the next lecture. The minute paper is not only a mode of learning for the students, it is also for the teacher a window into their learning, a method of establishing communication between teacher and student in large classes.

There are many other ways to use writing to learn assignments. John Bean, in *Engaging Ideas: The Professor's Guide to Integrating Writing, Critical Thinking, and Active Learning in the Classroom*, devotes chapter 6 to twenty-five varieties of what he calls "exploratory writing." These include versions of the journal and the minute paper as well as creative approaches (having students write an imaginary dialogue between historical figures) and practice pieces for what will eventually be graded writing (for example, dry run essay exams). Bean also answers the common objections teachers have to using this kind of writing (it will take too much time; students will regard it as busy work; if it's not corrected it will promote bad writing habits), and provides useful suggestions for responding to the assignments and managing the paper load.

Two major characteristics of WAC write-to-learn pedagogy should be clear by now. First, such pedagogy is student centered. College faculty who focus on and are concerned about their students' learning are those who pick up WAC techniques and use them successfully; they are quick to see the value of assignments like those described above that promote active learning and critical thinking. Second, it is reflective. These exploratory writing assignments are all ones that provide a feedback loop to the teacher as to the progress of student learning, allowing her or him to adjust the teaching accordingly. It also takes the teacher out of the role of judge for awhile, allowing her to play the role of coach. As the now-famous active learning mantra goes, the teacher moves from being the sage on the stage to the guide on the side.

Writing to Communicate

Writing to communicate is the other branch of WAC. It is closely related and interconnected with writing to learn, but has these important differences: it focuses on writing to an audience outside the self in order to inform that audience, and the writing therefore is revised, crafted, and polished. Writing to communicate is reader based rather than writer based, and uses the formal language of a particular discourse community to communicate information. This branch of WAC is sometimes called WID, writing in the disciplines. It is most closely identified with Elaine Maimon's WAC program at Beaver College, which started about the same time as Toby Fulwiler's program at Michigan Tech. Maimon's program, like Walvoord's and Fulwiler's, also grew out of a close collaboration of faculty colleagues, faculty talking to each other in a series of workshops about how to help students with their writing. Out of that program grew a textbook, *Writing in the Arts and Sciences,* now out of print.[4] In that text, Maimon (who invited Kenneth Bruffee, among others, to help lead the faculty workshops at her institution) articulates not only writing-to-learn principles, but also what has become known as the "social turn" in teaching writing: "Writing in every discipline is a form of social behavior in that discipline" (xii).

The notion of discourse communities is a commonplace now in the field of rhetoric and composition, but was not so obvious to composition teachers in the 1980s. In my own experience, at least, conversations with faculty in other disciplines helped me understand the nature of the differences in disciplinary discourses. Permit me another story. I was working with a group of graduate students in our American Studies program at my institution, students who shuttled back and forth between seminars in English and in history. Some of them were having mysterious difficulties with their papers for those classes; both history and English professors were circling their verbs and writing "tense" in the margins. The students were stumped. They had never had such problems as undergraduate history or English majors. I sat down with a history colleague, and together we discovered what should have been obvious. In English, we use the present tense to quote the words of authors long dead: "As Shakespeare says. . . ." For us, these authors live on in their texts; they are not of an age but for all time. But in history dates are very important, and one must mark the tense accordingly to indicate which authors are current and which are historical (e.g., dead). A historian would never write, "Gibbon says." The question was not just one of verb tense, but of epistemology.

WAC as writing to communicate, as differentiated from writing to learn, puts the teacher in a somewhat different but related pedagogical situation. The teacher is still a guide, but is focusing now on helping students learn the discourse of the discipline; the relationship is that of seasoned professional to apprentice, or in anthropological terms, of tribal elder to initiate. The person who knows best how to initiate the newcomer is not the composition teacher, but the teacher who is already grounded in the content of the field and who is fluent in the disciplinary discourse—the history teacher, the biology teacher, the math teacher.

This is not to say that we as writing teachers can't make students aware that there are different discourse communities and teach them some strategies for asking the right questions about discourse expectations in their other classes. Patricia Linton and her associates, in an excellent (and too little known) article on the role of the general composition course in WAC, describe how such a class might be set up: teaching students to observe disciplinary patterns in the way discourse is structured, helping them understand the various rhetorical moves that are accepted within particular discourse communities, explaining conventions of reference and of language. Composition teachers, the authors argue, are no strangers to teaching discourse analysis; we just need to enlarge our notions of what discourse we should be helping students analyze. Linton and her associates, this time with Madigan as the lead author,[5] demonstrate in another article how one might go about analyzing the language of psychology; in this article they suggest something far more complex than teaching students how to cite sources in APA as well as MLA style in first-year composition. Instead, they demonstrate convincingly that APA style is the embodiment of social science epistemology; the style reflects the values of the discipline. I think of a student I had recently, a theater major named Ginger, who was given to large dramatic gestures in class and double exclamation points in her prose. One day she brought in a draft of a paper she was writing in her introductory psychology class. She was researching child abuse in the United States, and had written "the statistics are horrifying." The teacher had circled the last word and written in the margin "diction." In a conference with the teacher Ginger had been told she couldn't use such a word in APA style. She came to me to vent: Why couldn't she???? What was wrong with saying that, since it was true???? After she had calmed down somewhat, we discussed some of the values of psychology, in particular the detached, objective tone. Although she wasn't happy about it, Ginger saw the point and changed "horrifying" to "cause for concern."

Having said that composition teachers can make students aware of disciplinary differences, of the fact that "good writing" (in academe as elsewhere) is a relative term, I must go on to state that such a course is only a first step toward helping students write to communicate in their own disciplines. The person who has the disciplinary knowledge base and writes the discourse as a mother tongue is the person who can best serve as mentor in this professional-apprentice relationship.[6]

The fact that academics are so grounded in their own disciplinary discourse conventions presents an immediate challenge, however, precisely because the conventions seem so natural to those fluent in them that it is difficult for them to see why students struggle as they learn them, or why writing in other disciplines has different but equally valid conventions. The psychology teacher is so used to the passive voice as a signal of objectivity in social science writing that she thinks of it as the norm, and of writing in the humanities as "flowery." I will say something in the final section about how WAC directors might approach this issue of disciplinary ethnocentrism in a WAC workshop; for now let us assume that faculty in the disciplines are aware of these differences and wish to demystify their own disciplinary discourse for students, helping them learn appropriate ways to write to those in their field as well as to audiences outside their field. How might they go about it?

There are various resources for teachers in the disciplines, many of them written by colleagues in those disciplines. I will mention just a few here. *Mathematical Writing*, edited by Donald Knuth and his associates and published by the Mathematical Association of America, is a book by and for mathematicians. It consists of lecture transcripts and handouts from a course of the same name offered at Stanford University in 1987. The course involved various star guest lecturers, and it focused on writing in computer science as well as in mathematics.[7] Robert Day's *How to Write and Publish a Scientific Paper* is a readable and lively book which at first glance seems to deal only with forms and formats, but in fact deals with the way knowledge is created in scientific fields; the chapter entitled "How to List the Authors," for example, deals with the thorny issue of who is really an "author" when a team of scientists has contributed to the findings. Perhaps the ultimate disciplinary discourse may be found in the foreign language curriculum, where the discourse to be learned is indeed an entirely different language. Claire Gaudiani's *Teaching Composition in the Foreign Language Curriculum* focuses on the issue of developing fluency in prose written in the target language, focusing on how learning to write in a foreign language differs considerably from learning to write in one's native language. Finally, there are a number of sites rapidly developing on the World Wide Web for teachers in the disciplines to consult. The most useful of these from my point of view is the WAC Clearinghouse at http://aw.colostate.edu/resource_list.htm. The site has answers to questions frequently asked about WAC and provides links to other WAC sites on the Web.

These and other resources like them for faculty in the disciplines may be thought of in light of genre theory. As Carol Berkenkotter and Thomas Huckin say in their book *Genre Knowledge in Disciplinary Communication*, "[g]enres are the media through which scholars and scientists communicate with their peers. Genres are intimately linked to a discipline's methodology, and they package information in ways that conform to a discipline's norms, values, and ideology" (1). Teaching the genres of the discourse community is therefore inseparable from teaching the disciplinary knowledge of the discipline. The pedagogy connected with such teaching is not one of forms and formats; it involves setting up various practice sessions for students to model the writing behaviors and practices they will need as members of particular discourse communities. This means doing away with the usual kinds of school assignments, writing only for the teacher as examiner, and having students try out as much as possible writing to real audiences for real professional purposes.

Teachers have known for some time that there is something wrong with the "school" writing assignment; in 1965, W. Earl Britton had this to say:

> I believe that in all too many instances, at least in college, the student writes the wrong thing, for the wrong reason, to the wrong person, who evaluates it on the wrong basis. That is, he writes about a subject he is not thoroughly informed upon, in order to exhibit his knowledge rather than explain something the reader does not understand, and he writes to a professor who already knows more than he does about the matter and who evaluates the paper, not in terms of what he has derived, but in terms of what he thinks the writer knows. In every respect, this is the converse of what happens in professional life, where the writer is the authority; he writes to transmit new or unfamiliar knowledge to someone who does not know but needs to, and who evaluates the paper in terms of what he derives and understands. (116)

The pedagogy of WAC as writing to communicate invites teachers to think about how they might place students in rhetorical situations that approximate those they will encounter as professionals in their fields and learn to use the appropriate genres and discourse conventions. For example, the College of Engineering at my institution has a capstone course in which students form teams that become consulting firms; they must go out into the community, find a client, and work up a project for that client, who then has a say in their final grade for the class. Business schools pioneered the use of the case method for situated learning, giving students a narrative describing a realistic scenario in which they might find themselves in their work and asking them to provide possible solutions to the problem described; this method has been used successfully by teachers in other disciplines to create writing assignments like the ones students will encounter in their professions.[8] Teachers in fields that are not charged with preparing students for such specific professions (for example, the liberal arts) are nevertheless able to create writing assignments that have audiences other than the teacher as examiner and have some purpose other than testing student knowledge and comprehension.

Genre theory also brings with it the promise of a pedagogical approach aimed at helping linguistically marginalized groups in academe—those whose home language is not standard English. Using a functional linguistics approach developed by M. A. K. Halliday at the University of Sydney (and promulgated by Gunther Kress in the United Kingdom), researchers in Australia have developed an "explicit pedagogy for inclusion and access" (Cope and Kalantzis 63), one that focuses explicitly on the teaching of genre as a way of teaching academic literacy. According to Bill Cope and Mary Kalantzis, this approach has been very successful with aboriginal children in Australia. Such a pedagogy is not without its critics, however; Berkenkotter and Huckin provide a useful examination of the issues in chapter 8 of *Genre Knowledge in Disciplinary Communication* (a chapter they title "Suffer the Little Children"). Their most telling critique is this: "It may be that a genre approach to the teaching of writing does not fit many language arts and composition teachers' conception of their role, given their training, ideological loyalties, and professional allegiances. If this is the case, rethinking the training of language arts and composition teachers as well as the current curricula in language arts and university writing courses may be what is called for" (163). Russell's article "Rethinking Genre in School and Society: An Activity Theory Analysis" also provides a useful overview of the issues involved in explicit teaching of genres.

Writing in the disciplines involves more than just learning genres and discourse conventions, however. It also involves learning the processes by which experts in the field develop and disseminate knowledge. Russell, in a 1993 article, argues the matter thus: "[Since writing is] a matter of learning to participate in some historically situated human activity that requires some kind(s) of writing, it cannot be learned apart from the problems, the habits, the activities—the subject matter—of some group that found the need to write in that way to solve a problem or carry on its activities" ("Vygotsky" 194).

What are some of the "habits and activities" Russell refers to that might be translated into pedagogical practice? One obvious answer is collaborative learning techniques, which are based on assumptions about the social nature of learning as well as of the collaborative construction of disciplinary knowledge. Donald Finkel and G. Stephen Monk's "Teachers and Learning Groups: Dissolution of the Atlas Complex" was an early resource for teachers in the disciplines. This piece encourages teachers to view their classrooms as social systems, and offers suggestions about how to get out of the two-person model of interaction (teacher-student) and encourage interaction among students that models the mode of debate and intellectual exchange among colleagues in the discipline. Finkel and Monk do not advocate exclusive use of group work, but differentiate among teaching functions (lecture, Socratic questioning, guided group work) and encourage teachers to think about which particular function suits each part of the course. Once teachers in the disciplines begin to see the teacher/student relationship as one of professional/apprentice, and once they also begin to view their classrooms as social systems that model the methods and the discourse of their particular discipline, it is not a large step for them to see that it makes sense for apprentices to follow the same process that the experts do when writing papers. If the experts draft papers and revise according to readers' and editors' comments, students should become familiar with this process. One of the most interesting quiet revolutions that has taken place on college campuses as a result of successful WAC programs is the use by many teachers in the disciplines of what we have come to think of as the "process approach" in teaching writing—not only allowing revision of student work, but requiring it, often using peer groups in the classroom to respond to drafts.

The increased use of peers for responding to student writing is most obvious in that now-familiar unit on campus, the writing center. It is not coincidental that WAC and writing centers have grown up together during the past twenty-five years, since they are natural partners and in many institutions mutually dependent on one another. One early (1984) article by Bruffee, "Peer Tutoring and the 'Conversation of Mankind,'" ties the theory of peer tutoring to the notion of the disciplinary conversation, showing how tutoring from a knowledgeable peer can help model the "habits and activities" (to use Russell's term again) of the knowledge-constructing processes in the disciplines. Ray Wallace's "The Writing Center's Role in the Writing Across the Curriculum Program: Theory and Practice" discusses not only theory but also gives some practical guidelines for tying the writing center firmly to a WAC program—including a helpful outline of a WAC tutor-training course.

Showing, Not Telling, at a Writing Workshop

I have borrowed the heading for the final section of this essay from Toby Fulwiler's early article on how a WAC faculty workshop should be run because it summarizes the main point to be made about all such workshops: they must model the pedagogy they are promulgating. Faculty don't like being told what to do in their own classrooms, and rightly so—not every technique is workable in every class. Faculty need to try out various techniques and decide for themselves how to adapt them to their own teaching and achieve their own pedagogical ends. Would-be facilitators of WAC faculty workshops should think carefully about how to use the pedagogical techniques they are suggesting in order to demonstrate their power. There are two rules of thumb: faculty should themselves write, and faculty should have opportunities to talk to each other about writing. Both writing-to-learn and writing-to-communicate pedagogies should be integral parts of every WAC faculty workshop. I said at the beginning that WAC programs grew out of cross-disciplinary faculty conversations, and that faculty workshops are at the heart of any WAC program. The reason for this is rather simple: faculty tend to teach as they were taught. The lecture mode is still one of the most common modes of instruction at research institutions, where faculty get their degrees. The faculty workshop is a place for faculty to learn other modes of instruction by experiencing these modes themselves and understanding from the inside out, as it were, how something other than a lecture-quiz approach to learning might work.

If you wish to set up and facilitate a faculty workshop, there are two sorts of resources available to you: those of the "how to" variety, which are of most use to the workshop facilitator, and those than can be used in the workshop as texts or resources for the workshop faculty. Fulwiler's article, mentioned earlier, is of the first sort, explaining how various types of workshops may be set up and managed. Anne Herrington's "Writing to Learn: Writing Across the Disciplines" also lays out some of the issues one needs to think about in planning a faculty workshop. For example, workshops often ask faculty to write out their course objectives and expected learning outcomes for one of their classes to bring to the workshop, so that they can design writing assignments connected to those course objectives. Often college faculty, most of whom have had no formal pedagogical training, find this small exercise one of the most useful parts of the workshop, since they have thought about course objectives and expected outcomes only tacitly. Joyce Magnotto and Barbara Stout have written the most direct and comprehensive piece on how to run a faculty workshop; it is full of advice on all aspects of such an event, and includes a sample syllabus. Some books that can be very helpful to the would-be WAC workshop leader are now available from commercial presses. The most useful of these is *The Harcourt Brace Guide to Writing Across the Curriculum* by Christopher Thaiss. Thaiss deals not only with conducting a workshop but also with how to launch a WAC program, WAC options for the curriculum, assessment, and research. It is the most compact, comprehensive book on WAC to date; this is not surprising, given the fact that Thaiss is the head of the Board of Consultants of the National Network of Writing Across the Curriculum Programs. The Board meets once a year as a Special Interest Group at the Conference on College Composition and Communication and consists of seasoned WAC directors who can be brought to campus as consultants.[9] If you are asked to start a WAC program on your campus, the outside consultant is a time-honored way of getting faculty involved. I should also mention here the book that I co-edited with Margot Soven, *Writing Across the Curriculum: A Guide to Developing Programs;* this book, with chapters from some of the members of the Board of Consultants of the National Network of WAC Programs, gives advice on starting and sustaining WAC programs and is intended for administrators as well as faculty.

There are several books that may be used as texts for a workshop and resources for teachers in the disciplines, books that have been written by experienced workshop facilitators and based in large part on their own versions of the WAC workshop. The earliest of these, *Improving Student Writing: A Guidebook for Faculty in All Disciplines* by Andrew Moss and Carol Holder, is short, affordable, and full of practical tips for teachers; its virtue is that parts of it (for example, the chapter on designing writing assignments) may be used as a basis for a segment of a seminar, but it is also a useful reference book for teachers after the seminar. True to its title, it really is a guidebook. More recently, Margot Soven has published a similar short guide, *Write to Learn: A Guide to Writing Across the Curriculum.* Soven's book provides instructions and models for academic assignments that are sequenced from journal writing to more formal academic assignments. (Bean's useful book, mentioned earlier, is a good resource for a faculty seminar, but probably too expensive to order copies for all participants.) Fulwiler's *Teaching with Writing* grew out of the many workshops Fulwiler has facilitated and may be used either as a text for a workshop or as a sort of workbook to be used by an individual teacher interested in learning more about using writing as a pedagogical tool.

As I said above, WAC workshop pedagogy should model both write-to-learn and write-to-communicate pedagogies. Let me give just two examples. I always begin a WAC faculty workshop with an exercise I saw modeled long ago at a WAC conference. First, I ask participants to write for a few minutes about the student writing problems they encounter; there is no lack of interest in this topic, and participants write busily. We then discuss what they have written and try to come to a consensus about the most important writing problems (the discussion invariably focuses on conceptual problems as being more important than the grammatical issues). I then give them a truly dreadful student paper and ask them to mark it as if it were a paper for one of their classes; then I ask them to tally up the sorts of marks they have made. Even though we have just discussed the fact that conceptual issues are more important than grammatical ones, they find that most of their marks are for spelling and punctuation errors. I then ask them to write for a few moments about how they might establish a hierarchy of problems to respond to in student writing, and we discuss possible grading rubrics. Finally, I ask them to step back and think about the way we used writing in this particular segment of the workshop—to begin the discussion, to think through the issue of responding to student papers, and we talk about possible applications to their own classes. We discuss writing to learn only after they have used it as a technique for their own thinking and learning.

To get at the issue of disciplinary discourse and get participants out of their disciplinary ethnocentrism a bit, I hand out a one-page student paper and ask faculty to grade it, using whatever criteria they wish—but they have to articulate their criteria for the rest of us. Invariably, teachers from the humanities grade it low, saying "lack of development" is the problem. Teachers from the sciences and from business grade it high, saying it is "concise." This always leads into a lively discussion of discourse values and of articulating those values for students. One of the more interesting discussions I have heard among faculty on this issue had to do with the use of headings: the engineering faculty member said he graded a paper down if it didn't have headings, since these were important signposts for the reader of technical material. Technical reports are not read front to back, but readers skip around to find the most important and relevant information. The history teacher said he graded papers down if they *did* have headings; history involves writing a careful, analytical narrative. Clearly, a student who relied on headings for this narrative hadn't yet learned how to use transitions gracefully. Hearing discussions like these helps teachers understand why students can be confused about disciplinary discourse conventions.

Final Thoughts: The Future of WAC

A recent thread on the Writing Program Administration listserv was titled "Is WAC dead?" A lively discussion ensued in cyberspace, with those of us who have been involved in WAC most of our professional lives saying "Of course not!" and pointing to the record attendance at the last (1997) national WAC conference.[10] But on reflection, I can see why the question was asked. In the early days of WAC, funding was readily available for programs; outside funding for WAC programs is now rare. Book publishers are no longer slapping a WAC subtitle on their more popular composition textbooks, hoping to push their sales higher. WAC is no longer the new initiative that deans want to claim on their CVs as they climb up the administrative ladder toward a position as provost.

But the interesting thing about the WAC reform movement is that over the decades it has been able to tie into and become part of whatever new initiative was thrust upon higher education. For example, the 1980s may be thought of as the decade of assessment and accountability in higher education. Institutions of higher learning were being pressured by legislators and by the taxpaying public to show that they were really doing what they claimed to do. Many of us involved in WAC programs had already developed extensive assessment tools to examine student writing; WAC and the assessment movement became allies in many universities. At my own institution, for example, we were called upon to present baseline data for freshmen writing skills, mid-point data, and end-of-program assessment data. Because our WAC program already involved a placement test for freshmen and a rising junior writing portfolio, we were able not only to provide the data but to track students longitudinally and show improvement in their writing between entry and mid-point assessment. I mentioned the book by Angelo and Cross earlier; that book is a good example of WAC techniques that are cast as assessment techniques—not necessarily in the sense of testing student knowledge but of assessing where students are, how well the instruction as well as the learning is progressing.

If the decade of the 1980s was one of assessment, that of the 1990s has been the decade of technology. Legislators and administrators alike are backing technology initiatives not only in the classroom but beyond; many institutions (my own included) are investing heavily in distance learning technologies, creating virtual classrooms and interacting with students on-line as well as (or often instead of) in person. WAC is part of this movement, although that fact may not be apparent. The most interesting recent WAC book doesn't even have the word "writing" in the title: it is called *Electronic Communication Across the Curriculum* (Reiss, Selfe, and Young). WAC has become ECAC.

What is the future of WAC? I am confident that it will continue as it has for the last twenty-five years, as an educational movement aimed at transforming college pedagogy and encouraging active learning as students understand and become part of the construction of knowledge in the disciplines. In the next twenty-five years, the term *writing across the curriculum* itself may disappear. Who cares? As long as there are teachers focusing on writing to learn and writing to communicate in the disciplines, WAC will continue to be part of the landscape of higher education.

Notes

[1] The educational reform movement now known as the National Writing Project began in 1974 as the Bay Area Writing Project; by 1976 it was a model for statewide staff development, and by 1979 it had become the National Writing Project. See Russell, *Writing* 280–82.

[2] James Britton and his associates called these "expressive" and "transactional" in his influential book *The Development of Writing Abilities (1–18)*.

[3] Although their book does not have WAC in its title, Angelo and Cross describe many pedagogical techniques and assignments that are drawn from WAC pedagogy.

[4] The book is available in some university libraries. Maimon is coauthoring a new text (with Janice Peritz), *College Research and Writing: A Guide and Handbook for Students*, that she says will be a second-generation *Writing in the Arts and Sciences*. It will be available in 2000 or 2001.

[5] Madigan is the psychologist of this interdisciplinary team; putting his name first is an example of the very style the authors are discussing, in which the lead author is put first to ensure that he or she will get the citation.

[6] Here I would be remiss if I did not mention my own mentors as I attempted to enter the discourse community of writing across the curriculum. When I set up my first WAC workshop, Carol Holder of California Polytechnic University, Pomona, was extremely generous with her time and materials, even coming down to run one session for me. Later, an administrator sent me to one of the meetings on WAC held at the University of Chicago to meet Elaine Maimon, who was a speaker at the meeting. In spite of her busy schedule, she met with me and gave me invaluable advice. Both Carol and Elaine urged me to call Toby Fulwiler, who likewise helped generously, coming out to my present institution when I started a WAC program here. I continue to be grateful to these three early leaders in WAC for their help and encouragement as I was learning my way in the field.

[7] Videotapes of the class sessions are in the Mathematical and Computer Sciences Library at Stanford.

[8] For further information about the case method, see Hutchings, *Using Cases to Improve College Teaching*.

[9] Thaiss may be contacted at the Department of English, George Mason University. Those interested in being involved in on-line conversations about WAC might want to join the WAC listserv. To subscribe, send a message to listserv@postoffice.cso.uiuc.edu. In the body of the message type: subscribe WAC-L ⟨your name⟩.

[10] The WPA list is archived on the Web at http://gcinfo.gc.maricopa.edu/~wpa/ The national WAC conferences (held every two years) are organized through Cornell University. For information about the next conference, contact Jonathan Monroe (jbm3@cornell.edu) or Katherine Gottschalk (kkg1@cornell.edu).

Bibliography

Angelo, Thomas A., and K. Patricia Cross. *Classroom Assessment Techniques: A Handbook for College Teachers*. 2nd ed. San Francisco: Jossey-Bass, 1993.

Bean, John. *Engaging Ideas: The Professor's Guide to Integrating Writing, Critical Thinking, and Active Learning in the Classroom*. San Francisco: Jossey-Bass, 1996.

Berkenkotter, Carol, and Thomas N. Huckin. *Genre Knowledge in Disciplinary Communication: Cognition/Culture/Power*. Hillsdale, NJ: Erlbaum, 1995.

Britton, James. *Language and Learning*. London: Penguin, 1970.

Britton, James, et al. *The Development of Writing Abilities (11–18)*. London: Macmillan, 1975.

Britton, W. Earl. "What Is Technical Writing?" *College Composition and Communication* 16 (1965): 113–16.

Bruffee, Kenneth A. "Collaborative Learning and the 'Conversation of Mankind.'" *College English* 46 (1984): 635–52.

———. "Peer Tutoring and the 'Conversation of Mankind.'" *Writing Centers: Theory and Administration*. Ed. Gary Olson. Urbana, IL: NCTE, 1984. 3–15.

Cope, Bill, and Mary Kalantzis. "The Power of Literacy and the Literacy of Power." *The Powers of Literacy: A Genre Approach to Teaching Writing*. Ed. Bill Cope and Mary Kalantzis. Pittsburgh: U of Pittsburgh P, 1993. 63–89.

Day, Robert. *How to Write and Publish a Scientific Paper.* Phoenix: Oryx, 1994.

Emig, Janet. "Writing as a Mode of Learning." *College Composition and Communication* 28 (1977): 122–28.

Finkel, Donald L., and G. Stephen Monk. "Teachers and Learning Groups: Dissolution of the Atlas Complex." *Learning in Groups.* Ed. Clark Bouton and Russell Y. Garth. New Directions for Teaching and Learning 14. San Francisco: Jossey-Bass, 1983. 83–97.

Fulwiler, Toby. *The Journal Book.* Portsmouth, NH: Boynton/Cook-Heinemann, 1987.

———. "Showing, Not Telling, at a Writing Workshop." *College English* 43 (1981): 55–63.

———. *Teaching with Writing.* Upper Montclair, NJ: Boynton/Cook, 1987.

Gaudiani, Claire. *Teaching Composition in the Foreign Language Curriculum.* Washington, DC: Center for Applied Linguistics, 1981.

Herrington, Anne J. "Writing to Learn: Writing Across the Disciplines." *College English* 43 (1984): 379–87.

Hutchings, Pat. *Using Cases to Improve College Teaching: A Guide to More Reflective Practice.* Washington, DC: American Association of Higher Education, 1993.

Knoblauch, C. A., and Lil Brannon. "Writing as Learning Through the Curriculum." *College English* 45 (1983): 465–74.

Knuth, Donald E., Tracy Larrabee, and Paul M. Roberts. *Mathematical Writing.* MAA Notes 14. Mathematical Association of America, 1989.

Linton, Patricia, Robert Madigan, and Susan Johnson. "Introducing Students to Disciplinary Genres: The Role of the General Composition Course." *Language and Learning Across the Disciplines* 1 (1994): 63–78.

Madigan, Robert, Susan Johnson, and Patricia Linton. "The Language of Psychology: APA Style as Epistemology." *American Psychologist* 50 (1995): 428–36.

Magnotto, Joyce Neff, and Barbara R. Stout. "Faculty Workshops." *Writing Across the Curriculum: A Guide to Developing Programs.* Ed. Susan H. McLeod and Margot Soven. Newbury Park, CA: Sage, 1992.

Mahala, Daniel. "Writing Utopias: Writing Across the Curriculum and the Promise of Reform." *College English* 53 (1991): 773–89.

Maimon, Elaine, et al. *Writing in the Arts and Sciences.* Cambridge, MA: Winthrop, 1981.

McLeod, Susan. "Writing Across the Curriculum: The Second Stage, and Beyond." *College Composition and Communication* 40 (1989): 337–43. Rpt. in *Landmarks in Writing Across the Curriculum.* Ed. David R. Russell and Charles Bazerman. Davis, CA: Hermagoras, 1994. 79–86.

McLeod, Susan H., and Margot Soven, eds. *Writing Across the Curriculum: A Guide to Developing Programs.* Newbury Park, CA: Sage, 1992.

Miraglia, Eric, and Susan H. McLeod: "Whither WAC?: Interpreting the Stories/Histories of Mature WAC Programs." *WPA: Writing Program Administration* (1997): 46–65.

Moss, Andrew, and Carol Holder. *Improving Student Writing: A Guidebook for Faculty in All Disciplines.* Dubuque, IA: Kendall Hunt, 1988.

Reiss, Donna, Dickie Selfe, and Art Young, eds. *Electronic Communication Across the Curriculum.* Urbana, IL: NCTE, 1998.

Russell, David R. "Rethinking Genre in School and Society: An Activity Theory Analysis." *Written Communication* 14 (1997): 504–54.

———. "Vygotsky, Dewey, and Externalism: Beyond the Student/Discipline Dichotomy." *Journal of Advanced Composition* 13 (1993): 173–97.

———. *Writing in the Academic Disciplines, 1870–1990.* Carbondale: Southern Illinois UP, 1991.

Soven, Margot K. *Write to Learn: A Guide to Writing Across the Curriculum.* Cincinnati: South-Western, 1996.

Thaiss, Christopher. *The Harcourt Brace Guide to Writing Across the Curriculum.* Fort Worth: Harcourt, 1998.

Wallace, Ray. "The Writing Center's Role in the Writing Across the Curriculum Program: Theory and Practice." *The Writing Center Journal* 8.2 (1988): 43–48. Rpt. in *Landmark Essays on Writing Centers.* Ed. Christina Murphy and Joe Law. Davis, CA: Hermagoras, 1995. 191–5.

Walvoord, Barbara Fassler. *Helping Students Write Well: A Guide for Teachers in All Disciplines.* New York: MLA, 1982. 2nd ed. 1986.

TEACHING WITH TECHNOLOGY

For more than a decade, the use of technology in writing classes has expanded exponentially. More and more of our students come to college with advanced computer skills and extensive experience with the Web and Internet and network-based communications. Across the country, institutions continue to invest substantial sums of money in computing facilities and in electronic classrooms of various kinds. Technology is not only changing classroom practices, but it is changing institutional structures and practices, too. The advent of distance- and distributed-learning initiatives has resulted in virtual classrooms and universities. Writing classes have been especially prominent sites for innovative applications of technology. Writing teachers are often at the center of instructional technology initiatives, integrating technology in their own classes and participating in institutional decision-making processes to plan and implement the use of instructional technology across the campus.

The articles included in this appendix recognize that teachers are technologically literate, and they address several crucial issues that writing teachers face in their ongoing attempts to use technology effectively.

- What choices do teachers have for using technology to teach writing? What factors should teachers consider as they plan writing courses that will require the use of technology?
- How is technology changing our understanding of genre, of publishing, of what it means to write?
- How can teachers use technology to enhance effective writing instruction? How can teachers be advocates for responsible uses of instructional technology in writing programs?

TECHNOLOGY AND THE TEACHING OF WRITING

Charles Moran

[From Gary Tate, Amy Rupiper, and Kurt Schick, eds. *A Guide to Composition Pedagogies.* New York: Oxford UP, 2000. 203–23.]

Professor of English at the University of Massachusetts at Amherst and co-director of the Western Massachusetts Writing Project, Charles Moran has been an active scholar, teacher, and leader in the field of composition for decades. He has earned awards for distinguished teaching and distinguished service. His articles have appeared in numerous journals, including *College English, College Composition and Communication, Journal of Basic Writing,* and *Journal of Teaching Writing.* He is coauthor of *Computers and the Teaching of Writing in American Higher Education, 1979–94: A History,* with Gail E. Hawisher, Paul LeBlanc, and Cynthia L. Selfe (1996); coeditor, with Anne Herrington, of *Writing, Teaching, and Learning in the Disciplines* (1992); and coeditor, with Elizabeth Penfield, of *Conversations: Contemporary Critical Theory and the Teaching of Literature* (1990).

In this article, Moran reminds us that we "need to know the medium that most of [our] writing students will be working with." Moran's thorough and extensive overview of technology and writing instruction not only informs us about technology, but can also help writing instructors to make informed choices about whether and how to use technology. The article provides a helpful overview of sources about teaching and technology, an especially useful section on "applications of computer technologies for writers and teachers," and a provocative closing section that challenges teachers to consider issues of difference and access as they consider using technology. Moran focuses on how teachers can use technology critically to enhance effective writing instruction.

As computer technology has evolved over the past two decades, writing teachers have found that they could adapt this emerging technology to radically different pedagogies. In the early 1980s, the "age of the microcomputer," technology seemed to support invention, writing, and revising, activities that defined process-based pedagogies. At the same time, however, this same technology supported microcomputer-based skill-and-drill exercises, which grew from the print-based workbooks that were a staple of the current-traditional curriculum. In the early 1990s, when local area networks and the Internet began to become more readily available, these new manifestations of computer-based technology supported a social, constructivist pedagogy. Today, as the Web captures our imaginations, we find that composing in hypermedia and adding graphics and sound to our writing seem increasingly appropriate activities in our writing courses, and as our students gain access to the Web, the research paper returns to the center of our consciousness, though perhaps in new forms.

Even though there is not a specific pedagogy associated with emerging technologies, writing teachers need to know about these technologies so that they may incorporate their use, or not, as they deem appropriate, into their classroom practice, and so that they may advise and teach those of their students who have access to these technologies and who are using them in their writing. I don't mean to suggest that we should all uncritically "dive in" to the new technology. As Cynthia L. Selfe pointed out in her Chair's address at the 1998 annual meeting of the Conference on College Composition and Communication, parents, taxpayers, and legislators seem to be willing to invest in educational technology even as they are disinvesting in public K–12 education. There is pressure on colleges and universities, too, to keep up with technology. If one does not, as the saying goes, one is roadkill on the information highway. This pressure on educators to use technology exists despite the fact that, as Todd Oppenheimer has noted, there is no proof yet that technology improves students' learning. In my own situation at the University of Massachusetts, we cheerfully spend money on computer-equipped classrooms, money that, if it were spent instead on direct instruction (teachers), would reduce our average class size significantly. Is spending our resources on technology cost effective? It depends on the calculus we use.

Whether we choose to dive in, or resist, or merely float along with the current, technology is affecting our work as writing teachers. Indeed, computers have entered the mainstream. No longer is computer talk the province of enthusiast publications like *Wired* or *Byte*. *The New York Times* now has a full section headed "Circuits" that it runs every Thursday, with, on August 13, 1998, articles on the ways in which computer vocabulary has moved into the lexicon of daily speech and writing, on new Web search engines, on an online textbook store for students, and on a present danger: the transmission of viruses through e-mail. A popular magazine on things scientific, *Discover*, now runs a "personal tech" column. Even *Consumer Reports* does what it can to review computers, modems, and software, and it now runs a regular section titled "Living with Technology," with, in its August 1998 issue, advice about finding and joining newsgroups and about dealing with problems you might be having with your Web browser. Computers invisibly schedule our air travel, conduct our financial transactions, and, as we drive our automobiles, control the engine's valve timing, spark advance, and fuel injection systems. In our field, our students will increasingly use computers to mediate their reading and writing; and as teachers we will increasingly use computers to mediate and support our students' learning.

At the moment, the "home computer" is the unit of currency, a large, clunky piece of machinery, obtrusively the staple of our computer-equipped writing classrooms. As liquid-crystal display (LCD) screens evolve and as computers continue to become smaller and power powerful, we will be teaching, and our students learning, assisted by technology that works for us unobtrusively, invisibly, as now is the case in our automobiles. It is my belief that technology will gradually infuse the work we writing teachers do, eventually becoming, in Mark Weiser's phrase, "ubiquitous computing," or, in the phrase adopted by the Carnegie-Mellon Institute for Complex Engineered Systems, "wearable computing" (Jannot). Whether this future is seen as "good" or "bad" depends on one's perspective. There are prophets of doom like Sven Birkirts, who see in the advent of screen text the end of civilization as we know it; there are prophet evangelists like Michael Joyce, who see the new text as inherently democratic, a medium that will release creativity and empower the individual. In this chapter, and in my own teaching, I take the pragmatic view: computers have altered our landscape. They have changed the medium in which some fraction of our students read and write. Therefore we, as writing teachers, need to pay attention to what is happening. On the basis of this knowledge, we will be able to make informed decisions about our use of technology in our teaching.

To make our subject manageable, I will begin with an overview of general bibliographic resources in our field. I will then move into the several applications of computer technology that writing teachers have included in their classroom practice: word processing, electronic mail, online chat programs, and the Web/hypertext/hypermedia. I make these divisions, knowing as I do that computer applications in our field are steadily converging: e-mail and the Web are now interrelated, and we can compose Web pages on word processors. But the taxonomy I have chosen, though not "true," will be useful, because it maps easily onto the activities that seem likely to continue to be the staples of our writing classrooms: writing, revising, and editing; class discussion; responding to writing; and research. In each of these sections I will summarize what we think we know about the implications of the application for our teaching practice. After these "applications" sections, I will describe a number of issues that confront us as we work with emerging technologies: the ways in which gender, race, and social class may affect our students as online writers; the implications of the new technology for writers who are second-language learners; and what we think and know about the ways in which the new technology affects basic writers. I will conclude with a section on an issue that includes and sharpens the others: our students' differential access to technology.

An Overview of Sources in the Field: Histories, Bibliographies, Online Resources

A great deal has been written in the past twenty-five years about the integration of computers into our work as writing teachers. For a review and history of much of this writing, I refer you to Gail Hawisher and colleagues'

Computers and the Teaching of Writing in American Higher Education, 1979–1994: A History (1996). This book, the first in the Ablex series titled New Directions in Computers and Composition Studies, approaches its subject chronologically: chapter 1 is headed "1979–1982: The Profession's Early Experience with Modern Technology"; chapter 2 "1983–1985: Growth and Enthusiasm"; chapter 3 "1986–1988: Emerging Research, Theory, and Professionalism"; chapter 4 "1989–1991: Coming of Age: The Rise of Cross-Disciplinary Perspectives and a Consideration of Difference"; and chapter 5 "1992–1994: Looking Forward." The final section is an edited transcript of an online discussion by young teacher/scholars then just entering the profession. Each of the five chapters opens with its period's scholarly and pedagogical context, then presents the technological context, then reviews the work of writing teachers and scholars who were using technology during this time, and concludes with an interview of a teacher/scholar who was particularly central to that period. The book is useful to the teacher who believes that the past may have value to those who will chart the future. It does not tell the whole story, as reviewers have pointed out: the book does not include the work that has been done in teaching writing to second-language learners; and it does not attempt to include a history of computer-assisted instruction (CAI).

For an update, one could turn to *Transitions: Teaching Writing in Computer-Supported and Traditional Classrooms* (1998), by Mike Palmquist and co-workers. This book includes as an appendix a fourteen-page "List of Related Readings" that is nicely divided into sections of selected titles under headings such as "Computers and Collaboration," "Human Factors Issues," "Computer Classroom Design," and "Software Selection, Evaluation, and Development." The list carries titles as recent as 1996. The book is addressed to teachers teaching in computer-supported classrooms, a topic that five years ago would have rated its own major heading, but today seems too specialized and potentially dated. The PC-filled room, though it may be with us in some places for some time, is a stage in our evolution as writing teachers. When and if most of our students have access to computers in dormitory room or home settings, the computer-equipped classroom will seem much less necessary than it now does to writing programs. Yet a number of us do teach writing in computer-supported facilities, and there is therefore a substantial literature on this subject. For the teacher who is contemplating a semester in a computer-supported writing classroom, *Transitions* is the best single source. The book draws on and summarizes previous research carried out in computer-equipped classrooms, and it adds to and updates earlier research through its authors' own research study. As is the case with all books and even most print articles on technology, the Web was an infant when the research was done, so the book is extremely light on Web-related pedagogy.

Both *Transitions* and *Computers and the Teaching of Writing in American Higher Education* are the work of a community of teachers/scholars that has grown up around a journal, *Computers and Composition*, that has been regularly published since November 1983, co-edited first by Cynthia L. Selfe and Kathleen E. Kiefer, and since 1988 (vol. 5, no. 3) by Selfe and Gail E. Hawisher. This group had its origins in the Conference on College Composition and Communication (CCCC) and in particular one of this conference's special interest groups, "The Fifth C." The group continues to meet at its own annual Computers and Writing Conference, a good place to meet fellow teachers/scholars and to hear papers that specifically address issues in this field. *Computers and Composition* is now a substantial journal, published triquarterly by Ablex. It is carried by major libraries, but if you have difficulty finding print copy, the journal, as of this writing, maintains a Web site, http://www.cwrl.utexas.edu/~ccjrnl, where you can find archived text from back issues, going back to volume 1, number 1. This Web site is accessible as well through the NCTE Web site, which may be a more permanent and reliable address: http://www.ncte.org. As of this writing, in October 1998, full texts of articles are online through volume 10 (1993), and abstracts are available through the current issue. The editors are adding full texts of articles, though it is not clear at this writing whether the print journal's publisher will smile on the project of publishing online issues that are still subject to copyright.

For other bibliographical sources, I'd suggest CCC Online, a Web site with a searchable archive (abstracts only) of articles and reviews in *College Composition and Communication* going back to 1991. The Council is in the process of deciding whether to move full texts online. You can reach CCC Online through the above-mentioned NCTE Web site. The "Annotated Bibliography of Research in the Teaching of English," published annually in the May issue of *Research in the Teaching of English,* is worth looking at, too. Its scope includes K–12 as well as postsecondary education. I do not suggest what might seem an obvious print source, the CCCC *Bibliography of Composition and Rhetoric,* because this bibliography, notoriously difficult to access by subject, has stalled at 1994, at least for the short term. At this writing, plans are afoot to update the bibliography and put it online. If and when this happens, it will be found through the NCTE Web site, most likely located at a revised CCC Online site. For the ways in which technology has changed the field of technical and professional writing, the best entry point is Patricia Sullivan and Jennie Dauterman's *Electronic Literacies in the Workplace.* The chapters in 1996 anthology look at corporate e-mail, classroom use of workplace simulation, online editing, and workplace writing with electronic tools. A further resource is the *IEEE Transactions on Professional Communication,* a journal sponsored by the Institute of Electrical and Electronics Engineers. Articles in this journal are abstracted in the IEEE Bibliographies Online, at http://www.ieee.org, though one has to be a member to use this resource.

Applications of Computer Technologies for Writers and Teachers

Word Processing

Depending on our situation, some, many, or all of our students will have access to word processing. These students may be composing differently on screen than they would on paper, though the evidence for this difference is not at all clear, and differences, where they exist, are likely to be determined by context more than they are by essential differences between screen and paper. Early research on online writers attempted to discover essential, global differences between writers who worked online and offline. In 1991 Elizabeth Klem and I summarized the best research in the field up to that time in a chapter titled "Computers and Instructional Strategies in the Teaching of Writing." In this summary we found that students might (Sudol) or might not (Daiute) be revising more online than they had on paper; that writers might be having difficulty seeing their text whole (Haas "Seeing"), might be spending less time planning before they wrote (Haas "Planning"), and might be helped (Kiefer and Smith) or hindered (Dobrin) by spell checkers and grammar checkers.

In retrospect it seems clear that looking for essential differences between screen text and print text is a dead end, because writers write differently, and even a given writer will write differently on different occasions. Yet these early studies alert us to the different ways in which writers may react to a move, forced or voluntary, from print to screen. And although these early studies focus on word processing, which is practically a transparent technology these days, until there is universal access technology—not a likely scenario—we will always be teaching students for whom writing online is a new or strange experience. So to a degree, as teachers of writing, we are teachers of word processing—not teachers of computer literacy, for that is not our job, but teachers who have read the relevant research and who, as online writers ourselves, have discovered helpful procedures. It may be, for example, that a particular student writer includes large swatches of unedited freewriting in her final draft. She will do this online, let us say, because cutting and pasting is so easy. She does her freewriting and then, without opening a new file, starts her essay by writing an introductory paragraph before the freewriting, which she includes whole and unedited in her final draft. She will need to be coached in a particular way: helped to preserve the generative power of her freewriting, while editing it toward the needs of a reader. Another student writer may revise by adding new material to the end of his piece. His editors suggest that he should include X in his piece, so he does—in a section tacked on to the end of his earlier draft. This student writer will need to be helped to plan, to outline, online, before writing or during. Yet another writer who is being intimidated by a grammar checker may need to be helped to understand that computers can't read and that most of the advice he is getting is not useful to him. This writer's desk partner, however, may be one whose sentences are habitually lengthy and complex and may be able to make good use of the information that the grammar checker can supply.

All student writers will need to be helped to understand that they can to a degree control their writing environment by manipulating the word processing program they are writing with. If auto-correct functions irritate, distract, or mislead, they can be turned off. If, as Haas suggests ("Seeing"), writers online have difficulty extrapolating the whole text from the segment that is on screen, then writers can be taught one or more of the word processing functions that help a writer navigate the digitized text: bookmarks, the search function, the keystrokes that move one swiftly to the beginning and end of the document, and Windows functions that make it possible to "see" more than one section of the text on the same screen. If it is the case for writers that the liveliest and most prestigious part of the screen is the menu bars and scroll bars that surround the text, as Stephen Bernhardt suggests, then they can be shown how to optimize their screens for writing by taking control of the screen through the "view" function on the toolbar. Some handbooks have sections titled "Working on a Word Processor," which give advice that is inevitably generic and qualified. Much better than generic handbook advice is the context-sensitive advice given by a teacher who knows the research in the field, has written online, and has reflected on that practice.

The best recent articles on the subject of computer-mediated writing are Bernhardt's "The Shape of Text to Come: The Texture of Print on Screens" and Carolyn Dowling's "Word Processing and the Ongoing Difficulty of Writing." Bernhardt gives us "nine dimensions of variation that help map the differences between paper and on-screen text" (151): relative to print on paper, online text tends to be more "situationally embedded," "interactive," "functionally mapped," "modular," "navigable," "hierarchically embedded," "spacious," "graphically rich," and "customizable and publishable" (151–52). This taxonomy of difference will be helpful to teachers and students as they themselves move between paper and screen. In "Word Processing and the Ongoing Difficulty of Writing" Dowling begins with the premise that writing is, simply, hard work, and that those who believe that the computer will somehow make this work easier are in for an unpleasant surprise. Indeed, if computers do seem to make writing easier, perhaps it is because some important writer work is being bypassed. Dowling notes that some writers report feeling "alienated" from their screen text; that others feel that when they write online they lose all sense of audience other than themselves; and that others find it difficult to come to closure when composing with text that can so easily be changed. Dowling's conclusion is extremely explicit, and, in my view, as close to the last word as we will find in this area: "The fact that writing continues to be perceived as a difficult activity . . . suggests the possibility that benefits of word processing might be counterbalanced . . . by aspects of the computing environment that render the activity, for some individuals, as fraught with problems in this medium as in others" (234).

Electronic Mail

Electronic mail (e-mail) makes it possible for teachers and students to communicate with one another during the intervals between their classes. E-mail is often included in the larger category of computer-mediated communication, or CMC, particularly in the field of distance learning, where students and teacher meet seldom, if at all, face to face. Writing teachers in campus settings may find that e-mail is a useful adjunct to their course, particularly if their class meets once each week and/or if students commute from a distance. Through e-mail, a teacher can construct a listserv for discussions; through e-mail a teacher can respond to student writing. The best present introduction to e-mail, for the writing teacher or for the student, is *English Online,* by Nick Carbone and Eric Crump. This handbook leads the reader gently through such e-mail-related topics as online conventions ("Netiquette"), e-mail acronyms and emoticons, signature files, mailing lists, telnet, and file transfer protocols (ftp).

If a writing teacher decides to use e-mail in a course, she or he needs to think about some of the characteristics of this medium. First, the language of e-mail bears a problematic relationship to American Standard English, a dialect that most of us believe we are privileging in our writing classes. Gail Hawisher and I summarized much of the research on the languages of e-mail in "The Rhetorics and Languages of Electronic Mail," a chapter in Ilana Snyder's *Page to Screen: Taking Literacy into the Electronic Era.* In this chapter we noted that the language of e-mail has been seen since its beginnings as related both to the written and spoken languages. We summarized recent studies of electronic language in Susan Herring's *Computer-mediated Communication: Linguistic, Social, and Cross-cultural Perspectives;* Collot and Belmore's analysis of the language used on bulletin board systems; Yates' analysis of the language of online conferences on the British conferencing network, CoSy; and Werry's analysis of the language used on what he terms Internet Relay Chat, something like real-time e-mail. All three studies found that in these rather different applications of e-mail, the language used has significant differences from both the written and spoken languages. Whether these differences signify a separate language or dialect is a matter of definition. What is clear is that writing in this medium is different from writing in print. The significance of this finding for teachers of writing is that we will find it difficult to insist that our students' e-mail writing conform to the standards we will apply to their formal essay writing.

Second, and certainly a contributor to the differences in language, is that the e-mail encounter is characteristically informal. Though I have received exquisitely formal e-mail from lawyers and from the occasional friend new to the medium, e-mail in the academic world tends to be chatty, invoking a relationship between correspondents that is casual and, in its ease and informality, potentially at odds with the conventional teacher-student relationship. Unlike the draft-by-draft revising that we encourage in our classes, e-mail is characteristically rapidly composed, uncensored, a species of freewriting. This is most true if the author composes online; with more advanced e-mail systems like Eudora, one can compose offline, at leisure, and then upload the message to the host computer. Yet even with Eudora correspondents, e-mail seems spontaneous, quick, and therefore open to dialogues that generate and exacerbate conflict.

Third, e-mail as a medium evokes intimacy, up to and including virtual, online sex. This sense of intimacy is a paradox because, unlike postal mail, e-mail has no envelope. E-mail is recorded and can, theoretically, be read by the system operator and anyone with system operator privileges. E-mail can also be copied and printed; it can be forwarded to other individuals without the author's knowledge; and it can be posted to lists. Most of us have been embarrassed at least once by a colleague who mistakenly posted to an entire department a message intended for one person's eyes only. This illusion of intimacy poses a problem for a teacher: How do we maintain appropriate authority online? As Gail Hawisher and I noted in 1997,

> In the conventional classroom, the teacher can draw on the students' previous experience—perhaps we should call it training?—of K–12 schooling. In the conventional classroom, this training has been associated with an array of visual cues that the teacher can use to signal expected behavior . . . the teacher's desk, the clock, the lectern, the gradebook, perhaps even the American flag! On-line, we usually have, for now, written language alone. In the new medium, the teacher and student together will have to establish what is, and what is not, appropriate behavior. (118)

Teachers who are considering online responding to students' writing should read what I consider the best recent book on the larger subject of responding to student writing generally: *Writing to Learn: Strategies for Assigning and Responding to Writing Across the Disciplines,* edited by Mary Deane Sorcinelli and Peter Elbow. This book includes, among others, chapters by Toby Fulwiler on the letter as response, by Art Young on response as "academic conversation," by Anne Herrington on "Developing and Responding to Major Writing Projects," and by Peter Elbow on high-stakes and low-stakes writing. For our particular subject, the Hawisher/Moran chapter titled "Responding to Writing On-Line" is directly pertinent, in that it brings together what we know about e-mail correspondence and applies it to the business of responding to student writing. The authors of this chapter argue that as a medium e-mail is so different from handwritten comments-in-the-margins that as we begin to respond online, we may be forced to rethink our assumptions about responding to student writing.

The teacher who incorporates e-mail in her pedagogy needs to remember that the digital "language" of e-mail is ASCII, the American Standard Code for Information Exchange. As Cynthia L. Selfe and Richard J. Selfe, Jr. have noted, ASCII is an ancient code that can handle only ninety-five characters. It can therefore cope only with lowercase and uppercase letters, numerals, and marks of punctuation: no diacritics or non-English characters. In our chapter on the rhetorics and languages of e-mail, Gail Hawisher and I build on the Selfes' work, noting that "to e-mail our friends Martín or Björn, we are obliged to 'english' their names, omitting the accents on the 'i' of Martín and the 'o' of Björn, leaving both somewhat Ellis-islanded, Americanised" (97). On e-mail, and in ASCII, all names are not considered equal. As teachers, we need to remember this. We can't change it, but we can make our students aware of the situation, and make it clear that as we use e-mail in our classes, we are unwittingly supporting the "English-only" movement that is today gaining ground in our country.

Finally, the teacher who considers using e-mail in her class needs to consider the extent to which her work load may increase as a result of this new practice. The great boon, and the great evil, of computer-mediated communication is that it makes it possible for us to be available twenty-four hours a day, seven days a week, in effect putting in unpaid hours for our employers. Offline, we have evolved strategies for limiting our availability: we post office hours when students can meet with us, and we have some way of screening our incoming telephone calls—either a secretary/receptionist or a voice-mail system. Online, until and unless we develop conventions that will protect us—such as telling our students that we don't read our e-mail on weekends—we can be reached at all hours, Monday through Sunday.

Online Discussion

Online, synchronous discussions are possible inside and outside computer-equipped classrooms: through distance-learning networks such as CoSy, through LAN-based software such as Daedalus *Interchange,* and through Web-based courseware like *Web-CT.* When LAN-based chat programs first appeared, they were hailed by writing teachers as an unalloyed good. Class discussions, it was argued, were now written, not oral, and therefore furthered our goals as writing teachers by increasing the amount of writing our students were doing. A number of researchers believed that these online discussions were more democratic than offline discussions: online, the argument was made, people who were marginalized in face-to-face group dynamics could and did move from the margins into the center (e.g., Faigley "Subverting the Electronic Workbook," *Fragments of Rationality).* Women in particular, it was widely believed, gained voice in the online forum. Later research, however, has discovered that we carry our culture with us as we move online. Two good sources on this topic are Susan Romano's "The Egalitarianism Narrative: Whose Story? Which Yardstick?" and Selfe and Paul Meyer's "Testing Claims for On-Line Conferences."

The issue of authority arises in online discussions, and in very much the same form as it did in our consideration of e-mail. Reduced to its simplest expression, the issue is this: Will students behave when they move online? A number of teachers have reported online discussions that moved rapidly off topic; others have reported that in the online discussion students are more likely to "flame" one another or to use language that is hurtful to others in the discussion. Why this happens is in doubt. Most researchers have adopted the "reduced social cues" hypothesis, arguing that because online we can't see or hear our correspondent, we are freed from social constraints that govern face-to-face communication and become asocial or antisocial in our behavior (e.g., Sproull and Kiesler). Others argue that in the absence of social cues we fall back on the cultural stereotypes that we have available to us, becoming, for example, the "aggressive male fraternity jock" (Spears and Lea). In this view, we are not freed from constraint, but are driven to accept narrowly defined and often inappropriate models of behavior. In either case the phenomenon is the same: online discourse can and does get out of hand, apparently more rapidly than face-to-face discourse. The teacher, therefore, needs to decide what kind of moderator she will be. Andrew Feenberg, in a useful chapter titled "The Written World: On the Theory and Practice of Computer Conferencing," argues for a "strong" moderator (33), one who both contextualizes the individual messages in the discussion and acts as a monitor. In my own practice, admittedly conservative, I follow Feenberg's advice, making as certain as I can that the online discussion has direction: a problem that the group must solve, a brainstorm session to generate material, or a chance for individual writers to update others on their progress on a particular assignment.

A full account of a class that fully utilized the online discussion capability of its computer-supported classroom is "Visible Conversation and Academic Inquiry" by Gregory G. Colomb and Joyce A. Simutis. This account carefully documents students' learning as they participate in extended Interchange sessions. As they report on their study, Colomb and Simutis squarely face the pedagogical, sociological, and psychological issues that I have outlined above, and they do so in a way that will be extremely helpful to the teacher who is considering adding online discussion to the curriculum.

The Web/Hypertext/Hypermedia

In what now seem the "old times," which is to say the early 1990s, it would have been possible to treat the Web, hypertext, and hypermedia separately. Indeed, there was in the early 1990s a powerful literature that defined *hypertext* as a new field. George Landow and others at Brown University reported on huge hypertexts that were developed in connection with literature courses (Delany and Landow). Michael Joyce, Stuart Moulthrop, and others developed and reported on *Storyspace*, a program for composing in hypertext designed for computer-supported classrooms. While *hypertext* was being used in English and in composition studies, in the larger world the defining term was *hypermedia*, as graphics, sound, and video were linked to text, and vice versa, in online help manuals and in CD-ROM encyclopedias and other reference works. Today the development of the Web browser and the consequent evolution of the Web have, for our purposes, subsumed the earlier technologies. At the moment I write this, hypertext seems a somewhat antique and limited conception, and hypermedia the very warp and woof of the Web.

For the writing teacher in today's classroom, knowing about these media is essential. A quick way in is Nicholas C. Burbules' chapter, "The Rhetorics of the Web." Burbules argues that reading on the Web is not the same as reading a book, despite the fact that the Web uses the page as its founding metaphor. When we read in a book, we will "link" what we read with previous reading or other experience. The links we make as we read print are our own links. One could argue, of course, that these links have been "made" by our prior experience: that we have already been written, linked. But still, if we grant the reader any agency at all, connections made in print are more the reader's than those discovered on the Web. When we read on the Web we click on links that have been made by others. Burbules argues therefore that we need to be teaching "critical hyperreading" (118): readers should

> know what goes into selecting material for a page, making links, organizing a cluster of separate pages into a hyperlinked Web site. . . . The more that one is aware of *how* this is done, the more one can be aware *that* it was done and that it *could* have been done otherwise. This discloses the apparent "naturalness" or invisibility of such designer/author choices, and grants the hyperreader the opportunity to stand outside them—to question, criticize, and imagine alternatives. (118–19)

Burbules notes as well that hypertextual reading habits include "surfing," which, if assumed as a reading practice, drives the need for the quick "hook," a dance on the surface, as opposed to a long read in which attention is sustained. He looks at links through "tropes" or "tools" of rhetoric: the link as metaphor, metonymy, antistasis—the link as a rhetorical device that is persuasive, not neutral.

The Web is not only a place where readers read; it is a place where student writers can, and if they can they will, do research. Unlike a college or university library, however, on the Web there is no librarian or print editor watching over the materials that are included in the collection. On the Web a search may turn up the home page of *The New York Times* and the home page of a 10-year-old preteen. Both will be presented by the screen as they are, with no indication that one is more authoritative than the other. So students and teachers will need to wrestle with the question of the authority of the writers' sources—not a new question, certainly, but one that we now have to ask more steadily. College/university librarians will be on top of this problem and are the teacher's first and best resource, though they may be unduly suspicious of the Web and its contents. Many libraries maintain "Internet toolboxes" on their Web sites, filled with links to search engines and advice about using and citing online sources. Both the MLA and APA lay out their conventions for online citation on their Web sites, and Diana Hacker's "Bedford Booklet," *Research and Documentation in the Electronic Age*, includes not only major library resources—indexes, encyclopedias, dictionaries, companions—but also major Web sites in the subdisciplines of the humanities, social sciences, and sciences, as well as advice on search engines, Internet search strategies, and ways of evaluating Internet sources.

Will the results of online research be fundamentally different from results of print research? The jury is out on this question. In "'Pulling Down' Books vs. 'Pulling Up' Files," Karen Ruhleder looks at what has happened to research in the field of classics since the widespread use of the *Thesaurus Linguae Grecae*, a CD-ROM-based, searchable database that contains the texts of classic Greek literature. She finds that in Classics "the textual landscape has become broader, but it has also become flatter" (187), as researchers trade the breadth of reference made possible by the searchable database for the depth that Ruhleder sees in scholarship that was the result of having spent years working with a single text. On the other hand, journalists tend to see the Web as a necessity for reporters and their writing, because its breadth and speed suit their work exactly.

An online resource for teachers who want to connect the Web with their pedagogies and with their classroom practice is *Kairos,* an electronic journal described by its editor, Greg Siering, as "designed to serve as a peer reviewed resource for teachers, researchers, and tutors of writing at the college and university level, including Technical Writing, Business Writing, Professional Communication, Creative Writing, Composition, and Literature." The editorial board describes their focus in these terms: "Our goal at *Kairos* is to offer a progressive and innovative online forum for the exploration of writing, learning, and teaching in hypertextual environments like the World Wide Web." Though Web sites come and go, I'm guessing that *Kairos* will persist. *Kairos'* Web address is http://english.ttu.edu/kairos.

Issues

Computers and "Difference"

In the previous sections we have looked at applications of computer technology without substantially considering how these applications might be used differently by, and have different effects on, different populations of students. It should be obvious that this technology is not neutral: as Selfe and Selfe have clearly demonstrated, computer interfaces, with their desktops, files, telephones, and faxes, reflect the values of the white collar professions; and as I noted above in the section on e-mail, the language of our computers is English, relegating all other languages and their cultures to second-class status. It should be intuitively obvious to us as well, however, that our students differ from one another: each brings to writing and reading, and to working with emerging technologies, a distinct history that helps determine how they will connect with the activity that we are trying to help them learn. If our intuition in this matter should need some support, it can be found in the work of Shirley Brice Heath, Lisa Delpit, and others who have studied the ways in which literacy functions in different cultures. But how can these differences be best described? Predicted? Understood? Clearly teachers who are planning to teach in computer classrooms need to know the best of what we now know about possible differences in the ways in which our students are connecting with technology. These differences can be seen along the axes of race, gender, and social class, and they can be seen in terms of the overlapping categories current in our field: the teaching of underprepared writers (basic writing) and the teaching of second-language learners (ESL instruction). In the paragraphs that follow, I will lay out what seems to me to be the best advice we can find as we begin to foreground the fact that technology is not neutral and that it may affect different people differently.

There has been a great deal of research on the ways in which women and men connect with computers. A good entry point to this subject is Emily Jessup's "Feminism and Computers in Composition Instruction." This 1991 study summarizes then-extant research on the gender gap in school computer use, where the computer is seen as a "boy's toy" (339). It gives statistics on computer camp attendance, subscriptions to computer magazines, and studies of computer user's confidence, all of which show a distinct gender gap. For the reader who wants to go further in the work of this time, the Fall 1990 issue of *Signs* is a rich lode. In this issue Ruth Perry and Lisa Greber look at the historical relationship between women and technology, argue that computers are bad for women in that they fragment work, isolate, and constitute a health hazard, and conclude that "as feminists we must decipher how and to what extent technologies reflect or reinforce the patriarchal order" (76). In "The Army and the Microworld," Paul N. Edwards reminds us of the close and continuing connection between computing and the military, still visible in the "abort-retry-fail" language that can surface even today when our computers "crash" or our applications and files are "killed." And in "Epistemological Pluralism: Styles and Voices Within the Computer Culture," Sherry Turkle and Seymour Papert report on their research into men's and women's programming styles. They see men generally using a "hard" programming style, what they call a "black box" formal approach: beginning with the big picture, planning. They see women programmers as at odds with this privileged mode, and wanting to program in a "soft" style: what Turkle and Papert, borrowing from Levi-Strauss, call "bricolage"—starting with bits and pieces and building up the program gradually (134–35).

For a more recent look at gender and computing, I suggest Gail Hawisher and Patricia Sullivan's "Women on the Networks," a chapter in *Feminism and Composition Studies*. Hawisher and Sullivan summarize the early research that claimed that online spaces were inherently egalitarian, and point to contemporary studies that see women as victims online, as they are, more often than men, offline. The authors summarize, too, the research that shows that even in apparently egalitarian online conferences, "women make fewer and shorter contributions than men and that both men and women respond more frequently to men's postings than to women's" (176). They turn from this summary, however, to document a "small group of academic women who persist." (176).

Though there is a great deal written about gender and technology, there is very little research explicitly on the ways in which race may make a difference in how students write and learn online. What we have suggests that race, by itself, is not a useful set of categories to work with. In "Race on the Superhighway: How E-mail Affects African American Student Writers," Teresa Redd and Victoria Massey find that African American students do not find enfranchisement online and that they "used fewer features of the African American oral tradition than we expected, fewer AAE grammatical forms and fewer 'styling' devices" (262). I can only speculate here, but it seems to me that the students studied knew that they were in school, under the watchful gaze of the teacher, and that they were writing to that audience, one that has traditionally disapproved of students' African American English in a classroom context. They were therefore, even on e-mail, on their best "school" behavior, perhaps experiencing what Keith Gilyard has called "a kind of enforced educational schizophrenia" (163) which he argues is a common element in the experience of African American students in America's schools. And Todd Taylor, in "The Persistence of Difference in Networked Classrooms," gives us a short case study of three African Americans in his technical writing class. Taylor finds practically no common ground among these students as online writers. From this study he concludes that we need to look beyond or through any stereotypes we might be moved to create, and consider our students as "individuals who defy tight demographic or cultural grouping" (177).

Research on computers in basic writing and ESL classrooms can be seen to be implicitly about race and social class, given the demographics of these courses in American postsecondary education, so this is another important thread for the writing teacher to follow. A good entry point for research on computers and basic writing students is Lisa Gerrard's ancient-but-still-useful chapter, "Computers and Basic Writers." Gerrard finds that basic writers who write on computers "enjoy using the computer, spend more time revising, feel more confident and in control of their writing, and socialize more with their classmates" (96). She argues that "these changes in attitude and practice provide conditions that foster learning," though she notes that the technology "seems to have had a more discernible impact on writers than on their prose" (97). A more recent study, Susan Stan and Terence G. Collins' "Basic Writing: Curricular Interactions with the New Technology," is not so careful in its claims. The authors give us a substantial overview of the field of basic writing: its history, its growth, its relation to the field of composition studies, and the ways in which technology has been brought into the work of teaching basic writing students. They survey teachers of basic writing to find the applications these teachers are making of emerging technologies. They summarize teacher reports and small-scale studies that report that basic writers' attitudes toward writing are more positive after a semester's work in computer-supported classrooms, that computers seem to help their revising practices, and that computers improve the appearance and content of student papers. It is hard not to share the authors' enthusiasm here, but I finally do not trust what seems to be their deepest argument, one that surfaces in their last paragraph but is implicit throughout: that if basic writing programs could only get access to enough technology, their students' transitions into the academic world would be easier and faster.

A good introduction to the use of computers in ESL classrooms is "The Wired World of Second-Language Education," by Michele Knobel and colleagues. The authors of this chapter are refreshingly aware of the extent to which "educators and learners alike face massive hype and pressure from commercial and political sources to 'technologise' teaching and learning" (21). They usefully describe the various applications of the new technology in ESL classrooms, and then zoom in on what they term "asynchronous communications": e-mail and discussion lists. They summarize the claims that have been made for the value of this particular application and then examine the studies that have tested these claims. They conclude that "the sketchy 'evidence' available from studies and projects we have investigated suggests that proponents of e-mail are longer on 'process' than they are on 'outcomes,' and tend to emphasize attitudes and feelings over downright competence in language use" (47). A short recent account is George Braine's "Beyond Word Processing: Networked Computers in ESL Writing Classes." Braine summarizes past studies of ESL writers on chat programs housed in local area networks in computer-supported classrooms, studies that have found that writing on chat programs has a positive effect on ESL writers' attitudes but not always on their writing. He reports as well on his own study, which compared the first draft and finished writing of students who peer edited and discussed their writing online with that of students who peer edited and discussed offline. Braine's study finds that the first drafts and final drafts written in the networked classroom were of higher quality than those written in a standard classroom, but that the improvement between drafts was marginally higher in the standard classroom.

Access

An important difference among our writing students is the degree to which they have access to emerging technologies. If we believe that word processing, e-mail, or the Web are in any way useful to writers, then our students' equitable access to computers becomes an important issue. In my first-year writing class in spring 1997, a few students had their own enormously powerful computer workstations in their dormitory rooms; several had their own modest Macs or IBM clones; but more than half had to borrow computer time from roommates or friends or seek out the very few public access terminals that the university provides. The students with the expensive computers produced papers with Web research and graphics downloaded from the Web. Some students without their own computers submitted drafts written in ink. I have learned not to require "typewritten" drafts, because there are, of course, no typewriters to be found. "Typed" today means composed on, or typed into, a computer and printed out on a laser printer. I have worked with the faculty at a local community college, where students have essentially no access to computers, at home or at the college. However, at the expensive private colleges in our area, students have practically unlimited access to computers. Access here is a function of wealth: not gender, not race, but wealth. Certainly these are overlapping categories: in America you are more likely to be poor if you are a person of color; you are most likely to be poor, and your children as well, if you are a single mother. Yet women at Smith College, just ten miles west of us, have more access to technology than do most men at the University of Massachusetts. As Americans, we are reluctant to admit that we are a nation divided by wealth and social class. But we are, and this wealth gap produces a technology gap, just as it produces a health care gap, or an access-to-legal-services gap, or a gap in access to all goods and services that can be bought and paid for.

Technology has made this wealth gap, always present in our writing classes, more dramatically visible. When I began teaching, I would always bring in extra pencils and paper, so that a student who did not have access to the then current writing technology would not be at a disadvantage in my class. It was my way of leveling the playing field. Because pencil and paper were cheap, my tactic did not cost me a great deal. Today, an up-to-date PC and printer cost $1,500 at the least. Web and e-mail access are additional costs, as are backup hardware, surge suppressors, software, maintenance, and depreciation. In a recent article in *Scientific American,* W. Wayt Gibbs estimates that it costs a corporation $13,000 per year to own a PC. It is hard to imagine that it costs an institution, or an individual, substantially less.

So how can I today level the playing field for my students? A typical answer in our profession is "By creating more public access terminals" (e.g., Palmquist et al., 191). To this, I respond by drawing a distinction between what I will call "home access" and "institutional access." Home access is when you have your computer at "home," perhaps a home office or a dormitory room. On this computer is your software, with your settings. The Web browser has your bookmarks, the word processor has your screen and page settings, and the cursor travels at a speed that you have chosen. On your computer's hard drive are your files: course notes, earlier papers written for this and other courses. On your e-mail program is your personal address list. Your CD collection is nearby, your coffeemaker at hand. You have constructed a work environment that is productive for you.

Institutional access, on the other hand, is traveling across campus to a computer, bringing with you your floppy disk with your files. Maybe it is February, and, in New England, after 4:30 p.m. it is dark. Has the trip been dangerous? Is the campus safe? Once you are at the lab, perhaps you have to wait for a computer, or perhaps not: this depends upon the hour and the academic calendar. If this is the week when papers are due in all courses, you will certainly have to wait. A sign on the wall reads "User time one hour. Be considerate!" Another sign reads "No Food or Drink in This Lab!" When you log on to the institution's terminal, you work with the institution's programs set in the way that the institution has determined. Perhaps in this lab the word processor's grammar-checker is on. If this disturbs you, you have to sort through "options" and "customize" menus to find out how to turn the program off. I'm painting a worst case scenario here, but it is not an unusual scenario. Some labs do allow food, some even allow or provide music. But the labs are still labs, not "home." And this is a great difference. Students with home access have a substantial advantage over students with institutional access.

What makes this access problem even more pressing for us than it may appear is that the wealth gap in America is increasing, and has been doing so for the past twenty years. This is a seemingly unstoppable trend: the rich get richer, the poor poorer. This topic does not get much press, despite the fact that a given issue of practically any national newspaper will contain articles about the "booming economy" and the "plight of the poor in America," often found in unintentionally ironic juxtaposition. A typical AP piece in our local newspaper, the *Daily Hampshire Gazette,* of May 12, 1998, begins, "Some 62,000 Massachusetts children younger than 12 go hungry during the year, despite the booming economy, according to the Physician Task Force on Child Hunger in Massachusetts" (10). A memorable issue of the Boston Sunday *Globe* of October 19, 1997, juxtaposed on its front page lead articles with these headlines: "Outgoing NU head tops in '96 Pay; Financial package for Curry near $1m," and "Rise seen in young homeless; Former wards of state swell ranks in shelters." The best book on the history, development, and causes of the American wealth gap is Paul Krugman's *Peddling Prosperity: Economic Sense and Nonsense in the Age of Diminished Expectations.* In the book he offers us this picture of what has been happening:

> Imagine two villages, each composed of one hundred families representing the percentiles of the family income distribution in a given year—in particular, a 1977 village and a 1989 village. According to CBO numbers, the total income of the 1989 village is about 10 percent higher than that of the 1977 village; but it is not true that the whole distribution is shifted up by 10 percent. Instead, the richest family in the 1989 village has twice the income of its counterpart in the 1977 village, while the bottom forty 1989 families actually have lower incomes than their 1977 counterparts. (138)

I wish that our field had written more on the question of access, but it has not. The best piece on the topic of access to computers is an early one, C. Paul Olson's chapter, "Who Computes?" in David Livingstone and colleagues' 1987 anthology, *Critical Pedagogy and Cultural Power.* In his chapter Olson considers the likely effect of computers on schooling, and argues that information technologies are likely to increase the wealth and power gap between rich and poor. In a chapter in the Hawisher and Selfe 1991 anthology titled *Evolving Perspectives on Computers and Composition Studies,* Mary Louise Gomez has argued for what she terms "equitable teaching" (320) with computers. She notes that even where there is sufficient software and hardware, "access and instruction are varied according to students' race, social class, and gender" (322). Other writers and researchers in our field either avoid this issue or give it a quick side glance and proceed. As I have said elsewhere, if as writing teachers we believe that writers are in any sense advantaged by technology, then access is the issue that drives all others before it.

Envoi

If you are a writing teacher, or a writing-teacher-in-training, you need to know the medium that most of your writing students will be working with. To the extent that these writers have access to technology, they will be using it. They will need, therefore, your best advice on moving between screen text and paper text as they compose and revise. If you are considering the use of e-mail or an online discussion as part of your course, or if you have students who will, whether you want them to or not, do their research on the Web, then you need to know about these scenes for writing. If you will be teaching in a computer-equipped classroom, then you need to think through your goals for your students' learning and consider the ways in which the available technology may help you and your students achieve these goals. Because your students are individuals, with different histories of experience, they will connect with the technology in different ways. To help them in their learning, you will need to know as much as you can about their access to, and attitudes toward, the technology that you will be asking them to use. Many of us early in our semesters have our students write their autobiographies as writers. In this way we hope to learn as much as we can about our students as writers, and we hope to help our students see themselves as writers. It is time now to add to this autobiography a new dimension: a question about the writing technologies your students use and their experience with, and attitudes toward, these technologies. In this way we will learn important information about our student writers, and we will help them become, as we are ourselves just now beginning to become, reflective and critical users of emerging technologies.

Bibliography

Bernhardt, Stephen A. "The Shape of Text to Come: The Texture of Print on Screens." *College Composition and Communication* 44 (1993): 151–75.

Birkirts, Sven. *The Gutenberg Elegies: The Fate of Reading in an Electronic Age.* New York: Ballantine, 1994.

Braine, George. "Beyond Word Processing: Networked Computers in ESL Writing Classes." *Computers and Composition* 14 (1997): 45–58.

Burbules, Nicholas C. "Rhetorics of the Web: Hyperreading and Critical Literacy." Snyder 102–22.

Carbone, Nick, and Eric Crump. *English Online.* Boston: Houghton Mifflin, 1997.

Colomb, Gregory G., and Joyce A. Simutis. "Visible Conversation and Academic Inquiry: CMC in a Culturally Diverse Classroom." Herring 201–22.

Daiute, Colette A. "Physical and Cognitive Factors in Revising: Insights from Studies with Computers." *Research in the Teaching of English* 20 (1986): 141–59.

Delany, Paul, and George P. Landow. *Hypermedia and Literary Studies.* Cambridge, MA: MIT P, 1990.

Delpit, Lisa. *Other People's Children.* New York: New Press, 1995.

Dobrin, David. "Style Analyzers Once More." *Computers and Composition* 3.3 (1986): 22–32.

Dowling, Carolyn. "Word Processing and the Ongoing Difficulty of Writing." *Computers and Composition* 11 (1994): 227–35.

Edwards, Paul N. "The Army and the Microworld: Computers and the Politics of Gender Identity." *Signs* 16.1 (1990): 102–27.

Faigley, Lester. *Fragments of Rationality.* Pittsburgh: U of Pittsburgh P, 1992.

———. "Subverting the Electronic Workbook: Teaching Writing Using Networked Computers." *The Writing Teacher as Researcher: Essays in the Theory and Practice of Class-based Research.* Ed. Donald A. Daiker and Max Morenberg. Portsmouth, NH: Boynton/Cook, 1990. 290–311.

Feenberg, Andrew. "The Written World: On the Theory and Practice of Computer Conferencing." *Mindweave.* Ed. Robin Mason and Anthony Kaye, Oxford: Pergamon, 1989. 22–39.

Gerrard, Lisa. "Computers and Basic Writers." Hawisher and Selfe, *Critical Perspectives* 94–108.

Gibbs, W. Wayt. "Taking Computers to Task." *Scientific American* 276.2 (1997): 82–89.

Gilyard, Keith. *Voices of the Self: A Study of Language Competence.* Detroit: Wayne State UP, 1991.

Gomez, Mary Louise. "The Equitable Teaching of Composition with Computers: A Case for Change." Hawisher and Selfe, *Evolving Perspectives* 318–35.

Haas, Christina. "How the Writing Medium Shapes the Writing Process: Effects of Word Processing on Planning." *Research in the Teaching of English* 23 (1989): 181–207.

———. "'Seeing It on the Screen Isn't Really Seeing It': Computer Writers' Reading Problems." Hawisher and Selfe, *Critical Perspectives* 16–29.

Hacker, Diana. *Research and Documentation in the Electronic Age.* Boston: St. Martin's P, 1998.

Hawisher, Gail E., Paul LeBlanc, Charles Moran, and Cynthia L. Selfe. *Computers and the Teaching of Writing in American Higher Education, 1979–1994: A History.* Norwood, NJ: Ablex, 1996.

Hawisher, Gail E., and Charles Moran. "Responding to Writing On-Line." *Writing to Learn: Strategies for Assigning and Responding to Writing Across the Disciplines.* Ed. Mary Deane Sorcinelli and Peter Elbow. San Francisco: Jossey-Bass, 1997. 115–26.

Hawisher, Gail E., and Cynthia L. Selfe, eds. *Critical Perspectives on Computers and Composition Instruction.* New York: Teachers College P, 1989.

———. *Evolving Perspectives on Computers and Composition Studies: Questions for the 1990's.* Urbana, IL: NCTE, 1991.

Hawisher, Gail E., and Patricia Sullivan. "Women on the Networks: Searching for E-Spaces of Their Own." *Feminism and Composition Studies.* Ed. Susan C. Jarratt and Lynn Worsham. New York: MLA, 1998. 172–97.

Heath, Shirley Brice. *Ways with Words: Language, Life, and Work in Communities and Classrooms.* New York: Cambridge UP, 1983.

Herring, Susan C. *Computer-mediated Communication: Linguistic, Social, and Cross-cultural Perspectives.* Amsterdam: Benjamins, 1996.

Jannot, Mark. "Future Ink." *Discover* 19.9 (1998): 44.

Jessup, Emily. "Feminism and Computers in Composition Instruction." Hawisher and Selfe, *Evolving Perspectives* 336–55.

Joyce, Michael. *Of Two Minds: Hypertext, Pedagogy, and Poetics.* Ann Arbor: U of Michigan P, 1995.

Kiefer, Kathleen E., and Charles R. Smith. "Textual Analysis with Computers: Tests of Bell Laboratories' Computer Software." *Research in the Teaching of English* 17 (1983): 201–14.

Klem, Elizabeth, and Charles Moran. "Computers and Instructional Strategies in the Teaching of Writing." Hawisher and Selfe, *Evolving Perspectives,* 132–49.

Knobel, Michele, et al. "The Wired World of Second-Language Education." Snyder 20–50.

Krugman, Paul. *Peddling Prosperity: Economic Sense and Nonsense in the Age of Diminished Expectations.* New York: W.W. Norton, 1994.

Moran, Charles, and Gail E. Hawisher. "The Rhetorics and Languages of Electronic Mail." Snyder 80–101.

Olson, C. Paul. "Who Computes?" *Critical Pedagogy and Cultural Power.* Ed. David W. Livingstone, et al. South Hadley, MA: Bergin and Garvey, 1987. 179–204.

Oppenheimer, Todd. "The Computer Delusion." *The Atlantic Monthly* 280.1 (1997): 45–62.

Palmquist, Mike, et al. *Transitions: Teaching Writing in Computer-supported and Traditional Classrooms.* Greenwich, CT: Ablex, 1998.

Perry, Ruth, and Lisa Greber. "Women and Computers: An Introduction." *Signs* 16.1 (1990): 74–101.

Redd, Teresa M., and Victoria W. Massey. "Race on the Superhighway: How E-mail Affects African American Student Writers." *Journal of Advanced Composition* 17.2 (1997): 245–66.

Romano, Susan. "The Egalitarianism Narrative: Whose Story? Which Yardstick?" *Computers and Composition* 10.3 (1993): 5–28.

Ruhleder, Karen. "'Pulling Down' Books vs. 'Pulling Up' Files: Textual Databanks and the Changing Culture of Classical Scholarship." The Cultures Star 181–195.

Selfe, Cynthia L., and Paul R. Meyer. "Testing Claims for On-Line Conferences." *Written Communication* 8.2 (1991): 163–92.

Selfe, Cynthia L., and Richard J. Selfe, Jr. "The Politics of the Interface." *College Composition and Communication* 45 (1994): 480–504.

Snyder, Ilana, ed. *Page to Screen: Taking Literacy into the Electronic Era.* Sydney: Allen and Unwin, 1997.

Sorcinelli, Mary Deane, and Peter Elbow, eds. *Writing to Learn: Strategies for Assigning and Responding to Writing Across the Disciplines.* San Francisco: Jossey-Bass, 1997.

Spears, Russell, and Martin Lea. "Social Influence and the Influence of the Social in Computer-mediated Communication." *Contexts of Computer-mediated Communication.* Ed. Martin Lea. New York: Harvester/Wheatsheaf, 1992. 30–65.

Sproull, Lee, and Sara Kiesler. *Connections: New Ways of Working in the Networked Organization.* Cambridge, MA: MIT P, 1991.

Stan, Susan, and Terence G. Collins. "Basic Writing: Curricular Interactions with the New Technology." *Journal of Basic Writing* 17.1 (1998): 18–41.

Star, Susan Leigh, ed. *The Cultures of Computing.* Oxford: Blackwell, 1995.

Sudol, Ronald A. "Applied Word Processing: Notes on Authority, Responsibility, and Revision in a Workshop Model." *College Composition and Communication* 36 (1985): 331–35.

Sullivan, Patricia, and Jennie Dauterman, eds. *Electronic Literacies in the Workplace: Technologies of Writing.* Urbana, IL: NCTE, 1996.

Taylor, Todd. "The Persistence of Difference in Networked Classrooms: Non-Negotiable Difference and the African American Student Body." *Computers and Composition* 14 (1997): 169–78.

Turkle, Sherry, and Seymour Papert. "Epistemological Pluralism: Styles and Voices within the Computer Culture." *Signs* 16.1 (1990): 128–57.

Weiser, Mark. "The Computer for the 21st Century." *Scientific American* 265.3 (1991): 94–104.

POSTINGS ON A GENRE OF E-MAIL

Michael Spooner and Kathleen Yancey

[*College Composition and Communication* 47 (May 1996): 252–78.]

Kathleen Blake Yancey is the R. Roy Pearce Professor of Professional Communication at Clemson University, and Michael Spooner is director of the Utah State University Press. These coauthors have written other unconventional articles together, published in print and/or online, addressing some of the same issues they raise in "Postings"—issues of textuality, technology, and collaboration. Some of their recent work is published under the joint pseudonym Myka Vielstimmig in the following books: *Passions, Pedagogies and 21st Century Technology* (1999), *The Subject is Reading* (2000), and *New Words New Worlds* (2001). Kathleen Yancey is well known for her work in writing assessment, and Michael Spooner is best known as an editor and publisher of books in composition studies.

Except for the use of word-processing software, perhaps the most pervasive and visible way that technology is integrated into writing courses is through the use of e-mail. Students and teachers use e-mail for informal communications, to exchange responses about work in progress, to deliver written assignments, and for a variety of other activities. In this innovative and provocative article, Spooner and Yancey present a dialogic exploration of e-mail as an academic genre, broadly conceived. They present a wide-ranging discussion of the various potential uses of e-mail (and by extension, technology) for teaching and for scholarly work.

> Kathleen, How does this grab
you for the opening? <mspooner>

I was talking with a novelist recently about various kinds of writing—nothing special, just happy-hour talk—and I found my earnest self assuring him that, oh yes, academic writing nowadays will tolerate a number of different styles and voices. (I should know, right? I'm in academic publishing.) He choked; he slapped my arm; he laughed out loud. I don't remember if he spit his drink back in the glass. Silly me, I was serious. And, among other things, I was thinking about this essay/ dialogue, in which we're turning dis- course conventions of the net—often a rather casual medium—to some fairly stuffy academic purposes.

Interesting that you call it an essay/dialogue (nice slide, that one). But many readers will expect a "real" essay here—or, betterworse, an academic essay. And we know what that means: a single voice, a single point (to which all the others are handmaidens), a coherence that's hierarchically anchored.

We couldn't say this in one voice. We—Griffin, Sabine, and Georgia notwithstanding—aren't one; we don't have identical points of view. This could have been an epistolary novel, were we novelists; it could have been a Platonic dialogue, except that most of Plato is single-minded essay in dialogic dress. This text takes the form of dialogue and is a dialogue.

Not just our own two voices here, either. Others interrupt us with commentary, obiter dicta, humor. All writers hear voices, but here we've made the convention/al choice to amplify those voices that in- form us (or contradict us). It's different from essay, article, paper, di- alogue, because this convention allows more juxtaposition with less predication. On the other hand, it's very like discourse on the net, but more coherent, more pre/pared. This has been done before, even in the academic world. It reminds one of Winston Weathers's "Gram- mar B" discussions (1980), though we're not being as artistic as the authors he has in mind. But there is something about e-mail that brings this out, and I'm predicting it will be commonplace within a very short time.

It's too much to claim that it's Bakhtin uncovered, but that's its tenor. E-mail seems to make this aspect of language more obvious. The point is that reading this piece is in some way like e-mailing, feeling the staccato effect of jumbled messages, the sense of the incoherent ready to envelop you, the quick as well as the sustained. Voices always populate; the transmission of them on e-mail is just more obvious—flagrant, almost—celebratory.

To use the tropes and gestures of the net seemed an obvious de- cision in an article about the discourse of the net. Natural, too, be- cause we've composed it entirely from e-mail exchanges. (In fact, I don't remember the last time I actually saw you: 1993?) Then there's the fact that we don't agree about the topic.

Our disagreement makes the blender- voice of many coauthored pieces virtually ;-) impossible for this one. Besides, the disagreement is part of the content. It's important to show that, while we do work toward each other, we finish feeling that there is still room for two separate soapboxes at the end. At least two.

I don't think we have an argument with each other so much, even though we do have more than a single point of view. But we write in different voices, and this is a problem if one insists on proper genres. Can't we just call it a text?

What is the difference between an article and an essay? A dialogue and a paper? Between hard copy and e-mail? Be- tween what we are submitting and what certain readers ex- pect? Those questions all center on genre—a central thread woven here. The essay genre becomes a place where genre it- self is the topic of inquiry, even of dispute.

*One thing we do agree about is that e-mail offers new ways of
representing intellectual life. This is one way.*

> :) This post has been smiley-captioned for the irony-impaired. :)
<skeevers>

The Digitized Word

E-mail is a floating signifier of the worst sort—whether it's called E-discourse,
or VAX conferences, or whatever. So the first task is to narrow the focus. Let's
look at these few dimensions.

- E-mail simple. Much like writing a letter, it is signalled by greetings, emoticons, closings, and other conventions; sometimes the author composes
  online, sometimes uploads a prepared text; author and topic are not unique,
  but audience is (as in letters). In its affective dimension, it feels like a hybrid
  form, combining elements one would expect in letters, on the phone, or in
  face-to-face conversation.
- E-mail on "lists"—electronic discussion groups. These groups have developed a new lexicon to cover unique rhetorical or technical functions online
  (e.g., flame wars, FTPs, lurkers, emoticons). Within the lists that I know,
  there is an evident territoriality (we who use the list, those who don't—be-
  nighted souls), but also an effort to democratize interaction. Some explicit
  conventions of interaction ("netiquettes") are established, others are in
  process, others implicit.
- E-mail in the classroom. Cooper and Selfe (1991) argue that democracy is
  closer in the computerized classroom. I wonder. I think a number of the
  features that seem to define lists do not obtain in the classroom—mostly
  authorial authority. But it does offer another kind of interaction, a chance to
  write differently, a different *opportunity* to learn.
- E-mail as resource. This is the networking function that Moran (1992) mentions—the thinking together that creates "a corporate, collaborative, collective 'self' that is more social and therefore more knowledgeable than the old."
- E-mail as mode of collaboration. As we write together/to(each)other,the author and audience elide; how does one represent that—in a single voice? in
  multiple voices? in CAPS? in multiple typefaces?

*It's easier to see these as discrete categories in theory than in
practice. For example, we've both taught students in at least the first
four of these five dimensions, overlapping freely. In many classrooms, they use the fifth one, too.*

*It is also worth pointing out that merely *composing* on a computer does *not* make your list here. It is clearly electronic writing,
but these days it has been absorbed into the normal. Not so long
ago, using a computer at all to teach writing was considered so
novel that many teachers bought books to help them do it (e.g., Rodrigues and Rodrigues, 1986). Now, many (I'd guess *most*) writing
teachers and students compose with computers routinely. And, while
electronic writing in the classroom offers some unique opportunities
that progressive teachers are exploring, it hasn't *required* a shift
in any single teacher's pedagogical
values: while some classes are models
of social constructivism, others are
still cranking out those five-paragraph
themes. That is, the machine will serve
the most progressive and the most traditional practice with equal indifference.*

On both counts, agreed. The second,
first: the fact that a pedagogy seems innovative or uses new technology does not
prevent it from simply reproducing the
prior paradigm. Aviva Freedman and
Peter Medway (1994) make this point
when talking about journals, which they see, all claims notwithstanding, not as a new genre, but as another and unacknowledged kind of test—a replication of the same game:

Although the writer's focus was now claimed to be solely on thinking about the topic, the rhetorical demands had not disappeared; they had simply taken a new form. Journals were, in our experience, still judged as *writing* and not just for the assistance they provided to the students' learning. The generic criteria were not made explicit, but, as Barnes and his colleagues found, clever students knew they were there. (18)

As to the first point about classroom e-mail practice *incorporating* many of the features articulated in the list above, again, agreed. But classroom e-mail is different in kind. Janet Eldred and Ron Fortune (1992) use classroom policy as the lens allowing us to see e-mail as its own type. Consider the case of the e-mail listserv group: subscribers presumably elect to subscribe, and there's no rule or convention or folkway that says they *must* participate. They may choose the Bartleby route, preferring not: they can lurk. But if an e-mail "discussion" group is a requirement of the course, lurking is not an option; it's forbidden.

The point? Classroom e-mail has a different set of conventions than other e-mails; precisely because it takes place in a different context, it inscribes a different ideology.

Vignette 1

They're mighty white, I think, as I wander into the IBM classroom. There are 18 of them, methods students and prospective teachers, and they're mighty female, too. On a second take, I see: they are all white, all women, and all anxious as they pose at keyboards, studiously avoiding them, carefully *not* touching them, collectively praying that our meeting in *this* classroom is a function of computer error. Computer error, after all, can be fixed.

Several tasks we have, I say. Write to Purdue's Online Writing Lab and secure some handouts that will help you. You are in groups, I say; here are the IDs. Read the Ednet discussions on grading, I tell them, as I hand out 13 pages of listserv discussions on grading.

Mimi says we shouldn't have to do this; we don't have any *real* students so we can't develop a grading philosophy *now*. Angie writes me an e-mail begging me to stop this exercise; it's too frustrating, and they already have too much to do.

They write, they cc to me. One group decides to number their posts to each other, in order to get a sense of chronology. They all greet each other as in a letter, and they all close: "See ya's!" and "Later's" predictably end the screen. They reassure each other that everyone is frustrated; they respond to each other's points, with varying detail. They share news. Kim writes, addressing me more as a friend than a teacher, remarking on the orange juice I might be drinking as I read her post. Through the opaque window of e-mail, she sees teacher as person. We begin to see each other a little differently, a little more fully. If the medium is the message, then affect is the medium.

Two weeks later a set of papers comes in. Sam's paper is among the best, and, to be honest, I'm a bit surprised at the quality of her work. Not that I thought she was incompetent, but she's the sort of student who's easy to overlook: compliant, not terribly vocal, older than the others—a "returning student." (And I admit: I'm troubled when she tells me, early on, that teaching will be *convenient,* easily slotted among motherhood, wifehood, the PTA, and Sunday school teaching.) More to the point perhaps, she's new to computers.

Sitting at the computer the first day of class was more stress and agony than I had imagined. I had never used a computer before, and now I was expected to write with one. When our class did a SneakerNet as an opening exercise, I did not know how to scroll the screen and there wasn't time to ask for help . . . .

Sam chooses to take her midterm on computer, earns the highest A in the class. During our 14-day e-mail cycle, she posts among the highest number of messages (ten of them) in the class and writes on various topics—including appropriate uses for technology in the classroom. After the e-mail cycle is over, she continues to post. Always, she is aware of how the computer is changing her world, changing her.

Hi, I saw something interesting in the Observer today. There was an article on computer-user language and do you know what "snail-mail" is? It refers to slower mail or any mail that is not e-mail! That meant something to me today but one week ago I wouldn't have understood that description.

Sam uses the occasion of composing her portfolio to look back— "Putting together the portfolio was actually a review of the course"—and to anticipate what she will do next—take more coursework in computer technology, with specific application to teaching and to using writing with the computer.

At the end of the term, I attempt to distribute the collections I have maintained, in my closet of an office, to trashcans and bookshelves and file cabinets, as students drop by to collect their portfolios. Sam arrives; we talk. She regrets that her e-mail has been cancelled. Oh, yes, they do that fast, I say, once the term is over. I can co-sign for you if you'd like to have another account, I say. Well, maybe next fall, she says. See you soon, we say.

Thirty minutes later, she's back, asking me to co-sign. Welcome to the net. ;)

Virtually Yours

The emotional boundaries of our encounter seemed to have been much expanded by the e-mail that preceded it.   – John Seabrook

If you have been in love, if your lover could write, you know what I mean: it appears every day. It's transactive—not plain exposition, not pure narrative. It's a letter, but then, not the sort of letter you get from the bank or university. It's more like conversation. It's not conversation: it's one-way, and it's written. And it's written in the knowledge that days may pass between the writing and the reading—that in fact (though heaven forbid) it may be lost before it reaches you. As you read it, it speaks in the familiar voice of news, disappointments, and desires. It's affectionate—full of affect. Sometimes it's telegraphic, sometimes oblique, sometimes it includes a sort of lover's code: silly abbreviations <imho> <rotfl>, smiley faces :), Xs and Os.

> loved your smiley run over by a truck: ..-_   <lffunkhouser>

I want to argue that what e-mail writers are doing on the net does not in essence or in genre differ from what writers do off line. In some cases, it looks like a business letter. Sometimes it's a bulletin, sometimes a broadside, sometimes a joke, a memo, a grafitto, a book. In many one-to-one postings, e-mail shows all the features of the lovers' correspondence you used to read (or did you write it?) every day.

So e-mail is like a letter, a personal letter that allows both cognition and affect: is that it?

Often, yes. But often otherwise. I send and receive formal letters (a different genre, by most accounts) via e-mail, too. Also announcements, assignments, essays, one-liners, poems, and dirty jokes. Just like paper and ink, this technology allows a wide range of genres. *That's* the point.

So it's not a genre, you say. Well. There are several ways to look at this question: we could try older, more literary definitions of genre, grounded in form; we could include more recent rhetorically based definitions, more oriented to the social dimension; and we could speak from the vantage point of literary theory so dominated by interest in the ideological workings of genre.

Or we could simply listen in on the thing itself:

>I found myself writing to a friend last night . . . and thinking how there *is* a difference between writing and this spontaneous posting that we do.   <mullanne>

>. . . our conversations seem much more like oral conversation than like written correspondence.   <newmann>

>. . . there is an element of spontaneity. And the essentials of conversation (as opposed to letter-writing) are there: a topic focus, a variety of voices, and statement-response structure. But unlike conversation, each of us can 1)edit and 2) speak without interruption.   <csjhs>

>. . . we all adopt a light, informal tone (and some real wit too) that is too often missing from letters typed on university letterhead.   <harrism>

>If writing on the net is a hybrid, what shall we call it? Well, it seems . . . to be kinda in between expressive writing . . . and transactional. . . . Maybe we could call it expractional? Or transpressive? Then, again, it gets downright poetic at times.   <ccrmitta>

These writers or speakers—or what shall we call them?—seem to share common perceptions about e-mail, about its friendliness, about its use for play as well as for thinking, about its novelty, about its inability to be categorized into any of the conventionalized schemes. I think this last point may serve as a place to start.

I don't seriously disagree with the consensus expressed by these folks, but there's something in it that troubles me: I wonder if we've truly come far enough in theorizing the electronic conference (whether one-on-one or in a group) to decide what these folks are deciding.

The consensus is not limited to this group, of course; it's repeated throughout the literature on computers and composition. And the consensus claims a great deal more than the comments above reveal. For example, we're told that the net is inherently non-hierarchical, "intrinsically communal," and that it is challenging the "hegemony of the teacher" (respectively: Zamierowski; Barker and Kemp; Cooper and Selfe). There's a fervor about this body of opinion.

> The Internet's glorious egalitarianism is one of its chief attractions for me.   <csjhs>

But these community-enhancing qualities of the net seem more *assumed* in the work on computers and composition than demonstrated, and I'm not sure we have examined our assumptions. Consider these few comments, selected from a single discussion thread on a single list (Cybermind).

> . . . however much I may like these identity-erasing facilities of the Net, my actual feelings of community are predicated on, and arise only with the revelation of, identities.   <malgosia>

> . . . my virtual communities are very dependent on gender and sexualities.   <lysana>

> Not everybody came here to form a community (maybe no one did; it wasn't on the agenda), and not everybody wants one.   <marius>

In Hawisher and LeBlanc's _Re-Imagining Computers and Composition: Teaching and Research in the Virtual Age_ (1992), Gail Hawisher acknowledges that ". . . as yet there are only a few studies of the electronic conference that have been conducted within composition studies" (84). She alludes to research in fields like distance education and information science, and she suggests that it supports the current heady consensus about computers in composition. In other publications, Hawisher has been careful not to overlook potential misuses of technology in pedagogy (e.g., 1991), and I don't necessarily doubt her here. There is surely research underway now specifically on issues in computers and composition, but in the meantime, should we rely on inference and extrapolation from other fields to give us the grounds for declaring utopia-at-hand in *writing*?

But is this *writing*?

Isn't it?

In the same collection, Paul Taylor effectively summarizes the consensus when he says "computer conferencing is evolving into a new genre, a new form of communication that has not been possible before now" (145). Not to single out Taylor, but, when he (as momentary speaker for all this enthusiasm) applies Carolyn Miller's (1984) criteria for genre identification to computer conferencing, immediately he has to fudge.

> First, the associated texts must exhibit similarity in form. Although computer-based messages are not yet exceptionally uniform, they do display several common features. . . . Second, Miller states that the genre must be based on all the rhetorical elements in recurring situations. Do computer conferences arise from a genuine exigence relative to a specific audience? Only if we begin to narrow the terms somewhat—if we begin to see computer conferencing not as a single genre, but as a collection of related genres. (145)

A genre of genres? Wishful thinking. And I wish he'd bluffed—held out for a vision of one E- Genre. After all, if we equivocate on any of Miller's criteria, the whole case caves in. And he has to equivocate on two.

The facts are, on the one hand, that computer-based messages (whether in conference or not) come in a *very* wide variety of forms

and, on the other hand, that they have common features with a zil-
lion forms of *non*-computer-based writing: e.g., the memo, the report, the bulletin, the note, the list, the valentine. One could argue
that the *only* distinctive feature of online writing is that it is transmitted via computer. And further, if we see computer conferencing
"not as a single genre, but as a collection of genres," we're tripped
again. Why gather them generically here? Why not let them individually stand where they were—with the memo, the report, the bulletin,
and the others—where they have both formal and rhetorical commonality? Just because we send them over the net? It seems to boil
down to that.

I can't see why the technology associated with a text is enough
to warrant the claim of a distinctive genre. To my mind, we have to
think of genres of writing as logically larger than the technologies
through which we convey them.

I agree that today's technology shows much of the wonder and
potential that these writers see in it. Perhaps the most careful, thorough exploration of this potential that I have read to date is in
Richard Lanham's _The Electronic Word_ (1993)—a portion of
which I actually received via e-mail from the publisher. This is the
hopeful claim of the rhetorician that the computer is intrinsically a
rhetorical device, and that through digitization it will inevitably democratize education in the liberal arts. Again, I don't much disagree
about the computer's potential here—until we start using words like
"intrinsic." Because it is quite clear that the same technology that
stirs hopes like Lanham's for a postmodern avatar of the Rhetorical
Paideia even now serves pedagogies of drill-and-skill, of Great
Books, and other rigid traditional paradigms. The same technology.

My point is simply this: we are seeing a transition in the technology that delivers our written genres, not an innovation in genres
themselves. And, in our enthusiasm for the (mere) technology, we
are mistaking transition for innovation.

Vignette 2

> These days nothing stays buried. . . .
> Particularly not on a computer.
> – Gail Colins

"Do you mind if we take notes on the computer?" asks Tara (a pseudonym). "It's easier for us, but I know the clattering distracts some
teachers."

These students are computer-literate—23 seniors in the Tech
Writing program. They are also white, most of them are women, middle-class, and they're from predominantly religious, politically conservative, semi-rural communities in the West. All right: they're
Mormon kids.

The computers are high-grade for the times (and for anywhere in
the college of humanities): twenty workstations outfitted with network software and several industry-standard programs. There's e-
mail with an uplink to Internet, and, oh yes, a couple of games. When
I boot up, my machine plays a clip from Pink Floyd. "Hey! Teacher!
Leave them kids alone!"

Like the others, Tara has never used the Internet, and she has
only a general concept of a listserv or newsgroup. But she shrugs.
It's just another network like the classroom LAN or the campus VMS.
After minimal instruction from me, she attacks the subscribe routine
through her workstation; she's an Internet list member within five
minutes.

*I ask the students to comment on the Internet discussions as well
as other matters in their online journals. They are used to the idea—
both writing such things and the process of saving their entries to a
common area on the network. They know how to check back later for
my replies. In one entry, Tara complains about how tedious the listserv of copyeditors can be.*

> I mean, it's interesting to see the comments on [whether
> to use] one space or two after a period, but is it really
> worth 25 postings?

*In another, she reflects on the topic of obscenity on e-mail—some-
one used the F-word in a realtime electronic conference in another
class.*

> Since the letter was sent to the entire class as instructed,
> everyone got the message. Some people were offended,
> others were not. One general argument was that if you
> don't want to read that kind of thing, don't—delete it!
> The other argument was: even if you decide to immedi-
> ately delete it, you have already been offended the in-
> stance [sic] the word hit your eyes.

*In her journal, Tara didn't make any comments about the differ-
ence between online writing and writing to a printed page. Where
she referred to online issues at all, she was concerned not with the
writing, but with matters of propriety—the choices and judgment of
individuals in relation to others—as in the two quotations above.*

*In other words, the technology was transparent to her. And, iron-
ically, this is best illustrated by an amusing twist from the end of the
quarter. Finals were over, students were gone, and I was clearing
the journal directory. There I found a long letter from Tara to one of
her classmates—evidently dropped into my space by mistake. Suddenly, I was a teacher picking up folded notes from the virtual classroom floor, somewhat stunned to see my best student write:*

> Well, I gotta go! Class is over! As you can see I find ways
> to entertain myself in class since I don't get anything
> out of the lectures!

Welcome to the net. ;)

A Virtual Genre

> If e-mail represents the renaissance of prose,
> why is so much of it so awful?
>
> – Philip Elmer-DeWitt

"Conceptual or substantive identity" and "procedural identity" are
key terms that Larson (1982) used in arguing that the research
paper as currently taught in freshman comp isn't a real paper. I
liked the terms, and I thought they might help me think about
genre—as having these kinds of identity.

Several articles composed via e-mail collaboration have been
published by now; how did the authors know how to write them?
How do we know what we're doing here? When I use e-mail in my
class this term, I want the students to write *this way*—but what
is this way? And what conventions should I point out to them
as accepted? Students have enough trouble trying to navigate
through "regular writing," yet if I want to extend the class and
show them how we are working (e.g., in this paper), I have to help
them do this. But *this* is still undefined.

>I just got a beep from you. Let me send this now, and I'll
read you, then finish.   <mspooner>

If you want to argue therefore that *this* is not a genre, that's
fine with me, but it doesn't absolve you of the need to show students how to put such a piece together. There is still a lot to be
learned here about composing.

And the medium allows us to claim what is ours—as it makes
the audience real. The fictionalized audience itself becomes a fiction, and the concept of author becomes
more collective. In other words, the
rhetorical situation is different—not theoretically so much as really, practically.
According to a definition of genre that is
oriented to purpose or to social action,
this should make a difference.

*I'm in accord with you on the need
for a social or purpose-oriented approach to genre. I'll accept Swales's
(1990) claim that "the principal criterial
feature that turns a collection of communicative events into a genre is some
shared set of communicative purposes" (51).*

*However, the mere fact that we can discover the several different
dimensions to electronic writing you described earlier is evidence to
me that we are not in the realm of a single rhetorical situation.
Among the five dimensions you listed are family resemblances, but
they do not represent a coherent set of communicative purposes, let
alone a coherent set of formal conventions. By the logic of the so-
cial/purposive approach to genre, electronic writing is no more one
genre than writing on clay tablets is one genre (cf. Swales on correspondence, p. 53). At best, we have a random clutch of communicative purposes and an enthusiasm for tech novelty.*

According to Swales, a genre is "a class of communicative
events, the members of which share some set of communicative
purposes" (58), and which can vary along three dimensions (at
least): complexity of rhetorical purpose; degree of advanced
preparation or construction; and medium or mode (62). Swales
also talks about pre-genres and multi-genres: the former too persuasive and fundamental to be generic, a place of "life" from
which other genres may emerge; and the latter, the multi-genre, a
larger category including several genres, as in letters vs letters-of-
condolence (58-61).

Could I get back to you by e-mail? I'm not comfortable dealing with you in voice mode.   — Anon.

Bakhtin seems to make the same distinction between pre-
generic and generic communications when he talks about primary and secondary genres: secondary genres "absorb and digest
primary (simple) genres that have taken form in unmediated
speech communication" (946). And as we might expect, he describes
secondary genres as arising "in more complex and comparatively
highly developed and organized cultural communication (primarily written) that is artistic, scientific, sociopolitical, and so on"
(946). But what Bakhtin has done in his formulation is to validate
as genre what Swales calls pre-genre, by classifying *all utter-
ances* as participating in genre, the distinction resting on the
same features later identified by Swales, especially organized
communication.

Others have made contributions to the definition that will help
us. Lloyd Bitzer (1968) discusses rhetorical situations, like genres,

and the role that recurrence plays: "The situations recur and, because we experience situations and the rhetorical responses to them, a form of discourse is not only established but comes to have a power of its own—the tradition itself tends to function as a constraint upon any new response in the form" (13). And, as Vincent Leitch (1991) says, the constraints—the conventions—helping to define genre act "as political instruments insuring order, effecting exclusions, and carrying out programs" (94). Genre is never innocent, he reminds us. Carolyn Miller (1984) makes the same point, but with greater attention to the role of social action in genre. Despite its ideological authority, however, genre is neither completely stable nor fixed. As Catherine Schryer (1993) observes, "Genres come from somewhere and are transforming into something else" (208).

To be able to create discourse that will count as a certain kind of action, one has to be able to produce a text with the features that distinguish it as belonging to a certain genre. One has to know that form to be able to perform. (Fahnestock 1993)

The English novel as developing genre helps illustrate the concept. Its beginnings, most literary historians agree, took place during the seventeenth and eighteenth centuries. According to Walter Allen (1954), this was in part a function of literary history. Elizabethan drama, with both tragedy and comedy, with realistic characters and plots, with audiences of ordinary people, played an unwitting role in preparing for a new genre. History itself, the recorded variety, played another; written accounts of events and people and places, buttressed by diaries and autobiographies—the latter genre also evolving at this time—provided material and context for the novel, as well as a kind of preparation for the acceptance of the realistic as opposed to the fantastic/romantic.

But it was during the nineteenth century that the novel in England flourished. Why? History and the pre-generic "novels" no doubt played their parts, but a critical factor was simply the material conditions of the time, particularly as they affected a possible audience. Given the rise of the middle class in the nineteenth century, the celebration of a middle-class conception of family, the opportunity for leisure and some resources to fund it, the novel easily found a home within the lives of a large group of people. And of course the novel itself was delivered in various forms—through the penny papers and through single editions (which often became different versions of the novel), through the silent reading of an adult, through the performative reading of a mother to spouse and children.

The episodic quality of the Victorian novel resulted, at least in part, from the penny paper distribution schedule. As important, the material conditions of the audience had everything to do with those forms. The point here is that the genre "novel" took more than one form, and the form had everything to do with the means of delivery.

We would say now that this blurred Romantic conceptions of writer and reader. And didn't the audience influence both form and content, in effect pressing the author and publisher to reproduce middle-class ideologies?

As they are today, as well, or why are we writing this?

Yes, in fact, arguably, both author and audience were influenced by merchants, publishers, and schools too.

So how is literary history relevant to our discussion? As a class of utterances, one could say, e-mail is "pregenre"—i.e., in the process of becoming genre. We can see analogies between this process and the process that gave us the novel:

- The material conditions of the late 20th century have enabled a group of generally well-educated, relatively affluent people to communicate in a new medium.
- Many of these people believe that this form of communication is new, is different, and that it enacts new relationships between authors and readers. There is, in other words, an ideology already at work here, and it entails social action.
- E-mail seems currently, however, to function as a primary utterance. The conventions that its advocates cite as defining it seem closer to those "constraining" a phone conversation, which is itself not a genre. And a lack of consensus governing this "netiquette" suggests that it doesn't yet exert the conserving force characteristic of genre. Through recurrence, however, these conventions will become more stabilized, and will in turn define more clearly what is acceptable, what the boundaries will be.
- E-mail does also, however, seem to be challenging what we have taken to be both the role/authority of the author as well as the relationship between author and audience. As Jay David Bolter (1991) suggests,

  The electronic medium now threatens to reverse the attitudes fostered by the [printing] press, by breaking down the barrier between author and reader. . . . Anyone can become an author and send his merest thoughts over one of the networks to hundreds of unwilling readers. His act of "publication" is neither an economic nor a social event. (101)

  If this observation is correct, then the rhetorical situation of e-mail is indeed different— something beyond and apart from other genres. Moreover, as it becomes more stabilized, particularly with reference to rhetorical intent, we should see more clearly the features defining it.

All of which leads me to suggest that e-mail may be a genre-in-the-making.

I'm of two minds about this. In the first place, though Bolter's book, _Writing Space_ (1991), is stunning, sometimes I think he is plain wrong about one thing; the "publication" he mentions is indeed a social event, and it may be an economic one as well (as, obviously, in the case of the many merest advertisements online). I would suggest further that such phenomena as flaming and "cancelling" (censoring) are evidence that the "barrier between reader and author" is still intact, if it ever was. Besides, "Anyone" has always been an author (i.e., anyone with the means— just like today), and has always been considered important or not at the discretion of the reader.

There's yet one more factor. In a recent piece on writing-in-geography as genre, Bill Green and Allison Lee (1994) focus, if implicitly, on the identity a genre requires of its authors. They locate school writing and curriculum as special contexts with special rhetorical situations producing school genres.

According to this formulation, curriculum work, as the provision of appropriate training in subject-disciplinary knowledge, has as part of its effect the projection and production of particular forms of student identity. This production is necessarily tied up with other major identity formations, such as gender, and connected to broader social power dynamics. For us, rhetoric is as much concerned with the formation of identities as the construction of texts. (210)

Another commentator on this scene, speaking of using e-mail in his own classes, also locates the identity issue as central. Russell Hunt (1994) sees e-mail as a device for forging and maintaining social relationships as well as for carrying on an intellectual discussion. The politics of e-mail, then, in the larger context are certainly those of the bourgeoisie, who—like other classes—seek to replicate their own ideology. Yes. But the politics are also those of the classroom, where identity formation is chief among its priorities.

I don't argue with the idea that rhetorical situations project and produce forms of identity—aside from my instinct that, for the sake of our postmodern anguish, we overstate this sort of thing. In any case, this doesn't establish that e-mail is a new rhetorical situation or genre; I believe Hunt could perceive the same identity effects by assigning a pen-pal unit. Exchange would be slower, but that has merely to do with the mechanics of the process. It's un-hip, I know, but I tend to believe that rhetorical situations are *not* defined by the mechanical process through which they travel, so much as by the social purposes of the rhetors. According to your sketch of the English novel, different media (penny papers, single editions) delivered a single genre. In that case, then (and I think in almost all cases), the genre is logically prior to the means of delivery. I don't doubt that new mechanics make new purposes possible (more about that in a minute), but I insist that we're overstating this effect. The purpose that an extant genre serves very rarely disappears at the appearance of a new mechanical device. More likely, the new device is bent to the old rhetorical purpose.

I think that's why most electronic communications are simply reproducing extant genres of writing instead of creating new ones. And for the same reason, I predict that we will see discourse communities online arrange themselves in terms of very familiar hierarchies and conventions. The page, the phone, the monitor is neither the utterance nor the context; it is merely the ground for them.

In fact, I see plenty of evidence on the net that this is true. The material conditions you mention fit here, I believe. One could argue that computer literacy lives within an even more elite socioeconomic hierarchy than does print literacy. But this is often quite forgotten by the users.

>Distributed technology is the antithesis of the totalitarian apparatus, seems to me. Freedom of speech for anybody who owns a modem.   <johnmc>

Leaving merely 90% of Americans disenfranchised. And how many Mexicans? How many Somalis and Burmese? In what may be a watershed article, even Selfe and Selfe, who have often led the optimism in the field of computers and composition, are now sounding a much-needed sobering note: "The rhetoric of technology obscures the fact that [computers] are not necessarily serving democratic ends" (1994).

We need to think of cyberspace as the commodity that it is, manufactured and marketed by today's captains of industry for the benefit of those who can afford it. So much of the "university view" of cyberspace seems naive on this point; we seem almost to believe in magic. As if this virtual reality we love were not constructed hammer-

and-tongs by grunts in computer factories, packaged and sold by slick marketeers. As if Bill Gates got richer than God by magic. Perhaps this is because we in the university usually don't have to pay our way—access is our caste privilege. Perhaps it's because Bill Gates looks like us: he's a baby boomer, and very very smart. But the cold gray truth is that cyberspace and its equipment are created in the real world by the same socioeconomic structures that gave us the railroad, the automobile, and the petroleum industry. It is merely our place in the hierarchy that conceals the hierarchy from us. "Let them use modems," we say, in all earnest charity.

Even within the online world, true democracy is a polite fiction. Zamierowski (1994) argues that power on lists (electronic conferences) is not hierarchical; it gravitates merely toward wit and erudition, he says, as if those were the great equalizers. But aren't these plain old bourgeois values, revealing their source in our larger social structures? Besides, <imho> even this is a weak version of the truth. Perhaps *especially* on academic/professional lists, power gravitates toward prestige—prestige in written dialect and opinion at least (common surrogates for wit and erudition); and where user addresses include institutional identifiers, power gravitates toward prestige institutions. Some users even perceive a hierarchy among different lists and networks:

>Subscription requests are not automatic for this list. Your request has been forwarded to ykfok@ttacs.ttu.edu for approval.
<listproc>

>In my experience, most of the regular post-ers on *interesting* lists are not academics. <artsxnet>

>Anti-AOL rantings routed to temp\trash\bigot\internet.
<lysana>

On less formal lists, power moves toward the most verbal and assertive users--whether they're witty and erudite or not. In other words, when people go online, they do not leave their biases behind. And, circling back, that's also why the "old" genres are being reproduced on the net instead of being replaced with new ones. If electronic communication is pre-generic, this is not because it's still young, but because it's indifferent: it is raw and mutable enough to handle the conflicted array of current genres just fine, thank you. And if you want to try a new one, that's fine, too.

When a new element such as e-mail enters the system that is our profession, it changes every element in that system. (Hawisher and Moran, 1993)

Among other things, postmodernism has concerned itself with the role of context in meaning. The strong position is that context *is* meaning, or that meaning is so context-bound that we cannot ascertain it apart from context. The literal sentence has become, quite literally, a dinosaur. We see the influence of this line of thinking on genre as well. Because genre occurs in context, it too derives meaning from the context, but—just as quickly—it shapes the context. (They are in dialogue.) As Freedman (1993) puts it: "genres themselves form part of the discursive context to which rhetors respond in their writing and, as such, shape and enable the writing; it is in this way that form is generative." (272). I think, then, that in order to declare something a genre, we'd have to describe the context in which it is likely to occur. How fixed is the context? How particularized? How quickly changing?

A Genre of Chaos

> To most users of the Internet, unbridled freedom, even anarchy, are guiding principles.　　　　　　　　　　　　　　　–Peter Lewis

In my second mind, I'm beginning to think that, insofar as e-mail can be said to make new approaches possible, it might offer most advantage to the anarchic. In many ways, the TV with a remote controller is analogous. If we think of the remote controller as keyboard, and the TV hour as text to be created, then the channel-surfing teenager may be the most creative artist yet undiscovered.

> *Armed with a remote control, stocked with a cableful of channels, the home viewer creates montages of unspeakable originality, editing parallel transmissions into an individual blend. This art form is rhythmic, improvisational, and ironic. (Wittig 1994)*

You get the idea. "Surrealism Triumphant," Wittig calls it (90), and it is founded in what is essentially a hermeneutic—or at least an aesthetic—of anarchy. Of course, it is worth noting that the TV artiste is improvising within a narrow range; he or she can only create from the very homogeneous values that TV offers. But at least the principle of random montage is evident.

When we recognize that the computer makes an analogous montaging potential available for the writer, we see some interesting new takes indeed on the scene of writing.

> >Moments in MOOspace where multithread conversations become recombinant and seem to take on a life of their own. Part of one thread responding with amazing aptness to part of another. A kind of gift.　　　　　　　　　　　　　　　<swilbur>

Eventually—perhaps within a decade—electronic writing and publication will be boringly normal. Predictions about what will then be possible abound: multimedia and hypertext figure prominently; information transfer and storage beyond our wildest dreams. Our technology even now can accommodate not only combined media (e.g., the "publications" on CD-ROM), but combined voices, epistemologies, even intelligences, juxtaposed into densely populated canvasses of electronic text. We may be seeing, in other words, a collapse of written and visual and aural genres back into the collage of raw experience. Only this time, it would be a prepared rhetoric of chaos, a genre of chaos, perhaps, designed to exploit more of our native ability to process many channels of information simultaneously.

But even this doesn't represent a raw new frontier of human communication; it only brings our technology closer to a capacity for what we already do daily, unassisted, in spades. What dinner-table parent isn't all too familiar with multi-tasking? What child isn't alive to two worlds at once? (I return to my student Tara, who does fine work in my class while sending notes online to her girlfriend. The sneak.)

The period we are entering . . . will see the ascendance of a new aesthetic animated by the vision of the cultural world as composed of mobile, *interchangeable* fragments— common property—messages constantly in motion, ready to be linked into new constellations. . . . A perfume, a broken muffler, the texture of a boot, two bird calls, and an electronic message will be understood to form an inseparable and organic whole. (Wittig, 95)

One issue, then, in this kind of discourse, is how to manage the multivocality and at the same time create enough coherence that a spectating conversationist can enter the fray, can discern what the fray is. *This* is what we need to teach our students.

Instead of hailing a brand-new genre, or speculating on pre-generic stases, perhaps we should reread your reference to Schryer: written forms have never been seamless wholes—they come from and point to many directions *at once.* And maybe we should acknowledge that in the postmodern age, the reader, not the writer, is the real tyrant: multi-tasking, channel-surfing, capricious and fickle, free to interpret, misread, manipulate, and (horrors) apply. We're all guilty; we start at the end, in the middle, we don't finish, we joyously juxtapose bits of what we read with other readings, other experiences. But the point is that this is our most natural process. Both reader and writer are engaged constantly in making knowledge from a very random world.

As our technology enables us to present multi-tasking in more and more tangible form, maybe we should be predicting not new genres, but the end of genre.

> >Communities in cyberspace are "real"—but it's important to keep in mind that they are only rhetorical; they have no other dimension.   <baldwine>

Last winter someone told me that on e-mail, when we argue in words, we argue. (Decades ago, Scott Momaday said that we are constructed of words.) Words are, apparently, all we have. But we are production editors now, as well as writers, changing fonts and adding borders and lines, managing a rhetoric of the document to energize the text. Through the technology, we can more easily than ever make the multilayered "postmodern" dimension of writing evident.

Which brings us round to the beginning again. The technologies through which this dialogue/text (and I sense we are no closer to an answer, but do we need one?) is composed has made possible (or made convenient—for all but Joe perhaps) the performative stances we're taking in it. It allows us to use unfamiliar conventions in the familiar context of academic publishing, and in so doing it highlights the joints and seams in the process of making meaning through writing.

To call it the end of genre was flippant and extreme, of course (and very Net—they'd love this on Cybermind), and it doesn't address all kinds of cognitive theory about our need for schemata in processing information. Implicit in my argument all along has been that extant genres are functional mental frames, and the rise of e-mail doesn't eliminate the need for them. I see e-mail as merely a kind of tablet with courier attached. As such, it serves only to deliver extant genres more efficiently than we could deliver them before, and hence I think e-mail itself doesn't destabilize current genres of writing.

But I still think e-mailing isn't writing—or not the discursive variety we're used to reading in academe. Our expectations will not the centre hold. This is the start of another kind of e-speech-that-is-writing: montage-like, quick, unpredictable in form and substance and tenor. That unpredictability, that flexibility, is its charm and thread. The linear and hierarchical, the neatly categorized, seen under erasure.

Well, yes. Where I wasn't being flip was in the sense that one can see e-mail as symbolic—I think you see it this way—as a harbinger, and multi-media as what it heralds. In that case, our tablet expands in many directions, and we see possibilities for combining text with graphics, with sound, with motion, in a wonderful stage-managed chaos of virtual communication. We become not only the production editors you mention, but the stars and directors of our own movies, or more likely (heaven help us) our own commercials.

Of course, montage and pastiche are increasingly chic now, partly as a function of a society that celebrates its difference by fragmentation. But it's also partly done in defense—to deconstruct before being deconstructed, partly to alleviate the anxiety of influence. In writing, electronic technology is the ideal medium for this. That is an important point, but it's one I think we don't fully comprehend yet. And it's one that is affecting us even as we write this, in ways we can't yet articulate. In other words, working on e-mail—constructing the messages within a pre-genre that is still being shaped itself—is constructing us, too.

We don't care. We have each other, on the Internet.   —Dave Barry

Works Cited

Allen, Walter. *The English Novel: A Short Critical History*. New York: Dutton, 1954.
<artsxnet>. "Hillbilly in Cyberspace." Cybermind Discussion List [online]. Available e-mail: CYBERMIND <LISTSERV@WORLD.STD.COM>. 6 July 1994.
Bakhtin, Mikhail. "The Problem of Speech Genres." *The Rhetorical Tradition*. Ed. Patricia Bizzell and Bruce Herzberg. Boston: Bedford, 1990. 944–64.
<baldwine>. "Define Cybermind." Cybermind Discussion List [online]. Available e-mail: CYBERMIND <LISTSERV@WORLD.STD.COM>. 6 July 1994.
Barker, Thomas, and Fred Kemp. "A Postmodern Pedagogy for the Writing Classroom." *Computers and Community*. Ed. Carolyn Handa. Portsmouth: Boynton, 1990. 1–27.
Barry, Dave. "Through Internet, Cybermuffin Shares Intimate Computer Secrets." Knight-Ridder Newspapers 6 Feb. 1994.
Bitzer, Lloyd. "The Rhetorical Situation." *Contemporary Rhetoric*. Ed. Douglas Ehninger. Glenview: Scott, 1972. 39–49.
Bolter, Jay David. *Writing Space*. Hillsdale: Erlbaum, 1991.
<ccrmitta>. "Email." Writing Center Discussion List [online]. Available e-mail: WCENTER <LISTPROC@UNICORN.ACS.TTU.EDU>. 1 Nov. 1993.
Colins, Gail. "The Freddy Krueger in Your Computer." *Working Woman* Apr. 1994: 62.
Cooper, Marilyn, and Cynthia Selfe. "Computer Conferences and Learning: Authority, Resistance, and Internally Persuasive Discourse." *College English* 52 (1991): 847–69.
<csjhs>. "Email." Writing Center Discussion List [online]. Available e-mail: WCENTER <LISTPROC@UNICORN.ACS.TTU.EDU>. 8 Nov. 1993.
———. "P\R." Writing Center Discussion List [online]. Available e-mail: WCENTER <LISTPROC@UNICORN.ACS.TTU.EDU>. 8 July 1994.
Eldred, Janet Cary, and Ron Fortune. "Exploring the Implications of Metaphors for Computer Networks and Hypermedia." Hawisher and LeBlanc 58–74.
Elmer-DeWitt, Philip. "Bards of the Internet." *Time* July 1994: 66–67.
Fahnestock, Jeanne. "Genre and Rhetorical Craft." *Research in the Teaching of English* 27 (1993): 265–71.
Freedman, Aviva. "Show and Tell? The Role of Explicit Teaching in the Learning of New Genres." *Research in the Teaching of English* 27 (1993): 222–52.
Freedman, Aviva, and Peter Medway, eds. *Learning and Teaching Genre*. Portsmouth: Boynton, 1994.
Green, Bill, and Allison Lee. "Writing Geography: Literacy, Identity, and Schooling." Freedman and Medway 207–24.
<harrism>. "Email." Writing Center Discussion List [online]. Available e-mail: WCENTER <LISTPROC@UNICORN.ACS.TTU.EDU>. 9 Nov. 1993.
Hawisher, Gail. "Electronic Meeting of the Minds: Research, Electronic Conferences, and Composition Studies." Hawisher and LeBlanc 81–101.
Hawisher, Gail, and Paul LeBlanc. *Re-Imagining Computers and Composition*. Portsmouth: Boynton, 1992.
Hawisher, Gail, and Charles Moran. "Electronic Mail and the Writing Instructor." *College English* 55 (1993): 627–43.
Hawisher, Gail, and Cynthia Selfe. "The Rhetoric of Technology and the Electronic Writing Class." *CCC* 42 (1991): 55–65.

Hunt, Russell. "Speech Genres, Writing Genres, School Genres, and Computer Genres." Freedman and Medway 243–62.

<johnmc>. "Elements of email Distribution." Megabyte University Discussion List [online]. Available e-mail: MBU-L <LISTPROC@UNICORN.ACS.TTU.EDU>. 5 July 1994.

Lanham, Richard. *The Electronic Word: Democracy, Technology, and the Arts.* Chicago: U of Chicago P, 1993.

Larson, Richard. "The 'Research Paper' in the Writing Course: A Non-Form of Writing." *College English* 44 (1982): 811–16.

Leitch, Vincent. "(De)Coding (Generic) Discourse." *Genre* 24 (Spring 91): 83–98.

Lewis, Peter H. "No More Anything Goes: Cyberspace Gets Censors." *New York Times* 29 June 1994: Business-Technology 3–4.

<lffunkhouser>. "Truck-Flattened Smiley." Copyediting Discussion List [online]. Available e-mail: COPYEDITING-L <LISTSERV@CORNELL.EDU>. 12 Feb. 1994.

<listproc>. "Subscribe CCCCC-L Michael S." Email to M. Spooner [online]. Available e-mail: <mspooner@cc.usu.edu>. 22 June 1994.

<lysana>. "Virtual Communities." Cybermind Discussion List [online]. Available e-mail: CYBERMIND <LISTSERV@WORLD.STD.COM>. 6 July 1994.

<malgosia>. "Virtual Communities." Cybermind Discussion List [online]. Available e-mail: CYBERMIND <LISTSERV@WORLD.STD.COM>. 4 July 1994.

<marius>. "Virtual Communities." Cybermind Discussion List [online]. Available e-mail: CYBERMIND <LISTSERV@WORLD.STD.COM>. 5 July 1994.

Miller, Carolyn R. "Genre as a Social Action." *Quarterly Journal of Speech* 70 (1984): 151–67.

Moran, Charles. "Computers and English: What Do We Make of Each Other?" *College English* 54 (1992): 193–98.

<mspooner>. "Early Final Thoughts." E-mail to K. Yancey [online]. Available e-mail: <mspooner@press.usu.edu>. 13 Dec. 1994.

<mullanne>. "Email." Writing Center Discussion List [online]. Available e-mail: WCENTER <LISTPROC@UNICORN.ACS.TTU.EDU>. 5 Nov. 1993.

<newmann>. "Email." Writing Center Discussion List [online]. Available e-mail: WCENTER <LISTPROC@UNICORN.ACS.TTU.EDU>. 29 Oct. 1993.

Rodrigues, Raymond, and Dawn Rodrigues. *Teaching Writing with a Word Processor.* Urbana: NCTE, 1986.

Schryer, Catherine. "Records as Genre." *Written Communication* 10 (1993): 200–34.

Seabrook, John. "E-mail from Bill." *The New Yorker* 10 Jan. 1994: 48–62.

———. "My First Flame." *The New Yorker* 6 June 1994: 70–79.

Selfe, Cynthia, and Richard J. Selfe, Jr. "The Politics of the Interface: Power and Its Exercise in the Electronic Contact Zone." *CCC* 45 (1994): 480–504.

<skeevers>. "Signature." Business Communication Discussion List [online]. Available e-mail: BIZCOM <LISTSERV@EBBS.ENGLISH.VT.EDU>. 6 June 1994.

Swales, John. *Genre Analysis: English in Academic and Research Discourse.* Cambridge: Cambridge UP, 1990.

<swilbur>. "Beauty in Cyberspace?" Cybermind Discussion List [online]. Available e-mail: CYBERMIND <LISTSERV@WORLD.STD.COM>. 5 July 1994.

Taylor, Paul. "Social Epistemic Rhetoric and Chaotic Discourse." Hawisher and LeBlanc 131–48.

Weathers, Winston. "Grammars of Style." *Rhetoric and Composition.* Ed. Richard L. Graves. Upper Montclair: Boynton, 1984. 133–47.

Wittig, Rob. *Invisible Rendezvous: Connection and Collaboration in the New Landscape of Electronic Writing.* Hanover: Wesleyan UP, 1994.

Zamierowski, Mark. "The Virtual Voice in Network Culture." *Voices on Voice: Perspectives, Definition, Inquiry.* Ed. Kathleen Yancey. Urbana: NCTE, 1994. 275–98.

DISTANT VOICES:
TEACHING AND WRITING IN A CULTURE OF TECHNOLOGY

Chris M. Anson

[*College English* 61.3 (1999): 261–80.]

Chris Anson is a professor in the Department of English at North Carolina State University, where he directs the campus writing and speaking program. He directed the university writing program at the University of Minnesota for eight years, where he was the Morse-Alumni Distinguished Teaching Professor. He is author, coauthor, or editor of many books, including *Under Construction: Working at the Intersections of Composition Theory, Practice, and Research* (1998), *Dilemmas in Teaching: Cases for Collaborative Faculty Reflection* (1998), *At the Center: Using Journals in the Classroom* (1995), *Scenarios for Teaching Writing: Contexts for Discussion and Reflective Practice* (1993), *Writing Across the Curriculum: An Annotated Bibliography* (1993), and *Writing and Response: Theory, Practice, and Research* (1989). His current interest is the integration of instruction in speech and writing across campus.

If twenty-first-century culture will be defined in part as a "culture of technology," how will the ongoing development of new technologies affect learning, teaching, and the conditions of our teaching? In this reflective piece, Anson explores this question, focusing specifically on two aspects: how technology is changing the face-to-face interactions between students and teachers and among students, and how technology makes possible the teaching of "classes" that meet only electronically, with students and teachers geographically distant. Anson asks teachers to consider carefully the ways that technology may threaten the hard-won advances in writing instruction and in working conditions, to the detriment of students and teachers. He offers several examples of the ways that technology currently challenges "best practices" of writing instruction, and he provides a list of provocative questions that teachers can consider as they make decisions about technology. Anson challenges teachers to recognize what they value about writing instruction and to consider how to use technology to enhance those practices and beliefs.

With the development of the Internet, and . . . networked computers, we are in the middle of the most transforming technological event since the capture of fire.
John Perry Barlow, "Forum: What Are We Doing Online?" (36)

August 3, Les Agettes, Switzerland. I am sitting on a veranda overlooking the town of Sion some three thousand feet below, watching tiny airplanes take off from the airstrip and disappear over the shimmering ridge of alps to the north. Just below us is another chalet, the home of a Swiss family. At this time of day, they gather at the large wooden table on the slate patio behind their home to have a long meandering lunch in the French Swiss tradition. Madame is setting the table, opening a bottle of Valais wine, which grandpère ritually pours out for the family and any friends who join them. As they sit to eat, the scene becomes for me a vision of all that is most deeply social in human affairs. They could not survive without this interconnectedness, this entwining of selves, the stories passed around, problems discussed, identities shared and nourished. For weeks, away from phones, TVs, computers, and electronic mail, a dot on the rugged landscape of the southern Alps, I have a profound sense of my own familial belonging, of how the four of us are made one by this closeness of being. Just now Bernard, the little boy who lives on the switchback above, has run down with his dog Sucrette to see if the kids can play. He is here, standing before us, his face smudged with dirt, holding out a toy truck to entice the boys. For now, it is his only way to communicate with them, poised here in all his Bernard-ness, his whole being telling his story.

Not long after writing this journal entry and reflecting on how different my life had become during a summer without access to computers, I came across an issue of *Policy Perspectives,* a periodical issued by the Pew Higher Education Roundtable, which was intriguingly titled "To Dance with Change." When the *Policy Perspectives* began in 1988, the roundtable members believed that "the vitality of education would be defined by its ability to control costs, its capacity to promote learning, and its commitment to access and equity" (1). Less than a decade later, they had shifted their attention to forces beyond academia, realizing that they had been thinking of the institution itself without considering its connection to broader social pressures and movements. They conclude that "among the changes most important to higher education are those external to it"—economic, occupational, and technological. In particular, the electronic superhighway

> may turn out to be the most powerful external challenge facing higher education, and the one the academy is least prepared to understand. It is not that higher education institutions or their faculties have ignored technology. The academy, in fact, is one of the most important supporters and consumers of electronic technology. . . . The problem is that faculty—and hence the institutions they serve—have approached technology more as individual consumers than as collective producers. For the most part the new capacities conferred by electronic means have not enhanced the awareness that teaching might be conceived as something other than one teacher before a classroom of students. While academicians appreciate the leverage that technology has provided in the library and laboratory, they have not considered fully how the same technology might apply to the process of teaching and learning—and they have given almost no thought to how the same technologies in someone else's hands might affect their markets for student-customers. The conclusion that has escaped too many faculty is that this set of technologies is altering the market for even the most traditional goods and services, creating not only new products but new markets and, just as importantly, new providers. (3A)

In the context of our beliefs about how students best learn to write, many educators are haunted, like the Pew members, by a sense that bigger things are happening around us as we continue to refine classroom methods and tinker with our teaching styles. Theorists or researchers or just plain teachers, we spend much of our time working within the framework of certain fairly stable educational conditions. These conditions include physical spaces that define the social and interpersonal contexts of teaching: classrooms where we meet large or small groups of students, offices where we can consult with students face-to-face, and tutorial areas such as writing centers. We expect students to come to these places—even penalizing them for not doing so—and also to visit other physical spaces on campus such as libraries, where they carry out work connected with our instruction. The textual landscape of writing instruction also has a long and stable history: students write or type on white paper of a standard size and turn in their work, adhering to various admonitions about the width of their margins and the placement of periphera such as names, dates, and staples. Teachers collect the papers, respond in predictable places (in the margins or in the spaces left at the end) and return the papers at the institutional site. Innovations like portfolios are extensions of the use of this textual space, but the spaces themselves remain the same.

While the Pew Roundtable members may be concerned that faculty are not attentive to the frenzy of innovation in computer technology, it is difficult for them to make the same claim about academic administrations. Searching the horizon for signs of educational and institutional reform, administrators are often the first to introduce new campus-wide initiatives to the professoriate, who react with delight, resistance, apathy, or outrage to various proposals for change. In the climate of burgeoning developments in technology that have far-reaching consequences for teaching and learning, such changes will no doubt challenge existing ideologies of writing instruction, in part because of the assumed stability on which we have based our curricula and pedagogies.

In this essay, I will consider two of the ways in which teaching and responding to student writing are pressured by rapidly developing technologies now being introduced into our institutions. The first—the increasing replacement of face-to-face contact by "virtual" interaction—is the product of multimedia technology, email communication systems, and the recently expanded capabilities of the World Wide Web. The second, somewhat more institutionally complex development is distance education, in which students hundreds or even thousands of miles apart are connected via interactive television systems. While these technologies offer an endless array of new and exciting possibilities for the improvement of education, they also frequently clash with some of our basic beliefs about the nature of classroom instruction, in all its communal richness and face-to-face complexity. Of even greater urgency is the need to understand the motivation for these developments. More specifically, new technologies introduced with the overriding goal of creating economic efficiencies and generating increased revenues may lead to even greater exploitation in the area of writing instruction, the historically maligned and undernourished servant of the academy. The key to sustaining our pedagogical advances in the teaching of writing, even as we are pulled by the magnetic forces of innovation, will be to take control of these technologies, using them in effective ways and not, in the urge for ever-cheaper instruction, substituting them for those contexts and methods that we hold to be essential for learning to write.

The Allure: Technology and Instructional Enhancement

Until recently, writing instruction has experienced the greatest technological impact from the personal computer, a tool that had an especially powerful effect on the teaching and practice of revision. The integration of the microcomputer into writing curricula seemed a natural outcome of our interests and prevailing ways of teaching: it offered students a screen on which they could manipulate texts, but they could still print out their writing and turn it in on paper.

Throughout the 1980s and 1990s, many writing programs experimented with labs or computerized classrooms where students could write to and with each other on local area networks. (For a historical account of computers in the teaching of writing, see Hawisher, Selfe, Moran, and LeBlanc.) Simultaneously, an array of computer-assisted instructional programs became available, allowing students to work through guided activities (typically alone) on a personal computer. Computer-generated questions could prompt students to invent ideas; style checkers could give them an index of their average sentence length or complexity; and outline programs could help them to map out the structure of their essays as they wrote. But even with all the cut-and-paste functions and floating footnotes that eased the writing process and facilitated revision, the "textuality" of academic essays remained relatively unchanged: students continued to meet in classrooms to work on their assignments, and teachers reacted to and assessed their products in conventional ways, by carrying the papers home and grading them. Personal computers offered students and teachers a new tool to practice the processes of writing, but the outcome still emerged, eventually, on paper.

In the field of composition studies, the development of more reasoned, theoretically informed methods of response to students' writing has been framed by assumptions about the perpetuation of these physical and textual spaces. Recent studies of response analyze marginal comments written on students' papers for various rhetorical or focal patterns (see, e.g., Straub; Straub and Lunsford; Smith). Studies that deliberately attend to the contextual factors that influence teachers' responses continue to do so within the traditional parameters of typed or handwritten papers turned in for (usually handwritten) response or assessment (e.g., Prior). While such work is much needed in the field, it largely ignores the sweep of change in the way that many students now create, store, retrieve, use, and arrange information (including text) in their academic work. Artificial intelligence expert Seymour Papert pictures a scenario in which a mid-nineteenth-century surgeon is time-warped into a modern operating theater. Bewildered, the doctor would freeze, surrounded by unrecognizable technology and an utterly transformed profession, unsure of what to do or how to help. But if a mid-nineteenth-century schoolteacher were similarly transported into a modern classroom, the teacher would feel quite at home. Recounting Papert's anecdote, Nicholas Negroponte points out that there is "little fundamental difference between the way we teach today and the way we did one hundred and fifty years ago. The use of technology is at almost at the same level. In fact, according to a recent survey by the U.S. Department of Education, 84 percent of America's teachers consider only one type of information technology absolutely 'essential' to their work—a photocopier with an adequate paper supply" (220). Yet most statistics show the use of computers, particularly by students in high school and college, increasing at lightning speed. Today, more than one-third of American homes already have a computer, and it is predicted that by 2005 Americans will spend more time on the Internet than watching TV.

That personal computers have done little to disrupt our decades-old habits of working with and responding to students' writing is partly because the channels of electronic media have been separate and discrete. Video has been kept apart from computer text, audio systems, and still pictures, requiring us to use different equipment for each technology (and allowing us to focus on computer text to the exclusion of other media). Whether teachers focus on text to the exclusion of other media is not really the point; as Pamela McCorduck points out, "knowledge of different kinds is best represented in all its complexity for different purposes by different kinds of knowledge representations. Choosing *la représentation juste* (words, images, or anything else) is not at all an obvious thing: in fact, it's magnificently delicate. But we have not had much choice until now because text, whether the best representation for certain purposes or not, has dominated our intellectual lives" (259).

The introduction of hypertext and multimedia refocused attention on the relationship between text and other forms of representation. Experimenting with new technology, teachers of literature dragged laptops and heavy projection equipment into their classrooms and displayed stored multimedia Web sites to students reading *Emma* or *King Lear,* linking such texts to their social and political contexts, revealing connections to pieces of art of the time, playing segments of music that the characters might have heard, or showing brief video clips of famous stage presentations. Early advocates of multimedia in teaching and learning clearly framed its advantages in terms that emphasized the process of absorbing information, however innovatively that information might be structured, and however freely the user might navigate through multiple, hierarchically arranged connections (see, for example, Landow). Multimedia was something *presented* and perhaps *explored,* but it was not "answerable." In all their activity as creators of their own knowledge, students remained relatively passive, now receiving deposits of knowledge from automatic teller machines that supplemented the more direct, human method.

But that situation, as Negroponte has suggested, is rapidly changing, creating potentially profound implications for the delivery and mediation of instruction in schools and colleges. Within a few years, the disparate channels of video, audio, and computerized text and graphics—channels that come to us via airwaves, TV cable, phone cable, CD-ROM and computer disks—will merge into a single set of bits sent back and forth along one electronic highway at lightning speed. Our equipment will selectively manipulate this information to produce various outputs, a process already visible in the rapidly developing multimedia capabilities of the World Wide Web. In turn, users can assemble information and send it back (or out) along the same highway. The effect on both the production and reception of writing may be quite dramatic. Modern newspapers, for example, which are already produced electronically, may largely disappear in their paper form:

> The stories are often shipped in by reporters as e-mail. The pictures are digitized and frequently transmitted by wire as well. And the page layout . . . is done with computer-aided design systems, which prepare the data for transfer to film or direct engraving onto plates. This is to say that the entire conception and construction of the newspaper is digital, from beginning to end, until the very last step, when ink is squeezed onto dead trees. This step is where bits become atoms. . . . Now imagine that the last step does not happen . . . but that the bits are delivered to you as bits. You may elect to print them at home for all the conveniences of hard copy. . . . Or you may prefer to download them into your laptop, palmtop, or someday into your perfectly flexible, one-hundredth-of-an-inch thick, full-color, massively high resolution, large-format, waterproof display. (Negroponte 56)

In the educational realm, the new capabilities emerging from multimedia technology offer many alternatives for teaching and learning, and for assigning and responding to writing, particularly as "papers" and "written responses" are replaced by electronic data. Imagine, for example, a college student (call her Jennifer) coming into the student union a few years from now. She pulls from her backpack a full-color, multimedia computer "tablet," just half an inch thick, plugs it into a slot on a little vending machine, puts three quarters into the machine, and downloads the current issue of *USA Today*. Over coffee, she reads the paper on the tablet, watching video clips of some events and listening to various sound bites. She finds a story of relevance to a project she is working on and decides to clip and save it in the tablet's memory. Then she deletes the paper.

Jennifer's first class of the day is still remembered as a "lecture course" in history, but the lecture material has been converted into multimedia presentations stored on CD-ROM disks (which the students dutifully buy at the bookstore or download onto massive hard drives from a server, paying with a credit card). Students experience the lectures alone and meet collectively only in recitation sections. Because her recitation begins in an hour and she did not finish the assignment the night before, Jennifer heads for one of the learning labs. There, she navigates through the rest of a multimedia presentation while handwriting some notes on her tablet and saving them into memory. She is impressed with the program, and justifiably: the institution is proud to have an exclusive contract with a world-famous historian (now living overseas) for the multimedia course.

The recitation is held in a room fully equipped for distance learning. Cameras face the students and teacher. Enormous, high-resolution monitors provide a view of two distant classes, each located a hundred miles away on smaller campuses. Jennifer sits at one of seventy-five computer stations. The first half of the class involves a discussion of some of the multimedia course material. The recitation coordinator (a non-tenure-track education specialist) brings the three sites together using artful techniques of questioning and response. After raising a number of issues which appear on a computerized screen from his control computer, the coordinator asks the three classes to discuss the issues. Students pair off electronically, writing to each other; some students at the main site pair with students at the distant sites, selected automatically by the instructor using an electronic seating chart and a program that activates the connections for each pair.

After the recitation, Jennifer remembers that she is supposed to send a revised draft of a paper to her composition instructor. She heads for another lab, where she accesses her electronic student file and finds a multimedia message from her instructor. The instructor's face appears on her screen in a little window, to one side of Jennifer's first draft. As Jennifer clicks on various highlighted passages or words, the instructor's face becomes animated in a video clip describing certain reactions and offering suggestions for revision. After working through the multimedia commentary and revising her draft, Jennifer then sends the revision back electronically to her instructor. Jennifer has never actually met her teacher, who is one of many part-time instructor/tutors hired by the semester to "telecommute" to the institution from their homes.

Because Jennifer is a privileged, upper-middle-class student who has a paid subscription to an online service, her own high-end computer system and modem, and the money to buy whatever software she needs for her studies, she can continue her schoolwork at home. There, she uses her multimedia computer to study for a psychology course offered by a corporation. On the basis of nationally normed assessments, the corporation has shown that its multimedia course achieves educational outcomes equal to or greater than those provided by many well-ranked colleges and universities. Jennifer will be able to transfer the course into her curriculum because the corporation's educational division has been recently accredited. She also knows that, as multimedia courses go, this one is first-rate: the corporation is proud to have an exclusive contract with its teacher-author, a world-famous psychologist. As she checks the courseline via email, she notices that a midterm is coming up. She decides to schedule it for an "off" day, since she will have to go to one of the corporation's nearby satellite centers to take the test at a special computer terminal that scores her answers automatically and sends the results to her via email.

Later that day, Jennifer decides to spend an hour doing some research for her history project. From her home computer, she uses various Internet search programs to find out more about the Civil War battle of Manassas. On her high-resolution, 30-inch monitor (which also doubles as a TV and video player), she reads text, looks at drawings, opens video and audio files, and locates bibliographic material on her topic. She also finds some sites where Civil War aficionados share information and chat about what they know. She sends and receives some messages through the list, then copies various bits of information and multimedia into her computer, hoping to weave them into her report, which itself may include photos, video clips, and audio recordings. Due in less than three weeks, the report must be added (quite simply) to a privately accessed course Web site so that one of the several teaching assistants can retrieve it, grade and comment briefly on it, and send it back to Jennifer with an assessment. Just before she quits her research to watch some rock videos from the massive archives in a subscription server, Jennifer locates a Web site at another college where the students had researched the Civil War. The site includes all twenty-six projects created by the students; one focuses for several electronic pages on the battle at Manassas. Intrigued, Jennifer copies the pages into her computer, intending to look at them carefully the next day and perhaps use parts of them in her own multimedia project.

While this scenario may seem futuristic, much of the technology Jennifer experiences is already here or soon to be. The Knight-Ridder Corporation, for example, has recently developed a prototype of Jennifer's multimedia news "tablet" weighing about two pounds (Leyden). The Web now has the capability to send software to the receiver along with the actual information requested, and this software enhances the user's capacities to work with the information. Programs are currently available that allow teachers to open a student's paper onscreen and scroll through it to a point where a comment might be made to the student. At that point, an icon can be deposited that starts up a voice-recording device. The teacher then talks to the student about the paper. Further marginal or intertextual icons encase further voice comments. Opening the paper on disk at home, the student notices the icons and, activating them, listens to the teacher's response and advice. Computers with tiny videocameras are already enabling a picture-in-picture window that shows the teacher's image talking to the student as if face-to-face. The technology that now provides teleconferencing, when merged with Web-like storage and retrieval devices, will easily facilitate "one-way" tutorials that project audio and video images from a teacher, superimposed over typed text on which marks, corrections, and marginal notes can be recorded "live," like the replay analyses during televised football games.

When demonstrated, such advances may dazzle teachers because we see them as a promise to simplify our lives and streamline our work. New technologies often seem to improve our working conditions and provide better ways to help our students (seasoned teachers, as they stand at the computer-controlled reducing/collating/stapling photocopier, have only to reminisce about the old fluid-and-ink ditto machines to feel these advantages quite tangibly). Teaching, too, seems if not eased, affected in ways that enhance students' experiences. Positive accounts already show that email can help students to form study groups, interact with their teachers, or carry on academic discussions with students at other locations all over the world. In one experiment, students in an all-black freshman composition course at Howard University teamed up with a class of predominantly white students in graphic design at Montana State University to create a 32-page publication, *On the Color Line: Networking to End Racism.* Using digital scanners and email, the students and teachers were able to bring together two classes 1,600 miles apart to critique each other's work, discuss race-related views, and collaboratively produce a pamphlet (Blumenstyk). Many other accounts of networked classrooms suggest increased participation among marginalized groups (see, for example, Selfe, "Technology"; Bump).

Curiously, these and other positive accounts almost always describe adaptations of new technologies as ancillary methods within classrooms where students interact with each other and with their teacher. In a typical computerized grade-school class, for example, a student might use email to ask kids around the world to rank their favorite chocolates as part of a project focusing on *Charlie and the Chocolate Factory;* but then the entire class tallies the results and shares the conclusions (Rector). At the college level, Rich Holeton describes his highly networked electronic writing classroom and its advantages, especially in the area of electronic groups and discussions, yet still sees face-to-face interaction as the "main action" of the course and electronic techniques as "supplementary." Similarly, Tom Creed discusses the many ways he integrates computer technology into his classrooms, but finds it essential to create cooperative learning groups and build in time for students to make stand-up presentations to the class. Electronic innovations, in other words, appear to be carefully controlled, integrated into the existing curriculum in principled ways that do not erode the foundations on which the teacher-experimenters already base their instructional principles. Recognizing the importance of this configuration, some educators much prefer the term "technology-enhanced learning" to other terms that imply a radical shift in the actual delivery of education, such as "technologized instruction."

Because of improvements in educational software and hardware, however, our profession will feel increased pressure to offer technologically enhanced "independent study" courses. Some campuses are already experiencing dramatic differences in students' use of communal spaces with the introduction of dorm-room email. Clifford Stoll, a former Harvard University researcher and author of *Silicon Snake Oil: Second Thoughts on the Information Highway,* claims that by turning college into a "cubicle-directed electronic experience," we are "denying the importance of learning to work closely with other students and professors, and developing social adeptness" (qtd. in Gabriel). Students may be psychodynamically separated from one another even while inhabiting the same campus or dorm building; even more profound effects may be felt when students and faculty use advanced technologies to link up with each other in a course without ever meeting in person. Although many studies and testimonials affirm the ways that Internet chat lines, listservs, email, and other "virtual spaces" can actually increase the social nature of communication, there is no doubt that the physical isolation of each individual from the others creates an entirely different order of interaction.

Distance, Independence, and the Transformation of Community

The teaching of writing, unlike some other disciplines, is founded on the assumption that students learn well by reading and writing with each other, responding to each other's drafts, negotiating revisions, discussing ideas, sharing perspectives, and finding some level of trust as collaborators in their mutual development. Teaching in such contexts is interpersonal and interactive, necessitating small class size and a positive relationship between the teacher and the students. At the largest universities, such classes taken in the first year are often the only place where students can actually get to know each other, creating and participating in an intimate community of learning. Large lecture courses, driven by the transmission and retrieval of information, place students in a more passive role. In her book on the effect of college entrance examinations on the teaching of English, Mary Trachsel points out that the "factory" model of education, which privileges standardized testing and the "input" of discrete bits of information, is at odds with our profession's instructional ideals, which align more comfortably with those of theorists like Paulo Freire:

> The model for [authentic education] is that of a dialogue in which hierarchical divisions are broken down so that teachers become teacher-learners, and learners become learner-teachers. Educational values are thus determined not by a mandate to perpetuate an established academic tradition but by local conditions and by the emerging purposes and realizations of educators and learners in social interaction with one another. This socially situated version of education stands in opposition to the "banking concept" of traditionally conceived schooling. (12)

For such ideological reasons, the teaching of writing by correspondence or "independent study" has always lived uneasily within programs that also teach students in classrooms. Although such instruction can be found at many institutions, few theorists strongly advocate a pedagogy in which students write alone, a guide of lessons and assignments at their elbows to provide the material of their "course," a remote, faceless grader hired by the hour to read assignments the students send through the mail and mail back responses. Next to classrooms with rich face-to-face social interaction—fueled by active learning, busy with small groups, energized by writers reading each other's work, powered by the forces of revision and response—independent study in writing appears misguided.

But in the context of our convictions about writing and response, new technologies now offer educational institutions the chance to expand on the idea of individualized learning. Online communication with students is an idea that seems stale by now but is by no means fully exploited; only some teachers eagerly invite email from students, and only some students end up using it when invited. Those faculty who value their autonomy and privacy find that email makes them better able to control when and where students enter their lives. Departments at many universities are requiring faculty to use email by giving them computers, hooking them up, offering workshops on how to use them, and then saying that faculty have no excuse for not voting on such and such an issue or not turning in their book orders on time. The results have already been felt on many campuses, as meetings give way to electronic communion, turning some departments into ghost haunts. Very few universities have developed policies that disallow the use of online office hours in place of physical presence on campus. As teachers across the country realize the tutorial potential of electronic media, such media may come to substitute for direct contact with students. For faculty busy with their own work, the gains are obvious: consultation by convenience, day or night; freedom from physical space; copyable texts instead of ephemeral talk.

From a more curricular perspective, the concept of independent study is rapidly changing from its roots in study manuals and the US Postal Service to a technology-rich potential for students to learn at their own pace, in their own style, with fingertip access to an entire world of information. Multimedia computers using text, sound, video, and photos provide opportunities to bring alive old-fashioned text-only materials. But it is not just independent-study programs, usually seen as ancillary to "real" education, that will change: multimedia could transform the very essence of classroom instruction. At many institutions, administrators are realizing that creating a state-of-the-art multimedia course out of, for example, "Introduction to Psychology," which may enroll up to five hundred students, represents a major improvement. The quality of faculty lectures is uneven; they come at a high cost; and they are often delivered in settings not conducive to learning—hot, stuffy lecture halls with poor sound systems and ailing TV monitors hung every few rows. In the converted version, a student can choose when to work through a multimedia presentation in a computer lab, can learn at her own pace, can review fundamental concepts, can download some information for later study, and can even test her developing knowledge as she learns. In such situations, as journalist Peter Leyden writes, "the time-honored role of the teacher almost certainly will change dramatically. No longer will teachers be the fonts of knowledge with all the answers that [students] seek. They can't possibly fill that role in the coming era" (2T).

In itself, multimedia technology has not directly challenged the field of composition. True, many educators are working on integrating into their research-paper units some instruction on citing electronic sources, searching the Web, or using online databases. The prospect of a teacherless and "community-less" course, however, creates much debate in the composition community, where many see computers as poor substitutes for old-fashioned forms of human interaction. In areas involving context-bound thinking, Stanley Aronowitz maintains, "knowledge of the terrain must be obtained more by intuition, memory, and specific knowledge of actors or geography than by mastering logical rules. . . . Whatever its psychological and biological presuppositions, the development of thinking is profoundly shaped and frequently altered by multiple determinations, including choices made by people themselves" (130–31). In the face of the trend to increasing "indirectness" of teaching, Charles Moran argues, "we will need to be more articulate than we have yet been in describing the benefits of face-to-face teaching, or what our British colleagues call 'live tuition'" (208).

New technologies are also giving a strong boost to distance learning. Like the concept of independent study, distance learning too may powerfully affect the way in which we teach and respond to students. In distance learning, students actually participate in the classroom—they are just not there, physically. Beamed in by cable or broadcast, their personae are represented on TV monitors, which, as the idea expands, are becoming larger and gaining in resolution. As classrooms become better equipped, students at several sites will work in virtual classrooms, writing to and for each other at terminals. Teachers can pair students, using small cameras and monitors at their desks, and then regroup the classes at the different sites for larger discussions using the bigger screens.

Institutions are attracted to the concept of distance education for reasons obvious in times of fiscal constraint. Students register for a single course from two or more sites, generating tuition revenue for the parent institution. A course previously taught by several salaried faculty (each on location, hundreds of miles apart) now needs only one main teacher, aided by a non-tenure-track staff "facilitator-graders" or teaching assistants hired inexpensively at the different locations. If small satellite sites are created, sometimes in available spaces such as public schools, community centers, or libraries, new revenue sources can be exploited in remote areas. Even after the cost of the interactive television equipment and link-up is calculated, distance education can generate profit for the institution at reduced cost, using its existing faculty resources as "lead teachers." Such an arrangement is especially attractive to institutions used to delivering instruction via the traditional "banking" model of lectures and objectively scorable tests.

Distance learning is also allowing some pairs or groups of institutions to consolidate resources by sharing programs with each other. Imagine that University A realizes that its Swahili language program does not have the resources to compete with the Swahili language program at University B; but it does have a nationally recognized Lakota language program. Unfortunately, the Lakota program is not very cost-effective, in spite of its standing, because its student cohort is so small. Likewise, University B recognizes that its own Lakota language program pales by comparison with University A's, yet it boasts a particularly strong Swahili program similarly suffering from its inability to generate profits for the school. Using sophisticated interactive television and multimedia resources, the two institutions team up to exchange programs, swapping the tuition revenues along with their instructional programs. As technology keeps expanding and becoming refined, collaborations like these will become increasingly popular, even necessary. In part, these ideas save money. In part, they also respond to growing competition from non-academic providers of education, a major threat to our present institutions. By collaborating to deliver the "best" programs possible, the institutions protect themselves against the intrusion of industry, of what the Pew Roundtable calls "high-quality, lower-cost educational programming conjoined with the rising demand for postsecondary credentials that creates the business opportunity for higher education's would-be competitors" (3). But the result is almost certain to be a continued reduction in full-time, tenure-track faculty and an increased reliance on modes of instructional delivery that physically distance students from each other and from their mentors.

Practically speaking, the idea of distance learning seems reasonable in the context of Lakota and Swahili—it saves duplication of effort, it cuts costs, it may lead to increased institutional collaboration, and it offers students at different locations the chance to be taught, in some sense of the word, by high-quality teachers. It is when the prospect of fully interactive, technologically advanced distance learning conflicts with our most principled educational theories that we feel an ideological clash. Long privileged in composition instruction, for example, is the interactive teaching style. Writing teachers arrange and participate in small groups in the classroom, talk with students before and after class, walk with them to other buildings, meet them in offices, and encourage students to respond to each other instead of through the teacher. Distance learning has yet to overcome the virtuality of its space to draw all students into such interpersonal relationships. Teachers often report feeling detached from the students at the distant sites, unable to carry on "extracurricular" conversations with them. The savings promised by distance education come from the elimination of trained professionals who reduce teacher-student ratios and offer meaningful consultation with students, face to face. If distance learning becomes the norm in fields where general education courses are usually delivered in large lectures with little chance for students to learn actively or interact with each other or the teacher, it will not be long before writing programs are encouraged to follow suit.

In exploring the concept of humans in cyberspace, we can find, as Anna Cicognani has found, many of the same conditions as those we experience in physical space: social interaction; logical and formal abstractions; linguistic form; corresponding organizations of time; the possibility for rhetorical action; and so on. But it is, finally, a "hybrid space, a system which is part of another but only refers to itself and its own variables." It belongs to the main system of space, but "claims independence from it at the same time." Cicognani's representation of cyberspace as a hybrid, which still allows communities to form and develop but relies for its existence on the physical space from which it has been created, offers a useful metaphor for the continued exploration of the relationships between education and computer technology, as the latter is carefully put to use in the improvement of the former. Yet to be considered, however, are broader questions about the role of teachers in technology-rich educational settings.

Response, Technology, and the Future of Teaching

The quality of faculty interaction with students is a product of our *work*—our training, the material conditions at our institutions, how much support we get for developing our teaching and keeping up on research. While to this point, we have been reflecting on the possible effects of new technologies on the quality of students' learning experiences and contexts, we must also consider ways in which colleges and universities, as places of employment, may change.

Teachers of composition continue to argue that writing programs provide an important site for active and interactive learning in higher education. Our national standards have helped to keep classes small; our lobbying continues to call attention to the exploitation of part-time faculty. We argue the need for support services, such as writing centers, tutors, and ESL programs. And, in writing-across-the-curriculum programs, we have helped to integrate the process approach in various disciplines and courses with considerable success. But the current cost-cutting fervor will continue to erode these principles. Massy and Wilger argue, for example, that "most faculty have yet to internalize the full extent of the economic difficulties facing higher education institutions, both public and private. . . . [F]ew faculty take seriously the current fiscal constraints. Most believe that the problems are not as significant as administrators and others warn, or that the conditions are only temporary" (25).

As teachers, our own occupational space is clearly defined. We "belong" to a particular institution, which pays us, and the students get our instruction, consultation, expertise, and time in exchange for their tuition or, in public schooling, the revenues generated by local taxes and other local, state, and federal funds. Yet technology will soon change not only how we work within our institutions but also how "attached" we may be to an institution, particularly if we can work for several institutions at some physical (but not electronic) remove from each other. In an article in the Information Technology Annual Report of *Business Week*, Edward Baig lists by category the percentage of sites that plan additional "telecommuters"—"members of the labor force who have chosen to, or have been told to, work anywhere, anytime—as long as it's not in the office" (59). Higher education is placed at the very top of the heap, with over 90 percent of sites planning to increase telecommuting.

Universities once looked upon computer technology as an expense and a luxury; increasingly it is now seen as an investment that will lead to increased revenues and reduced expenses. The standards of work defined by the Conference on College Composition and Communication have not anticipated a new vision of writing instruction involving low-paid reader-responders, tutorial "assistants" for CD-ROM courses taken "virtually" by independent study, or coordinators at interactive television sites where students from many campuses link to a single site requiring only one "master professor." Robert Heterick, writing for Educom, predicts a major shift in resource allocation across institutions of higher education:

> The infusion of information technology into the teaching and learning domain will create shifts in the skill requirements of faculty from instructional delivery to instructional design . . . with faculty being responsible for course content and information technologists being responsible for applying information technology to the content. These changes will increase the number of students the institutions can service without corresponding increases in the need for student daily-life support facilities. (3)

In the area of composition, part-time telecommuters, supplied with the necessary equipment, could become the primary providers of instruction to many students. At some locations, private industry is already exploring the possibility of supplying writing instruction, using technology, to institutions interested in "outsourcing" this part of their curriculum. In the *Adjunct Advocate*, a newsletter for part-time and temporary writing teachers, instructors have expressed considerable concern about administrators' requests that they teach sections of introductory composition via the Internet (see Lesko; Wertner). The "profound change in work" represented by advanced technology may also further isolate women. Although the computer once promised to level gender discrimination by removing direct identity from online forums, some social critics are now seeing the potential for new inequities in the labor force. In her contribution to Susan Leigh Star's *The Cultures of Computing*, for example, Randi Markussen takes up the question of "why gender relations seem to change so little through successive waves of technological innovation" (177). Technology promises the "empowerment" of workers, but it also reinforces and more strongly imposes the measurement of work in discrete units. In her analysis of the effects of technology on practicing nurses, Markussen notes that instead of "empowering" employees by making their work more visible or supporting their demands for better staffing and pay, new computer technology actually places greater demands on nurses to account for their work in "categories of work time," decreasing the need for "interpersonal task synchronization" and cooperation with other people. "The transformation of work," Markussen writes, "puts new demands on nurses in terms of relating the formalized electronic depiction of work to caregiving activities, which may still be considered residual and subordinate" (172).

Like nursing, composition has been positively constructed through its preoccupation with the development of the individual and the creation of an engaging, student-focused classroom. Yet composition likewise suffers from higher education's continued attitude that it serves a "residual and subordinate" role, necessary for "remediation." This gross misconception of the value of writing instruction is directly linked to employment practices at hundreds of colleges and universities, where large numbers of "service professionals," a majority of them women, are hired into low-paid, non-tenurable positions with poor (or no) benefits. With the potential for the further automation of writing instruction through the use of telecommuting and other technology-supported shifts in instructional delivery, composition may be further subordinated to the interests of powerful subject-oriented disciplines where the conception of expertise creates rather different patterns of hiring and material support.

Our key roles—as those who create opportunities and contexts for students to write and who provide expert, principled response to that writing—must change in the present communications and information revolution. But we cannot let the revolution sweep over us. We need to guide it, resisting its economic allure in cases where it weakens the principles of our teaching. The processes of technology, even when they are introduced to us by administrations more mindful of balancing budgets than enhancing lives, will not threaten us as long as we, as educators, make decisions about the worth of each innovation, about ways to put it to good use, or about reasons why it should be rejected out of hand. More sustained, face-to-face discussions—at conferences and seminars, at faculty development workshops, and in routine departmental and curricular meetings—can give us hope that we can resist changes that undermine what we know about good teaching and sound ways of working. Such discussions are often difficult. They are highly political, painfully economic, and always value-laden and ideological. But as teachers of writing and communication, we have an obvious investment in considering the implications of technology for working, teaching, and learning, even as that technology is emerging.

Because technology is advancing at an unprecedented rate, we must learn to assess the impact of each new medium, method, or piece of software on our students' learning. Most of the time, such assessments will take place locally (for example, as a genetics program decides whether it is more effective for students to work with real drosophila flies or manipulate a virtual drosophila world using an interactive computer program). But we also urgently need broader, institution-wide dialogues about the effect of technology on teaching, particularly between students, faculty, and administrators. Deborah Holdstein has pointed out that as early as 1984 some compositionists were already critiquing the role of computers in writing instruction; "caveats regarding technology . . . have always been an important sub-text in computers and composition studies, the sophistication of self-analysis, one hopes, maturing with the field" (283). Among the issues she proposes for further discussion are those of access, class, race, power, and gender; she questions, for example,

> those who would assert without hesitation that email, the Net, and the Web offer us, finally, a nirvana of ultimate democracy and freedom, suggesting that even visionaries such as Tuman and Lanham beg the question of access, of the types of literacies necessary to even gain access to email, much less to the technology itself. What *other* inevitable hierarchies—in addition to the ones we know and understand . . . —will be formed to order us as we "slouch toward cyberspace"? (283)

While it is impossible to overlook not only that advanced learning technologies are here to stay but that they are in a state of frenzied innovation, Holdstein's admonishments remind us of the power of thoughtful critique and interest punctuated by caution. In addition to the issues she raises, we can profit by engaging in more discussions about the following questions:

1. What will multimedia do to alter the personae of teachers and students as they respond to each other virtually? How do new communication technologies change the relationships between teachers and students? Recent research on small-group interaction in writing classes, for example, shows labyrinthine complexity, as demonstrated in Thomas Newkirk's study of students' conversational roles. What do we really know about the linguistic, psycho-social, and pedagogical effects of online communication when it replaces traditional classroom-based interaction? (See Eldred and Hawisher's fascinating synthesis of research on how electronic networking affects various dimensions of writing practice and instruction.)

2. How might the concept of a classroom community change with the advent of new technologies? What is the future of collaborative learning in a world in which "courseware" may increasingly replace "courses"?

3. What are the consequences of increasing the distance between students and teachers? Is the motivation for distance education financial or pedagogical? Will the benefits of drawing in isolated clients outweigh the disadvantages of electronically "isolating" even those who are nearby?
4. What will be the relationship between "human" forms of response to writing and increasingly sophisticated computerized responses being developed in industry?
5. How will the conditions of our work change as a result of increasing access to students via telecommunications? Who will hire us to read students' writing? Will we work at home? Will educational institutions as physical entities disappear, as Alvin Toffler is predicting, to be replaced by a core of faculty who can be commissioned from all over the world to deliver instruction and response via the electronic highway? What new roles will teachers, as expert responders, play in an increasingly electronic world?
6. What are the implications of telecommuting for the hiring and support of teachers? Could technology reduce the need for the physical presence of instructors, opening the door to more part-time teachers hired at low wages and few benefits?
7. How will writing instruction compete with new, aggressive educational offerings from business and industry? What will be the effects of competing with such offerings for scarce student resources?

If we can engage in thoughtful discussions based on questions such as these, we will be better prepared to make principled decisions about the effect of new technologies on our students' learning and the conditions of our teaching. And we will be more likely, amid the dazzle of innovation, to reject those uses of technology that will lead to bad teaching, poor learning, unfair curricular practices, and unjust employment.

August 21, Les Agettes, Switzerland. I have met the family below. They tell me grandpère has lost some of his memory. He often spends part of the day breaking up stones, clack, clack, clack, behind the chalet. It's not disturbing, they hope. We haven't noticed, I say. We talk almost aimlessly, wandering around topics. Have we met the priest who rents an apartment below the chalet? Can they tell me what the local school is like? We talk about learning, about computers. As if scripted by the ad agency for IBM, they tell me they are interested in the Internet; their friends have computers, and they may get one too, soon. Later, gazing down toward the bustling town of Sion, I wonder how their lives will change. I imagine them ordering a part for their car over the computer without ever catching up on news with Karl, the guy at the garage near the river. Yet I'm also optimistic. They will use email someday soon, and I can get their address from my brother and write them messages in bad French, and they can share them during their long lunches on the patio, where they still gather to eat and laugh, turning my text back into talk.

Works Cited

Aronowitz, Stanley. "Looking Out: The Impact of Computers on the Lives of Professionals." Tuman 119–38.

Baig, Edward C. "Welcome to the Officeless Office." *Business Week* (Information Technology Annual Report, International Edition) 26 June 1995: 59–60.

Barlow, John Perry, Sven Birkerts, Kevin Kelly, and Mark Slouka. "Forum: What Are We Doing Online?" *Harper's Magazine* Aug. 1995: 35–46.

Blumenstyk, Goldie. "Networking to End Racism." *Chronicle of Higher Education* 22 Sept. 1995: A35–A39.

Bump, Jerome. "Radical Changes in Class Discussion Using Networked Computers." *Computers and the Humanities* 24 (1990); 49–65.

Cicognani, Anna. "On the Linguistic Nature of Cyberspace and Virtual Communities." <http://www.arch.usyd.edu.au/~anna/papers/even96.htm>

Creed, Tom. "Extending the Classroom Walls Electronically." *New Paradigms for College Teaching.* Ed. William E. Campbell and Karl A. Smith. Edina, MN: Interaction, 1997. 149–84.

Eldred, Janet Carey, and Gail E. Hawisher. "Researching Electronic Networks." *Written Communication* 12.3 (1995): 330–59.

Gabriel, Trip. "As Computers Unite Campuses, Are They Separating Students?" *Minneapolis Star Tribune* 12 Nov. 1996: A5.

Hawisher, Gail E., Cynthia L. Selfe, Charles Moran, and Paul LeBlanc. *Computers and the Teaching of Writing in American Higher Education, 1979–1994: A History.* Norwood, NJ: Ablex, 1996.

Heterick, Robert. "Operating in the 90's." <http://ivory.educom.edu:70/00/educom.info/html>

Holdstein, Deborah. "Power, Genre, and Technology." *College Composition and Communication* 47.2 (1996): 279–84.

Holeton, Rich. "The Semi-Virtual Composition Classroom: A Model for Techn-Amphibians." *Notes in the Margins* Spring 1996: 1, 14–17, 19.

Landow, George. "Hypertext, Metatext, and the Electronic Canon." Tuman 67–94.

Lesko, P. D. "Adjunct Issues in the Media." *The Adjunct Advocate* March/April 1996: 22–27.

Leyden, Peter. "The Changing Workscape." Special Report, Part III. *Minneapolis Star Tribune* 18 June 1995: 2T–6T.

Markussen, Randi. "Constructing Easiness: Historical Perspectives on Work, Computerization, and Women." *The Cultures of Computing.* Ed. Susan Leigh Star. Oxford: Blackwell, 1995. 158–80.

Massy, William F., and Andrea K. Wilger. "Hollowed Collegiality: Implications for Teaching Quality." Paper presented at the Second AAHE Annual Conference on Faculty Roles and Rewards, New Orleans, 29 Jan. 1994.

McCorduck, Pamela. "How We Knew, How We Know, How We Will Know." Tuman 245–59.

Moran, Charles. "Review: English and Emerging Technologies." *College English* 60.2 (1998): 202–9.

Negroponte, Nicholas. *Being Digital.* New York: Knopf, 1995.

Newkirk, Thomas. "The Writing Conference as Performance." *Research in the Teaching of English* 29.2 (1996): 193–215.

Pew Higher Education Roundtable. "To Dance with Change." *Policy Perspectives* 5.3 (1994): 1A–12A.

Prior, Paul. "Contextualizing Writing and Response in a Graduate Seminar." *Written Communication* 8 (1991): 267–310.

———. "Tracing Authoritative and Internally Persuasive Discourses: A Case Study of Response, Revision, and Disciplinary Enculturation." *Research in the Teaching of English* 29 (1995): 288–325.

Rector, Lucinda. "Where Excellence is Electronic." *Teaching and Technology* Summer 1996: 10–14. <http://www.time.com/teach>

Selfe, Cynthia. "Literacy, Technology, and the Politics of Education in America." Chair's Address, Conference on College Composition and Communication, Chicago, 2 April 1998.

———. "Technology in the English Classroom: Computers Through the Lense of Feminist Theory." *Computers and Community: Teaching Composition in the Twenty-First Century.* Ed. Carolyn Handa. Portsmouth, NH: Boynton/Cook, 1990. 118–39.

Smith, Summer. "The Genre of the End Comment: Conventions in Teacher Responses to Student Writing." *College Composition and Communication* 48.2 (1997): 249–68.

Stoll, Clifford. *Silicon Snake Oil: Second Thoughts on the Information Highway.* New York: Doubleday, 1995.

Straub, Richard. "The Concept of Control in Teacher Response: Defining the Varieties of 'Directive' and 'Facilitative' Commentary." *College Composition and Communication* 47.2 (1996): 223–51.

Straub, Richard, and Ronald F. Lunsford. *Twelve Readers Reading: Responding to College Student Writing.* Cresskill: Hampton, 1995.

Trachsel, Mary. *Institutionalizing Literacy.* Carbondale, IL: Southern Illinois UP, 1992.

Tuman, Myron C., ed. *Literacy Online: The Promise (and Peril) of Reading and Writing with Computers.* Pittsburgh: U of Pittsburgh P, 1992.

Wertner, B. "The Virtual Classroom" (letter to the editor). *The Adjunct Advocate* May/June 1996: 6.

BIBLIOGRAPHY FOR FURTHER READING

This bibliography points out further books and articles related to the variety of topics discussed in *Background Readings*. For convenience, it follows the organization of *Background Readings*.

Part One: The Writing Process

Booth, Wayne C. "The Rhetorical Stance." *College Composition and Communication* 14 (1963): 139–45.

Coe, Richard M. "If Not to Narrow, Then How to Focus: Two Techniques for Focusing." *College Composition and Communication* 32 (1981): 272–77.

Cooper, Marilyn. "The Ecology of Writing." *College English* 48 (1986): 364–75.

Ede, Lisa, and Andrea Lunsford. "Audience Addressed/Audience Invoked: The Role of Audience in Composition Theory and Pedagogy." *College Composition and Communication* 35 (1984): 155–71. Rpt. in *The Writing Teacher's Sourcebook*. 3rd ed. Ed. Gary Tate, Edward P. J. Corbett, and Nancy Meyers. New York: Oxford UP, 1994. 243–47.

Elbow, Peter. "Closing My Eyes as I Speak: An Argument for Ignoring Audience." *College English* 49 (1987): 50–69.

Emig, Janet. *The Composing Processes of Twelfth Graders*. NCTE Research Report No. 13. Urbana: NCTE, 1971.

Flower, Linda, and John R. Hayes. "A Cognitive Process Theory of Writing." *College Composition and Communication* 32 (1981): 365–87.

Fulwiler, Toby, ed. *The Journal Book*. Portsmouth, NH: Boynton/Cook, 1987.

Hillocks, George, Jr. "The Composing Process: A Model." *Teaching Writing as Reflective Practice*. New York: Teachers College P, 1995. 76–95.

Kinneavy, James L. *A Theory of Discourse*. New York: Norton, 1980. 17–40, 48–68.

Kroll, Barry. "Writing for Readers: Three Perspectives on Audience." *College Composition and Communication* 35 (1984): 172–85.

Marsella, Joy, and Thomas L. Hilgers. "Exploring the Potential of Freewriting." *Nothing Begins with N: New Investigations of Freewriting*. Ed. Pat Belanoff, Peter Elbow, and Sheryl L. Fontaine. Carbondale: Southern Illinois UP, 1991. 93–110.

Perl, Sondra. "Understanding Composing." *College Composition and Communication* 31 (1980): 363–69.

Porter, James E. *Audience and Rhetoric*. Englewood Cliffs: Prentice, 1992.

Pratt, Mary Louise. "Arts of the Contact Zone." *Profession* 91 (1991): 33–40.

Rafoth, Bennet A. "Discourse Community: Where Writers, Readers, and Texts Come Together." *The Social Construction of Written Communication*. Ed. Bennet A. Rafoth and Donald L. Rubin. Norwood, NJ: Ablex, 1988. 131–46.

Reynolds, Mark. "Make Freewriting More Productive." *College Composition and Communication* 39 (1988): 81–82.

Roth, Robert G. "The Evolving Audience: Alternatives to Audience Accommodation." *College Composition and Communication* 38 (1987): 47–55.

Selzer, Jack. "Exploring Options in Composing." College Composition and Communication 35 (1984): 276–84.

Shafer, Gregory. "Using Letters for Process and Change in the Basic Writing Class." *Teaching English in the Two-Year College* 28 (2000): 285–92.

Tobin, Lad, and Thomas Newkirk, eds. *Taking Stock: The Writing Process Movement in the '90s*. Portsmouth, NH: Boynton/Cook, 1994.

Young, Richard, and Yameng Liu, eds. *Landmark Essays on Rhetorical Invention in Writing*. Davis, CA: Hermagoras, 1994.

Planning, Drafting, and Revising

Bishop, Wendy. "Helping Peer Writing Groups Succeed." *Teaching English in the Two-Year College* 15 (1988): 120–25.

Bruffee, Kenneth A. "Writing and Collaboration." *Collaborative Learning: Higher Education, Interdependence, and the Authority of Knowledge.* Baltimore: Johns Hopkins UP, 1993. 52–62.

Butts, Elizabeth A. "Overcoming Student Resistance to Group Work." *Teaching English in the Two-Year College* 28 (2000): 81–83.

Elbow, Peter. *Writing with Power: Techniques for Mastering the Writing Process.* New York: Oxford UP, 1981.

Faigley, Lester, and Stephen Witte. "Analyzing Revision." *College Composition and Communication* 32 (1981): 400–14.

Flower, Linda, et al. "Detection, Diagnosis, and the Strategies of Revision." *College Composition and Communication* 37 (1986): 16–55.

Fulkerson, Richard. "On Imposed versus Imitative Form." *Journal of Teaching Writing* 7 (1988): 143–55.

Gorrell, Donna. "Central Question for Prewriting and Revising." *Teaching English in the Two-Year College* 23 (1996): 34–38.

Harris, Muriel. "Collaboration Is Not Collaboration Is Not Collaboration: Writing Center Tutorials vs. Peer-Response Groups." *College Composition and Communication* 43 (1992): 369–83.

Healy, Dave, and Murray Jensen. "Using Feedback Groups and an Editorial Board in a WAC Classroom." *Teaching English in the Two-Year College* 23 (1996): 57–63.

Hilbert, Betsy S. "It Was a Dark and Nasty Night It Was a Dark and You Would Not Believe How Dark It Was a Hard Beginning." *College Composition and Communication* 43 (1992): 75–80.

Horning, Alice S. "Reflection and Revision: Intimacy in College Writing." *Composition Chronicle* 9 (1997): 4–7.

Lawrence, Sandra M., and Elizabeth Sommers. "From the Park Bench to the [Writing] Workshop Table: Encouraging Collaboration among Inexperienced Writers." *Teaching English in the Two-Year College* 23 (1996): 101–11.

Lindemann, Erika. *A Rhetoric for Writing Teachers.* 3rd ed. New York: Oxford UP, 1995. 21–34.

Moran, Mary Hurley. "Connections between Reading and Successful Revision." *Journal of Basic Writing* 16.2 (1997): 76–89.

Murray, Donald. *The Craft of Revision.* 2nd ed. Orlando: Harbrace, 1995.

Raymond, Richard C. "Teaching Students to Revise: Theories and Practice." *Teaching English in the Two-Year College* 16 (1989): 49–58.

Willis, Meredith Sue. *Deep Revision: A Guide for Teachers, Students, and Other Writers.* New York: Teachers and Writers Collaborative, 1993.

Responding to Student Writing

Beach, Richard. "Demonstrating Techniques for Assessing Writing in the Writing Conference." *College Composition and Communication* 37 (1986): 56–65.

Blau, Susan R., John Hall, and Tracy Strauss. "Exploring the Tutor/Client Conversation: A Linguistic Analysis." *Writing Center Journal* 19.1 (1998): 19–48.

Garrison, Roger. "One-to-One: Tutorial Instruction in Freshman Composition." *New Directions for Community Colleges* 2 (Spring 1974): 55–84.

Gay, Pamela. "Dialogizing Response in the Writing Classroom: Students Answer Back." *Journal of Basic Writing* 17.1 (1998): 3–17.

Harris, Muriel. "The Ins and Outs of Conferencing." *The Writing Instructor* 6 (1987): 87–96.

——. *Teaching One-to-One.* Urbana: NCTE, 1986.

Krest, Margie. "Monitoring Student Writing: How Not to Avoid the Draft." *Journal of Teaching Writing* 7 (1988): 27–39.

Murray, Donald M. "Teaching the Other Self: The Writer's First Reader." *College Composition and Communication* 33 (1982): 140–47.

O'Neill, Peggy. "From the Writing Process to the Responding Sequence: Incorporating Self-Assessment and Reflection in the Classroom." *Teaching English in the Two-Year College* 26 (1998): 61–70.

Robertson, Michael. "Is Anybody Listening?" *College Composition and Communication* 37 (1986): 87–91.

Sherwood, Steve. "Censoring Students, Censoring Ourselves: Constraining Conversations in the Writing Center." *Writing Center Journal* 20.1 (1999): 51–60.

Smith, Summer. "The Genre of the End Comment: Conventions in Teacher Responses to Student Writing." *College Composition and Communication* 48 (1997): 249–68.

Straub, Richard. "The Concept of Control in Teacher Response: Defining the Varieties of 'Directive' and 'Facilitative' Commentary." *College Composition and Communication* 47 (1996): 223–51.

Straub, Richard, and Ronald F. Lunsford. *Twelve Readers Reading: Responding to College Student Writing.* Cresskill, NJ: Hampton, 1995.

Sweeney, Marilyn Ruth. "Relating Revision Skills to Teacher Commentary." *Teaching English in the Two-Year College* 27 (1999): 213–18.

Thompson, Jan C. "Beyond Fixing Today's Paper: Promoting Metacognition and Writing Development in the Tutorial through Self-Questioning." *Writing Lab Newsletter* 23.6 (1999): 1–6.

White, Edward M. *Assigning, Responding, Evaluating: A Writing Teacher's Guide.* 3rd ed. New York: St. Martin's, 1995.

Paragraphs

Bamberg, Betty. "What Makes a Text Coherent?" *College Composition and Communication* 34 (1983): 417–29.

Braddock, Richard. "The Frequency and Placement of Topic Sentences in Expository Prose." *Research in Teaching Writing* 8 (Winter 1974): 287–304.

Brostoff, Anita. "Coherence: 'Next to' is Not 'Connected to'" *College Composition and Communication* 32 (1981): 278–94.

Christensen, Francis. "A Generative Rhetoric of the Paragraph." *Notes toward a New Rhetoric.* New York: Harper, 1967. 52–81.

D'Angelo, Frank. "The Topic Sentence Revisited." *College Composition and Communication* 37 (1986): 431–41.

Haswell, Richard H. "Textual Research and Coherence: Findings, Intuition, Application." *College English* 51 (1989): 305–19.

Laib, Nevin. "Conciseness and Amplification." *College Composition and Communication* 41 (1990): 443–59.

Lindemann, Erika. *A Rhetoric for Writing Teachers.* 3rd ed. New York: Oxford UP, 1995. 141–57.

Popken, Randell L. "A Study of Topic Sentence Use in Academic Writing." *Written Communication* 4 (1987): 209–28.

Witte, Stephen P., and Lester Faigley. "Coherence, Cohesion, and Writing Quality." *College Composition and Communication* 32 (1981): 189–204.

Part Two: Document Design

Anderson, W. Steve. "The Rhetoric of the Résumé." Annual Meeting of the Coll. English Assn. Clearwater Beach, FL. 12–14 Apr. 1984. ERIC. CD-ROM. Silver Platter. 1995.

Andrews, Deborah C., and Marilyn Dyrud, eds. "Document Design: Part 1." Spec. issue of *Business Communication Quarterly* 59.3 (1996): 65–76.

Bernhardt, Stephen A. "The Shape of Text to Come: The Texture of Print on Screens." *College Composition and Communication* 44 (1993): 151–75.

Ellis, Shelley M. "Up Close and Personal: A Real-World Audience Awareness Assignment." *Teaching English in the Two-Year College* 26 (1999): 286–90.

Hall, Dean G., and Bonnie A. Nelson. "Initiating Students into Professionalism: Teaching the Letter of Inquiry." *Technical Writing Teacher* 14 (1987): 86–89.

Hawisher, Gail E., and Charles Moran. "Electronic Mail and the Writing Instructor." *College English* 55 (1993): 627–43.

Heba, Gary. "Hyper Rhetoric: Multimedia, Literacy, and the Future of Composition." *Computers and Composition* 14 (1997): 19–44.

Humphreys, Donald S. "Making Your Hypertext Interface Usable." *Technical Communication* 40 (1993): 754–61.

Kostelnick, Charles. "The Rhetoric of Text Design in Professional Communication." *Technical Writing Teacher* 17 (1990): 189–202.

Kress, Gunther. "'English' at the Crossroads: Rethinking Curricula of Communication in the Context of the Turn to the Visual." *Passions, Pedagogies, and 21st Century Technologies.* Ed. Gail E. Hawisher and Cynthia L. Selfe. Logan: Utah State UP, 1999. 66–88.

Lanham, Richard A. *Revising Business Prose.* 3rd ed. New York: Prentice, 1991.

Lay, Mary M. "Nonrhetorical Elements of Layout and Design." *Technical Writing: Theory and Practice.* Ed. Bertie E. Fearing and W. Keats Sparrow. New York: MLA, 1989. 72–85.

Mansfield, Margaret A. "Real World Writing and the English Curriculum." *College Composition and Communication* 44 (1993): 69–83.

Markel, Mike. "What Students See: Word Processing and the Perception of Visual Design." *Computers and Composition* 15 (1998): 373–86.

Matalene, Carolyn B., ed. *Worlds of Writing: Teaching and Learning in Discourse Communities of Work.* New York: McGraw, 1989.

Mendelson, Michael. "Business Prose and the Nature of the Plain Style." *Journal of Business Communication* 24 (Spring 1987): 3–18.

Norman, Rose. "Resumex: A Computer Exercise for Teaching Résumé Writing." *Technical Writing Teacher* 15 (1988). 162–66.

Odell, Lee, and Dixie Goswami, eds. *Writing in Nonacademic Settings.* New York: Guilford, 1986.

Parker, Roger C. *Looking Good in Print: A Guide to Basic Design for Desktop Publishing.* 2nd ed. Chapel Hill: Ventana, 1990.

Shenk, Robert. "Ghost Writing in Professional Communications." *Journal of Technical Writing and Communication* 18 (1988): 377–87.

Singh-Gupta, Vidya, and Eileen Troutt-Ervin. "Preparing Students for Teamwork through Collaborative Writing and Peer Review Techniques." *Teaching English in the Two-Year College* 23 (1996): 127–36.

Parts Three and Four: Clear Sentences and Word Choice

Clear Sentences

Carkeet, David. "Understanding Syntactic Errors in Remedial Writing." *College English* 38 (1977): 682–86, 695.

Christensen, Francis. "A Generative Rhetoric of the Sentence." *College Composition and Communication* 14 (1963): 155–61. Rpt. In *Notes toward a New Rhetoric.* New York: Harper, 1967. 1–22.

Connors, Robert J. "The Erasure of the Sentence." *College Composition and Communication* 52 (2000): 96–128.

Corbett, Edward P. J. *Classical Rhetoric for the Modern Student.* 3rd ed. New York: Oxford UP, 1990. 398–403, 404–23.

Crowhurst, Marion. "Sentence Combining: Maintaining Realistic Expectations." *College Composition and Communication* 34 (1983): 62–72.

Elbow, Peter. "The Challenge for Sentence Combining." *Sentence Combining: A Rhetorical Perspective.* Ed. Don Daiker, Andrew Kerek, and Max Morenberg. Carbondale: Southern Illinois UP, 1985. 232–45.

Faigley, Lester. "Names in Search of a Concept: Maturity, Fluency, Complexity, and Growth in Written Syntax." *College Composition and Communication* 31 (1980): 291–300.

Freeman, Donald C. "Linguistics and Error Analysis: On Agency." *The Territory of Language.* Ed. Donald A. McQuade. Carbondale: Southern Illinois UP, 1986. 165–73.

Frischkorn, Craig. "Style in Advanced Composition: Active Students and Passive Voice." *Teaching English in the Two-Year College* 26 (1999): 415–18.

Graves, Richard L. "Symmetrical Form and the Rhetoric of the Sentence." *Rhetoric and Composition: A Sourcebook for Teachers and Writers.* Ed. Richard L. Graves. Upper Montclaire, NJ: Boynton/Cook, 1984. 119–27.

Jordan, Michael P. "Unattached Clauses in Technical Writing." *Journal of Technical Communication* 29.1 (1999): 65–93.

Kolln, Martha. *Understanding English Grammar.* 4th ed. New York: Macmillan, 1994. 349–90.

Laib, Nevin. "Conciseness and Amplification." *College Composition and Communication* 41 (1990): 443–59.

Latham, Richard. *Style: An Anti-Textbook.* New Haven: Yale UP, 1978.

Noguchi, Rei R. *Grammar and the Teaching of Writing: Limits and Possibilities.* Urbana: NCTE, 1991. 38–58.

Pixton, William H. "The Dangling Gerund: A Working Definition." *College Composition and Communication* 24 (1973): 193–99.

Robinson, William S. "Sentence Focus, Cohesion, and the Active and Passive Voices." *Teaching English in the Two-Year College* 27 (2000): 440–45.

Scriven, Karen. "Actively Teaching the Passive Voice." *Teaching English in the Two-Year College* 16 (1989): 89–93.

Shaughnessy, Mina P. *Errors and Expectations: A Guide for the Teacher of Basic Writing.* New York: Oxford UP, 1979. 44–89.

Walker, Robert L. "The Common Writer: A Case for Parallel Structure." *College Composition and Communication* 21 (1970): 373–79.

Walpole, Jane R. "The Vigorous Pursuit of Grace and Style." *Writing Instructor* 1 (1982): 163–69.

Weaver, Constance. *Teaching Grammar in Context.* Portsmouth, NH: Boynton/Cook, 1996. 102–47.

Williams, James D. *Preparing to Teach Writing.* Mahwah, NJ: Eribaum, 1996. 301–02, 306.

Williams, Joseph. *Style: Ten Lessons in Clarity and Grace.* 5th ed. New York: Longman, 1997. 140–44.

Word Choice

Balester, Valerie M. *Cultural Divide: A Study of African-American College-Level Writers.* Portsmouth, NH: Boynton/Cook, 1993. 77–151.

Corbett, Edward P. J. *Classical Rhetoric for the Modern Student.* 3rd ed. New York: Oxford UP, 1990. 438–47.

Devet, Bonnie. "Bringing Back More Figures of Speech into Composition." *Journal of Teaching Writing* 6 (1987): 293–304.

Frank, Francine Wattman, and Paula A. Treichler. *Language, Gender, and Professional Writing: Theoretical Approaches and Guidelines for Nonsexist Usage.* New York: MLA, 1989.

Giannasi, Jenefer M. "Language Varieties and Composition." *Teaching Composition.* Ed. Gary Tate. Rev. ed. Fort Worth: Texas Christian UP, 1987.

Kari, Daven M. "A Cliché a Day Keeps the Gray Away." *Teaching English in the Two-Year College* 19.6 (1992): 128–33.

Labov, William. *Language in the Inner City: Studies in the Black English Vernacular.* Philadelphia: U of Pennsylvania P, 1972.

Lanham, Richard A. *Revising Prose.* 3rd ed. New York: Prentice, 1991.

Lutz, William. *The New Doublespeak: Why No One Knows What Anyone's Saying Anymore.* New York: Harper, 1996.

Quarterly Review of Doublespeak. Urbana: NCTE.

Williams, James D. "Nonstandard English." *Preparing to Teach Writing.* Mahwah, NJ: Eribaum, 1996. 160–76.

Part Five: Grammatical Sentences

Bamberg, Betty. "Periods Are Basic: A Strategy for Eliminating Comma Faults and Run-on Sentences." *Teaching the Basics—Really!* Ed. Ouida Clapp. Urbana: NCTE, 1977. 97–99.

Bryony, Shannon. "Pronouns: Male, Female, and Undesignated." *ETC: A Review of General Semantics* 45 (Winter 1998): 334–36.

Carroll, Joyce Armstrong, and Edward E. Wilson. *Acts of Teaching: How to Teach Writing.* Englewood, CO: Teaching Ideas, 1993.

Connors, Robert J. *Composition-Rhetoric: Backgrounds, Theory, and Pedagogy.* Ithaca: Cornell UP, 1997. 112–70.

Devet, Bonnie. "Errors as Discoveries: An Assignment for Prospective English Teachers." *Journal of Teaching Writing* 15.1 (1996): 129–39.

Epes, Mary. "Tracing Errors to the Sources: A Study of the Encoding Processes of Adult Basic Writers." *Journal of Basic Writing* 41 (1985): 4–33.

Harris, Joseph. *A Teaching Subject: Composition since 1966.* Upper Saddle River, NJ: Prentice, 1997. 76–90.

Hull, Glynda. "Constructing Taxonomies for Error." *A Sourcebook for Basic Writing Teachers.* Ed. Theresa Enos. New York: McGraw, 1987. 231–44.

Kagan, Dona M. "Run-on and Fragment Sentences: An Error Analysis." *Research in the Teaching of English* 14 (1980): 127–38.

Kolln, Martha. "Everyone's Right to Their Own Language." *College Composition and Communication* 37 (1986): 100–02.

Kroll, Barry M., and John C. Schaefer. "Error Analysis and the Teaching of Composition." *College Composition and Communication* 29 (1978): 242–48.

Lu, Min-Zhan. "Conflict and Struggle: The Enemies or Preconditions of Basic Writing?" *College English* 54 (1992): 887–913.

Mathews, Alison, and Martin S. Chodorow. "Pronoun Resolution in Two-Clause Sentences: Effects of Ambiguity, Antecedent Location, and Depth of Imbedding." *Journal of Memory and Language* 27 (June 1988): 245–60.

Moskovit, Leonard. "When Is Broad Reference Clear?" *College Composition and Communication* 34 (1983): 454–60.

Noguchi, Rei R. *Grammar and the Teaching of Writing: Limits and Possibilities.* Urbana: NCTE, 1991.

Shaughnessy, Mina P. *Errors and Expectations: A Guide for the Teacher of Basic Writing.* New York: Oxford UP, 1979. 16–43, 135.

Sklar, Elizabeth S. "The Tribunal of Use: Agreement in Indefinite Constructions." *College Composition and Communication* 39 (1988): 410–22.

Williams, Joseph M. "The Phenomenology of Error." *College Composition and Communication* 32 (1981): 152–68.

Wolfram, Walt, and Ralph W. Fasold. *The Study of Social Dialects in American English.* Upper Saddle River, NJ: Prentice, 1974.

Part Six: English as a Second Language

Anzaldúa, Gloria. "How to Tame a Wild Tongue." *Borderlands/La Frontera.* San Francisco: Aunt Lute, 1987. 53–64.

Bizzell, Patricia, and Bruce Herzberg. "Teaching English as a Second Language." *The Bedford Bibliography for Teachers of Writing.* Boston: Bedford/St. Martin's, 2000. 170–78.

Celce-Murcia, Marianne, Diane Larsen-Freeman, and Stephen Thewlis. *The Grammar Book: An ESL/EFL Teacher's Course.* 2nd ed. Boston: Heinle, 1999.

Chappel, Virginia A., and Judith Rodby. "Verb Tense and ESL Composition: A Discourse Level Approach." Annual Convention of Teachers of English to Speakers of Other Languages. Honolulu. 1–6 May 1982. ERIC. CD-ROM. SilverPlatter. 1995.

Cook, Lenora, and Helen C. Lodge, eds. "Voices in English Classrooms: Honoring Diversity and Change." *Classroom Practices in Teaching English* 28. Urbana: NCTE, 1996.

Cooper, Charles R., and Lee Odell, eds. *Evaluating Writing: The Role of Teachers' Knowledge about Text, Learning, and Culture.* Urbana: NCTE, 1999.

Dean, Terry. "Multicultural Classrooms, Monocultural Teachers." *College Composition and Communication* 40 (1989): 23–37.

Fox, Helen. *Listening to the World: Cultural Issues in Academic Writing.* Urbana: NCTE, 1994.

Harris, Muriel, and Tony Silva. "Tutoring ESL Students: Issues and Options." *College Composition and Communication* 44 (1995): 525–37.

Leki, Ilona. "Coaching from the Margins: Issues in Written Response." *Second Language Writing: Research Insights for the Classroom.* Ed. Barbara Kroll. Cambridge: Cambridge UP, 1990. 57–68.

Master, Peter. "Teaching the English Articles as a Binary System." *TESOL Quarterly* 24 (1990): 461–78.

Nelson, Gayle L., and John M. Murphy. "Peer Response Groups: Do L2 Writers Use Peer Comments in Revising Their Drafts?" *TESOL Quarterly* 27 (1993). 135–41.

Rinnert, Carol, and Mark Hansen. "Teaching the English Article System." Japan Association of Language Teachers' International Conference on Language, Teaching, and Learning. Seiri Gakuen, Hamamatsu, Japan. 22–24 Nov. 1986. *ERIC.* CD-ROM. Silver Platter. 1995.

Robinson, William S. "ESL and Dialect Features in the Writing of Asian American Students." *Teaching English in the Two-Year College* 22 (1995): 303–09.

Schlumberger, Ann, and Diane Clymer. "Tailoring Composition Classes to ESL Students' Needs." *Teaching English in the Two-Year College* 16 (1989): 121–28.

Zamel, Vivian. "Strangers in Academia: The Experiences of Faculty and ESL Students across the Curriculum." *College Composition and Communication* 46 (1995): 506–21.

Part Seven and Eight: Punctuation and Mechanics

Punctuation

Bruthiaux, Paul. "Knowing When to Stop: Investigating the Nature of Punctuation." *Language and Communication* 13 (1993): 27–43.

———. "The Rise and Fall of the Semicolon: English Punctuation Theory and English Teaching Practice." *Applied Linguistics* 16 (1995): 1–14.

Dawkins, John. "Teaching Punctuation as a Rhetorical Tool." *College Composition and Communication* 46 (1995): 533–48.

Hassett, Michael. "Toward a Broader Understanding of the Rhetoric of Punctuation." *College Composition and Communication* 47 (1996): 419–21.

Meyer, Charles F. *A Linguistic Study of American Punctuation.* New York: Lang, 1987.

———. "Teaching Punctuation to Advanced Writers." *Journal of Advanced Composition* 6 (1985–86): 117–29.

Shaughnessy, Mina P. *Errors and Expectations: A Guide for the Teacher of Basic Writing.* New York: Oxford UP, 1979. 14–43.

Vasallo, Phillip. "'How's the Weather?': Ice-Breaking and Fog-Lifting in Your Written Messages." *ETC: A Review of General Semantics* 50 (1993–94): 494–91.

Mechanics

Dobie, Ann R. "Orthographical Theory and Practice, or How to Teach Spelling." *Journal of Basic Writing* 5 (Fall 1986): 41–48.

Martin, Charles L., and Dorothy E. Ranson. "Spelling Skills of Business Students: An Empirical Investigation." *Journal of Business Communication* 27.4 (1990): 377–400.

Meyer, Emily, and Louise Z. Smith. *The Practical Tutor.* New York: Oxford UP, 1987. 286–96.

Shaughnessy, Mina P. *Errors and Expectations: A Guide for the Teacher of Basic Writing.* New York: Oxford UP, 1979. 36–38, 160–86.

"Vygotsky and the Bad Speller's Nightmare." *English Journal* 80.8 (1991): 65–70.

White, Linda F. "Spelling Instruction in the Writing Center." *Writing Center Journal* 12 (1991): 34–47.

Part Nine: Critical Thinking

Bator, Paul. "Aristotelian and Rogerian Rhetoric." *College Composition and Communication* 31 (1980): 427–32.

Bean, John C. *Engaging Ideas: The Professor's Guide to Integrating Writing, Critical Thinking, and Active Learning in the Classroom.* San Francisco: Jossey-Bass, 1996.

Bizzell, Patricia. "The 4th of July and the 22nd of December: The Function of Cultural Archives in Persuasion, as Shown by Frederick Douglass and William Apess." *College Composition and Communication* 48 (1997): 44–60.

Browne, M. Neil, and Stuart M. Keeley. *Asking the Right Questions: A Guide to Critical Thinking.* 6th ed. Englewood Cliffs: Prentice, 2000.

Browne, Neil M., Kari E. Freeman, and Carrie L. Williamson. "The Importance of Critical Thinking for Student Use of the Internet." *College Student Journal* 3.3 (Spring 2000): 391–98.

Carella, Michael J. "Philosophy as Literacy: Teaching College Students to Read Critically and Write Cogently." *College Composition and Communication* 34 (1983): 57–61.

Clark, John H., and Arthur W. Biddle, eds. *Teaching Critical Thinking: Reports from across the Curriculum.* Englewood Cliffs: Prentice, 1993.

Dyrud, Marilyn A. "Teaching Logic." Oregon Council of Teachers of English Spring Conf. Bend, OR. 6–7 Apr. 1984. *ERIC.* CD-ROM. SilverPlatter, 1995.

Fahnestock, Jeanne, and Marie Secor. "Teaching Argument: A Theory of Types." *College Composition and Communication* 34 (1983): 20–30.

Fishman, Stephen M., and Lucille Parkinson McCarthy. "Teaching for Student Change: A Deweyan Alternative to Radical Pedagogy." *College Composition and Communication* 47 (1996): 342–66.

Fulkerson, Richard. *Teaching the Argument in Writing.* Urbana: NCTE, 1996.

———. "Technical Logic, Comp-Logic, and the Teaching of Writing." *College Composition and Communication* 39 (1988): 436–52.

Galotti, Kathleen M. "Valuing Connected Knowing in the Classroom." *The Clearing House* 71.5 (May/June 1998): 281–83.

Kaufer, David S., and Christine M. Neuwrith. "Integrating Formal Logic and the New Rhetoric: A Four Stage Heuristic," *College English* 45 (1983): 380–89.

Lamb, Catherine E. "Beyond Argument in Feminist Composition." *College Composition and Communication* 42 (1991): 11–24.

Lazere, Donald. "Teaching the Political Conflicts: A Rhetorical Schema." *College Composition and Communication* 43 (1992): 194–213.

Marzano, Robert J. "What Are the General Skills of Thinking and Reasoning and How Do You Teach Them?" *The Clearing House* 71.5 (May/June 1998): 268–73.

McCleary, William J. "A Case Approach for Teaching Academic Writing." *College Composition and Communication* 36 (1985): 203–23.

Rapkin, Angela A. "The Uses of Logic in the College Freshman English Classroom." *Activities to Promote Critical Thinking: Classroom Practices in Teaching English.* Urbana: NCTE, 1986. 130–35. *ERIC.* CD-ROM. SilverPlatter, 1995.

Secor, Marie J. "Recent Research in Argumentation Theory." *Technical Writing Teacher* 14 (1987): 337–54.

Smith, Paul C. "Countering Uncritical Skepticism." *College Teaching* 45 (Spring 1997): 78.

Sorapure, Madeleine, Pamela Inglesby, and George Yatchisin. "Web Literacy: Challenges and Opportunities for Research in the New Medium." *Computers & Composition* 15.3 (1998): 409–24.

Sosnoski, James. "Hyper-Readers and Their Reading Engines." *Passions, Pedagogies, and 21st Century Technologies.* Logan: Utah State UP, 1999. 161–77.

Trail, George Y. "Teaching Argument and the Rhetoric of Orwell's 'Politics of the English Language.'" *College English* 57 (1995): 570–83.

Zeller, Robert. "Developing the Inferential Reasoning of Basic Writers." *College Composition and Communication* 38 (1987): 343–45.

Part Ten: Researched Writing

Bean, John C. "Encouraging Engagement and Inquiry in Research Papers." *Engaging Ideas: The Professor's Guide to Integrating Writing, Critical Thinking, and Active Learning in the Classroom.* San Francisco: Jossey-Bass, 1996. 197–214.

Brent, Doug. *Reading as Rhetorical Invention: Knowledge, Persuasion, and the Teaching of Research-Based Writing.* Urbana: NCTE, 1992.

Chamberlain, Lori. "Bombs and Other Exciting Devices, or the Problem of Teaching Irony." *College English* 51 (1989): 29–40.

Coon, Anne C. "Using Ethical Questions to Develop Autonomy in Student Researchers." *College Composition and Communication* 40 (1989): 85–89.

Dellinger, Dixie G. "Alternatives to Clip and Stitch: Real Research and Writing in the Classroom." *English Journal* 78 (1989): 31–38.

Dixon, Deborah. *Writing Your Heritage: A Sequence of Thinking, Reading, and Writing Assignments.* Berkeley: Natl. Writing Project, 1993.

Dragga, Sam. "Collaborative Interpretation." *Activities to Promote Critical Thinking: Classroom Practices in Teaching English.* Urbana: NCTE, 1986. 84–87. *ERIC.* CD-ROM. Silver-Platter, 1995.

Gillette, Mary Anne, and Carol Videon. "Seeking Quality on the Internet: A Case Study of Composition Student's Works Cited." *Teaching English in the Two-Year College* 26.2 (1998): 189–94.

Grobman, Laurie. "'I Found It on the Web, So Why Can't I Put It in My Paper?': Authorizing Basic Writers." *Journal of Basic Writing* 18.2 (Fall 1999): 76–90.

Herrington, Anne. J. "Teaching, Writing, and Learning: A Naturalistic Study of Writing in an Undergraduate Class." *Writing in Academic Disciplines.* Ed. David Jolliffe. Norwood, NJ: Ablex, 1988. 133–66.

Hull, Glynda, and Mike Rose. "'This Wooden Shack Place': The Logic of an Unconventional Reading." *College Composition and Communication* 41 (1990): 287–98.

Isakesen, Judy L., Tim Waggoner, Nancy Christensen, and Dianne Fallon. "World Wide Web Research Assignments." *Teaching English in the Two-Year College* 26.2 (1998): 196–98.

Kantz, Margaret. "Helping Students Use Textual Sources Persuasively." *College English* 52 (1990): 74–91.

Kennedy, Mary Lynch. "The Composing Process of College Students Writing from Sources." *Written Communication* 2 (1985): 434–56.

Klausman, Jeffrey. "Teaching Plagiarism in the Age of the Internet." *Teaching English in the Two-Year College* 27.2 (1999): 209–12.

Kleine, Michael. "What Is It We Do When We Write Papers like This One—and How Can We Get Students to Join Us?" *Writing Instructor* 6 (1987): 151–61.

Kroll, Barry M. "How College Freshmen View Plagiarism." *Written Communication* 5 (1988): 203–21.

Lazere, Donald. "Teaching the Political Conflicts: A Rhetorical Schema." *College Composition and Communication* 43 (1992): 194–213.

Lynn, Steven. "A Passage into Critical Theory." *College English* 52 (1990): 258–71.

Macrorie, Ken. *The I-Search Paper.* Rev. ed. of *Searching, Writing.* Portsmouth, NH: Boynton/Cook, 1988.

Marino, Sarah R., and Elin K. Jacob, "Questions and Answers: The Dialog between Composition Teachers and Reference Librarians." *Reference Librarian* 37 (1992): 129–42.

Neverow-Turk, Vara. "Researching the Minimum Wage: A Moral Economy for the Classroom." *College Composition and Communication* 42 (1991): 477–83.

Page, Miriam Dempsey. "'Thick Description' and a Rhetoric of Inquiry: Freshmen and the Major Fields." *Writing Instructor* 6 (1987): 141–50.

Penrose, Ann M., and Cheryl Geisler. "Reading and Writing without Authority." *College Composition and Communication* 45 (1994): 505–20.

Profozich, Richard. "Coping with the Research Paper." *Teaching English in the Two-Year College* 24.4 (1997): 304–07.

Rose, Shirley K. "'What's Love Got to Do with It?' Scholarly Citation Practices as Courtship Rituals." *Language and Learning Across the Disciplines* 1.3 (1996): 34–48.

Roskelly, Hepzibah. "Writing to Read: The Stage of Interpretation." 1988. *ERIC.* CD-ROM. SilverPlatter. 1995.

Schmersahl, Carmen B. "Teaching Library Research: Process, Not Product." *Journal of Teaching Writing* 6 (1987): 231–38.

Shapiro, Jeremy J., and Shelley K. Hughes. "Information Literacy as a Liberal Art." *Educom Review* 31.2 (1996): 31–35.

Sherrard, Carol. "Summary Writing: A Topographical Study." *Written Communication* 3 (1986): 324–43.

St. Onge, Keith R. *The Melancholy Anatomy of Plagiarism.* Lanthan, MD: UP of America, 1988.

Strickland, James. "The Research Sequence: What to Do before the Term Paper." *College Composition and Communication* 37 (1986): 233–36.

Sutton, Brian. "Writing in the Disciplines, First-Year Composition, and the Research Paper." *Language and Learning Across the Disciplines* 2.1 (1997): 46–57.

Tyryzna, Thomas N. "Research outside the Library: Learning a Field." *College Composition and Communication* 37 (1986): 217–23.

Williams, Nancy. "Research as a Process: A Transactional Approach." *Journal of Teaching Writing* 7 (1988): 193–204.

Zebroski, James Thomas. "Using Ethnographic Writing to Construct Classroom Knowledge." *Thinking through Theory*. Portsmouth, NH: Boynton/Cook, 1994: 31–43.

Zemelman, Steven, and Harvey Daniels. "Collaborative Research and Term Papers." *A Community of Writers*. Portsmouth, NH: Boynton/Cook, 1988. 256–67.

Part Eleven: Grammar Basics

Baron, Dennis. *Grammar and Good Taste: Reforming the American Language*. New Haven: Yale UP, 1982.

Connors, Robert J. "Grammar in American College Composition: An Historical Overview." *The Territory of Language: Linguistics, Stylistics, and the Teaching of Composition*. Ed. Donald A. McQuade. Carbondale: Southern Illinois UP, 1986. 3–22.

Crowley, Sharon. "Linguistics and Composition Instruction: 1950–1980." *Written Communication* 6 (1989): 21–41.

Harris, Muriel, and Katherine E. Rowan. "Explaining Grammatical Concepts." *Journal of Basic Writing* 8.2 (1989): 21–41.

Lindemann, Erika. *A Rhetoric for Writing Teachers*. 3rd ed. New York: Oxford UP, 1995. 68–86.

Noguchi, Rei R. *Grammar and the Teaching of Writing: Limits and Possibilities*. Urbana: NCTE, 1991.

Parker, Frank, and Kim Sydow Campbell. "Linguistics and Writing: A Reassessment." *College Composition and Communication* 44 (1993): 295–314.

Quirk, Randolph, and Sidney Greenbaum. *A Concise Grammar of Contemporary English*. New York: Harcourt, 1973.

Sedgwick, Ellery. "Alternatives to Teaching Formal, Analytical Grammar." *Journal of Developmental Education* 12.3 (1980): 8+.

Weaver, Constance. *Teaching Grammar in Context*. Portsmouth, NH: Boynton/Cook, 1996.

Appendix A: Writing in the Disciplines

Anderson, W. Steve. "The Rhetoric of the Résumé." Annual Meeting of the Coll. English Assn. Clearwater Beach, FL. 12–14 Apr. 1984. *ERIC*. CD-ROM. Silver Platter, 1995.

Andrews, Deborah C., and Marilyn Dyrud, eds. "Document Design: Part 1." Spec. issue of *Business Communication Quarterly* 59.3 (1996): 65–76.

Beach, Richard. *A Teacher's Introduction to Reader-Response Theories*. Urbana: NCTE, 1993.

Biddle, Arthur W., and Toby Fulwiler, eds. *Reading, Writing, and the Study of Literature*. New York: McGraw, 1989.

Commeyras, Michelle. "Using Literature to Teach Critical Thinking." *Journal of Reading* 32 (1989): 703–07.

Daemmrich, Ingrid. "A Bridge to Academic Discourse: Social Science Research Strategies in the Freshman Composition Course." *College Composition and Communication* 40 (1989): 343–48.

Ellis, Shelley M. "Up Close and Personal: A Real-World Audience Awareness Assignment." *Teaching English in the Two-Year College* 26 (1999): 286–90.

Gibson, Craig. "Research Skills across the Curriculum: Connections with Writing-across-the-Curriculum." *Writing across the Curriculum and the Academic Library: A Guide for Librarians, Instructors, and Writing Program Directors*. Ed. Jean Sheridan. Westport: Greenwood, 1995. 55–70.

Gould, Christopher. "Literature in the Basic Writing Course: A Bibliographic Survey." *College English* 49 (1987): 558–74.

Hall, Dean G., and Bonnie A. Nelson. "Initiating Students into Professionalism: Teaching the Letter of Inquiry." *Technical Writing Teacher* 14 (1987): 86–89.

Healy, Dave, and Murray Jensen. "Using Feedback Groups and an Editorial Board in a WAC Classroom." *Teaching English in the Two-Year College* 23 (1996): 57–63.

Holman, C. Hugh, and William Harmon. *A Handbook to Literature*. 7th ed. New York: Macmillan. 1996.

Jeske, Jeff. "Borrowing from the Sciences: A Model for the Freshman Research Paper." *Writing Instructor* 6 (1987): 62–67.

Kirscht, Judy, Rhonda Levine, and John Reiff. "WAC and the Rhetoric of Inquiry." *College Composition and Communication* 45 (1994): 369–80.

Kostelnick, Charles. "The Rhetoric of Text Design in Professional Communication." *Technical Writing Teacher* 17 (1990): 189–202.

Lanham, Richard A. *Revising Business Prose*. 3rd ed. New York: Prentice, 1991.

Lentricchia, Frank, and Thomas McLaughlin, eds. *Critical Terms for Literary Study*. 2nd ed. Chicago: U of Chicago P, 1995.

Lindemann, Erika. "Freshman Composition: No Place for Literature." *College English* 55 (1993): 311–16.

Lutzker, Marilyn. *Research Projects for College Students: What to Write across the Curriculum*. Westport: Greenwood, 1988.

MacDonald, Susan Peck, and Charles R. Cooper. "Contributions of Academic and Dialogic Journals to Writing about Literature." *Writing, Teaching, and Learning in the Disciplines*. Ed. Anne Herrington and Charles Moran. New York: MLA, 1992: 137–55.

Mansfield, Margaret A. "Real World Writing and the English Curriculum." *College Composition and Communication* 44 (1993): 69–83.

Matalene, Carolyn B., ed. *Worlds of Writing: Teaching and Learning in Discourse Communities of Work*. New York: McGraw, 1989.

Mendelson, Michael. "Business Prose and the Nature of the Plain Style." *Journal of Business Communication* 24 (Spring 1987): 3–18.

Meyer, Emily, and Louise Z. Simthy. "Reading and Writing about Literature." *The Practical Tutor*. New York: Oxford UP, 1987. 256–85.

Moran, Charles, and Elizabeth F. Penfield. *Conversations: Contemporary Critical Theory and the Teaching of Literature*. Urbana: NCTE, 1990.

Norman, Rose. "Resumex: A Computer Exercise for Teaching Résumé Writing." *Technical Writing Teacher* 15 (1988). 162–66.

Odell, Lee, and Dixie Goswami, eds. *Writing in Nonacademic Settings*. New York: Guilford, 1986.

Oster, Judith. "Seeing with Different Eyes: Another View of Literature in the ESL Class." *TESOL Quarterly* 23 (1989): 85–102.

Reilly, Jill M., et al. "The Effects of Prewriting on Literary Interpretation." Annual Meeting of the Amer. Educ. Research Association. San Francisco. 16–20 Apr. 1986. *ERIC*. CD-ROM. SilverPlatter. 1995.

Steinberg, Erwin R., et al. "Symposium: Literature in the Composition Classroom." *College English* 57 (1995): 265–318.

Sutton, Brian. "Writing in the Disciplines, First-Year Composition, and the Research Paper." *Language and Learning Across the Disciplines* 2.1 (1997): 46–57.

Swope, John W., and Edgar H. Thompson. "Three R's for Critical Thinking about Literature: Reading, 'Riting, and Responding." *Activities to Promote Critical Thinking: Classroom Practices in Teaching English*. Urbana: NCTE, 1986. 75–79. *ERIC*. CD-ROM. SilverPlatter. 1995.

Tate, Gary. "A Place for Literature in Freshman Composition." *College English* 55 (1993): 317–21.

Wentworth, Michael. "Writing in the Literature Class." *Journal of Teaching Writing* 6 (1987): 155–62.

Young, Art, and Toby Fulwiler, eds. *When Writing Teachers Teach Literature: Bringing Writing to Reading*. Portsmouth, NH: Boynton/Cook, 1995.

Appendix B: Teaching with Technology

Bernhardt, Stephen A. "The Shape of Text to Come: The Texture of Print on Screens." *College Composition and Communication* 44 (1993): 151–75.

Crew, Louie. "The Style-Checker as Tonic, Not Tranquilizer." *Journal of Advanced Composition* 8 (1988): 66–70.

Gillette, Mary Anne, and Carol Videon. "Seeking Quality on the Internet: A Case Study of Composition Student's Works Cited." *Teaching English in the Two-Year College* 26.2 (1998): 189–94.

Hawisher, Gail E., and Charles Moran. "Electronic Mail and the Writing Instructor." *College English* 55 (1993): 627–43.

Heba, Gary. "Hyper Rhetoric: Multimedia, Literacy, and the Future of Composition." *Computers and Composition* 14 (1997): 19–44.

Holdstein, Deborah H., and Cynthia L. Selfe, eds. *Computers and Writing: Theory, Research, Practice.* New York: MLA, 1990.

Isakesen, Judy L. Tim Waggoner, Nancy Christensen, and Dianne Fallon. "World Wide Web Research Assignments." *Teaching English in the Two-Year College* 26.2 (1998): 196–98.

Klausman, Jeffrey. "Teaching Plagiarism in the Age of the Internet." *Teaching English in the Two-Year College* 27.2 (1999): 209–12.

Kress, Gunther. "'English' at the Crossroads: Rethinking Curricula of Communication in the Context of the Turn to the Visual." *Passions, Pedagogies, and 21st Century Technologies.* Ed. Gail E. Hawisher and Cynthia L. Selfe. Logan: Utah State UP, 1999. 66–88.

Markel, Mike. "What Students See: Word Processing and the Perception of Visual Design." *Computers and Composition* 15 (1998): 373–86.

Shapiro, Jeremy J., and Shelley K. Hughes. "Information Literacy as a Liberal Art." *Educom Review* 31.2 (1996): 31–35.

Sorapure, Madeleine, Pamela Inglesby, and George Yatchisin. "Web Literacy: Challenges and Opportunities for Research in the New Medium." *Computers & Composition* 15.3 (1998): 409–24.

Sosnoski, James. "Hyper-Readers and Their Reading Engines." *Passions, Pedagogies, and 21st Century Technologies.* Logan: Utah State UP, 1999. 161–77.

Webb, Patricia R. "Changing Writing / Changing Writers: The World Wide Web and Collaborative Inquiry in the Classroom." *Weaving a Virtual Web: Practical Approaches to New Information Technologies.* Ed. Sybille Gruber. Urbana: NCTE, 2000. 123–36.

Acknowledgments (continued from page ii)

Rick Eden and Ruth Mitchell, "Paragraphing for the Reader." From *College Composition and Communication*, December 1986. Copyright © 1986 by the National Council of Teachers of English. Reprinted with permission.

Peter Elbow, "Ranking, Evaluation and Liking: Sorting Our Three Forms of Judgment." From *College English* 55, February 1993. Copyright © 1993 by The National Council of Teachers of English. Reprinted with permission.

Lester Faigley, "Competing Theories of Process: A Critique and a Proposal." From *College English* 48, October 1986. Copyright © 1986 by the National Council of Teachers of English. Reprinted with permission.

Kristie S. Fleckenstein, "An Appetite for Coherence: Arousing and Fulfilling Desires." From *College Composition and Communication* 43, February 1992. Copyright © 1987 by the National Council of Teachers of English. Reprinted with permission.

Tina Lavonne Good, "Individual Student Conferences and Community Workshops: Is There a Conflict?" From *In Our Own Voice: Graduate Students Teach Writing* by Tina Lavonne Good and Leanne B. Warshauer, eds. Copyright © 2000 by Tina Lavonne Good and Leanne B. Warshauer. Reprinted with the permission of Allyn & Bacon.

Diana Hacker, "Following the Tao." From *Teaching English in the Two-Year College*. Copyright © 2000 by the National Council of Teachers of English. Reprinted with permission.

Joseph Harris, "Community." From *A Teaching Subject: Composition Since 1966*. Copyright © 1997 by Joseph Harris. Reprinted with the permission of Pearson Education, Inc., Upper Saddle River, NJ 07458.

Muriel Harris, "Composing Behaviors of One-and Multi-Draft Writers." From *College English* 51, February 1989. Copyright © 1989 by the National Council of Teachers of English. Reprinted with permission.

Patrick Hartwell, "Grammar, Grammars, and the Teaching of Grammar." From *College English* 47, January 1985. Copyright © 1985 by The National Council of Teachers of English. Reprinted with permission.

Joan Hawthorne, "'We Don't Proofread Here': Revisioning the Writing Center to Better Most Students Needs." From *The Writing Lab Newsletter* 23.8. Reprinted with permission.

Charles Kostelnick, "Visual Rhetoric: A Reader-Oriented Approach to Graphics and Designs." From *Technical Writing Teacher* 16.1 (1989). Reprinted with permission.

David Lang, "Critical Thinking in Web Courses: An Oxymoron?" From *Syllabus* 14.2. (2000). Copyright © 2000 by Syllabus Press. Reprinted with permission.

Susan G. LeJeune, "Writing for the Ignorant Reader." From *Teaching English in the Two-Year College*, December 1998. Copyright © 1998 by National Council of Teachers of English. Reprinted with permission.

Ilona Leki, "Classroom Expectations and Behaviors." From *Understanding ESL Writers: A Guide for Teachers* by Ilona Leki. Copyright © 1990 by Ilona Leki. Reprinted with permission of the publisher.

Erika Lindemann, "Prewriting Techniques," "Responding to Student Writing," "Teaching about Sentences." From *A Rhetoric for Writing Teachers*, Third Edition. Copyright © 1995 by Erika Lindemann. Used by permission of Oxford University Press.

Dennis A. Lynch, Diana George, and Marilyn M. Cooper. "Moments of Argument: Agonistic Inquiry and Confrontational Cooperation." From *College Composition and Communication*, February 1997. Copyright © 1997 by the National Council of Teachers of English. Reprinted with permission.

Steven Lynn, "A Passage into Critical Theory." From *College English*, March 1990. Copyright © 1990 by the National Council of Teachers of English. Reprinted with permission.

Susan McLeod, "The Pedagogy of Writing Across the Curriculum." From *A Guide to Composition Pedagogies* by Gary Tate, Amy Rupiper and Kurt Schick, editors. Copyright © 2001 by Gary Tate, Amy Rupiper and Kurt Schick. Used by permission of Oxford University Press.

Casey Miller and Kate Swift, "Introduction: Change and Resistance to Change." From *The Handbook of Nonsexist Writing*, Second Edition. Originally published by HarperCollins

Publishers (1988). Copyright © 1988 by Casey Miller and Kate Swift. Reprinted by permission of Kate Swift. Identical text is available online from www.iuniverse.com.

Ruth Mirtz, "A Conversation about Small Groups." From *Small Groups in Writing Workshops: Invitations to a Writer's Life* edited by Robert Brooke, Ruth Mirtz, and Rich Evans. Copyright © 1994 by the National Council of Teachers of English. Reprinted with permission.

Charles Moran, "Technology and the Teaching of Writing." From *A Guide to Composition Pedagogies* by Gary Tate, Amy Rupiper, and Kurt Schick, eds. Copyright © 2001 by Gary Tate, Amy Rupiper, and Kurt Schick, eds. Used by permission of Oxford University Press.

Stephen North, "The Idea of the Writing Center." From *College English* 46.5 (1984). Copyright © 1984 by the National Council of Teachers of English. Reprinted with permission.

Douglas B. Park, "Analyzing Audiences." From *College Composition and Communication* 37, December 1986. Copyright © 1986 by the National Council of Teachers of English. Reprinted with permission.

William Peirce, "Online Strategies for Teaching Thinking." From *Syllabus* 14.2 (2000). Copyright © 2000 by Syllabus Press. Reprinted with permission.

D.R. Ransdell, "Directive versus Facilitative Commentary." From *Teaching English in the Two-Year College*, March 1999. Copyright © 1999 by the National Council of Teachers of English. Reprinted with permission.

Alan Rea and Doug White, "The Changing Nature of Writing: Prose or Code in the Classroom." From *Computers and Composition* 16 (1999). Copyright © 1999 Elsevier Science. Reprinted with the permission of the publisher.

Mike Rose,"Rigid Rules, Inflexible Plans, and the Stifling of Language: A Cognitivist Analysis of Writer's Block." From *College Composition and Communication*, December 1980. Copyright © 1980 by the National Council of Teachers of English. Reprinted with permission.

Mariolina Salvatori, "Conversations with Texts: Reading in the Teaching of Composition." From *College English*, April 1996. Copyright © 1996 by the National Council of Teachers of English. Reprinted with permission.

Nancy Sommers, "Responding to Student Writing." From *College Composition and Communication*, May 1982. Copyright © 1982 by the National Council of Teachers of English. "Revision Strategies of Student Writers and Experienced Adult Writers." From *College Composition and Communication*, December 1980. Copyright © 1980 by the National Council of Teachers of English. Reprinted with permission.

Michael Spooner and Kathleen Yancey, "Postings on a Genre of E-mail." From *College Composition and Communication*, May 1996. Copyright © 1996 by the National Council of Teachers of English. Reprinted with permission.

Elizabeth Tebeaux, "The Trouble with Employees' Writing May be Freshman Composition." From *Teaching English in the Two-Year College*, February 1988. Copyright © 1998 by the National Council of Teachers of English. Reprinted with permission.

"WPA Outcomes Statement for First-Year Composition" From *WPA: Writing Program Administration* 23½ (Fall/Winter 1999). Later published in *College English* 63.3, January 2000.